ACCOUNTING
FOR
MANAGEMENT
CONTROL
An Introduction

CHARLES T. HORNGREN

Ph.D., C.P.A.
Stanford University

PRENTICE-HALL, INC., ENGLEWOOD CLIFFS, NEW JERSEY

third edition

ACCOUNTING FOR MANAGEMENT CONTROL

An Introduction

Library of Congress Cataloging in Publication Data

Horngren, Charles T
    Accounting for management control.

    Bibliography:
    1. Cost accounting.   2. Accounting.   3. Management.
I. Title.
HF5686.C8H586   1974   658.1′5   73-22124
ISBN 0-13-001081-2

**ACCOUNTING
FOR
MANAGEMENT
CONTROL**
An Introduction

third edition
by Charles T. Horngren

PRINTED IN THE UNITED STATES OF AMERICA

PRENTICE-HALL INTERNATIONAL, INC., London
PRENTICE-HALL OF AUSTRALIA, PTY. LTD., Sydney
PRENTICE-HALL OF CANADA, LTD., Toronto
PRENTICE-HALL OF INDIA PRIVATE LIMITED, New Delhi
PRENTICE-HALL OF JAPAN, INC., Tokyo

To Joan
Scott
Mary
Susie
Cathy

Preface

This book is an introduction to internal accounting—most often called *management accounting*. The important topics with which it deals are those that all students of business should study. The book is written primarily for undergraduates who have had one or two terms of basic accounting. It is appropriate for a one-term course in managerial accounting at either the undergraduate or graduate level. It is also appropriate for executive educational programs of varying lengths in which the students have had no formal training in accounting. My twin goals have been to choose relevant subject matter and to present it clearly.

A student of business will be educationally short-changed unless he acquires a knowledge and appreciation of the ways in which accounting can help managers to operate effectively. Because accounting is so pervasive, an understanding of its usefulness—and its limitations—is desirable whether the student eventually becomes a company president, a production manager, a public accountant, a sales manager, a controller, a hospital administrator, or a politician. The study of accounting for planning and control can be especially fruitful because it is viewed through the eyes of the managers who are subject to accounting measures of performance and who are often heavily dependent on accounting information for guidance in decision making. There is no escaping the linkage of accounting and management. That is why the study of internal accounting is important. That is why such courses are increasingly required of all undergraduate students of business.

This book attempts a balanced, flexible approach. For example, it deals as much with retail, wholesale, selling, and administrative situations as it does with manufacturing. The fundamental accounting concepts and techniques for planning and control are applicable to all types and functions of organizations, not just to manufacturing. This more general approach makes it easier for the student to relate the book's examples and problems to his particular interests. Moreover, many valuable concepts (for example, master budgets) are more easily grasped if they are not complicated by intricate manufacturing situations.

Stress is on planning and control, not on product costing for purposes of inventory valuation and income determination. This approach, which excludes the troublesome but unimportant complications introduced by changes in inventory levels, simplifies the presentation of planning and control techniques in the classroom. Instead of the simultaneous discussion of costs for control and for product costing found in most texts, this text presents control thoroughly without dwelling on product costing at all until Chapter 15. At that point, the implications of overhead application for product costing may be considered in perspective and in relation to management policy decisions regarding the "best" inventory valuation method.

The major changes in this revision attempt to enhance the clarity of the material on planning and control systems:

1. The material on variations in cost behavior patterns, which had been sprinkled throughout old Chapters 8 and 10, has been concentrated in one place, Chapter 10.

2. Chapter 8 now focuses on basic terminology and the traditional and contribution approaches to income statements.

3. Chapter 9 is an almost completely new approach to flexible budgets and standards that emphasizes the trail between the original static budget and the final results actually encountered. It tries to maintain an overall perspective and to minimize the confusing proliferation of terms used in variance analysis.

4. Chapter 10 in the old edition dealt with various fixed costs, work measurement, and an analysis of fixed overhead that imposed a flock of new variances. The latter has been dropped, and the new Chapter 10 concentrates on distinctions among engineered, discretionary, and committed cost behavior patterns, work measurement, and some approaches to determining how costs behave.

5. Chapter 11 has been extensively rewritten and has combined some ideas on goal congruence and motivation, which were in the old Chapter 12, with responsibility accounting and problems of cost allocation.

6. The material on motivation in old Chapter 12 is now in Chapter 11, and the material on divisional performance is now in a new Chapter 16 because it is covered more deeply. Because of the shifting of the material in old Chapter 12 to other chapters, old Chapters 13, 14, and 15 have now become Chapters 12, 13, 14.

7. Chapter 15 is a new chapter that deals with overhead application: direct and absorption costing. It replaces old Chapters 16 and 17, which dealt with cost bookkeeping under actual cost systems as well as with

standard cost systems. These old chapters were rough going for many students, primarily because so many alternatives and new terms were covered in a small space.

The new Chapter 15 is an extension of Chapter 9. It focuses on two major variations of standard product costing, even though there are several product costing methods that do not employ standard costs. This approach was chosen for the following reasons:

a. The instructor has the option of following Chapter 9, which introduces flexible budgets and standards for planning and control purposes, with Chapter 15, which introduces the product costing purpose. This maximizes flexibility in using the book. Some instructors, like myself, prefer to concentrate solely on planning and control before considering product costing; that is why the material is in Chapter 15 instead of earlier. However, there are also good arguments for jumping directly to new Chapter 15 after finishing Chapter 9. This leap can be accomplished smoothly now, without being bogged down by too much detail and too many alternatives.

b. The student is not swamped with bookkeeping details and various non-standard cost systems. This is no great loss because an understanding of the standard product costing in Chapter 15 is readily transferable to any other product costing system that may be encountered.

8. Because old Chapters 16 and 17 have been replaced by new Chapter 15, old Chapter 18, the final chapter, is now Chapter 17.

Another major revision is Chapter 2, which deals with basic accounting concepts and techniques. It has been divided into two major parts. Part One covers the fundamentals without employing bookkeeping techniques, whereas Part Two pursues the ideas in Part One in more depth and does use bookkeeping devices. If little time is available, and the students have no background in elementary accounting, I confine my coverage of Chapter 2 to Part One.

The book has three major sections. Section One introduces, interprets, and appraises basic accounting. These chapters form a unified package that covers all elementary financial accounting in capsule form with heavy stress on interpretation and uses and, except in Chapter 2, with little attention given to the accumulation of the information. In my view, a major objective of basic financial accounting should be to equip the student with enough fundamental concepts and terminology so that he can reasonably comprehend any industrial corporate annual report. Chapters 3–5, including their assignment material, stress the income statement rather than the balance sheet.

Chapters 2-5 may be skipped entirely or may be used in a variety of ways:

1. In courses or executive programs where the students have *no* accounting background but where the main emphasis is on management rather than financial accounting.

2. In courses where the chapters may be used as a quick review by students who have had some financial accounting previously.

3. In courses where one or two of Chapters 2-5 may be chosen to remedy weaknesses or gaps in the background of the students.

Chapters 2-5 need not be used in total, page by page or topic by topic. The teacher is free to pick and choose those topics (particularly in Chapter 5) that seem most suitable for his students.

On the other hand, some teachers may want to use these chapters to teach the fundamentals of financial accounting to students with no prior background in accounting. Classroom testing has shown that such teaching can be done successfully, provided that the homework material is chosen carefully.

Section Two is the nucleus of the book. It emphasizes the attention-directing and problem-solving functions of accounting in relation to current planning and control, evaluation of performance, special decisions, and long-range planning. Stress is on cost analysis rather than on cost record keeping.

Section Three contains chapters on income tax planning, product costing, and quantitative techniques. These topics are important, but the decision to study them will depend on the teacher's preferences and on the students' background.

Two special features contribute to the clarity of the book's over-all presentation. First, every chapter has at least one "Summary Problem for Your Review," followed by a complete solution in which the chapter's important concepts and techniques are stressed. The student should: (1) study the chapter; (2) attempt to solve the review problem; (3) consult the solution after making an honest attempt to achieve his own solution; and (4) solve the homework problems. This plan provides a built-in check of the student's comprehension, helps his preparation for class, and minimizes the classroom discussion of issues which can bog down the session. More material can therefore be covered in a single session, and a more thorough course is possible. Profuse suggestions for the use of this material are in the solutions manual.

Second, the homework problems have been carefully prepared and fully tested in the classroom. The choice and development of appropriate, stimulating problems have been regarded as a key phase of this book's preparation. First-rate homework material is crucial to the success of any accounting course.

ALTERNATIVE WAYS OF USING THIS BOOK

How much time should be spent on each of the various chapters? The answer to such a question must always be tentative, because the backgrounds of students vary and because teachers never completely agree on the relative importance of various topics or on the proper sequence of

ALTERNATE SUGGESTED ASSIGNMENT SCHEDULES

| Alternative 1* | | | | Alternative 2† | | | |
| SEQUENCE A | | SEQUENCE B | | SEQUENCE A | | SEQUENCE B | |
Chapter	Sessions	Chapter	Sessions	Chapter	Sessions	Chapter	Sessions
1	.5	1	.5	1	.5	1	.5
2–5	skip	2–5	skip	2	2.0	2	2.0
6	1.5	6	1.5	3	2.0	3	2.0
7	1.0	7	1.0	4	2.0	6	2.0
8	3.0	8	2.0	5‖	1.0	7	1.0
9	4.0	9	4.0	6	2.0	8	2.5
10	3.0	15‖	4.0	7	1.0	9	4.0
11	4.0	10	3.0	8	2.5	10	2.0
12	3.0	11	4.0	9	4.0	11	2.5
13	3.0	16	2.5	10	2.0	16	1.5
14	1.5	12	3.0	11	2.5	12	2.5
15–17‖	5.5	13	3.5	12	2.5	13	3.5
		14	1.0	13	3.5	14	1.0
		17	Optional	14	1.0	4	2.0
				16	1.5	5‖	1.0
Total	30.0¶		30.0		30.0		30.0

*For students with a relatively strong background in elementary accounting, perhaps two terms taken immediately prior to this course.

†For students with a relatively weak background in elementary accounting, perhaps only one term, or when there has been a substantial lapse of time between elementary accounting and this course.

‖ All or part can be omitted. However, some instructors may wish to stress this material.

¶ Thirty sessions used for illustrative purposes; for fewer or more sessions, the relative time devoted to each topic would be unchanged.

Note: Students with no background in accounting will need to spend more time on Chapters 2 and 5 than is suggested in the above tables.

presentation. This book is flexible enough to permit the instructor to use a variety of chapter sequences and to place emphasis on varying assignments. Alternative schedules for assignment material are shown above. Various combinations of these alternatives are also possible.

Some instructors may be able to cover all the chapters in one term. In my view, Alternative 1, Sequence A: (Chapter 1 plus Parts Two and Three) will provide the basis for a course that is aimed wholly at the management uses of accounting.

The instructor can, if he wishes, employ any of the following variations: (1) assign Chapter 15 (Product Costing) at any point after Chapter 9; (2) assign appropriate sections on income tax planning from Chapter 14 simultaneously with the sections on capital budgeting in Chapter 13; (3) skip or dwell on various parts of Chapters 2–5, depending on the students' backgrounds; (4) omit Chapter 15 in classes where the techniques of inventory valuation are not as important as other topics; and (5) assign Chapter 16 immediately after Chapter 11.

In short courses, such as those in continuing education programs for managers, I favor the following sequence: Chapters 7, 8, 12, 13, 14 (first part), 9, 10, 11, and 16. Chapters 12-14 are considered earlier because they have innate utility and provide a quick glimpse of the attention-directing and problem-solving qualities of accounting.

ACKNOWLEDGMENTS

I have received ideas, assistance, miscellaneous critiques and assorted assignment material in conversations and by mail from many students and professors. Each has my gratitude, but the list is too long to enumerate here.

Professor Dudley W. Curry (Southern Methodist) has my special thanks for offering many helpful suggestions and for preparing the quiz and examination material and a student guide that are available as supplementary material.

The following professors supplied helpful reviews of the previous edition or drafts of this edition: Dennis Gordon, John Helmkamp, and Alfred Roberts.

Cristina Faragher has my appreciation for her cheerful and skillful typing and related help. The following students ably performed assorted editorial chores: Michael Garton, Thomas Keltner, and Carl Stern.

My thanks to the American Institute of Certified Public Accountants (problem material designated as CPA), the National Association of Accountants (NAA), the Society of Industrial Accountants of Canada (SIA), and the Institute of Management Accounting (CMA) for their generous permission to use some of their problems and to quote from their publications.

And finally, my thanks to Garret White and Fred Dahl at Prentice-Hall.

Comments from users are welcome.

CHARLES T. HORNGREN

Contents

PART TWO
THE CORE
OF ACCOUNTING
FOR PLANNING
AND CONTROL

PART THREE
SELECTED TOPICS
FOR FURTHER STUDY

**PART FOUR
APPENDICES**

SCOREKEEPING, STEWARDSHIP, AND EVALUATION

Perspective: Scorekeeping, Attention Directing, and Problem Solving

1

As the preface indicates, the objective of this book is to develop your knowledge and appreciation of how accounting helps managers to execute their responsibilities. Accounting and management are inextricably linked. That is why the study of internal accounting is important, regardless of whether you ultimately become an accountant or a manager.

The objective of this chapter is to view the accountant's role in an organization in perspective. We shall see that the accountant must fulfill three jobs simultaneously: scorekeeping, attention directing, and problem solving.

DISTINCTIVE PURPOSES OF ACCOUNTING FOR PLANNING AND CONTROL

Three Broad Purposes of an Accounting System

The accounting system is the major quantitative information system in almost every organization. An effective accounting system provides information for three broad purposes: (1) internal reporting to managers, for use in planning and controlling current operations; (2) internal reporting to managers, for use in strategic planning, that is, the making of special decisions and in the formulating of overall policies and long-range plans; and (3) external reporting to stockholders, government, and other outside parties.

Both management (internal parties) and the external parties share an interest in all three important purposes, but the emphases of financial accounting and of management (internal) accounting differ. Financial accounting has been mainly concerned with the third purpose and has traditionally been oriented toward the historical, stewardship aspects of external reporting. The distinguishing feature of management (internal) accounting—of accounting for planning and control—is its emphasis on the first and second purposes. Internal accounting is concerned with the accumulation, classification, and interpretation of information that assists individual executives to fulfill organizational objectives as revealed explicitly or implicitly by top management.

Types of Information Supplied by Accounting

What information should the management accountant supply? The types of information needed have been neatly described in a study of seven large companies with geographically dispersed operations, made by H. A. Simon and his associates. Their approach would probably prove fruitful to any company:

> By observation of the actual decision-making process, specific types of data needs were identified at particular organizational levels—the vice-presidential level, the level of the factory manager, and the level of the factory head [foreman], for example—each involving quite distinct problems of communication for the accounting department.[1]

The Simon research team found that three types of information, each serving a different purpose, often at various management levels, raise and help to answer three basic questions:

1. **Scorecard questions:** Am I doing well or badly?

2. **Attention-directing questions:** What problems should I look into?

3. **Problem-solving questions:** Of the several ways of doing the job, which is the best?

The scorecard and attention-directing uses of data are closely related. The same data may serve a scorecard function for a foreman and an attention-directing function for his[2] superior. For example, many accounting systems provide performance reports in which actual results are compared with previously determined budgets or standards. Such a performance report often helps to answer scorecard questions and attention-

---

[1] H. A. Simon, *Administrative Behavior,* 2nd ed. (New York: The Macmillan Company), p. 20.

[2] "He" and "his" are used throughout this book rather than "he or she" or "his or hers" or "person." This is done for *convenience,* not as a gesture of male chauvinism.

directing questions simultaneously. Furthermore, the actual results collected serve not only control purposes but also the traditional needs of financial accounting, which is chiefly concerned with the answering of scorecard questions. This collection, classification, and reporting of data is the task that dominates day-to-day accounting.

Problem-solving data may be used in long-range planning and in making special, nonrecurring decisions, such as whether to make or buy parts, replace equipment, add or drop a product, etc. These decisions often require expert advice from specialists such as industrial engineers, budgetary accountants, statisticians, and others.

In sum, the accountant's task of supplying information has three facets:

1. *Scorekeeping*. The accumulation of data. This aspect of accounting enables both internal and external parties to evaluate organizational performance and position.

2. *Attention directing*. The reporting and interpreting of information that helps managers to focus on operating problems, imperfections, inefficiencies, and opportunities. This aspect of accounting helps managers to concern themselves with important aspects of operations promptly enough for effective action either through perceptive planning or through astute day-to-day supervision. Attention directing is commonly associated with current planning and control and with the analysis and investigation of recurring, routine internal-accounting reports.

3. *Problem solving*. This aspect of accounting involves the concise quantification of the relative merits of possible courses of action, often with recommendations as to the best procedure. Problem solving is commonly associated with nonrecurring decisions, situations that require special accounting analyses or reports.

The above distinctions sometimes overlap or merge. Consequently, it is often difficult to pinpoint a particular accounting task as being scorekeeping, attention directing, or problem solving. Nevertheless, attempts to make these distinctions provide insight into the objectives and tasks of both accountants and managers.

Management Accounting and the
Overall Information System

These three uses of data may be related to the broad purposes of the accounting system. The business information system of the future is likely to be a single, multiple-purpose system with a highly selective reporting scheme. It will be tightly integrated and will serve three main purposes: (1) routine reporting to management, primarily for planning and controlling current operations (scorekeeping and attention directing); (2) special reporting to management, primarily for strategic planning (problem solving); and (3) routine reporting on financial results, primarily for external parties (scorekeeping). Although such a system can probably be designed in a self-contained, integrated manner to serve routine purposes simultaneously, its function of providing information about special problems will always entail preparing much data that will not lie within the system.

THE MANAGEMENT PROCESS

Nature of Planning and Controlling

The manager needs to have an overall perspective, a perception of the goals of the organization as a whole and of the goals of his own department within that organization. He needs a plan for attaining these objectives. He needs to execute the plan and to follow it up with an appraisal of how well actual performance conformed to his plan. Then he can formulate new plans based on his experience and on contemplated new conditions.

The nucleus of the management process is decision making, the purposeful choosing from among a set of alternative courses of action in light of some objective. These decisions range from the nonroutine (the

EXHIBIT 1-1

Accounting Framework for Planning and Control

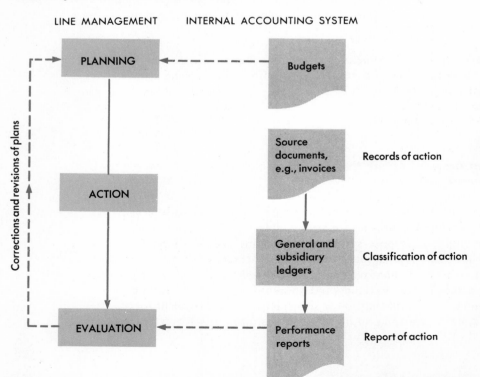

launching of a new product line) to the routine (whether to answer the correspondence today or tomorrow).

Decision making underlies the commonly encountered two-fold division of the management process into (1) planning and (2) control. The left-hand side of Exhibit 1-1 clearly demonstrates the planning and control cycle of current operations. *Planning* (the top box) means the selecting of objectives and the means for their attainment. It provides the answers to two questions: What is desired? When and how is it to be accomplished? *Controlling* (the two boxes labeled "Action" and "Evaluation" immediately below) means implementation of plans and the use of feedback so that objectives are optimally obtained. Planning and controlling are so intertwined that it seems artificial to draw rigid lines of separation between them; yet at times we will find it useful to concentrate on one or the other phase of the planning-control cycle.

The right-hand side of Exhibit 1-1 shows that accounting formalizes plans by expressing them in the language of figures as **budgets.** Accounting formalizes control as **performance reports** (the last box), which compare results with plans and which spotlight exceptions (i.e., deviations or variances from plans). Exhibit 1-2 shows the form of a simple performance report.

EXHIBIT 1-2
Performance Report

	BUDGETED AMOUNTS	ACTUAL AMOUNTS	DEVIATIONS OR VARIANCES	EXPLANATION
Sales	xxx	xxx	xx	—
Various expenses	xxx	xxx	xx	—
Net income	xxx	xxx	xx	—

Such reports spur investigation of exceptions. Operations are then brought into conformity with the plans, or the plans are revised. This is an example of management by exception.

Management by exception means that the executive's attention and effort are concentrated on the significant deviations from expected results and that the information system highlights the areas most in need of investigation. Management should not ordinarily be concerned with results that conform closely to plans.

Well-conceived plans incorporate enough discretion or flexibility so that the manager may feel free to pursue any unforeseen opportunities. That is—and this is important—the definition of control does not mean that managers should blindly cling to a preexisting plan when unfolding events indicate the desirability of actions that were not authorized specifically in the original plan.

*Illustration of the Budget and the
Performance Report*

An assembly department constructs electric fans. The assembly of the parts and the installation of the electric motor are basically hand operations. Each fan is inspected before being transferred to the painting department. In light of the present sales forecast, a production schedule of 4,000 window fans and 6,000 table fans is planned for the coming month. Cost classifications are shown in Exhibit 1-3, the Assembly Department Budget.

EXHIBIT 1-3

Assembly Department Budget for the Month
Ending March 31, 19x1

Material (detailed by type: metal stampings, motors, etc.)	$ 38,000
Assembly labor (detailed by job classification, number of workers, etc.)	73,000
Other labor (foremen, inspectors)	12,000
Utilities, maintenance, etc.	7,500
Supplies (small tools, lubricants, etc.)	2,500
Total	$133,000

The operating plan (the department budget) for the coming month is prepared in conferences attended by the foreman, his supervisor, and an accountant. Each of the costs subject to the foreman's control is scrutinized. Its average amount for the past few months is often used as a guide, especially if past performance has been reasonably efficient. However, the budget is a **forecast** of costs. Each cost is projected in the light of trends, price changes, alterations in product mix, specifications, labor methods, and changes in production volume from month to month. The budget is then formulated, and it becomes the foreman's target for the month.

As actual factory costs are incurred during the month, the accounting department collects them and classifies them by departments. At the end of the month (or perhaps weekly, or even daily, for such key items as materials or assembly labor), the accounting department prepares an Assembly Department Performance Report (Exhibit 1-4). In practice, this report may be very detailed and contain explanations of variances from the budget.

The foreman and his superiors use this report to help appraise performance. The spotlight is cast on the variances—the deviations from the budget. It is through management's investigation of these variances that better ways of doing things are discovered. The budget is an aid to planning; the performance report is the tool that aids controlling. The accounting system thus helps to direct managerial attention to the excep-

EXHIBIT 1-4

Assembly Department Performance Report for the
Month Ending March 31, 19x1

	BUDGET	ACTUAL	VARIANCE
Material (detailed by type: metal stampings, motors, etc.)	$ 38,000	$ 39,000	$1,000U
Assembly labor (detailed by job classification, number of workers, etc.)	73,000	74,300	1,300U
Other labor (foremen, inspectors)	12,000	11,200	800F
Utilities, maintenance, etc.	7,500	7,400	100F
Supplies (small tools, lubricants, etc.)	2,500	2,600	100U
Total	$133,000	$134,500	$1,500U

U = Unfavorable
F = Favorable

tions. Exhibit 1-1 shows that accounting does *not* do the controlling. Controlling consists of action performed by the managers and their workmen and of the evaluation that follows action. Accounting assists the managerial control function by providing a prompt record of the action and by systematically pinpointing trouble spots. This management-by-exception approach frees managers from needless concern with those phases of operations that are functioning effectively.

ROLE OF THE ACCOUNTANT IN THE ORGANIZATION

Line and Staff Authority

Except for exerting line authority over his own department, the chief accounting executive generally fills a staff role in his company, as contrasted with the line roles of sales and production executives. Most companies have the production and sale of goods as their basic objectives. Line managers are *directly* responsible for attaining these objectives as efficiently as possible.

Staff elements of organizations arise when the scope of the line manager's responsibility and duties enlarges to such a degree that he needs specialized help to operate effectively. When a department's primary task is advice and service to other departments, it is a staff department. Staff authority is *indirectly* related to the major objectives of the organization.

The accounting function is usually a staff function. The accounting department has responsibility for providing line managers, and also other staff managers, with specialized service, including advice and help in budgeting, controlling, pricing, and the making of special decisions. The

9

EXHIBIT 1-5
Organization Chart of a Manufacturing Company

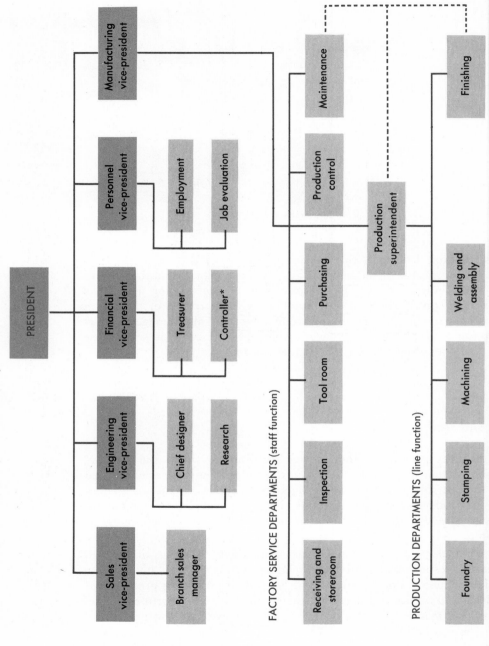

FACTORY SERVICE DEPARTMENTS (staff function)

PRODUCTION DEPARTMENTS (line function)

*For detailed organization of a controller's department, see Exhibit 1-6.

Dotted line represents staff authority.

EXHIBIT 1-6

Organization Chart of a Controller's Department

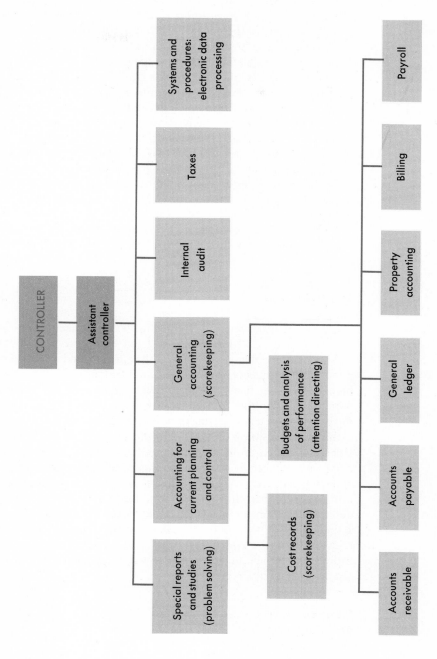

accounting department does not exercise direct authority over line departments: its authority to prescribe uniform accounting and reporting methods is delegated to the controller by top-line management. The uniform accounting procedure is authorized by the company president and is installed for him by the controller. When the controller prescribes the line department's role in supplying accounting information, he is not speaking as the controller, a staff man; he is speaking for top-line management.

Theoretically, the controller's decisions regarding the best accounting procedures to be followed by line people are transmitted to the president. In turn, the president communicates these procedures through a manual of instructions which comes down through the line chain of command to all people affected by the procedures. In practice, the daily work of the controller, and his face-to-face relationships with the production manager or foreman, may require him to direct how production records should be kept or how work tickets should be completed. The controller usually holds delegated authority from top line management over such matters.

Exhibit 1-5 shows the general organizational relationship described above. Exhibit 1-6 shows how a controller's department may be organized.

The Controller

The title of controller is applied to various accounting positions, the stature and duties of which vary from company to company. In some firms, the controller is little more than a glorified bookkeeper who compiles data, primarily for conventional balance sheets and income statements. In other firms (General Electric), he is a key executive who aids managerial planning and control in over 160 company subdivisions. In most firms, he has a status somewhere between these two extremes. For example, his opinion on the tax implications of certain management decisions may be carefully weighed, yet his opinion on other aspects of these decisions may not be sought. In this book, **controller** means the chief accounting executive. We have already seen that the modern controller does not do any controlling in terms of line authority, except over his own department. Yet the modern concept of controllership maintains that, in a special sense, the controller *does* control: by reporting and interpreting relevant data, the controller exerts a force or influence or projects an attitude that impels management toward logical decisions which are consistent with its objectives.

Distinctions between Controller and Treasurer

Many people confuse the offices of controller and treasurer. The Financial Executives Institute, an association of corporate treasurers and controllers, distinguishes their functions as follows:

Controllership	*Treasurership*
1. Planning for control	1. Provision of capital
2. Reporting and interpreting	2. Investor relations
3. Evaluating and consulting	3. Short-term financing
4. Tax administration	4. Banking and custody
5. Government reporting	5. Credits and collections
6. Protection of assets	6. Investments
7. Economic appraisal	7. Insurance

Note how management accounting is the controller's primary *means* of implementing the first three functions of controllership.

We shall not dwell at length on the treasurer's functions. As the seven points indicate, he is concerned mainly with financial, as distinguished from operating, problems. The exact division of various accounting and financial duties obviously varies from company to company.

The controller has been compared to the ship's navigator. The navigator, with the help of his specialized training, assists the captain. Without the navigator, the ship may flounder on reefs or miss its destination entirely, but the captain exerts his right to command. The navigator guides and informs the captain as to how well the ship is being steered. This navigator role is especially evident in points 1 through 3 of the seven functions.

TWO IMPORTANT PARTS OF MANAGEMENT ACCOUNTING

Decision Analysis and Implementation

Management accounting has been a growth industry over the past fifteen to twenty years. Courses and books that bear managerial or management accounting labels were rare indeed in the early 1950s. Now almost every business school teaches such accounting, and the techniques taught therein are becoming useful fixtures in organizations throughout the world. We shall study techniques like the contribution approach to allocating costs and evaluating performance, responsibility accounting, market-based transfer pricing, cost-volume-profit analysis, relevant cost analysis for special decisions, discounted cash flow analysis, flexible budgets, and standards.

A few of these topics, such as budgets and standards, were discussed in accounting courses long before 1950; however, in general, accounting for management planning and control did not receive nearly as much attention before 1950 as it has since.

Many of the analytical tools enumerated above largely represent applications of economic analysis. Management accounting has been concerned with spanning the gap between managerial economics and accounting. In a sense, management accounting in the 1950s was pragmatic managerial economics and little more.

The view of accounting as pragmatic managerial economics is too limiting; it provides an incomplete picture of the scope of management accounting. The results of economic analysis must be implemented in human organizations. Implementation is primarily a behavioral problem, not an economic problem. Thus, management accounting has two equally important parts: (a) decision analysis and choice, which often uses well-defined methods of choice known as **decision models;** and (b) implementation of the actions chosen in (a), which uses a variety of men and machines to assure that (a) is achieved.

Cost and Value of Information

Although decision analysis and implementation may be separated for analytical purposes, in practice they are interwoven so that managers often foresee behavioral implications and temper their choices beforehand to make them workable. The accountant and the manager must be concerned with both analysis and implementation as a unified whole. For example, a manager may wish to install an elaborate computerized inventory-control system at the retail level. There may be no doubt in his mind that with the help of this system he could make more profitable decisions regarding the timing, variety, and amounts of inventory purchases. Nevertheless, he may reject the system because its prospective value (benefits) is exceeded by the measurable and unmeasurable costs of implementation, including the costs of educating personnel and of operating a more elaborate system. Sometimes these costs are hard to pinpoint; for instance, the extra time taken by clerks for record keeping may exceed the patience of customers and result in the loss of some sales.

Managers and accountants must repeatedly make decisions about whether a change in an accounting system is worth undertaking. They must compare the expected cost and expected value of information to see whether the change is economically feasible (justifiable). Often, the "value" of the information is measured by the expected savings or extra income that might be generated by using an improved accounting system or a more elaborate decision model. But the cost of the information is usually measured in the implementation phase. Again, this illustrates why decision analysis and implementation must be considered simultaneously. Unless implementation is explicitly considered, the accountant and the manager will have an incomplete picture of the scope of the management process and its accompanying accounting-information system.

This weighing of the cost and value of information, which is often called *information economics,* provides a central framework for designing management-accounting systems. Managers and accountants should incessantly ask whether any suggested changes in a given system will generate net benefits. Note how the choice of what information should be supplied is a separate decision that, in turn, hinges on perceptions of how the information may affect a manager's decisions.

15

Perspective

SUMMARY

An understanding of the overall purposes of the accounting system provides perspective for the study of the usefulness of accounting to management. The accounting system of the future is likely to be a multiple-purpose system with a highly selective reporting scheme. It will be highly integrated and will serve three main purposes: (1) routine reporting to management, primarily for planning and controlling current operations (scorekeeping and attention directing); (2) special reporting to management, primarily for long-range planning and nonrecurring decisions (problem solving); and (3) routine reporting on financial results, oriented primarily for external parties (scorekeeping). The first two purposes are the distinguishing characteristics of internal accounting for planning and control.

Internal accounting is interwoven with management itself. Accounting is a service function. Internal accounting is not management as ordinarily conceived, but it helps management do a better job.

The chief of internal accounting is usually called the *controller*. His responsibilities usually encompass all phases of accounting, including income taxes and routine reporting to outside parties. But accounting techniques for planning and control are his main tools for helping managers to get things done. Besides being a combination scorekeeper, attention director, and problem solver, he must constantly exert an objective influence without seizing or accepting line authority. The human or organizational facets of his work often provide his most challenging and delicate tasks.

Management accounting encompasses both decision analysis and implementation. The behavioral impact of accounting techniques and systems deserves more attention than it has received in the past. The choice of an information system should be based on a weighing of the value of the information against its cost. The "value" of information largely depends on perceptions of its effects on managers' decisions.

SUMMARY PROBLEMS FOR YOUR REVIEW

(Try to solve these problems before examining the solutions that follow.)

Problem One

The scorekeeping, attention-directing, and problem-solving duties of the accountant have been described in this chapter and elsewhere in literature. The accountant's usefulness to management is said to be directly influenced by how good an attention director and problem solver he is.

Evaluate this contention by specifically relating the accountant's duties to the duties of operating management.

Problem Two

Using the organization charts in this chapter (Exhibits 1-5 and 1-6) answer the following questions:

1. Do the following have line or staff authority over the machining foreman: maintenance foreman, manufacturing vice-president, production superintendent, purchasing agent, storekeeper, personnel vice-president, president, chief budgetary accountant, chief internal auditor?

2. What is the general role of service departments in an organization? How are they distinguished from operating or producing departments?

3. Does the controller have line or staff authority over the cost accountants? The accounts receivable clerks?

4. What is probably the *major duty* (scorekeeping, attention directing, or problem solving) of the following:

Payroll clerk	Budgetary accountant
Accounts receivable clerk	Cost analyst
Cost record clerk	Head of special reports and studies
Head of general accounting	Head of accounting for planning and control
Head of taxes	Controller
Head of internal auditing	

Solution to Problem One

Operating managers may have to be good scorekeepers, but their major duties are to concentrate on the day-to-day problems that most need attention, to make longer-range plans, and to arrive at special decisions. Accordingly, because the manager is concerned mainly with attention directing and problem solving, he will obtain the most benefit from the alert internal accountant who is a useful attention director and problem solver.

Solution to Problem Two

1. The only executives having line authority over the machining foreman are the president, the manufacturing vice-president, and the production superintendent.

2. A typical company's major purpose is to produce and sell goods or services. Unless a department is directly concerned with producing or selling, it is called a service or staff department. Service departments exist only to help the production and sales departments with their major tasks: the efficient production and sale of goods or services.

3. The controller has line authority over all members of his own department, all those shown in the controller's organization chart (Exhibit 1-6).

4. The major duty of the first five—through the head of taxes—is typically scorekeeping. Attention directing is probably the major duty of the next three. Problem solving is probably the primary duty of the head of special reports and

studies. The head of accounting for planning and control and the controller should be concerned with all three duties: scorekeeping, attention directing, and problem solving. However, there is a perpetual danger that day-to-day pressures will emphasize scorekeeping. Therefore, accountants and managers should constantly see that attention directing and problem solving are also stressed. Otherwise, the major management benefits of an accounting system may be lost.

ASSIGNMENT MATERIAL

The assignment material for each chapter is divided into two groups: *fundamental* and *additional*. The first group consists of carefully designed, relatively straightforward material aimed at conveying the essential concepts and techniques of the particular chapter. These assignments provide a solid introduction to the major concepts of accounting for management control.

The first question in each chapter usually concerns terminology, an extremely important and often troublesome phase of the learning process. A fuzzy understanding of terms hampers the learning of concepts. Many instructors will not require written answers to the question on terminology; in this case, the reader should check his comprehension of new terms by consulting the Glossary at the end of the book.

The second group of assignment material in each chapter should not be regarded as inferior to the fundamental group. Many of these problems can be substituted for ones in the fundamental group.

Fundamental Assignment Material

1-1. Terminology. Define the following terms: *scorekeeping; attention directing; problem solving; management by exception; planning; controlling; performance report; budget; variance; line authority; staff authority; controller; comptroller; source document.*

1-2. Role of the accountant in the organization: line and staff functions.

1. Of the following, who have line authority over a cost record clerk: budgetary accountant; head of accounting for current planning and control; head of general accounting; controller; storekeeper; production superintendent; manufacturing vice-president; president; production control chief?

2. Of the following, who have line authority over an assembler: stamping foreman; assembly foreman; production superintendent; production control chief; storekeeper; manufacturing vice-president; engineering vice-president; president; controller; budgetary accountant; cost record clerk?

1-3. Scorekeeping, attention directing, and problem solving. For each of the following, identify the function the accountant is performing—i.e., scorekeeping, attention directing, or problem solving. *Also state* whether the departments mentioned are service or production departments.

1. Processing the weekly payroll for the maintenance department.

2. Explaining the welding foreman's performance report.

3. Analyzing the costs of several different ways to blend raw materials in the foundry.

4. Tallying sales, by branches, for the sales vice-president.

5. Analyzing, for the president, the impact on net income of a contemplated new product.

6. Interpreting why a branch did not meet its sales quota.

7. Interpreting variances on a machining foreman's performance report.

8. Preparing the budget for research and development.

9. Adjusting journal entries for depreciation on the personnel manager's office equipment.

10. Preparing a customer's monthly statement.

Additional Assignment Material

1-4. "The accounting system is intertwined with operating management. Business operations would be a hopeless tangle without the paperwork that is so often regarded with disdain." Do you agree? Explain, giving examples.

1-5. What are the three broad purposes of an accounting system?

1-6. "The emphases of financial accounting and management accounting differ." Explain.

1-7. Distinguish among scorekeeping, attention directing, and problem solving.

1-8. Give examples of special nonrecurring decisions and of long-range planning.

1-9. Briefly describe the probable business information system of the future.

1-10. "Planning is much more vital than control." Do you agree? Explain.

1-11. Distinguish among a source document, a subsidiary ledger, and a general ledger.

1-12. Distinguish among a budget, a performance report, and a variance.

1-13. "Management by exception means abdicating management responsibility for planning and control." Do you agree? Explain.

1-14. "Good accounting provides automatic control of operations." Do you agree? Explain.

1-15. Distinguish between line and staff authority.

1-16. "The controller does control in a special sense." Explain.

1-17. "The importance of accurate source documents cannot be overemphasized." Explain.

1-18. Organization chart. Draw an organization chart for a single-factory company with the following personnel. Which represent factory service departments? Producing departments?

Punch press foreman	Personnel vice-president
Vice-president and controller	Maintenance foreman
Storekeeper	Sales vice-president
Drill press foreman	Production control chief
Production superintendent	Production planning chief
Chairman of the board	Assembly foreman
Engineering vice-president	Purchasing agent
Manufacturing vice-president	Secretary and treasurer
President	

1-19. Scorekeeping, attention directing, and problem solving. Internal (management) accounting tends to emphasize the attention-directing and problem-solving functions of accounting. However, there are many companies that have accounting systems that are oriented almost exclusively to scorekeeping. For example, one critic has stated:

> Very few people in business have had the opportunity to reflect on the way in which the accounting model developed, particularly on how an instrument well adapted to detect fraud and measure tax liability has gradually been used as a general information source. Having become accustomed to information presented in this form, business people have adapted their concepts and patterns of thought and communication to it rather than adapting the information to the job or person. When one suggests the reverse process, as now seems not only logical but well within economic limits, he must expect a real reluctance to abandon a pattern of behavior that has a long history of working apparently quite well.[3]

Considering the introductory material in this chapter, comment on this quotation, particularly on the meaning and implications of the last quoted sentence for today's and tomorrow's controllers.

[3]William R. Fair, "The Next Step in Management Controls," in Donald G. Malcom and Alan J. Rowe, eds., *Management Control Systems* (New York: John Wiley & Sons, Inc.), pp. 229–30.

Basic Accounting: Concepts, Techniques and Conventions

2

The purpose of this chapter is to provide an overview of the accounting process for individuals with little or no background in accounting and for those who want to review some fundamental ideas. We shall become acquainted with some terminology and with what financial statements say and do not say. Knowing what financial statements do *not* communicate is just as important as knowing what they do communicate. We shall be mainly concerned with how to measure the managers' custodial or stewardship responsibilities for the assets entrusted to them. This is basically a scorekeeping task.

This chapter is divided into two major parts. Part One covers the fundamentals without employing some of the bookkeeping techniques (e.g., T-accounts) and language (e.g., debit and credit) that are commonplace in accounting. Part One should be thoroughly understood before studying Part Two, which pursues the ideas in Part One in more depth and which employs T-accounts and debits and credits.

PART ONE

First, let us consider the essence of profit-making activities and how the accountant portrays them. As we examine what the accountant does, we shall introduce the principles and conventions that he uses.

The Accounting Process

Managers, investors, and other interested groups usually want the answers to two important questions about an organization: How well did the organization perform for a given period of time? Where does the organization stand at a given point in time? The accountant answers these questions with two major financial statements—an income statement and a balance sheet. To obtain these statements, he continually records the history of an organization or entity. Through the financial accounting process, he accumulates, analyzes, quantifies, classifies, summarizes, and reports the seemingly countless events and their effects on the entity.

Economic Activity

Most organizations exist to serve a need for some type of goods or services. Whether they are profit seeking or not, they typically follow a similar, somewhat rhythmic, cycle of economic activity. Consider the following example. A retail business usually engages in some version of the following "operating cycle" in order to earn profits:

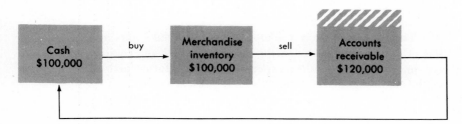

The Accounts Receivable (amounts owed to the business by customers) box is bigger than the other two boxes because the objective is to sell goods at a price higher than acquisition cost. Retailers and nearly all other businesses buy goods and services and perform acts (such as placing them in a convenient location or changing their form) that merit selling prices that hopefully will yield a profit. The total amount of profit earned during a particular period heavily depends on the size of the selling prices in relation to the costs of the goods and services (the markup) and on the speed of the operating cycle (turnover).

For example, Retailer No. 1, as illustrated above, may earn an operating income of $20,000 in, say, one month. His competitor, Retailer No. 2, may have lower prices, realizing in each cycle only $110,000 in sales instead of $120,000. But his lower prices attract three times as many customers in the same span of a month. He will earn $30,000 (sales of $330,000 minus the cost of merchandise sold, $300,000) because his lower prices have resulted in a turnover of merchandise three times faster than that of Retailer No. 1. This is the fundamental approach of the owner of the discount store. He trades off lower prices for quicker turnover with the hope that he will earn larger profits than the conventional retailer.

Financial Statements

The accountant records these acts and other events and measures their financial effects on the organization. Financial statements, which are summarized reports of these financial activities, can be produced at any instant and can apply to any span of time. Suppose that Retailer No. 1 began business as a corporation on March 1. An opening balance sheet (more accurately called **statement of financial position** or **statement of financial condition**) follows:

RETAILER NO. 1
Balance Sheet (Statement of Financial Position)
As of March 1, 19x1

Assets		*Equities*	
Cash	$100,000	Capital stock (issued as evidence of ownership)	$100,000

The balance sheet is a photograph of financial status at an instant of time. It has two counterbalancing sections—assets and equities. Assets are economic resources that are expected to benefit future activities. Equities are the claims against, or interests in, the assets.

The accountant conceives of the balance sheet as an equation:

$$\text{Assets} = \text{Equities}$$

The equities side of this fundamental equation is often divided as follows:

$$\text{Assets} = \text{Liabilities} + \text{Ownership Equity}$$

The liabilities are the economic obligations of the entity. The ownership equity is the excess of the assets over the liabilities. For a corporation, the ownership equity is called **stockholders' equity.** In turn, the stockholders' equity is composed of the ownership claim against or interest in the total assets arising from any paid-in investment (**capital stock**), plus the ownership claim arising as a result of profitable operations (**retained income or retained earnings**).

The following is a summary of the **transactions** that occurred in March. A transaction is any event that affects the financial position of the organization, and that requires recording:

1. Initial investment by owners, $100,000 cash.

2. Acquisition of inventory at a cost of $110,000 for $75,000 in cash plus an open account agreement with suppliers for the balance of $35,000. A purchase (or a sale) on open account is an agreement whereby the buyer pays cash sometime after the date of sale, often in thirty days. Amounts owed on open accounts are usually called **accounts payable.**

3. Merchandise carried in inventory at a cost of $100,000 were sold on open account for $120,000. These open customer accounts are called **accounts receivable.**

4. Collections of accounts receivable, $30,000.

5. Payments of accounts payable, $10,000.

6. On March 1, $3,000 cash was disbursed for store rent for March, April, and May. Rent is $1,000 per month, payable quarterly in advance, beginning March 1.

Note that these are indeed *summarized* transactions. For example, all the sales will not take place at once, nor will purchases of inventory, collections from customers, or disbursements to suppliers. A vast number of repetitive transactions occur in practice, and specialized data collection techniques are used to monitor their effects on the entity.

The above transactions can be analyzed using the balance sheet equation, as shown in Exhibit 2-1.

Transaction 1 has been explained previously. Note that capital stock represents the claim arising from the total initial investment in this illustration.[1]

Transaction 2, the purchase of inventory, is a step toward the ultimate goal—the earning of a profit. But stockholders' equity is not affected. That is, no profit is realized until a sale is made.

Transaction 3 is the sale of $100,000 of inventory for $120,000. Two things happen simultaneously: A new asset, Accounts Receivable, is acquired (3a) in exchange for the giving up of Inventory (3b).

Transaction 4, the collection, is an example of an event that has no impact on stockholders' equity. It is merely the transformation of one asset (Accounts Receivable) into another (Cash).

Transaction 5, the payment, also has no effect on stockholders' equity—it affects assets and liabilities only. In general, collections from customers and payments to suppliers of the *principal* amounts of debt have no direct impact on stockholders' equity. Of course, as will be seen in a subsequent section, *interest* on debt does affect stockholders' equity as items of revenue and expense.

Transaction 6, the rent disbursement, is made to acquire the right to

---

[1]Stock certificates usually bear some nominal "par or stated value" that is far below the actual cash invested. For example, the par or stated value of the certificates might be $10,000; if so, the ownership claim arising from the investment might be split between two ownership equity claims, one for $10,000 "capital stock, at par" and another for $90,000 "paid-in capital in excess of par value of capital stock."

EXHIBIT 2-1

RETAILER NO. 1

Analysis of Transactions for March, 19x1 (in dollars)

	ASSETS				=	LIABILITIES +	STOCKHOLDERS' EQUITY	
	CASH	+ ACCOUNTS RECEIVABLE	+ INVENTORY	+ PREPAID RENT	=	ACCOUNTS PAYABLE	CAPITAL STOCK	+ RETAINED INCOME
Transaction								
1.	+100,000				=		+100,000	
2.	−75,000		+110,000		=	+35,000		
3a.		+120,000			=			+120,000 (revenue)
3b.			−100,000		=			−100,000 (expense)
4.	+30,000	−30,000			=			
5.	−10,000				=	−10,000		
6a.	−3,000			+3,000	=			
6b.				−1,000	=			− 1,000 (expense)
Balance, March 31	+42,000	+90,000	+10,000	+2,000	=	+25,000	+100,000	+19,000

24

use store facilities for the next three months. At March 1, the $3,000 measures the future benefit from these services, so the asset Prepaid Rent is created (6a). At the end of March, one-third of these rental services have expired, so the asset is reduced and stockholders' equity is also reduced by $1,000 as rent expense (6b).

For simplicity, we have assumed no expenses other than cost of goods sold and rent. The accountant would ordinarily prepare at least two financial statements:

RETAILER NO. 1
Balance Sheet
As of March 31, 19x1

Cash	$ 42,000	Liabilities: Accounts payable		$ 25,000
Accounts receivable	90,000	Stockholders' equity:		
Inventory	10,000	Capital stock	$100,000	
Prepaid rent	2,000	Retained income	19,000	119,000
Total assets	$144,000	Total equities		$144,000

RETAILER NO. 1
Income Statement
For the Month Ending March 31, 19x1

Sales (revenue)		$120,000
Expenses:		
Cost of goods sold	$100,000	
Rent	1,000	
Total expenses		101,000
Net income		$ 19,000

Relationship of Balance Sheet and Income Statement

The income statement has measured the operating performance of the corporation by matching its accomplishments (revenue from customers, which usually is called *sales*) and its efforts (cost of goods sold and other expenses). The balance sheet shows the financial position at an instant of time, but the income statement measures performance for a span of time, whether it be a month, a quarter, or longer. The income statement is the major link between balance sheets:

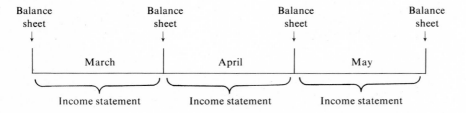

Examine the changes in stockholders' equity in Exhibit 2-1. The accountant records revenue and expense so that they represent increases (revenues) and decreases (expenses) in the ownership claims. At the end of a given period, these items are summarized in the form of an income statement.

In the above example, the outflows of assets are represented by decreases in the Inventory and Prepaid Rent accounts and corresponding decreases in stockholders' equity in the form of Cost of Goods Sold and Rent Expense. Expense accounts are basically negative stockholders' equity accounts. Similarly, the Sales (revenue) account, a stockholders' equity account, is increased because the inflow of Accounts Receivable (an asset) had a positive effect on stockholders' equity.

Accrual Basis and Cash Basis

The process of determining income and financial position is anchored to the **accrual basis** of accounting, as distinguished from the **cash basis.** In accrual accounting, the impact of events on assets and equities is recognized in the time periods when services are rendered or utilized instead of when cash is paid or received. For example, Transaction 3a in Exhibit 2-1 recognizes revenue when sales are made on credit. Similarly, Transactions 3b and 6b show that expenses are recognized as efforts are expended or services utilized to obtain the revenue (regardless of when cash is disbursed). Therefore, income is affected by measurements of noncash resources and obligations. The accrual basis is the principal conceptual framework for matching accomplishments (revenue) with efforts (expenses).

If the **cash basis** were used instead of the accrual basis, revenue and expense would depend on the timing of various cash receipts and disbursements. In our Retailer No. 1 example, the March income statement would contain the following:

Revenue (cash collected from customers)		$ 30,000
Expenses:		
Cash disbursed for merchandise ($75,000 in Transaction 2 plus $10,000 in Transaction 5)	$85,000	
Cash disbursement for rent	3,000	
Total expenses		88,000
Net loss		−$58,000

The March 31 balance sheet would have:

Cash	$42,000	Capital stock	$ 100,000
		Retained income	– 58,000
		Stockholders' equity	$ 42,000

The cash basis is used widely by individuals when they measure their income for personal income tax purposes. For this limited purpose, the cash basis often gives a good approximation of what might also be reported on the accrual basis. Long ago, however, accountants and managers found cash basis financial statements such as those above to be unsatisfactory as a measure of both performance and position. Now more than 95 percent of all business is conducted on a credit basis; cash receipts and disbursements are not the critical transactions as far as the recognition of revenue and expense is concerned. Thus, the accrual basis evolved in response to a need for a more accurate report of the financial impact of various events.

Adjusting Entries

To measure income under the accrual basis, certain **adjusting entries** must be made. An example of an adjusting entry is Transaction 6b in Exhibit 2-1. Earlier, we mentioned that a "transaction" is any economic event that should be recorded by the accountant. Note that this definition is not limited to market transactions, which are explicit exchanges between the entity and another party. Transactions also include internal conversions (such as raw materials into finished goods), losses of assets from fire or theft, and any other changes in assets and equities that occur because of the passage of time or some other event. The latter changes, such as the expiration of Prepaid Rent, are generally recognized formally in the accounts at periodic intervals—when the financial statements are about to be prepared—through the use of these adjusting entries.

The principal adjusting entries concern prepayments, accruals, deferrals, and depreciation (the periodic write-off of the original costs of long-lived physical assets such as equipment). All have an important common characteristic. They reflect implicit transactions, in contrast to the explicit transactions that trigger nearly all of the day-to-day routine entries.

To illustrate: Entries for sales, purchases, cash receipts, and cash disbursements are supported by explicit evidence. This evidence is usually in the form of source documents (for example, sales slips, purchase invoices, employee time records, cash receipts, or cash payments). On the other hand, adjusting entries for accrued interest, accrued wages, prepaid insurance, subscriptions collected in advance, depreciation, and the like are prepared from special schedules or memoranda that recognize events (like the passage of time) that are ignored in day-to-day recording procedures.

Adjusting entries refine the accountant's accuracy and provide a more meaningful measure of efforts, accomplishments, and financial position. They are an essential part of accrual accounting.

The Measurement of Expenses: Assets Expire

Transactions 3b and 6b demonstrate how assets may be viewed as bundles of economic services awaiting future use or expiration. It is helpful to think of assets, other than cash and receivables, as prepaid or stored costs (for example, inventories or plant assets) that are carried forward to future periods rather than immediately charged against revenue:

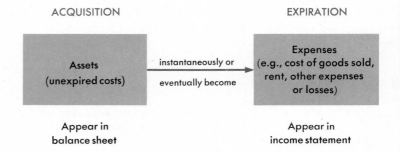

ACQUISITION   EXPIRATION

Assets (unexpired costs) — instantaneously or eventually become → Expenses (e.g., cost of goods sold, rent, other expenses or losses)

Appear in balance sheet   Appear in income statement

Expenses are used-up assets. Thus assets are unexpired costs held back from the expense stream and carried in the balance sheet to await expiration in future periods.

The analysis of the inventory and rent transactions in Exhibit 2-1 maintains this distinction of acquisition and expiration. The unexpired costs of inventory and prepaid rent are assets until they are used up and become expenses.

Sometimes services are acquired and utilized almost instantaneously. Examples are advertising services, interest services (the cost of money, which is a service), miscellaneous supplies, and sales salaries and commissions. Conceptually, these costs should, at least momentarily, be viewed as assets upon acquisition before being written off as expenses. For example, suppose there was a seventh transaction in Exhibit 2-1, whereby newspaper advertising was acquired for $1,000 cash. To abide by the acquisition-expiration sequence, the transaction would be analyzed in two phases:

Trans-action	Cash	+	Other assets	+	Unexpired advertising	=	Capital stock	+	Retained income
7a.	−1,000				+1,000	=			
7b.					−1,000	=			−1,000 (expense)

Assets = Liabilities + Stockholders' Equity

Frequently, services are acquired and used up so quickly that accountants do not bother opening an asset account such as Unexpired

Advertising or Prepaid Rent for them. Instead, a shortcut is taken:

Transaction	Cash	+ Other assets	= Liabilities	+ Capital stock	+ Retained income
7.	−1,000		=		−1,000 (expense)

Making the entry in two steps instead of one may seem cumbersome, and it is—from a practical bookkeeping viewpoint. But our purpose is not to learn how to be efficient bookkeepers. We want an orderly way of thinking about what the manager does. He acquires goods and services, not expenses *per se*. These goods and services become expenses as they are utilized in obtaining revenue.

Some of the most difficult issues in accounting center on when an unexpired cost expires to become an expense. For example, some accountants believe that research and development costs should be accounted for as unexpired costs (often found on balance sheets as "Deferred Research and Development Costs") and written off (amortized) in some systematic manner over a period of years. Other accountants believe that nearly all such costs have vague future benefits that are difficult to measure and thus favor writing them off as expenses immediately; in cases such as this, they would never be found on balance sheets.

Retained Income

Retained income, retained earnings, undistributed earnings, or reinvested earnings is the accumulated increase in stockholders' equity arising from profitable operations. As a company grows, this account can soar enormously if dividends are not paid. Retained income can easily be the largest stockholders' equity account.

Retained income is *not* a pot of cash that is awaiting distribution to stockholders. Consider the following illustration:

Step 1. Assume an opening balance sheet of:

Cash	$100	Capital stock	$100

Step 2. Purchase inventory for $50 cash. The balance sheet now reads:

Cash	$ 50	Capital stock	$100
Inventory	50		
	$100		

Step 3. Now sell the inventory for $80:

Cash	$130	Capital stock	$100
		Retained income	30
			$130

At this stage, the retained income might be reflected by a $30 increase in cash. But the $30 in retained income connotes only a general claim against total assets. This may be clarified by the transaction which follows.

Step 4. Purchase equipment and inventory, in the amounts of $40 and $50, respectively. Now:

Cash	$ 40	Capital stock	$100
Inventory	50	Retained income	30
Equipment	40		$130
	$130		

Where is the $30 in retained income reflected? Is it reflected in Cash, in Inventory, or in Equipment? The answer is indeterminate. This example helps to explain the nature of the Retained Income account. It is a *claim,* not a pot of gold. Retained income is increased by profitable operations, but the cash inflow from sales is an increment in assets (see Step 3). When the cash inflow takes place, management will use the cash, most often to buy more inventory or equipment (Step 4). Retained income is a *general* claim against or undivided interest in *total* assets, *not* a preferred claim against cash or against any other asset.

The term **earned surplus** is sometimes found in stockholders' equity sections. Fortunately, its use is fading fast. Earned surplus is an interchangeable term for retained income. The trouble with the term is that *surplus* is misleading. It connotes something superfluous or unessential or left over; therefore, consequent misunderstandings of the term might be expected. As the above example shows, earned surplus (retained income) is not an asset, nor does it represent an unnecessary ownership interest.

Dividends are distributions of assets which reduce ownership claims. The cash assets that are distributed typically arose from profitable operations. Thus, dividends or withdrawals are often spoken of as "distributions of profits" or "distributions of retained income." Dividends are often erroneously described as being "paid *out of* retained income." **In reality, cash dividends are distributions of assets and liquidate a portion of the ownership claim. The distribution is made possible by profitable operations.**

The amount of cash dividends declared by the board of directors of a company is dependent on many factors, the least important of which is the balance in Retained Income. Although profitable operations are generally essential, dividend policy is also influenced by the company's cash position and future needs for cash to pay debts or to purchase additional assets. It is also influenced by whether the company is committed to a stable dividend policy or to a policy that normally ties dividends to fluctuations in net income. Under a stable policy, dividends may be paid consistently even if a company encounters a few years of little or no net income.

"Principles" Is a Misnomer

The balance sheet and income statement[2] of publicly-held corporations and many other corporations are subject to an independent audit which forms the basis for a professional accounting firm's opinion that includes the following key phrasing:

> In our opinion, the accompanying financial statements present fairly the financial position of the *ABC* Company at December 31, 19x1, and the results of its operations for the year then ended, in conformity with generally accepted accounting principles applied on a basis consistent with that of the preceding year.

The auditor's opinion, usually appearing at the end of annual reports, is often mistakenly relied on as an infallible guarantee of financial truth. Somehow accounting is thought to be an exact science, perhaps because of the aura of precision that financial statements possess. But accounting is more art than science. The financial reports may appear accurate because of their neatly integrated numbers, but they are the results of a complex measurement process that rests on a huge bundle of assumptions and conventions called **accounting principles.**

What are these generally accepted accounting principles? This technical term covers much territory. It includes both broad concepts or guidelines and detailed practices. It includes all conventions, rules, and procedures that together make up accepted accounting practice at any given time.

Accounting principles become "generally accepted" by agreement. Such agreement is not influenced solely by formal logical analysis. Experience, custom, usage, and practical necessity contribute to the set of principles. Accordingly, it might be better to call them **conventions,** because **principles** connotes that they are the product of airtight logic.

During the 1960's and 1970's, generally accepted accounting principles have been most heavily influenced by the Accounting Principles Board (hereafter often referred to as the APB) and its successor body, the Financial Accounting Standards Board (FASB). These Boards have been financially supported by various professional accounting associations. In addition, these Boards have had the general backup of the Securities and Exchange Commission, which has had legal authority over most financial reporting to investors. In other words, the public body (the SEC) has informally delegated much rule-making power regarding accounting theory to the private bodies (the APB and FASB). These Boards

---

[2]Another key financial statement, the statement of changes in financial position, is discussed in Chapter 4.

have rendered a series of pronouncements on various accounting issues. Independent auditing firms, which prepare reports with respect to the fairness of corporate financial statements, are required to see that corporate statements do not depart from these pronouncements.

There are three broad measurement or valuation conventions (principles) that establish the basis for implementing accrual accounting: realization (when to recognize revenue), matching (when to recognize expense), and the stable dollar (what unit of measure to use).

Realization

The realization concept usually pertains to the recording of revenue from sales of products and services to customers. When is revenue realized—when the inventory is acquired, when the order is received, when the order is put into process, when it is finished, when it is delivered, or when the sales proceeds are collected? Generally, the accountant has maintained that revenue is realized when the goods or services are delivered, despite the fact that delivery is only one of a series of events related to the sale. He defends this entrenched practice by pointing out that, for most businesses, delivery is the occasion which validates a legal claim against the customer for goods or services rendered. He maintains that although the importance of purchasing, production, and distribution may differ from business to business, revenue is generally regarded as an indivisible totality. In this sense, revenue cannot be allocated in bits and pieces to individual business functions.

In sum, to be realized, revenue must meet the following two tests: First, the earning process must be virtually complete in that the goods or services must be fully rendered. Second, an exchange of resources evidenced by a market transaction must occur.

There are two major exceptions to the notion that an exchange (delivery, in most cases) is needed to justify the realization of revenue. First, long-run construction contracts often necessitate a percentage-of-completion method. For example, the builder of an ocean liner or a huge office building may portray his performance better by spreading prospective revenues, related costs, and resulting net income over the life of the contract in proportion to the work accomplished. Otherwise, all of the net income would appear in one chunk upon completion of the project, as if it were earned on a single day. Second, in exceptionally rare cases (such as in the retail sales of undeveloped lots), where receivables are collectible over an extended period of time and there is no reliable basis for estimating the degree of collectibility, revenue is regarded as being realized under such long-run installment contracts in proportion to the cash collections. In the first instance, revenue is realized earlier than under the general realization test; in the second instance, revenue is realized later.

Matching

The matching process has already been described. Many accountants claim that the principal concern of accounting is the periodic matching of accomplishments (as measured by the selling prices of goods and services rendered) with efforts (as measured by the cost of the goods and services rendered). Much of the accountant's work deals with the difficult measurement problems to be overcome in the evaluation of an organization's performance—the relationship between efforts and accomplishments—during a given period.

Stable Dollar

The monetary unit (the dollar in the United States and Canada) is the principal means for measuring assets and equities. It is the common denominator for quantifying the effects of a wide variety of transactions. Accountants record, classify, summarize, and report in terms of the dollar.

Such measurement assumes that the principal counter—the dollar—is an unchanging yardstick. Yet we all know that a 1975 dollar does not have the same purchasing power as a 1965 or 1955 dollar. Therefore, accounting statements that include different dollars must be interpreted and compared with full consciousness of the limitations of the basic measurement unit. (For an expanded discussion, see Chapter 5.)

Accountants have been extensively criticized for not making explicit and formal adjustments to remedy the defects of their measuring unit. In the face of this, they maintain that price-level adjustments would lessen objectivity and would add to general confusion. They claim that the price-level problem has been exaggerated, and that the adjustments would not significantly affect the vast bulk of corporate statements because most accounts are in current or nearly current dollars.

On the other hand, inflation has been steady and its effects are sometimes surprisingly pervasive. We can expect to see increasing experimentation with reporting that measures the effects of changes in the price level. The most troublesome aspect, however, is how to interpret the results after they are measured. Investors and managers are accustomed to the conventional statements. The intelligent interpretation of statements adjusted for changes in the price level will require extensive changes in the habits of users.

Additional Conventions

The foregoing conventions of measurement are only three of many conventions that heavily influence generally accepted accounting principles. We shall now consider **entity, going concern, consistency, objectivity, conservatism, disclosure, materiality, and economic feasibility.**

The Entity

The accounting process focuses upon events as they affect an *entity,* which is a specific area of accountability. This entity may be a single corporation, a tax district, a department, a paper-making machine, or a consolidated group of many interrelated corporations. The concept of an entity helps the accountant relate events to a sharply defined unit of activity. He separates *business* transactions from *personal* transactions. A purchase of groceries for inventory is an accounting transaction for a grocery store (the entity), but the owner's alimony payment by personal check is not.

Going Concern

Many accountants would regard this term as a fact of life rather than as a convention or assumption. To view an entity as a going concern is to assume that it will continue indefinitely or at least that it will not be liquidated in the near future. This notion implies that existing *resources,* such as plant assets, *will be used* to fulfill the general purposes of a continuing concern, *rather than sold* in tomorrow's real estate or equipment markets. It also implies that existing liabilities will be paid at maturity in an orderly manner.

Consistency

In reporting information, accountants are often free to select any one of a variety of procedures, all of which conform to "generally accepted accounting principles." There are, for example, various inventory cost-flow assumptions and various methods of allocating depreciation. Unless they are informed otherwise, users of financial statements assume that the particular procedures adopted by a given organization are consistent from year to year. If consistency could not be assumed, chaos would result. An organization could, for example, switch at whim from a first-in, first-out accounting of inventory to a last-in, first-out accounting, and back again.

Although consistency is desirable, it does not in itself constitute virtue. An accounting procedure can be consistently wrong. A company could, for example, consistently write off all acquisitions of plant assets as expenses in the year of purchase. What is desired is described as "generally accepted accounting principles applied on a basis consistent with that of the preceding year." Where such consistency is not maintained, adequate disclosure and explanation should be mandatory.

Objectivity or Verifiability

Users want assurance that the numbers in the financial statements are not fabricated by management or by accountants in order to mislead or to falsify the financial position and performance. Consequently, accountants seek and prize objectivity as one of their principal strengths and regard it as an essential characteristic of measurement. Objectivity results in accuracy that is supported by convincing evidence which can be verified by independent accountants. It is a relative rather than an absolute concept. Some measurements can be extremely objective (such as cash in a cash register) in the sense that the same measurement would be produced by each of a dozen CPAs. But there are gradations of objectivity. A dozen CPAs are less likely to arrive at the same balances for receivables, inventories, plant and equipment, and intangible assets, respectively. Yet they strive for measurement rules that will produce results which are subject to independent check. That is why accountants are generally satisfied with existing tests of realization; requiring an exchange to occur before revenue is realized helps assure verifiability.

Many critics of existing accounting practices want to trade objectivity (accuracy) for what they conceive as more relevant or valid information. For example, the accounting literature is peppered with suggestions that accounting should attempt to measure "economic income," even though objectivity may be lessened. This particular suggestion often involves introducing asset valuations at replacement costs, when these are higher than historical costs. The accounting profession has generally rejected these suggestions, even when reliable replacement price quotations are available, because no evidence short of a bona fide sale is regarded as sufficient to justify income recognition.

Conservatism

In a technical sense, conservatism means selecting that method of measurement which yields the gloomiest immediate results. This attitude is reflected in such working rules as: "Anticipate no gains, but provide for all possible losses," and "If in doubt, write it off."

Accountants regard the historical costs of acquiring an asset as the ceiling for its valuation. Assets may be written up only upon an exchange, but they may be written down without an exchange. For example, consider lower-of-cost-or-market procedures. Inventories are written down when replacement costs decline, but they are never written up when replacement costs increase.

Conservatism has been criticized as being inherently inconsistent. If replacement market prices are sufficiently objective and verifiable to justify write-downs, why aren't they just as valid for write-ups? Furthermore, the critics maintain, conservatism is not a fundamental concept. Accounting reports should try to present the most accurate picture possible—neither too high nor too low. Accountants defend their attitude by saying that erring in the direction of conservatism has less severe economic consequences than erring in the direction of overstating assets and net income.

Disclosure

Accountants are obliged to transmit all significant financial data, preferably in the body of the financial reports but also in explanatory footnotes. Especially since they may disagree about which particular inventory or depreciation method is best, accountants should disclose all the major facts so that the user can make his own adjustments and comparisons. The need for ample disclosure is paramount. There is no rule against providing supplementary information on price-level adjustments, depreciation methods, or market values. A working rule should be: "When in doubt, disclose." Disclosure is perhaps one of the most important of the underlying conventions.

Materiality

Because accounting is a practical art, the practitioner often tempers accounting reports by applying the convention of materiality. Many outlays that theoretically should be recorded as assets are immediately written off as expenses because of their lack of significance. For example, many corporations have a rule that immediately writes off all outlays under a specified minimum of, say, $100 to expense, regardless of the useful life of the asset acquired. In such a case, coat hangers may be acquired which may last indefinitely but which may never appear in the balance sheet as assets. The resulting $100 understatement of assets and stockholders' equity would be too trivial to worry about.

When is an item material? There probably will never be a universal clear-cut answer. What is trivial to General Motors may be material to Joe's Tavern. An item is material if its omission or misstatement would tend to mislead the user of the financial statements under consideration. A working rule is that an item is material if its proper accounting will affect the decision of a knowledgeable user. The continued emphasis in the stock market on earnings per share has lowered this threshold to 3 percent or lower in some cases. For example, if reporting earnings per share would drop from $1.00 to $.97, the item in question is material. In sum, materiality is an important convention. But it is difficult to use anything other than prudent judgment to tell whether an item is material.

Economic Feasibility

Accounting systems vary in complexity from the minimum crude records kept to satisfy governmental authorities to the sophisticated budgeting and feedback schemes that are at the heart of management planning and controlling. As a system is changed, its potential benefits usually must exceed its additional costs. Often the benefits are difficult to measure, but this cost-benefit criterion at least implicitly underlies the decisions about the design of accounting systems. The reluctance to adopt suggestions for new ways of measuring financial position and performance is frequently because of inertia, but it is often because the apparent benefits do not exceed the obvious costs of gathering and interpreting the information.

PART TWO

The previous sections offered some insight into the overall approach of the accountant to the measuring of economic activity. But we now take a more careful look to obtain a better understanding as Part Two focuses on the accounting process.

A CLOSER LOOK AT THE ACCOUNTING PROCESS

Illustration of Analysis and Measurement

Suppose that a corporation is formed to sell used cars. Its initial capital is cash of $20,000. The accountant could prepare a balance sheet after this initial event:

SINCERE COMPANY
Balance Sheet
March 1, 19x1

Assets		Equities	
Cash (in checking account)	$20,000	Capital stock	$20,000

During March, the corporation had a total of only three transactions: (1) the initial investment was $20,000; (2) three cars were acquired as inventory for $2,000 cash; and (3) seven more cars were acquired for $8,000 ($3,000 in cash plus $5,000 on open account to be paid in thirty days).

These transactions could be analyzed using the balance sheet equation, as was done in Exhibit 2-1. (You may wish to test your comprehension by using the equation approach of Exhibit 2-1.) However, as you can see, changes in the balance sheet equation may be made several times daily. In large businesses such as in a department store, hundreds of repetitive transactions occur hourly. An **account** is used to keep track of how the transactions affect the balance sheet equation. Our three previous transactions could be recorded in simple T-accounts as follows:

	Cash				Inventory	
Increases		Decreases		Increases		Decreases
(1) 20,000		(2) 2,000		(2) 2,000		
		(3) 3,000		(3) 8,000		
3/31 Bal. 15,000				3/31 Bal. 10,000		

	Accounts Payable				Capital Stock	
Decreases		Increases		Decreases		Increases
		(3) 5,000				(1) 20,000

Each account summarizes the changes in a particular asset or equity. A balance is computed by deducting the smaller amount from the bigger and placing the remainder on the side with the bigger amount.   These accounts can be kept in various forms, from fancy account paper with pen and ink to magnetic computer tape. Whatever their form, their objective is to keep an up-to-date summary of the changes in a specific asset or equity account.

The ending balances in the accounts provide the information needed for the balance sheet as of March 31:

SINCERE COMPANY
Balance Sheet
March 31, 19x1

Assets		Equities	
Cash	$15,000	Liabilities:	
		Accounts payable	$ 5,000
Inventory	10,000	Stockholders' equity:	
		Capital stock	20,000
Total assets	$25,000	Total equities	$25,000

Summarized Transactions for April

Consider a summary of transactions for April. If you do not wish to get immersed in the rudiments of bookkeeping, then concentrate solely on Exhibit 2-2, which uses the basic approach as in Exhibit 2-1. If you want a deeper understanding, also examine Exhibit 2-3, which uses T-accounts. This material requires careful step-by-step study to develop full understanding. First, look at the description of the transaction. Then examine its effect on the balance sheet equation (Exhibit 2-2).   Then examine the entry in the T-accounts (Exhibit 2-3).

These transactions are numbered as a follow-up to Transactions 1 through 3, which occurred in March.

EXHIBIT 2-2
Effects of Transactions on Balance Sheet Equation

DESCRIPTION OF CHANGES	ASSETS (A)	=	LIABILITIES (L) +	STOCKHOLDERS' EQUITY (SE)
4a. Sale	Cash +4,000 Accounts receivable +5,000	=		Sales (revenue) + 9,000
4b. Cost of goods sold	Inventory −6,000	=		Cost of goods sold (expense) −6,000
5a. Rental services acquired	Cash −2,000 Prepaid rent +2,000	= 0		
5b. Rental services expired	Prepaid rent −1,000	=		Rent expense −1,000
6a. Furniture and fixtures acquired	Cash −2,600 Furniture and fixtures +3,600	=	Note payable +1,000	
6b-1. Depreciation	Furniture and fixtures − 30	=		Depreciation expense − 30
6b-2. Interest services acquired	Unexpired interest + 5	=	Accrued interest payable +5	
6b-3. Interest services expired	Unexpired interest − 5	=		Interest expense − 5
7a. Advertising services acquired	Cash −300 Unexpired advertising + 300	= 0		
7b. Advertising services expired	Unexpired advertising − 300	=		Advertising expense − 300
8a-1. Salaries services acquired	Cash −900 Unexpired salaries and commissions + 900	= 0		
8b-1. Salaries services acquired	Unexpired salaries and commissions + 200	=	Accrued salaries and commissions payable +200	
8b-2. Salaries services expired	Unexpired salaries and commissions −1,100	=		Salaries and commission expense −1,100
9a. Rent collected in advance	Cash + 100	=	Deferred rent revenue +100	
9b. Rent earned	0	=	Deferred rent revenue − 50	Rent revenue + 50

EXHIBIT 2-3

Accounts of SINCERE COMPANY

ASSETS: INCREASES ON LEFT DECREASES ON RIGHT		EQUITIES: DECREASES ON LEFT INCREASES ON RIGHT			

CASH

3/31 Bal. 15,000	(5a)	2,000
(4a)	4,000	(6a)	2,600
(9a)	100	(7a)	300
		(8a-1)	900
4/30 Bal. 13,300		

ACCOUNTS PAYABLE

	3/31 Bal. 5,000

DEFERRED RENT REVENUE

(9b)	50	(9a)	100

ACCRUED SALARIES AND COMMISSIONS PAYABLE

	(8a-2)	200

NOTE PAYABLE

	(6a)	1,000

ACCRUED INTEREST PAYABLE

	(6b-2)	5

CAPITAL STOCK

	3/31 Bal. 20,000

RETAINED INCOME

	4/30 Bal.	615 *

ACCOUNTS RECEIVABLE

(4a)	5,000

EXPENSE AND REVENUE ACCOUNTS

INVENTORY

3/31 Bal. 10,000	(4b)	6,000

PREPAID RENT

(5a)	2,000	(5b)	1,000

FURNITURE AND FIXTURES

(6a)	3,600	(6b-1)	30

UNEXPIRED INTEREST

(6b-2)	5	(6b-3)	5

UNEXPIRED ADVERTISING

(7a)	300	(7b)	300

UNEXPIRED SALARIES AND COMMISSIONS

(8a-1)	900	(8b)	1,100
(8a-2)	200		

COST OF GOODS SOLD

(4b)	6,000

RENT EXPENSE

(5b)	1,000

DEPRECIATION EXPENSE

(6b-1)	30

INTEREST EXPENSE

(6b-3)	5

ADVERTISING EXPENSE

(7b)	300

SALARIES AND COMMISSIONS EXPENSE

(8b)	1,100

SALES

	(4a)	9,000

RENT REVENUE

	(9b)	50

*The details of the revenue and expense accounts appear in the income statement. Their net effect appears in Retained Income in the balance sheet.

Note: Ending balances should be drawn in each account, but they are not here because they can be computed mentally.

4. The Sincere Company sold six cars during April for $9,000 including $5,000 on open accounts receivable. These cars were carried in inventory at a cost of $6,000. The two phases of this summary transaction are 4a, the inflow of assets, which increased stockholders' equity by $9,000 (revenue); and 4b, the outflow of assets, which decreased stockholders' equity by $6,000 (expense). The latter method of accounting for inventory is called the **perpetual method,** whereby the inventory account is immediately reduced as sales are made.

5a. Effective April 1, the company rented a building on a quarter-to-quarter basis. Rent for April and May, totaling $2,000, was paid in cash on April 1. The payment is to acquire rental services. At April 1, the $2,000 measures the future benefit from those services and the asset Prepaid Rent is created.

5b. This benefit expires as time elapses. Therefore, at April 30, the accountant should recognize that the services of the asset have been utilized to the extent of $1,000, one month's rent. Entry 5b shows how the asset expires with a corresponding negative effect on stockholders' equity (rent expense).

6a. The company bought some furniture and fixtures on April 1 for $2,600 cash plus a three-month promissory note payable of $1,000 with interest payable at an annual rate of 6 percent. Note that the total outright cash outlay equivalent cost is the measure of the asset, not just the cash payment at the date of acquisition.

6b-1. The furniture and fixtures are expected to be useful for ten years. Part of the original cost should be allocated to each month's operations as depreciation expense. Because no scrap value is expected, the entire $3,600 cost is spread over ten years, or 120 months, at a rate of $3,600 ÷ 120, or $30 monthly.

6b-2. The company has had the service benefit of a $1,000 loan for one month. The creditor is now owed $\frac{1}{12} \times .06 \times \$1,000$, or $5, for these interest services. The amount is insignificant, but the idea is important. The acquisition of these services is recorded as an asset, Unexpired Interest, or Unexpired Interest Services, with a corresponding increase in a liability, Accrued Interest Payable.

6b-3. The interest services have expired because the company has had the benefit of a $1,000 loan for one month. Therefore, the asset is immediately written off and Interest Expense is recognized.

7a. Advertising services of $300 for the month are paid in cash. The acquisition is recognized by the asset Unexpired Advertising, or Unexpired Advertising Services.

7b. The benefits from the advertising have expired by the end of the month, so the asset is written off and Advertising Expense is recognized.

8a-1. Salaries and commissions services of $900 were paid in cash. The acquisition is recognized by the asset Unexpired Salaries and Commission Services.

8b-1. Additional salaries and commissions of $200 were unpaid at the end of April. The acquisition is recognized as in Transaction 8a-1, except that a liability is created for the unpaid amount.

8b-2. All the benefits of the services are deemed to have been received in April, so the asset is written off and Salaries and Commissions Expense is recognized.

9a. On April 15, the company subleased two of its offices for two months at $100 per month. The first month's rent was received in cash. Note that this is a payment in advance of services rendered. It is often called **deferred income;** a more accurate description is **unearned revenue** or **deferred revenue.** It is a liability, a claim by an outside party, until the service is rendered.

9b. As the service is rendered, revenue is recognized by decreasing the liability, Deferred Rent Revenue, and recognizing Rent Revenue (often called **Rent Income**) in the amount of $50, half of the rent received on April 15.

Financial Statements

Exhibit 2-4 is a so-called single-step form of income statement for the month of April. An alternative multiple-step presentation (Exhibit 2-5) draws a subtotal, the **gross profit** (or **gross margin**), which is the excess of sales over the cost of the inventory that was sold. This figure is often of interest to managers and others because its size can be an indication of how the pricing markup over cost is being maintained through time and in comparison with competitors.

The balance sheet as of April 30 is shown in Exhibit 2-6.

EXHIBIT 2-4
SINCERE COMPANY
Single-Step Income Statement for the
Month Ending April 30, 19x1

Revenue:		
Sales	$9,000	
Rent revenue	50	$9,050
Expenses:		
Cost of goods sold	$6,000	
Depreciation	30	
Rent expense	1,000	
Advertising	300	
Salaries and commissions	1,100	
Interest expense	5	8,435
Net income (before income taxes)		$ 615

The Analytical Power of the Balance Sheet Equation

As you study Exhibits 2-2 and 2-3, the following points should become clearer about how accountants use the fundamental balance sheet equation as their framework for analyzing and reporting the effects of transactions.

1. $$\text{Assets}\,(A) = \text{Liabilities}\,(L) + \text{Stockholders' equity}\,(SE) \qquad (1)$$

SE equals original ownership claim plus the increase in ownership claim due to profitable operations. That is, SE equals the claim arising from paid-in capital plus the claim arising from retained income.

EXHIBIT 2-5
SINCERE COMPANY
Multiple-Step Income Statement for the
Month Ending April 30, 19x1

Sales		$9,000
Cost of goods sold		6,000
Gross profit		$3,000
Operating expenses:		
Depreciation	$ 30	
Rent expense	1,000	
Advertising	300	
Salaries and commissions	1,100	2,430
Net operating profit		$ 570
Other revenue (and expenses):		
Rent revenue	$ 50	
Interest expense	(5)	45
Net income (before income taxes)		$ 615

EXHIBIT 2-6
SINCERE COMPANY
Balance Sheet
April 30, 19x1

ASSETS		EQUITIES		
Cash	$13,300	Liabilities:		
Accounts receivable	5,000	Accounts payable		$ 5,000
Inventory	4,000	Notes payable		1,000
Prepaid rent	1,000	Accrued interest payable		5
Furniture and fixtures	3,570	Accrued salaries and		
		commissions payable		200
		Deferred rent revenue		50
		Total liabilities		$ 6,255
		Stockholders' equity:		
		Capital stock	$20,000	
		Retained income	615	
		Total stockholders' equity		20,615
Total assets	$26,870	Total equities		$26,870

Therefore, $A = L +$ Capital stock $+$ Retained income   (2)

But, ignoring dividends for the moment, Retained income equals Revenue minus Expenses.

Therefore, $A = L +$ Capital stock $+$ Revenue $-$ Expenses   (3)

The accountant often talks about his entries in a technical way:

Transposing, $A +$ Expenses $= L +$ Capital stock $+$ Revenue   (4)

Finally,   Left $=$ Right   (5)
                                Debit $=$ Credit

   2. *Debit* **means one thing and one thing only—"left" (not "bad," "something coming," etc.).** *Credit* **means one thing and one thing only—"right" (not "good," "something owed," etc.). The word** *charge* **is often used instead of** *debit*.

For example, if you asked an accountant what entry to make for Transaction 6a, his answer would be: "I would debit (or charge) Furniture and Fixtures for $3,600; and I would credit Cash for $2,600 and credit Notes Payable for $1,000." Note that the total debits (entries on the left side of the account(s) affected) will **always** equal the total credits (entries on the right side of the account(s) affected) because the whole accounting system is based on an equation. The symmetry and power of this analytical debit-credit technique is indeed impressive.

   3. *Revenue* and *expense accounts* are nothing more than subdivisions of stockholders' equity—temporary stockholders' equity accounts, as it were. Their purpose is to summarize the volume of sales and the various expenses, so that management is kept informed of the reasons for the constant increases and decreases in stockholders' equity in the course of ordinary operations. In this way comparisons can be made, standards or goals can be set, and control can be better exercised.

   4. Assets are traditionally carried as left-hand balances. Why do assets and expenses both carry debit balances? They carry left-hand balances for different reasons. *Expenses* **are temporary stockholders' equity accounts. Decreases in stockholders' equity are entered on the left side of the accounts because they offset the normal (i.e., right-hand) stockholders' equity balances. Because expenses decrease stockholders' equity, they are carried as left-hand balances.**

SUMMARY

There is an underlying structure of concepts, techniques, and conventions that provides a basis for accounting practice. The major ideas that guide accountants in their recording, classifying, and reporting are *entity, going concern, realization, matching, stable dollar, consistency, objectivity, con-*

servatism, disclosure, materiality, and last but not least, *economic feasibility.*

Accountants have precise meanings for their terms. Among the more important terms are *revenue, assets, expired costs, expense, income, accrual basis,* and *retained income.*

The word *value,* used alone, is vague; it should be used cautiously and always with a descriptive modifier, such as in the term *replacement value.* Accountants measure assets in terms of their historical cost. Therefore, it is more precise to refer to the *costs* of plant, equipment, and inventories rather than to their *values.*

SUMMARY PROBLEMS FOR YOUR REVIEW

The first two problems are based on Part One of the chapter; the third problem is based on Part Two.

Problem One

The Retailer No. 1 transactions for March were analyzed early in this chapter. The balance sheet showed the following balances as of March 31, 19x1:

Cash	$ 42,000	
Accounts receivable	90,000	
Inventory	10,000	
Prepaid rent	2,000	
Accounts payable		$ 25,000
Capital stock		100,000
Retained income		19,000
	$144,000	$144,000

The following is a summary of the transactions that occurred during April:

1. Collections of accounts receivable, $88,000.
2. Payments of accounts payable, $24,000.
3. Acquisitions of inventory on open account, $80,000.
4. Merchandise carried in inventory at a cost of $70,000 were sold on open account for $85,000.
5. Adjustment for recognition of rent expense for April.
6. Wages (which were ignored for simplicity in March) earned and paid in cash in April were $6,000. The acquisition of these employee services was recognized by the asset Unexpired Wages Services.
7. Additional wages of $2,000 were unpaid at the end of April. The acquisition is recognized as in Transaction 6, except that a liability is created for the unpaid amount. (Note that unpaid wages are a type of outsider claim—that is, all employees, including officers, are creditors of a corporation in the amount of unpaid wages.)
8. All the benefits of the services acquired in Transactions 6 and 7 are deemed to have been received in April, so the asset is written off and Wages Expense is recognized.

9. Some customers paid $3,000 in advance for merchandise they ordered but that is not expected in inventory until mid-May. (What asset must rise? Does this transaction increase liabilities or stockholders' equity?)

10. Cash dividends declared and disbursed to stockholders on April 29 equalled $18,000. (What account besides cash is affected?)

Required:

1. Using the accrual basis of accounting, prepare an analysis of transactions, employing the equation approach demonstrated in Exhibit 2-1. To have plenty of room for new accounts, put your analysis sideways.

2. Prepare a balance sheet as of April 30, 19x1, and an income statement for the month of April. Also prepare a new report, the Statement of Retained Income, which should show the beginning balance, followed by a description of any major changes, and end with the balance as of April 30, 19x1.

3. Using the cash basis of accounting, prepare an income statement for April. Compare the net income with that computed in Requirement 2. Which net income figure do you prefer as a measure of the economic performance for April? Why?

Problem Two

The following interpretations and remarks are sometimes encountered with regard to financial statements. Do you agree or disagree? Explain fully.

1. "If I purchase 100 shares of the outstanding common stock of General Motors Corporation (or Sincere Company), I invest my money directly in that corporation. General Motors must record that transaction."

2. "Sales shows the cash coming in from customers and the various expenses show the cash going out for goods and services. The difference is net income."

3. "Why can't that big steel company pay higher wages and dividends too? It can use its hundreds of millions of dollars of retained income to do so."

4. "The total stockholders' equity measures the amount that the shareholders would get today if the corporation were liquidated."

5. "Conservatism is desirable because investors will be misled if the financial report is too rosy."

Problem Three

The balance sheet in Exhibit 2-6 (page 43) shows the following balances as of April 30, 19x1:

Cash	$13,300	
Accounts receivable	5,000	
Inventory	4,000	
Prepaid rent	1,000	
Furniture and fixtures	3,570	
Accounts payable		$ 5,000
Notes payable		1,000
Accrued interest payable		5
Accrued salaries and commissions payable		200
Deferred rent revenue		50
Capital stock		20,000
Retained income		615
	$26,870	$26,870

The operations that were begun in March and April continued in May. The following is a summary of the transactions that occurred in May:

1. A dividend of $200 was declared and paid in cash.
2. Seven more cars were purchased for $8,000; $2,000 was paid in cash and the remainder was an open account on thirty-day terms.
3. Advertising services for May were $1,000 on open account.
4. Ten cars that cost $10,000 were sold for $14,000. A down payment was made. The balance, $10,800, of the sales proceeds was received in the form of notes receivable, principal due in full in one year, plus 10 percent interest. Assume that the notes were in effect for the full month of May and recognize accrued interest receivable.
5. Prepaid rent expired.
6. Depreciation was $30 for the month.
7. Accounts payable of $5,300 were paid in cash.
8. Accounts receivable of $4,800 were collected.
9. (a) Salaries and commissions of $500 were paid in cash on May 5, including the $200 unpaid as of April 30, 19x1. (b) On May 25, additional salaries and commissions of $400 were paid. (c) On May 31, the company owed $800 for additional salaries and commissions. (d) The total salaries and commissions expired during May was $1,500.
10. (a) On May 15, office rent of $100 was received. (b) On May 31, the rent revenue earned for May was recognized.

Required:

1. Using the accrual basis of accounting, prepare an analysis of transactions, employing the equation approach demonstrated in Exhibit 2-2. Place your analysis sideways. (Are there any adjustments not mentioned above?)
2. Make entries for May in T-accounts. Key your entries for handy reference.
3. Prepare an income statement, a balance sheet, and a reconciliation of retained income. The latter explains the changes in the retained income during a span of time.

Solution to Problem One

Part 1. See Exhibit 2-7.

Part 2. See Exhibits 2-8, 2-9, and 2-10. Note that deferred sales revenue is a liability because the retailer is obligated to refund the money if the goods on order are not delivered. Note, too, that cash dividends are not expenses like rent and wages. They are unrelated to the generation of sales or the conduct of operations. Cash dividends are distributions of assets that reduce an ownership claim, retained income, which arose because of profitable operations. Moreover, although the amount of a dividend often is some fraction of net income, dividends are not necessarily tied to current net income, as this illustration shows.

Part 3. See Exhibit 2-11. The net income is $61,000 on the cash basis, but only $6,000 on the accrual basis. Accountants prefer the accrual basis because it provides a more precise measurement of economic performance, a better matching of accomplishments with efforts. In particular, the timing of disbursements to reduce accounts payable obviously is not as closely related to sales in April as the cost of inventory that was sold.

EXHIBIT 2-7
RETAILER NO. 1
Analysis of Transactions (in dollars)
For April, 19x1

Transaction	CASH	+ ACCOUNTS RECEIVABLE	+ INVENTORY	+ PREPAID RENT	+ UNEXPIRED WAGES SERVICES	=	ACCOUNTS PAYABLE	+ ACCRUED WAGES PAYABLE	+ DEFERRED SALES REVENUE*	+ CAPITAL STOCK	+ RETAINED INCOME
Bal. 3/31/x1	+42,000	+90,000	+10,000	+2,000		=	+25,000			+100,000	+19,000
1.	+88,000	−88,000				=					
2.	−24,000					=	−24,000				
3.			+80,000			=	+80,000				
4a.		+85,000				=					+85,000 (revenue)
4b.			−70,000			=					−70,000 (expense)
5.				−1,000		=					− 1,000 (expense)
6.	− 6,000				+6,000	=					
7.					+2,000	=		+2,000			
8.					−8,000	=					− 8,000 (expense)
9.	+ 3,000					=			+ 3,000*		
10.	−18,000					=					−18,000 (dividend)
Bal. 4/30/x1	+85,000	+87,000	+20,000	+1,000	0	=	+81,000	+2,000	+3,000	+100,000	+ 7,000

*Some managers and accountants would call this account "Customer Deposits" or "Advances from Customers."

EXHIBIT 2-8
RETAILER NO. 1
Balance Sheet
As of April 30, 19x1

ASSETS		EQUITIES		
Cash	$ 85,000	Liabilities:		
Accounts receivable	87,000	Accounts payable	$ 81,000	
Inventory	20,000	Accrued wages		
Prepaid rent	1,000	payable	2,000	
		Deferred sales		
		revenue	3,000	$ 86,000
		Stockholders' equity:		
		Capital stock	$100,000	
		Retained income	7,000	107,000
Total assets	$193,000	Total equities		$193,000

EXHIBIT 2-9
RETAILER NO. 1
Income Statement (Multiple-Step)*
For the Month Ending April 30, 19x1

Sales		$85,000
Cost of goods sold		70,000
Gross profit		$15,000
Operating expenses:		
Rent	$1,000	
Wages	8,000	9,000
Net income		$ 6,000

*A "single-step" statement would not draw the gross profit figure, but would merely list all the expenses—including cost of goods sold—and deduct the total from sales.

EXHIBIT 2-10
RETAILER NO. 1
Statement of Retained Income
For the Month Ending April 30, 19x1

Balance, March 31, 19x1	$19,000
Net income for April	6,000
Total	$25,000
Cash dividends	18,000
Balance, April 30, 19x1	$ 7,000

EXHIBIT 2-11
RETAILER NO. 1
Income Statement (Cash Basis)
For the Month Ending April 30, 19x1

Sales (collections from customers, including advance payments)		$91,000
Expenses:		
Disbursements for merchandise	$24,000	
Wages	6,000	30,000
Net income		$61,000

Solution to Problem Two

1. Money is invested directly in a corporation only upon original issuance of the stock. For example, 100,000 shares of stock may be issued at $80 per share, bringing in $8,000,000 to the corporation. This is a transaction between the corporation and the stockholders. It affects the corporate financial position:

   Cash $8,000,000   Stockholders' equity $8,000,000

   In turn, 100 shares of that stock may be sold by an original stockholder (A) to another individual (B) for $130 per share. This is a private transaction; no funds come to the corporation. Of course, the corporation records the fact that 100 shares originally owned by A are now owned by B, but the corporate financial position is unchanged. Accounting focuses on the business entity; the private dealings of the owners have no direct effect on the financial position of the entity and hence are unrecorded except for detailed records of the owners' identities.

   In sum, B invests his money in the shares of the corporation when he buys them from A. However, individual dealings in shares already outstanding have no direct effect on the financial position of the corporation.

2. Cash receipts and disbursements are not the fundamental basis for recognizing revenue and expenses. Credit, not cash, lubricates the economy. Therefore, if services or goods have been rendered to a customer, a legal claim to cash in the form of a receivable is deemed sufficient justification for recognizing revenue; similarly, if services or goods have been used up, a legal obligation in the form of a payable is justification for recognizing expense.

   This approach to the measurement of net income is known as the accrual method. Revenue is recognized as it is earned by (a) goods or services rendered and (b) an exchange in a market transaction. Expenses or losses are recognized when goods or services are used up in the obtaining of revenue or when such goods or services cannot be justifiably carried forward as an asset because they have no potential future benefit. The expenses and losses are deducted from the revenue, and the result of this matching process is net income, the net increase in stockholders' equity from the conduct of operations.

Depreciation is probably the best example of an expense that does not entail a cash outlay at its time of recognition.

3. As the chapter indicated, retained income is not cash. It is a stockholders' equity account that represents the accumulated increase in ownership claims due to profitable operations. This claim or interest may be partially liquidated by the payment of cash dividends, but a growing concern will reinvest cash in sustaining the added investments in receivables, inventories, plant, equipment, and other assets so necessary for expansion. As a result, the ownership claims become "permanent" in the sense that, as a practical matter, they will never be liquidated as long as the company remains a going concern.

This linking of retained income and cash is only one example of fallacious interpretation. As a general rule, there is no direct relationship between the individual items on the two sides of the balance sheet.

4. Stockholders' equity is a difference, the excess of assets over liabilities. If the assets were carried at their liquidating value today, and the liabilities were carried at the exact amounts needed for their extinguishment, the remark would be true. But such valuations would be coincidental because assets are carried at historical cost expressed in an unchanging monetary unit. Intervening changes in markets and general price levels in inflationary times may mean that the assets are woefully understated. Investors may make a critical error if they think that balance sheets indicate current values.

5. Conservatism is an entrenched practice among accountants, and it is also favored by many managers and investors. However, it has some ramifications that should be remembered. Conservatism will result in fast write-offs of assets with consequent lower balance sheet values and lower net incomes. But later years may show higher net incomes because of the heavier write-offs in early years.

So being conservative has some long-run countereffects because, for any asset, early fast write-offs will lighten expenses in later years. This countervailing effect is especially noteworthy when a company is having trouble making any net income. In such cases, the tendency is to wipe the slate clean by massive write-offs which result in an enormous net loss for a particular year. Without such assets to burden future years, the prospects brighten for reporting future net profits rather than net losses.

Conservatism has another boomerang effect. The understatement of assets and net income may prompt anxious stockholders to sell their shares when they should hold them. A dreary picture may be every bit as misleading as a rosy one.

Solution to Problem Three

Part 1. See Exhibit 2-12.

Part 2. See Exhibit 2-13.

Part 3. See Exhibits 2-14, 2-15, and 2-16.

EXHIBIT 2-12
Effects of Transactions on Balance Sheet Equation

DESCRIPTION OF CHANGES	ASSETS (A)	=
1. Cash dividend	Cash − 200	=
2. Acquisition of inventory	Cash − 2,000 Inventory + 8,000	=
3a. Advertising services acquired	Unexpired advertising + 1,000	=
3b. Advertising services used up	Unexpired advertising − 1,000	=
4a. Revenue earned by sales	Cash + 3,200 Notes receivable + 10,800	=
4b. Cost of inventory given up	Inventory − 10,000	=
4c. Interest earned during May	Accrued interest receivable + 90	=
5. Rent expired	Prepaid rent − 1,000	=
6. May depreciation	Furniture and fixtures − 30	=
7. Payments on accounts payable	Cash − 5,300	=
8. Collections of accounts receivable	Cash + 4,800 Accounts receivable − 4,800	=
9a. Reduction of liability and acquisition of services	Cash − 500 Unexpired salaries and commissions + 300	=
9b. Acquisition of more services for cash	Cash − 400 Unexpired salaries and commissions + 400	=
9c. Acquisition of more services on credit	Unexpired salaries and commissions + 800	=
9d. Expiration of services	Unexpired salaries and commissions − 1,500	=
10a. Rent collected in advance	Cash + 100	=
10b. Rent revenue earned for May		=
11a. Interest services acquired	Unexpired interest + 5	=
11b. Interest services expired	Unexpired interest − 5	=

LIABILITIES (L)	+	STOCKHOLDERS' EQUITY (SE)
		Retained income — 200
Accounts payable +6,000		
Accounts payable +1,000		
		Advertising expense — 1,000
		Sales +14,000
		Cost of goods sold — 10,000
		Interest revenue + 90
		Rent expense — 1,000
		Depreciation expense — 30
Accounts payable — 5,300		
Accrued salaries and commissions payable — 200		
Accrued salaries and commissions payable +800		
		Salaries and commissions expense — 1,500
Deferred rent revenue +100		
Deferred rent revenue — 100		Rent revenue + 100
Accrued interest payable +5		
		Interest expense — 5

EXHIBIT 2-13

Accounts of SINCERE COMPANY

ASSETS: INCREASES ON LEFT DECREASES ON RIGHT	EQUITIES: DECREASES ON LEFT INCREASES ON RIGHT	

CASH

4/30 Bal. 13,300	(1)		200
(4a)	3,200	(2)	2,000
(8)	4,800	(7)	5,300
(10a)	100	(9a)	500
		(9b)	400
5/31 Bal. 13,000			

ACCOUNTS PAYABLE

(7)	5,300	4/30 Bal. 5,000	
		(2)	6,000
		(3a)	1,000
		5/31 Bal. 6,700	

NOTES PAYABLE

	4/30 Bal. 1,000

ACCRUED INTEREST PAYABLE

	4/30 Bal.	5
	(11a)	5

ACCOUNTS RECEIVABLE

4/30 Bal. 5,000	(8)	4,800

DEFERRED RENT REVENUE

(10b)	100	4/30 Bal.	50
		(10a)	100

CAPITAL STOCK

	4/30 Bal. 20,000

NOTES RECEIVABLE

(4a)	10,800

ACCRUED SALARIES AND COMMISSIONS PAYABLE

(9a)	200	4/30 Bal.	200
		(9c)	800

RETAINED INCOME

(1)	200	4/30 Bal.	615
		Net income	655
			*

ACCRUED INTEREST RECEIVABLE

(4c)	90

REVENUE AND EXPENSE ACCOUNTS

INVENTORY

4/30 Bal. 4,000	(4b)	10,000	
(2)	8,000		

COST OF GOODS SOLD

(4b)	10,000

SALES

	(4a)	14,000

PREPAID RENT

4/30 Bal. 1,000	(5)	1,000

RENT EXPENSE

(5)	1,000

RENT REVENUE

	(10b)	100

FURNITURE AND FIXTURES

4/30 Bal. 3,570	(6)	30

DEPRECIATION EXPENSE

(6)	30

INTEREST REVENUE

	(4c)	90

UNEXPIRED INTEREST

(11a)	5	(11b)	5

INTEREST EXPENSE

(11b)	5

*The details of the revenue and expense accounts appear in the income statement. Their net effect appears in Retained Income in the balance sheet.

UNEXPIRED ADVERTISING

(3a)	1,000	(3b)	1,000

ADVERTISING EXPENSE

(3b)	1,000

UNEXPIRED SALARIES AND COMMISSIONS

(9a)	300	(9d)	1,500
(9b)	400		
(9c)	800		

SALARIES AND COMMISSIONS EXPENSE

(9d)	1,500

Note: Ending balances should be drawn for each account, but they are not here because they can be computed mentally.

EXHIBIT 2-14

SINCERE COMPANY
Income Statement*
For the Month Ending May 31, 19x1

Sales		$14,000
Cost of goods sold		10,000
Gross profit		$ 4,000
Operating expenses:		
Depreciation	$ 30	
Rent Expense	1,000	
Advertising	1,000	
Salaries and commissions	1,500	3,530
Net operating profit		$ 470
Other revenue (and expense):		
Rent revenue	$ 100	
Interest revenue	90	
Interest expense	(5)	185
Net income (before income tax)		$ 655

*This is the multiple-step format. The single-step format, which is illustrated in Exhibit 2-4, would be acceptable.

EXHIBIT 2-15

SINCERE COMPANY
Reconciliation of Retained Income
For the Month Ending May 31, 19x1

Retained income, April 30, 19x1	$ 615
Net income for May	655
Total	$1,270
Dividends paid in cash	200
Retained income, May 31, 19x1	$1,070

EXHIBIT 2-16
SINCERE COMPANY
Balance Sheet
As of May 31, 19x1

ASSETS		EQUITIES		
Cash	$13,000	Liabilities:		
Accounts receivable	200	Accounts payable		$ 6,700
Notes receivable	10,800	Notes payable		1,000
Accrued interest		Accrued interest payable		10
receivable	90	Accrued salaries and		
Inventory	2,000	commissions payable		800
Furniture and fixtures	3,540	Deferred rent revenue		50
		Total liabilities		$ 8,560
		Stockholders' equity:		
		Capital stock	$20,000	
		Retained income	1,070	
		Total stockholders'		
		equity		21,070
Total assets	$29,630	Total equities		$29,630

ASSIGNMENT MATERIAL

The assignment material for this chapter is divided into the two parts that correspond to Parts One and Two in the chapter.

ASSIGNMENT MATERIAL FOR PART ONE

Fundamental Assignment Material

2-1. Analysis of transactions and preparation of financial statements. The Retailer No. 1 transactions for April were analyzed in Problem One of the Summary Problems for Your Review. The balance sheet as of April 30 is shown in Exhibit 2-8. The following is a summary of transactions that occurred during May:

1. Collections of accounts receivable, $80,000.
2. Acquisitions of inventory on open account, $90,000.
3. Payments of accounts payable, $84,000.
4. Merchandise carried in inventory at a cost of $78,000 was sold on open account for $97,000.
5. In addition to the Transaction 4, Retailer No. 1 delivered inventory that cost $2,000 to customers who had paid $3,000 in advance. This represented the complete fulfillment of these customer orders.
6. Adjustment for rent expense for May.
7. Paid $4,000 cash on May 31 for a fire and burglary insurance policy covering the next twelve months.

Before analyzing transactions 8 through 11, review entries 6 through 8 in Exhibit 2-7, page 48.

57

Basic Accounting

8. Wages of $3,000 were paid in cash on May 5, including the $2,000 unpaid as of April 30, 19x1.
9. During the rest of May, additional wages of $6,000 were paid.
10. On May 31, the company owed $3,000 for additional wages.
11. All the benefits of the employee services acquired during May are deemed to have expired in May, so the asset is written off and Wages Expense is recognized.
12. On May 31, Retailer No. 1 received $2,000 in advance as a year's rental payment from a costume jewelry vendor who will occupy some space within the store.
13. On May 31, cash dividends of $4,000 were declared and disbursed to stockholders.

Required:

1. Using the accrual basis of accounting, prepare an analysis of May transactions, employing the equation approach demonstrated in Exhibit 2-7. Place your analysis sideways. To save space, make all entries in thousands of dollars. Allow room for new accounts.
2. Prepare a balance sheet as of May 31, 19x1, and an income statement and a statement of retained income for May.
3. Using the cash basis of accounting, prepare an income statement for May. Compare the net income with that computed in Requirement 2. Which net income figure do you prefer as a measure of the economic performance for May? Why?
4. Examine the balance sheet. Based on the limited information available what advice would you, as a consultant, be inclined to give the manager? What additional information would you seek before giving your advice with more assurance?

Additional Assignment Material

2-2. Describe the usual "operating cycle" of a business.

2-3. Give five examples of accounting entities.

2-4. Define *going concern*.

2-5. What is the major criticism of the dollar as the principal accounting measure?

2-6. Define *consistency*.

2-7. What is a major exception to the idea that an exchange is needed to justify the realization of revenue?

2-8. What does the accountant mean by *objectivity?*

2-9. Define *conservatism*.

2-10. How important is disclosure in relation to other fundamental accounting concepts?

2-11. Criticize: "Assets are things of value owned by the entity."

2-12. Criticize: "Net income is the difference in the ownership capital amount balances at two points in time."

2-13. Distinguish between the accrual basis and the cash basis.

2-14. How do adjusting entries differ from routine entries?

2-15. Why is it better to refer to the *costs*, rather than *values*, of assets like plant or inventories?

2-16. Give at least two synonymous terms for each of the following: *balance sheet; income statement; assets.*

2-17. Give at least three other terms for *retained earnings.*

2-18. Criticize: "As a stockholder, I have a right to more dividends. You have millions stashed away in retained earnings. It's about time that you let the true owners get their hands on that pot of gold."

2-19. Criticize: "Dividends are distributions of profits."

2-20. Explain why advertising should be viewed as an asset upon acquisition.

2-21. What is the role of economic feasibility in the development of accounting principles?

2-22. If gross profit is 60 percent, express the relationship of cost of goods sold to gross profit in percentage terms.

2-23. Balance sheet effects. The Wells Fargo Bank showed the following items (among others) on its balance sheet at December 31, 19x1:

Cash	$ 947,000,000
Total deposits	$6,383,000,000

Required:
1. Suppose that you made a deposit of $1,000 in the Wells Fargo Bank. How would the bank's assets and equities be affected? How would your personal assets and equities be affected? Be specific.
2. Suppose that the bank makes a $1,000 loan to a local merchant. What would be the effects on the bank's assets and equities immediately after the loan is made? Be specific.
3. Suppose that you borrowed $10,000 from the Wells Fargo Bank on a personal loan. How would such a transaction affect your personal assets and equities?

2-24. Pinpointing the entity. Manuel Colón Lebron, a successful professional auto-racing driver, decided that fifteen years of competition was enough. So he quit racing, returned to his native Puerto Rico, and began an automobile repair shop, named Manuel Colón Lebron Auto Repairs Company. Colón (he was called Colón by his friends) was a skillful manager, but he lacked knowledge of accounting. At the end of his first year in business, he asked you to prepare financial statements for his company, and you collected the following data:

1. Colón did not conduct his business as a corporation. He had one checking account which he used to pay all bills, including $37,000 for personal and

family items. Total checks drawn for all purposes amounted to $220,000. The balance in the checking account at January 2, 19x5, his first day in business, was $100,000.

2. At December 31, 19x5, he owed $40,000 on a long-term mortgage on his home, which he had acquired with a $20,000 cash down payment on December 29, 19x5, $45,000 to various suppliers to his repair company, $2,000 to employees for accrued wages, and $1,000 to a local appliance dealer for a television set and refrigerator for his home.

3. Customers owed his company $16,000 on open accounts receivable. His brother also owed him $200 for a used television set and refrigerator that Colón had sold to him.

4. One of the checks was a $300 Christmas gift to his church.

5. Cash receipts from customers during 19x5 were $200,000.

6. He acquired $40,000 of equipment in early 19x5 on open account. However, all this equipment was fully paid for by the end of 19x5. You decide to write this equipment off over five years on a straight-line basis.

7. His repair building was rented on a month-to-month basis.

Required:

Prepare an income statement and an ending balance sheet for Colón's repair company. If you are unsure about how to account for some items, state your assumptions and account for them anyway.

2-25. Fundamental transaction analysis and preparation of statements. Joan Biner entered a new luncheon counter business in a large metropolitan hospital. She and some relatives invested $7,000 in a new checking account in the name of the business, which she incorporated on June 1, 19x4 as Biner Foods, Inc. Joan and her relatives owned all the capital stock. The following is a summary of the many individual transactions that occurred during the first month's operations:

1. Equipment and fixtures were immediately acquired in exchange for a $1,800 cash down payment plus a $3,000 note payable at the end of six months.

2. Food inventory was immediately purchased for $2,500 cash.

3. Additional food was purchased during the month for $2,400 cash and $4,100 on open account.

4. Sales, all for cash, were $15,000.

5. The cost of the food sold was $7,000.

6. The total rent for three months of $1,500 was paid in cash to the hospital at the start of the month.

7. Wages of Joan and other employees were paid in cash, $3,000.

8. Miscellaneous services of $2,500 were paid for in cash.

9. At the end of the month, employees were owed $600 for wages.

10. Interest is payable at maturity of the note payable at a rate of 12 percent per annum.

11. Depreciation on the equipment and fixtures is straight-line and based on zero-expected residual value. Their expected useful life is four years.

12. The expiration of rent was recognized for June.

13. As of June 30, creditors were owed $500 for miscellaneous services such as utilities, consulting, and so on. (Set up a liability account for miscellaneous payables.)

14. Interest, wages, and all miscellaneous services acquired were regarded as expenses in June.

15. Cash dividends of $400 were paid.

Required:

Ignore income taxes.

1. Using the accrual basis of accounting, prepare an analysis of transactions, employing the equation approach demonstrated in Exhibits 2-1 and 2-7. To have plenty of room for new accounts, put your analysis sideways.
2. Prepare a balance sheet, an income statement, and a statement of retained income.

2-26. Comparison of cash and accrual basis. Refer to Assignment 2-25. Suppose the cash basis of accounting were used instead of the accrual basis. Prepare an income statement, but assume that 20 percent of the sales was uncollected at the end of the month. Which income statement, accrual or cash basis, is more indicative of economic performance? Why?

2-27. Balance sheet equation; solving for unknowns. Compute the unknowns (X, Y, and Z) in each of the individual cases, Columns a through g.

Given	a	b	c	d	e	f	g
Assets at beginning of period		$10,000				Z	$ 8,200
Assets at end of period		11,000					9,600
Liabilities at beginning of period		6,000				$12,000	4,000
Liabilities at end of period		Y					6,000
Stockholders' equity at beginning of period	$5,000						X
Stockholders' equity at end of period	X	5,000				10,000	
Sales			$15,000		X	14,000	20,000
Inventory at beginning of period			6,000	$ 8,000		Y	
Inventory at end of period			7,000	6,000		7,000	
Purchases			10,000	10,000		6,000	
Gross profit			Y		2,000	6,000	
Cost of goods sold			X	X	4,500	X	Z
Other expenses			4,000			4,000	5,000
Net profit	3,000	X	Z				Y
Dividends	1,000					1,500	400
Additional investments						5,000	

2-28. Effects on balance sheet equation. Given below is a list of effects of accounting transactions on the basic accounting equation: assets equal liabilities plus stockholders' equity.

1. Increase in assets, increase in liabilities.
2. Increase in assets, decrease in liabilities.
3. Increase in assets, increase in stockholders' equity.
4. Increase in assets, decrease in assets.
5. Decrease in assets, decrease in liabilities.
6. Increase in liabilities, decrease in stockholders' equity.
7. Decrease in assets, increase in liabilities.
8. Decrease in liabilities, increase in stockholders' equity.
9. Decrease in assets, decrease in stockholders' equity.
10. None of these.

Which of the above relationships defines the accounting effect of each of the following?

1. The adjusting entry to record accrued salaries.
2. The adjusting entry to record accrued interest receivable.
3. The collection of interest previously accrued.
4. The settlement of an account payable by the issuance of a note payable.
5. The earning of income previously collected. A Deferred Income account was credited when collection was made.
6. The recognition of an expense which had been paid for previously. A "prepaid" account was debited upon payment.
7. The adjusting entry to recognize periodic depreciation.

2-29. Measuring income for tax and other purposes. The following are the summarized transactions of Dr. Cristina Faragher, a dentist, for 19x7, her first year in practice:

1. Acquired equipment and furniture for $50,000. Its expected useful life is five years. Straight-line depreciation will be used.
2. Fees collected, $80,000. These fees included $2,000 paid in advance by some patients on December 31, 19x7.
3. Rent is paid at the rate of $500 monthly, payable on the twenty-fifth of each month for the following month. Total disbursements during 19x7 for rent were $6,500.
4. Fees billed but uncollected, December 31, 19x7, $15,000.
5. Utilities expense paid in cash, $600. Additional utility bills unpaid at December 31, 19x7, $100.
6. Salaries expense of dental assistant and secretary, $16,000 paid in cash. In addition, $1,000 was earned but unpaid on December 31, 19x7.

Dr. Faragher may elect either the cash basis or accrual basis of measuring income for income tax purposes, provided that she uses it consistently in subsequent years. Under either alternative, the original cost of the equipment and furniture must be written off over its five-year useful life rather than being regarded as a lump-sum expense in the first year.

Required:

1. Prepare a comparative income statement on both the cash and accrual bases, using one column for each basis.
2. Which basis do you prefer as a measure of Dr. Faragher's performance? Why? What is the justification for the government allowing the use of the cash basis?

2-30. Timing of recognition of revenue. Massive Enterprises, a huge conglomerate company, has recently acquired the Galaxy Publishing Company.

The president of Massive, Martin Mass, is surprised that the Galaxy income statement assumes that an equal proportion of the revenue is earned with the publication of every issue of the company's magazines: "The critical event in the process of earning revenue in the magazine business is the cash sale of the subscription. Therefore, why can't most of the revenue be realized in the period of sale?"

Required:

Discuss the propriety of timing the recognition of revenue in relation to: (1) the cash sale of the subscription, (2) the publication of magazines every month, (3) both events—by recognizing a portion of the revenue with the cash sale of the magazine subscription and a portion of the revenue with the publication of the magazine every month.

2-31. Nature of research costs. Maria Gersteli, a distinguished scientist of international repute, had developed many successful drugs for a well-established pharmaceutical company. Having an entrepreneurial spirit, she persuaded the board of directors that she should resign her position as vice-president of research and launch a subsidiary company to produce and market some powerful new drugs for treating arthritis. However, she did not predict overnight success. Instead, she expected to gather a first-rate research team that might take three to five years to generate any marketable products. Furthermore, she admitted that the risks were so high that conceivably no commercial success might result. Nevertheless, she had little trouble obtaining an initial investment of $5 million. The Gersteli Pharmaceuticals Company was 80 percent owned by the parent and 20 percent by Maria.

Maria acquired a team of researchers and began operations. By the end of the first year of the life of the new subsidiary, $2 million had been expended on research activities, mostly for researchers' salaries, but also for related research costs.

No marketable products had been developed, but Maria and other top executives were extremely pleased about overall progress and were very optimistic about getting such products within the next three or four years.

Required:

How would you account for the $2 million? Would you write it off as an expense in Year 1? Carry it indefinitely? Write it off systematically over three years or some longer span? Why? Explain, giving particular attention to the idea of an asset as an unexpired cost.

2-32. Choosing the entity: an example from the petroleum industry. The entity may be a consolidated group of many interrelated corporations, a single corporation, a tax district, a department, or a machine. The concept of an entity helps the accountant relate events to a sharply defined unit of activity.

Drilling for oil is a highly risky operation. For example, in 1973, only 14.6

percent of the exploratory holes drilled were successful. The vast majority of petroleum companies write off to expense all drilling costs applicable to dry holes. The reason given is that such costs have no future benefit and that the current fiscal period should bear the charge for them.

A few companies carry such costs as an asset. The reason is that all nonproductive exploratory activities are unavoidable in the search for and development of oil and gas reserves. Therefore, such costs should be carried as assets and related to future production in order to match revenues and expenses. The supporters of this "full-costing" approach also point out that a manufacturing company with a history of spoilage or rejects will include these costs in the costs of the "good" products.

Tenneco, Inc., uses these full-costing methods. A footnote in its annual report reads:

"The Company and its subsidiaries capitalize all productive and nonproductive well drilling costs applicable to the exploration for and development of oil and gas reserves. Depreciation, depletion, and amortization of producing and undeveloped oil and gas properties is provided on a composite basis using the unit-of-production method.... A rate is determined for each production area by dividing the total unrecovered book cost of all producing and undeveloped oil and gas properties by the total quantity of remaining reserves."

Required:

Evaluate these arguments; attempt to use the accountant's notion of an entity in judging the issues. Which method do you favor? Why?

2-33. Effects of errors. Assume a going concern. Indicate the effect of each of the following situations on net income for the year ended December 31, 19x1. Choose one of three answers: The error described resulted in net income being understated (u), overstated (o), or no effect (n):

1. On December 4, some merchandise was acquired on open account. The bookkeeper debited Land and credited Accounts Payable. The merchandise was still on hand as of December 31.
2. A purchase of equipment on February 2 was erroneously debited to Accounts Payable. The credit was correctly made to Cash.

2-34. Accrual to cash basis. The Simon Athletic Club provided the following data from its comparative balance sheets:

| | December 31 | |
	19x5	19x6
Dues receivable	$25,000	$30,000
Deferred dues revenue	10,000	—

The income statement for 19x6, which was prepared on an accrual basis, showed dues revenue earned of $200,000.

Required:

How much cash was received in 19x6 for dues?

2-35. **Accrual basis of accounting.** Mary Stern runs a small consulting-engineering firm that specializes in designing and overseeing the installation of environmental-control systems. However, even though she is the president, she has had no formal training in management. She has been in business one year and has prepared the following income statement for her fiscal year ended June 30, 19x4:

STERN CONSULTING ENGINEERS, INC.
Income Statement
For the Year Ended June 30, 19x4

Fees collected in cash		$500,000
Expenses paid in cash except for depreciation:		
Rent	$ 12,500	
Utilities	10,000	
Wages	200,000	
President's salary	46,000	
Office supplies	14,000	
Travel	40,000	
Miscellaneous	80,000	
Depreciation	10,000	412,500
Operating income		$ 87,500

Stern realized that the entire $50,000 cost of the equipment acquired on July 1, 19x3 should not be an expense of one year. She predicted a useful life of five years and deducted $10,000 as depreciation for the first year.

Stern is thinking about future needs for her expanding business. For example, although she now uses rented space in an office building, she is considering buying a small building. She showed her income statement to a local banker, who reacted: "Mary, this statement may suffice for filing income tax forms, but the bank will not consider any long-term financing until it receives a balance sheet and income statement prepared on the accrual basis of accounting. Moreover, the statements must be subjected to an audit by an independent certified public accountant."

As a CPA, you are asked to audit her records and fulfill the bank's request.

The following data are gathered:

1. On July 1, 19x3, Mary Stern invested $25,000 cash, and two friends each invested $2,000 cash in the firm in return for capital stock.
2. Stern acquired $50,000 of equipment on July 1, 19x3. A down payment of $20,000 cash was made. A $30,000 two-year note bearing an annual interest rate of 15 percent was signed. Principal plus interest were both payable at maturity.
3. On June 30, 19x4, clients owed Stern $95,000 on open accounts.
4. Salaries are paid on the fifteenth of every month. As business expanded throughout the fiscal year, additional employees were added. The total payroll paid on June 15, 19x4, including the president's monthly salary of $4,000, was $40,000.
5. Rent was paid in advance on the fifteenth of every month. An initial payment of $1,500 covered July 1, 19x3–August 15, 19x4. Payments of $1,000 monthly were paid beginning August 15, 19x3.

6. Office supplies on hand on June 30, 19x4, were $5,000.
7. On April 1, 19x4, a local oil refinery gave Stern a retainer fee of $60,000 cash in exchange for twelve months of consulting services beginning at that date.

Required:

1. Using the accrual basis of accounting, prepare an income statement for the fiscal year. Submit supporting computations properly labeled.
2. Prepare a balance sheet, dated June 30, 19x4. Assume that the cash balance is $106,500.

2-36. Reconstruct the cash account in Assignment 2-35. Show a summary analysis of the cash flow in 2-35 that proves that the ending cash balance is indeed $106,500. Label your analysis fully.

2-37. The case of the president's wealth. From the *Chicago Tribune,* August 20, 1964:

> Accountants acting on President Johnson's orders today reported his family wealth totaled $3,484,098.
>
> The statement of capital, arrived at through conservative procedures of evaluation, contrasted with a recent estimate published by *Life* magazine, which put the total at 14 million dollars.
>
> The family fortune, which is held in trust while the Johnsons are in the White House, was set forth in terms of book values. The figures represent original cost rather than current market values on what the holdings would be worth if sold now.
>
> Announced by the White House press office, but turned over to reporters by a national accounting firm at their Washington branch office, the financial statement apparently was intended to still a flow of quasi-official and unofficial estimates of the Johnson fortune. . . .

Assets

Cash	$ 132,547
Bonds	398,540
Interest in Texas Broadcasting Corp.	2,543,838
Ranch properties and other real estate	525,791
Other assets, including insurance policies	82,054
Total assets	$3,682,770

Liabilities

Note payable on real estate holding, 5 percent due 1971	$ 150,000
Accounts payable, accrued interest, and income taxes	48,672
Total liabilities	$ 198,672
Capital	$3,484,098

The report apportions the capital among the family, with $378,081 credited to the President; $2,126,298 to his wife Claudia T., who uses the name Lady Bird; $490,141 to their daughter Lynda Bird; and $489,578 to their daughter Luci Baines.

The statement said the family holdings—under the names of the President, his wife, and his two daughters, Lynda Bird and Luci Baines—had increased from $737,730 on January 1, 1954, a year after Johnson became Democratic leader of the Senate, to $3,484,098 on July 31 this year, a gain of $2,746,368. . . .

A covering letter addressed to Johnson said the statement was made "in conformity with generally accepted accounting principles applied on a consistent basis."

By far the largest part of the fortune was listed as the Johnsons' interest in the Texas Broadcasting Corporation, carried on the books as worth $2,543,838.

The accountants stated that this valuation was arrived at on the basis of the cost of the stock when the Johnsons bought control of the debt-ridden radio station between 1943 and 1947, plus accumulated earnings ploughed back as equity, less 25 percent capital gains tax.

Editorial, *Chicago Tribune,* August 22, 1964:

An accounting firm acting on Mr. Johnson's instructions and employing what it termed "generally accepted auditing standards" has released a statement putting the current worth of the Lyndon Johnson family at a little less than $3\frac{1}{2}$ million dollars. . . .

Dean Burch, chairman of the Republican National Committee, has remarked that the method used to list the Johnson assets was comparable to placing the value of Manhattan Island at $24, the price at which it was purchased from the Indians. The Johnson accounting firm conceded that its report was "not intended to indicate the values that might be realized if the investment were sold."

In fact, it would be interesting to observe the response of the Johnson family if a syndicate of investors were to offer to take Texas Broadcasting off the family's hands at double the publicly reported worth of the operation. . . .

Evaluate the criticisms, making special reference to fundamental accounting concepts or "principles."

ASSIGNMENT MATERIAL FOR PART TWO

Fundamental Assignment Material

2-38. Using T-accounts. Refer to Assignment 2-1. Make entries for May in T-accounts. Key your entries and check to see that the ending balances agree with the financial statements.

Additional Assignment Material

2-39. Debits and credits. Determine for the following transactions whether the account *named in parentheses* is to be debited or credited.

1. Sold merchandise (Merchandise Inventory), $1,000.
2. Paid Johnson Associates $3,000 owed them (Accounts Payable).
3. Bought merchandise on account (Merchandise Inventory), $2,000.
4. Received cash from customers on accounts due (Accounts Receivable), $1,000.
5. Bought merchandise on open account (Accounts Payable), $5,000.
6. Borrowed money from a bank (Notes Payable), $10,000.

2-40. True or false. Use *T* or *F* to indicate whether each of the following statements is true or false.

1. Debit entries must always be recorded on the left.
2. Decreases in accounts must be shown on the debit side.
3. The bank balance is the best evidence of stockholders' equity.
4. Both increases in liabilities and decreases in assets should be entered on the right.
5. From a single balance sheet you can find stockholders' equity for a period of time but not for a specific day.
6. Money borrowed from the bank should be credited to Cash and debited to Notes Payable.
7. Purchase of inventory on account should be credited to Inventory and debited to Accounts Payable.
8. It is not possible to determine change in the condition of a business from a single balance sheet.
9. Decreases in liability accounts should be recorded on the right.
10. Increases in asset accounts must always be entered on the left.
11. Increases in stockholders' equity always should be entered as credits.
12. Equipment purchases for cash should be debited to Equipment and credited to Cash.
13. Asset credits should be on the right and liability credits on the left.
14. Payments on mortgages should be debited to Cash and credited to Mortgages Payable.
15. Retained Earnings should be accounted for as a current asset item.
16. Cash should be classified as a stockholders' equity item.
17. Machinery used in the business should be recorded as a fixed asset item.

2-41. Using T-accounts. Refer to Problem One of the Summary Problems for Your Review. Make entries in T-accounts and check to see that the ending balances agree with the financial statements in Exhibits 2-8, 2-9, and 2-10.

2-42. Analysis of transactions using T-accounts. Refer to Assignment 2-25. Prepare an analysis of all transactions using T-accounts. Check to see that the ending balances agree with the financial statement.

2-43. Entries in T-accounts and preparation of financial statements. The Sincere Company in Problem Three of Summary Problems for Your Review continues operations in June. The following is a summary of the transactions that occurred in June:

1. Rent of $2,000 for June and July was paid in cash.
2. A cash dividend of $500 was declared and paid.
3. Ten more cars were purchased for $11,000; $5,000 was paid in cash and the remainder was on open account on thirty-day terms.

4. Twelve cars that cost $11,500 were sold for $15,500. Of the sales proceeds, $12,000 was received in the form of notes receivable, due in full in one year plus 12 percent interest. Assume that the notes were in effect for the full month of June. Interest on the old notes continued to accrue.

5. Depreciation was $30 for the month.

6. Accounts payable of $6,300 were paid in cash.

7. Accounts receivable of $100 were collected.

8. Advertising services for June were $1,320 on open account.

9. (a) Salaries and commissions of $1,100 were paid in cash on June 4, including the $800 unpaid on May 31, 19x1. (b) On June 22, additional salaries and commissions of $600 were paid. (c) On June 30, the company owed $1,000 in salaries and commissions.

10. Office rent revenue earned during June was recognized.

11. Interest on the note payable continued to accrue.

12. On June 30, the three-month note payable was paid in full.

Required:

1. Using the accrual basis of accounting, prepare an analysis of transactions, employing the equation approach demonstrated in Exhibit 2-12. Place your analysis sideways. Many month-end adjustments are implied by these transactions, and they should be made.

2. Make entries for June in T-accounts. Key your entries.

3. Prepare an income statement, reconciliation of retained income, and balance sheet.

4. Compare May and June statements. What conclusions seem warranted? Explain in detail. This is more important than Requirements 1 and 2.

2-44. Fundamental transaction analysis and preparation of statements. Three women who were college classmates have decided to pool a variety of work experiences by opening a women's clothing store. The business has been incorporated as Sartorial Choice, Inc. The following transactions occurred during April:

1. On April 1, 19x1, each women invested $9,000 in cash in exchange for 1,000 shares of stock each.

2. The corporation quickly acquired $50,000 in inventory, half of which had to be paid for in cash. The other half was acquired on open accounts which were payable after thirty days.

3. A store was rented for $500 monthly. A lease was signed for one year on April 1. The first two months' rents were paid in advance. Other payments were to be made on the second of each month.

4. Advertising during April was purchased on open account for $3,000 from a newspaper owned by one of the stockholders. Additional advertising of $6,000 was acquired for cash.

5. Sales were $65,000. The average markup above the cost of the merchandise was two-thirds of cost. Eighty percent of the sales were on open account.

6. Wages and salaries paid in April amounted to $5,000. In addition, $6,000 was owed at April 30.

7. Miscellaneous services paid for in cash were $1,410.

8. On April 1, fixtures and equipment were purchased for $6,000 with a down payment of $1,000 plus a $5,000 note payable in one year. The annual interest

rate was 9.6 percent, payable when the note matures; recognize the interest effects for April. The estimated useful life of the fixed assets was ten years. Depreciation is taken on a straight-line basis.

9. Cash dividends of $300 were declared and disbursed to stockholders on April 29.

Required:

1. Using the accrual basis of accounting, prepare an analysis of transactions, employing the equation approach demonstrated in Exhibit 2-12. Place your analysis sideways.
2. Make entries for April in T-accounts. Key your entries for convenient reference.
3. Prepare a balance sheet and income statement. Also prepare a statement of retained income.
4. What advice would you give the owners based on the information compiled in the financial statements?

Understanding Corporate Annual Reports— Part One

3

Accounting has often been called the language of business. But it is a language with a special vocabulary aimed at conveying the financial story of organizations. To understand corporate annual reports, a reader must learn at least the fundamentals of the language. This chapter presents the basic meanings of the terms and relationships used in the financial statements found in annual reports.

Accounting is commonly misunderstood by laymen as being a precise discipline which produces exact measurements of a company's financial position and performance. As a result, many laymen regard accountants as little more than mechanical tabulators who grind out financial reports after processing an imposing amount of detail in accordance with stringent predetermined rules. Although accountants take methodical steps with masses of data, their rules of measurement allow much room for judgment. Managers and accountants who exercise this judgment have more influence on financial reporting than is commonly believed.

Exhibits 3-1, 3-2, and 3-3 are the principal financial statements that appear in annual reports. Their degree of complexity is representative of the typical report. This chapter will be the first of two that attempt to make such statements comprehensible.

Current Assets

Assets are usually grouped in the manner shown in Exhibit 3-1. The current assets are cash plus those assets which are reasonably expected to be

EXHIBIT 3-1
GOLIATH CORPORATION
Consolidated Balance Sheets
As of December 31
(In millions of dollars)

ASSETS	19x3	19x2	CHANGE	EQUITIES	19x3	19x2	CHANGE
Current Assets:				Current liabilities:			
Cash	$ 90	$ 56		Accounts payable	$100	$ 84	
Marketable securities at cost				Notes payable	10	—	
(which approximates market				Accrued expenses payable	32	22	
value)	—	28		Accrued income taxes			
Accounts receivable (less al-				payable	34	38	
lowance for doubtful ac-				Total current liabilities	176	144	32
counts of $2,000,000 and				Long-term liabilities:			
$2,100,000 at their respec-				First mortgage bonds, 5%			
tive dates)	91	95		interest, due Dec. 31, 19x6	25	25	
Inventories at average cost	120	130		Subordinated debentures,			
Total current assets	301	309	(8)	6% interest, due Dec. 31,			
Investments in unconsolidated				19x9	30	20	10
subsidiaries	63	55	8	Total long-term liabilities	55	45	
Property, plant, and equipment:				Deferred income*	12	9.3	2.7
Land at original cost	60	48	12	Outside stockholders' interest in			
Plant and				subsidiaries (minority			
equipment 19x3 19x2				interests)	6	5.7	0.3
Original				Total liabilities	249	204	
cost $192 $135			57	Stockholders' equity:			
Accumulated				Preferred stock, 100,000			
depre-				shares $30 par†	3	3	
ciation 126 112			(14)	Common stock, 1,000,000			
Net plant and equipment	66	23		shares, $1 par	1	1	
Total property, plant, and				Paid-in capital in excess of par	55	55	
equipment	126	71		Retained income	200	192	8
Other assets:				Total stockholders' equity	259	251	
Franchises and trademarks	15	16		Total equities	$508	$455	53
Deferred charges and pre-							
payments	3	4					
Total other assets	18	20	(2)				
Total assets	$508	$455	53				

*Advances from customers on long-term contracts. Other examples are collections for rent and subscriptions, which often are classified as current liabilities.

†Dividend rate is $5 per share; each share is convertible into two shares of common stock. The shares were originally sold for $100. The excess over par is included in "paid-in capital in excess of par." Liquidating value is $100 per share.

EXHIBIT 3-2

GOLIATH CORPORATION

Consolidated Income Statements

For the Year Ending December 31

(000's omitted)

	19x3	19x2
Net sales and other operating revenue	$500,000	$600,000
Cost of goods sold and operating expenses, exclusive of depreciation	468,750	554,550
Depreciation	14,000	11,000
Total operating expenses	482,750	565,550
Operating income before share of unconsolidated net income	17,250	34,450
Pro-rata share of unconsolidated subsidiary net income	8,000	10,000
Total income before interest expense and income taxes	25,250	44,450
Interest expense	2,450	2,450
Income before income taxes	22,800	42,000
Income taxes	12,000	21,900
Income before minority interests	10,800	20,100
Outside stockholders' interest (minority interests) in consolidated subsidiaries' net income	300	600
Net income to Goliath Corporation*	10,500	19,500
Preferred dividends	500	500
Net income to Goliath Corporation common stock	$ 10,000	$ 19,000
Earnings per share of common stock:		
On shares outstanding (1,000,000 shares)†	$10.00	$19.00
Assuming full dilution, reflecting conversion of all convertible securities (1,200,000 shares)	$ 8.75	$16.25

*This is the total figure in dollars that the accountant traditionally labels net income. It is reported accordingly in the financial press.

†This is the figure most widely quoted by the investment community.

converted to cash or sold or consumed during the normal operating cycle. They are the assets directly involved in the operating cycle, including cash; temporary investments in marketable securities; receivables of nearly all kinds, including installment accounts and notes receivable if they conform to normal industry practice and terms; inventories, and prepaid expenses.

Several operating cycles may occur during one year. But some businesses need more than one year to complete a single cycle. The distillery, tobacco, and lumber industries are examples. Inventories in such industries are nevertheless regarded as current assets. Similarly, installment accounts and notes receivable are typically classified as current assets even though they will not be fully collected within one year.

Some comments on specific kinds of current assets follow:

Cash consists of bank deposits plus money on hand.

Marketable securities is a misnomer, although the term is encountered frequently. Strictly speaking, marketable securities may be held for either a short-term purpose or a long-term purpose. A better term would be **temporary or short-term investments** (as distinguished from **long-term investments** in capital stock or bonds of other companies, which are not current assets). They represent an investment of excess cash not needed immediately. The idea is to get earnings on otherwise idle cash. The money is typically invested in highly liquid (which means quickly and easily convertible into cash), relatively stable securities such as short-term notes or government bonds. These securities are usually shown at cost or market price, whichever is lower. The market price is disclosed parenthetically if it is above cost, as Exhibit 3-1 demonstrates.

Accounts receivable is the total amount owed to the company by its customers. Because some accounts will ultimately be uncollectible, the total is reduced by an allowance or provision for doubtful accounts (possible bad debts). The difference represents the net amount that probably will be collected.

EXHIBIT 3-3
GOLIATH CORPORATION
Consolidated Statement of Retained Income
For the Year Ending December 31
(000's omitted)

	19x3	19x2
Balance beginning of year	$192,000	$176,000
Add: Net income to Goliath Corporation	10,500	19,500
Total	202,500	195,500
Deduct:		
Cash dividends on preferred stock		
(also shown in Exhibit 3-2)	500	500
Cash dividends on common stock	2,000	3,000
Total dividends	2,500	3,500
Balance, end of year	$200,000	$192,000

Inventories consist of merchandise, finished products of manufacturers, goods in the process of being manufactured, and raw materials.

These are frequently carried at cost or market (defined as replacement cost), whichever is lower. Cost of manufactured products normally is composed of raw material plus other costs of production (direct labor and manufacturing overhead).

Once the cost is defined, how should it be allocated between the goods sold (an expense) and goods still on hand (an asset)? This is easy to do if the products are readily identifiable, like used cars or expensive jewelry. But it is infeasible to have an elaborate identification system for goods that are purchased and sold in vast numbers and variety. Therefore, some version of average cost is often used.[1]

Investments

This classification is discussed in the final section of the chapter.

Property, Plant, and Equipment

Property, plant, and equipment are sometimes called **plant assets** or **fixed assets.** They are physical items that can be seen and touched and are also often called **tangible assets.** They represent future services to be used over a prolonged span of time. In general, their measure of usefulness at the time of acquisition is cost: the invoice amount, plus freight and installation, less cash discounts. The major difficulties of measurement center about the choice of a pattern of depreciation—that is, the allocation of the original cost to the particular periods or products that benefit from the utilization of the assets.

Accountants often stress that depreciation is a process of **allocation of the original cost** of acquisition; it is not a process of valuation in the layman's sense of the term. The ordinary balance sheet presentation does *not* show replacement cost, resale value, or the price changes since acquisition.

The amount of original cost to be allocated over the total useful life of the asset as depreciation is the difference between the total acquisition cost and the estimated scrap or disposal value. The depreciation allocation to each year may be made on the basis of time or service. The estimate of useful life, which is an important factor in determining the yearly allocation of depreciation, is influenced by estimates of physical wear and tear, technological change, and economic obsolescence.

Suppose that equipment with an estimated useful life of four years is acquired for $41,000. Its estimated scrap value is $1,000. Exhibit 3-4 shows how the asset would be displayed in the balance sheet if a straight-line method of depreciation were used. The annual depreciation expense that would appear on the income statement would be:

---

[1]First-in, first-out and last-in, first-out methods are discussed in Chapter 5.

Annual straight-line depreciation expense

$$= \frac{\text{Original cost} - \text{Estimated disposal value}}{\text{Years of useful life}}$$

$$= \frac{\$41,000 - \$1,000}{4} = \$10,000 \text{ per year}$$

An understanding of how the accountant reports plant assets and depreciation will highlight the limitations of financial statements. Professor William A. Paton, a leading scholar in accounting for more than fifty years, once compared accounting for fixed assets with a boy's acquisition of a jelly-filled doughnut (the original cost, $41,000). The boy is so eager to taste the jelly that he licks it and creates a hole in the center of the doughnut (the accumulated depreciation of $10,000 at the end of Year 1). He continues his attack on the doughnut, and the hole enlarges. The hole is the **accumulated depreciation.** The **net book value** of the asset diminishes as the hole gradually becomes larger throughout the useful life of the doughnut. At the end of the useful life, the book value consists of the original doughnut ($41,000) less its gaping hole ($40,000), leaving a crumbly $1,000.

If you remember that accumulated depreciation is like a hole in a doughnut, you will be less likely to fall into the trap of those who think that accumulated depreciation is a sum of cash being accumulated for the replacement of plant assets. Accumulated depreciation is not cash; if specific cash is being accumulated for the replacement of assets, such cash will be an asset specifically labeled as a **cash fund for replacement and expansion** or a **fund of marketable securities for replacement and expansion.** Such funds are rare because most companies can earn better returns by invest-

EXHIBIT 3-4
Straight-Line Depreciation*

	BALANCES AT END OF YEAR			
	1	2	3	4
Plant and equipment (at original acquisition cost)	$41,000	$41,000	$41,000	$41,000
Less: Accumulated depreciation (that portion of original cost which has already been charged to operations as expense)	10,000	20,000	30,000	40,000
Net book value (that portion of original cost which will be charged to future operations as expense)	$31,000	$21,000	$11,000	$ 1,000

*Other patterns of depreciation are discussed in Chapter 4.

ing any available cash in ordinary operations rather than in special funds. Companies will use or acquire cash for the replacement and expansion of plant assets as specific needs arise.

Other Assets

Intangible assets are a fuzzy class of long-lived assets that are not physical in nature. Examples are goodwill, franchises, patents, trademarks, and copyrights. Goodwill, which is discussed in more detail in Chapter 5, is defined as the excess of the cost of an acquired company over the sum of the market value of its identifiable net assets. For example, suppose Company *A* acquires Company *B* at a cost to *A* of $10,000,000 and can assign only $9,000,000 to various identifiable assets like receivables, plant, and patents; the remainder, $1,000,000, is goodwill. Identifiable intangible assets, like franchises and patents, may be acquired singly but goodwill cannot.

Intangible assets are accounted for like plant and equipment—that is, the acquisition costs are capitalized as assets and then written off over their estimated useful lives, which, because of obsolescence, are often much shorter than their legal lives. For instance, a patent might be written off over five or ten years rather than its seventeen-year legal life. This periodic write-off, called **amortization**, is similar to depreciation of plant and equipment.

Although many managers and accountants maintain that some franchises, trademarks, and goodwill have perpetual lives, the APB concluded otherwise. The Board ruled that the value of intangible assets eventually disappears. Therefore, the costs of all intangible assets must be amortized in a straight-line manner over the periods benefited. In no case should the useful lives exceed forty years.

Prepayments and deferred charges are frequently lumped together. They are usually unimportant in relation to other assets. Strictly speaking, short-term prepayments or advance payments to suppliers belong in the current asset category as prepaid expenses. Examples are short-term prepaid expenses like rent, operating supplies, and insurance which will be used up within the current operating cycle. They belong in current assets because if they were not present more cash would be needed to conduct current operations.

Deferred charges have long-term benefits. For example, research and development costs, large advertising campaigns to introduce new products, and factory relocation or assembly line rearrangement costs may be carried forward as assets and amortized over, say, a three- to five-year period.

Accountants tend to be extremely conservative about intangible assets (including deferred charges), and most intangibles are swiftly amortized. The contrast between the accounting for tangible and intangible long-lived assets raises some provocative and knotty theoretical issues. Accountants are sometimes overly concerned with physical objects or contractual rights, tending to overlook the underlying reality of future economic benefits.

This preoccupation with physical evidence often results in the expensing of outlays that should be treated as assets. Thus, expenditures for research, advertising, employee training, and the like are usually expensed, although it seems clear that in an economic sense such expenditures represent expected future benefit. The difficulty of measuring future benefits is the reason usually advanced for expensing these items.

Liabilities

Current liabilities are those that fall due within the coming year or within the normal operating cycle if longer than a year. **Accounts payable** are amounts owed to suppliers who extended credit for purchases on open account. These open account purchases from trade creditors are ordinarily supported by signatures on purchase orders or similar business documents. **Notes payable** are backed by formal promissory notes held by a bank or business creditors.

Accrued expenses payable are recognized for wages, salaries, interest, and similar items. The accountant tries to recognize expenses as they occur in relation to the operations of a given time period regardless of when they are paid for in cash. Federal **income taxes payable** is a special accrued expense of enough magnitude to warrant a separate classification.

Long-term liabilities are those that fall due beyond one year. Bonds payable are formal certificates of indebtedness that are accompanied by a promise to pay interest at a specified annual rate.

Mortgage bonds are supposed to provide some additional safety for the bondholders in case the company is unable to meet its regular obligations on the bonds. If such an undesirable event occurs, the bondholders will have a prior lien on a specific asset(s). This means that such an asset may be sold and the proceeds used to liquidate the obligations to the bondholders. If no such lien exists, the bondholders would have no special claims against the assets beyond the general claim against the *total* assets enjoyed by the general creditors such as trade creditors.

Subordinated debentures are like any long-term debt except that *subordinated* means such bondholders are junior to the other general creditors in exercising claims against assets, and *debenture* means a general claim against all unencumbered assets rather than a specific claim against particular assets.

The following example should clarify these ideas. Suppose a company is liquidated. **Liquidation** means converting assets to cash and terminating outside claims:

	Proceeds		*Owed*
Cash and other assets	$ 10,000	Accounts payable	$ 30,000
Building	100,000	First mortgage bonds payable	90,000
	$110,000	Subordinated debentures payable	40,000
		Stockholders' equity	(50,000)
			$110,000

The mortgage bonds would be paid in full, the trade creditors would get paid two-thirds on the dollar ($20,000 for a $30,000 claim), and the other claimants would get nothing. If the debentures were **unsubordinated,** the $20,000 left over after paying $90,000 to the mortgage holders would be distributed as follows:

To trade creditors	$\frac{3}{7} \times \$20,000 =$	$ 8,571
To debenture holders	$\frac{4}{7} \times \$20,000 =$	11,429
Total cash distributed		$20,000

Deferred income (better called **unearned** or **deferred revenue**) is revenue collected in advance which has not been earned as yet. Rent and magazine subscriptions are examples. This kind of revenue will generate income only later as it is earned through delivery of goods or services. Deferred income or revenue is classified as either a current or long-term liability, depending on the length of the commitment.

Deferred income taxes, which arise because the timing of income tax payments is delayed beyond the current operating cycle, are not shown in Exhibit 3-1, but are commonly found in the annual reports of American companies. These deferrals are discussed in Chapter 5.

Stockholders' Equity

Stockholders' equity (also called **ownership equity** or **capital** or **net worth**) as an overall class is the total residual interest in the business. It is a difference, the excess of total assets over total liabilities. There may be many subclasses. It arises from two main sources: (1) contributed or paid-in capital and (2) retained income.

Paid-in capital typically comes from owners who invest in the business in exchange for stock certificates, which are issued as evidence of shareholder rights. It is often composed of a number of classes of capital stock with a variety of different attributes. **Preferred stock** typically has some priority over other shares regarding dividends or the distribution of assets upon liquidation. A **cumulative** preferred stock means that if a specified annual dividend of, say, $5 per share is not paid, this preferred claim accumulates and must be paid in full before any dividends are paid to any other classes of stock. Preferred shareholders do not ordinarily have voting privileges regarding the management of the corporation.

Stock frequently has a designated **par** or **legal** or **stated** value that is printed on the face of the certificate. For preferred stock (and bonds), par is a basis for computing the amount of dividends or interest. Many preferred stocks have $100 par values; therefore, a 5 percent, $100-par preferred stock would be entitled to a $5 annual dividend. Similarly, a 5 percent bond usually means that the investor is entitled to annual interest of $50 because most bonds have par values of $1,000. **Par value of common stock has no practical importance.** Historically, it was used for establishing the maximum legal liability of the stockholder in case the corporation could not pay its debts. Currently, it is set at a nominal amount (for example, $5) in relation to the market value of the stock upon issuance (for example, $80). It is generally illegal to sell an original issue of common stock below par. Common shareholders typically have **limited liability**, which means that creditors cannot resort to them as individuals if the corporation itself cannot pay its debts.

Common stock has no predetermined rate of dividends and is the last to obtain a share in the assets when the corporation is dissolved. Common shares usually have voting power in the management of the corporation. Common stock is usually the riskiest investment in a corporation, being unattractive in dire times but attractive in prosperous times because, unlike other stocks, there is no limit to the stockholder's potential participation in earnings.

Capital surplus or **paid-in surplus** (better called **paid-in capital in excess of par**) is the excess received over the par or stated or legal value of the shares issued. Common shares are often issued at a price substantially greater than par. The balance sheet effects of selling 100,000 shares of $5 par common at $80 per share would be:

Cash	$8,000,000	Common stock	$ 500,000
		Paid-in capital in excess of par	7,500,000
		Stockholders' equity	$8,000,000

Retained income is also called **retained earnings** or **reinvested earnings.** It is the increase in stockholders' equity due to profitable operations. It is explained more fully in Chapter 2. Retained income is the dominant item of stockholders' equity for most companies. For instance, as of January 27, 1973, J. C. Penney Company had a stockholders' equity of $1,138 million, of which $864 million was retained income.

Treasury stock is outstanding stock that has subsequently been repurchased by the company. Such repurchase is a liquidation of an ownership claim: It should appear on a balance sheet as a deduction from total stockholders' equity. For example, if treasury stock—common—costing $2 million were held at December 31, 19x3, in Exhibit 3-1, the stockholders' equity would appear as follows (in millions of dollars):

Preferred stock	$ 3
Common stock	1
Paid-in capital in excess of par	55
Retained income	200
Subtotal	$259
Deduct: Cost of common shares held in treasury	2
Stockholders' equity	$257

The stock is not retired; it is held temporarily in the treasury to be distributed later as a part of an employee stock purchase plan or as an executive bonus. Cash dividends are not paid on shares held in the treasury; cash dividends are distributed only to the shares outstanding, and treasury stock is not outstanding stock. Treasury stock is usually of minor significance.

Meaning of Stockholders' Equity Section: Stock Splits and Stock Dividends

Distinguishing among the par or stated value, capital surplus, and retained income has little practical importance. It is simpler to think of stockholders' equity as a lump sum.

Many companies occasionally split their stock. A stock split or split-up refers to the issuance of additional shares for no consideration and under conditions indicating that the objective is to increase the number of outstanding shares for the purpose of reducing their unit market price. This encourages wider distribution and a higher total price for the same ownership interest. Corporate management naturally wants the stock to be as attractive as possible because this will ease the task of raising additional investment capital when needed. For a given ownership interest, the higher the market price, the more capital can be raised for each additional share issued.

Stock split-ups can be achieved by issuing new shares for old shares or simply by issuing additional shares to conform to the size of the split. Suppose that Company *A* has the following stockholders' equity section:

	Before 2-for-1 Split	Changes	After 2-for-1 Split
Common stock, 100,000 shares @ $10 par	$1,000,000	200,000 shares @ $5 par	$1,000,000
Paid-in capital in excess of par	4,000,000		4,000,000
Retained income	6,000,000		6,000,000
Stockholders' equity	$11,000,000		$11,000,000
Overall market value of stock @ assumed $150	$15,000,000	@ assumed $80	$16,000,000

There is no effect on total stockholders' equity. A person who previously owned 1,000 shares (a 1 percent interest) now owns 2,000 shares (still a 1 percent interest). Professor Willard Graham explained a stock split as being akin to taking a gallon of whiskey and pouring it into five individual bottles. The resulting packaging will attract a price for each fifth that will produce a higher total value than if the gallon were not split (less the amount spilled when pouring into the five bottles— that's the legal, printing, and clerical costs). Therefore, Company *A* splits its stock with the hope that the market value of the total ownership interest will increase from $15,000,000 to $16,000,000 because one share that previously sold for $150 will now be in the form of two shares that might sell for $80, or a total of $160.

Stock dividends is a misnomer because such dividends are totally different from cash dividends. A stock dividend is a distribution of additional certificates of any class of the distributing company's stock. The most frequently encountered type of stock dividend is the distribution of additional common stock to existing holders of common stock already outstanding; usually anywhere from 1 to 10 percent of the number of common shares already outstanding are distributed.

In substance, stock dividends are not dividends at all, as the term is usually understood. The shareholders' proportionate interest in the corporation is unchanged, and the market value of each share tends to decline in response to the additional shares outstanding without any corresponding infusion of new capital. Again, an example may clarify. Suppose the market price of common stock is $80:

	Before 5% Stock Dividend	Changes	After 5% Stock Dividend
Common stock, 200,000 shares @ $5 par	$ 1,000,000	+ (10,000 shares @ $5 par)	$ 1,050,000
Paid-in capital in excess of par	4,000,000	+ [10,000 shares @ ($80 − $5)]	4,750,000
Retained income	6,000,000	− (10,000 @ $80)	5,200,000
Stockholders' equity	$11,000,000		$11,000,000
Fractional ownership interest of a stockholder	2,000 shares 1%	100 shares	2,100 shares Still 1%

First, note that the individual shareholder receives no assets from the corporation. Moreover, his fractional interest is unchanged; if he sells his dividend shares, his proportionate ownership interest in the company will decrease.

Second, the company records the transaction by transferring the market value of the additional shares from retained income to common stock and "paid-in capital in excess of par." This entry is often referred to as being a "capitalization of retained income." It is basically a signal to the shareholder that $800,000 of retained income will not be reduced via cash dividends.

Stock dividends are prime examples of have-your-cake-and-eat-it-too manipulations that in substance are meaningless but that seemingly leave all interested parties happy. The company pays a "dividend" but gives up no assets. The stockholder thinks he's getting a dividend even though to realize it in cash he must sell some of his fractional interest in the company.

The stock dividend device is particularly effective where a low percentage, such as 1 or 2 percent, of additional shares are issued which may have an imperceptible effect on the market price. The recipient, who is not particularly concerned about his fractional ownership interest anyway, may hold 100 shares @ $80 before the dividend and 101 shares @ $80 after the dividend. His reaction is likely to be favorable because he is $80 richer because of the dividend. Why? Because the peculiarities of the stock market somehow avoided the logical lowering of the market price per share, and not because the corporation gave him anything directly.

A stock split is often achieved via the use of the stock dividend device by issuing an enormous stock "dividend" of 50 or 100 percent or more. The use of such high-percentage stock dividends is merely another way of obtaining a stock split. Such a transaction should not really be called a stock dividend; it would be better to call it a "split-up effected in the form of a stock dividend." This requires a decrease in Retained Income and an increase in Common Stock in the amount of the par value (rather than the market value) of the additional shares. For example, if the two-for-one split described earlier were achieved through a 100 percent stock dividend, the total stockholders' equity would be unaffected. However, its composition would change:

Common stock, 200,000 shares @ $10 par	$ 2,000,000
Paid-in capital in excess of par	4,000,000
Retained income	5,000,000
Stockholders' equity	$11,000,000

Reserves and Funds

Accountants frequently use the term **reserve** in their reports. To a layman, reserve normally means setting aside a specific amount of cash or securities for a special purpose such as vacations, illness, Christmas gifts, and so on. The accountant *never* uses the word reserve to describe such an amount; instead he calls such assets a *fund*. For example, a **pension fund** is cash or other highly liquid assets segregated for meeting the pension obligations. Similarly, a **sinking fund** is usually cash or securities segregated for meeting obligations on bonded debt.

The word *reserve* is on the wane, but it is used frequently enough to warrant an acquaintance with its three broad meanings in accounting:

1. **Retained income reserve.** A restriction of dividend-paying power denoted by a specific subdivision of retained income. The term **appropriated** or

restricted is better terminology than reserve. Examples are reserves for contingencies (which can refer to any possible future losses from such miscellany as foreign devaluations of currency, lawsuits, natural disasters, and so on) and reserves for self-insurance (which refer to possible future losses from fires or other casualty losses). (This reserve is *not* a reduction of total retained income; it is merely an earmarking or subdividing of part of retained income.)

2. **Asset valuation.** An offset to an asset. Examples: reserves for depreciation, depletion, uncollectible accounts, reduction of inventory, or investments to market. "Allowance for . . ." is much better terminology.

3. **Liability.** An estimate of a definite liability of indefinite or uncertain amount. Examples: reserves for income taxes, warranties, pensions, and vacation pay. "Estimated liability for . . ." is much better terminology.

Note that asset valuation reserves and liability reserves are created by charges to expense (and, hence, reductions of stockholders' equity).

Alternate Form of Balance Sheet

The balance sheet in Exhibit 3-1 is sometimes presented in a different format. The most popular alternative is to deduct current liabilities from current assets. The difference is called **net working capital,** which measures the ownership equity (or net investment) in the current assets. The only change in Exhibit 3-1 would be that the current liabilities would appear on the left side as negative assets:

	As of December 31, 19x3
Current assets (detailed)	$301
Less current liabilities (detailed)	176
Net working capital	125
Investment in unconsolidated subsidiaries	63
Property, plant, and equipment (detailed)	126
Other assets (detailed)	18
Total assets, less current liabilities	$332

INCOME STATEMENT

Use of Subtotals

Income statements are much more important than balance sheets because most investors are vitally concerned about the company's ability to produce long-run earnings and dividends. The income statement is straightforward and, for the most part, is stated in terms of current dollars. Revenue is shown first; this represents the total sales value of products delivered and services rendered to customers. Expenses are then listed and deducted. Subtotals often highlight certain relationships. For example, sometimes cost of goods sold is deducted from sales to show a gross profit. This indicates the size of the markups above costs that the company was able to command. Federal taxes are frequently deducted as a separate item instead of being included with operating expenses.

Earnings per Share and Dilution

The earnings (net income) applicable to each share of common stock is perhaps the single most-quoted figure in an annual report, primarily because investors are so heavily interested in the effect of such earnings on the market price of the stock. At first glance, earnings per share is a deceptively simple idea. Merely divide net income by the number of common shares outstanding. However, where preferred stock exists, as in Exhibit 3-2, the preferred dividends must be deducted in order to compute the net income applicable to common stock. The computation of earnings per share usually stops at this point because most companies have relatively simple capital structures.

However, a lone earnings per share figure is inadequate when companies have complex capital structures. Until the 1960's, there was a sharp traditional distinction between common shares and senior securities (i.e., bonds and preferred stock). But the decade of the sixties was marked by the widespread popularity of convertible securities—bonds and stock that could be transformed into common shares at the option of the holder. Consider the following example, which has been incorporated in Exhibit 3-2:

	Outstanding
5% convertible preferred stock, $100 par, each share convertible into two common shares	100,000 shares
Common stock	1,000,000 shares
Computation of earnings per share:	
Net income	$10,500,000
Preferred dividends	500,000
Net income to common stock	$10,000,000
Earnings per share of common stock ($10,000,000 ÷ 1,000,000 shares)	$ 10.00
But if all shares were converted:	
Net income	$10,500,000
Preferred dividends	—
Net income to common stock	$10,500,000
Earnings per share of common stock— assuming full dilution ($10,500,000 ÷ 1,200,000 shares)	$ 8.75

Where there is potential material dilution of earnings per share, a supplementary, fully diluted earnings per share must be reported along with the regular earnings per share, shown at the bottom of the income statement with an additional footnote, as follows:

Earnings per common share (Note A)	$10.00
Earnings per common share assuming full dilution (Note B)	$ 8.75

Note A: Per share data are based on the average number of common shares outstanding during each year, after recognition of the dividend requirements on the 5% preferred stock.

Note B: Per share data based on the assumption that the outstanding preferred stock was converted into common shares at the beginning of the year, reflecting the 200,000 shares issuable on conversion and eliminating the preferred dividend requirements.

Extraordinary Items

Extraordinary transactions often produce a gain or loss that should be reported as a separate item because they are distinguished by their *unusual nature* and by the *infrequency of their occurrence.* In 1973, the APB concluded that an event or transaction should be presumed to be an ordinary and usual activity unless the evidence clearly supports its classification as an extraordinary item. Therefore, the classification of an item as extraordinary rather than as ordinary will be rarer than in the early 1970's. An example of an extraordinary event is an earthquake, as distinguished from ordinary events such as the sale or abandonment of plant or equipment or exchange gains or losses from fluctuations in foreign currencies held by multi-national companies.

Extraordinary gains or losses are shown net of income tax effects and are an integral part of the computation of net income for the year. For example, if there were an extraordinary loss from the expropriation of a segment of a business of, say, $4 million, which also resulted in savings of $2.1 million income taxes, the income statement in Exhibit 3-2 would be modified as shown in Exhibit 3-5.

The intelligent investor will interpret any net income figure in light of the future prospects of each of its determinants and with a view to company plans and obligations. The subdividing of earnings per share to isolate extraordinary effects, as Exhibit 3-5 illustrates, should help to alert the investor to the idea that earnings per share needs interpretation. The presence of four earnings per share figures in Exhibit 3-5 indicates the complexity of the accountant's task.

RECONCILIATION OF RETAINED INCOME

A reconciliation of retained income (Exhibit 3-3) summarizes the changes in stockholders' equity arising from net income and dividends. This statement is often incorporated as the bottom section in a combined income statement and reconciliation of retained income.

EXHIBIT 3-5
Recommended Format for Income Statement
Having Extraordinary Loss

Net income to Goliath Corporation before extraordinary item (from Exhibit 3-2)	$10,500,000
Extraordinary loss from the expropriation of a segment of a business, net of applicable income tax of $2,100,000	1,900,000
Net income to Goliath Corporation	$ 8,600,000
Preferred dividends	500,000
Net income to Goliath Corporation common stock	$ 8,100,000
Net income per share of common stock (1,000,000 shares):	
Income before extraordinary item*	$ 10.00
Extraordinary item, net of tax	(1.90)
Net income	$ 8.10
Earnings per common share—assuming full dilution (1,200,000 shares):	
Income before extraordinary item	$ 8.75
Extraordinary item, net of tax	(1.58)
Net income	$ 7.17

*$10,500,000 − $500,000 preferred dividends = $10,000,000 or $10 per share, as is shown in Exhibit 3-2.

The inclusion of extraordinary items in the computation of net income was not necessarily required before 1967. Instead, these items were often buried in the reconciliation of retained income because they were viewed as not being representative of the firm's "normal" earning power. However, there were questionable inconsistencies. Several companies did not hesitate to insert extraordinary gains in the income statement to boost earnings per share, but extraordinary losses were tucked away in the reconciliation of retained income to avoid hurting earnings per share. The Accounting Principles Board now requires nearly all extraordinary items to appear in the income statement.

CONSOLIDATED FINANCIAL STATEMENTS

Reasons for Use

A publicly-held business is typically composed of two or more separate legal entities that constitute a single overall economic unit. This is almost always a parent-subsidiary relationship where one corporation (the parent) owns more than 50 percent of the outstanding voting shares of another corporation (the subsidiary).

Why have subsidiaries? Why not have the corporation take the form of a single legal entity? The reasons include limiting the liabilities in a risky venture, saving income taxes, conforming with government regulations with respect to a part of the business, doing business in a foreign country, and expanding in an orderly way. For example, there are often tax advantages in acquiring the capital stock of a going concern rather than its individual assets.

Consolidated statements combine the financial positions and earnings reports of the parent company with those of various subsidiaries into an overall report as if they were a single entity. The aim is to give the reader better perspective than could be obtained by his examining a large number of separate reports on individual companies.

Minority Interests

As Exhibit 3-1 shows, a consolidated statement usually includes an account called **Outside Stockholders' Interest in Subsidiaries,** often also termed simply **Minority Interests.** It arises because the consolidated balance sheet is a combination of all the assets and liabilities of a subsidiary. If the parent owns, for example, 90 percent of the subsidiary stock, then outsiders to the consolidated group own the other 10 percent. The account Outside Stockholders' Interest in Subsidiaries is a measure of this minority interest. The following diagram shows the area encompassed by the consolidated statements; it includes all the subsidiary assets, item by item. The creation of an account for minority interests, in effect, corrects this overstatement.

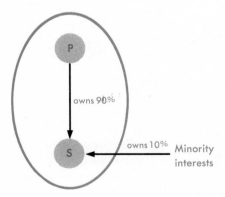

The following table, using assumed figures, shows the overall approach to a consolidated balance sheet, where *P* owns 90 percent of the stock of *S*:

	P	S	Intercompany Eliminations	Consolidated
Investment in S	$ 63,000	$ —	$(63,000)	$ —
Other assets	437,000	100,000		537,000
Total assets	$500,000	$100,000	$(63,000)	$537,000
Liabilities to creditors	$200,000	$ 30,000		$230,000
Minority interests	—	—		7,000
Stockholders' equity	300,000	70,000	(63,000)	300,000
	$500,000	$100,000	$(63,000)	$537,000

Company P's investment in Company S and 90 percent of Company S's stockholders' equity are eliminated because they are reciprocal. They do not belong on a consolidated balance sheet because all intercompany accounts usually are of no interest to investors who are trying to grasp an overall picture of a consolidated entity. As Exhibit 3-1 shows, the minority interest typically appears just above the stockholders' equity section.

Similarly, the income statement must recognize the minority interest:

	P	S	Consolidated
Sales	$900,000	$300,000	$1,200,000
Expenses	800,000	250,000	1,050,000
Income before minority interests	$100,000	$ 50,000	$ 150,000
Outside interest in consolidated subsidiaries' net income	—	—	5,000
Net income to consolidated entity	—	—	145,000
Total accounted for	$100,000	$ 50,000	150,000

Exhibit 3-2 shows how the minority interest in net income is deducted as if it were an expense of the consolidated entity.

Investment in Unconsolidated Subsidiaries

Sometimes there is justification for not consolidating subsidiaries whose business is totally different from the parent and other subsidiaries. Examples are subsidiary finance companies and insurance companies. For instance, a consolidated statement of Sears Roebuck and Allstate Insurance Company would produce a meaningless hodgepodge, so the Allstate statements are shown as an Investment on the Sears consolidated balance sheet. A separate set of Allstate statements is included in the Sears annual report.

Investments in domestic unconsolidated subsidiaries are carried in the balance sheet at original cost plus the consolidated group's share of accumulated retained income since acquisition. This is sometimes called the **equity method.**

The use of the equity method necessitates recognition of the parent's share of unconsolidated subsidiary net income. Exhibit 3-2 is an example of how this income usually appears as a separate item in the consolidated income statement. Note also that the beginning balance of the Investment account in Exhibit 3-1 was $55 million. It has risen by $8 million for the year because of the consolidated enterprise's share in the subsidiary net income.

Another way that investments have been carried is at cost. Suppose in our Goliath example that the unconsolidated subsidiary were purchased on January 1, 19x3, for $55 million. Under the cost method, such an investment would be carried indefinitely at $55 million regardless of the profits made by the subsidiary. Dividends received from the subsidiary would be recognized as parent company income.

Exhibits 3-1 and 3-2 indicate that the unconsolidated subsidiary did not declare dividends during 19x3. But suppose that the parent received $6 million in dividends. The equity method would have the following effects:

Equity method:
Original investment	$55	
Share of subsidiary net income	8	→ Same as now appears in the
Balance	$63	income statement in
Dividends received	6	Exhibit 3-2
Balance, December 31, 19x3	$57	

The $6 million dividend does not appear in the income statement because it would represent a double-counting. Instead, it is regarded as a partial liquidation of the $63 million ownership "claim" as measured in the Investment account. Thus, net income of the subsidiary increases this claim and dividends reduce this claim.

In contrast, the cost method would not tamper with the original $55 million balance in the investment account. Instead, the net income of the subsidiary is ignored and the dividends are viewed as the realization of net income by the parent. This means that under the cost method Goliath would show $6 million in income from the subsidiary instead of the $8 million now shown in Exhibit 3-2.

The most striking difference between the two methods is how they permit management to influence reported net income. Under the cost method, the net income of the parent can be directly affected by the dividend policies of the subsidiary. Under the equity method, the manipulation of dividend policies cannot influence the reported net income.

The equity method is now required for all long-term investments in unconsolidated domestic subsidiaries. In 1970, the required use of the equity method was extended beyond the ordinary parent-subsidiary relationship. It now ordinarily covers long-term domestic investments of 20 percent or more of the outstanding voting securities of the investee.

Investments in foreign subsidiaries are often carried at cost because of a long-standing reluctance to recognize gains prior to the receipt of a corresponding amount of funds from the foreign subsidiaries. This conservative approach is an outgrowth of many unhappy experiences with wars, expropriations of assets, devaluations of currencies, and currency restrictions.

RECAPITULATION OF ACCOUNTING FOR INVESTMENTS

As we have seen, the accounting for investments in common stock depends on the nature of the investment:

1. Except for those subsidiaries in insurance and finance activities, nearly all investments that represent more than a 50 percent ownership interest are usually consolidated. A subsidiary is a corporation controlled by another corporation. The usual condition for control is ownership of a majority (more than 50 percent) of the outstanding voting stock.

2. (a) If the subsidiary is not consolidated, it is carried by the parent under the equity method, which is cost at date of acquisition adjusted for the investor's share of the earnings or losses of the investee subsequent to the date of investment. Dividends received from the investee reduce the carrying amount of the investment.

   (b) The equity method is also generally used for a 20 through 50 percent interest because such a level of ownership is regarded as a presumption that the owner has the ability to exert significant influence.

   (c) Investments in corporate joint ventures should also be accounted for under the equity method. "Corporate joint ventures" are corporations owned and operated by a small group of businesses (the "joint venturers") as a separate business or project for the mutual benefit of the members of the group. Joint ventures are common in the petroleum and construction industries.

3. All other investments are generally carried at cost, unless there is evidence that there has been a decline in market value below the carrying amount which is deemed to be permanent rather than temporary.

SUMMARY

This chapter explained the meaning of the account titles most often found in corporate annual reports. Accountants have special meanings for many of their terms, including *funds, reserves, surplus, consolidated, unconsolidated, net working capital, depreciation, earnings per share,* and many others. Unless these terms are understood, the user is likely to misinterpret financial reports.

Problem One

"The net book value of plant assets is the amount that would be spent to-day for their replacement." Do you agree? Explain.

Problem Two

On December 31, 19x1, a magazine publishing company receives $300,000 in cash for three-year subscriptions. This is regarded as deferred revenue. Show the balances in that account at December 31, 19x2, 19x3, and 19x4. How much revenue would be earned in each of those three years?

Problem Three

B Company splits its $10 par common stock 5 for 1. How will its balance sheet be affected? Its earnings per share?

Problem Four

C Company distributes a 2 percent stock dividend on its 1,000,000 out-standing $5 par common shares. Its stockholders' equity section before the dividend was:

Common stock, 1,000,000 shares @ $5 par	$ 5,000,000
Paid-in capital in excess of par	20,000,000
Retained income	75,000,000
	$100,000,000

The common was selling on the open market for $150 per share when the dividend was distributed.

How will the stockholders' equity section be affected? If net income were $10,200,000 next year, what would earnings per share be before considering the effects of the stock dividend? After considering the effects of the stock dividend?

Problem Five

C Company has net income of $20,000,000 and 500,000 shares of 4% convertible preferred stock $50 par. What is the net income per share of common stock if 2,000,000 shares are outstanding? What is the fully diluted net income per share reflecting conversion if each share of preferred is convertible into one share of common?

Problem Six

"A reserve for depreciation provides cash for the replacement of fixed assets." Do you agree? Explain.

Problem Seven

"A reserve for taxes is cash set aside in a special bank account so that the cash is readily available when taxes are due." Do you agree? Explain.

Problem Eight

"A reserve for contingencies is cash earmarked for use in case of losses on lawsuits or fires." Do you agree? Explain.

Problem Nine

(a) Consider the following for *D* Company as of December 31, 19x4:

	Parent	*Subsidiary**
Assets	$700,000	$200,000
Liabilities to creditors	$200,000	$ 80,000
Stockholders' equity	500,000	120,000
Total equities	$700,000	$200,000

*80 percent owned by parent

The $700,000 of assets of Parent include a $96,000 investment in the subsidiary. Prepare a consolidated balance sheet.

(b) The income statements for the above companies for 19x4 follow:

	Parent	*Subsidiary*
Sales	$1,000,000	$800,000
Operating expenses	900,000	760,000
Net income	$ 100,000	$ 40,000

Prepare a consolidated income statement.

Solution to Problem One

Net book value of the plant assets is the result of deducting accumulated depreciation from original cost. This process does not attempt to capture all the technological and economic events that may affect replacement value. Consequently, there is little likelihood that net book value will approximate replacement cost.

Solution to Problem Two

The balance in Deferred Revenue would decline at the rate of $100,000 yearly; $100,000 would be recognized as earned revenue in each of three years.

Solution to Problem Three

Total stockholders' equity would be unaffected, but there would be five times more outstanding shares than previously at $2 par rather than $10 par. Earnings per share would be one-fifth of that previously reported, assuming no change in total net income applicable to the common stock.

Solution to Problem Four

Stockholders' equity:

	Before 2% Stock Dividend	Changes	After 2% Stock Dividend
Common stock 1,000,000 shares @ $5 par	$ 5,000,000	+ (20,000 @ $5)	$ 5,100,000
Paid-in surplus	20,000,000	+ [20,000 @ ($150 − $5)]	22,900,000
Retained income	75,000,000	− (20,000 @ $150)	72,000,000
	$100,000,000		$100,000,000

Earnings per share before considering the effects of the stock dividend would be 10,200,000 ÷ 1,000,000, or $10.20. After the dividend: 10,200,000 ÷ 1,020,000 or $10.00.

Note that the dividend has no effect on net income, the numerator of the earnings per share computation. But it does affect the denominator and causes a mild dilution which, in theory, should be reflected by a slight decline in the market price of the stock.

Solution to Problem Five

Net income	$20,000,000
Preferred dividends 4% × (500,000 × $50 par)	1,000,000
Net income to common stock	$19,000,000

Earnings per share $19,000,000 ÷ 2,000,000 = $9.50
Fully diluted earnings per share $20,000,000 ÷ 2,500,000 = $8.00

Note that preferred dividends are not deducted when computing fully diluted earnings per share.

Solution to Problem Six

Reserve for depreciation is a synonym for accumulated depreciation. It is a negative asset, an offset to or deduction from original cost. It is a "hole in a doughnut" and in no way represents a direct stockpile of cash for replacement.

Solution to Problem Seven

Reserve for taxes is a liability reserve, not a fund gathered for a particular purpose. It is a misleading label because it means "estimated income taxes payable." This does not preclude the establishment of a special *fund* if one is desired.

Solution to Problem Eight

Reserve for contingencies is a retained income reserve, a formal restriction of dividend-paying power often made voluntarily by a board of directors. Its purpose is to warn stockholders that future dividend-paying possibilities are constrained by future possible events which might bear sad economic consequences.

Often restrictions on dividend-paying power are the result of legal agreements with bondholders or other creditors who do not want resources paid to shareholders in the form of dividends until creditor claims are met.

Solution to Problem Nine

(a)

D COMPANY
Consolidated Balance Sheet
As of December 31, 19x4

Assets	$804,000	Liabilities to creditors	$280,000
		Minority interests	24,000
		Total liabilities	$304,000
		Stockholders' equity	500,000
		Total equities	$804,000

(b)

D COMPANY
Consolidated Income Statement
For the Year Ending December 31, 19x4

Sales	$1,800,000
Operating expenses	1,660,000
Income before minority interests	$ 140,000
Outside stockholders' interest in consolidated subsidiary's net income (20% × $40,000)	8,000
Net income to D Company	$ 132,000

ASSIGNMENT MATERIAL

Fundamental Assignment Material

3-1. Net book value of land and building. Y Company purchased an office building twenty years ago for $1 million, $200,000 of which was attributable to land. The mortgage has been fully paid. The current balance sheet follows:

Cash		$400,000	Stockholders'	
Land		200,000	equity	$750,000
Building at cost	$800,000			
Accumulated depreciation	650,000			
Net book value		150,000		
Total assets		$750,000		

The company is about to borrow $1,800,000 on a first mortgage to modernize and expand the building. This amounts to 60 percent of the combined appraised value of the land and building before the modernization and expansion.

Required:

Prepare a balance sheet after the loan is made and the building is expanded and modernized. Comment on its significance.

3-2. Earnings per share. The Koss Corporation reported earnings per share of $5 for 19x4. The company had outstanding 4,000,000 common shares and 200,000 shares of 4% convertible preferred stock, $100 par, each share convertible into four common shares.

Required:

1. Net income for 19x4.
2. Earnings per share on a fully diluted basis.

3-3. Equity method of accounting for unconsolidated subsidiaries. Trans World Airlines owns 100 percent of Hilton International Company. The hotel operations are not consolidated with the airline operations for financial reporting purposes. The following data are extracted from the TWA 1972 annual report (in millions):

From statement of consolidated income:

Income from airline operations	(5.3)
Income from hotel operations	8.8
Net income for the year	$ 3.5

From consolidated balance sheet:	12-31-72	12-31-71
Investments: equity in Hilton International	$47.0	$38.2

Required:

If Hilton International had paid cash dividends of $4.1 million in 1972, how would the payment have affected TWA net income for the year? How would it have affected the investment balance at December 31, 1972?

3-4. Fundamentals of consolidated financial statements. Fresno Company (the parent) owns 100 percent of the common stock of Grand Company (the subsidiary). Their financial statements follow:

Income Statements for the year Ended December 31, 19x3

	Parent	Subsidiary
Sales	$40,000,000	$10,000,000
Expenses	38,000,000	9,000,000
Net Income	$ 2,000,000	$ 1,000,000

Balance Sheets, December 31, 19x3

Assets	$10,000,000	$ 4,000,000
Liabilities to creditors	$ 4,500,000	$ 1,000,000
Stockholders' equity	5,500,000	3,000,000
Total equities	$10,000,000	$ 4,000,000

Required:

1. The $10,000,000 of assets of the parent company include a $3,000,000 investment in the subsidiary. Prepare a consolidated balance sheet.
2. Suppose that the Fresno Company owned 60 percent of the Grand Company. The $10,000,000 in assets of the parent company include a $1,800,000 investment in the subsidiary. Prepare a consolidated balance sheet and a consolidated income statement.

3-5. **Prepare classified financial statements.** The Crown Company has the following balances in accounts and miscellaneous data (in millions of dollars) that pertain to operations for 19x2 or to December 31, 19x2:

Minority interests	$ 10
Cash	10
Capital surplus	30
Revenue received in advance	5
Franchise at amortized cost	9
Reserve for contingencies	5
Plant and equipment—at original cost	100
Outside stockholders' interest in consolidated subsidiaries' net income	1
Depreciation expense	10
Land—at current realizable value	70
Preferred stock, not convertible	20
Unappropriated reinvested earnings	35
Accounts payable	20
Prepaid rent	1
Net sales and other operating revenue	200
Inventories at average cost	50
Income taxes	23
Preferred dividends	1
Prepaid insurance	1
Accounts receivable	39
Accumulated depreciation	30
Cost of goods sold and operating expenses, exclusive of depreciation	144
Temporary investments in marketable securities—at cost	14
Notes payable	10
Treasury common stock—at cost	3
Accrued wages payable	4
Interest expense	2
Land—at original cost	9
Pro-rata share of unconsolidated subsidiary net income	2
Trademarks—at amortized cost	10
Accrued income taxes payable	5
Common stock	40
Deferred charges (e.g., research and development costs)	2
Plant and equipment—current replacement cost	110
Long-term debt	45
Investments in unconsolidated subsidiaries	12
Franchise—at current realizable value	13
Accrued interest payable	1

The company had issued 10,150,000 shares of common stock, of which 150,000 have been repurchased and held in the treasury. Note that all the above data need not necessarily appear in the financial statements as prepared under generally accepted accounting principles.

Required:

Prepare a formal consolidated balance sheet and income statement. Include appropriate classifications of the various accounts.

Additional Assignment Material

3-6. "Asset valuation reserves are created by charges to stockholders' equity." Do you agree? Explain.

3-7. What criterion is used to determine whether a parent-subsidiary relationship exists?

3-8. Why have subsidiaries? Why not have the corporation take the form of a single legal entity?

3-9. What is a minority interest?

3-10. When is there justification for not consolidating subsidiaries in accounting reports?

3-11. What is the equity method?

3-12. Contrast the cost method and the equity method.

3-13. Define *current assets*.

3-14. Why is the term *marketable securities* a misnomer?

3-15. Define *depreciation*.

3-16. "Accumulated depreciation is a hole in a doughnut." Explain.

3-17. "Accumulated depreciation is a sum of cash being accumulated for the replacement of fixed assets." Do you agree? Explain.

3-18. "Goodwill may have nothing to do with the personality of the manager or employees." Do you agree? Explain.

3-19. Why should short-term prepaid expenses be classified as current assets?

3-20. Why are intangible assets and deferred charges usually swiftly amortized?

3-21. Define *current liabilities*.

3-22. What is a subordinated debenture?

3-23. "Mortgage bonds are always safer investments than debentures." Do you agree? Explain.

3-24. What is the role of a par value of stock or bonds?

3-25. "Common shareholders have limited liability." Explain.

3-26. "Treasury stock is negative stockholders' equity." Do you agree? Explain.

3-27. What is a stock split?

3-28. What is a stock dividend?

3-29. How can a stock split be achieved via the use of a stock dividend?

3-30. What are convertible securities?

3-31. What is a reconciliation of retained income?

3-32. What are the three major types of reserves?

3-33. Enumerate the items most commonly classified as current assets.

3-34. "Sometimes 100 shares of stock should be classified as current assets and sometimes not." Explain.

3-35. What is the proper measure for an asset newly acquired through an exchange (e.g., an exchange of land for securities)? Explain.

3-36. Criticize: "Depreciation is the loss in value of a fixed asset over a given span of time."

3-37. What factors influence the estimate of useful life in depreciation accounting?

3-38. "Accountants sometimes are too concerned with physical objects or contractual rights." Explain.

3-39. How may the distinction between contributed and accumulated capital be blurred by traditional accounting?

3-40. Traveler's checks. The American Express Company had $1 billion of traveler's checks outstanding on December 31, 1972. Each May, the First National City Bank of New York conducts a special sale of its traveler's checks whereby up to $5,000 of its checks can be purchased for a flat fee of $2.00.

Required:

When a company issues $1,000 of its traveler's checks, how are its assets and equities affected? Describe how profits might be made in the traveler's checks business.

3-41. Classification on balance sheet. The following accounts appeared in the annual report of the Jewel Companies, Inc.:

1. Accumulated earnings—reserved for self-insured losses and general contingencies
2. Long-term indebtedness, due within one year
3. Investments: minority interest in foreign affiliates (at cost)
4. Prepaid expenses and supplies
5. Dividends payable
6. Treasury stock at cost

Required:

Indicate in detail in what section of the balance sheet each account should appear.

3-42. Meaning of account descriptions. The following account descriptions were found in various annual reports:

Montgomery Ward: Net earnings of subsidiaries not consolidated
Tenneco: Equity in undistributed earnings of 50% owned companies
St. Regis Paper: Equity in net earnings of subsidiaries not consolidated and associated companies

In your own words, explain what this account represents.

3-43. Advances and deposits. Airlines typically have accounts such as Customer Deposits and Advance Ticket Sales on their balance sheets. Customer deposits often are required from large customers who have not yet established a credit rating. This money is ordinarily fully refunded at a later date. (In the bottling business, customer deposits typically are refundable when the containers are returned.) Advance ticket sales means that cash has been received from customers who have not yet used their tickets.

Required:

In what section of the balance sheet would such accounts appear? Why? Explain in detail how the balances are usually extinguished, including their effects on the income statement.

3-44. Consolidated financial statements. The Parent Company owns 90 percent of the common stock of Company S-1 and 60 percent of the common stock of Company S-2. The balance as of December 31, 19x4 in the condensed accounts follow:

	(In thousands of dollars)		
	Parent	S-1	S-2
Sales	300,000	80,000	100,000
Investment in subsidiaries*	72,000	—	—
Other assets	128,000	90,000	20,000
Liabilities to creditors	100,000	20,000	5,000
Expenses	280,000	90,000	95,000
Stockholders' equity, including current net income	100,000	70,000	15,000

*Carried at equity in subsidiaries.

Required:

Prepare a consolidated balance sheet as of December 31, 19x4, and a consolidated income statement for 19x4.

3-45. Preparing individual statements from consolidated and other information. Using the following, prepare individual balance sheets and income statements for P and S. P owns 60 percent of the stock of S and carries its investment at its underlying equity in Company S. All figures are expressed in millions of dollars:

Total minority interest	10
Consolidated assets	141
Outside interest in consolidated subsidiaries' net income	2
Consolidated liabilities	55
Consolidated sales	371
Consolidated expenses	360
Company P sales	301
Company P total assets	125

3-46. Franchises and trademarks. The 19x9 annual report of the ABC Corporation contained the following account at the bottom of the asset side of the consolidated balance sheet:

Franchises and trademarks $2,347,900

Explain how this account probably arose. Will it be carried indefinitely on the balance sheet? Why?

3-47. Stock dividends. The St. Regis Paper Company had 13,700,000 shares of $5 par value common stock issued and outstanding in 19x8 when a 2 percent stock dividend was issued. The market value of the stock at the time was $36 per share.

Required:

Indicate what accounts would be affected by the issuance of the dividend and by how much.

3-48. Effects on stockholders' equity. Indicate the effect ($+$, $-$, or 0) on *total* stockholders' equity of General Motors Corporation of each of the following:

1. Declaration of a cash dividend.
2. Payment of (1).
3. Declaration of a stock dividend (common on common).
4. Issuance of a stock dividend (common on common).
5. Failing to declare a regular dividend on cumulative preferred stock.
6. Sale of 100 shares of General Motors by David Rockefeller to Tom Jones.
7. Operating loss for the period.
8. Purchase of ten shares of treasury stock for $1,000 cash.
9. Sale of treasury stock, purchased in (8), for $1,200.
10. Sale of treasury stock, purchased in (8), for $900.
11. Creation of a reserve for contingencies.
12. Creation of a construction fund.
13. Creation of a reserve for current income taxes.
14. Creation of a reserve for depreciation.

3-49. Creation and disposition of reserves. Show how the items listed below are created and disposed of, using the following letters:

For Creation	*For Disposition*
A. By debit to an asset	*A*. Usually written off against the related asset
E. By debit to an expense	*I*. Carried indefinitely
R. By debit to retained earnings	*L*. Written off when the liability is liquidated
	R. Restored to retained earnings when its purpose is fulfilled
	O. Credited as other income to current net income

Each item below will have two answers, one for creation and one for disposition.

1. Reserve for holiday pay.
2. Reserve for contingencies.
3. Reserve for possible future price declines in inventory.
4. Reserve for redemption of S & H green merchandise savings stamps.
5. Reserve for bad debts.
6. Reserve for plant expansion.
7. Reserve for bond-sinking fund.

8. Reserve for depletion.
9. Reserve for income taxes.
10. Reserve to reduce inventories from acquisition cost to current market price.

3-50. Balance sheet classification of reserves and funds. Designate whether each of the following is essentially an asset account (*A*); asset valuation account (*AV*); liability account (*L*); or retained earnings account (*R*).

1. Reserve for sinking fund.
2. Reserve for vacation pay.
3. Reserve for possible future losses in foreign operations.
4. Sinking fund for retirement of bonds.
5. Reserve for employees' bonuses.
6. Reserve for purchases of other companies.
7. Construction fund.
8. Reserve for impending economic recession.
9. Reserve for replacement of facilities at higher price levels.
10. Reserve to reduce investments from cost to market.

3-51. Distinction between fund and reserve. On January 1, 1970, the firm issued bonds for cash in the amount of $10,000,000, payable at maturity on January 1, 1990. The bonds carried a coupon interest rate of 7 percent. Interest is payable semiannually on July 1 and January 1.

The contract with the bondholders also contained the following two provisions:

1. By December 31 of each year the firm must contribute enough cash so that a sinking fund (a fund used to redeem the bonds) accumulates over the twenty-year period at the rate of $500,000 per year.
2. At the end of each year the board of directors must formally "restrict" or "appropriate" an amount of $500,000 of retained earnings. The amount must be segregated in a special stockholders' equity account called "Reserve for Sinking Fund." (*Note:* The purpose of this latter provision is *not* to set aside cash in order to provide funds for the eventual retirement of the bonds. Rather the purpose is to restrict dividend-paying powers so as to assure the bond-holders that the corporation will not be drained of the current assets which generate profits as they are "turned over" in day-to-day operations. In other words, if the current assets are kept in the business rather than being paid out in dividends, then the likelihood of the corporation's being able to meet its yearly interest and sinking *fund* obligations will be enhanced. This distinction between a Sinking *Fund* and a *Reserve* for Sinking Fund is fundamental and is an example of the very special meanings that accountants have for these terms.)

Required:

1. a. How much interest expense would appear in the income statement for 1970?
   b. Indicate what accounts and amounts would appear on the balance sheet as of December 31, 1970, as a result of the above description. Also indicate whether the item is a current asset, a long-term investment, a current liability, a long-term liability, or a stockholders' equity account.
2. Repeat all of Requirement 1 for the year 1979. Assume that the interest earned and received in cash by the trustee on sinking fund investments in 1979 was $225,000.
3. How would the transactions at January 1, 1990, be analyzed assuming that the bonds are paid at maturity? Show T-account entries and amounts.

3-52. Accounting for Casualty Item. A fully insured oil tanker owned by the Murphy Oil Company sank in the Gulf of Mexico in March, 1969. It has been fully depreciated and hence its carrying value was zero at the time of the disaster. The insurance company paid Murphy $300,000 in cash, a material amount. How should this transaction be reported in the financial statements? Why? Be specific.

3-53. Investments in equity securities. Clark Equipment Company is a multinational corporation with subsidiaries and affiliations throughout the world. Its annual report for 1972 showed total assets of $633.3 million. Investments in companies in which Clark owned 20 percent or more minority interest was $13.5 million. The remaining investments in companies in which Clark owned less than 20 percent amounted to $6.7 million.

Required:

How did Clark report the investments in which it owned more than 50 percent interest? Indicate briefly how the following three classes of investments should be accounted for: (a) greater than 50 percent interest; (b) 20 percent through 50 percent interest; and (c) less than 20 percent interest.

3-54. Stock split. The 19x7 annual report of Essex International Corporation included the following in the statement of consolidated retained earnings:

Charge relating to stock split in May, 19x7 $4,392,800

The comparative balance sheets showed:

| | December 31 | |
	19x7	19x6
Common stock $1.00 par value	$8,785,600	$4,392,800

Required:

Define *a stock split*. What did Essex International do to achieve its stock split? Does it conflict with your definition? Explain fully.

3-55. Stock dividends and stock splits. The 19x7 annual report of Grumann Aircraft Engineering Corporation contained the following:

Balance sheet items:

| | December 31 | |
	19x7	19x6
Shareholders' equity		
Preferred stock—authorized 1,000,000 shares of $1 par value; non issued		
Common stock—authorized 10,000,000 shares of $1 par value; issued: 19x7, 7,106,933 shares; 19x6, 7,039,621 shares (Note)	30,960,744	27,577,729
Earnings retained for use in the business	100,125,893	86,683,379
	131,086,637	114,261,108
Less cost of 15,300 shares of common stock in treasury	399,616	399,616
	130,687,021	113,861,492
	$315,335,231	$286,251,315

A footnote stated:

Changes in the common stock account during 19x7 (shares restated for the stock split described below) were as follows:

	Shares	Amount
Balance, January 1, 19x7	7,039,621	$27,577,729
Proceeds from exercise of employees' stock options	67,312	1,030,373
Amount transferred from earnings retained for use in the business in connection with three-for-two stock split (at $1 par value per share distributed)	—	2,352,642
Balance, December 31, 19x7	7,106,933	$30,960,744

Options held by executives and key employees under the terms of the Company's Incentive Stock Option Plan were outstanding at December 31, 19x7, for the purchase of 236,209 shares. Option prices are not less than the fair market value of the shares at the dates options were granted. In accordance with the provisions of the Plan, the number of shares and option prices per share, as to which options are outstanding, have been proportionately adjusted to reflect the three-for-two stock split on March 31, 19x7. No options were granted in 19x7, and no additional options may now be granted under the Plan.

From the statement of retained earnings for the years ended December 31:

	19x7	19x6
Earnings retained for use in the business, January 1	86,683,379	68,150,661
	108,134,237	95,772,913
Deduct:		
Cash dividends	5,655,702	4,580,505
Amount transferred to common stock in connection with three for two stock split	2,352,642	—
Stock dividends, 2% (92,021 shares at $49 per share, market value at declaration date)	—	4,509,029
	8,008,344	9,089,534
Earnings retained for use in the business, December 31	$100,125,893	$86,683,379

Required:

1. Assuming that no options were exercised during 19x6 and that there were no additional shares issued or repurchased for cash, estimate the dollar balance of the "common stock" account on December 31, 19x5. (Show calculations.)
2. Describe briefly all the events that took place during 19x7 which affected shareholders' equity.
3. In what other way could the 19x7 stock split have been accounted for?

3-56. **Meaning of stock dividends.** A *Wall Street Journal* story stated:

The Securities and Exchange Commission moved to bolster its control over companies that use stock dividends to misrepresent their operating results.

The agency proposed a rule generally prohibiting a company from distributing stock to its shareholders unless it has enough "earned surplus" to cover the "fair value" of the distributed shares and has transferred that amount from its earned surplus to its capital accounts.

The SEC said the proposed rule wouldn't affect traditional stock splits involving the distribution of at least an additional share for each share outstanding. It applies to distributions made "on a pro-rata basis and without consideration."

The Commission said a number of companies use stock dividends to create the impression "that a distribution is being made out of the earned surplus . . . without the drain on current assets that would result from the distribution of a cash dividend."

It added that some instances have occurred "recently" where "such distributions were utilized by companies having little or no earned surplus, thus creating a misleading impression concerning the results of operations of the company."

Required:

Suppose that *A* Company owned 10,000 common shares of *B* Company, which declared a 3 percent dividend in common stock. The market price of the shares before the dividend was $50. *B* Company had the following stockholders' equity before declaring the stock dividend:

Capital stock, 100,000 shares issued and outstanding, par value $10 per share	$1,000,000
Paid-in capital in excess of par value	2,000,000
Retained income	3,000,000
	$6,000,000

1. How would the stockholders' equity of *B* Company be changed upon issuance of the dividend? Assuming that 3,000 additional shares of $10 par value would be issued? Give dollar amounts.
2. How would the accounts of *A* Company be affected? Give dollar amounts.
3. What are the overall dollar effects on the total assets and total stockholders' equity of *A* Company? *B* Company?

3-57. **Cash and stock dividends.** In 1969, a merger was proposed between Boise Cascade and Ebasco whereby Ebasco common shareowners would receive Boise stock under one of the two possible offers described in the following excerpt from a communication to Ebasco shareowners:

Based on continuation of the 1968 dividend on the common stock of Boise Cascade of 25 cents per share in cash and 2% in stock, Ebasco shareowners would receive annually per share of existing Ebasco stock, on the assumption that the value of the Boise Cascade stock is approximately equivalent to its market price on June 16, 1969 (66¼):

On the All Common Stock Offer
Cash dividend	$0.3125	(1¼ shares × $0.25 dividend per share)
Market value of stock dividend	$1.6562	(1¼ shares × 2% of 66¼)
Total	$1.9687	per share of Ebasco stock.

On the Combined Preferred and Common
Stock Offer
Cash dividend:		
On preferred	$1.20	(⁴⁄₁₀ share × $3.00)
On common	0.1625	(⁶⁵⁄₁₀₀ share × $0.25 dividend per share)
Total cash	$1.3625	
Market value of stock dividend	$0.8612	(⁶⁵⁄₁₀₀ share × 2% of 66¼)
Total	$2.2237	per share of Ebasco stock.

Each of the foregoing compares with the present cash dividend of Ebasco of $2.00 per share. It should be noted that the formula for computation of the value of the stock dividend does not reflect, for shareowners who choose to sell the stock dividend, the cost of selling or any possible effect of the stock dividend upon the market price of the Boise Cascade stock.

Required:

Evaluate the communication. Be specific.

3-58. Valuation of intangible assets of football team. New owners acquired the Los Angeles Rams football team in 1962 for $7.2 million. They valued the contracts of their forty players at a total of $3.5 million. For income tax purposes, the Rams amortized the $3.5 million over five years; therefore, they took a tax deduction of $700,000 annually.

The Internal Revenue Service challenged the deductions. It maintained that only $300,000 of the $7.2 million purchase price was attributable to the player contracts and that the bulk of the purchase price was attributable to the league franchise rights. Such franchise rights are regarded by the Internal Revenue Service as a valuable asset with an indefinite future life; therefore, no amortization is permitted for tax-reporting purposes.

Required:

Reports to stockholders by American companies do not have to adhere to the same basis used for income tax purposes. Assume that the operating income reported to stockholders (before considering any possible amortization of the $3.5 million cost) was $1,000,000 each year. There may have been additional amortization deducted in arriving at the $1,000,000 figure, but ignore such amortization for purposes of this problem. That is, concentrate solely on the effects of accounting for the $3.5 million in dispute. Also assume that $300,000 is identified with the player contracts and $3.2 million with the franchise rights. Under generally accepted accounting principles as now existing rather than those that existed in the 1960s, by how much would the annual operating income reported to stockholders be changed for each of the five years in question? Comment on your answer; that is, do you think that your answer is an appropriate measure of operating income? Why? By how much would taxable income increase if the IRS position is upheld?

Understanding Corporate Annual Reports— Part Two

4

This chapter continues the discussion of corporate annual reporting begun in Chapter 3. It examines the statement of changes in financial position and the uses of financial ratios for interpreting financial statements.

STATEMENT OF CHANGES IN FINANCIAL POSITION

Concept and Format of Funds Statement

In 1971, in *Opinion No. 19,* the Accounting Principles Board added an additional financial report to its requirements. A statement of changes in financial position must be presented as a basic financial statement in corporate annual reports. Before 1971, the statement was most widely known as a statement of sources and applications of funds. For brevity in the ensuing discussion, the statement will frequently be called a **funds statement.**

The funds statement summarizes the financing and investing activities of the enterprise. The statement shows directly information that can otherwise be obtained only by makeshift analysis and interpretation of balance sheets and statements of income and retained earnings.

There has been long-standing disagreement on the concept and format of the funds statement. The most popular approach has been to view the statement as an explanation of how net working capital (the excess of current assets over current liabilities) has changed for a given period.

Therefore, most funds statements have displayed the sources and applications of net working capital, as follows:

Sources of funds:

Operations (excess of revenue over charges against revenue requiring funds)
Sale of noncurrent assets (plant, equipment, long-term stocks and bonds)
Issuance of long-term debt
Issuance of capital stock

Applications of funds:

Declaration of dividends
Purchase of noncurrent assets (plant, equipment, long-term stocks and bonds)
Redemption of long-term debt
Repurchase of outstanding capital stock

Financial analysts have cited the following information as being revealed by a funds statement: the major sources from which funds have been obtained (that is, profitable operations, borrowing, sale of capital stock); clues as to the financial management habits of the executives (that is, management attitudes toward spending and financing); the proportion of funds applied to plant, dividends, debt retirement, etc.; indications of the impact of fund flows upon future dividend-paying probabilities; and an indication of the company's trend toward general financial strength or weakness.

Example of Funds Statement

The preparation of a funds statement can become complex, but the basic ideas are straightforward. Generally, as the example will show, a funds statement can be prepared from visual inspection of the changes in balance-sheet items, the availability of a few additional facts, and a familiarity with the typical components of the funds statement.

Consider the example of the *B* Company, which had net income of $43,000 in 19x2. Sales were $200,000, expenses requiring working capital, $140,000, and depreciation, $17,000. The *B* Company had the following balance sheets (in thousands of dollars):

	December 31				*December 31*	
	19x2	*19x1*			*19x2*	*19x1*
Current assets:				Current		
Cash	$ 5	$ 25		liabilities	$100	$ 10
Net receivables	45	25		Long-term debt	105	5
Inventories	100	60		Stockholders'		
Total current assets	$150	$110		equity	425	315
Plant assets, net of				Total equities	$630	$330
accumulated depreciation	480	220				
Total assets	$630	$330				

In 19x2, the company issued long-term debt and capital stock for cash of $100,000 and $87,000, respectively. Cash dividends were $20,000. New plant and equipment was acquired for $277,000 cash.

Because the funds statement explains the *causes* for the change in net working capital, the first step is to compute such a change (which represents the effects):

| | December 31 | |
	19x2	19x1
Current assets	$150	$110
Current liabilities	100	10
Net working capital	$ 50	$100
Net decrease		$50

When business expansion occurs, as in this case where there is a strong net-working-capital position at the outset, net working capital will probably decline because maximum use of current trade credit limits is likely. Cash balances will also fall to a bare minimum because the cash is needed for investment in miscellaneous business assets.

The statement in Exhibit 4-1 gives a direct picture of where the funds came from and where they went. In this instance, the excess of applications over sources reduced net working capital by $50,000. Without the statement of funds, the reader would have to conduct his own analysis of the balance sheets, income statement, and statement of retained income to get a grasp of the financial management decisions.

Role of Depreciation

The most perplexing aspect of a funds statement is how depreciation and other expenses and revenue which do not require net working capital relate to the flow of funds (net working capital). There is widespread misunderstanding of the role of depreciation in financial reporting, so let us examine this point in detail.

Accountants view depreciation as an allocation of historical cost to expense which does not entail an outflow of current resources. Exhibit 4-2 shows the typical relationship of current operations to the production of net working capital. Net income is a residual; by itself, it provides no funds. Sales to customers is almost always *the* major source of funds. The excess of sales over the expenses that require outflows of funds is called **net funds provided by operations,** which is labeled as a major source of funds. This figure can be computed and shown in a funds statement in two ways, as Exhibit 4-2 indicates. The most straightforward way is to begin with the total sales figure and then deduct all the operating expenses that drained working capital ($A - B$ in Exhibit 4-2). Because a detailed listing of such operating expenses is a cumbersome way of arriving at

EXHIBIT 4-1

B COMPANY

Statement of Sources and Applications of Funds
(Net Working Capital)
For the Year Ending December 31, 19x2

Sources of net working capital:		
Net income	$ 43,000	
Add charges against income not requiring net working capital:		
depreciation	17,000	
Funds provided by operations		$ 60,000
Issuance of long-term debt ($105,000 − $5,000)		100,000
Issuance of additional capital stock*		87,000
Total sources		$247,000
Applications of net working capital:		
Acquisition of plant and equipment†	$277,000	
Payment of cash dividends	20,000	
Total applications		297,000
Decrease in net working capital		$ (50,000)

*In this example, the amounts of inflows and outflows were given. In cases where the exact amounts of inflows or outflows are not explicitly given, they can usually be computed by analyzing the changes in the beginning and ending balances of the accounts in question:

Let X = amount of additional capital stock issued

$315,000 beginning balance + $43,000 net income

$$- \$20,000 \text{ dividends} + X = \$425,000 \text{ ending balance}$$
$$\$338,000 + X = \$425,000$$
$$X = \$ 87,000$$

†There were two changes in the plant asset accounts, an increase from new acquisitions and a decrease from depreciation.

Let X = amount spent for new acquisitions

$220,000 beginning balance − $17,000 depreciation + X = $480,000 ending balance
$$X = \$277,000$$

EXHIBIT 4-2

Analysis of Income Statement to Show Effects of
Operations on Net Working Capital

Sales	$200,000	(A)
Less: All expenses requiring working capital (detailed)	140,000	(B)
Net funds provided by operations	$ 60,000	(C)
Less: Depreciation	17,000	(D)
Net income	$ 43,000	(E)

Note: Figures are from the preceding example. In this example, depreciation is the only expense not requiring net working capital.

funds provided by operations, accountants and financial analysts use a shortcut. Instead of beginning with the Sales total and working down, accountants usually start with Net Income and work up ($E + D$ in Exhibit 4-2) by adding back all charges not requiring working capital. The funds statement usually presents this shortcut computation as follows:

Sources:		
Net income		$43,000
Add charges not requiring working capital:		
Depreciation	$17,000	
Other (amortization of patents, etc.)	—	17,000
Total funds provided by operations		$60,000
Other sources		xx

Unfortunately, the use of this shortcut method creates an erroneous impression that depreciation is, by itself, a source of funds. If that were really true, a corporation could merely double or triple its depreciation charges when funds are badly needed. What would happen? Funds provided by operations would be unaffected. Suppose that depreciation in Exhibit 4-2 is doubled:

Sales	$200,000
Less: All expenses requiring working capital (detailed)	140,000
Net funds provided by operations	$ 60,000
Less: Depreciation	34,000
Net income	$ 26,000

The doubling affects depreciation *and* net income, but it has no direct influence on funds provided by operations.

Effects of Different Patterns of Depreciation

Federal income tax laws permit faster write-offs for depreciation than were previously allowed. The pattern of depreciation has a direct effect on reported net income. Exhibit 4-3 is a comparison of the annual depreciation produced by three methods. Note how income taxes can be affected substantially by the depreciation method chosen.

Depreciation, Income Taxes, and Cash Flow

One of the reasons for the liberalizing of these deductions for depreciation has been "to provide more funds for industrial expansion." The business press and financial analysts' reports are replete with such phrasing as "cash provided by depreciation" or "funds generated by depreciation."

EXHIBIT 4-3

Annual Depreciation Expense: Three Methods
Assume equipment costs $85,000, no scrap value,
five-year life.

YEAR	STRAIGHT-LINE*	DECLINING BALANCE AT TWICE THE STRAIGHT-LINE RATE†	SUM-OF-YEARS DIGITS**
1	$17,000	$34,000	$28,333
2	17,000	20,400	22,667
3	17,000	12,240	17,000
4	17,000	7,344	11,333
5	17,000	4,406	5,667
Total	$85,000	$78,390	$85,000

*20% of $85,000 each year.

†40% of $85,000; 40% of ($85,000 − $34,000); etc. This method will never fully depreciate the existing balance. Therefore, in the later years of asset's life, companies typically switch to a straight-line method.

**Sum of digits is 1 + 2 + 3 + 4 + 5 = 15. Then 5/15 × $85,000: 4/15 × $85,000; etc.

Accountants quarrel with such phrasing because depreciation in itself is not a direct source of funds, as we saw in the previous section.

The use of faster depreciation permits larger deductions in the computation of income taxes and thus reduces the outflow of funds for current income taxes. So faster depreciation conserves funds by reducing current income tax disbursements:

	Straight-Line Depreciation	Double Declining Balance Depreciation
(C) Income before depreciation	$60,000	$60,000
Depreciation deduction on income tax return	17,000	34,000
Income before income taxes	$43,000	$26,000
(T) Income taxes @ 40%	17,200	10,400
Net income	$25,800	$15,600

Net after-tax inflow from operations:

C − T = $60,000 − $17,200 = $42,800

= $60,000 − $10,400 = $49,600

As the tabulation shows, the effect of more depreciation on fund flows is indirect; it reduces income taxes by 40 percent of the extra de-

111

preciation deduction of $17,000, or $6,800, and therefore keeps more funds in the business for a longer period of time because of the postponement of income taxes.

Alternative Concepts and Formats

Critics of the net-working-capital approach have stressed that it excludes the disclosure of some important financing and investing activities that do not entail the direct use of net working capital but that belong in any statement of changes in financial position. Consequently, *Opinion No. 19* requires disclosure of all the important aspects of financing and investing activities "regardless of whether cash or other elements of working capital are directly affected." For example, acquisitions of property by issuance of securities or in exchange for other property should be appropriately reflected on the statement. In our *B* Company example (Exhibit 4-1), suppose that some plant and equipment were acquired in exchange for the issuance of capital stock having a market value of $87,000. Strictly interpreted, the net working capital concept of funds would exclude that transaction from the statement in Exhibit 4-1 because there was no impact on net working capital. However, *Opinion No. 19* would include the issuance as a source and the acquisition as an application.

The disadvantages of defining funds as working capital have led to a variety of substitute definitions. Among them are "cash," "net liquid assets, exclusive of inventories," and "all financial resources." All have various strengths and weaknesses. The broader coverage of the funds statement required by *Opinion No. 19* has been accompanied by flexibility (some commentators might say fuzziness) in form, content, and terminology. The statement of changes in financial position may be in balanced form (i.e., total sources equal total uses) or in a form ending with the net change in financial position "in terms of cash, of cash and temporary investments combined, of all quick assets, or of working capital."

Cash Flow

Sometimes a statement of sources and applications of cash is found in an annual report. For practical purposes, **cash** in many of these instances is **loosely** defined so that it is equivalent to net working capital. Therefore, statements of sources and applications of cash are essentially another type of funds statement.

Some companies like to stress a cash flow per share figure as well as an earnings per share figure. Cash flow per share and funds provided by operations per share are usually equivalent. Net income is an attempt to summarize management performance. Cash flow or funds provided by operations gives an incomplete picture of that performance because it ignores noncash expenses that are just as important as cash expenses for judging overall company performance. Because they give an incomplete picture, cash flow per share figures can be downright misleading. They should be interpreted cautiously.

ANALYSIS OF FINANCIAL STATEMENTS

Financial statements should facilitate comparison and prediction, the two major analytical tasks of both internal and external users. In this section, we consider some techniques and ratios commonly used in financial analysis and interpretation. Although internal and external users share an interest in these techniques, our present emphasis is on external uses, particularly because internal uses—evaluation of management performance —are discussed at length in subsequent chapters. The techniques discussed in this chapter will be helpful both to managers and to investors.

Focus of Interest and Sources of Information

Published financial statements are properly oriented toward the long-term investor, who is mainly interested in long-term earning power. Short-term creditors, such as major suppliers or banks, are usually more interested in the short-run ability of the corporation to satisfy its obligations as they mature. The amount of time allotted by the analyst and the quantity of information he seeks depend directly on the size of the investment he is considering and on his general familiarity with the company. Financial analysts usually use a company's annual report as the springboard for their review.

Ideally, of course, the best possible set of financial statements would be those that directly portray the future. Such statements would show budgeted figures for as far ahead as could be reliably predicted. After all, the analyst is a predictor. Lacking budgeted statements, he must rely on financial history to help obtain clues as to future performance.

Comparison is an essential step in the prediction process—comparison of changing overall economic conditions, comparison of industries, comparison of firms within industries, comparison of divisions within firms, and comparison of specific company financial data through the months or years.

The following is a summary of the financial analysts' approach to financial data:

1. Analysts look for trends and changes in major items. They compare years, products, and similar firms. Their figures are condensed.

2. The income statement is regarded as the most important reflector of the operations of the firm. There is a definite tendency to think in terms of "normal earning power," but all components of the statement are examined carefully. The items of greatest interest include: sales and sales breakdowns; cost of goods sold, inventory valuations, and gross margin;

operating expenses, such as research, long-term rentals, and depreciation; extraordinary gains and losses; foreign operations; income taxes; and net income.

3. The analysts' concern with the balance sheet centers about the current working capital position. The long-term investor wants assurance that the company is not on the brink of bankruptcy. Hence, he wants to know if there is sufficient net working capital to sustain smooth operations.

The investor is also interested in the existing composition of long-term debt and stockholders' equity. He wants to assess the likelihood of and need for future issuances of bonds and stocks. He also wants to appraise the impact on earnings per common share of the possible conversion of debt and preferred stock. Of course, the reporting of fully diluted earnings per share on the income statement helps him with that task.

Character of Income

The analyst focuses on income because the company's earning power is a primary basis for judging the market value of its stock. In the long run, without earnings there can be no dividends, no growth, and ultimately no existence. Therefore, the analyst concentrates on various factors that might affect net income.

In studying revenue, the analyst considers each product line in the light of the following factors: capital investment needs, pricing changes, stability, research productivity, competitive situation, and general business conditions. In studying expenses, he considers questions like the following: What are the cost behavior patterns? Are some expenses postponable? Which expenses vary with volume and which do not? Which types of expense may be eliminated if there is a drastic decrease in revenue? What is the ratio between expenses and sales in various product lines? What about labor conditions and cost-control techniques? What about research outlays and attitudes toward research?

USE OF RATIOS IN INTERPRETATION

Do Ratios Provide Answers?

Some analysts maintain that financial ratios merely provide clues that necessitate deeper probing to discover underlying causes. However, there is a growing body of evidence that shows that ratios can be directly helpful as a basis for making predictions. The most commonly used ratios, numbered one through seventeen, are presented on the following pages.

There are two major purposes of financial-statement analysis: (1) solvency determination and (2) profitability evaluation. Solvency determination is the assessment of the likelihood of a firm's ability to meet its financial obligations as they mature. Profitability evaluation is the assessment of the likelihood of a future rate of return on a given security. Empirical studies have shown that ratios related to income (the ratios in Equations 1 through 13) possess the highest predictive power for both purposes.[1] In contrast, the liquidity and turnover ratios (in Equations 14 through 17) are poor predictors.

Our illustrative analysis will focus on one or two years. This is sufficient as a start, but a series of years should be examined to get the best overall perspective. That is why annual reports typically contain a table of comparative statistics for five or ten years.

Operating Performance

An important measure of overall accomplishment is the rate of return on invested capital:

$$\text{Rate of return on investment} = \frac{\text{Income}}{\text{Invested capital}} \qquad (1)$$

On the surface, this measure is straightforward, but its ingredients may differ according to the purpose it is to serve. What is Invested Capital, the denominator of the ratio? What income figure is appropriate?

Management functions may usefully be divided into **operating** (i.e., utilizing a given set of assets) and **financing** (i.e., obtaining the needed capital). The best managements perform both functions superbly. However, some companies are marked by superior operating management and inferior financial management, or vice versa.

The measurement of operating performance (i.e., how profitably assets are employed) should not be influenced by the management's financial decisions (i.e., how assets are obtained). Operating performance is best measured by the rate of return on total assets:

$$\begin{array}{l}\text{Pretax operating rate} \\ \text{of return on total assets}\end{array} = \frac{\begin{array}{c}\text{Income before} \\ \text{interest expense and income taxes}\end{array}}{\text{Average total assets available}} \qquad (2)$$

The right-hand side of Equation 2 consists, in turn, of two important ratios:

$$\frac{\begin{array}{c}\text{Income before} \\ \text{interest expense and income taxes}\end{array}}{\text{Average total assets available}} = \frac{\begin{array}{c}\text{Income before} \\ \text{interest expense and income taxes}\end{array}}{\text{Sales}} \times \frac{\text{Sales}}{\begin{array}{c}\text{Average total} \\ \text{assets available}\end{array}} \qquad (3)$$

[1] For a summary of these studies, see William H. Beaver, "Financial Statement Analysis," in Sidney Davidson, ed., *Handbook of Modern Accounting* (New York: McGraw-Hill Book Company, 1970), pp. 5–12 to 5–17.

EXHIBIT 4-4

THE GREEN CO.
Balance Sheet
(In thousands of dollars)

ASSETS	DECEMBER 31 19x1	DECEMBER 31 19x0
Current assets:		
Cash	$ 2,600	$ 2,200
Marketable securities	600	600
Receivables, net	5,300	5,100
Inventories at cost	14,600	14,400
Prepayments	600	600
Total current assets	$23,700	$22,900
Plant assets:		
Land	$ 300	$ 300
Buildings and equipment, net	7,000	5,800
Total plant assets	$ 7,300	$ 6,100
Total assets	$31,000	$29,000
EQUITIES		
Current liabilities:		
Notes payable	$ 3,900	$ 2,800
Accounts payable	3,200	2,400
Accrued expenses	1,600	1,700
Income taxes payable	500	400
Total current liabilities	$ 9,200	$ 7,300
5% bonds payable	$16,000	$16,000
Stockholders' equity:		
Preferred stock, 6%, $100 par value,		
$100 liquidating value	$ 1,600	$ 1,600
Common stock, $10 par value	2,000	2,000
Additional paid-in capital	1,000	1,000
Retained earnings	1,000	900
Reserve for contingencies	200	200
Total stockholders' equity	$ 5,800	$ 5,700
Total equities	$31,000	$29,000

Using Exhibits 4-4 and 4-5, we may compute the following 19x1 results for Green Company:

$$\frac{\$3,100,000}{\frac{1}{2}(\$31,000,000 + \$29,000,000)} = \frac{\$3,100,000}{\$55,000,000} \times \frac{\$55,000,000}{\$30,000,000}$$

The right-hand terms in Equation 3 are often called the **margin percentage on sales** and the **total asset turnover,** respectively. Equation 3 may be re-expressed:

Pretax operating rate of return on total assets
$\quad\quad$ = Margin percentage on sales × Total asset turnover
$\quad$ 10.33% = 5.64% × 1.833 times $\quad\quad\quad\quad\quad\quad\quad\quad\quad$ (4)

If ratios are used to evaluate operating performance, they should exclude extraordinary items because they are regarded as nonrecurring items which do not reflect normal performance.

EXHIBIT 4-5
THE GREEN CO.
Statement of Income and Reconciliation of Retained Earnings
For the Year Ending December 31, 19x1
(In thousands of dollars)

Sales		$55,000
Cost of goods sold		40,000
Gross profit on sales		$15,000
Other operating expenses:		
$\quad$ Selling expenses	$8,900	
$\quad$ Administrative expenses	2,000	
$\quad$ Depreciation	1,000	11,900
Operating income		$ 3,100
Interest expense		800
Income before income taxes		$ 2,300
Income taxes		1,150
Net income after income taxes		$ 1,150
Dividends on preferred stock		96
Net income for holders of common stock		$ 1,054
Dividends on common stock		954
Net income retained		$ 100
Retained earnings, December 31, 19x0		900
Retained earnings, December 31, 19x1		$ 1,000
Earnings per share of common stock:		
$\quad$ $1,054,000 ÷ 200,000 shares		$ 5.27

A scrutiny of Equation 4 shows that there are two basic factors in profit making: operating margin percentages and turnover. An improvement in either will, by itself, increase the rate of return on total assets. This phase of performance measurement is discussed fully in Chapter 16.

The ratios used can also be computed on the basis of figures after taxes. However, the peculiarities of the income tax laws may sometimes distort results—for example, the tax rate may change, or losses carried back or forward might eliminate the tax in certain years.

Trading on the Equity

Another measure of invested capital is stockholders equity:

After-tax rate of return on stockholders' equity

$$= \frac{\text{Net income after taxes}}{\text{Average total stockholders' equity}}$$

$$= \frac{\$1,150,000}{\frac{1}{2}(\$5,800,000 + \$5,700,000)} = 20.0\% \quad (5)$$

This ratio focus on the ultimate rate of return being earned by the preferred and common stockholders.

Equation 5 can be refined to compute the rate of return on common equity:

Rate of return on common equity

$$= \frac{\text{Net income after taxes} - \text{Preferred dividends}}{\text{Average total stockholders' equity} - \text{Liquidating value of preferred equity}}$$

$$= \frac{\$1,150,000 - \$96,000}{\$5,750,000 - \$1,600,000} = 25.4\% \quad (6)$$

This rate of return is higher than the 20 percent rate in Equation 5 because the holders of preferred shares are entitled to a limited return based on the 6 percent preferred dividend rate.

Note that the capitalization structure provides limited returns to bondholders and preferred shareholders. This means that common shareholders enjoy the benefits from all income in excess of interest and preferred dividends. When the overall rate of return on total assets exceeds the 5 and 6 percent rates needed to pay interest and preferred dividends, the rate of return to the common shareholders will be magnified. This is an example of *trading on the equity.*

Trading on the equity, which is also referred to as **using financial leverage,** generally means using borrowed money at fixed interest rates and/or paying preferred dividends in the hope of enhancing the rate of return on common stockholders' equity.

Exhibit 4-6, regarding hypothetical companies, shows that results

EXHIBIT 4-6

Trading on the Equity: Effects of Debt
on Rates of Return
(In thousands of dollars)

	ASSETS	BONDS PAYABLE	STOCKHOLDERS' EQUITY	INCOME BEFORE INTEREST	5% INTEREST	NET INCOME	RETURN ON INVESTED CAPITAL ASSETS	RETURN ON INVESTED CAPITAL EQUITY
Year 1								
Co. A	$80,000	$30,000	$50,000	$12,000	$1,500	$10,500	15.0%	21.0%
Co. B	80,000	—	80,000	12,000	—	12,000	15.0	15.0
Year 2								
Co. A	80,000	30,000	50,000	4,000	1,500	2,500	5.0	5.0
Co. B	80,000	—	80,000	4,000	—	4,000	5.0	5.0
Year 3								
Co. A	80,000	30,000	50,000	2,000	1,500	500	2.5	1.0
Co. B	80,000	—	80,000	2,000	—	2,000	2.5	2.5

differ, depending on whether the version of invested capital used is total assets or stockholders' equity. Borrowing is a two-edged sword. In Year 1, Company *A* paid 5 percent for the use of $30,000,000, which in turn earned 15 percent. This method of financing benefited the stockholders handsomely, resulting in an ultimate return on equity of 21 percent, compared with the 15 percent earned by debt-free Company *B*.

In Year 3, the picture is reversed. When a company is unable to earn at least the interest rate on the funds it borrows, the return on equity will be lower than for the debt-free company.

Real estate promoters are classical examples of traders on the equity. They use layers of mortgage debt, a minimum amount of ownership capital, and enjoy very high returns on investment as long as revenues are ample. Obviously, the more stable the business, the less dangerous it is to trade on the equity. Moreover, the *prudent* use of debt is part of intelligent financial management. Managers who brag about having no long-term debt may not be obtaining the maximum return on equity. On the other hand, too much debt can cause financial disaster when operations become unprofitable.

Common Stock Statistics

Because stock market prices are quoted on a per share basis, many of the popular ratios are expressed per share (and after taxes). Some of the more important of these ratios follow:

Earnings per share of common stock

$$= \frac{\text{Net income} - \text{Preferred dividends}}{\text{Number of shares outstanding}}$$

$$= \frac{\$1,150,000 - \$96,000}{200,000} = \$5.27 \tag{7}$$

Price/earnings ratio

$$= \frac{\text{Average market price per share of common stock}}{\text{Earnings per share of common stock}}$$

$$= \frac{\$63.25 \text{ (assumed)}}{\$5.27} = 12 \text{ times} \tag{8}$$

Dividend-payout ratio

$$= \frac{\text{Common dividends per share}}{\text{Common earnings per share}}$$

$$= \frac{\$4.77}{\$5.27} = 90.5\% \tag{9}$$

Dividend-yield ratio

$$= \frac{\text{Common dividends per share}}{\text{Average market price per share of common stock}}$$

$$= \frac{\$4.77}{\$63.25} = 7.5\% \tag{10}$$

The above ratios focus on net income and dividends per share—by far, the two factors which most influence investors. When earnings are materially affected by an extraordinary charge, they are reported both before and after the extraordinary charge. Equation 8, the price/earnings ratio (sometimes called an **earnings multiple**), generally measures how much the investing public is willing to pay for the company's prospects for earnings. Note especially that the price/earnings ratio is a consensus of the marketplace. This earnings multiplier may differ considerably for two companies within the same industry. It may also change for the same company through the years. Glamor stocks often have astronomical ratios. In general, a high price/earnings ratio indicates that investors are optimistic about the prospective stability and growth of the company's net income. The dividend ratios may be of particular importance to investors in common stock who seek regular cash returns on their investments. For example, an investor who favors high current returns would not buy stock in growth companies. Growth companies have conservative dividend policies because they are using their resources to help finance expansion.

Another oft-quoted statistic is **book value:**

Book value per share of common stock

$$= \frac{\text{Stockholders' equity } - \text{ Liquidating value of preferred stock}}{\text{Number of common shares outstanding}}$$

$$= \frac{\$5,800,000 - \$1,600,000}{200,000} = \$21.00 \qquad\qquad (11)$$

Note the low book value as compared with market value. The shareholders are paying for earning power rather than for assets *per se.* The usefulness of this computation is highly questionable, except in the cases of investment companies. Supposedly, if a stock's market price is below its book value, the stock is attractively priced. The trouble is that market prices are geared to forecasted earnings and dividends—not to book values, which are based on balance-sheet values. Consequently, some companies may perpetually have market prices in excess of book values, and vice versa. Book value may, however, be pertinent when companies have heavy investments in liquid assets and are contemplating liquidation.

Senior Securities and Safety

Long-term bonds and preferred stocks are sometimes called **senior securities.** Investors who buy senior securities want assurance that future operations will easily provide funds sufficient to pay bond interest, make repayments of principal on bonds, and pay dividends on preferred stock. Senior securities often have protective provisions, such as mortgage liens on real estate or restrictions on dividend payments to holders of common stock, but these are of minor importance compared with prospective earnings. Bondholders don't care for the trouble and inconvenience of foreclosure; they would rather receive a steady stream of interest and repayments of principal. The guiding rule regarding investments in senior securities is to look to **earnings coverage,** not to liens or legal restrictions on common stock dividends, for protection. The presence of restrictive clauses in bond or preferred stock agreements is secondary; sole reliance on them as justification for investment is foolhardy.

The most informative way to calculate earnings coverage is:

Times bond interest earned

$$= \frac{\text{Net income before bond interest and extraordinary items}}{\text{Bond interest expense}}$$

$$= \frac{\$3,100,000}{\$800,000} = 3.88 \text{ times} \qquad\qquad (12)$$

Times interest and preferred dividends earned

$$= \frac{\text{Net income before interest, extraordinary items, and taxes}}{\text{Bond interest} + (\text{Preferred dividends} \div 1 \text{ minus tax rate})}$$

$$= \frac{\$3,100,000}{\$800,000 + (\$96,000 \div .5)}$$

$$= \frac{\$3,100,000}{\$800,000 + \$192,000} = 3.13 \text{ times} \qquad (13)$$

Equation 12 is self-explanatory. One rule of thumb for adequate safety of an industrial bond is that the interest charges should be earned at least five times in the poorest year in a span of seven to ten years which might be under review. The numerator does not deduct income taxes because interest expense is deductible for income tax purposes. In effect, income taxes have a lower priority than interest. For example, if the numerator were only $800,000, interest would be paid, leaving a net taxable income of zero. This tax deductibility feature is a major reason why bonds are used so much more widely than preferred stock.

Equation 13 highlights the difference between bonds and preferred stock. Because interest payments precede both taxes and preferred dividends, the coverage of preferred dividends is affected by both interest and taxes. The denominator must include an adjustment of preferred dividends for the income tax rate to determine the amount of pretax income needed to cover the taxes and the preferred dividends. The minimum amount of income needed is $992,000, which can be proven as follows:

Income before interest and taxes	$992,000
Interest	800,000
Income before taxes	$192,000
Income taxes	96,000
Net income	$ 96,000
Preferred dividends	96,000
Net income to common stock	0

Short-Term Credit Analysis

Although all investors are interested in any clues that may yield insights into the operating and financial outlook for a company, the short-term lender is naturally more concerned with immediate prospects than with whether bonds due in 2010 will be paid. The direct way for him to obtain his answers is from a **budgeted statement of cash receipts and disbursements** (discussed in Chapter 6). The indirect way is to rely on the following ratios:

$$\text{Current ratio} = \frac{\text{Current assets}}{\text{Current liabilities}}$$

$$= \frac{\$23,700,000}{\$9,200,000} = 2.58 \text{ to } 1 \qquad (14)$$

Acid-test ratio or Quick ratio

$$= \frac{\text{Cash} + \text{Receivables} + \text{Short-term investments}}{\text{Current liabilities}}$$

$$= \frac{\$8,500,000}{\$9,200,000} = .92 \text{ to } 1 \qquad (15)$$

Inventory turnover

$$= \frac{\text{Cost of goods sold}}{\text{Average inventory}}$$

$$= \frac{\$40,000,000}{\frac{1}{2}(\$14,600,000 + \$14,400,000)} = 2.76 \text{ times} \qquad (16)$$

Average collection period

$$= \frac{\text{Average accounts receivable}}{\text{Sales on account}} \times 365 \text{ (or 360) days}$$

$$= \frac{\$5,200,000}{\$55,000,000^*} \times 365 = 34.5 \text{ days} \qquad (17)$$

*Assumed all on account.

The current ratio (Equation 14), although it is probably as widely used as any ratio, is subject to many criticisms. For example, a high current ratio may be due to increases in inventories that have not been selling well. A low current ratio may be traceable to a high current liability for income taxes because of a prosperous year. An increase in the current ratio does not necessarily mean that the business is currently doing well, or vice versa. In other words, changes in current ratios are difficult to interpret. (The current ratio is often called the **working capital ratio.**)

The acid-test ratio (Equation 15), or quick ratio, attempts to show the ability of the company to pay its current liabilities without having to liquidate its inventory. The time-honored rules of thumb are that a company is below standard if (1) its quick ratio is not at least 1 to 1 and (2) its current ratio is not at least 2 to 1.

These rules of thumb are, of course, subject to countless exceptions, depending on a specific industry's or company's financial picture.

Inventory turnover (Equation 16, the number of times a given amount of stock is sold in a year), computed for classes of inventory, is a useful technique for discovering slow-moving items, for comparing present with past performance, and for spotting possible pricing problems. All these factors are related to the gross profit associated with each turnover.

Turnover standards also differ from industry to industry. Turnovers are faster in grocery stores than in jewelry stores, for example, and turnover traditionally receives more attention in retail than in manufacturing companies.

The average collection period (Equation 17) is a crude indicator of how well the credit terms are being enforced. The shorter the collection period, the better the quality of the receivables. On the other hand, too-stringent credit terms may result in the loss of credit sales and thus may adversely affect profits. Again, variations from rule-of-thumb ratios may mean only that a company performs differently, not less effectively.

SUMMARY

Statements of changes in financial position, also called **funds statements,** are increasing in importance because they yield direct insights into the financial management policies of a company. They also directly explain why a company with high net income may nevertheless be unable to pay dividends because of the weight of other financial commitments to plant expansion or retirement of debt.

There are many aids to the intelligent analysis of statements. Financial ratios are widely used as a basis for prediction. Above all, financial analysts want to assess future earnings and dividend-paying prospects. If analysts are investigating senior securities, they are concerned with the adequacy with which earnings cover interest payments and related yearly cash requirements. Short-term creditors are less interested in long-run earning power. They want to know the immediate outlook for smooth payment.

Earnings per share seems to be the single number that gets the widest attention as a measure of company performance. Its surface appeal is probably attributable to its deceptive simplicity. However, the difficulties of measuring net income plus the complexities of modern capitalization structures mean that both the numerator and denominator are far from being simple computations.

SUMMARY PROBLEMS FOR YOUR REVIEW

Problem One

1. Using Exhibits 4-4 and 4-5 (pages 116–117), prepare a statement of sources and applications of net working capital for the Green Company.

2. In your own words, explain why net working capital declined. What other
   sources of funds are likely to be available?

Problem Two

1. Using Exhibits 3-1, 3-2, and 3-3 (pages 71–73), prepare the following ratios:
   (a) Pretax operating rate of return on total assets.
   (b) Divide your answer in Requirement 1 into two components: margin percentage on sales, and total asset turnover.
   (c) After-tax rate of return on total stockholders' equity.
   (d) Rate of return on common equity.
   (e) Average market price of common stock was $52\frac{1}{2}$. What was the price/earnings ratio?
   (f) Dividend yield ratio.
   (g) Book value per share of common stock.

Solution to Problem One

1.

GREEN CO.
Statement of Sources and Applications of Net Working Capital
For the Year Ending December 31, 19x1

Sources:

Net income	$1,150,000	
Add charges against income not requiring net		
working capital: depreciation	1,000,000	
Funds provided by operations		$ 2,150,000
Other sources		—
Total sources		$ 2,150,000
Applications:		
Purchases of plant and equipment	$2,200,000	
Cash dividends:		
On preferred stock	96,000	
On common stock	954,000	
Total applications		3,250,000
Net decrease in net working capital		
(Note A)		$(1,100,000)

Note A:

Net working capital, December 31, 19x1, $23,700,000 − $9,200,000 = $14,500,000
Net working capital, December 31, 19x0, $22,900,000 − $7,300,000 = 15,600,000

Net decrease to be explained. $ (1,100,000)

2. The decline in net working capital came from the inability to generate enough
   funds from operations to cover expenditures for plant and equipment and
   dividends. In view of the pressure on working capital, one may question the
   wisdom of paying a $954,000 cash dividend to common shareholders. Other
   sources of funds might be sales of long-term investments, if any; sales of plant
   and equipment; issuance of long-term debt; or sale of capital stock.

Solution to Problem Two

From Equation 2 in text:
(a)

$$\text{Pretax operating rate of return} = \frac{\$25,250,000 \text{ (from Exhibit 3-2)}}{\frac{1}{2}(\$508,000,000 + \$455,000,000)}$$

$$= 5.2\%$$

(b) From Equation 3:

$$\text{Pretax rate of return} = \text{Margin percentage on sales} \times \text{total asset turnover}$$

$$5.2\% = \frac{\$25,250,000}{\$500,000,000} \times \frac{\$500,000,000}{\$481,500,000}$$

$$= 5.05\% \qquad \times \quad 1.04$$

(c) From Equation 5:

$$\text{After-tax rate of return} = \frac{\$10,500,000}{\frac{1}{2}(\$259,000,000 + \$251,000,000)}$$

$$= 4.12\%$$

(d) From Equation 6:

Rate of return on common equity

$$= \frac{\$10,500,000 - (\$5 \times 100,000 \text{ shares})}{\$255,000,000 - (\$100 \times 100,000 \text{ shares})} = 4.08\%$$

Note that the preferred stockholders get a dividend of 5 percent based on the liquidating value of $100 per share. This explains why the rate of return on common declines slightly between parts (4) and (5). The decline is almost imperceptible in this instance because the preferred stock component of stockholders' equity is relatively insignificant.

Suppose that there were two million shares of preferred stock outstanding instead of only 100,000. Then the rate of return on common stock would be only 1 percent:

Rate of return on common equity

$$= \frac{\$10,500,000 - (\$5 \times 2 \text{ million shares})}{\$255,000,000 - (\$100 \times 2 \text{ million shares})}$$

$$= \frac{\$500,000}{\$55,000,000} = 1\% \text{ (rounded)}$$

(e) From Equation 8:

$$\text{Price/earnings ratio} = \frac{\$52.50}{\$10.00} = 5.25 \text{ times}$$

$$\text{On a fully diluted basis} = \frac{\$52.50}{\$8.75} = 6.00 \text{ times}$$

(f) From Equation 10:

$$\text{Dividend yield ratio} = \frac{\$2.00}{\$52.50} = 3.8\%$$

(g) From Equation 11:

$$\text{Book value} = \frac{\$259,000,000 - \$10,000,000}{1,000,000 \text{ shares}} = \$249 \text{ per share}$$

The high book value and the low market value again demonstrate the heavy influence of earning power, not balance sheet values, on market prices per share. Without more facts, it is dangerous to jump to conclusions, but there is some indication that the company may be worth more dead than alive—particularly if the book value is a crude index of what a piecemeal liquidation of assets may generate after full payment of liabilities.

Bargain-hunting investors frequently view companies with high book values and low market values as candidates for closer scrutiny in their attempts to uncover companies which are undervalued. To this limited extent, the computation of book value may have a useful function.

APPENDIX: CONVERTIBLE SECURITIES AND THE COMMON STOCK EQUIVALENT CONCEPT

The popularity of convertible securities in the 1960s prompted the Accounting Principles Board (APB) to abandon the time-honored legal distinctions between common stock and senior securities for purposes of computing earnings per share. Convertible securities are most often issued with the full intention and expectation of their eventually being transformed into common stock. In this sense, a convertible bond can be regarded as a sort of "deferred common stock" rather than as debt because, unlike straight debt, it will probably never reach maturity and never be retired via a cash payment. The APB was alarmed that investors might be misled by an overstatement of the earnings per share figure because its denominator did not include the potential common shares as well as the actual common shares outstanding.

As we saw in Chapter 3, the Board now requires the disclosure of a fully diluted earnings per share figure. But that is not enough. In its *Opinion No. 15* (paragraph 25), the APB also took a position that drastically affects the denominator for computing the basic or primary earnings per share figure. The denominator now provides for any convertible security that is in substance equivalent to common stock:

The holders of these securities can expect to participate in the appreciation of the value of the common stock resulting principally from the earnings and earnings potential of the issuing corporation. This participation is essentially the same as that of a common stockholder except that the security may carry a specified dividend or interest rate yielding a return different from that received by a common stockholder. The attractiveness of this type of security to investors is often based principally on this potential right to share in increases in the earnings potential of the issuing corporation rather than on its fixed return or other senior security characteristics.

As a practical matter, the APB defined convertible securities as having common stock equivalence if the cash yield to the holder at time of issuance is significantly below what would be a comparable rate[2] for a similar security of the issuer without the conversion option.

Suppose in our Green Company illustration that upon issuance the bonds payable were convertible into 200,000 shares of common stock and had a cash yield of 5 percent. Comparable bonds without the conversion feature were selling for an 8 percent yield. Such a convertible security clearly is a common stock equivalent. The APB would require earnings per share for the Green Company to be computed as follows:

Operating income	$3,100,000
Interest expense	—
Income before income taxes	$3,100,000
Income taxes @ 50%	1,550,000
Net income	$1,550,000
Dividends on preferred stock	96,000
Net income for common shares and common equivalent shares	$1,454,000*
Divide by 400,000 shares instead of 200,000 shares	
Earnings per common share and common equivalent share	$3.64

*Alternatively, this may be computed by adding back the $800,000 interest, less the $400,000 applicable income tax effect or $400,000, to the $1,054,000 of net income for holders of common stock shown in Exhibit 4-5: $1,054,000 + $400,000 = $1,454,000.

Note particularly that the above analysis is the computation of a financial statistic; it is not a different form of income statement. That is, the income statement in Exhibit 4-5 would be unaffected except for the bottom line, which would be: Earnings per common share and common equivalent share (Note a) $3.64.

Note (a) would contain the following:

Earnings per share is based on the earnings applicable to the total of outstanding shares of common shares plus shares of common stock which would be issuable upon the conversion of the convertible bonds, which are regarded as common stock equivalents. In this computation, the interest (less applicable income tax effect) has been added back to the earnings applicable to common stock.

In this computation, any interest (or preferred dividends) on convertible bonds (or convertible preferred stocks) which are regarded as common stock equivalents are added back (less any applicable income tax effects) because the earnings per share figure is really an "as if" computation. That is, these securities are viewed as if they were common stock, not as bonds (or preferred stock). If so, the earnings per share figure should be predictive of what will occur when no interest (or

[2]Where it is impossible to ascertain such comparable rates, the Board concluded, as a practical approximation, that a convertible security should be considered a common stock equivalent upon issuance if, based on its market price, it has a cash yield of less than $66\frac{2}{3}$ percent of the then current bank prime-interest rate.

preferred dividends) must be paid. In this example, only the convertible bonds qualified as common stock equivalents; preferred stock did not so qualify.

Note that $3.64 is $1.63 less than the $5.27 reported on the legalistic basis in Equation 7. In effect, this common stock equivalence approach broadens the notion of a common stock to include all convertible securities that upon issuance have "valuable" conversion rights. The mere existence of such rights upon issuance makes the convertible security a common stock equivalent by definition.

The practical impact of this APB position is to make the computation of earnings per share more complex than ever. This may be troublesome and hard to understand, but perhaps any accounting practice is desirable if it warns the investor that a single earnings per share figure is not a simple wrapup of a company's performance. Business is too complicated to be summarized by one number or ratio.

To check your understanding of these ideas, examine Exhibit 3-2. Suppose that the convertible preferred stock was clearly a common stock equivalent upon issuance. How would Exhibit 3-2 be changed regarding net income per share? The Accounting Principles Board would require that earnings per share be presented as follows:

Earnings per common share and common equivalent share:

Outstanding	1,000,000	common shares
Preferred shares, 100,000 shares,		
convertible into	200,000	common shares
Total	1,200,000	residual shares
Earnings per share		$8.75
Earnings per common share, assuming		
full dilution, reflecting conversion of		
all convertible securities		$8.75

Note the difference between Exhibit 3-2 and this presentation. This presentation abandons the legalistic interpretation of what is common stock and results in a *primary* earnings per share figure that, in this case, happens to be the same as the fully diluted figure.

In many instances, however, a company may have several classes of convertible securities outstanding, some qualifying as common stock equivalents and some not. This would result in a primary figure that also abandons the legalistic notion, plus a fully diluted figure that would differ from the primary figure. Does this seem complex? It is. The major point is that earnings per share looks deceptively simple, but it is really bewilderingly complicated when corporations have several classes of securities. The watchword to investors is beware.

ASSIGNMENT MATERIAL

Fundamental Assignment Material

4-1. Funds statement. The *D* Company has the following balance sheets (in millions of dollars):

	As of December 31			As of December 31	
	19x4	*19x3*		*19x4*	*19x3*
Current assets (detailed)	$ 90	$ 80	Current liabilities (detailed)	$ 50	$ 45
Fixed assets (net of depreciation)	60	40	Long-term debt	5	—
Goodwill	5	10	Stockholders' equity	100	85
	$155	$130		$155	$130

Net income was $25 million. Cash dividends paid were $10 million. Depreciation was $7 million. Half the goodwill was amortized. Fixed assets of $27 million were purchased.

Required:

Prepare a statement of sources and applications of net working capital.

4-2. Funds statement and analysis of growth. The Denny Company has the following balance sheets (in millions):

	December 31			December 31	
	19x7	*19x6*		*19x7*	*19x6*
Current assets:			Current liabilities (detailed)	$105	$ 30
Cash	$ 2	$ 10			
Receivables, net	60	30	Long-term debt	150	—
Inventories	100	50	Stockholders' equity	207	160
Total current assets	$162	$ 90	Total equities	$462	$190
Plant assets (net of accumulated depreciation)	300	100			
Total assets	$462	$190			

Net income was $54 million. Cash dividends paid were $7 million. Depreciation was $20 million. Fixed assets were purchased for $220 million, $150 million of which was financed via the issuance of long-term debt outright for cash.

Denny Alain, the president and majority stockholder, was a superb operating executive. He was an imaginative, aggressive marketing man and an ingenious, creative production man. But he had little patience with financial matters. After examining the most recent balance sheet and income statement he muttered, "We've enjoyed ten years of steady growth; 19x7 was our most profitable ever. Despite such profitability, we're in the worst cash position in our history. Just look at those current liabilities in relation to our available cash! This whole picture of the more you make, the poorer you get just does not make sense. These statements must be cockeyed."

Required:

1. Prepare a statement of sources and applications of funds.

2. Using the funds statement and other information, write a short memorandum to Mr. Alain, explaining why there is such a squeeze on cash.

4-3. Depreciation, income taxes, and cash flow. The Howell Company has purchased special-purpose automated machinery for the production of electronic gear. The useful life of this machinery is four years because rapid technological and market changes make the products obsolete by that time. The scrap value will be negligible. The original cost is $100,000.

The company expects annual sales of $2.0 million and annual operating expenses other than depreciation of $1.8 million.

Required:
1. Show a tabulation of net income and funds provided by operations for each of the four years using (a) straight-line depreciation and (b) sum-of-the-years'-digits depreciation. Ignore income taxes.
2. Assume an income tax rate of 40 percent. Show a tabulation of net income before income taxes, income taxes, net income after taxes, and net after-tax funds provided by operations for (a) straight-line depreciation and (b) sum-of-the-years'-digits depreciation.
3. In your own words, express as precisely as possible the effects on fund flows of using the sum-of-the-years'-digits method rather than the straight-line method.

4-4. Effects of transactions on financial statements. For each of the following numbered items, select the lettered transaction which indicates its effect on the corporation's financial statements. If a transaction has more than one effect, list all applicable letters. Assume that the total current assets exceed the total current liabilities both before and after every transaction described.

Numbered Transactions
1. The appropriation of retained earnings as a reserve for contingencies.
2. Issue of new shares in a three-for-one split of common stock.
3. Issuance of additional common shares as a stock dividend.
4. Sale and leaseback of factory building at a selling price which substantially exceeds the book value.
5. The destruction of a building by fire. Insurance proceeds, collected immediately, slightly exceed book value.
6. Payment of trade account payable.
7. Purchase of inventory on open account.
8. Collection of account receivable.
9. Sale on account (ignore related cost of goods sold).

Lettered Effects
a. Increases current ratio.
b. Decreases current ratio.
c. Increases net working capital.
d. Decreases net working capital.
e. Increases total stockholders' equity.
f. Decreases total stockholders' equity.
g. Increases the book value per share of common stock.
h. Decreases the book value per share of common stock.
i. Increases total retained earnings.
j. Decreases total retained earnings.

Additional Assignment Material

4-5. What is solvency determination?

4-6. What are the major sources of funds? Applications?

4-7. What type of insights are provided by a funds statement?

4-8. Define *a funds statement.*

4-9. What is net working capital?

4-10. What are some examples of expenses and losses not affecting working capital?

4-11. What are the two major ways of computing funds provided by operations?

4-12. "The ordinary purchase of inventory has no effect on working capital." Why?

4-13. "Net losses mean drains on working capital." Do you agree? Explain.

4-14. "Depreciation is usually a big source of funds." Do you agree? Explain.

4-15. What are some weaknesses of the idea that funds are net working capital?

4-16. Give other definitions of funds.

4-17. What is the major difference between a funds statement and a cash flow statement?

4-18. Criticize the following presentation of part of a funds statement:

Sources:	
Sales	$100,000
Less expenses requiring working capital	70,000
Funds provided by operations	$ 30,000

4-19. The gain on the sale of a fixed asset represents part of the funds received by the X Company. How should this item be presented on a funds statement? Why?

4-20. What are the effects on funds flows of the following transaction: The purchase of fixed assets at a cost of $100,000, of inventories at a cost of $200,000, and of receivables at a cost of $50,000, paid for by the assumption of a $70,000 mortgage on the fixed assets and the giving of a ninety-day promissory note for $280,000.

4-21. The net income of the Lear Company was $1,500,000. Included on the income statement are the following:

Uninsured loss of inventory, by flood	$100,000
Gain on the sale of equipment	200,000
Dividend income	10,000

Interest income, including $5,000 not	
yet received	20,000
Amortization of patents	50,000
Depreciation	400,000

Compute the funds provided by operations, assuming that interest and dividend income are a part of operating income.

4-22. What are the major analytical tasks of internal and external users of financial statements?

4-23. What is the financial analyst's most important single source of financial information?

4-24. What are some of the items in the income statement which most interest the analyst?

4-25. What sections of the balance sheet are of major interest to him?

4-26. What questions do the analysts attempt to answer when examining revenues and expenses?

4-27. How does the analyst approach depreciation?

4-28. "Ratios are mechanical and incomplete." Explain.

4-29. "Trading on the equity means exchanging bonds for stock." Do you agree? Explain.

4-30. "Borrowing is a two-edged sword." Do you agree? Explain.

4-31. "Senior securities are all those issued before 1940." Do you agree? Explain.

4-32. What is the guiding rule for investing in senior securities?

4-33. "Sale and leasing back entails invisible debt." Explain.

4-34. "The objective of credit management is to avoid credit losses." Do you agree? Explain.

4-35. What is the argument for departing from the use of historical cost as a basis of recording depreciation of fixed assets?

4-36. "Depreciation may be viewed in at least two different ways." Explain.

4-37. What are the most pressing problems of financial reporting?

4-38. Cash flow and reported income. The owner of a small manufacturing company is mystified by his accounting statements. His accountant has informed him that the company's net income hovers around zero each year. Cash has increased steadily since the inception of the business six years ago, so the owner believes that the company must be profitable. Inventories, receivables, payables, long-term debt, and capital stock have not changed perceptibly. No dividends have been paid.

Explain briefly why cash has increased in the face of zero profits. Give illustrations of transactions that would clarify your explanation.

4-39. Format of funds statement. Criticize the following excerpts from actual annual reports:

FMC Corporation:

Source of funds:	
Net income	$ 60,822,770
Provision for depreciation and amortization	49,296,594
Cash flow from operations	$110,119,364

Trans World Airlines:

Source of funds (amounts in millions):	
Operations:	
Net income for the year	$ 21.5
Add noncash expense:	
Depreciation and amortization	83.3
Total from operations	$104.8

Tenneco, Inc.:

Source of funds:	
Net income	$166,931,748
Depreciation, depletion and amortization	156,901,757
Preferred stock sold	30,000,000
Disposal of properties	50,506,439
Etc.	Etc.

St. Regis Paper Company:

Source:	
Operations:	
Net earnings	$ 34,022,000
Expenses which did not require outlay of cash:	
Depreciation	36,365,000
Deferred items	6,101,000
Other	1,569,000
Total	$ 78,057,000

4-40. Depreciation, income taxes, and cash flow. Mr. Hawtrey, president of the Vaunt Transportation Company, had read a newspaper story which stated: "The Zenith Steel Company had a cash flow last year of $1,500,000, consisting of $1,000,000 of net income plus $500,000 of depreciation. New plant facilities helped the cash flow, because depreciation was 25 percent higher than in the preceding year."

Hawtrey was encouraged by the quotation because the Vaunt Company had just acquired a vast amount of new transportation equipment. These acquisitions had placed a severe financial strain on the company. Hawtrey was heartened because he thought that the added cash flow provided by the depreciation on the new equipment should ease the financial pressures on the company.

The income before income taxes of the Vaunt Company last year (19x2) was $200,000. Depreciation was $200,000. It will also be $200,000 on the old equipment in 19x3.

In 19x3, the new equipment is expected to help increase revenue by $1,000,000. However, operating expenses other than depreciation will increase by $800,000.

Required:

1. Suppose that depreciation on the new equipment for financial reporting purposes is $100,000. What would be the "cash flow" from operations (funds provided by operations) for 19x3? Show computations. Ignore income taxes.
2. Repeat Requirement 1, assuming that the depreciation on the new equipment is $50,000. Ignore income taxes.
3. Assume an income tax rate of 40 percent. (a) Repeat Requirement 1; (b) repeat Requirement 2. Assume that the same amount of depreciation is shown for tax purposes and for financial-reporting purposes.
4. In your own words, state as accurately as possible the effects on "cash flow" of depreciation. Comment on Requirements 1, 2, and 3 above in order to bring out your points. This is a more important requirement than Requirements 1, 2, and 3.

4-41. Financial ratios: multiple choice. The transactions listed below relate to Jekyll Chemicals, Inc. You are to assume that, on the date on which each of the transactions occurred, the corporation's accounts showed only common stock ($100 par value) outstanding, a current ratio of 2.5 to 1, and a substantial net income for the year to date (before giving effect to the transaction concerned). On that date the book value, per share of stock, was $146.48.

Each numbered transaction *is to be considered completely independently of all the others,* and your answer should be based on the effect of that transaction alone. Assume that all numbered transactions occurred during 19x7 and that the amount involved in each case is sufficiently material to distort reported net income, if it were *improperly* included in the determination of net income. Assume further that each transaction was recorded in accordance with generally accepted accounting principles.

Required:

For each of the numbered transactions, decide whether it:

a. Increased the corporation's 19x7 net income.
b. Decreased the corporation's 19x7 net income.
c. Increased the corporation's total retained earnings *directly* (i.e., *not* via net income).
d. Decreased the corporation's total retained earnings *directly.*
e. Increased the corporation's current ratio.
f. Decreased the corporation's current ratio.
g. Increased each stockholder's total *owner's equity.*
h. Decreased each stockholder's total *owner's equity.*
i. Increased each stockholder's equity *per share* of stock.
j. Decreased each stockholder's equity *per share* of stock.
k. Had none of the above effects.

Answer by selecting as many letters as you deem appropriate to reflect the effect(s) of each transaction as of the date of the transaction.

Transactions

(1) In January, the board directed the write-off of certain patent rights which had suddenly and unexpectedly become worthless.
(2) Treasury stock, originally repurchased and carried at $101 per share, was sold for cash at $103.50 per share.
(3) The corporation sold, at a profit, land and a building which had been idle for

some time. Under the terms of the sale, the corporation immediately received a portion of the sales price in cash. The balance is to mature at six-month intervals.

(4) The corporation called in all its outstanding shares of stock and exchanged them for new shares on a two-for-one basis, at the same time reducing the par value to $50 per share.

(5) The corporation paid a cash dividend, the declaration of which had previously been recorded in the accounts.

(6) Litigation involving Jekyll Chemicals, Inc., as defendant, was settled in the corporation's favor, with the plaintiff paying all court costs and legal fees. In 19x6, the corporation had appropriated retained earnings for a special contingency reserve for this court action, and the board directs abolition of the reserve.

(7) The corporation received a check from the company which insures it against theft of trucks. No entries concerning the theft have been made. The proceeds reduce, but do not completely cover, the loss.

4-42. Financial ratios, inventories, costing. (CPA adapted.) In the cases cited below, five different conditions are possible when X is compared with Y. These possibilities are as follows:

a. X equals Y.
b. X is greater than Y.
c. X is less than Y.
d. X is equal to or greater than Y.
e. X is equal to or less than Y.

Required:

Show the relationship between X and Y for each of the following independent statements [Questions (1) through (5)].

An example of the manner in which the questions should be answered is shown in the following illustration:

Question	*Answer*
(0) The Effee Company declared a cash dividend. Compare the amount of the stockholders' equity before the declaration of the cash dividend (X) with the amount of the stockholders' equity after the payment of the cash dividend (Y).	*b*

(1) The working capital ratio of the Zeno Company is two-for-one. If cash is used to pay a current liability, compare the ratio before payment (X) with the ratio after payment of the current liability (Y).

(2) The cash sale of a fixed asset has resulted in a loss. Compare the working capital ratio before the sale (X) with the ratio after the sale (Y).

(3) The authorized capital stock of the K Corporation consisted of one million shares of $5 par value common, of which 800,000 shares were issued and outstanding. The balance in the retained earnings account was $1,260,000. A 10 percent stock dividend was declared and issued when the market value of the stock was $7.50 per share. Compare the total net worth before the issuance of the stock dividend (X) with the total net worth after the issuance of the stock dividend (Y).

(4) The following data concerning the sales and collections of Company A and Company B were compiled from their records. Compare the average collection period of Company A's accounts receivable (X) with that of Company B (Y).

	Company A	Company B
Sales	$245,000	$90,000
Accounts receivable, January 1	20,000	4,000
Accounts receivable, December 31	15,000	8,000

(5) The following data concerning Company A and Company B were compiled from their records. Compare Company A's inventory turnover (X) with that of Company B(Y).

	Company A	Company B
Sales	$100,000	$400,000
Gross profit percentage:		
Based on cost price	25	
Based on selling price		30
Initial inventory	30,000	160,000
Ending inventory	34,000	90,000

4-43. Computation of financial ratios. You are given the financial statements of the Maxim Co.

Required:

Compute the following for the 19x2 financial statements:

1. Pretax operating rate of return on total assets.
2. Divide your answer in Requirement 1 into two components: margin percentage on sales and total asset turnover.
3. After-tax rate of return on total stockholders' equity.
4. Rate of return on common equity. Did the common stockholders benefit from the existence of preferred stock? Explain fully.
5. Earnings per share.
6. Suppose the preferred stock were convertible into common on a basis of ten shares of common for each share of preferred. What would be the "fully diluted" earnings per share?
7. The average market price of the stock was $9\frac{3}{8}$. What was the price/earnings ratio?
8. Dividend yield ratio. Explain why cash dividends might be so high.
9. Book value per share of common stock.

THE MAXIM CO.
Balance Sheet
(In thousands of dollars)

	December 31 19x2	December 31 19x1
Assets		
Current assets:		
Cash	$ 1,000	$ 1,000
Marketable securities		1,000
Receivables, net	5,000	4,000
Inventories at cost	12,000	9,000
Prepayments	1,000	1,000
Total current assets	$19,000	$16,000
Plant and equipment, net	22,000	23,000
Total assets	$41,000	$39,000

Equities

Current liabilities:		
Accounts payable	$10,000	$ 6,000
Accrued expenses	500	500
Income taxes payable	1,500	1,500
Total current liabilities	$12,000	$ 8,000
4% bonds payable	$10,000	$10,000
Stockholders equity:		
Preferred stock, 6% par value and liquidating		
value are $100 per share	$ 5,000	$ 5,000
Common stock, $10 par value	8,000	8,000
Premium on common stock	4,000	4,000
Retained earnings	1,000	3,000
Reserve for plant expansion	1,000	1,000
Total stockholders' equity	$19,000	$21,000
Total equities	$41,000	$39,000

THE MAXIM CO.
Statement of Income and Reconciliation of Retained Earnings
For the Year Ended December 31, 19x2
(In thousands of dollars)

Sales (all on credit)		$40,000
Cost of goods sold		30,100
Gross profit on sales		$ 9,900
Other operating expenses:		
Selling expenses	$ 5,000	
Administrative expenses	2,000	
Depreciation	1,000	8,000
Net operating income		$ 1,900
Interest expense		400
Net income before income taxes		$ 1,500
Income taxes		700
Net income after income taxes		$ 800
Dividends on preferred stock		300
Net income for common stockholders		$ 500
Dividends on common stock		2,500
Net income retained		$ (2,000)
Retained earnings, December 31, 19x1		3,000
Retained earnings, December 31, 19x2		$ 1,000

4-44. Financial ratios. You are given the financial statements shown on pages 139–140.

Required:

Compute the following for the 19x3 financial statements:

1. Pretax operating rate of return on total assets.
2. Divide your answer in Requirement 1 into two components: margin percentage on sales and total asset turnover.

3. After-tax rate of return on total stockholders' equity.
4. Rate of return on common equity. Did the common stockholders benefit from trading on the equity? Explain fully.
5. Earnings per share.
6. Suppose the preferred stock were convertible into common on a basis of ten shares of common for each share of preferred. What would be the "fully diluted" earnings per share?
7. The average market price of the stock was 15. What was the price/earnings ratio?
8. Dividend yield ratio.
9. Book value per share of common stock.

FED CONTRACTORS, INC.
Consolidated Balance Sheets
As of December 31
(In millions of dollars)

Assets	19x3	19x2	Change
Current assets:			
Cash and U.S. government securities	$ 12.1	$ 9.8	
Notes and accounts receivable	23.2	28.8	
Unreimbursed costs and fees under cost-plus contracts	26.5	33.7	
Inventories	43.9	43.6	
Prepaid expenses	1.1	.8	
Total current assets	$106.8	$116.7	$ −9.9
Long-term investments in unconsolidated subsidiaries	$ 13.2	$ 12.0	+1.2
Property, plant, and equipment, net of accumulated depreciation	$ 20.8	$ 35.5	−14.7
Total assets	$140.8	$164.2	$−23.4

Equities	19x3	19x2	Change
Current liabilities:			
Notes payable to banks	$ 26.8	$ 39.0	
Accounts payable	27.5	17.4	
Accrued wages, interest, etc.	12.3	14.0	
Income taxes payable	2.1	—	
Total current liabilities	$ 68.7	$ 70.4	$ −1.7
Long-term debt (mostly debentures)	$ 34.6	$ 64.2	−29.6
Stockholders' equity:			
Preferred stock, 150,000 shares, $30 par value; liquidating value is $31.50, dividend rate is $1.35 per share	$ 4.5	$ 4.5	
Common stock, 2,800,000 shares and capital surplus	7.3	7.3	
Retained earnings	25.7	17.8	
Total stockholders' equity	$ 37.5	$ 29.6	+7.9
Commitments and contingencies (see Note)			
Total equities	$140.8	$164.2	$−23.4

Note: The annual report contains a long footnote about possible liabilities in relation to government price renegotiations. Notice the decrease in fixed assets. In December, 19x3, machinery and equipment were sold and leased back, under two leases, for periods of five and ten years. Proceeds were applied to the redemption of long-term debt. The annual minimum rental obligations on these and other facilities are approximately $4,700,000 in 19x4, between $4,300,000 and $3,900,000 for the next four years, and between $1,500,000 and $1,400,000 for the succeeding five years.

FED CONTRACTORS, INC.
Consolidated Income Statements
As of December 31
(In millions of dollars)

	19x3	*19x2*
Net sales	$331.3	$326.0
Cost of goods sold	$250.0	$240.0
Research and development	13.6	9.6
Other operating expenses	47.0	56.2
Depreciation	5.7	5.7
Total operating expenses	$316.3	$311.5
Net income from operations	$ 15.0	$ 14.5
Interest expense	4.6	5.8
Net income before income taxes	$ 10.4	$ 8.7
Income taxes (after deducting loss carried forward)	3.3	—
Net income before extraordinary charge	$ 7.1	$ 8.7
Extraordinary charge for loss on notes receivable related to discontinued operations, net of specific income tax deductibility effect ($1.8 loss minus savings in income taxes)	.9	—
Net income	$ 6.2	$ 8.7

	Dividends		
	Total	*Per Share*	*Shares Outstanding*
Preferred	$202,500	$1.350	150,000
Common	350,000	.125	2,800,000

4-45. Short-term ratios. Refer to Problem 4-44. Compute (1) current ratio, (2) acid-test or quick ratio, (3) inventory turnover, and (4) average collection period of receivables outstanding.

4-46. Prepare funds statement. Refer to Problem 4-44. Based on the data available, prepare a funds statement for Fed Contractors, Inc. Comment on what additional information you would need to prepare a more complete statement.

4-47. Short-term ratios. Refer to Problem 4-43. Compute (1) current ratio, (2) acid-test or quick ratio, (3) inventory turnover, and (4) average collection period of receivables outstanding.

4-48. Prepare funds statement. Refer to Problem 4-43. Prepare a statement of sources and applications of funds.

4-49. Funds statement. (This is more difficult than the other problems on the funds statement.) Using Exhibits 3-1, 3-2, and 3-3, prepare a consolidated statement of sources and applications of funds for the Goliath Corporation.

4-50. Financial analysis: multiple choice. (Prepared by David Green, Jr.)

THE OIL COMPANY OF CALIFORNIA
Consolidated Financial Position

	December 31	
	19x9	*19x8*
Current Assets		
Cash in banks and on hand	$ 16,736,501	$ 22,126,407
U.S. government securities (at cost, which is below market)	14,168,267	308,569
Marketable securities (at cost, which is below market)	1,202,697	2,118,046
	$ 32,107,465	$ 24,553,382
Accounts and notes receivable, less allowance of $385,007 and $409,722, respectively, for uncollectible accounts	$ 25,324,924	$ 25,869,068
Inventories:		
Crude oil	4,437,762	5,989,870
Petroleum products (at first-in, first-out cost)	22,785,488	19,351,417
Materials and supplies	2,087,598	3,269,241
Total current assets	$ 86,743,237	$ 79,032,978
Less Current Liabilities		
Amounts payable for oil purchases, lessor's royalties, employees' wages, construction projects, material and supplies, utilities, etc.	$ 15,464,937	$ 15,790,355
Motor fuel and other sales and excise taxes collected from customers for governmental agencies	3,382,528	2,841,330
Cash dividend payable on common shares	2,633,135	2,916,419
Interest accrued on long-term debt	290,903	92,292
Portion of debentures to be retired within one year, as required by sinking fund provisions	300,000	200,000
Amounts payable for property and miscellaneous taxes	2,813,722	2,487,388
Amounts provided for estimated federal and other income taxes	3,187,049	7,075,658
Total current liabilities	$ 28,072,274	$ 31,403,442
Working capital	$ 58,670,963	$ 47,629,536

THE OIL COMPANY OF CALIFORNIA
Consolidated Financial Position (cont'd)

| | December 31 | |
	19x9	19x8

Properties
Gross investment in oil lands and wells,
pipelines, tankships, refineries, marketing
facilities, etc.

Gross investment in oil lands and wells, pipelines, tankships, refineries, marketing facilities, etc.	$503,631,629	$431,124,879
Less: Related accumulated charges for depletion and depreciation, etc., representing exhaustion of oil properties, wear and tear on facilities, and obsolescence	254,259,360	234,525,287
Net investment in properties	$249,372,269	$196,599,592

Other Assets

Investment in capital stocks of, and advances ($2,000,000 on Dec. 31, 19x9) to controlled companies	$ 5,313,593	$ 3,378,569
Investment in other securities (at cost); long-term receivables; and royalty and other advances	3,717,823	2,109,782
	$ 9,031,416	$ 5,488,351
Less: Allowance for losses	2,565,056	1,965,056
	$ 6,466,360	$ 3,523,295
Proceeds from 8.80 percent promissory note invested in U.S. government securities (transferred to current assets in 19x9)		$ 14,907,433
Taxes and insurance paid in advance	$ 2,941,794	$ 2,778,764
Other prepaid expense and deferred charges	2,023,837	1,573,841
Total other assets	$ 11,431,991	$ 22,783,333
Total working capital, properties, and other assets	$319,475,223	$267,012,461

Less: Long-term debt outstanding, after deducting amounts to be retired within one year (see current liabilities)

8.75% promissory notes, due 19x5 to 19x4	$ 40,000,000	
8.80% promissory notes, due 19x3 to 19x2	15,000,000	$ 15,000,000
8.75% debentures, due 19x1 to 19x0	24,700,000	25,000,000
9% debentures, maturing 19x0 (redeemed in 19x9)		14,400,000
Total long-term debt	$ 79,700,000	$ 54,400,000
Reserve for self-insurance	1,670,512	1,508,259
Total long-term debt and reserve	$ 81,370,512	$ 55,908,259

Shareholders' Ownership, consisting of outstanding preferred and common shares; premium from sale, and credit arising from retirement of, capital stock; and net income retained in business

	$238,104,711	$211,104,202

Required:

Questions (1) through (11) refer to the accompanying balance sheets for The Oil Company of California. You are to use exclusively the information on these balance sheets in selecting your responses. Any information which you have —of this company, the industry, or the general business picture—should not influence your answer. Accept these financial statements as being correctly prepared and in proper order.

For the following Questions (1) through (11), select answer *a, b, c, d,* or *e.*

a. True, without reservation.
b. Probably true, but additional information is needed to eliminate any reservation.
c. False, without reservation.
d. Probably false, but additional information is needed to eliminate any reservations.
e. The data are *insufficient* to indicate the probable truth or falsity of the statement.

Questions for The Oil Company of California

(1) During the year 19x9, the company acquired U.S. government securities at a cost of at least $13,859,698.
(2) Market price appreciation of $113,278 in marketable securities was taken into income in 19x9.
(3) Dollar purchases of materials and supplies in 19x9 exceeded the dollar amounts of these items used during the year.
(4) The company anticipated serious declines in the market prices of crude oil and petroleum products in the coming year, 19x0.
(5) The current ratio, on December 31, 19x9, was 3.1 to 1.
(6) The amount of notes and bonds retired during 19x9 was $14,700,000.
(7) Some of the company's long-term debt has interest payment dates other than December 31.
(8) Investments in capital stocks of controlled companies in the amount of $64,976 were charged to the Allowance for Losses account in 19x9.
(9) Total assets, on December 31, 19x9, amounted to $319,475,223.
(10) On December 31, 19x9, the company had funds of $1,670,512 segregated to take care of the replacement of noninsured properties.
(11) The number of shares of common stock outstanding was decreased during 19x9.

4-51. The concept of common stock equivalents and earnings per share. (The appendix must be studied before solving this problem.) The Lyding Company has the following securities outstanding:

4% subordinated debentures, convertible into common shares at the rate of 50 shares for each $1,000 bond—outstanding	$10,000,000
5% preferred stock $50 par, convertible into common shares at the rate of 5 common shares for each preferred share— 100,000 preferred shares outstanding, par value	$ 5,000,000
Common stock, $5 par—1,600,000 shares outstanding, par value	$ 8,000,000

The income statement showed:

Operating income	$4,200,000
Interest expense	400,000
Net income before income taxes	$3,800,000
Income taxes at 50%	1,900,000
Net income	$1,900,000
Dividends on preferred stock	250,000
Net income for common stockholders	$1,650,000

Required:

1. Compute earnings per share on outstanding common shares and on a fully diluted basis.

2. Upon issuance, the preferred stock sold for $50 per share. Comparable straight preferred stock (that is, comparable shares without the conversion feature) are currently selling for $31¼ per share. Therefore, under the rules of the Accounting Principles Board, this preferred stock would be deemed a common stock equivalent because its yield of 5 percent "is less than 66⅔ percent of what would be a comparable rate for a similar security of the issuer without the conversion option."

   Compute earnings per share of common stock and common stock equivalents. Under these rules, what earnings per share figures would appear on the face of the income statement? Why?

Difficulties in Measuring Net Income

5

The income statement summarizes the performance of a company. This chapter examines how a selected few of the major accounting practices affect the determination of net income. Unless these effects are understood, the user of an income statement will be unable to interpret it intelligently.

This discussion attempts to focus on the major issues without getting bogged down in techniques. First, various concepts of income are explored. Then various generally accepted alternative accounting methods are inspected to highlight their divergent effects on income. The aim is to alert the reader to the imprecision of a reported net income figure and to the need for awareness of the assumptions and limitations of generally accepted accounting measurements. The issues discussed include inventory methods, mergers, the investment credit, and deferral of income taxes. There are, of course, many other issues unsettled in accounting, including, for example, accounting for long-term leases, pensions, stock options, research and development costs, intangible exploratory drilling costs, foreign currency revaluation, reporting of diversified companies, and whether companies should publish financial forecasts. However, space limitations preclude our discussion of these accounting controversies.

VARIOUS CONCEPTS OF INCOME

Universality of Accrual Basis

Net income is a measure of organizational performance, of accomplishments and efforts for a given period of time. The accuracy of that measure is subject to dispute among managers, accountants, and investors. This section examines some of the major reasons for the lack of agreement as to what constitutes net income.

The crudest concept, that of matching cash receipts and disbursements, has been generally rejected in favor of the accrual concept which was discussed in Chapter 2. To demonstrate this, nearly all so-called "cash basis" income measurement systems have at least been modified to provide for depreciation. After all, depreciation is central to an accrual method. The accrual basis is universally applicable to all the variations in the concepts of income discussed below.

Various Concepts of Income

There are many approaches to income measurement.[1] The historical cost approach has already been explained: Income is the excess of realized revenue over the historical costs of assets used in obtaining the revenue (without regard to intervening changes in the general purchasing power of money). In contrast, under assorted versions of the current value approach, net income is a net increase in wealth as achieved by operations plus changes in the current value of assets held. Current value is used here to describe the fundamental basis for valuing the assets. However, current value is a general term that embraces several variations. Be on guard as to its meaning in a particular situation. Sometimes current value is used to represent replacement (entry) cost, and other times it is used to represent realizable (exit) value. In any event, to measure income under the current value approach, some version of these values is chosen and consistently used.

Under the replacement cost version of the current value approach, net income is often presented in two major parts: operating income and holding gains. Operating income in this context is the excess of revenue over the *replacement costs* of the assets consumed in obtaining that revenue. **Holding gains** (or **losses**) are the increases (or decreases) in the prices of the assets held during the current period. This differs sharply from the historical-cost basis because it abandons the well-entrenched concept of realization; it includes "unrealized" gains in net income.[2]

Consider the following example. Company *A* buys 12,000 units of Product *Y* for $10 each, a total cost of $120,000. It sells 10,000 of the units for $15 each, a total revenue of $150,000. Other expenses were $12,000. The replacement cost of these items soared to $13 each almost immediately after they were acquired. The price is still $13. The two approaches would show the following:

---

[1]For an elaboration, see the section called Alternatives to Historical Cost in Chapter 16.

[2]As Chapter 2 pointed out, under the historical-cost basis, an exchange transaction is nearly always necessary before revenue or gains are realized.

	Historical Cost		Replacement Cost
Revenue	$150,000	Revenue	$150,000
Cost of goods sold @ $10	$100,000	Cost of goods sold @ $13	$130,000
Other expenses	12,000	Other expenses	12,000
Total expenses	$112,000	Total expenses	$142,000
Net income	$ 38,000	Operating income	$ 8,000
		Holding gain*	36,000
		Net income	$ 44,000

*Consisting of $30,000 on goods sold (10,000 × $3) plus $6,000 (2,000 × $3) on goods held in inventory.

The distinction between operating income and holding gain is not essential to the replacement-cost approach. The same net income would be computed by taking the net income under the historical-cost approach and adding the effects of the price rise on the ending inventory:

Net income under historical-cost approach	$38,000
Unrealized gain on ending inventory, 2,000 @ $3	6,000
Net income under replacement-cost approach	$44,000

The proponents of showing the $44,000 as being composed of operating income of $8,000 and a holding gain of $36,000 claim that this distinction helps to sharpen the focus on two major functions of management: to get trading profits in excess of replacement costs and to invest wisely in assets. This distinction may be important in many organizations. Note that the measuring of cost of goods sold at replacement cost permits the distinction between operating income and holding gains. Under this view, the goods or services utilized must be replenished substantially in kind before operating income can result.

In the context of a corporation, the operating income is an approximation of "distributable" income. That is, the company in our example could pay dividends in an amount of $8,000, leaving enough resources to allow for replenishment of the inventory that has just been sold. The $38,000 figure is misleading because it does not reflect the net increment in distributable assets. If a $38,000 dividend were paid, the company would be unable to continue operations at the same level as before.

As the above example shows, most proponents of the replacement notion of operating income would implement their proposals by departing from historical cost as a measure of expense. This could be accomplished by either (a) using current replacement prices and appraisal values or (b) using specific price-index numbers for various classes of assets (e.g., a construction index or an index for a particular raw material). Such an approach would also necessitate computing depreciation on replacement costs rather than on historical costs. Note especially that the use of **specific** price indexes is a method for implementing a current value basis for computing net income.

The distinction between historical-cost and replacement-cost bases for computing net income becomes most vivid in plant asset accounting. It is self-evident that, in capital-goods industries, depreciation is almost always significant. And even when depreciation is but a small fraction of total expenses, it may be an important figure in comparison to net income. Those who argue against using historical cost as a basis for recording the depreciation of plant assets usually maintain that depreciation based on the historical cost of a plant built ten or twenty years ago is an understatement of current expenses and an overstatement of current net income. The extent of the error is the difference between depreciation computed on the basis of replacement cost and depreciation computed on the basis of historical-acquisition cost.

Deficiences of Historical Costs

Accountants in the United States and Canada use the dollar as their measuring rod. However, a 1970 dollar has a different general purchasing power than a 1950 dollar, and financial statements, particularly in the capital goods industries, are conglomerations of different dollars. Critics have been disturbed by the defects of the dollar as a yardstick and have suggested modifications of accounting and financial reporting to compensate for the effects of changing price levels.

If the price level remained perfectly stable, net income would be a meaningful mirror of overall changes in physical resources and purchasing power (e.g., cash, inventory, production capacity). In practice, reported net income is often the result of equating 19x1 dollars with 19x9 dollars. When purchasing power is declining over the long run, a company cannot pay out in dividends an amount equal to net income without eroding its stock of physical assets. Thus, an increase in reported net income may not always indicate enhancement of distributable assets.

One remedy, the use of current values, would entirely abandon the idea of matching historical costs with revenue. Another remedy is not nearly as radical. It maintains that all historical costs to be matched against revenue should be adjusted or restated on some common dollar basis, so that all revenue and all expenses can be expressed in dollars of the same (usually current) purchasing power. The point is that such adjustments do not represent a departure from historical costs; the **adjusted figures** *are* **historical costs,** expressed in common dollars via the use of a general price index (e.g., a consumer price index). An example of such an index is the gross national product implicit price deflator, which is a more general index than the consumer price index. See Exhibit 5-1.

EXHIBIT 5-1

Gross National Product Implicit Price Deflator

Annual Averages 1940–1972

YEAR	DEFLATOR (1958 = 100)	PERCENT INCREASE (DECREASE) FROM PREVIOUS YEAR	YEAR	DEFLATOR (1958 = 100)	PERCENT INCREASE (DECREASE) FROM PREVIOUS YEAR
1940	43.9	1.6	1957	97.5	3.7
1941	47.2	7.5	1958	100.0	2.6
1942	53.0	12.3	1959	101.6	1.6
1943	56.8	7.2	1960	103.3	1.7
1944	58.2	2.5	1961	104.6	1.3
1945	59.7	2.6	1962	105.7	1.1
1946	66.7	11.7	1963	107.1	1.3
1947	74.6	11.8	1964	108.9	1.7
1948	79.6	6.7	1965	110.9	1.8
1949	79.1	(.6)	1966	113.9	2.7
1950	80.2	1.4	1967	117.5	3.1
1951	85.6	6.7	1968	122.3	4.4
1952	87.5	2.2	1969	128.2	4.6
1953	88.3	.9	1970	135.2	5.5
1954	89.6	1.5	1971	141.6	4.7
1955	90.9	1.5	1972	146.1	3.1
1956	94.0	3.4	1973	154.3	5.3

Use of General Price Indexes

Anyone who has lived long enough to be able to read this book is aware
that the purchasing power of the dollar is unstable. Index numbers are
used to gauge the relationship between current conditions and some norm
or base condition. For our purposes, a general price index compares the
average price of a group of goods and services at one date with the average price of a similar group at another date. A price index is an average;
it does not measure the behavior of the individual component prices.
Some individual prices may move in one direction and some in another
direction. The general consumer price level may soar while the prices of
eggs and chickens decline.

For example, suppose a parcel of land was acquired for $10,000
during 19x1, a **base period** when the price index is 100. In 19x4, another
parcel was purchased for $10,000, after prices in general rose 25 percent.
In 19x6, a third parcel was bought for $10,000 after prices in general fell to
75 percent of the 19x1 level. If the figures are not restated, the $30,000

cost of land will be composed of three $10,000 segments of widely different meaning.[3]

The restatement requires expressing each $10,000 purchase in terms of a common dollar. The current dollar is usually used because users of financial statements tend to think in such terms. Suppose it is 19x9 and the current index is 200:

Purchase	Not Restated Cost	Multiplier	Restated Cost
19x1	$10,000	$\frac{200}{100}$	$20,000
19x4	10,000	$\frac{200}{125}$	16,000
19x6	10,000	$\frac{200}{75}$	26,667
	$30,000		$62,667

The restated amounts indicate the relative sacrifice in acquiring each parcel and the relative significance to the seller of the amounts received.

Restated Cost Is Not Current Value

The foregoing example used a general price-level index, not appraisal value or a specific price index. Moreover, nothing was mentioned about the quantity or the comparative current values of the land at the time of each acquisition. The results of a general price-level adjustment and a specific price-level adjustment would agree only by coincidence.

Consider the additional facts in Exhibit 5-2. The comparison of not restated average cost, restated average cost, and average current value shows that general price-level adjustments merely express the original cost of the land in current dollars and cannot be labeled as an adoption of current appraisal value. If the appraisal value of the land had gone down rather than up, the restated cost would be unaffected.

EXHIBIT 5-2
Various Values of Land

PURCHASE	ACRES	PRICE PER ACRE	GENERAL PRICE INDEX
19x1	10	$1,000	100
19x4	15	667	125
19x6	5	2,000	75
	30		
19x9		3,000	200

[3]Adapted from Accounting Research Study No. 6, *Reporting the Financial Effects of Price-Level Changes* (New York: American Institute of CPAs), pp. 27ff.

Not restated average cost:

$$\$30,000 \div 30 = \$1,000 \text{ per acre}$$

General price level restated average cost:

$$\$62,667 \text{ (from preceding tabulation)} \div 30 = \$2,089 \text{ per acre}$$

Average appraisal value:

$$\$90,000 \div 30 = \$3,000 \text{ per share}$$

In short, general indexes are used to express past measures in *common dollars,* but specific indexes adhere to the *current value* basis for income measurement. The point is that general indexes can be coupled with either the historical cost basis or the *current value* basis of income measurement.

For example, suppose that at December 31, 19x2, a parcel of land is acquired for $100,000. Half of it is sold on December 31, 19x3, for $80,000. The remaining half is sold on December 31, 19x4, for $90,000. The general price level rose 10 percent the first year and 20 percent the second year. There are at least four possible ways to measure net income for each year. Exhibit 5-2a shows that the choice of historical cost or *current value* affects the timing of the recognition of the gains. The use of a general index merely restates all measures in common dollars.

Maintenance of Invested Capital

The adjusted historical cost approach harmonizes with the concept of maintaining "general invested capital" in total rather than maintaining "specific invested capital," item by item. *Reporting the Financial Effects of Price-Level Changes* expresses the idea as follows:

> . . . generally accepted accounting principles do not call for the replacement of existing facilities or the maintenance of an existing level of production to be financed out of revenue before a profit can be said to have been earned. Instead, in accordance with the requirements and standards of the business community, they call for accounting measurements to determine if the "capital" (money cost) embodied in the resources of the business (including its depreciable assets) has been maintained, increased, or decreased. Furthermore, there is not even a requirement that the "capital" be held in any particular form, but merely that we know whether it has been maintained in total.
>
> If the general price level has not changed, the entire excess of replacement cost over original cost represents an additional capital requirement which should be treated as such. If the general price level has risen, it is proper to insist that all operating costs should be stated in comparable dollars; any excess of replacement cost over the adjusted original cost then becomes the additional capital requirement.[4]

[4]*Ibid.,* p. 37.

EXHIBIT 5-2a

Four Ways to Measure Income

	NOT RESTATED FOR GENERAL INDEX		RESTATED FOR GENERAL INDEX	
	HISTORICAL COST	CURRENT VALUE	HISTORICAL COST	CURRENT VALUE
19x3				
Selling price	$80,000	$80,000	$80,000	$80,000
Current value at Dec. 31, 19x2;		50,000		
adjusted for general price level change				
($50,000 × 1.10)				55,000
Historical cost	50,000		55,000	
Gain on parcel sold	$30,000	$30,000	$25,000	$25,000
Land not sold:				
Current value of land held at Dec. 31, 19x3		$80,000		$80,000
Current value at Dec. 31, 19x2		50,000		55,000
Gain on land not sold	—	$30,000	—	$25,000
Total gain recognized	$30,000	$60,000	$25,000	$50,000
19x4				
Selling price	$90,000	$90,000	$90,000	$90,000
Current value at Dec. 31, 19x3;		80,000		
adjusted for general price level change				
($80,000 × 1.20)				96,000
Historical cost	50,000		66,000	
Gain (loss) on parcel sold	$40,000	$10,000	$24,000	$ (6,000)
Cumulative gain:				
Two years together (Note A)	$70,000	$70,000		

Note A: The essential difference between the historical cost basis and the current value basis is one of timing. The total gain for the two years is the same. In order to compare current with past net income figures, the past must be restated in terms of current dollars.

Two-year summary of income:

19x3 restated in terms of 19x4 general purchasing power;		
$25,000 × 1.20 and $50,000 × 1.20	$30,000	$60,000
19x4 gain	24,000	(6,000)
Two years together	$54,000	$54,000

Current Status and Outlook

Inflation seems here to stay. If so, it is only a matter of time before accountants formally recognize its existence by adjusting financial statements for changes in the general price level. The Accounting Principles Board issued Statement No. 3 in 1969 and it may have a significant long-run effect on financial reporting. Its purpose is to encourage the preparation and presentation of supplementary financial statements restated for general price-level changes as they affect all accounts rather than only particular accounts such as plant assets. In 1973, the United Kingdom Accounting Steering Committee tried but failed to require the issuance of adjusted statements as supplementary statements by all companies having a quotation on a stock exchange. Moreover, in the United States in 1973 only one corporation, Indiana Telephone, published adjusted financial statements.

UNIFORMITY VS. FLEXIBILITY

Despite the weaknesses of historical cost, generally accepted accounting principles in the United States and Canada continue to view it as the primary basis for determining net income. Even within the historical-cost framework, there are many ways of computing net income. Given the same set of facts, two companies within the same industry may have accounting policies that show quite different results. The use of different patterns of depreciation is one example.

The user of financial statements wants to make comparisons over time and among companies. He is obviously hampered by the lack of uniformity in accounting. Uniformity does not mean rigid adherence to a detailed encyclopedia of stringent rules. It does mean that variations should be eliminated that cannot be justified by differences in circumstances. The trouble is that managers and accountants interpret "differences in circumstances" in a variety of ways.

Almost everybody is for narrowing the differences in accounting as long as flexibility is not inhibited. Such a position is self-contradictory because flexibility must be reduced to obtain more uniformity, and vice versa. It is hard to assail the idea that differences in circumstances may justify differences in accounting. The key need is to define what "differences in circumstances" means. So far, the authoritative professional bodies have not directly discussed that issue. Nevertheless, some progress is being made. *Opinion No. 11,* on deferred income taxes, which is discussed later in this chapter, narrowed the differences even though many accountants felt strongly that the method supported was not defensible accounting theory.

The remainder of this chapter will examine the possible effects of alternative accounting methods on financial statements with particular stress on net income computed on the historical-cost basis.

INVENTORY METHODS

Fifo and Lifo

Accountants argue vigorously about the theoretical merits of two widely used inventory-costing methods that entail totally different cost-flow assumptions:

1. **First-in, first-out** (**Fifo**). The stock acquired earliest is assumed to be used first; the stock acquired latest is assumed to be still on hand.

2. **Last-in, first-out** (**Lifo**). The stock acquired earliest is assumed to be still on hand; the stock acquired latest is assumed to have been used immediately. In the Lifo method, the most recent, or last, inventory costs are considered to be the cost of goods used or sold. The attempt is to match the current cost of materials against current sales. As compared to Fifo, the Lifo technique of valuing inventory usually results in the reporting of less income when prices are rising and more income when prices are falling.

If unit prices did not fluctuate, all inventory methods would show identical results. But prices change, and these changes appear in the financial records in different ways, depending on the specific inventory methods used. Under Lifo, current purchase prices immediately affect current operating results; under Fifo, recognition of price effects is delayed. If prices are volatile, year-to-year incomes may differ dramatically under the two approaches to inventory valuation.

Balance sheet presentations are also affected by the choice of Lifo or Fifo. Under the Lifo method, older and older, and hence meaningless, inventory prices are shown, especially if stocks grow through the years. Under the Fifo method, the balance sheet tends to reflect current prices.

When prices are rising, Lifo shows less income than Fifo, thus minimizing current taxes. Also, Lifo permits the immediate influencing of net income by the timing of purchases, a feature that has not received the attention it deserves. For example, if prices are rising and a company desires, for income tax or other reasons, to show less income in a given year, all it need do is to buy a large amount of inventory near the end of the year—thus releasing, as expenses, higher costs than would ordinarily be released.

Note that neither the Fifo nor the Lifo approach isolates and measures the effects of price fluctuations as special managerial problems. As Exhibit 5-3 shows, Fifo buries rises in price in the regular income figure and Lifo excludes the effects of price changes from the income statement. The $50 increase in the cost of merchandise (which is attributable to the 1,000 units in ending inventory @ $.05) is buried in the $300 Fifo gross margin figure and ignored in the $250 Lifo gross margin figure. In contrast, the replacement cost method pinpoints price effects by isolating them as holding gains. Keep in mind that the replacement cost method is not allowed under generally accepted accounting principles as now practiced.

The continued inflation in the United States since 1940 has generally encouraged the adoption of Lifo. Almost one-third of the 600 companies whose practices are tabulated in the annual volume *Accounting Trends and Techniques*[5] use Lifo. The major theoretical justification hinges on the matching of current costs with current revenues. By so doing, the result-

[5]Published by American Institute of CPAs, New York.

EXHIBIT 5-3

Comparison of Lifo, Fifo, and Replacement Cost

	LIFO			FIFO			REPLACEMENT COST		
	UNITS	UNIT PRICE	TOTAL	UNITS	UNIT PRICE	TOTAL	UNITS	UNIT PRICE	TOTAL
Sales	5,000	$.22	$1,100	same		$1,100	same		$1,100
Beginning inventory	1,000	.10	$ 100	same		$ 100			
Purchases	5,000	.15	750	same		750			
Available for sale	6,000		$ 850	same		$ 850			
Ending inventory	1,000	.10	100	1,000	.15	150			
Cost of goods sold	5,000	.15	$ 750	{1,000 / 4,000}	{.10 / .15}	$ 700	5,000	.15	$ 750*
Gross profit			$ 350			$ 400			$ 350
Other expenses			100			100			100
Net income			250			$ 300			
Operating income									$ 250
Holding gain 1,000 units @ $.05									50
Net income									$ 300

*Under the replacement cost method, cost of goods sold is computed by multiplying the number of units sold times the unit replacement cost.

ing net income is a better reflection of the increase in "distributable" assets. Thus, Lifo achieves this goal better than Fifo. For instance, Exhibit 5-3 shows that if $300 were paid out in dividends instead of $250, a company using Fifo would not have enough funds to replenish its stocks to sustain sales of 5,000 units again during the next period. In contrast, Lifo would be more likely to conserve sufficient funds:

	Lifo	Fifo
Revenue	$1,000	$1,000
Dividends equal to net income	250	300
Funds left for replenishment of stock to maintain sales of 5,000 units next period	750	$ 700
Funds needed, 5,000 units @ $15	$ 750	$ 750
Shortage of funds		$ −50

This argument has some appeal, but it is not really the reason why companies have adopted Lifo. Dividend payouts are not made before considering many of their financial ramifications. The fundamental reason is that Lifo became acceptable for income tax purposes. If prices rise and if inventory quantities are maintained, current taxable income will be less under Lifo than Fifo and income taxes will be postponed; intelligent financial management would therefore be very tempted to adopt Lifo.

Lower of Cost or Market

When the concept of the market price is superimposed upon a cost method, the combined method is often called the lower-of-cost-or-market method. That is, the current market price is compared to cost (derived by Fifo, average, or other method), and the lower of the two is selected as the basis for the valuation of goods at a specific inventory date. **Market** generally means the current replacement cost or its equivalent. It does not mean the ultimate selling price to customers.

Assume that an ending inventory is valued at $10,000 at cost and $7,000 at market. If the lower market price is indicative of lower ultimate sales prices, an inventory write-down of $3,000 is in order. Of the cost, $3,000 is considered to have expired during the current period because it cannot be justifiably carried forward to the future. Furthermore, the decision to purchase was probably made during the current period, but unfortunate fluctuations occurred in the replacement market during the same period. These downward price fluctuations caused the inventory to lose some utility, some revenue-producing power. (On the other hand, if **selling prices** are not also likely to fall, the revenue-producing power of the inventory will be maintained and no write-down would be justified.)

The new $7,000 valuation is what is left of the original cost of the inventory. In other words, the new market price becomes, for accounting purposes, the new cost of the inventory.

Compared to a strict cost method (see Exhibit 5-4), the lower-of-cost-or-market method reports less net income in the current period and more net income in the future period. Assuming that there are no sales in

EXHIBIT 5-4

Effects of Lower of Cost or Market

	COST		LOWER OF COST OR MARKET	
	PERIOD 1	PERIOD 2	PERIOD 1	PERIOD 2
Net sales	$100,000	$11,000	$100,000	$11,000
Cost of goods available	$ 80,000	$10,000	$ 80,000	$ 7,000
Ending inventory after write-down	10,000	—	7,000	—
Cost of goods sold*	$ 70,000	$10,000	$ 73,000	$ 7,000
Gross profit	$ 30,000	$ 1,000	$ 27,000	$ 4,000

*Cost of goods sold is increased by the $3,000 inventory write-down in this example. Many accountants favor isolating the write-down and deducting it separately after the ordinary gross profit.

inventory in question, total income for both periods will be the same (ignoring income tax). Note that the total gross profit for the two periods is $31,000, under both methods. The lower-of-cost-or-market method has been termed a conservative valuation method. However, it results in a favorable impact upon the net income of the next period.

ACCOUNTING FOR MERGERS AND GOODWILL

Mergers Are Acquisitions

Many companies merged during the 1960's. So-called "conglomerate" companies—such as Litton Industries and Ling-Temco-Vought—became very popular with investors. A conglomerate company is one with widely diversified product lines that might vary from pork chops to guided missiles. How do accountants record these mergers? There were many confusing but acceptable methods during the 1960's. However, in 1970, the Accounting Principles Board issued an Opinion that reduced the variety.

The APB stipulated that, in general, a purchaser be identified in each merger. The net assets obtained should be recorded at acquisition cost—that is, at the amount of cash disbursed or the fair value of other assets distributed. If the purchaser issues capital stock for the assets required, cost is usually considered as being either the fair value of the stock or the fair value of the assets received, whichever is the more clearly evident.

Allocating the total purchase price among individual assets is an important but difficult problem. All identifiable assets and liabilities should be recorded whether or not previously recorded by the acquired company. The excess of the total purchase price over the sum of the fair values of the identifiable individual assets less the liabilities is "purchased goodwill." This account is more accurately called "excess of cost over net identifiable assets of businesses acquired."

Exhibit 5-5 shows how a merger is accounted for. *X* paid $120 million to *Y* stockholders for all of their stock and then dissolved *Y*. Note particularly that the plant assets of *Y* are brought into the combined enterprise at current value. Note also that the book value of *Y* was 80, the market value of the individual assets was 120, and that any excess paid over 120 would be labeled as purchased goodwill.

Nature of Goodwill

Goodwill would be carried as an intangible asset on the balance sheet. Goodwill is frequently misunderstood. The layman often thinks of goodwill as the friendly attitude of the neighborhood store manager. Goodwill may have nothing to do with the personality of the managers or employees. A company may be willing to pay more than the current values of the individual assets received because the acquired company is able to

EXHIBIT 5-5

Merger Accounting

Cash Purchase of Y by X

(In millions of dollars)

	COMPANY X	COMPANY Y	COMBINED		
Cash	150	20	150 + 20 − 120	=	50
Inventories	60	30	60 + 30	=	90
Plant assets, net	60	30	60 + (30 + 40)†	=	130
Total assets	270	80			270
Common stock and paid-in capital	70	30	Company X balance only		70
Retained income	200	50	Company X balance only		200
Total equities	270	80			270
Current net income	20	12*			

*After depreciation of 6.

†The current market value of Y plant assets is 70, an increase of 40 over the old book value.

    Note on goodwill: If X decided that the fair value of Y exceeded 120, an additional amount of cash would be needed to acquire Y. For example, if X were willing to pay 140 rather than 120, "purchased goodwill" of 20 would be recorded as an additional asset of the combined enterprise.

generate abnormally high earnings. This excess earning power may be traceable to:

1. Saving in time and costs by purchasing a corporation having a share of the market in a type of business or in a geographical area where the acquiring corporation planned expansion;

2. Excellent general management skills or a unique product line;

3. Potential efficiency by combination, rearrangement, or elimination of duplicate facilities and administration.

Of course, "goodwill" is originally generated internally. For example, a happy combination of advertising, research, management talent, and timing may give a particular company a dominant market position for which another company is willing to pay dearly. This ability to command a premium price for the total business is goodwill. Nevertheless, such goodwill is never recorded by the selling company. Goodwill is generally recognized as an asset only when one company is purchased by another. The acquiring company then must show in its accounts and financial statements the purchased goodwill.

Goodwill must be amortized by systematic charges in the income statement over the period estimated to be benefited. The maximum amortization period should not exceed forty years. (Before 1970, amortization was not required.) Managers, investors, and accountants tend to be uncomfortable about the presence of goodwill on the balance sheet. Somehow, it is regarded as an inferior asset even though management decided that it was valuable enough to warrant a total outlay in excess of the total current value of the individual assets. As a practical matter, many accountants feel that the income-producing factors of goodwill are unlikely to have a value in perpetuity even though expenditures may be made to maintain their value.

As already mentioned, the allocation of a total purchase price among individual assets is often a difficult task. Before 1970, some managers were inclined to take advantage of the fuzziness in this area by insisting that goodwill be loaded with a heavy share of the total purchase price. In this way, future earnings would bear lighter charges because the individual assets would have lower assigned acquisition costs and the goodwill would not be amortized. The requirement for mandatory amortization of goodwill should reduce this type of abuse.

THE INVESTMENT TAX CREDIT

Although Congress may suspend or alter its provisions from time to time, the investment tax credit is highly likely to continue to affect financial reporting for many years. The United States Internal Revenue Code has allowed **investment tax credits** (hereafter called *investment credits,* for brevity) that are equal to various percentages of the original costs of the depreciable assets acquired (up to 7 percent if the useful life is eight years or more). These credits are used as direct reductions of income taxes. For example, suppose that a company spends $100,000 for an asset with an estimated useful life of ten years. If the expenditure qualifies for a 7 percent tax credit, the company is permitted to deduct $7,000 from its liability for income taxes and is also permitted to deduct the full $100,000 in the form of depreciation through the years of useful life, provided, of course, that there is no predicted scrap value at the end of the useful life. Many observers maintain that these credits are equivalent to discounts on the purchase of assets.

How should this credit be accounted for? Should the beneficial effects on net income of the $7,000 credit be recognized in full for the year of purchase (the **flow-through** method)? Or should the effects be reflected in net income over the productive life of the asset (the **deferral method**)? What do you think? There is no uniform agreement on this issue. In many industries (such as airlines and others which have heavy capital expenditures), the method chosen will have a material effect on reported net income. Exhibit 5-6 compares the two methods.

The proponents of the flow-through method claim that the investment credit is a selective tax reduction in the year in which taxes otherwise payable are reduced by the credit. It is not a determinant of cost of acquisition or use of the related assets. The majority of companies use

EXHIBIT 5-6

Effects of Investment Tax Credit on Net Income

Assumptions: Net income before considering investment credit of $7,000 is $50,000 annually. The asset acquired for $100,000 will be used ten years and have no scrap value.

YEAR	(1) NET INCOME BEFORE INVESTMENT CREDIT EFFECT	FLOW-THROUGH EFFECTS		DEFERRAL EFFECTS	
		(2) FLOW-THROUGH	(3) (1) + (2) NET INCOME	(4) DEFERRAL	(5) (1) + (4) NET INCOME
1	$50,000	$7,000	$57,000	$700	$50,700
2	50,000	—	50,000	700	50,700
3	50,000	—	50,000	700	50,700
4	50,000	—	50,000	700	50,700
5	50,000	—	50,000	700	50,700
	Etc. through Year 10				

this method. Note that if a company is expanding, its current reported net income will benefit greatly from the flow-through method in comparison with the deferral method.

Supporters of the deferral method are particularly critical of the idea that net income can be directly affected by the amount spent for depreciable assets in a given year. Within constraints, the more the company buys, the more it earns. This conflicts with the generally accepted concept that net income is earned only via using assets in the production of revenue from customers. The deferral method prevents current net income from being so significantly affected by unrelated management actions in buying depreciable assets.

The advocates of deferral also maintain that the amount of the investment credit is primarily associated with the use of the property qualifying for the credit. In addition, the property must be held for a minimum period of time. Deferral of the credit and its subsequent amortization associates the credit with the useful life of the related property. This matching is consistent with the objectives of income measurement because it spreads a purchase discount over the useful life of the asset purchased.

The investment credit is an excellent example of the existence of alternative accounting methods not justified by changes in underlying circumstances. This provision of the Internal Revenue Code affects all companies alike, and there seems little reason for permitting two such diametrically different accounting methods.

In recent years, American companies have had increasing opportunities to postpone disbursements for income taxes. For example, the Internal Revenue Service permits companies to use accelerated methods of depreciation when computing taxable income even though straight-line methods of depreciation are used in annual reports to stockholders. Therefore, as the top of Exhibit 5-7 shows, income tax payments are lower in the early years of the useful life of the asset and higher in the later years than they would be if straight-line depreciation were used for both tax and stockholder reporting purposes.

These differences in the timing of cash payments for income tax purposes have spurred great controversy regarding how income should be measured for stockholder-reporting purposes. An example should clarify the issues. Suppose that B Company purchases an asset for $15 million with an estimated useful life of five years and an estimated scrap value of zero. The sum-of-the-years'-digits-depreciation (SYD) method is used for tax purposes. The straight-line method is used for financial reporting purposes. Prospective annual net income before depreciation and income taxes is $10 million. The income tax rate is 60 percent. Exhibit 5-7 shows the effect on net income after tax if (1) no income tax allocation is used and (2) allocation is used.

As Method 1 in Exhibit 5-7 shows, some accountants believe that the income tax expense on the income statement should be the actual amount paid to the government for the year in question—no more, no less. Again note that the favorable effect of lower taxes on net income in earlier years is offset by higher taxes in later years. This method has been outlawed in favor of Method 2 as a basis for reporting to stockholders.

As Method 2 in Exhibit 5-7 shows, the APB (after heated debate) concluded in favor of interperiod allocation of income taxes, "both in the manner in which tax effects are initially recognized and in the manner in which deferred taxes are amortized in future periods." Method 2 demonstrates that the effect for a particular asset would be to regard any reported income as if it were subject to the full current tax rate even though a more advantageous accounting method were used for tax purposes. As Exhibit 5-7 shows, this results in a smoothing effect on income in these particular circumstances when the year-by-year effects are viewed over the five-year span.

The deferred income tax payable is a deferred credit in the sense that it is intended to offset the income tax expense in future years. Years 4 and 5 show how the credit is utilized to bring the reported tax expense down to a lower amount. More fundamentally, the deferred tax payable is a liability (rather than a part of stockholders' equity) that should be recognized under the accrual basis of accounting. Proponents of allocation maintain that failure to allocate is tantamount to retrogressing to a cash basis of accounting. Therefore, deferred income taxes should be recognized as a legitimate claim on the assets of the enterprise; it is an

EXHIBIT 5-7

Comparison of Alternative Reporting Practices
For Depreciation and Income Taxes

Facts: Purchase asset for $15 million; five-year life; 60 percent tax rate. Company takes SYD for tax purposes, but uses straight-line depreciation for financial reporting purposes.

		REPORTING FOR TAX PURPOSES			
YEAR	INCOME BEFORE DEPRECIATION AND TAXES	SYD DEPRECIATION	INCOME BEFORE TAX	INCOME TAX PAID	NET INCOME AFTER TAX
1	$10	$\frac{5}{15} \times \$15 = \$ 5$	$ 5	$ 3.0	$ 2.0
2	10	$\frac{4}{15} \times \$15 = 4$	6	3.6	2.4
3	10	$\frac{3}{15} \times \$15 = 3$	7	4.2	2.8
4	10	$\frac{2}{15} \times \$15 = 2$	8	4.8	3.2
5	10	$\frac{1}{15} \times \$15 = 1$	9	5.4	3.6
Cumulative	$50	$15	$35	$21.0	$14.0

obligation to the government that arises because the firm elects to postpone some income tax payments from the present to some future date.

For growing companies, these deferred income tax accounts are likely to accumulate to enormous amounts that will never diminish unless the company starts reducing the level of its operations. For example, in Exhibit 5-7, if the company spent $15 million each year for more plant assets, the additional deferrals in each of these years would more than offset the decline in deferrals in Years 4 and 5 associated with the original $15 million outlay. Exhibit 5-8 summarizes this point.

The objectors to the deferral method point out that tax-allocation procedures should not apply to the recurring differences between taxable income and pretax accounting income in Exhibit 5-8 if there is a relatively stable or growing investment in depreciable assets. This results in an indefinite postponement of the additional tax, a mounting deferred taxes payable that may never be reduced, and a consequent understatement of net income. Note from Year 6 in Exhibit 5-8 that the income taxes payable will never decline unless the company fails to maintain its $15 million annual expenditure each year. Furthermore, if the company continued to grow at the rate of $15 million per year, the expenditure in Year 6 would be $30 million and the deferred income tax account would soar even more.

EXHIBIT 5-7 (cont.)

REPORTING TO STOCKHOLDERS

1. Straight-Line Depreciation and No Tax Allocation

YEAR	INCOME BEFORE DEPRECIATION AND TAXES	STRAIGHT-LINE DEPRECIATION	INCOME BEFORE TAX	INCOME TAX EXPENSE	NET INCOME AFTER TAX	BALANCE SHEET EFFECT: DEFERRED INCOME TAXES
1	$10	$ 3	$ 7	$ 3.0	$ 4.0	—
2	10	3	7	3.6	3.4	—
3	10	3	7	4.2	2.8	—
4	10	3	7	4.8	2.2	—
5	10	3	7	5.4	1.6	—
Cumulative	$50	$15	$35	$21.0	$14.0	

2. Straight-Line Depreciation and Tax Allocation

YEAR	INCOME BEFORE DEPRECIATION AND TAXES	STRAIGHT-LINE DEPRECIATION	INCOME BEFORE TAX	INCOME TAX EXPENSE			NET INCOME AFTER TAX	BALANCE SHEET EFFECT: DEFERRED INCOME TAXES*
				TAX PAID	TAX ALLOCATED	TOTAL TAX EXPENSE		
1	$10	$3	$ 7	$ 3.0	$ 1.2	$ 4.2	$ 2.8	$1.2
2	10	3	7	3.6	0.6	4.2	2.8	1.8
3	10	3	7	4.2	0	4.2	2.8	1.8
4	10	3	7	4.8	−0.6	4.2	2.8	1.2
5	10	3	7	5.4	−1.2	4.2	2.8	0
Cumulative	$50		$35	$21.0	$ 0	$21.0	$14.0	—

*This would ordinarily appear in the liability section of the balance sheet as a separate item just above the stockholders' equity section.

The proponents of deferral reject the growing firm argument as fallacious. The ever-increasing aggregate amount of deferred income taxes is an example of a phenomenon that affects many other accounts in a growing firm. For example, accounts payable and liabilities for product warranties may also grow, but that is not justification for assuming that liabilities for these obligations are unnecessary.

Whatever your reactions to these conflicting arguments, the Board's action on deferred income taxes has reduced the number of available accounting alternatives and increased comparability. The Board supports the view that the amount of taxes payable for a given period does not necessarily measure the appropriate income tax expense related to transactions for that period as measured and reported to stockholders. Income tax expense includes any accrual, deferral, or estimation necessary to

EXHIBIT 5-8

Analysis of Growing Firm and Deferred Income Taxes

Facts: Same as in Exhibit 5-7, except that $15 million is spent each year for additional assets and income increases $10 million each year. In Year 6, the $15 million represents a replacement of the asset originally purchased in Year 1.

		REPORTING FOR TAX PURPOSES				
YEAR	INCOME BEFORE DEPRECIATION AND TAXES	SYD DEPRECIATION		NET INCOME BEFORE TAX	INCOME TAX PAID	NET INCOME AFTER TAX
1	$10	$5		$ 5	$ 3.0	$ 2.0
2	20	4 + 5 = 9		11	6.6	4.4
3	30	3 + 4 + 5 = 12		18	10.8	7.2
4	40	2 + 3 + 4 + 5 = 14		26	15.6	10.4
5	50	1 + 2 + 3 + 4 + 5 = 15		35	21.0	14.0
6	50	1 + 2 + 3 + 4 + 5 = 15		35	21.0	14.0

		REPORTING TO STOCKHOLDERS Straight-Line Depreciation and Tax Allocation						
				INCOME TAX EXPENSE				BALANCE SHEET EFFECT
YEAR	INCOME BEFORE DEPRECIATION AND TAXES	STRAIGHT-LINE DEPRECIATION	NET INCOME BEFORE TAX	TAX PAID	TAX ALLOCATED	TOTAL TAX EXPENSE	NET INCOME AFTER TAX	DEFERRED INCOME TAXES PAYABLE
1	$10	$ 3	$ 7	$ 3.0	$1.2	$ 4.2	$ 2.8	$1.2
2	20	6	14	6.6	1.8	8.4	5.6	3.0
3	30	9	21	10.8	1.8	12.6	8.4	4.8
4	40	12	28	15.6	1.2	16.8	11.2	6.0
5	50	15	35	21.0	—	21.0	14.0	6.0
6	50	15	35	21.0	—	21.0	14.0	6.0

adjust the amount of income taxes payable for the period to measure the tax effects of all revenue and expenses included in the pretax income reported to stockholders. As *Opinion No. 11*, paragraph 29, states:

> Those supporting comprehensive allocation believe that the tax effects of initial timing differences should be recognized and that the tax effects should be matched with or allocated to those periods in which the initial differences reverse [Years 4 and 5 in Exhibit 5-7]. The fact that when the initial differences reverse other initial differences may offset any effect on the amount of taxable income [Years 4, 5, and 6 in Exhibit 5-8] does not . . . nullify the fact

of the reversal.... These initial differences do reverse, and the tax effects thereof can be identified as readily as can those of other timing differences. While new differences may have an offsetting effect, this does not alter the fact of the reversal; without the reversal there would be different tax consequences. Accounting principles cannot be predicated on reliance that offsets will continue.

SUMMARY

The matching of historical costs with revenue is the generally accepted means of measuring net income. But basing such computations on some version of current values has been proposed as a better gauge of the corresponding net increase in net wealth.

General price indexes are used to adjust historical costs so that all expenses are measured in current dollars of the same purchasing power. Such adjustments do not represent a departure from historical cost. In contrast, specific price indexes are often used to implement the current-value approach to measuring net income.

Within the historical-cost framework, there is an immense diversity of accounting alternatives that have quite different impacts on net income. Examples include Fifo and Lifo inventory methods and accounting for the investment tax credit on a flow-through or deferral basis.

There is a need for more uniformity in accounting where underlying circumstances are the same.

SUMMARY PROBLEMS FOR YOUR REVIEW

Problem One

In 1930, a parcel of land was purchased for $1,200. An identical parcel was purchased today for $3,600. The general price-level index has risen from 100 in 1930 to 300 now. Fill in the blanks:

Parcel	*(1)* *Historical Cost* *Measured in 1930* *Purchasing Power*	*(2)* *Historical Cost* *Measured in Current* *Purchasing Power*	*(3)* *Historical Cost* *As Originally* *Measured*
1			
2			
Total			

1. Compare the figures in the three columns. Which total presents a non-sense result. Why?

2. Does the write-up of Parcel 1 in Column 2 result in a gain? Why? Assume that these parcels are the only assets of the business. There are no liabilities. Prepare a complete balance sheet for each of the three columns.

Problem Two

Suppose that a parcel of land is acquired for $1,000 on December 31, 19x1, when the general index is 100. The general price level rose 20 percent during 19x2 and 10 percent during 19x3. The land is sold on December 31, 19x3, for $3,000; it could have been sold on December 31, 19x2, for $1,800.

1. Using four columns, show the balance sheet amount for land plus net income for 19x2 and 19x3 under (1) historical cost—not restated, (2) historical cost—restated, (3) current value—not restated, and (4) current value restated for general price-level effects.

2. At the bottom of your presentation in Requirement 1 show comparative income statistics for the two years and the cumulative gain for the two years.

3. What major points can be learned from the tabulations in Requirements 1 and 2?

Problem Three

"Depreciation somehow is a source of funds: it is used to pay for new fixed assets." Do you agree? Explain.

Problem Four

"When prices are rising, Fifo results in fool's profits because more resources are needed to maintain operations than previously." Do you agree? Explain.

Problem Five

"The lower-of-cost-or-market method is inherently inconsistent." Do you agree? Explain.

Problem Six

Examine Exhibit 5-5. Suppose that only $60 million rather than $70 million of the total purchase price of $120 million could be logically assigned to the plant assets. How would the combined accounts be affected if the merger were accounted for as a purchase?

Problem Seven

Examine Exhibit 5-6. The flow-through method would reduce income taxes by $7,000 in Year 1. How would the relevant balance-sheet and income-statement accounts be affected by the deferral method? Show accounts and amounts for each of the first three years. Assume that income taxes before considering the investment tax credit were $52,000.

Problem Eight

Examine Exhibit 5-8. In Year 7 suppose that $30 million were spent on depreciable assets with five-year lives and that income before depreciation and taxes reached $60 million. For Year 7, fill in all the columns in Exhibit 5-8.

1.

Parcel	*(1)* Historical Cost Measured in 1930 Purchasing Power	*(2)* Historical Cost Measured in Current Purchasing Power	*(3)* Historical Cost as Originally Measured
1	$1,200	$3,600	$1,200
2	1,200	3,600	3,600
Total	$2,400	$7,200	$4,800

The addition in Column 3 produces a nonsense result. In contrast, the other sums are the results of applying a standard unit of measure. The computations in Columns 1 and 2 are illustrations of a restatement of historical cost in terms of a common dollar, a standard unit of measure. Such computations have been frequently termed as adjustments for changes in the general price level. Whether the restatement is made using the 1930 dollar or the current dollar is a matter of personal preference; Columns 1 and 2 yield equivalent results. The preponderance of opinion seems to favor restatement in terms of the current dollar (Column 2) because the current dollar has more meaning to the reader of the financial statements.

The mere restatement of identical assets in terms of different but equivalent measuring units cannot be regarded as a gain. The expression of Parcel 1 as $1,200 in Column 1 and $3,600 in Column 2 is like expressing Parcel 1 in terms of, say, either 1,200 square yards or 10,800 square feet. Surely, the "write-up" from 1,200 square yards to 10,800 square feet is not a gain; it is merely another way of measuring the same asset. The 1,200 square yards and the 10,800 square feet are equivalent; they are different ways of describing the same asset. That is basically what general price-level accounting is all about. It says you cannot measure one plot of land in square yards and another in square feet and add them together before converting to some common measure. Unfortunately, Column 3 fails to perform such a conversion before adding the two parcels together; hence, the total is internally inconsistent.

2. Note especially that write-ups under general price-level accounting do not result in the recognition of gains. They are restatements of costs in dollars of equivalent purchasing power. The balance sheets would be:

	(1)	*(2)*	*(3)*
Land	$2,400	$7,200	$4,800
Stockholders' equity	$2,400	$7,200	$4,800

Solution to Problem Two

1.

	(1) Historical Cost	(2)	(3) Current Value	(4)
	Not Restated	Restated	Not Restated	Restated
Balance-sheet amount of land:				
Dec. 31, 19x1	$1,000	$1,000	$1,000	$1,000
Dec. 31, 19x2	1,000	1,200	1,800	1,800
Dec. 31, 19x3, before sale	1,000	1,320	3,000	3,000
Income-statement gains reported:				
19x2:				
Current value	$ —	$ —	$1,800	$1,800
Historical cost				
Not restated			1,000	
Restated, 120% of				
1,000				1,200
Gain	—	—	$ 800	$ 600
19x3:				
Selling price	$3,000	$3,000	$3,000	$3,000
Historical cost				
Not restated	1,000			
Restated		1,320		
Current value				
Not restated			1,800	
Restated, 110% of				
$1,800				1,980
Gain	$2,000	$1,680	$1,200	$1,020
2. Two-year comparative summary:				
19x2	$ —	$ —	$ 800	$ 660*
19x3	2,000	1,680	1,200	1,020
Cumulative	$2,000	$1,680	$2,000	$1,680

*When statements are recast for the general price level, to compare current with past net income figures, the past net income must be restated in terms of current dollars: $600 × 1.10 = $660.

3. (a) Column 1 depicts the concept of income as usually applied in practice. General price-level accounting as recommended (but not required) by the Accounting Principles Board is concerned with the income concept demonstrated in Column 2; it is *not* concerned with current value concepts of income.

(b) The choices among accounting measures are often expressed as either historical-cost accounting or general price-level accounting or specific price-level (current value) accounting. *But this is an inaccurate and confusing statement of choices.* A correct statement would be that general price-level accounting may be combined with either historical cost accounting (Column 2) or current value accounting (Column 4).

(c) The difference between current value and historical cost concepts of income is primarily the *timing* of the recognition of income. The cumulative effects of both concepts on income are identical.

Solution to Problem Three

By now, it should be clear that depreciation can be usefully viewed in two lights. Accountants view depreciation as a systematic and rational allocation to operations of the cost of plant assets. Many accounting professors abhor any other interpretation. They become visibly upset when a student or a professor of finance uses sloppy terminology such as "depreciation is a source of funds" or "cash flow from depreciation last year was a million dollars." Given the accountant's definition, such terminology is inaccurate and is likely to be misleading.

Financial analysts often view depreciation differently. An analyst looks upon depreciation as that portion of incoming *funds from customers* which is, or should be, devoted to replacing or expanding plant assets or to retirements of long-term debt that arose from past outlays for plant assets. In short, a part of the funds provided by operations is considered to be the recovery of past outlays for plant assets. There is no harm in this line of thought as long as the act of recording depreciation is not considered, by itself, as the act of generating cash or funds, and also as long as the amount of depreciation recorded is not considered to be the amount required to replace the assets.

Solution to Problem Four

The merit of this position is directly dependent on the concept of income favored. As Exhibit 5-3 shows, Lifo does give a better measure of "distributable" income than Fifo. Fifo increases profits by the $50 difference in ending inventory valuation (1,000 units @ 5¢). The $50 in a sense is "tied up" in maintaining the same inventory level as previously; therefore, it cannot be distributed as a cash dividend without contracting the current level of operations.

Solution to Problem Five

The inconsistency is the willingness of accountants to have replacement costs used as a basis for write-downs below historical costs, even though a market exchange has not occurred, but the unwillingness to have replacement costs used as a basis for write-ups above historical costs. Historical cost is an upper limit for valuation under generally accepted accounting principles.

Solution to Problem Six

Accounting as a purchase would necessitate recognizing a new asset, goodwill, at $10 million. Plant assets would be carried at $120 million rather than the $130 million shown in Exhibit 5-5 because the newly acquired plant assets are now $60 million instead of $70 million.

Solution to Problem Seven

The deferral method would appear as follows in each of the three years:

		Year One		Each of Years Two and Three	
Income before taxes					
($50,000 + $52,000)			$102,000		$102,000
Income tax expenses:					
Taxes paid	($52,000 − $7,000)	$45,000		$52,000	
Taxes allocated to this year		6,300		700	
Total income tax expense			51,300		51,300
Net income			$ 50,700		$ 50,700

The balance sheet at the end of the first year would show a deferred credit of $7,000 − $700, or $6,300. This balance would decline by $700 annually as the beneficial effects of the investment credit are spread out over the useful life of the asset in the form of an annual reduction of income taxes. At the end of Year 3, the balance in deferred income taxes would be $7,000 − 3($700), or $4,900.

Solution to Problem Eight

For tax purposes:

Income Before Depreciation and Taxes	SYD Depreciation	Net Income Before Tax	Income Tax Paid	Net Income After Tax
$60	$1 + 2 + 3 + 4 + 5 + 5 = $20	$40	$24	$16

For stockholders:

Income Before Depreciation and Taxes	Straight-line Depreciation	Net Income Before Tax	Income Tax Expenses Paid	Income Tax Expenses Allocated	Income Tax Expenses Total	Net Income After Tax	Balance Sheet Effect: Deferred Income Taxes Payable
$60	$18	$42	$24	$1.2	$25.2	$16.8	$7.2

ASSIGNMENT MATERIAL

Note: These problems are generally grouped sequentially in accordance with the topical coverage of the chapter.

5-1. What are the two polar approaches to income measurement?

5-2. Explain how net income is measured under the market-value approach.

5-3. What is *distributable income?*

5-4. Explain what a general price index represents.

5-5. Distinguish between general indexes and specific indexes.

5-6. Enumerate four ways to measure income.

5-7. What does uniformity mean in accounting?

5-8. Briefly distinguish the difference between Fifo and Lifo.

5-9. Does Fifo or Lifo isolate and measure the effects of price fluctuations as special management problems?

5-10. What is meant by the term *market* in inventory accounting?

5-11. What are the relative effects on net income of a strict-cost method and the lower-of-cost-or-market method?

5-12. Why has Lifo been so widely adopted?

5-13. "Lifo reflects current prices in the financial statements." Do you agree? Explain.

5-14. How does goodwill usually arise in accounting?

5-15. "Lifo consistently results in less net income than Fifo." Do you agree? Explain.

5-16. What is an investment tax credit?

5-17. What are the two most widely used methods for accounting for the investment tax credit?

5-18. Which of the two methods of accounting for the investment credit will benefit current income the most?

5-19. Why do deferred federal income taxes arise?

5-20. In brief, why did the Accounting Principles Board favor deferral of income taxes?

5-21. "General price-level accounting is a loose way of achieving replacement cost income accounting." Do you agree? Explain.

5-22. Meaning of general index applications and choice of base year. Mays Company acquired land in mid-1946 for $2,000,000. In mid-1973 it acquired a substantially identical parcel of land for $4,000,000. The gross national product implicit price deflator annual averages were:

$$1973—160.0 \qquad 1958—100.0 \qquad 1946—66.7$$

Required:

1. In four columns, show the computations of the total cost of the two parcels of land expressed in (a) costs as traditionally recorded, (b) dollars of 1973 purchasing power, (c) 1958 purchasing power, and (d) 1946 purchasing power. For ease of computations, round all adjusted figures to the nearest hundred thousand dollars.
2. Explain the meaning of the figures that you computed in Requirement 1.

5-23. Concepts of income. Suppose that on December 31, 19x2, a parcel of land has a' historical cost of $100,000 and a current value (measured via use of a specific price index) of $300,000; the general price level had doubled since the land was acquired. Suppose also that the land is sold on December 31, 19x3, for $360,000. The general price level rose by 5 percent during 19x3.

Required:

1. Compute net income for 19x3 on the historical-cost basis, the current value basis, the historical-cost basis adjusted for changes in the general price level, and the current-value basis also so adjusted.
2. In your own words, explain the meaning of each net income figure.

5-24. Four ways to compute income. Suppose that a parcel of land is acquired at the end of 19x3 for $100,000 when the general price index is 100. Its current value at the end of 19x4 is $140,000; the general price index is 115. There are at least four ways to portray these events:

(1) Historical cost—not restated for general price-level effects.
(2) Historical cost—restated for general price-level effects.
(3) Current value (specific price level)—not restated for general price-level effects.
(4) Current value (specific price level)—restated for general price-level effects.

Required:

1. Using the above four ways as column headings, tabulate the amounts to be shown at the end of 19x4 for land, original capital, retained earnings, and "gain" on the income statement.
2. Suppose that one more year transpires with absolutely no change in either the general price level or in the specific price of the land. Suppose that the land is sold for $140,000 cash. Repeat Requirement 1 for 19x5.
3. Explain the composition of the gain that you show in Requirements 1 and 2. What other major points flow from the tabulations in Requirements 1 and 2?

5-25. Four ways to compute a gain. Land was purchased in Year 1 for $20,000. Market price did not change in Year 1. It was held during Year 2, and its market price increased to $26,000. It was sold for $33,000 at the end of Year 3. The GNP deflator indexes were 100, 110, and 120 for the successive years. There are at least four ways to measure these events:
(1) Historical cost—not restated for general price-level effects.
(2) Historical cost—restated for general price-level effects.
(3) Current value—not restated for general price-level effects.
(4) Current value—restated for general price-level effects.

Required:

1. Using the above four ways as column headings, tabulate the amounts to be shown for land on the balance sheet at the end of Year 1, Year 2, and before the sale at the end of Year 3. Also show the gains to be reported in the income statement for each year.
2. Explain the composition of the gains shown in Requirement 1. What other major points flow from the tabulations?

5-26. Depreciation and the general price level. An accounting research study[6] examined the following facts. Suppose that $100,000 is invested in a group of assets with an expected life of five years with no scrap value, that the straight-line method of depreciation is used, that the general price index is 120 for the year of acquisition, and that the index increases ten points a year during the next four years. The results follow:

Year	Price-Level Index	Unadjusted Depreciation	Multiplier	Adjusted Depreciation As Recorded
1	120	$ 20,000	$\frac{120}{120}$	$20,000
2	130	20,000	$\frac{130}{120}$	21,667
3	140	20,000	$\frac{140}{120}$	23,333
4	150	20,000	$\frac{150}{120}$	25,000
5	160	20,000	$\frac{160}{120}$	26,667
		$100,000		

[6]Accounting Research Study No. 6, *op. cit.*, pp. 35–37.

The figures in the last column show the results of applying a general price index. Their sum, $116,667, is meaningless because it combines five different types of dollars.

Required:

1. Convert the figures in the last column so that they are comparable and are expressed in terms of fifth-year dollars.
2. Suppose in Requirement 1 that revenue easily exceeds expenses for each year and that funds equal to the annual depreciation charge were invested in a non-interest-bearing cash account. If amounts equal to the unadjusted depreciation charge were invested each year, would sufficient funds have accumulated to equal the general purchasing power of $100,000 invested in the assets five years ago? If not, what is the extent of the total financial deficiency?
3. Suppose in Requirement 2 that amounts equal to the adjusted depreciation for each year were used. What is the extent of the total financial deficiency?
4. Suppose in Requirement 3, that the amounts were invested each year in assets which increased in value at the same rate as the increase in the general price level. What is the extent of the total financial deficiency?

5-27. Depreciation and price-level adjustments. The Klaman Company purchased a computer for $260,000. It has an expected life of four years and an expected residual value of zero. Straight-line depreciation is used. The general price index is 100 at the date of acquisition; it increases 20 points annually during the next three years. The results follow:

Year	Price-Level Index	Unadjusted Depreciation	Multiplier	Adjusted Depreciation As Recorded
1	100	$ 65,000	$\frac{100}{100}$	$ 65,000
2	120	65,000	$\frac{120}{100}$	78,000
3	140	65,000	$\frac{140}{100}$	91,000
4	160	65,000	$\frac{160}{100}$	104,000
		$260,000		

Required:

1. Convert the figures in the last column so that they are expressed in terms of fourth-year dollars.
2. Suppose in Requirement 1 that revenue easily exceeds expenses for each year and that cash equal to the annual depreciation charge was invested in a noninterest-bearing cash account. If amounts equal to the unadjusted depreciation charge were invested each year, would sufficient cash have accumulated to equal the general purchasing power of $260,000 invested in the asset four years ago? If not, what is the extent of the total financial deficiency measured in terms of fourth-year dollars?
3. Suppose in Requirement 2 that amounts equal to the adjusted depreciation for each year were used. What is the extent of the total financial deficiency?
4. Suppose in Requirement 3 that the amounts were invested each year in assets which increased in value at the same rate as the increase in the general price level. What is the extent of the total financial deficiency?

5-28. Monetary and nonmonetary items and changes in the general price level.
The risks of inflation—of the decline in the general purchasing power of the dollar
—are borne by the holders of monetary assets and monetary liabilities. Monetary
items (for example, cash or accounts receivable or accounts payable) are those that
have prices which cannot change and their amounts therefore remain fixed in
terms of numbers of dollars regardless of changes in specific prices or in the general price level. In contrast, nonmonetary items (for example, inventory, equipment, or stockholders' equity) have prices that can change.

Required:

1. Suppose that a company had $100,000 in cash in 1940 and held this in a safety
   deposit box until today. Meanwhile the general price-level index has risen
   from 100 to 200.
   Fill in the blanks:

	(1) Measured in 1940 Purchasing Power	*(2)* Measured in Current Purchasing Power	*(3)* As Conventionally Measured
Cash balance—1940	_____	_____	_____
Cash balance— today	_____	_____	_____
General price-level loss from holding monetary item	_____	_____	_____

2. Suppose that the $100,000 were invested in a parcel of land in 1940 that had
   been held intact since. Prepare a three-column statement similar to that in
   Requirement 1. Compare the two tabulations; what do they tell you?

5-29. Monetary versus nonmonetary assets and price-level changes. The
Sloan Company owns land acquired for $100,000 one year ago, when the general
price index was 100. It also owns $100,000 of government bonds acquired at the
same time. The index today is 110. Operating expenses and operating revenue,
including interest income, resulted in net income (and an increase of cash) of
$4,000 measured in historical-dollar terms. Assume that all income and expense
transactions occurred yesterday. The Sloan Company has no other assets and no
liabilities. Its cash balance one year ago was zero.

Required:

1. Prepare comparative balance sheets for the two instants of time plus an income
   statement summary based on historical costs. Then prepare such statements on
   a basis restated for changes in the general price level.
2. This is a more important requirement. In your own words, explain the meaning of the price-level-adjusted statement. Why should the holding of a monetary asset generate a monetary loss while the holding of land causes neither a
   loss nor a gain?

5-30. Monetary and nonmonetary items. The Stone Company has the following summarized balance sheet accounts at December 31, 19x2:

	Historical Cost	Restated for General Price Level		Historical Cost	Restated for General Price Level
Monetary assets	$ 20,000	$ 20,000	Monetary liabilities*	$ 30,000	$ 30,000
Nonmonetary assets	80,000	110,000	Stockholders' equity	70,000	100,000
	$100,000	$130,000		$100,000	$130,000

*Includes long-term debt.

Required:

1. Suppose that monetary holdings and debts were constant through the year 19x2. The general price-level index was 110 at December 31, 19x2, and 100 at December 31, 19x1. What was the purchasing power gain or loss? Explain.
2. Suppose that nonmonetary holdings have also remained constant. What was the purchasing power gain or loss on these nonmonetary accounts? Explain.

5-31. Case study of price-level adjustments. The Indiana Telephone Company is the only American company that publishes financial statements restated for changes in the purchasing power of the dollar. The annual report of the company contains two sets of columnar statements, which are too voluminous to reproduce here. Column A presents statements based on historical cost. Column B presents the restated statements.

The Auditor's Opinion included the following:

In our opinion, the accompanying financial statements shown under Column A present fairly the financial position of the Corporation as of December 31, 1973, and the results of its operations and the changes in its financial position for the year then ended, in conformity with generally accepted accounting principles applied on a basis consistent with that of the preceding year.

In our opinion, however, the accompanying financial statements shown under Column B more fairly present the financial position of the Corporation and the results of its operations since appropriate recognition has been given to changes in the purchasing power of the dollar . . .

ARTHUR ANDERSEN & CO.

Required:

Do you agreee that the Column B figures "more fairly" present ITC's financial position and results of operations? Explain.

5-32. Lifo and Fifo. The inventory of the Kiner Coal Company on June 30 shows 1,000 tons at $6 per ton. A physical inventory on July 31 shows a total of 1,200 tons on hand. Revenue from sales of coal for July totals $30,000. The following purchases were made during July:

July 5	2,000 tons @ $7 per ton
July 15	500 tons @ $8 per ton
July 25	600 tons @ $9 per ton

Required:

Compute the inventory value, as of July 31, using:

a. Lifo: last-in, first-out
b. Fifo: first-in, first-out

5-33. Lower of cost or market. The company uses cost or market, whichever is lower. There were no sales or purchases during the periods indicated, and there has been no change in the salability of the merchandise. At what amount would you value merchandise on the dates listed below:

	Invoice cost	Replacement cost
December 31, 19x1	$100,000	$ 80,000
April 30, 19x2	100,000	90,000
August 31, 19x2	100,000	105,000
December 31, 19x2	100,000	65,000

5-34. Multiple choice: comparison of inventory methods. The Byron Corporation began business on January 1, 19x4. Information about its inventories under different valuation methods is shown below. Using this information, you are to choose the phrase which best answers each of the following questions. For each question, insert on an answer sheet *the number which identifies the answer you select.*

			Inventory	
	Lifo Cost	Fifo Cost	Market	Lower of Specifically Identified Cost or Market
December 31, 19x4	$10,200	$10,000	$ 9,600	$ 8,900
December 31, 19x5	9,100	9,000	8,800	8,500
December 31, 19x6	10,300	11,000	12,000	10,900

1. The inventory basis which would show the *highest net income for 19x4* is: (a) Lifo cost; (b) Fifo cost; (c) market; (d) lower of cost or market.
2. The inventory basis which would show the *highest net income for 19x5* is: (a) Lifo cost; (b) Fifo cost; (c) market; (d) lower of cost or market.
3. The inventory basis which would show the *lowest net income for the three years combined* is: (a) Lifo cost; (b) Fifo cost; (c) market; (d) lower of cost or market.
4. For the year 19x5, how much higher or lower would profits be on the *Fifo-cost basis* than on the *lower-of-cost-or-market basis?* (a) $400 higher; (b) $400 lower; (c) $600 higher; (d) $600 lower; (e) $1,000 higher; (f) $1,000 lower; (g) $1,400 higher; (h) $1,400 lower.
5. On the basis of the information given, it appears that *the movement of prices* for the items in the inventory was: (a) up in 19x4 and down in 19x6; (b) up in both 19x4 and 19x6; (c) down in 19x4 and up in 19x6; (d) down in both 19x4 and 19x6.

5-35. Fifo and Lifo. Two companies, the Lifo Company and the Fifo Company, are in the scrap metal warehousing business as arch-competitors. They are about the same size and in 19x1 coincidentally encountered seemingly identical operating situations.

Their beginning inventory was 10,000 tons; it cost $50 per ton. During the year, each company purchased 50,000 tons at the following prices:

20,000 @ $70
30,000 @ $90

Each company sold 45,000 tons at average prices of $100 per ton. Other expenses in addition to cost of goods sold but excluding income taxes were $700,000. The income tax rate is 60 percent.

Required:

1. Compute net income for the year for both companies. Show your calculations.
2. As a manager, which method would you prefer? Why? Explain fully. Include your estimate of the overall effect of these events on the cash balances of each company, assuming that all transactions during 19x1 were direct receipts or disbursements of cash.

5-36. Eroding the Lifo base. Many companies on Lifo occasionally are faced with strikes or material shortages that necessitate a reduction in their normal inventory levels in order to satisfy current sales demands. A few years ago several large steel companies requested special legislative relief from the additional taxes that ensued from such events.

A news story stated:

As steelworkers slowly streamed back to the mills this week, most steel companies began adding up the tremendous losses imposed by the longest strike in history. At a significant number of plants across the country, however, the worry wasn't losses but profits—"windfall" bookkeeping profits that for some companies may mean painful increases in corporate income taxes.

These outfits have been caught in the backfire of a special mechanism for figuring up inventory costs on tax returns. It's known to accountants as Lifo, or last in, first out. Ironically, it's designed to slice the corporate tax bill in a time of rising prices.

Biggest Bite—Most of the big steel companies—16 out of the top 20 —as well as 40 percent of all steel warehousers, use Lifo accounting in figuring their taxes. But the tax squeeze from paper Lifo profits won't affect them all equally. It will put the biggest bite on warehousers that kept going during the strike—and as a result, the American Steel Warehouse Assn. may ask Congress for a special tax exemption on these paper profits. . . .

Companies such as Ryerson and Castle have been caught because they have had to strip their shelves bare in order to satisfy customer demands during the strike. And they probably won't be able to rebuild their stocks by the time they close their books for tax purposes.

To see how this can happen, consider the following example. Suppose that a company adopted Lifo in 19x1. At December 31, 19x8, its Lifo inventory consisted of three "layers":

From 19x1:	100,000 units @ $1.00	$100,000
From 19x4:	50,000 units @ 1.10	55,000
From 19x7:	30,000 units @ 1.20	36,000
		$191,000

In 19x9, prices rose enormously. Data follow:

Sales	500,000 units @ $3.00 =	$1,500,000
Purchases	340,000 units @ 2.00 =	680,000
Operating expenses		500,000

A prolonged strike near the end of the year resulted in a severe depletion of the normal inventory stock of 180,000 units. The strike was settled on December 28, 19x9. The company intended to replenish the inventory as soon as possible.

The applicable income tax rate is 60 percent.

Required:

1. Compute the income taxes for 19x9.
2. Suppose that the company had been able to meet the 500,000-unit demand out of current purchases. Compute the income taxes for 19x9 under those circumstances.

5-37. Lifo inventories and replacement costs. J. L. Castleman & Company is a metals distributor carrying some 20,000 different sizes, shapes, and grades of metal in inventory. Purchases are made in large quantities and standardized mill sizes from the basic producers of the metals. Sales are made in relatively small quantities to meet specific needs of more than 30,000 customers.

The current assets section of the balance sheets contained in J. L. Castleman & Company's 19x8 and 19x9 annual report included:

	19x9	*19x8*
Inventories of merchandise, at lower of cost (principally on last-in, first-out basis which is approximately $2,440,000 under cost at December 31, 19x9, and $2,150,000 under cost at December 31, 19x8) or market	$15,969,183	$13,545,931

Assume that J. L. Castleman & Company was considering measuring year-end inventories at current replacement cost, as advocated by some accountants and managers.

Required:

1. Indicate the effect on total current assets at December 31, 19x9, if inventories were measured at replacement cost.
2. If inventories had been consistently measured at current replacement cost, at what amount would the cost of material sold have been measured in the 19x9 income statement? The 19x9 income statement, as reported, measured cost of material sold at $50,049,464.
3. Assume that J. L. Castleman uses the average cost of inventory purchases made during the year to determine the cost of any Lifo layer (the difference between the ending and beginning inventory balances) added. Can you determine from the financial statements if the 19x9 average inventory purchase costs were greater, less than, or equal to the replacement costs on December 31, 19x9? Explain.

5-38. Lifo, Fifo, purchase decisions, and earnings per share. Suppose that a company with one million shares of common stock outstanding has had the following transactions during 19x1, its first year in business:

Sales:	1,000,000 units @ $5
Purchases:	800,000 units @ $2
	300,000 units @ $3

The current income tax rate is a flat 50 percent; the rate next year is expected to be 40 percent. Prices on inventory are not expected to decline next year.

It is December 20, and as the president, you are trying to decide whether you should buy the 600,000 units you need for inventory now or early next year. The current price is $4 per unit. Prices on inventory are expected to remain stable; in any event, no decline in prices is anticipated.

You have not chosen an inventory method as yet, but you will pick either Lifo or Fifo.

Other expenses for the year will be $1,400,000.

Required:

1. Using Lifo, prepare a comparative income statement assuming the 600,000 units (a) are not purchased (b) are purchased. The statement should end with reported earnings per share.
2. Repeat Requirement 1, using Fifo.
3. Comment on the above results. Which method would you choose? Why? Be specific.
4. Suppose in Year 2 that the tax rate drops to 40 percent, that prices remain stable, that 1,000,000 units are sold @ $5, that enough units are purchased at $4 so that the ending inventory will be 700,000 units, and that other expenses are reduced to $800,000.
   a. Prepare a comparative income statement for the second year showing the impact of each of the four alternatives on net income and earnings per share for the second year.
   b. Explain any difference in net income that you encounter among the four alternatives.
   c. Why is there a difference in ending inventory values under Lifo even though the same amount of physical inventory is in stock?
   d. What is the total cash outflow for income taxes for the two years together under the four alternatives?
   e. Would you change your answer in Requirement 3 now that you have completed Requirement 4? Why?

5-39. Effects of Lifo on purchase decisions. The Bjork Corporation is nearing the end of its first year in business. The following purchases of its single product have been made:

	Units	Unit Price	Total Cost
January	1,000	$10	$10,000
March	1,000	10	10,000
May	1,000	11	11,000
July	1,000	13	13,000
September	1,000	14	14,000
November	1,000	15	15,000
	6,000		$73,000

Sales for the year will be 5,000 units for $120,000. Expenses other than cost of goods sold will be $20,000.

The president is undecided about whether to adopt Fifo or Lifo for income tax purposes. The company has ample storage space for up to 7,000 units of inventory. Inventory prices are expected to stay at $15 per unit for the next few months.

Required:

1. If the president decided to purchase 4,000 units @ $15 in December, what would be the net income before taxes, the income taxes, and the net income after taxes for the year under: (a) Fifo; and (b) Lifo? Income tax rates are 30 percent on the first $25,000 of net taxable income and 50 percent on the excess.
2. If the company sells its year-end inventory in Year 2 @ $24 per unit and goes out of business, what would be the net income before taxes, the income taxes, and the net income after taxes under: (a) Fifo; and (b) Lifo? Assume that other expenses in Year 2 are $20,000.
3. Repeat Requirements 1 and 2, assuming that 4,000 units, @ $15, were not purchased until January of the second year. Generalize on the effect on net income of the timing of purchases under Fifo and Lifo.

5-40. Effects of Lifo and Fifo. (Adapted from a problem originated by George H. Sorter.) The Cado Company is starting in business on December 31, 19x0. In each *half year,* from 19x1 through 19x4, they expect to purchase 1,000 units and sell 500 units for the amounts listed below. In 19x5, they expect to purchase no units and sell 4,000 units for the amount indicated below.

	19x1	*19x2*	*19x3*	*19x4*	*19x5*
Purchases:					
First 6 months	$ 2,000	$ 4,000	$ 6,000	$ 6,000	0
Second 6 months	4,000	9,000	6,000	8,000	0
Total	$ 6,000	$13,000	$12,000	$14,000	0
Sales (at selling price)	$10,000	$10,000	$10,000	$10,000	$40,000

Assume that there are no costs or expenses other than those shown above. The tax rate is 60 percent, and taxes for each year are payable on December 31 of each year. Cado Company is trying to decide whether to use periodic Fifo or Lifo throughout the five-year period.

Required:

1. What was net income after taxes under Fifo for each of the five years? Under Lifo? Show calculations.
2. Explain briefly which method, Lifo or Fifo, seems more advantageous, and why.

5-41. Purchase and goodwill. Examine Exhibit 5-5. Suppose that only $50 million rather than $70 million of the total purchase price of $120 million could logically be assigned to the plant assets.

Required:

1. How would the combined accounts be affected if the merger were accounted for as a purchase?

2. Assume a straight-line depreciation rate of 20 percent. What would be the net income for the next year after the purchase, where goodwill is not amortized? After the purchase, where goodwill is amortized over a five-year period? Over a forty-year period?

5-42. Purchases and goodwill. The B Company and the Y Company have neither debt nor preferred stock outstanding. The accounts at December 31, 19x1 are:

	B	Y
Net assets	$99,000,000	$27,000,000
Stockholders' equity	$99,000,000	$27,000,000
Net income	$10,000,000	$10,000,000

B combined with Y by issuing stock with a market value of $67,000,000 in exchange for the shares of Y. Assume that the book value and the current value of the individual assets of Y were equal.

Required:

1. Show the balance-sheet accounts and immediate net income for the combined companies as they would appear if the merger were accounted for as a $67,000,000 purchase with recognition of purchased goodwill. Assume that goodwill is not amortized.
2. How would net income in Requirement 1 above be affected if goodwill were amortized on a straight-line basis over five years? Comment on the results.

5-43. Allocating total purchase price to assets. Two companies had the following balance-sheet accounts as of December 31, 19x1 (in millions):

	Grey-mont	Para-delt		Grey-mont	Para-delt
Cash and			Current liabilities	$ 50	$ 20
receivables	$ 30	$ 22	Common stock	100	10
Inventories	120	3	Retained income	150	90
Plant assets, net	150	95	Total equities	$300	$120
Total assets	$300	$120			
Net income for					
19x1	$ 19	$ 4			

On January 4, 19x2, these companies merged. Greymont issued $180 million of its shares (at market value) in exchange for all of the capital stock of Paradelt, a motion picture company. The inventory of films acquired through the merger had been fully amortized on Paradelt's books.

During 19x2, Greymont entered into many television distribution contracts that called for $21 million in film rentals over a prolonged span of years. These rentals were to be collected over this period of time, but the contracts were used as support for immediate recognition of revenue (and consequent net income).

Greymont earned $20 million on its other operations during 19x2. Paradelt broke even on its other operations during 19x2.

Required:

1. Prepare a consolidated balance sheet for the merged company immediately after the merger on a purchase basis. Assume that on a purchase basis $80 million would be assigned to the inventory of films.
2. Prepare a comparison of net income between 19x1 and 19x2 where 25 percent of the cost of the film inventories would be properly matched against the revenue from the television contracts. What would be the net income for 19x2 if the $80 million were assigned to goodwill rather than to the library of films, and goodwill were amortized over forty years?

5-44. Accounting for the purchase of another company. The following are excerpts from the 1973 annual report of the Champion Spark Plug Company. The following footnote describes Champion's acquisition of 74 percent of the common stock of the DeVilbiss Company:

> In 1973, the Company acquired approximately 74 percent of the common stock of The DeVilbiss Company at a cost of $38,887,364 which was paid in cash ($28,404,824) and by issuing its 6% notes for the remainder. The notes, which are due to former shareholders of the subsidiary in the amounts of $5,438,640 and $5,043,900, are due on April 10, 1974 and April 10, 1975, respectively. The statement of consolidated earnings includes the operations of DeVilbiss and its consolidated subsidiaries from July 1, 1973, the approximate date of acquisition.
>
> The Company has elected to amortize the excess of cost over equity acquired over a twenty-year period.
>
> As a result of the above transaction, the Company changed its consolidation policy from the inclusion of only wholly-owned subsidiaries to also include the accounts of its other majority-owned subsidiaries. The consolidated financial statements for the year ended December 31, 1972 have been restated to include the subsidiaries previously omitted.

Other pertinent items are:

	December 31	
	1973	*1972*
From balance sheet:		
Included in intangible assets, at amortized cost:		
Excess of cost over equity acquired in subsidiary company	$17,464,993	—
Minority interest in subsidiary companies	9,901,657	1,591,359
Included in income statement for 1973, amortization of excess cost	431,685	

Required:

1. The balance sheet for Champion Spark Plug Company includes an item called "Excess of cost over equity acquired in subsidiary company." Briefly describe the nature of this item. (Assume it relates entirely to the DeVilbiss Company.)
2. What was the approximate book value of the total net assets of DeVilbiss at July 1, 1973? Show all calculations.
3. The 1973 annual report of the DeVilbiss Company revealed a net income of $3,968,579 for the year ended December 31, 1973. Assuming that the net in-

come of DeVilbiss was evenly distributed throughout 1973, how much of the net income of DeVilbiss is included in Champion's retained earnings at December 31, 1973?

4. The 1973 annual report of the DeVilbiss Company also revealed a total stockholder's equity of $29,559,780 at December 31, 1973: How much of the "Minority Interest in Subsidiary Companies" shown on Champion's consolidated balance sheet at December 31, 1973, represents the equity of minority interests of DeVilbiss?

5-45. Investment credit. The Scott Company purchased machinery for $300,000. Its estimated useful life is eight years; its expected scrap value is zero. Net income (after taxes but before considering the investment credit) is $160,000 annually. Income taxes before considering the investment credit were $100,000.

Required:

1. Net income for Year One under the flow-through method.
2. Net income for Years 1, 2, and 3 under the deferral method. Show how the income statement and balance-sheet accounts will be affected by the deferral method for each of the first three years.

5-46. Computer leasing companies and the materiality of the investment credit. The following news item appeared in the *Wall Street Journal:*

Even suggesting elimination of the 7% investment tax credit for corporations —as some Senators have done—is enough to send analysts running to their profit tables. . . . The possibility warrants a close look at one prominent group of tax credit beneficiaries—computer leasing companies.

The contribution of the tax credit to earnings also could shrink if the companies decrease purchases of new computer equipment, as some have indicated they may do. "It will be necessary to substitute purchases of equivalent capital goods if the companies don't wish to lose the benefits of the credit," the analysts say.

Here's how they list the tax-credit portion, compared with per-share profit of leading companies, all traded on the American exchange:

Dearborn Computer, 56 cents of the $1.50 in the year ended last Sept. 30.

Data Processing Financial, 64 cents of $1.81 in the nine months ended Feb. 28.

Granite Equipment, 17 cents of the 50 cents in the six months ended last Aug. 30.

Levin-Townsend, 64 cents of the $2.22 in the eight months ended last Nov. 30.

Randolph Computer, 15 cents of the $1.82 in the year ended Dec. 31.

Leasco Data, 10 cents on the 32 cents earned on computer operations in the year ended last Sept. 30.

Required:

How do the above facts influence your judgment as to whether flow-through or deferral is the "better" accounting method for the investment credit?

5-47. Investment credit and airlines. Suppose that United Airlines purchases ten new airplanes for $7,000,000 each. Their estimated useful life is fourteen years.

Ignore scrap value. Net earnings before considering the investment credit are averaging $50 million annually. Twenty million common shares are outstanding.

Required:

1. For the first four years, show how net income and earnings per share would differ between flow-through and deferral of the investment credit.
2. Repeat Requirement 1, but assume that $70 million is spent in each of the four years to replace ten worn-out airplanes that were originally not subject to the investment credit.
3. Suppose there is a severe economic recession. To encourage investment, Congress increases the investment tax credit from 7 percent to 40 percent for a duration of one year. Repeat Requirement 1. Which of the two computations of net income "present fairly" the results of operations? Why?
4. Examine the results in Requirements 1 and 2. If United Airlines steadily expands, how will net income be affected under the two methods? Compute the difference for Years 1 and 2 if United spent $105 million on new equipment in Year 2.

5-48. Analysis of deferral method for investment credit and earnings per share. The following excerpts are from the annual report of Rational Airlines for the fiscal year ending June 30, 1973:

	June 30, 1973	June 30, 1972
Balance sheet: Deferred investment tax credits	$14,566,587	$5,868,000

Income statement:	Year ended June 30, 1973
Income before income taxes	$39,773,586
Income taxes	18,648,000
Net income	$21,125,586
Shares outstanding (rounded), 8,400,000	
Earnings per share	$2.51

A footnote stated:

Federal income tax payments for fiscal 1973 were $6,065,000 after deduction of investment tax credits in the amount of $6,083,000. In addition, $4,159,000 of investment tax credits were utilized for refund of federal income taxes paid in prior years and such amount is included in Accounts Receivable at June 30, 1973.

For corporate financial reporting purposes, the investment tax credit is amortized over the depreciable lives of the related assets. Such amortization reduced income tax expenses by $1,544,000 in fiscal 1973. A balance of $14,566,000 of investment tax credit is available for reduction of income tax expense in future years.

This note highlights an aspect of the investment credit not discussed in the text. The investment credit may be used to offset up to a maximum of 50 percent of the tax otherwise payable. For example, if the available investment credit is $10 million and income taxes payable for 19x9 are $12 million, the maximum credit allowable for that year is $6 million. However, any amount not usable in the current year because of these limitations may be "carried back" to the preceding three years and carried forward to the next five years.

Required:

1. Prepare an analysis of the deferred investment tax credits of Rational Airlines. Begin with the opening balance, add the credits received and utilized this year, and deduct the amortization for fiscal 1973 to arrive at the ending balance.
2. If Rational had flowed-through their credits, what would earnings per share have been? Show your computations.
3. The following are excerpts from the 1973 annual report of Uniter Airlines:

	1973	1972
Net earnings	$41,750,000	$72,819,000
Net earnings per common share (rounded)	$ 2.20	$ 4.28
Shares outstanding (rounded)	19,000,000	17,000,000

A footnote stated: "Investment tax credits reduced income tax provisions for 1973 by $3,793,000 ($18,337,000 in 1972)."

What is the impact on earnings per share of the investment tax credits for each year?

4. Another part of the Rational report stated:

These investment tax credits were derived from acquisition of the 23 Boeing 727's and two DC8's during the year . . .

For stockholder reporting purposes we are depreciating our new jet fleet on a straight-line basis over a 12-year life despite the trend of many others to use longer periods.

This is not a trivial point. For example, a footnote in the 1973 report of RWA stated:

Effective January 1, 1973 the depreciable lives of Boeing jet aircraft were extended from 11 to 12 years, as to aircraft equipped with nonfan engines and to 14 years, as to aircraft equipped with fan engines. . . . This had the effect of increasing net income for the year ended December 31, 1973 by $14,000,000.

RWA reported earnings per share of $1.96.

Net income	$21,537,000
Preferred dividends	1,923,000
Net income for common shares	$19,614,000
Common shares (rounded)	10 million
Earnings per share	$1.96

What was the effect of the change in depreciation on earnings per share?

5. If you wished to compare the earnings of Uniter and Rational what major information concerning equipment and taxes would you seek for a reliable comparison of operating performance?

5-49. Effect of flow-through on earnings per share. The 1973 annual report of Southern Pacific Company contained the following footnote: "Federal income taxes charged to income have been reduced by approximately $19,000,000 in 1973 and $10,000,000 in 1972 by application of the 7 percent investment credit for property additions." In 1973 net income per share was $3.26; in 1972, $2.70. There were about 27 million common shares outstanding in each year.

Required:

Compute the effect on earnings per share if flow-through were not used.

5-50. Deferred income taxes. Examine Exhibit 5-8. Suppose in Year 7 that $45 million were spent on fixed assets with five-year lives and that income before depreciation and taxes reached $70 million. For Year 7, fill in all the columns in Exhibit 5-8.

5-51. Fundamentals of income tax allocation. Suppose that the Norfolk & Western Railroad purchases a group of highly specialized freight cars for $2.1 million dollars. They will have a six-year life and no residual value. The company uses sum-of-the-years'-digits depreciation for tax purposes and straight-line depreciation for financial reporting purposes.

The income of this division before depreciation and taxes is $1.0 million. The applicable income tax rate is 40 percent.

Required:

1. For the six years, tabulate the details of how these facts would influence the Norfolk & Western reporting for tax purposes and for reporting to stockholders. Ignore the investment tax credit.
2. How will the Deferred Income Taxes account be affected if capital expenditures are the same each year? Grow each year?

5-52. Installment sales and deferred income taxes. On January 2, 19x1, Retail Appliance Company sold a refrigerator for $540 on an installment sale basis. The sales contract required no down payment and thirty-six payments of $15 per month plus interest on the unpaid balance. The gross margin was 20 percent of the sales price. For purposes of this problem, ignore interest and any carrying charges.

Required:

1. For financial reporting purposes, what is the pretax gross profit on the sale? The Internal Revenue Code gives the retailer the option of using either the accrual or the installment method, whereby 20 percent of each installment payment would be taxable in the period received. Under this method, what would be the pretax gross profit for each of the three years?
2. Assume a 50 percent tax rate. Prepare a table for three years showing the effects of income tax deferral. Use the following columns: pretax gross profit, tax paid, tax allocated, total tax expense, net income after tax, and balance-sheet effect: deferred income taxes.
3. Repeat Requirement 2, assuming that a refrigerator is sold for the same price and terms on January 2, 19x2, and also on January 2, of 19x3, 19x4, and 19x5. Extend the analysis through Year 5.
4. Repeat Requirement 3, assuming that two units are sold on January 2, 19x2, 3 in 19x3, four in 19x4, and five in 19x5.
5. Study the results in the above parts. What conclusions can you draw about the long-run effects of income tax allocation on financial statements?

5-53. **Decline in balance of deferred income taxes.** The following are excerpts from the 1973 annual report of American Machine and Foundry Company (AMF):

	December 31	
	1973	1972
Included in current liabilities:		
Federal income taxes (including deferred		
taxes applicable to installment obligations:		
1973—$5,223,000, 1972—$9,636,000)	$12,769,618	$28,405,310
As a separate item above stockholders' equity:		
Deferred federal income taxes (due princi-		
pally to accelerated depreciation)	16,533,000	20,413,000
In the income statement for the year ending		
December 31:		
Federal taxes on income	19,467,000	19,052,000

Required:

1. Explain the accounting options in the areas of installment sales and depreciation accounting which would give rise to the deferred tax liabilities.
2. The deferred tax liabilities declined between 1972 and 1973. What specific underlying relationship(s) would yield this result?
3. Estimate the profit reported by AMF on its federal tax return in 1973. (For purposes of this estimate, assume a 50 percent tax rate.) Show all your calculations.

5-54. **Investment credit and deferred taxes.** The Wonder Steel Company had used accelerated depreciation for both financial reporting and tax purposes. It had also amortized the investment credit for financial reporting purposes. After enjoying steady growth in earnings for several years, the company encountered severe competition from foreign sources. This had a leveling effect on reported earnings per share.

In 19x8, the company invested $50 million in a mammoth plant construction program. This resulted in an investment credit of $3.5 million for 19x8. Management is seriously considering changing its method of reporting from Requirements 2a to 2d below. Other data:

Useful life of $50 million investment, 20 years with no scrap value

Double declining balance depreciation rate of 10 percent used for tax purposes

Net income before depreciation on new assets and income taxes and investment credit effects, $20 million

Depreciation on new assets for 19x8:

Straight-line	$2.5 million
Double-declining balance	$5 million
Income tax rate, 60 percent	

Required:

1. Compute net taxable income and the total income taxes for 19x8.
2. Suppose that the Wonder Steel Company has 10,000,000 common shares outstanding and no preferred shares outstanding. For financial-reporting purposes, compute net income and earnings per share where:

a. The company uses accelerated depreciation and defers the investment credit.
b. The company uses accelerated depreciation and "flows through" the investment credit.
c. The company uses straight-line depreciation and defers the investment credit.
d. The company uses straight-line depreciation and "flows through" the investment credit.

5-55. Effects of various accounting methods on net income. You are the manager of Drivo Company, a profitable new company that has high potential growth. It is nearing the end of your first year in business and you must make some decisions regarding accounting policies for financial reporting to stockholders. Your controller and your certified public accountant have gathered the following information (in thousands):

Revenue	$30,000
Beginning inventory	-0-
Purchases	14,000
Ending inventory—Lifo	4,000
Ending inventory—Fifo	5,000
Depreciation—straight-line	1,000
Depreciation—double-declining balance	2,000
Research and development	2,000
Research and development amortized amount	400
Other expenses	4,000
Common shares outstanding (in thousands)	1,000
Income tax rate	50%
Investment credit—total received on tax returns this year	500
Investment credit—amortized amount per year	50

Double-declining balance depreciation and flow-through of the investment credit will be used for tax purposes regardless of the method chosen for reporting to stockholders. For all other items, assume that the same method is used for tax purposes and for financial reporting purposes.

Required:

1. Prepare a columnar income statement. In Column 1 show the results using Lifo, double-declining balance depreciation, direct write-off of research and development, and amortization of the investment credit. Show earnings per share as well as net income. In successive columns, show the separate effects on net income and earnings per share of: 2) Fifo inventory, 3) straight-line depreciation, 4) amortization of research and development, 5) flow-through of investment credit. In Column 6, show all the effects of choosing 2 through 5. Note that in Columns 2 through 5 only single changes in Column 1 should be shown; that is, Column 3 does not show the effects of 2 and 3 together, nor does Column 4 show the effects of 2, 3, and 4 together.
2. As the manager, which accounting policies would you adopt? Why?

THE CORE
OF ACCOUNTING
FOR PLANNING
AND CONTROL

The Master Budget: The Overall Plan

6

Management—and many investors and bank loan officers—has become increasingly aware of the merits of formal business plans. This chapter provides a condensed view of the overall business plan for the forthcoming year (or less)—the **master budget.** The major technical work of the budgetary accountant involves expected future data rather than historical data. There is also a major philosophical difference: The advocates of budgeting maintain that the process of preparing the budget forces executives to become better administrators. Budgeting puts planning where it belongs—in the forefront of the manager's mind.

This chapter provides a bird's-eye view of planning for the organization as a whole. We will see that planning requires all the functions of a business to blend together. We will see the importance of an accurate sales forecast. Most of all, we should begin to appreciate why budgeting is helpful. Budgeting is primarily attention directing, because it helps managers to focus on operating or financial problems early enough for effective planning or action.

This book stresses how accounting helps the **operating** performance of management (how effectively assets are acquired and utilized). But the **financing** function (how funds for investment in assets are obtained) is also important. That is why this chapter examines cash budgets as well as operating budgets. Successful organizations are usually characterized by both superior operating management *and* financial management. Business failures are frequently traceable to management's shirking of the financial aspects of its responsibilities.

Definition of Budget

A budget is a formal quantitative expression of management plans. The master budget summarizes the goals of all subunits of an organization—sales, production, distribution, and finance. It quantifies targets for sales, production, net income, and cash position, and for any other objective that management specifies. The master budget usually consists of a statement of expected future income, a balance sheet, a statement of cash receipts and disbursements, and supporting schedules. These statements are the culmination of a series of planning decisions arising from a detailed, rigorous look at the organization's future.

Advantages of Budgets

Many skeptics who have never used budgets are quick to state, "I suppose budgeting is okay for the other fellow's business, but *my* business is different. There are too many uncertainties and complications to make budgeting worthwhile for me." But the same managers, when prodded for details, usually reveal that they are planning incessantly. Perhaps the best way to combat such a short-sighted attitude is to name others in the same industry who are zealous about budgeting and who, inevitably, are among the industry's leaders. An organization which adopts formal budgeting usually becomes rapidly convinced of its helpfulness and would not consider regressing to its old-fashioned, nonbudgeting days. The benefits of budgeting almost always clearly outweigh the cost and the effort.

Some kind of budget program is bound to be useful to any organization, regardless of its size or its uncertainties. The major benefits are:

1. Budgeting, by formalizing their responsibilities for planning, compels managers to think ahead.

2. Budgeting provides definite expectations that are the best framework for judging subsequent performance.

3. Budgeting aids managers in coordinating their efforts, so that the objectives of the organization as a whole harmonize with the objectives of its parts.

Formalization of Planning

The principal advantage of budgeting is probably that it forces managers to think ahead—to anticipate and prepare for changing conditions. The budgeting process makes planning an explicit management responsibility. Too often, managers operate from day to day, extinguishing one business brush fire after another. They simply have no time for any tough-minded thinking beyond the next day's problems. Planning takes a back seat or is actually obliterated by workaday pressures.

      The trouble with the day-to-day approach to managing an organization is that objectives are never crystallized. Without goals, company operations lack direction, problems are not foreseen, and results are hard to interpret. Advocates of budgeting correctly maintain that most business emergencies can be avoided by careful planning.

Expectations as a Framework for Judging Performance

As a basis for judging actual results, budgeted performance is generally regarded as being better than past performance. The news that a company had sales of $10 million this year, as compared with $8 million the previous year, may or may not indicate that the company has been effective and has achieved maximum success. Perhaps sales should have been $11 million this year. The major drawback of using historical data for judging performance is that inefficiencies may be concealed in the past performance. Moreover, the usefulness of comparisons with the past is also limited by intervening changes in economic conditions, technology, competitive maneuvers, personnel, etc.

      Another benefit of budgeting is that key personnel are informed of what is expected of them. Nobody likes to drift along, not knowing what his boss expects or hopes to achieve.

Coordination and Communication

Coordination is the meshing and balancing of an organization's resources so that its overall objectives are attained—so that the goals of the individual manager harmonize with goals of the organization as a whole. The budget is the means for communicating overall objectives and for blending the objectives of all departments.

      Coordination requires, for example, that purchasing officers integrate their plans with production requirements, and that production officers use the sales budget to help them anticipate and plan for the manpower and plant facilities they will require. The budgetary process obliges executives to visualize the relationship of their department to other departments, and to the company as a whole.

      A budget is not a cure-all for existing organizational ills. It will not solve the problems created by a bumbling management or a faulty information system. The budget is a device whose value depends on its being administered astutely in conjunction with an information system that is tuned to a coordinated organization.

Middle management's attitude toward budgets will be heavily influenced by the attitude of top management. The chief executives must offer wholehearted support if a budgetary program is to achieve maximum benefits.

The ability to adhere to a budget is often an important factor in judging a manager's performance, and naturally, budgets are usually not the most popular feature of a manager's business life. Budgets pinpoint a manager's performance and direct his superior's attention to trouble spots. Few individuals are ecstatic about any techniques used by the boss to check their performance. Budgets are therefore commonly regarded by middle management as embodiments of nickel-nursing, restrictive, negative top-management attitudes.

These misconceptions can be overcome by persuasive education and salesmanship. The budget should not be an unpleasant instrument for harassing the employee. Properly used, it will be a positive aid in setting standards of performance, in motivating toward goals, in metering results, and in directing attention to the areas that need investigation. **The budget is inanimate;** however, its administration is a delicate task because everyone it affects must understand and accept the notion that the budget is primarily designed to help, not hinder.

The supreme importance of the human relations aspects of budgeting cannot be overemphasized. Too often, top management and its accountants are overly concerned with the mechanics of budgets, whereas the effectiveness of any budgeting system depends directly on whether the managers it affects understand it and accept it. Ideally, managers should be cooperative and cost-conscious. This subject is explored more fully in Chapter 11.

TYPES OF BUDGETS

Time Span

The planning horizon for budgeting may vary from a year or less to many years, depending on budget objectives and on the uncertainties involved. Long-range budgets, called **capital budgets,** are often prepared for particular projects such as equipment purchases, locations of plant, and additions of product lines. **Master budgets,** which consolidate an organization's overall plans for a shorter span of time, are usually prepared on an annual basis. The annual budget may be subdivided on a month-to-month basis, or perhaps on a monthly basis for the first quarter and on a quarterly basis for the three remaining quarters.

Continuous budgets are increasingly used. These are master budgets which perpetually add a month in the future as the month just ended is dropped. Continuous budgets are desirable because they compel managers to think specifically about the forthcoming twelve months and thus maintain a stable planning horizon.

Classification of Budgets

The terms used to describe assorted budget schedules vary from company to company. Sometimes budgets are called **pro-forma** statements because they are forecasted financial statements.

Budgets, accompanied by subsidiary schedules, may be classified as follows:

1. Master budget
   a. Operating budget
      (1) Sales budget
      (2) Production budget (for manufacturing companies)
         (a) Materials used and material purchases
         (b) Direct labor
         (c) Indirect manufacturing overhead
         (d) Changes in inventory levels
      (3) Cost-of-goods-sold budget (for merchandising and manufacturing companies)
      (4) Selling expense budget
      (5) Administrative expense budget
   b. Financial budget
      (1) Cash budget: cash receipts and disbursements
      (2) Budgeted balance sheet
      (3) Budgeted statement of sources and applications of funds (net working capital) or budgeted statement of changes in financial position
2. Special budget reports
   a. Performance reports (comparisons of results with plans)
   b. Capital budgets (long-range expectations for specific projects)

ILLUSTRATION OF PREPARATION OF A MASTER BUDGET

Description of Problem

Try to prepare the budget schedules required for the solution of this illustrative problem. Use the basic steps described after the problem. Do not rush. This is a comprehensive illustration which will require some step-by-step thinking and some reflection before a full understanding can be achieved. Although this illustration may seem largely mechanical, remember that the master-budgeting process generates key decisions regarding pricing, product lines, capital expenditures, research and development, personnel assignments, and so forth. Therefore, the first draft of a budget leads to decisions that prompt subsequent drafts before a final

EXHIBIT 6-1
R COMPANY
Balance Sheet
March 31, 19x1

ASSETS		
Current assets:		
Cash	$10,000	
Accounts receivable,		
net (.4 × March sales of $40,000)	16,000	
Merchandise inventory,		
$20,000 + .8 (.7 × April sales of $50,000)	48,000	
Unexpired insurance	1,800	$ 75,800
Plant:		
Equipment, fixtures, and other	$37,000	
Accumulated depreciation	12,800	24,200
Total assets		$100,000

EQUITIES		
Current liabilities:		
Accounts payable		
(.5 × March purchases of $33,600)	$16,800	
Accrued wages and commissions payable		
($1,250 + $3,000)	4,250	$ 21,050
Owners' equity		78,950
Total equities		100,000

budget is chosen. Suppose that *R* Company is a retailer of a wide variety of household items. The company rents a number of retail stores and also has a local door-to-door sales force.

The *R* Company's newly hired accountant has persuaded management to prepare a budget to aid financial and operating decisions. Because this is the company's first attempt at formal budgeting, the planning horizon is only four months, April through July. In the past, sales have increased during the spring season. Collections lag behind and cash is needed for purchases, wages, and other operating outlays. In the past, the company has met this cash squeeze with the help of six-month loans from banks.

Exhibit 6-1 is the closing balance sheet for the fiscal year just ended.

Sales in March were $40,000. Monthly sales are forecasted as follows:

April	$50,000	June	$60,000	August	$40,000
May	$80,000	July	$50,000		

Sales consist of 60 percent cash and 40 percent credit. All credit accounts are collected in the month following the sales. The accounts receivable on March 31 represent credit sales made in March (40 percent of $40,000). Bad debts are negligible and may be ignored.

At the end of any month, the R Company wishes to maintain a basic inventory of $20,000 plus 80 percent of the cost of goods to be sold in the following month. The cost of merchandise sold averages 70 percent of sales. Therefore, the inventory, on March 31, is $20,000 + .8 (.7 × April sales of $50,000) = $20,000 + $28,000 = $48,000. The purchase terms available to the R Company are net, 30 days. Fifty percent of a given month's purchases is paid during that month and 50 percent during the following month.

Wages and commissions are paid semimonthly, half a month after they are earned. They are divided into two portions: monthly fixed wages of $2,500 and commissions, equal to 15 percent of sales, which are uniform throughout each month. Therefore, the March 31 balance of Accrued Wages and Commissions Payable consists of (.5 × $2,500) + .5 (.15 × $40,000) = $1,250 + $3,000 = $4,250. This $4,250 will be paid on April 15. A delivery truck will be purchased for $3,000 cash in April.

Other monthly expenses are:

Miscellaneous expenses	5% of sales, paid as incurred
Rent	$2,000, paid as incurred
Insurance	$200
Depreciation, including new truck	$500

The company desires to maintain a minimum cash balance of $10,000 at the end of each month. Money can be borrowed or repaid in multiples of $1,000, at an interest rate of 6 percent per annum. Management does not want to borrow any more cash than necessary and wants to repay as promptly as possible. Interest is computed and paid when the principal is repaid. Assume that borrowing takes place at the beginning, and repayment at the end, of the months in question.

Required:
1. Using the data given, prepare the following detailed schedules:
   a. Sales forecast.
   b. Cash collection from customers.
   c. Purchases.
   d. Disbursements for purchases.
   e. Wages and commissions.
   f. Disbursements for wages and commissions.

2. Using the data given and the schedules you have compiled, prepare the following major statements:

	March	April	May	June	July	April–July Total
Schedule *a: Sales Forecast*						
Credit sales, 40%	$16,000	$20,000	$ 32,000	$24,000	$20,000	
Cash sales, 60%	24,000	30,000	48,000	36,000	30,000	
Total sales, 100%	$40,000	$50,000	$ 80,000	$60,000	$50,000	$240,000
Schedule *b: Cash Collections*						
Cash sales this month		$30,000	$ 48,000	$36,000	$30,000	
100% of last month's credit sales		16,000	20,000	32,000	24,000	
Total collections		$46,000	$ 68,000	$68,000	$54,000	

	March	April	May	June	July	April–July Total
Schedule *c: Purchases*						
Ending inventory	$48,000	$64,800	$ 53,600	$48,000	$42,400	
Cost of goods sold	28,000*	35,000	56,000	42,000	35,000	$168,000
Total needed	$76,000	$99,800	$109,600	$90,000	$77,400	
Beginning inventory	42,400**	48,000	64,800	53,600	48,000	
Purchases	$33,600	$51,800	$ 44,800	$36,400	$29,400	
Schedule *d: Disbursements for Purchases*						
50% of last month's purchases		$16,800	$ 25,900	$22,400	$18,200	
50% of this month's purchases		25,900	22,400	18,200	14,700	
Disbursements for merchandise		$42,700	$ 48,300	$40,600	$32,900	

*.7 × March sales of $40,000 = $28,000.
**$20,000 + .8(.7 × March sales of $40,000) = $20,000 + $22,400 = $42,400.

	March	April	May	June	July	April–July Total
Schedule *e: Wages and Commissions*						
Wages, all fixed	$ 2,500	$ 2,500	$ 2,500	$ 2,500	$ 2,500	
Commissions (15% of current month's sales)	6,000	7,500	12,000	9,000	7,500	
Total	$ 8,500	$10,000	$ 14,500	$11,500	$10,000	$ 46,000

	April	May	June	July
Schedule *f: Disbursements for Wages and Commissions*				
50% of last month's expenses	$ 4,250	$ 5,000	$ 7,250	$ 5,750
50% of this month's expenses	5,000	7,250	5,750	5,000
	$ 9,250	$ 12,250	$13,000	$10,750

a. Budgeted income statement for four months ending July 31, 19x1.
b. Budgeted statement of cash receipts and disbursements by months, including details of borrowings, repayments, and interest.
c. Budgeted balance sheet as of July 31, 19x1.

The Master Budget: The Overall Plan

For consistency with the numbering scheme used in this book, label your responses to Requirement (2) as Exhibits 6-2, 6-3, and 6-4, respectively. Note that Schedules *a, c,* and *e* will be needed to prepare Exhibit 6-2, and Schedules *b, d,* and *f* will be needed to prepare Exhibit 6-3.

Basic Steps in Preparing Master Budget

The basic steps in preparing budgeted financial statements follow. Use the steps to prepare your own schedules. Then examine the schedules in the Solution.

Step 1. The sales forecast (Schedule *a*) is the starting point for budgeting, because inventory levels, purchases, and operating expenses are generally geared to the rate of sales activity.

Step 2. After sales are budgeted, the purchases budget (Schedule *c*) may be prepared. The total merchandise needed will be the sum of the desired ending inventory plus the amount needed to fulfill budgeted sales demand. The total need will be partially met by the beginning inventory; the remainder must come from planned purchases. Therefore, these purchases are computed as follows: Purchases = Desired ending inventory + Cost of goods sold − Beginning inventory.

EXHIBIT 6-2
R COMPANY
Budgeted Income Statement
For the Four Months Ending July 31, 19x1

		DATA	SOURCE OF DATA
Sales		$240,000	Schedule a
Cost of goods sold		168,000	Schedule c
Gross margin		$ 72,000	
Operating expenses:			
Wages and commissions	$46,000		Schedule e
Rent	8,000		Exhibit 6-3
Miscellaneous expenses	12,000		Exhibit 6-3
Insurance	800		Given
Depreciation	2,000	68,800	Given
Income from operations		$ 3,200	
Interest expense		220	Exhibit 6-3
Net income		$ 2,980	

EXHIBIT 6-3
R COMPANY
Budgeted Statement of Cash Receipts and Disbursements
For the Four Months Ending July 31, 19x1

	APRIL	MAY	JUNE	JULY
Cash balance, beginning	$10,000	$10,550	$10,990	$10,240
Cash receipts:				
Collections from customers (Schedule b)	46,000	68,000	68,000	54,000
w.* Total cash available for needs, before financing	56,000	78,550	78,990	64,240
Cash disbursements:				
Merchandise (Schedule d)	42,700	48,300	40,600	32,900
Wages and commissions (Schedule f)	9,250	12,250	13,000	10,750
Miscellaneous expenses, 5% of sales	2,500	4,000	3,000	2,500
Rent	2,000	2,000	2,000	2,000
Truck purchase	3,000	—	—	—
x . Total disbursements	59,450	66,550	58,600	48,150
Minimum cash balance desired	10,000	10,000	10,000	10,000
Total cash needed	69,450	76,550	68,600	58,150
Excess (deficiency) of total cash available over total cash needed before current financing	(13,450)	2,000	10,390	6,090
Financing:				
Borrowings (at beginning)	14,000**		3 mos	
Repayments (at end)	—	(1,000)	(10,000)	(3,000)
Interest (at 6% per annum)	—	2 mos (10)	(150)	(60)
y . Total effects of financing	14,000	(1,010)†	(10,150)	(3,060)
z . Cash balance, ending (w + y − x)	$10,550	$10,990	$10,240	$13,030

Note: Expired insurance and depreciation do not entail cash outlays.

*Letters are keyed to the explanation in the text.

**Borrowings and repayments of principal are made in multiples of $1,000, at an interest rate of 6 percent per annum.

†$2,000 is not repaid here because the repayment, plus interest of $20, would result in an ending cash balance of $9,980, which—strictly interpreted—is insufficient.

Step 3. The budgeting of operating expenses is dependent on various factors. Many operating expenses are directly influenced by month-to-month fluctuations in sales volume. Examples are sales commissions and delivery expenses. Other expenses are not directly influenced (e.g., rent, insurance, depreciation, certain types of payroll). In this solution, Schedule *e* should be prepared for wages and commissions. The other operating expenses may be entered directly in the pertinent major exhibits.

Step 4. Steps 1 through 3 will provide enough information for a budgeted income statement (Exhibit 6-2).

Step 5. Predict the month-to-month effects on the cash position of

EXHIBIT 6-4

R COMPANY
Budgeted Balance Sheet
July 31, 19x1

ASSETS		
Current assets:		
Cash (Exhibit 6-3)	$13,030	
Accounts receivable (.40 × July sales of $50,000) (Schedule a)	20,000	
Merchandise inventory (Schedule c)	42,400	
Unexpired insurance ($1,800 old balance − $800 expired)	1,000	$ 76,430
Plant:		
Equipment, fixtures, and other ($37,000 + truck, $3,000)	$40,000	
Accumulated depreciation ($12,800 + $2,000 depreciation)	14,800	25,200
Total assets		$101,630

EQUITIES		
Current liabilities:		
Accounts payable (.5 × July purchases of $29,400) (Schedule d)	$14,700	
Accrued wages and commissions payable ($1,250 + $3,750)	5,000	$ 19,700
Owners' equity ($78,950 + $2,980 net income)		81,930
Total equities		$101,630

Note: Beginning balances were used as a start for the computations of Unexpired Insurance, Plant, and Owners' Equity.

the level of operations summarized in Exhibit 6-2. The preparation of the cash budget (Exhibit 6-3) is explained below.

Step 6. In a budgeted balance sheet (Exhibit 6-4), each item is projected in the light of the details of the business plan as expressed in the previous schedules. For example, Unexpired Insurance is $1,800 (the balance on March 31) minus $800 (i.e., $200 × 4 months), or $1,000.

Explanation of Cash Budget

The cash budget (budgeted statement of cash receipts and disbursements, Exhibit 6-3) has the following major sections:

w. The beginning cash balance plus cash receipts yield the total cash available for needs, before financing. Cash receipts depend on collections from customers' accounts receivable and cash sales (Schedule b) and on other operating sources such as miscellaneous rental income. Studies of the collectibility of accounts receivable are a prerequisite to accurate forecasting. Key factors include bad-debt experience and average time lag between sales and collections.

x. Cash disbursements:

(1) Purchases depend on the credit terms extended by suppliers and the bill-paying habits of the buyer (Schedule *d*).

(2) Payroll depends on wage, salary, or commission terms and on payroll dates (Schedule *f*).

(3) Other costs and expenses depend on timing and credit terms. **Note that depreciation does not entail a cash outlay.**

(4) Other disbursements include outlays for fixed assets, long-term investments, installment payments on purchases.

y. Financing requirements depend on how the total cash available *w* (in Exhibit 6-3) compares with the total cash needed. Needs include the disbursements *x* plus the ending cash balance *z* desired. The financing plans will depend on the relationship of cash available to cash sought. If there is an excess, loans may be repaid or temporary investments made. The pertinent outlays for interest expenses are usually contained in this section of the cash budget.

z. The ending cash balance $z = w + y - x$. Financing *y* may have a positive (borrowing) or a negative (repayment) effect on the cash balance. The illustrative cash budget shows the pattern of short-term, self-liquidating financing. Seasonal peaks often result in heavy drains on cash, for merchandise purchases and operating expenses, before the sales are made and cash collected from customers. The resulting loan is self-liquidating—that is, the borrowed money is used to acquire merchandise for sale, and the proceeds from the sale are used to repay the loan. This "working capital cycle" moves from cash to inventory to receivables and back to cash.

Cash budgets help management to avoid having unnecessary idle cash, on the one hand, and unnecessary nerve-racking cash deficiences, on the other. An astutely mapped financing program keeps cash balances in reasonable relation to needs.

THE DIFFICULTIES OF SALES FORECASTING

As you have seen in the foregoing illustration, the sales forecast is the foundation of the entire master budget. The accuracy of estimated production schedules and of cost to be incurred depends on the detail and accuracy, in dollars and in units, of the forecasted sales.

The sales forecast is usually prepared under the direction of the top sales executive. All of the following factors are important: (1) past patterns of sales; (2) the estimates made by the sales force; (3) general economic and competitive conditions; (4) specific interrelationships of sales and economic indicators, such as gross national product or industrial production indexes; (5) changes in prices; (6) market research studies; and (7) advertising and sales promotion plans.

Sales forecasting usually combines various techniques. Opinions of the sales staff are sought. Statistical methods are often used. Correlations between sales and economic indicators help make sales forecasts more reliable. In most cases, the quantitative analysis provided by economists and members of the market research staff provide valuable help but not outright answers. The opinions of line management heavily influence the final setting of sales forecasts.

Pricing policies can have pronounced effects on sales. Management's assessment of price elasticities (the effect of price changes on the physical volume sold) will influence the sales forecast. A company may not offer a single unit price to all customers. In such cases, a detailed analysis of both units to be sold as well as dollar sales is needed for each price category before a final sales forecast can be aggregated.

Sales forecasting is still somewhat mystical, but its procedures are becoming more formal and are being viewed more seriously because of the intensity of competitive pressures. Although this book does not encompass a detailed discussion of the preparation of the sales budget, the importance of an accurate sales forecast cannot be overstressed.

In recent years, the formal use of statistical probabilities has been applied to the problem of sales forecasting. (See Chapter 17 for an elaboration.) Moreover, financial planning models and simulation have enabled managers to get a quantitative grasp on the ramifications of various sales strategies.

FINANCIAL PLANNING MODELS AND SIMULATION

In most cases, the master budget is the best practical approximation to a formal model of the total organization: its objectives, its inputs, and its outputs. If the master budget serves as a "total decision model" for top management, then decisions about strategies for the forthcoming period may be formulated and altered during the budgetary process. Traditionally, this has been a step-by-step process whereby tentative plans are gradually revised as executives exchange views on various aspects of expected activities.

In the future, much of the interaction and interdependence of the decisions will probably be formalized in mathematical simulation models —"total models" that are sometimes called **financial-planning models.**[1] These models are mathematical statements of the relationships in the organization among all the operating and financial activities, and of other major internal and external factors that may affect decisions.

Financial models include all the ingredients for preparing a master budget. However, they can also be used for long-range planning decisions. For example, if managers want to predict the impact of adding a new product line, they can obtain budgeted financial statements for many future years.

Some companies have prepared computerized versions of the master budget. For example, the Sun Oil Company[2] has expressed its processes

---

[1] Vincent R. LoCascio, "Financial Planning Models," *Financial Executive,* Vol. XL, No. 3.

[2] George W. Gershefski, "Building a Corporate Financial Model," *Harvard Business Review,* Vol. 47, No. 4, 61–72.

and accounting as a series of equations that can be manipulated by the computer. The working version required thirteen man-years to complete: ten man-years of analytical time and three of computer coding. An additional ten man-years were devoted to educating management at many levels regarding use of the model.

Many models are constructed and working. They are used for budgeting, for revising budgets with little incremental effort, and for comparing a variety of decision alternatives as they affect the entire firm. The models speed the budgetary process because the sensitivity of income and cash flows to various decisions can be tested promptly via a simulation. Management can react quickly to events and to revisions in predictions of various aspects of operations. Moreover, mathematical probabilities can be incorporated in these models, so that uncertainty can be dealt with explicitly rather than informally.

SUMMARY

The master budget expresses management's overall operating and financing plan. It outlines company objectives and steps for achieving them. The budgetary process compels managers to think ahead and to prepare for changing conditions. Budgets are aids in setting standards of performance, motivating personnel toward goals, measuring results, and directing attention to the areas that most need investigation.

The human factors in budgeting are more important than the mechanics. Top management must support a budgetary program wholeheartedly. The job of educating personnel and selling them on the budget is everlasting, but essential, if those who are affected by the budget are to understand it and accept it. The master budget should be a powerful aid to the most crucial decisions of top management. Often, it falls far short of that role because its potential is misunderstood. Instead of being regarded as a management tool, in many cases the budget is unfortunately looked upon as a necessary evil.

The cornerstone of the budget is the sales forecast. All current operating and financial planning is generally tied to the expected volume of sales.

SUMMARY PROBLEM FOR YOUR REVIEW

Problem

Before attempting to solve the homework problems, review the R Company illustration in this chapter.

Fundamental Assignment Material

6-1. Terminology. Define *master budget; continuous budget; pro-forma statements;* and *cash budget.*

6-2. Prepare master budget. (Problem 6-23 may be substituted for this problem.) The Loebl Company wants a master budget for the next three months, beginning January 1, 19x2. It desires an ending minimum cash balance of $4,000 each month. Sales are forecasted at average selling prices of $4 per unit. Inventories are supposed to equal 125 percent of the next month's sales in units, except for the end of March. The March 31 inventory in units should be 75 percent of the next month's sales. Merchandise costs are $2 per unit. Purchases during any given month are paid in full during the following month. All sales are on credit, payable within thirty days, but experience has shown that 40 percent of current sales are collected in the current month, 40 percent in the next month, and 20 percent in the month thereafter. Bad debts are negligible.

Monthly operating expenses are as follows:

Wages and salaries	$12,000
Insurance expired	100
Depreciation	200
Miscellaneous	2,000
Rent	100 + 10% of sales

Cash dividends of $1,000 are to be paid quarterly, beginning January 15, and are declared on the fifteenth of the previous month. All operating expenses are paid as incurred, except insurance, depreciation, and rent. Rent of $100 is paid at the beginning of each month, and the additional 10 percent of sales is paid quarterly on the tenth of the month following the quarter. The next settlement is due January 10.

The company plans to buy some new fixtures, for $2,000 cash, in March.

Money can be borrowed or repaid in multiples of $500, at an interest rate of 6 percent per annum. Management wants to minimize borrowing and repay rapidly. Interest is computed and paid when the principal is repaid. Assume that borrowing takes place at the beginning, and repayments at the end, of the months in question. Money is never borrowed at the beginning and repaid at the end of the *same* month. Compute interest to the nearest dollar.

Assets as of December 31:		Liabilities as of December 31:	
Cash	$ 4,000	Accounts payable	
Accounts receivable	16,000	(merchandise)	$28,750
Inventory	31,250	Dividends payable	1,000
Unexpired insurance	1,200	Rent payable	7,000
Fixed assets, net	10,000		$36,750
	$62,450		

Recent and forecasted sales:

| October | $30,000 | December $20,000 | February $60,000 | April $36,000 |
| November | 20,000 | January 50,000 | March 30,000 | |

Required:

1. Prepare a master budget, including a budgeted income statement, balance sheet, statement of cash receipts and disbursements, and supporting schedules.
2. Explain why there is a need for a bank loan and what operating sources provide the cash for the repayment of the bank loan.

Additional Assignment Material

6-3. What are the major benefits of budgeting?

6-4. Why is budgeted performance better than past performance, as a basis for judging actual results?

6-5. What is coordination?

6-6. "Education and salesmanship are key features of budgeting." Explain.

6-7. "Capital budgets are plans for managing long-term debt and common stock." Do you agree? Explain.

6-8. "*Pro-forma* statements are those statements prepared in conjunction with continuous budgets." Do you agree? Explain.

6-9. What is the difference between an operating budget and a financial budget?

6-10. Why is the sales forecast the starting point for budgeting?

6-11. What is a self-liquidating loan?

6-12. What is the principal objective of a cash budget?

6-13. What factors influence the sales forecast?

6-14. "There are too many uncertainties and complications to make budgeting worthwhile in my business." Do you agree? Explain.

6-15. What is the major technical difference between historical and budgeted financial statements?

6-16. **Cash budget.** Kay Sharon is the manager of an extremely successful gift shop, Gifts for Charities, that is operated for the benefit of local charities. From the data below, she wants a cash budget showing expected cash receipts and disbursements for the month of April, and the cash balance expected as of April 30, 19x1:

Bank note due April 10, $100,000 plus $5,000 interest.

Depreciation for April, $3,000.

Two-year insurance policy due April 14 for renewal: $3,000, to be paid in cash.

Planned cash balance, March 31, 19x1: $100,000.

Merchandise purchases for April: $700,000, 40% paid in month of purchase, 60% paid in next month.

Customer receivables as of March 31: $100,000 from February sales, $600,000 from March sales.

Payrolls due in April, $120,000.

Other expenses for April, payable in April: $60,000.

Accrued taxes for April, payable in June: $9,000.

Sales for April: $1,400,000, half collected in month of sale, 40% in next month, 10% in third month.

Accounts payable, March 31, 19x1: $600,000.

Required:

Prepare the cash budget.

6-17. Importance of sales forecast. A retail department of a local chain of department stores sells a plain and a fancy pound box of hard candy. The candy is purchased in bulk from a local candy manufacturer, and two types of pound containers are purchased from a local container manufacturer. The store clerks use a back room for packaging the candy, as the need arises. Purchasing and selling prices have been stable, and no price changes are anticipated.

It is near the end of October. Orders must be placed today for delivery by November 1. These orders are to provide sufficient stock to last through the Christmas season.

Federal Reserve statistics for the local area show retail department store sales to be 2 percent over last year, for the period January 1–September 30. The store's top management anticipates an increase of 1 percent in dollar sales of ordinary items and of 10 percent in dollar sales of luxury items this year, as compared with last year.

Other data are:

	Last Year		This Year	
	November	December	Inventory Oct. 31	Target Inventory Dec. 31
Selling price per pound, $1.50 fancy and $1.00 plain				
Pounds sold:				
Plain	4,000	7,000		
Fancy	4,000	12,000		
Pounds			1,000	600
Number of containers:				
Plain			200	100
Fancy			500	100
Purchase costs:				
Candy, per pound $.40				
Container, plain $.05				
Container, fancy $.20				

Required:

Prepare the following:

1. Budgeted sales of plain candy, in pounds and in total dollars, for November and December.

2. Budgeted sales of fancy candy, in pounds and in total dollars, for November and December.
3. Pounds and total cost of needed candy purchases.
4. Number and total cost of needed plain containers.
5. Number and total cost of needed fancy containers.

6-18. Sales forecasting. In each of the diagrams *a* through *e* on page 209, the dollar value of a sales order is contrasted with the quantity of product or service sold. Assume a single product in each case.

Required:

1. What pricing policy is reflected by these order patterns (assuming that all customers are rational)?
2. Why are these patterns relevant to a sales forecast?

6-19. Comprehensive budgeting for a college. (CPA adapted). DeMars College has asked your assistance in developing its budget for the coming 19x1–x2 academic year. You are supplied with the following data for the current year:

a.

	Lower Division (Freshman– Sophomore)	Upper Division (Junior– Senior)
Average number of students per class...............	25	20
Average salary of faculty member	$10,000	$10,000
Average number of credit hours carried each year per student	33	30
Enrollment including scholarship students	2,500	1,700
Average faculty teaching load in credit hours per year (10 classes of 3 credit hours).................	30	30

For 19x1–x2, lower division enrollment is expected to increase by 10 percent, while the upper division's enrollment is expected to remain stable. Faculty salaries will be increased by a standard 5 percent, and additional merit increases to be awarded to individual faculty members will be $90,750 for the lower division and $85,000 for the upper division.

b. The current budget is $210,000 for operation and maintenance of plant and equipment; this includes $90,000 for salaries and wages. Experience of the past three months suggests that the current budget is realistic, but that expected increases for 19x1–x2 are 5 percent in salaries and wages and $9,000 in other expenditures for operation and maintenance of plant and equipment.

c. The budget for the remaining expenditures for 19x1–x2 is as follows:

Administrative and general.........$240,000
Library 160,000
Health and recreation................ 75,000
Athletics............................. 120,000
Insurance and retirement 265,000
Interest 48,000
Capital outlay....................... 300,000

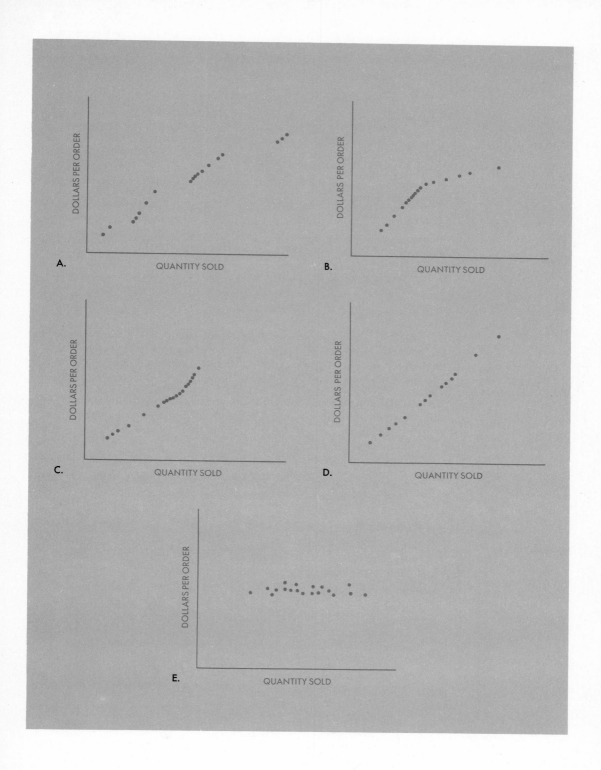

A.

QUANTITY SOLD

DOLLARS PER ORDER

B.

QUANTITY SOLD

DOLLARS PER ORDER

C.

QUANTITY SOLD

DOLLARS PER ORDER

D.

QUANTITY SOLD

DOLLARS PER ORDER

E.

QUANTITY SOLD

DOLLARS PER ORDER

d. The college expects to award twenty-five tuition-free scholarships to lower division students and fifteen to upper division students. Tuition is $22 per credit hour and no other fees are charged.

e. Budgeted revenues for 19x1–x2 are as follows:

Endowment income.........................$114,000
Net income from auxiliary services.......... 235,000
Athletics.................................... 180,000

The college's remaining source of revenue is an annual support campaign held during the spring.

Required:

1. Prepare a schedule computing for 19x1–x2 by division (a) the expected enrollment, (b) the total credit hours to be carried and (c) the number of faculty members needed.
2. Prepare a schedule computing the budget for faculty salaries by division for 19x1–x2.
3. Prepare a schedule computing the tutition revenue budget by division for 19x1–x2.
4. Assuming that the faculty salaries budget computed in part "2" was $2,400,000 and that the tuition revenue budget computed in part "3" was $3,000,000, prepare a schedule computing the amount which must be raised during the annual support campaign in order to cover the 19x1–x2 expenditures budget.

6-20. Sales quotas and budgets. For the past few years the Sexton Company has budgeted sales in its various territories. In addition, the company sets ambitious target quota volumes, despite the fact that actual performance will not meet the quotas assigned.

For the coming year, the following budget has been formulated for Districts *A* and *B*.

	District A	*District B*
Gross sales	$5,000,000	$8,000,000
Returns and allowances	$ 100,000	$ 120,000
Sales discounts (not cash discounts)	250,000	480,000
Freight-out allowance*	250,000	80,000
Total deductions	$ 600,000	$ 680,000
Net sales	$4,400,000	$7,320,000

*Sexton's plants are located in the center of each district, but local competitors' plants have freight advantages that Sexton must allow for in setting competitive prices.

The *quotas* for *net sales* in District *A* and District *B* have been set at $5,000,000 and $8,000,000, respectively.

Required:

1. Use the given data as a basis for describing the principal differences in selling in Districts *A* and *B*.

2. What figures should be used for formulating the master financial budget? Why?
3. Evaluate the Sexton method of setting quotas. Why doesn't Sexton simply use currently attainable net sales as a quota?

6-21. **Multiple choice.** (CPA adapted.) Choose the best answer for each item. Give supporting computations.

The Dilly Company marks up all merchandise at 25 percent of gross purchase price. All purchases are made on account with terms of 1/10, net/60. Purchase discounts, which are recorded as miscellaneous income, are always taken. Normally, 60 percent of each month's purchases are paid for in the month of purchase while the other 40 percent are paid during the first ten days of the first month after purchase. Inventories of merchandise at the end of each month are kept at 30 percent of the next month's projected cost of goods sold.

Terms for sales on account are 2/10, net/30. Cash sales are not subject to discount. Fifty percent of each month's sales on account are collected during the month of sale, 45 percent are collected in the succeeding month, and the remainder are usually uncollectible. Seventy percent of the collections in the month of sale are subject to discount while 10 percent of the collections in the succeeding month are subject to discount.

Projected sales data for selected months follow:

	Sales on Account—Gross	Cash Sales
December.........	$1,900,000	$400,000
January...........	1,500,000	250,000
February	1,700,000	350,000
March	1,600,000	300,000

1. Projected gross purchases for January are
   a. $1,400,000.   c. $1,472,000.   e. None of the above.
   b. $1,470,000.   d. $1,248,000.
2. Projected inventory at the end of December is
   a. $420,000.   c. $552,000.   e. None of the above.
   b. $441,600.   d. $393,750.
3. Projected payments to suppliers during February are
   a. $1,551,200.   c. $1,528,560.   e. None of the above.
   b. $1,535,688.   d. $1,509,552.
4. Projected sales discounts to be taken by customers making remittances during February are
   a. $5,250.   c. $30,500.   e. None of the above.
   b. $15,925.   d. $11,900. $ 13,250
5. Projected total collections from customers during February are
   a. $1,875,000.   c. $1,511,750.   e. None of the above.
   b. $1,861,750.   d. $1,188,100.

Hints: 1/10, net/60 means that one percent of the gross purchase price may be deducted as a purchase discount if payment is made within ten days. In any event, the invoice is payable within sixty days. Similar reasoning applies to sales terms. This problem requires painstaking attention to detail.

6-22. **Cash budget.** Prepare a statement of estimated cash receipts and disbursements for October 19x2, for the Rourk Company, which sells one product.

On October 1, 19x2, part of the trial balance showed:

Cash	$ 6,000	
Accounts receivable	19,500	
Allowance for bad debts		$2,400
Merchandise inventory	12,000	
Accounts payable, merchandise		9,000

The company's purchases are payable within ten days. Assume that one-third of the purchases of any month are due and paid for in the following month.

The unit invoice cost of the merchandise purchased is $10. At the end of each month it is desired to have an inventory equal in units to 50 percent of the following month's sales in units.

Sales terms include a 1 percent discount if payment is made by the end of the calendar month. Past experience indicates that 60 percent of the billings will be collected during the month of the sale, 30 percent in the following calendar month, 6 percent in the next following calendar month. Four percent will be uncollectible. The company's fiscal year begins August 1.

Unit selling price	$ 15
August actual sales	15,000
September actual sales	45,000
October estimated sales	36,000
November estimated sales	27,000
Total sales expected in the fiscal year	450,000

Exclusive of bad debts, total budgeted selling and general administrative expenses for the fiscal year are estimated at $68,500, of which $21,000 is fixed expense (inclusive of a $9,000 annual depreciation charge). These fixed expenses are incurred uniformly throughout the year. The balance of the selling and general administrative expenses vary with sales. Expenses are paid as incurred.

6-23. **Master budget.** (Alternate to 6-2.) A retailing subsidiary of a widely diversified company has a strong belief in using highly decentralized management. You are the new manager of one of its small "Apex" stores (Store No. 82). You know much about how to buy, how to display, how to sell, and how to reduce shoplifting. However, you know little about accounting and finance.

Top management is convinced that training for higher management should include the active participation of store managers in the budgeting process. You have been asked to prepare a complete master budget for your store for April, May and June. You are responsible for its actual full preparation. All accounting is done centrally, so you have no expert help on the premises. In addition, tomorrow the branch manager and the assistant controller will be here to examine your work; at that time they will assist you in formulating the final budget document. The idea is to have you prepare the budget a few times so that you gain more confidence about accounting matters. You want to make a favorable impression on your superiors, so you gather the following data as of March 31, 19x1:

		Recent and projected sales:		**213**

Cash	$ 11,000		
Inventory	300,000		
Accounts receivable	261,000	February	$200,000
Net furniture and fixtures	150,000	March	250,000
Total assets	$722,000	April	500,000
		May	300,000
Accounts payable	$340,000	June	300,000
Owner's equity	382,000	July	200,000
Total equities	$722,000		

Credit sales are 90 percent of total sales. Credit accounts are collected 80 percent in the month following the sale and 20 percent in the next following month. Assume that bad debts are negligible and may be ignored. The Accounts Receivable on March 31 are the result of the credit sales for February and March: $(.20 \times .90 \times \$200,000 = \$36,000) + (1.00 \times .90 \times \$250,000 = \$225,000)$. The average gross profit on sales is 40 percent. *∴ CGS = 60% of sales.*

The policy is to acquire enough inventory each month to equal the following month's projected sales. All purchases are paid for in the month following purchase.

Salaries, wages, and commissions average 20 percent of sales; all other expenses, excluding depreciation, 4 percent of sales. Fixed expenses for rent, property taxes, and miscellaneous payroll and other items are $40,000 monthly. Assume that these expenses require cash disbursements each month. Depreciation is $2,000 monthly.

In April, $40,000 is going to be disbursed for fixtures acquired in March. The March 31 balance of Accounts Payable includes this amount.

Assume that a minimum cash balance of $10,000 is to be maintained. Also assume that all borrowings are effective at the beginning of the month and all repayments are made at the end of the month of repayment. Interest is paid only at the time of repaying principal. Interest rate is 8 percent per annum; round out interest computations to the nearest ten dollars. All loans and repayments of principal must be made in multiples of a thousand dollars.

Required:

1. Prepare a budgeted income statement for the coming quarter, a budgeted statement of monthly cash receipts and disbursements (for the next three months) and a budgeted balance sheet for June 30, 19x1. All operations are evaluated on a before-income-tax basis. Also, because income taxes are disbursed from corporate headquarters, they may be ignored here.
2. Explain why there is a need for a bank loan and what operating sources supply cash for repaying the bank loan.

SUGGESTED READINGS

Welsch, G., *Budgeting: Profit Planning and Control,* 3rd ed. (Englewood Cliffs, N.J.: Prentice-Hall, Inc., 1971).

The following references pertain especially to the difficult problem of sales forecasting:

Green, Paul E., and Donald S. Tull, *Research for Marketing Decisions,* 2nd ed. (Englewood Cliffs, N.J.: Prentice-Hall, Inc., 1970). Chapter 16 covers sales forecasting.

Wolfe, Harry D., *Business Forecasting Methods* (New York: Holt, Rinehart & Winston, Inc., 1966).

Cost Behavior: Volume-Profit Relationships

7

In the previous chapter, we saw that planning entails the selection of an organization's profit objective and the mapping of the ways to reach that objective. The importance of an accurate sales forecast was stressed because the overall master plan is built upon contemplated volume levels.

But what if the planned-for sales are not achieved? What will be the impact of different sales volumes on net income? On financial needs? Furthermore, suppose costs change. This can also affect net income. Managers must know how an assortment of costs behaves as the volume of sales expands or contracts. The study of the interrelationships of sales, costs, and net income is usually called **cost-volume-profit analysis.**

Cost-volume profit analysis provides attention-directing and problem-solving background for important planning decisions such as selecting distribution channels, pricing, special promotions, and personnel hiring. "Know your costs" is an essential theme for any manager. And cost-volume-profit analysis helps to direct managerial attention to important problems and paves the way to their solution.

Of course, we will be considering simplified versions of the real world. Are these simplifications defensible? The answer depends on the facts in a particular case. The simplifications are justified if they lead to the same or better decisions than might be provided by more realistic, complex, and costly models.

VARIABLE COSTS AND FIXED COSTS

Variable costs and fixed costs are usually defined in terms of how a total cost changes in relation to fluctuations in the quantity of some selected activity. Activity bases are diverse: They may be the number of orders processed, the number of lines billed in a billing department, the number of admissions to a theater, the number of pounds handled in a warehouse, the hours of labor worked in an assembly department, the number of rides in an amusement park, the seat-miles on an airline, the dollar sales in a grocery store, or some other index of volume.

If Watkins Products pays its door-to-door salesmen a 40 percent straight commission, then the total cost of sales commissions should be 40 percent of the sales dollars. If a garden shop buys bags of weed killer at $2 each, then the total cost of weed killer should be $2 times the number of bags. These are variable costs. They are uniform *per unit,* but their *total* fluctuates in direct proportion to the total of the related activity or volume. These relationships are depicted graphically in Exhibit 7-1. The cost of most merchandise, materials, parts, and supplies, of many types of labor, and of commissions is variable.

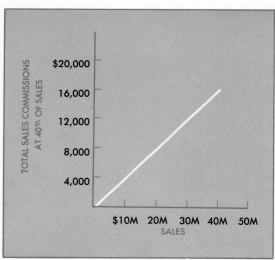 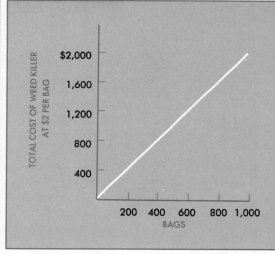

EXHIBIT 7-1
Variable Cost Behavior

If a manufacturer of picture tubes for color television rents a factory for $100,000 per year, then the unit cost of rent applicable to each tube will depend on the total number of tubes produced. If 100,000 tubes are produced, the unit cost will be $1; if 50,000 tubes are produced, $2. This is an example of a fixed cost, a cost that does not change in *total* but becomes progressively smaller on a *per unit* basis as volume increases. Real estate taxes, real estate insurance, many executive salaries, and straight-line depreciation charges are fixed costs.

COMPARISON OF VARIABLE AND FIXED COSTS

Note carefully from the foregoing examples that the "variable" or "fixed" characteristic of a cost relates to its *total dollar amount* and not to its per unit amount. A variable cost (e.g., the 40 percent sales commission) is constant per unit, and its total dollar amount changes proportionally with changes in activity or volume. A fixed cost (e.g., the factory rent), on a per unit basis, varies inversely with activity or volume changes, but is constant in total dollar amount.

Relevant Range

A fixed cost is fixed only in relationship to a given period of time—the budget period—and a given, though wide, range of activity called the "relevant range." Fixed costs may change from budget year to budget year solely because of changes in insurance and property tax rates, executive salary levels, or rent levels. But these items are highly unlikely to change within a given year. In addition, the total budgeted fixed costs may be formulated on the basis of an expected activity level (i.e., volume), say, within a relevant planning range of 40,000 to 85,000 units of production per month. However, operations on either side of the range will result in major salary adjustments or in the layoff or hiring of personnel. In Exhibit 7-2, the total monthly fixed cost within the relevant range is $100,000. If operations fell below 40,000 units, changes in personnel and salaries would slash fixed costs to $60,000. If operations rose above 85,000 units, increases in personnel and salaries would raise fixed costs to $115,000.

These assumptions—a given time period and a given range—are shown graphically at the top of Exhibit 7-2. The possibility that operations will be outside the relevant range is usually remote. Therefore, the three-level refinement at the top of Exhibit 7-2 is usually not graphed. A single horizontal line is usually extended through the plotted activity levels, as at the bottom of the exhibit.

Some Simplifying Assumptions

Nearly every organization has some variable costs and some fixed costs. As you may suspect, it is often difficult to classify a cost as exactly variable or exactly fixed. Many complications arise, including the possibility of costs behaving in some nonlinear way and of costs being simultaneously affected by more than one activity base. For example, the costs of ship-

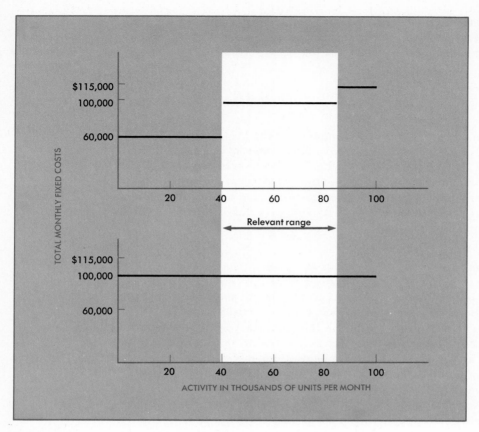

EXHIBIT 7-2
Fixed Costs and the Relevant Range

ping labor may be affected by both the weight and the number of units handled. We shall investigate various facets of this problem in succeeding chapters; for now, we shall assume that any cost may be classified as either variable or fixed.

UNIT COSTS AND TOTAL COSTS

The preceding section concentrated on the behavior patterns of total costs in relation to chosen activity levels. Generally, the decision maker should take a straightforward, analytical approach by thinking in terms of total costs rather than unit costs. As we shall see momentarily, unit costs must be interpreted carefully. Nevertheless, the use of unit costs is essential in many decision contexts. For example, the chairman of the social committee of a fraternity or a senior class may be trying to decide whether to hire a prominent musical group for a forthcoming party. The total fee may be predicted with certainty at $1,000. This knowledge is essential for the decision, but it may not be enough.

Before a decision can be reached, the decision maker must predict both the total cost and the probable number of persons who will attend. Without knowledge of both, he cannot decide intelligently on a possible admission price or even on whether to have a party at all. So he computes a unit cost by dividing the total cost by the expected number of persons who will attend. If 1,000 people attend, the unit cost is $1; if 100 attend, the unit cost soars to $10 per person. Unless the total cost is "unitized," the $1,000 cost is difficult to interpret; so the unit cost combines the total cost and the number of persons in a handy communicative way.

In management accounting, different measurement bases (denominators) may be used as units, depending on the circumstances. Generally, *unit costs should be expressed in terms most meaningful to the people who are responsible for incurring the costs.* The unit in question is not always a physical product; the unit (base) should be that objectively definable statistic of activity that is most closely correlated with cost incurrence. Thus, the base may differ between departments; it may be machine-hours in a factory department, pounds handled in the shipping department, and number of invoices processed or lines billed in the billing department.

The unit cost of making a finished good is sometimes computed by accumulating manufacturing costs and then dividing the total by the number of units produced. For example:

Total costs of manufacturing 1,000 units	$3,800
Divided by the number of units produced	÷ 1,000
Equals a cost per unit	= $3.80

Suppose that 800 units are sold and 200 units remain in ending inventory. The unit-cost idea facilitates the assignment of a total cost to various accounts:

Cost of goods sold, 800 units × $3.80	= $3,040
Ending inventory of finished goods, 200 units × $3.80 =	760

Unit costs are averages, and they must be interpreted with caution. For example, what does it mean to say that the unit cost for the musicians is $1 if 1,000 persons attend? A $1 unit cost would be valid for predicting total costs if the musicians indeed charged a fee at the rate of $1 per person, so that the total cost would be $800 if only 800 persons actually attended. However, the total cost is a lump sum, $1,000, and in this instance the unit cost is strictly dependent on the size of the denominator. As we shall discuss more fully in Chapters 8 and 15, unit costs often represent the averaging of a fixed-cost, a lump-sum total (the musicians' fee). Such unit costs must be interpreted quite differently from variable costs, where the unit costs are indeed valid indicators of how a total cost fluctuates in relation to the denominators; for example, the total costs of tires acquired and used will increase as the number of autos manufactured increases. One of the most common mistakes in cost analysis is to regard all unit costs indiscriminately—as if the total costs to which they are related are variable costs. Changes in activity (the denominator) will affect total variable costs, but not total fixed costs.

ILLUSTRATION OF COST-VOLUME-PROFIT ANALYSIS

The following situation will be used to demonstrate the techniques and the analytical power of cost-volume-profit analysis. This problem is based on the actual analysis used by a midwestern company in locating outlets.

A chain of gasoline stations which sell premium gasoline only is centrally owned. The stations are rented. The decision at hand is the desirability of opening another station which would have the following revenue and expense relationships:

	Per Gallon	Percent of Sales
Sales price	$ .50	100%
Cost of gasoline, including taxes and delivery	.40	80%
Gross profit (also the contribution margin in this case)	$ .10	20%
Monthly fixed expenses:		
Rent	$1,000	
Electricity for 24-hour operation	300	
Wages	3,800	
Payroll fringe costs	700	
Other fixed costs	200	
Total fixed costs	$6,000	

Required:

1. Express the monthly break-even point in number of gallons and in dollar sales.
2. Graph the cost-volume-profit relationships in Requirement 1.
3. If the rent were doubled, what would be the monthly break-even point:
   a. In number of gallons?
   b. In dollar sales?
4. Assume that the rent is unchanged.
   a. If the station manager is paid 1¢ per gallon as commission, what is the monthly break-even point in number of gallons? In dollar sales?
   b. If the selling price fell from 50¢ to 45¢, and the original variable expenses were unchanged, what is the monthly break-even point, in number of gallons? In dollar sales?
5. Refer to the original data. If the company considered $480 per month the minimum acceptable net income, how many gallons would have to be sold to warrant the opening of the station? Convert your answer into dollar sales.

6. Refer to the original data. Management is trying to decide whether a 24-hour operation is desirable. The closing of the station from 11:00 p.m. to 7:00 a.m. would reduce electricity costs by $120, and payroll and payroll fringe costs (one man) by $700. However, monthly sales would decline by 10,000 gallons. Should the 24-hour operation be continued? Assume that current sales on a 24-hour basis are:
   a. 62,000 gallons.
   b. 90,000 gallons.

1. Break-even Point—
Two Analytical Techniques

The study of cost-volume-profit relationships is often called **break-even analysis.** The latter is a misnomer because the break-even point—the point of zero net income—is often only incidental to the planning decision at hand. Still, knowledge of the break-even point provides insights into the possible riskiness of certain courses of action.

There are three basic techniques for computing a break-even point: equation, contribution margin, and graphing. The graphical technique is shown in the solution to Requirement 2.

a. Equation technique. This is the most general form of analysis, the one that may be adapted to any conceivable cost-volume-profit situation. You are familiar with a typical income statement. Any income statement can be expressed in equation form, as follows:

$$\text{Sales} = \text{Variable expenses} + \text{Fixed expenses} + \text{Net income} \quad (1)$$

$$\text{Let } X = \text{Number or gallons to be sold to break even}$$

$$\text{Then } \$.50X = \$.40X + \$6,000 + 0$$

$$\$.10X = \$6,000 + 0$$

$$X = \frac{\$6,000 + 0}{\$.10}$$

$$X = 60,000 \text{ gallons}$$

Total sales in the equation is a price-times-quantity relationship. In the above equation, this was expressed as $\$.50X$. Of course, the dollar sales answer in this case could be obtained in shortcut fashion by multiplying 60,000 gallons by 50¢, which also yields the break-even dollar sales of $30,000. However, you should study the equation method of getting answers in dollars, because often no information on the number of units or unit selling price is given. Most companies sell more than one product, and the overall break-even point is often expressed in sales dollars because of the variety of product lines. For example, although radios and television sets cannot be meaningfully added, their sales prices provide an automatic common denominator.

The same equation, this time using percentage relationships, may be used to obtain the sales in dollars:

Let X = Sales in dollars needed to break even

$$X = .80X + \$6,000$$
$$.20X = \$6,000 + 0$$

$$X = \frac{\$6,000 + 0}{.20}$$

$$X = \$30,000$$

b. **Contribution-margin technique.** If algebra is not one of your strong points, you may prefer to approach cost-volume-profit relationships in the following common-sense arithmetic manner. Every unit sold generates a contribution margin or marginal income, which is the excess of the sales price over the variable expenses pertaining to the unit in question:

Unit sales price	$.50
Unit variable expenses	.40
Unit contribution margin to fixed expenses and net income	$.10

The $.10 unit contribution is divided into total fixed expenses plus a target net profit to obtain the number of units which must be sold to break even: ($6,000 + 0) ÷ $.10 = 60,000 gallons.

The computation in terms of dollar sales is similar:

Sales price	100%
Variable expenses as a percentage of dollar sales	80%
Contribution-margin ratio	20%

Therefore, 20 percent of each sales dollar is the amount available for the recovery of fixed expenses and the making of net income: ($6,000 + 0) ÷ .20 = $30,000 sales needed to break even.

c. **Relationship of the two techniques.** Reflect on the relationship between the equation technique and the contribution-margin technique. The contribution-margin technique is merely a shortcut version of the equation technique. Look at the second-last line in the solutions to Equation 1. They read:

Target Volume

In Units	*In Dollars*
$.10X = \$6,000 + 0$	$.20X = \$6,000 + 0$
$X = \dfrac{\$6,000 + 0}{\$.10}$	$X = \dfrac{\$6,000 + 0}{.20}$

This gives us the shortcut general formulas:

$$\text{Target volume in units} \ = \ \frac{\text{Fixed expenses} \ + \ \text{Net income}}{\text{Contribution margin per unit}} \qquad (2)$$

$$\text{Target volume in dollars} \ = \ \frac{\text{Fixed expenses} \ + \ \text{Net income}}{\text{Contribution-margin ratio}} \qquad (3)$$

Which should you use, the equation or the contribution-margin technique? Use either; the choice is a matter of personal preference.

2. Graphical Technique

The relationships in this problem may be depicted on a graph. The break-even point is represented by the intersection of the sales line and the total expenses line in Exhibits 7-3 and 7-4.

Exhibit 7-4 was constructed by using a sales line and a total expenses line that combined variable and fixed expenses. The procedure (see Exhibit 7-3) is as follows:

Step 1. Plot the revenue (i.e., Sales) line.

Step 2. Determine where the line showing the Fixed Portion of expenses should intersect the vertical axis. Insert a dashed horizontal line to represent fixed expenses.

Step 3. Determine the Variable Portion of expenses at any single level of activity other than zero. Plot this on top of the fixed expenses. Draw a line between this point and the fixed cost intercept of the vertical axis. This is the Total Expenses line.

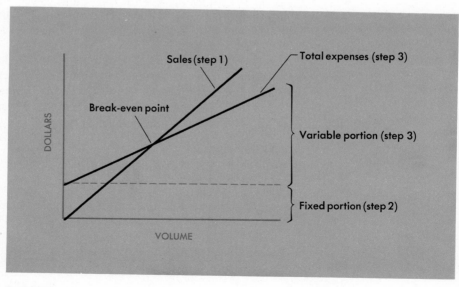

EXHIBIT 7-3
Cost-Volume-Profit Graph

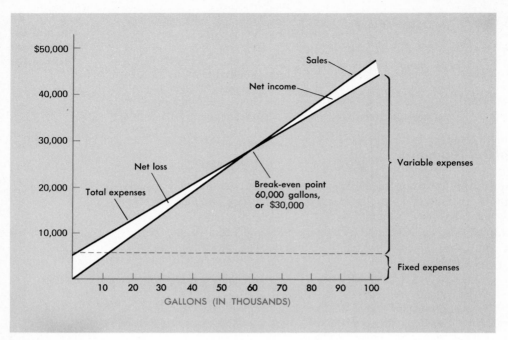

EXHIBIT 7-4
Complete Cost-Volume-Profit Chart

Exhibit 7-4 is the complete break-even chart. The break-even point is only one facet of this cost-volume-profit chart, which shows the profit or loss at any rate of activity. At any given volume, the vertical distance between the sales line and the total expenses line measures the net income or net loss.

The chart portrays only one of a number of methods for picturing cost-volume-profit variable expenses relationships. The chart often has educational advantages because it shows potential profits over a wide range of volume more easily than numerical exhibits. Whether graphs or other types of exhibits are used depends largely on management's preference.

3. Changes in Fixed Expenses

Reread and try to complete Requirement 3 on page 220 before reading on. The fixed expenses would increase from $6,000 to $7,000. Then:

$$\text{Target volume in units} = \frac{\text{Fixed expenses} + \text{Net income}}{\text{Contribution margin per unit}} = \frac{\$7,000}{\$.10} = \frac{70,000}{\text{gallons}} \quad (2)$$

$$\text{Target volume in dollars} = \frac{\text{Fixed expenses} + \text{Net income}}{\text{Contribution-margin ratio}} = \frac{\$7,000}{.20} = \$35,000 \quad (3)$$

Note that a one-sixth increase in fixed expenses altered the break-even point by one-sixth: from 60,000 to 70,000 gallons and from $30,000 to $35,000.

4. Changes in Contribution Margin per Unit

Reread and try to complete Requirement 4 on page 220 before reading on.

a. The variable expenses would be 41¢, the unit contribution margin would be 9¢, and the contribution-margin ratio would be 18 percent (9¢ ÷ 50¢).
The original fixed expenses of $6,000 would be unaffected, but the denominators are changed as compared with the denominators used in the solutions to Requirements 1 and 3. Thus:

$$\text{Break-even point in units} = \frac{\$6,000}{\$.09} = 66,667 \text{ gallons} \qquad (2)$$

$$\text{Break-even point in dollars} = \frac{\$6,000}{.18} = \$33,334 \qquad (3)$$

b. A change in unit contribution margin can also be caused by a change in selling price. If the selling price fell from 50¢ to 45¢, and the original variable expenses were unchanged, the unit contribution would still be 5¢ (i.e., 45¢ − 40¢) and the break-even point would soar to 120,000 gallons. The break-even point in dollars would also change, because the selling price and contribution-margin ratio change: the contribution-margin ratio would be 11.11 percent (5¢ ÷ 45¢). The break-even point, in dollars, would be $54,000 (120,000 gallons × 45¢), or using the formula:

$$\text{Break-even point in dollars} = \frac{\$6,000}{.1111} = \$54,000 \qquad (3)$$

5. Target Net Profit and an Incremental Approach

If the company considered $480 per month as the minimum acceptable net income, how many gallons would have to be sold to warrant the opening of the new station? What is your answer in terms of sales dollars?

$$\text{Target sales volume in units} = \frac{\text{Fixed expenses} + \text{Net income}}{\text{Contribution margin per unit}}$$

$$= \frac{\$6,000 + \$480}{\$.10} = 64,800 \text{ gallons} \qquad (2)$$

Another way of getting the same answer is to use your knowledge of the break-even point and adopt an incremental approach. If 60,000 gallons is the break-even point, all fixed expenses would be recovered at that volume. Therefore, every gallon beyond 60,000 would represent a unit contribution to *net profit* of 10¢. If $480 were the target net profit, $480 ÷ 10¢ would show that the target volume must exceed the break-even volume by 4,800 gallons.

The answer, in terms of dollar sales, can then be computed by multiplying 64,800 gallons by 50¢, or by using the formula:

$$\text{Target sales volume in dollars} = \frac{\text{Fixed expenses} + \text{Net income}}{\text{Contribution margin ratio}}$$

$$= \frac{\$6,000 + \$480}{.20} = \$32,400 \qquad (3)$$

In the alternative incremental approach, the break-even point, $30,000, is a frame of reference. Every sales dollar beyond that point contributes 20¢ to net profit. Divide $480 by 20¢. The dollar sales must exceed the break-even volume by $2,400 to produce a net profit of $480.

6. Multiple Changes in the Key Factors

Reread and try to complete Requirement 6 on page 221 before reading on.

First, whether 62,000 or 90,000 gallons are being sold is irrelevant to the decision at hand. The analysis of this situation consists of constructing and solving equations for conditions that prevail under either alternative and selecting the volume level that yields the highest net profit. However, the incremental approach is much quicker. What is the essence of this decision? We are asking whether the prospective savings in cost exceed the prospective loss in contribution margin:

Lost contribution margin, 10,000 gallons @ $.10	$1,000
Savings in fixed expenses	820
Prospective decline in net income	$ 180

Regardless of the current volume level, whether it be 62,000 or 90,000 gallons, the closing of the station from 11:00 P.M. to 7:00 A.M., if we accept the prediction that sales will decline by 10,000 gallons as accurate, will decrease the profit by $180:

	Decline from 62,000 to 52,000 gallons		Decline from 90,000 to 80,000 gallons	
Gallons	62,000	52,000	90,000	80,000
Sales	$31,000	$26,000	$45,000	$40,000
Variable expenses	24,800	20,800	36,000	32,000
Contribution margin	6,200	5,200	$ 9,000	$ 8,000
Fixed expenses	6,000	5,180	6,000	5,180
Net profit	$ 200	$ 20	$ 3,000	$ 2,820
Change in net profit		($180)		($180)

USES AND LIMITATIONS OF COST-VOLUME ANALYSIS

Optimum Combination of Factors

The analysis of cost-volume-profit relationships is one of management's paramount responsibilities. The knowledge of patterns of cost behavior offers insights valuable in planning and controlling short- and long-run operations. This is a major theme of this book, so we should regard the current material as introductory. Our purpose in this chapter is to provide perspective, rather than to impart an intimate knowledge of the niceties of cost behavior.

The example of the gasoline station demonstrated some valuable applications of cost-volume-profit analysis. One of management's principal duties is to discover the most profitable combination of the variable and fixed cost factors. For example, a sales force may be expanded to reach markets directly, instead of through wholesalers, thereby increasing unit sales prices. Or automated machinery may be purchased, to reduce labor cost per unit. On the other hand, it may be wise to reduce fixed costs in order to obtain a more favorable combination. Thus, direct selling by a salaried sales force may be supplanted by the use of manufacturers' agents.

Generally, companies which spend heavily for advertising have high contribution margins (e.g., cigarette and cosmetic companies). Companies with low advertising and sales promotion outlays do not usually have high contribution margins (e.g., manufacturers of industrial equipment). The size of the contribution margin influences such outlays. Obviously, a company with a volume of 100,000 units and a contribution margin of 10¢ per unit is not going to risk the same promotional outlay to obtain, say, a 10 percent increase in volume as a company with a contribution margin of 90¢ per unit.

Therefore, when the contribution-margin ratio is low, great increases in volume are necessary before noticeable increases in net profits can occur. As sales exceed the break-even point, a high contribution-margin ratio increases profits faster than a small contribution-margin ratio.

Limiting Assumptions

The notion of **relevant range,** which was introduced when fixed expenses were discussed, is applicable to the entire break-even chart. Almost all break-even charts have lines extending back to the vertical axis. This is misleading, because the relationships depicted in such graphs are valid only within the relevant range that underlies the construction of the graph. Exhibit 7-5(B), a modification of the conventional break-even chart, partially demonstrates the multitude of assumptions that must be made in constructing the typical break-even chart.

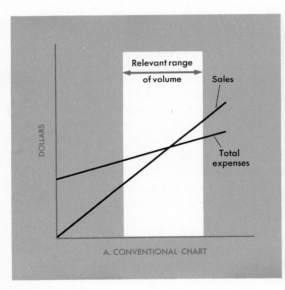 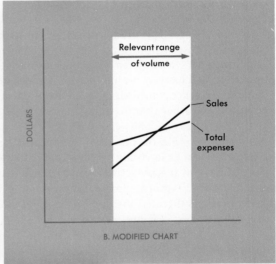

EXHIBIT 7-5
Conventional and Modified Break-even Charts

Some of these assumptions are:

1. The behavior of revenues and expenses is accurately portrayed and is linear over the relevant range. The principal difference between the accountant's break-even chart and the economist's are: (a) The accountant's sales line is drawn on the assumption that prices do not change with production or sales, and the economist assumes that price changes may be needed to spur sales; (b) the accountant usually assumes a constant variable expense per unit, and the economist assumes that variable expense changes with production.

2. Expenses may be classified into variable and fixed categories. Total variable expenses vary directly with volume. Total fixed expenses do not change with volume.

3. Efficiency and productivity will be unchanged.

4. Sales mix will be constant. The **sales mix** is the relative combination of quantities of a variety of company products that compose total sales.

5. The difference in inventory level at the beginning and at the end of a period is insignificant. (The impact of inventory changes on cost-volume-profit analysis is discussed in Chapter 15.)

SUMMARY

An understanding of cost behavior patterns and cost-volume-profit relationships can help guide a manager's decisions.

Variable costs (and expenses) and fixed costs (and expenses) have contrasting behavior patterns. Their relationship to sales, volume, and net profit is probably best seen on a cost-volume-profit chart. However, the chart should be used with great care. The portrayal of all profit-influencing factors on such a chart entails many assumptions that may hold over only a relatively narrow range of volume. As a tool, the chart may be compared to a meat-ax rather than to a surgeon's scalpel. Cost-volume-profit analysis, as depicted on a chart, is a framework for analysis, a vehicle for appraising overall performance, and a planning device.

The assumptions that underlie typical cost-volume-profit analysis are static. A change in one assumption (e.g., total fixed cost or the unit price of raw materials) will affect all the cost-volume-profit relationships on a given chart. The static nature of these assumptions should always be remembered by the managers who use this valuable analytical technique.

SUMMARY PROBLEM FOR YOUR REVIEW

Problem

The income statement of Wiley Company is summarized as follows:

Net revenue	$800,000
Less: Expenses, including $400,000 of fixed expenses	880,000
Net loss	$ (80,000)

The manager believes that an increase of $200,000 in advertising outlays will increase sales substantially. His plan was approved by the chairman of the board.

Required:
1. At what sales volume will the company break even?
2. What sales volume will result in a net profit of $40,000?

Solution

1. Note that all data are expressed in dollars. No unit data are given. Most companies have many products, so the overall break-even analysis deals with dollar sales, not units. The variable expenses are $880,000 − $400,000, or $480,000. The variable expense ratio is $480,000 ÷ $800,000, or .60. Therefore, the contribution-margin ratio is .40.

$$\text{Let } S = \text{Break-even sales, in dollars}$$

$$\text{Then } S = \text{Variable expenses} + \text{Fixed expenses} + \text{Net profit} \quad (1)$$

$$S = .60S + (\$400,000 + \$200,000) + 0$$

$$.40S = \$600,000 + 0$$

$$S = \frac{\$600,000 + 0}{.40} = \frac{\text{Fixed expenses} + \text{Target net profit}}{\text{Contribution-margin ratio}} \quad (3)$$

$$S = \$1,500,000$$

2.
$$\text{Required sales} = \frac{\text{Fixed expenses} + \text{Target net profit}}{\text{Contribution-margin ratio}} \quad (3)$$

$$\text{Then Required sales} = \frac{\$600,000 + \$40,000}{.40} = \frac{\$640,000}{.40}$$

$$\text{Required sales} = \$1,600,000$$

Alternatively, we can use an incremental approach and reason that all dollar sales beyond the $1,500,000 break-even point will result in a 40 percent contribution to net profit. Divide $40,000 by .40. Sales must be $100,000 beyond the $1,500,000 break-even point in order to produce a net profit of $40,000.

APPENDIX:
THE P/V CHART AND SALES MIX ANALYSIS

The P/V Chart

Exhibit 7-4 can be recast in simpler form as a so-called P/V chart (a profit-volume graph). This form is preferred by many managers who are interested mainly in the impact of changes in volume on net income. The first graph in Exhibit 7-6 illustrates the chart, using the data in our example. The chart is constructed as follows:

1. The vertical axis is net income in dollars. The horizontal axis is volume in units (or in sales dollars, in many cases).

2. At zero volume, the net loss would be approximated by the total fixed costs—$6,000 in this example.

3. A contribution margin line will slope upward from the −$6,000 intercept at the rate of the unit contribution margin of 10¢. The line will intersect the volume axis at the break-even point of 60,000 gallons. Each unit sold beyond the break-even point will add 10¢ to net income.

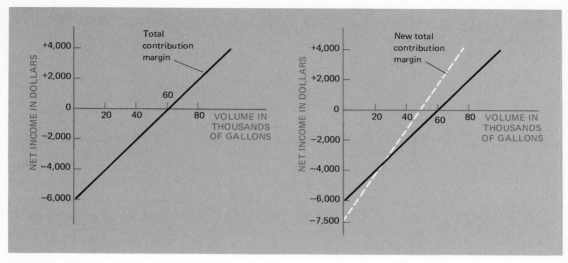

EXHIBIT 7-6
P/V Chart

The P/V chart provides a quick, condensed comparison of how alternatives on pricing, variable costs, or fixed costs may affect net income as volume changes. For example, the second graph in Exhibit 7-6 shows how net income and the break-even point would be affected by an increase in selling price from 50¢ to 55¢ and a $1,500 increase in rent. The unit contribution would become 15¢, and the break-even point would fall from 60,000 gallons to 50,000 gallons:

$$\text{New break-even point} = \$7,500 \div \$.15$$

$$= 50,000 \text{ gallons}$$

Note also that the net income will increase at a much faster rate as volume increases.

Effects of Sales Mix

The cost-volume-profit analysis in this chapter has focused on single products. In multiproduct firms, sales mix is an important factor in calculating an overall company break-even point. If the proportions of the mix change, the cost-volume-profit relationships also change. When managers choose a sales mix, it can be depicted on a break-even chart or P/V chart by assuming average revenues and costs for a given mix.

For example, suppose that a two-product company has a unit contribution margin of $1 for Product *A* and $2 for Product *B*, and that fixed costs are $100,000. The break-even point would be 100,000 units if only *A* were sold and 50,000 units if only *B* were sold. Suppose that the planned mix is three units of *A* for each unit of *B*. The contribution margin for each "package" of products would be 3 × $1 plus 1 × $2, or $5. The average contribution margin per unit of product would be $5 ÷ 4 units in each package = $1.25. The break-even point, assuming that the mix is maintained, would be:

$$\$100,000 \div \$1.25 = 80,000 \text{ units (consisting of 60,000 units of } A$$
$$\text{and 20,000 of } B)$$

These relationships are shown in Exhibit 7-7. The slopes of the solid lines depict the unit contribution margins of each product. The slope of the broken line depicts the average contribution per unit. Suppose that the total planned sales are 160,000 units, consisting of 120,000 units of *A* and 40,000 of *B*. Exhibit 7-7 shows that if overall unit sales and mix targets are achieved, net income would be $100,000. However, if the mix changes, net income may be much greater because the proportion of sales of *B* might be higher than anticipated. The opposite effect would occur if *A* sold in a higher proportion than expected. When the sales mix changes, the break-even point and the expected net income at various sales levels are altered.

EXHIBIT 7-7
P/V Chart and Sales Mix

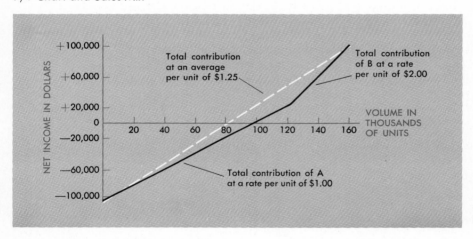

ASSIGNMENT MATERIAL

Fundamental Assignment Material

7-1. Terminology. Define: *fixed cost; relevant range; contribution margin; marginal income;* and *variable cost.*

7-2. Cost-volume-profits and vending machines. The Pickit Company operates and services cigarette vending machines located in restaurants, gas stations, factories, etc. The vending machines are rented from the manufacturer. In addition, Pickit must rent the space occupied by its machines. The following expense and revenue relationships pertain to a contemplated expansion program of twenty machines.

Fixed monthly expenses:

Machine rental: 20 machines @ $26.75	$ 535
Space rental: 20 locations @ $14.40	288
Wages to service the additional 20 machines	660
Payroll fringe costs: 10%	66
Other fixed costs	41
Total monthly fixed costs	$1,590

Other data:

	Per Package	*Per $100 of Sales*
Selling price	$.50	100%
Cost of cigarettes	.40	80%
Contribution margin	$.10	20%

Required:

These questions relate to the above data unless otherwise noted. Consider each question independently.

1. What is the monthly break-even point in dollar sales? In number of packages?
2. If 20,000 packages were sold, what would be the company's net income?
3. If the space rental were doubled, what would be the monthly break-even point in dollar sales? In number of packages?
4. If, in addition to the fixed rent, the vending machine manufacturer is also paid 1¢ per package sold, what is the monthly break-even point in dollar sales? In number of packages? Refer to the original data.
5. If, in addition to the fixed rent, the machine manufacturer is paid 1¢ for each package sold in excess of the break-even point, what would Pickit's net income be if 20,000 packages were sold? Refer to the original data.

7-3. The Thorp Trucking Company specializes in long-haul intercity transportation. Pertinent budget data for next year are as follows:

Sales volume	1,000,000 miles*
Average selling price (revenue)	25¢ per mile*
Fixed expenses	$40,000
Average variable expenses	20¢ per mile*

Miles is an abbreviation for "intercity-vehicle mile."

Compute the new profit for each of the following changes. (Consider each case independently.)

a. A 10 percent increase in sales volume.
b. A 10 percent decrease in sales volume.
c. A 4 percent increase in selling price.
d. A 4 percent decrease in selling price.
e. A 1¢ per mile increase in variable expenses.
f. A 1¢ per mile decrease in variable expenses.
g. A 10 percent increase in fixed costs.
h. A 10 percent decrease in fixed costs.

i. A decrease in variable expenses of 1c per mile and a decrease in selling price of 4¢.

j. A decrease in selling price of 4c and an increase in miles of sales volume at 10 percent.

k. A 10 percent increase in fixed costs and 10 percent increase in miles of sales volume.

Additional Assignment Material

7-4. What is meant by unit cost?

7-5. Why is "break-even analysis" a misnomer?

7-6. Distinguish between the equation technique and the unit contribution technique.

7-7. What is the difference between conventional and modified break-even charts?

7-8. What are the principal differences between the accountant's and the economist's break-even charts?

7-9. What is the sales mix?

7-10. What is the general guide for expressing unit costs?

7-11. What is meant by an optimum combination of factors?

7-12. **Fixed costs and relevant range.** Zayre Engineering Consultants has a substantial year-to-year fluctuation in billings. Top management has the following policy regarding the employment of key personnel and staff engineers:

Number of Engineers	Engineers' Salaries	Gross Annual Billings
4	$52,000	$100,000 or less
5	$70,000	$100,000–$200,000
6	$88,000	$200,001 or more

For the past four years, gross annual billings have fluctuated between $120,000 and $180,000. You are preparing a budget for the coming year. Expectations are that gross billings will be between $165,000 and $185,000. What amount should be budgeted for engineers' salaries? Graph the relationships on an annual basis using the two approaches illustrated in Exhibit 7-2. Indicate the relevant range on each graph. You need not use graph paper; simply approximate the graphical relationships.

7-13. **Effects of change in channels of distribution.** Mavis Company, a television manufacturer, has always sold its products through distributors. In 19x1, its sales were $50,000,000 and its net income was 10 percent of sales. Fixed expenses were $10,000,000.

Because television sets are increasingly being sold through discount houses and huge outlets, Mavis is considering the elimination of its distributors and selling directly to retailers. This would cause a 20 percent drop in sales, but net income would be $4,800,000 because of the elimination of the middleman. Fixed expenses would increase to $11,200,000 because of the additional warehouses and distribution facilities required.

Required:

1. What was the break-even point (in dollars) under the situation prevailing in 19x1?
2. What would be the break-even point under the proposed situation?
3. What dollar sales volume must be obtained under the proposed plan to make as much net income as last year?

7-14. **Nature of variable and fixed costs.** "As I understand it, costs such as the salary of the vice-president of transportation operations are variable because the more traffic you handle the less your unit cost. In contrast, costs such as fuel are fixed because each ton-mile should entail consumption of the same amount of fuel and hence bear the same unit cost." Do you agree? Explain.

7-15. **Distribution of beer.** A large brewery circulated a written explanation of break-even analysis to its wholesalers. The explanation had the following assumptions for a typical wholesaler:

		Per Unit
Sales price		$4.00
Variable expenses:		
Cost of beer	$3.20	
Variable selling and other expenses	.30	3.50
Contribution margin		$ .50

The brewery used cost-volume-profit analysis to stress the desirability of high-volume operations. The typical wholesaler presently has annual fixed expenses of $35,000 and sells 100,000 cases per year.

Required:

1. Compute the break-even volume in number of cases.
2. Compute the net income for a volume of 100,000 cases. If the wholesaler increases volume by 20,000 cases, what would be the change in net income in both dollar and percentage terms?
3. The brewery suggests that the wholesaler could easily bear a special promotional expense, say, $4,000, because the increase in volume would still leave an attractive increase in income for the wholesaler. If the $4,000 expense generated a 20 percent increase in sales volume, what would be the increase in net income in dollars and in percent?
4. If the contribution margin were only 20¢ a case instead of 50¢, would the promotional expense of $4,000 be justified? Why?
5. What is probably the most critical or sensitive assumption underlying the cost-volume-profit analysis in Requirements 1 through 4?

7-16. **Promotion of entertainment.** George Doherty, a theatrical promoter, is trying to decide whether to engage The Bugs, a very popular singing group, for a one-night appearance at the local arena, which has a salable capacity of 5,000 seats. He has gathered the following data:

Rental, including ushering and cleanup service	$ 4,000
Advertising	3,000
Ticket service and ticket printing	1,000
Miscellaneous expenses	2,000
Entertainers' fee	10,000
Total	$20,000

Sales and entertainment taxes are 10 percent of the price (excluding the tax) on each ticket, and ticket prices include this tax. That is, if the price of the ticket is $5.00 (excluding taxes), the total price is $5.50. Therefore, the tax is one-eleventh of the total price of the ticket.

Required:

All prices include the sales and entertainment taxes.

1. What is the average price for each ticket that is needed for Doherty to break even, assuming that the arena can be filled to capacity?
2. Suppose that Doherty thinks that he can maximize his return by pricing as follows: 1,000 seats @ $10; 1,000 @ $8; 1,000 @ $6; and 2,000 @ $4. If the house were sold out, how much net income would be produced for Doherty at such prices?
3. Suppose that The Bugs appeal mainly to young people who are unlikely to pay high prices. Suppose further that 300 seats are sold @ $10; 700 @ $8; 900 @ $6; and 2,000 @ $4. (a) How much net income would Doherty make? (b) What is the average price of the sold tickets? How does it compare with your answer in Requirement 1? In your own words, explain the difference.
4. (a) The Bugs' agent phoned Doherty and offered an alternate arrangement for compensation: $5,000 plus $1 per ticket sold regardless of the ticket price. How would this arrangement affect your answers to Requirements 1, 2, and 3a? Show your computations. (b) If you were Doherty, which arrangement would you prefer? Why? (c) Would your answer to (b) change if the compensation were based on $1.20 per ticket rather than $1.00? Why?

7-17. Cost-volume-profit chart and sales mix. A firm sells two products, A and B, at unit prices of $9.24 and $7.69, respectively. The sales of A and B are simultaneous, and always in a 1-to-4 ratio. The overall contribution margin ratio is 40 percent, and the break-even point is 15,000 units.

Required:

1. Given the above conditions, what are the dollar amounts appropriate to points x, y, and z in the graph at the top of page 237.
2. How many units, in total together, of A and B must be sold in order to arrive at a profit of $24,000 if:
   a. The selling prices now prevailing are maintained.
   b. By incurring some extra shipping and sales commission costs, the company can boost volume. The incidence of these costs would be an extra $1.24 per unit for each unit of product A sold in excess of 3,000 per year and an extra 69¢ per unit for each unit of product B sold in excess of 12,000 units per year.
3. Assume that the break-even point is 15,000 units under either Plan 2a or Plan 2b. Beyond the break-even point, the total units sold under Plan 2b will exceed the total under Plan 2a by 40 percent. Which pricing plan is more profitable, 2a or 2b? Show computations to support your answer.

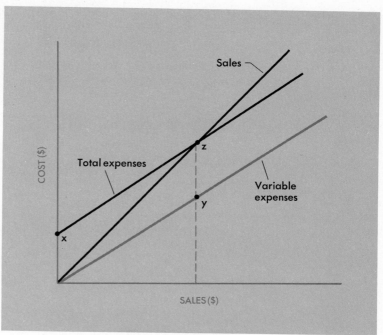

Graph axes: vertical axis labeled "COST ($)", horizontal axis labeled "SALES ($)". Lines labeled "Sales", "Total expenses", and "Variable expenses". Points labeled x, y, z.

7-18. Hospital cost-volume-profit relationships. Dr. Brown and Dr. Black, the two radiologists of the San Susi Hospital, have submitted the following costs for operating the Department of Radiology:

Radiologists' salaries	30% of gross receipts
Technicians' and clerical salaries	$70,000
Supplies (fixed)	80,000
Depreciation	60,000

This year, the department processed 65,000 films with three 200-milliampere X-ray machines. (Their original cost was $200,000 each, their life ten years.) For these processed films, the average charge was $6. The 65,000 films represent maximum volume possible with the present equipment.

Drs. Brown and Black have submitted a request for two new 300-milli-ampere X-ray machines. (The cost will be $250,000 each machine, their life expectancy, ten years.) They will increase the capacity of the department by 35,000 films per year. Because of their special attachments (i.e., fluoroscopes) it will be possible to take more intricate films, for which a higher charge will be made. The average charge to the patient for each of these additional 35,000 films is estimated at $10. In order to operate the new machines, one highly trained technician must be hired at an annual salary of $15,000. The added capacity will increase the cost of supplies by $20,000.

Required:

1. Determine the break-even point in films for the three 200-milliampere X-ray machines. How much do they contribute to the hospital's overall profits?

2. Determine the break-even point if the two new 300-milliampere X-ray machines are added to the department. How much will be contributed to the hospital's overall profit, assuming they are operated at maximum volume?

7-19. Estimating cost behavior patterns. The Mideastern Railroad showed the following results (in millions of dollars):

	19x3	*19x2*
Operating revenues	$218	$196
Operating expenses:		
Transportation	$ 87	$ 84
Maintenance of way and structures	34	32
Maintenance of equipment	37	34
Traffic	7	6
General	12	11
Payroll taxes	9	9
Property taxes	7	7
Equipment and other rentals	13	12
Total operating expenses	$206	$195
Net railway operating income	$ 12	$ 1

Required:

Based solely on your analysis of these figures, what is the percentage relationship of variable operating expenses to operating revenue? Explain any assumptions that underlie your answer.

7-20. The case of the advertising agency. Three advertising men, Smith, Cummings, and Combs, have formed an agency in which they are to be equal stockholders. The new agency advises its customers on the media for their ads and submits copy, layout, and rough design for approval. The Smith, Cummings, and Combs Agency charges the standard 15 percent of media billings for their services. For example, an advertisement that is billed by *Time* magazine for $10,000 would be subject to a 15 percent agency commission. The agency would be billed by *Time,* would pay $8,500, and in turn would bill the client for the full $10,000. Total charges to customers include:

Billings (media costs, including 15% agency commission)		xxx
Production charges (work done outside the agency):		
Finished art work	xx	
Typesetting	xx	
Engraving	xx	xxx
Total charges		xxx

To help serve the nucleus of customers who have followed the owners from their previous employments, two account executives are hired. The two, Brand and Reed, are each paid $4,000 per year plus three-fourths of 1 percent of all the agency's media billings. Brand, Reed, and the three owners entertain the agency's clients at a fishing lodge maintained, for that purpose, at an annual cost of $900. In addition, the agency pays $1,400 annually for memberships in clubs where clients are entertained. Other annual costs are:

Office rent	$ 4,800
Subscriptions to readership surveys and service publications	470
Clerical and administrative expenses	14,500
Production chief's salary	8,700
Copywriters' salary (2 @ $9,400)	18,800
Property tax and insurance	480
Salaries of Smith, Cummings, and Combs	81,000

Required:

1. What media billings are needed to break even?
2. Smith, Cummings, and Combs believe they can expand their services and profits if they set up their own art department. The art department would use a converted storage room adjacent to the offices. Rent would be $75 a month, and insurance and property tax would be another $30 per annum. For $130 annually, a messenger service would ferry art work between agency and clients. Materials are expected to cost 1 percent of art work charges. The partners agree to charge $6 per hour for work done in the art department.
   a. Cummings estimates that the art break-even point is billings of $14,454. How much per hour does he plan to pay the artists?
   b. Smith has determined that art-work billings of $25,914 will yield a profit of $3,000, with a contribution-margin ratio of .157. How much per hour does Smith plan to pay the artists?

7-21. **Traveling expenses.** (Prepared by Professor Alfred R. Roberts.) Harold Nuget is a traveling salesman for the Goody Candy Company. He uses his own car and the company reimburses him at 10¢ per mile. Harold claims he needs 12¢ per mile just to break even.

George Barr, the district manager, decides to look into the matter. He is able to compile the following information about Harold's expenses:

Oil change every 3,000 miles	$ 6.00
Maintenance (other than oil) every 6,000 miles	78.00
Yearly insurance	400.00
Auto cost $4,500 with an average cash trade-in value of $600; has a useful life of three years.	
Gasoline is approximately 48¢ per gallon and Harold averages 12 miles per gallon.	

When Harold is on the road, he averages 120 miles a day. The manager knows that Harold does not work Saturdays or Sundays, has ten working days vacation, six holidays, and spends approximately fifteen working days in the office.

Required:

1. How many miles a year would the salesman have to travel to break even at the current rate of reimbursement?
2. What would be an equitable mileage rate?

7-22. **Pricing by auto dealers.** Many automobile dealers have an operating pattern similar to Lance Motors, a dealer in Ohio. Each month, Lance initially aims at a unit volume quota that approximates a break-even point. Until the break-even point is reached, Lance has a policy of relatively lofty pricing, whereby the "minimum deal" must contain a sufficiently high markup to assure a contribution to profit of no less than $250. After the break-even point is attained, Lance tends to quote lower prices for the remainder of the month.

Required:

What is your opinion of this policy? As a prospective customer, how would you react to this policy?

7-23. Pricing strategy. The Dreker Company has the following cost behavior pattern for the unique ashtrays that it manufactures and sells:

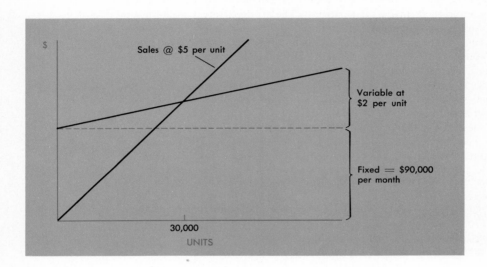

Required:

1. What is the break-even point in units?
2. If sales were at 40,000 units, would you then be inclined to cut the selling price? Why?
3. If sales were at 20,000 units, would you then be inclined to cut the selling price? Why?

7-24. P/V chart and sales mix. The Hartnett Company has three products—*A*, *B*, and *C*—having contribution margins of $3, $2, and $1, respectively. The president is planning to sell 200,000 units in the forthcoming period, consisting of 20,000 *A*, 100,000 *B*, and 80,000 *C*. The company's fixed costs for the period are $255,000.

Required:

1. What is the company break-even point in units, assuming that the given sales mix is maintained?
2. Prepare a P/V chart for a volume of 200,000 units. Have a broken line represent the average contribution margin per unit and have a solid line represent the contribution margins of each product. What is the total contribution margin at a volume of 200,000 units? Net income?
3. What would net income become if 20,000 units of *A*, 80,000 units of *B*, and 100,000 units of *C* were sold?

7-25. Break-even analysis and the product mix assumption. Suppose that a consulting company has the following budget data for 19x1 for the Warner Company:

| | Product | | |
	X	Y	Total
Selling price	$3	$6	
Variable expenses	1	2	
Contribution margin	$2	$4	
Total fixed expenses	$100,000	$120,000	
Number of units to be sold to break even	?	?	?
Number of units expected to be sold	30,000	50,000	80,000

Required:

1. Compute the break-even point for each product.
2. Suppose that Products X and Y were made in the same plant. Assume that a prolonged strike at the factory of the sole supplier of raw materials prevented the production of X for all of 19x1. Suppose also that the Warner fixed costs were unaffected.
   a. What is the break-even point for the company as a whole, assuming that no X is produced?
   b. Suppose instead that the shortage applied so that only X and no Y could be produced. In that case, what is the break-even point for the company as a whole?
3. Draw a break-even chart for the company as a whole, using an average selling price and an average variable expense per unit. What is the break-even point under this aggregate approach? What is the break-even point if you add together the individual break-even points that you computed in Requirement 1? Why is the aggregate break-even point different from the sum of the individual break-even points?

7-26. Effects of shift in sales mix. Assume that budgeted sales of the NAA Company of $6,000 (000's omitted here and in the tabulation below) represents sales of four products which are expected to be sold in the mixture shown below, a budgeted profit of $630 and break-even sales of $4,200 result:

| | Product | | | | |
	A	B	C	D	Totals
Sales	$2,000	$2,500	$1,000	$500	$6,000
Percentage of total sales	$33\frac{1}{3}\%$	$41\frac{2}{3}\%$	$16\frac{2}{3}\%$	$8\frac{1}{3}\%$	100%
Variable cost	1,200	1,700	800	200	3,900
Contribution-margin balance	$ 800	$ 800	$ 200	$300	$2,100
Contribution-margin ratio	40%	32%	20%	60%	35%
Fixed costs					$1,470
Operating profit					$ 630

Break-even sales: $\dfrac{\$1,470}{0.35}$ is $4,200

Suppose actual sales are:

A—$1,500, B—$2,200, C—$2,000, and D—$300.

Required:

1. Prepare a tabulation of actual results that is similar to the one shown above.
2. Explain why the operating profit and break-even point have changed.

Cost Behavior and Income Statements

8

In this chapter, we shall examine some commonly encountered costs and two major ways of formulating an income statement. We shall continue to confine our cost behavior classification to variable and fixed costs, and we shall see how these costs are often subdivided among business functions such as manufacturing, selling, and general administration. After studying this chapter, you should be acquainted with many new cost terms and also with the two basic approaches of an income statement: the functional approach and the contribution approach.

FUNCTIONAL OR TRADITIONAL APPROACH

Merchandising and Manufacturing

Some form of cost accounting is applicable to manufacturing companies, retail stores, insurance companies, medical centers, and nearly all organizations. We shall consider both nonmanufacturing and manufacturing organizations throughout this book, but we shall start with the manufacturing company because it is the most general case—embracing production, marketing, and general administration functions. You can then apply this overall framework to any organization.

Manufacturing is the transformation of materials into other goods through the use of labor and factory facilities. In contrast, retailers or wholesalers sell goods without changing their basic form. Balance sheets of manufacturers and merchandisers differ with respect to inventories.

The merchandise inventory account is supplanted in a manufacturing concern by three inventory classes: **direct-material inventory; work-in-process inventory** (cost of uncompleted goods still on the production line containing appropriate amounts of the three major manufacturing costs: direct material, direct labor, and factory overhead); and **finished goods** (fully completed goods). The only essential difference between the structure of the balance sheet of a manufacturer and that of the balance sheet of a retailer would appear in their respective current-asset sections:

Current-Asset Sections of Balance Sheets

Manufacturer			Merchandiser	
Cash		$ 4,000	Cash	$ 30,000
Receivables		5,000	Receivables	70,000
Finished goods	$12,000			
Work in process	2,000			
Direct material	3,000			
Total inventories		17,000	Merchandise inventories	100,000
Other current assets		1,000	Other current assets	3,000
Total current assets		$27,000	Total current assets	$203,000

In the income statements, the detailed reporting of selling and administrative expenses is typically the same for manufacturing and retailing organizations, but the cost of goods sold is different:

Retailer or Wholesaler	*Manufacturer*
Merchandise cost of goods sold, usually composed of the purchase cost of items, including freight in, that are acquired and then resold.	Manufacturing cost of goods produced and then sold, usually composed of the three major elements of cost explained below.

Explanation of Manufacturing Costs

There are three major elements in the cost of a manufactured product:

1. **Direct material.** This includes all raw material which is an integral part of the finished goods and which may be conveniently assigned to specific physical units (e.g., sheet steel, subassemblies). These materials are usually specified on a list of materials or on a blueprint. Certain minor materials, such as glue or nails, may be considered supplies, or indirect material, rather than direct material, because of the impracticality of

tracing such items to specific physical units of product. They are usually included in indirect manufacturing costs.

2. **Direct labor.** This includes all labor which is obviously related to and easily traceable to a specific product (e.g., the labor of machine operators and assemblers). This type of labor is usually specified on a Master Operations List or Routing sheet (Exhibit 8-1). Much labor (e.g., of material handlers, janitors, and plant guards) is considered indirect labor because of the difficulty or impracticality of assigning the cost of such work to specific physical units. These wages are therefore included in indirect manufacturing costs.

3. **Indirect manufacturing costs.** These include all manufacturing costs other than direct material and direct labor. Other terms used to describe this category are: **factory overhead, factory burden, manufacturing overhead,**

EXHIBIT 8-1
Master Operations List

MASTER OPERATIONS LIST				
Part name: Fuel pump body with bushings			Part number: B-489	
Stock specifications: Grey iron casting			Standard quantity: 200	

Operation Number	Department Number	Standard Time Allowed in Minutes		Description of Operation
		Setup	Operation Per Unit	
20	27	90	10.2	Drill, bore, face, chamfer and ream
25	29	18	.7	Face and chamfer hub
30	29	12	1.5	Mill eng. fit pad
35	31	18	8.0	Drill and tap complete
40	29	12	1.5	Mill clearance
45	29	–	1.8	Clean and grind hose connection
50	29	12	2.3	Press in 2 bushings G-98 and face flange on mandrel
	13			Inspect
	21			To stockroom

and **manufacturing expenses.** There are two major types of indirect manufacturing costs:

a. **Variable factory overhead.** The two principal examples are supplies
and most indirect labor. Whether the cost of a specific category of indirect labor is variable or fixed depends on its behavior in a given company. In this book, unless we specify otherwise, indirect labor will be
considered a variable rather than a fixed cost.

b. **Fixed factory overhead.** Examples are supervisory salaries, property
taxes, rent, insurance, and depreciation.

Indirect manufacturing costs is a more accurate descriptive term than
factory overhead, but the latter will be used throughout this book because
it is briefer. The term *overhead* is peculiar; its origins are unclear. Some
accountants have wondered why such costs are not called "underfoot"
rather than "overhead" costs.

Admittedly, the area of manufacturing costs contains a thicket of
new terms. One of your main tasks in studying this chapter is to assimilate these terms.

Direct and Indirect Costs

To guide his decisions, the manager needs data pertaining to a variety of
objectives. He needs the cost of *something.* It may be an activity, a product, a product group, a plant, a territory, a labor-hour, a machine-hour,
a customer, an order, a project, an X-ray, a class-hour, a welfare case, and
so forth. We shall call this "something" a cost object or object of costing,
and define it as any action or activity or part of an organization for which
a separate determination of costs is desired.

The terms *direct* and *indirect* have no meaning unless they are related to an object of costing. Traceability is the essence of the distinction.
The word *direct* refers to the practicable, obvious, physical tracing of cost
as incurred to a given cost object. A cost may be direct with respect to an
activity but indirect with respect to a product. For example, the salary
cost of a foreman may be a direct charge to a department, but an indirect
charge to a variety of products being manufactured in that department.

As you undoubtedly have gathered, whether a particular cost is
direct or indirect is often a slippery issue. The same cost may be regarded
as direct by one company and indirect by another company. For example,
if many job orders are being assembled, where batches of unique goods
are manufactured (for instance, furniture, jewelry, printing), the miscellaneous supplies used, the material-handling labor that transports items
from one part of a department to another, and the assembly foreman's
salary may be accounted for as indirect costs. In contrast, these costs may
be viewed as direct costs in a mixing department that works on long runs
of one product—such as in flour milling or canning.

The distinction between direct and indirect costs can be illustrated as
follows:

Nature of Classification	Producing Department or Function	Products
Materials used	D	D
Supplies used	D	D or I*
Assembly labor	D	D
Material-handling labor	D	D or I*
Depreciation—building	I	I
Assembly foreman's salary	D	D or I*
Building and grounds supervisor's salary	I	I

D = direct   I = indirect

*Whether such costs are direct or indirect depends on the types of products in question, as explained below.

Subdivisions of Labor Costs

The terminology for labor costs is usually the most confusing. Each organization seems to develop its own interpretation of various labor-cost classifications. We shall begin by considering some commonly encountered labor-cost terminology.

For our purposes, we shall categorize the terminology as follows:

Direct labor (already defined)
Indirect labor:
    Fork-lift truck operators (internal handling of materials)
    Janitors
    Plant guards
    Rework labor (time spent by direct laborers redoing spoiled work)
    Overtime premium paid to *all* factory workers
    Idle time
Payroll fringe costs

All factory labor costs, other than those for direct labor, are usually classified as **indirect labor costs,** a major component of indirect manufacturing costs. The term *indirect labor* is usually divided into many subsidiary classifications. The wages of fork-lift truck operators are generally not commingled with janitors' salaries, for example, although both are regarded as indirect labor.

Costs are classified in a detailed fashion primarily in an attempt to associate a specific cost with its specific cause, or reason for incurrence. Two classes of indirect labor need special mention: **overtime premium** and **idle time.**

Overtime premium paid to all factory workers is usually considered a part of overhead. If a lathe operator earns $3 per hour for straight time, and time and one-half for overtime, his premium is $1.50 per overtime hour. If he works forty-four hours, including four overtime hours, in one week, his gross earnings would be classified as follows:

Direct labor: 44 hours × $3	$132
Overtime premium (factory overhead): 4 hours × $1.50	6
Total earnings	$138

(handwritten note in margin: — possible overtime not budgeted)

Why is overtime premium considered an indirect cost rather than direct? After all, it can usually be traced to specific batches of work. It is usually not considered a direct charge because the scheduling of production jobs is generally random. For example, assume that Jobs No. 1 through 5 are scheduled for a specific workday of ten hours, including two overtime hours. Each job requires two hours. Should the job scheduled during hours 9 and 10 be assigned the overtime premium? Or should the premium be prorated over all the jobs? The latter approach does not penalize a particular batch of work solely because it happened to be worked on during the overtime hours. Instead, the overtime premium is considered to be attributable to the heavy overall volume of work and its cost is thus regarded as indirect manufacturing costs (factory overhead).

Another subsidiary classification of indirect labor costs is *idle time*. This cost typically represents wages paid for unproductive time caused by machine breakdowns, material shortages, sloppy production scheduling, and the like. For example, if the same lathe operator's machine broke down for three hours during the week, his earnings would be classified as follows:

Direct labor: 41 hours × $3	$123
Overtime premium (factory overhead): 4 hours × $1.50	6
Idle time (factory overhead): 3 hours × $3	9
Total earnings	$138

The classification of factory **payroll fringe costs** (e.g., employer contributions to social security, life insurance, health insurance, pensions, and miscellaneous other employee benefits) differs from company to company. In most companies, these are classified as indirect manufacturing costs. In some companies, however, the fringe benefits related to direct labor are charged as an additional direct labor cost. For instance, a direct laborer, such as a lathe operator whose gross wages are computed on the basis of $3 an hour, may enjoy payroll fringe benefits totaling, say, 75¢ per hour. Most companies tend to classify the $3 as direct labor cost and the 75¢ as factory overhead. Other companies classify the entire $3.75 as direct labor cost. The latter approach is preferable because most of these costs are also a fundamental part of acquiring labor services.

EXHIBIT 8-2

Relationships of Balance Sheets
and Income Statements

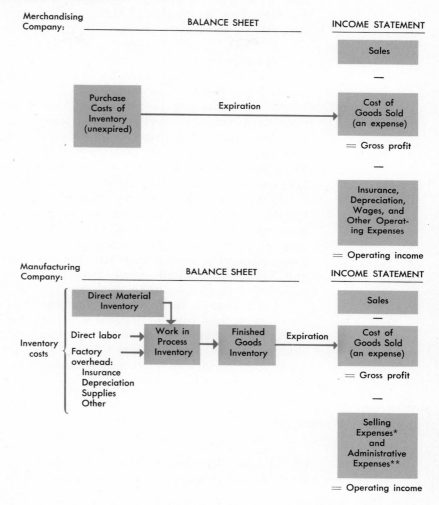

*Examples: insurance on salesmen's cars, depreciation on salesmen's cars, salesmen's salaries.

**Examples: insurance on corporate headquarters building, depreciation on office equipment, clerical salaries.

Note particularly that where insurance and depreciation relate to the manufacturing function, they are inventoriable; but where they relate to selling and administration, they are not inventoriable.

Unexpired and Expired Costs

Costs may be classified as **unexpired** and **expired.** Unexpired costs are those costs, including inventory costs and miscellaneous deferred or prepaid costs such as insurance premiums or research outlays, that are associated with (charged against) the revenue of *future* periods. Unexpired costs are measures of assets. In contrast, expired costs are measures of expenses. They are those costs, including the manufacturing cost of goods sold, that are associated with the revenue of the *current* period in question.

Exhibit 8-2 depicts the relationships between the balance sheets and income statements of a merchandising (retailer or wholesaler) company and a manufacturing company. To obtain perspective, stop and examine the exhibit and review the terminology.

In manufacturing accounting, many unexpired costs (assets) are transferred from one classification of unexpired costs to another before becoming expired costs (expense). Examples are direct material, factory insurance, depreciation on plant, and wages of production workers. These items are held back as product costs (inventory costs); they are later released to expense as part of cost of goods sold (an expense). The reader should distinguish sharply between the merchandising accounting and the manufacturing accounting for such costs as insurance, depreciation, and wages. In merchandising accounting, such items are generally treated as costs that mostly expire immediately; whereas, in manufacturing accounting, most of such items are related to production activities and thus are inventoriable costs—costs that do not expire (become expense) until the goods to which they relate are sold.

In this chapter, we shall not dwell on the intricacies of product costing—that is, how costs are related to inventories and how they flow through the accounts. In Chapter 15, we shall consider these matters and also such controversial points as whether fixed factory overhead should be excluded from the inventory cost of manufactured products.

CONTRIBUTION APPROACH

Contribution Approach Versus Traditional Approach

The major difference between the traditional and the contribution approaches is the tendency of the traditional approach to emphasize a *functional-cost* classification as opposed to a classification by *cost behaviors*. Hence, the traditional income statement has the following pattern:

Sales	xx
Less manufacturing cost of goods sold (including fixed manufacturing overhead)	xx
Gross profit	xx
Less selling and administrative expenses	xx
Operating income	xx

In contrast, the contribution approach stresses cost behavior as the primary classification scheme:

Sales		xx
Less variable costs:		
Manufacturing	xx	
Selling	xx	
Administrative	xx	xx
Contribution margin		xx
Less fixed costs:		
Manufacturing	xx	
Selling	xx	
Administrative	xx	xx
Operating income		xx

Note that the traditional statement does not show any contribution margin. Although the manufacturing-, selling-, and administrative-cost

EXHIBIT 8-3
Comparison of Contribution Approach
with Traditional (Functional) Approach

SAMSON COMPANY Contribution Income Statement For the Year Ending December 31, 19x2 (In thousands of dollars)			SAMSON COMPANY Traditional (Functional) Income Statement For the Year Ending December 31, 19x2 (In thousands of dollars)		
Sales		$20,000	Sales		$20,000
Less **variable** expenses:			Less **manufacturing** cost of		
Direct material	$ 7,000		goods sold:		
Direct labor	4,000		Direct material	$7,000	
Variable indirect manufacturing			Direct labor	4,000	
(Schedule 1)	1,000		Indirect **manufacturing costs**		
Total **variable** manufacturing			(Schedules 1–6—total)	4,000	15,000
cost of goods sold	$12,000		**Gross profit**		$ 5,000
Variable selling expenses			**Selling** expenses (Schedule 3)	$3,000	
(Schedule 3)	1,000		**Administrative** expenses		
Variable administrative expenses			(Schedule 4)	1,000	
(Schedule 4)	100		Total **selling** and		
Total **variable** expenses		13,100	**administrative** expenses		4,000
Contribution margin		$ 6,900	Operating income		$ 1,000
Less **fixed** expenses:					
Manufacturing (Schedule 2)	$ 3,000				
Selling (Schedule 3)	2,000				
Administrative (Schedule 4)	900	5,900			
Operating income		$ 1,000			

Note: Schedules 1 and 2 are in Exhibit 8-4. Schedules 3 and 4 are in Exhibit 8-5.

classifications could also be further subdivided to show variable and fixed classifications, this subdivision is not typical. The omission of a contribution margin raises analytical difficulties in the computation of the impact on net income of changes in sales. Fixed manufacturing overhead, under traditional procedures, is unitized and assigned to products. Hence, unit costs and gross-profit figures include fixed overhead that must be removed for a short-run cost-volume-profit analysis.

The contribution approach stresses the lump-sum amount of fixed costs to be recouped before net income emerges. This highlighting of total fixed costs helps to attract management attention to fixed-cost behavior and control when both short-run and long-run plans are being made. Keep in mind that advocates of this contribution approach *do not maintain that fixed costs are unimportant or irrelevant;* but they do stress that the distinctions between behaviors of variable and fixed costs are crucial for certain decisions.

Exhibit 8-3 shows how the same data can be used to prepare two different financial statements, according to the approach used. Variable and fixed subclassifications are shown in the Schedules of Indirect Manufacturing Costs (Exhibit 8-4) in order to facilitate comparison. In practice, such labeling is rare under the traditional approach. The figures are assumed. In addition, the units produced are assumed to equal the units

EXHIBIT 8-4
SAMSON COMPANY
Schedules of Indirect Manufacturing Costs
For the Year Ending December 31, 19x2
(In thousands of dollars)

Schedule 1: Variable Costs		
Supplies (lubricants, expendable tools, coolants, sandpaper)	$ 150	
Indirect labor (material transfer, idle time, setup costs)	700	
Repairs	100	
Power	50	$1,000
Schedule 2: Fixed Costs		
Foremen's salaries	$ 200	
Employee training	90	
Factory picnic and holiday party	10	
Supervisory salaries, except foremen's salaries	700	
Depreciation, plant and equipment	1,800	
Property taxes	150	
Insurance	50	3,000
Total indirect manufacturing costs		$4,000

EXHIBIT 8-5

SAMSON COMPANY

Schedules of Selling and Administrative Expenses

For the Year Ending December 31, 19x2

(In thousands of dollars)

Schedule 3: Selling Expenses		
Variable:		
Sales commissions	$ 700	
Shipping expenses	300	$1,000
Fixed:		
Advertising	$ 700	
Sales salaries	1,000	
Other	300	2,000
Total selling expenses		$3,000
Schedule 4: Administrative Expenses		
Variable:		
Some clerical wages	$ 80	
Computer time rented	20	$ 100
Fixed:		
Office salaries	$ 100	
Other salaries	200	
Depreciation on office facilities	100	
Public-accounting fees	40	
Legal fees	100	
Other	360	900
Total administrative expenses		$1,000

sold—that is, there is no change in inventory levels. In this way, we avoid some complications that are unnecessary and unimportant at this stage. These complexities are discussed in Chapter 15.

Advantages of Contribution Margins and Ratios

The advantages of knowing the contribution margins and ratios of divisions and product lines may be summarized as follows:

1. *Contribution-margin ratios* often help management decide on which products to push and which to de-emphasize or tolerate only because of the sales benefits that relate to other products.

2. *Contribution margins* are essential for helping management to decide whether a product line should be dropped. In the short run, if a

product recovers more than its variable costs, it may be making a contribution to overall profits. This information is provided promptly by the contribution approach. Under the traditional approach, the relevant information is not only difficult to gather, but there is a danger that management may be misled by reliance on unit costs that contain an element of fixed overhead.

3. Contribution margins may be used to appraise alternatives that arise with respect to price reductions, special discounts, special advertising campaigns, and the use of premiums to spur sales volume. Decisions such as these are really determined by a comparison of the added costs with the prospective additions in sales revenue. Ordinarily, the higher the contribution-margin ratio, the better the opportunity for sales promotion; the lower the ratio, the greater the increase in volume that is necessary to recover additional sales-promotion commitments.

4. When desired profits are agreed upon, their attainability may be quickly appraised by computing the number of units that must be sold to secure the wanted profits. The computation is easily made by dividing the fixed costs plus desired profits by the contribution margin per unit.

5. Decisions must often be made as to how to utilize a given set of resources (for example, machines or materials) most profitably. The contribution approach furnishes the data for a proper decision, because the latter is determined by the product that makes the largest total contribution to profits. (However, the solution to the problem of calculating the maximum contribution is not always intuitively obvious. This point is amplified in Chapters 12 and 17.)

6. The contribution approach is helpful where selling prices are firmly established in the industry, because often the principal problem for the individual company is how much variable cost is allowable (a matter most heavily affected in many companies by design of products) and how much volume can be obtained.

7. Pricing will be discussed at greater length in Chapter 12. Ultimately, maximum prices are set by customer demand. Minimum short-run prices are sometimes determined by the variable costs of producing and selling. Advocates of a contribution approach maintain that the compilation of unit costs for products on a contribution basis helps managers understand the relationship among costs, volume, prices, and profits, and hence leads to wiser pricing decisions.

Troublesome Terminology

There are many terms that have very special meanings in accounting. The meanings often differ from company to company; each organization seems to develop its own distinctive and extensive accounting language. This is why you will save much confusion and wasted time if you always find out the exact meanings of any strange jargon that you encounter.

This chapter and the preceding chapter have merely hinted at the vast number of classifications of costs that have proven useful for various purposes. Among other categories, classifications can be made by:

1. Time when computed
   a. Historical costs
   b. Budgeted or predetermined costs (via cost "prediction")

2. Behavior in relation to fluctuations in activity
   a. Variable-cost behavior
   b. Fixed-cost behavior
   c. Other cost behavior

3. Degree of averaging
   a. Total costs
   b. Unit costs

4. Management function
   a. Manufacturing costs
   b. Selling costs
   c. Administrative costs

5. Ease of traceability to some object of costing
   a. Direct costs
   b. Indirect costs

6. Timing of charges against revenue
   a. Unexpired costs
   b. Expired costs

SUMMARY

The most important aspect of intelligent cost planning and control is an understanding of cost behavior patterns and influences. The most basic behavior pattern of costs may be described as either variable or fixed. The contribution approach to preparing an income statement emphasizes this distinction and is a natural extension of the cost-volume-profit analysis used in decisions. In contrast, the traditional approach emphasizes the distinction between three major business functions: manufacturing, selling, and administration.

Many new terms were introduced in this chapter. You should review them to make sure you know their exact meanings.

SUMMARY PROBLEM FOR YOUR REVIEW

Problem

The following information is taken from the records of the Levander Company for the year ending December 31, 19x2. There were no beginning or ending inventories.

Sales	$10,000,000	Long-term rent, factory	$ 100,000
Sales commissions	500,000	Factory superintendent's	
Advertising	200,000	salary	30,000
Shipping expenses	300,000	Foremen's salaries	100,000

Administrative executive salaries	100,000	Direct material used	4,000,000
Administrative clerical salaries (variable)	400,000	Direct labor	2,000,000
		Cutting bits used	60,000
		Factory methods research	40,000
Fire insurance on factory equipment	2,000	Abrasives for machining	100,000
		Indirect labor	800,000
Property taxes on factory equipment	10,000	Depreciation on equipment	300,000

Required:

1. Prepare a contribution income statement and a traditional (functional) income statement. If you are in doubt about any cost behavior pattern, decide on the basis of whether the total cost in question will fluctuate substantially over a wide range of volume. Prepare a separate supporting schedule of indirect manufacturing costs subdivided between variable and fixed costs.

2. Suppose that all variable costs fluctuate directly in proportion to sales, and that fixed costs are unaffected over a very wide range of sales. What would operating income have been if sales had been $10,500,000 instead of $10,000,000? Which income statement did you use to help get your answer? Why?

Solution

1.

LEVANDER COMPANY
Contribution Income Statement
For the Year Ending
December 31, 19x2
(In thousands of dollars)

Sales			$10,000
Less variable expenses:			
Direct material		$4,000	
Direct labor		2,000	
Variable indirect manufacturing costs (1)*		960	
Total variable manufacturing cost of goods sold		$6,960	
Variable selling expenses			
Sales commissions	$500		
Shipping expenses	300	800	
Variable clerical salaries		400	
Total variable expenses			8,160
Contribution margin			$ 1,840
Less fixed expenses:			
Manufacturing (2)*		$ 582	
Selling (advertising)		200	
Administrative— executive salaries		100	
Total fixed expenses			882
Operating income			$ 958

LEVANDER COMPANY
Functional Income Statement
For the Year Ending
December 31, 19x2
(In thousands of dollars)

Sales			$10,000
Less manufacturing cost of goods sold:			
Direct material		$4,000	
Direct labor		2,000	
Indirect manufacturing costs (from schedules)		1,542	7,542
Gross profit			$ 2,458
Selling expenses:			
Sales commissions	$500		
Advertising	200		
Shipping expenses	300	$1,000	
Administrative expenses:			
Executive salaries	$100		
Clerical salaries	400	500	1,500
Operating income			$ 958

*Keyed to accompanying schedules.

LEVANDER COMPANY
Schedules 1 and 2
Indirect Manufacturing Costs
For the Year Ending December 31, 19x2
(In thousands of dollars)

Schedule 1: Variable costs

Cutting bits	$ 60	
Abrasives for machining	100	
Indirect labor	800	$ 960

Schedule 2: Fixed costs

Foremen's salaries	$100	
Factory methods research	40	
Long-term rent, factory	100	
Fire insurance on equipment	2	
Property taxes on equipment	10	
Depreciation on equipment	300	
Factory superintendent's salary	30	582
Total indirect manufacturing costs		$1,542

2. Operating income would increase from $958,000 to $1,050,000, computed as follows:

Increase in revenue	$ 500,000
Increase in contribution margin:	
Contribution-margin ratio in Contribution Income Statement is	
$1,840 ÷ $10,000 = .184	
Ratio times revenue is .184 × $500,000 =	$ 92,000
Increase in fixed expenses	-0-
Operating income before increase	958,000
New operating income	$1,050,000

The above analysis is readily calculated by using data from the contribution income statement. In contrast, the data in the traditional (functional) income statement must be analyzed and divided into variable and fixed categories before the effect on operating income can be estimated.

ASSIGNMENT MATERIAL

Fundamental Assignment Material

8-1. Terminology. Define: *direct material; direct labor; idle time; overtime premium; indirect labor; indirect manufacturing costs; factory overhead; factory burden; manufacturing overhead; manufacturing expenses;* and *contribution approach.*

8-2. Contribution and traditional income statements. (An alternate problem is 8-15.) The Del Prado Company had the following data for the year 19x1. Assume that inventories are unchanged and that they may therefore be ignored:

Shipping expenses	$ 70,000	Fire insurance on	
Factory rent	50,000	equipment	$ 3,000
Sales	1,400,000	Material-handling labor	40,000
Administrative expenses	100,000	Lubricants and coolants	3,000
Property taxes on		Idle time	10,000
equipment	4,000	Miscellaneous indirect	
Sales commissions	60,000	labor	40,000
Depreciation–Equipment	40,000	Overtime premium	20,000
Sandpaper used	1,000	Direct material used	380,000
Direct labor	300,000	Sales salaries	200,000

Required:

1. Prepare a contribution income statement and a traditional (functional) income statement. Prepare a separate supporting schedule of indirect manufacturing costs subdivided between variable and fixed costs. If you are in doubt about any cost behavior pattern, decide on the basis of whether the individual cost in question will fluctuate substantially over a wide range of volume.

2. Suppose that total variable costs fluctuate directly in proportion to sales. Also suppose that total fixed costs are unaffected over a wide range of sales. What would operating income have been if sales had amounted to (a) $1,300,000 instead of $1,400,000? (b) $1,500,000 instead of $1,400,000? Which income statement did you use to arrive at your answer? Why?

8-3. **Variable costs and fixed costs; manufacturing and other costs.** For each of the numbered items, choose the appropriate classification for a job-order manufacturing company (e.g., custom furniture, job printing). If in doubt about whether the cost behavior is basically variable or fixed, decide on the basis of whether the total cost will fluctuate substantially over a wide range of volume. Most items have two answers from among the following possibilities:

a. Variable cost	*d.* Selling cost
b. Fixed cost	*e.* Manufacturing costs, direct
c. General and administrative cost	*f.* Manufacturing costs, indirect
	g. Other (specify)

Sample answers:

Direct material.	*a, e*
President's salary.	*b, c*
Bond interest expense.	*b, g* (financial expense)

Items for your consideration:

1. Sandpaper.
2. Supervisory salaries, production control.
3. Supervisory salaries, assembly department.
4. Supervisory salaries, factory storeroom.
5. Company picnic costs.
6. Overtime premium, punch press.
7. Idle time, assembly.
8. Freight out.
9. Property taxes.
10. Factory power for machines.
11. Salesmen's commissions.
12. Salesmen's salaries.
13. Welding supplies.
14. Fire loss.
15. Paint for finished products.
16. Heat and air conditioning, factory.
17. Material-handling labor, punch press.
18. Straight-line depreciation, salesmen's automobiles.

8-4. Distinguish between supplies and direct material.

8-5. "Glue or nails become an integral part of the finished product, so they would be direct material." Do you agree? Explain.

8-6. What is the advantage of the contribution approach as compared to the traditional approach?

8-7. Distinguish between manufacturing and merchandising.

8-8. "Departments are not cost objects or objects of costing." Do you agree? Explain.

8-9. "Manufacturing cost of goods sold is a special category of expense." Do you agree? Explain.

8-10. "Unexpired costs are always inventory costs." Do you agree? Explain.

8-11. "Miscellaneous supplies are always indirect costs." Do you agree? Explain.

8-12. Variable or fixed indirect costs. Many indirect manufacturing costs do not fall easily into the categories of variable and fixed costs. Nevertheless, for the following costs, indicate whether each is more widely to have a variable (use V) or fixed (use F) behavior pattern over a wide range of volume:

1. Supplies
2. Depreciation
3. Patent amortization
4. Taxes on real estate
5. Fuel
6. Purchased power
7. Overtime premium
8. Wages, building employees
9. Hauling within plant
10. Taxes on plant equipment
11. Supervision
12. Small tools
13. Insurance, property
14. Royalties
15. Cost accounting department costs
16. Salaries, production executives
17. Research and development
18. Receiving costs
19. Rework operations
20. Indirect labor

8-13. Classification of manufacturing costs. Classify each of the following as direct or indirect (D or I) with respect to product, and as variable or fixed (V or F) with respect to whether the cost fluctuates in total as activity or volume changes over wide ranges of activity. You will have two answers, D or I and V or F, for *each* of the ten items:

1. Food for a factory cafeteria.
2. Factory rent.
3. Salary of a factory storeroom clerk.
4. Foreman training program.
5. Abrasives (sandpaper, etc.).
6. Cutting bits in a machinery department.
7. Workmen's compensation insurance in a factory.
8. Cement for a roadbuilder.
9. Steel scrap for a blast furnace.
10. Paper towels for a factory washroom.

8-14. Cost behavior patterns and planning. The McCovey Company has a maximum production capacity of 20,000 units per year. At that level, fixed costs are $280,000 annually; variable costs per unit are $30 at all production levels.

For the ensuing year, the company has orders of 24,000 units at $50. If the company desired to make a minimum overall net income of $148,000 on these 24,000 units, what maximum unit purchase price would McCovey Company be willing to pay to a subcontractor for 4,000 units? Assume that the subcontractor would act as McCovey's agent and deliver the units to customers directly, bearing all related costs of manufacture, delivery, and so on. The customers, however, would pay McCovey directly as goods are delivered.

8-15. Contribution and traditional income statement. (Alternate to 8-2.) The Colone Corporation was incorporated on January 1, 19x1. The controller has given you the following information pertaining to the company's operations for the year ending December 31, 19x1. There are no ending inventories. During a discussion with the sales manager, he informs you that the company's three salesmen are paid a base salary of $10,000 each, plus 2 percent of their sales.

Sales	$3,050,000	Salesmen's compensation	$ 91,000
Training program,		Advertising and	
factory	50,000	promotion	150,000
Direct material	1,000,000	Direct labor	750,000
Shipping expense		Manufacturing manager's	
(a selling expense)	37,000	salary	25,000
Administrative and		Indirect labor	200,000
clerical salaries		Engineering consultants	
(variable)	28,000	on factory operations	70,000
Depreciation, factory	90,000	Foremen's salaries	125,000
Miscellaneous factory		Rental of factory	
supplies	10,000	equipment on long-	
Time and motion studies		term lease	75,000
of factory operations	12,000	Property taxes on factory	18,000
Administrative executive		Fire insurance on factory	4,000
salaries	135,000		

Required:

1. Prepare a traditional income statement and a contribution income statement for the Colone Corporation for the year ending December 31, 19x1. Include a separate statement of indirect manufacturing costs. Assume that the foremen's salaries are fixed costs.
2. Assume that total variable costs fluctuate directly in proportion to sales, and that total fixed costs are unaffected over a wide range of sales. What would operating income have been if sales had amounted to $3,200,000 instead of $3,050,000? Which income statement did you use to arrive at your answer? Why?

8-16. Contribution analysis. (CMA adapted.) The Justa Corporation produces three products, A, B, and C, which are sold in a local market and in a regional market. At the end of the first quarter of the current year, the following income statement has been prepared:

	Total	Local	Regional
Sales	$1,300,000	$1,000,000	$300,000
Cost of goods sold	1,010,000	775,000	235,000
Gross margin	$ 290,000	$ 225,000	$ 65,000
Selling expenses	$ 105,000	$ 60,000	$ 45,000
Administrative expenses	52,000	40,000	12,000
	$ 157,000	$ 100,000	$ 57,000
Net income	$ 133,000	$ 125,000	$ 8,000

Management has expressed special concern with the regional market because of the extremely poor return on sales. This market was entered a year ago because of excess capacity. It was originally believed that the return on sales would improve with time, but after a year no noticeable improvement can be seen from the results as reported in the above quarterly statement.

In attempting to decide whether to eliminate the regional market, the following information has been gathered:

	Products		
	A	B	C
Sales	$500,000	$400,000	$400,000
Variable manufacturing expenses as a percentage of sales	60%	70%	60%
Variable selling expenses as a percentage of sales	3%	2%	2%

	Sales by Markets	
Product	Local	Regional
A	$400,000	$100,000
B	300,000	100,000
C	300,000	100,000

All administrative expenses and fixed manufacturing expenses are common to the three products and the two markets and are fixed for the period. Remaining selling expenses are fixed for the period and separable by market. All fixed expenses are based upon a prorated yearly amount.

Required:

1. Prepare the quarterly income statement showing contribution margins by markets.
2. Assuming there are no alternative uses for the Justa Corporation's present capacity, would you recommend dropping the regional market? Why or why not?
3. Prepare the quarterly income statement showing contribution margins by products.
4. It is believed that a new product can be ready for sale next year if the Justa Corporation decides to go ahead with continued research. The new product can be produced by simply converting equipment presently used in producing

Product *C*. This conversion will increase fixed costs by $10,000 per quarter. What must be the minimum contribution margin per quarter of the new product to make the changeover financially feasible?

8-17. **Dropping or adding products.** (CPA adapted). The officers of Bradshaw Company are reviewing the profitability of the company's four products and the potential effect of several proposals for varying the product mix. An excerpt from the income statement and other data follow:

	Totals	Product P	Product Q	Product R	Product S
Sales	$62,600	$10,000	$18,000	$12,600	$22,000
Cost of goods sold	44,274	4,750	7,056	13,968	18,500
Gross profit	18,326	5,250	10,944	(1,368)	3,500
Operating expenses	12,012	1,990	2,976	2,826	4,220
Income before income taxes	$ 6,314	$ 3,260	$ 7,968	$ (4,194)	$ (720)
Units sold		1,000	1,200	1,800	2,000
Sales price per unit		$ 10.00	$ 15.00	$ 7.00	$ 11.00
Variable cost of goods sold per unit		$ 2.50	$ 3.00	$ 6.50	$ 6.00
Variable operating expenses per unit		$ 1.17	$ 1.25	$ 1.00	$ 1.20

Each of the following proposals is to be considered independently of the other proposals. Consider only the product changes stated in each proposal; the activity of other products remains stable. Ignore income taxes.

1. If Product *R* is discontinued, the effect on income will be
   a. a $900 increase. c. a $12,600 decrease. e. None of the above.
   b. a $4,194 increase. d. a $1,368 increase.
2. If Product *R* is discontinued and a consequent loss of customers causes a decrease of 200 units in sales of *Q*, the total effect on income will be
   a. a $15,600 decrease. c. a $2,044 increase. e. None of the above.
   b. a $2,866 increase. d. a $1,250 decrease.
3. If the sales price of Product *R* is increased to $8 with a decrease in the number of units sold to 1,500, the effect on income will be
   a. a $2,199 decrease. c. a $750 increase. e. None of the above.
   b. a $600 decrease. d. a $2,199 increase.
4. The plant in which *R* is produced can be utilized to produce a new product, *T*. The total variable costs and expenses per unit of *T* are $8.05, and 1,600 units can be sold at $9.50 each. If *T* is introduced and *R* is discontinued, the total effect on income will be
   a. a $2,600 increase. c. a $3,220 increase. e. None of the above.
   b. a $2,320 increase. d. a $1,420 increase.
5. Part of the plant in which *P* is produced can easily be adapted to the production of *S*, but changes in quantities may make changes in sales prices advisable. If production of *P* is reduced to 500 units (to be sold at $12 each) and production of *S* is increased to 2,500 units (to be sold at $10.50 each), the total effect on income will be
   a. a $1,765 decrease. c. a $2,060 decrease. e. None of the above.
   b. a $250 increase. d. a $1,515 decrease.

6. Production of *P* can be doubled by adding a second shift, but higher wages must be paid, increasing variable cost of goods sold to $3.50 for each of the additional units. If the 1,000 additional units of *P* can be sold at $10 each, the total effect on income will be

 a. a $10,000 increase.   c. a $6,500 increase.   e. None of the above.
 b. a $5,330 increase.   d. a $2,260 increase.

Note: Ignore fixed costs. Be careful when you compute differences—it is easy to get algebraic signs confused. Note how the contribution approach facilitates getting the solution.

8-18. **Contribution analysis.** (CMA adapted.) R. A. Ro and Company, maker of quality handmade pipes, has experienced a steady growth in sales for the past five years. However, increased competition has led Mr. Ro, the president, to believe that an aggressive advertising campaign will be necessary next year to maintain the company's present growth.

To prepare for next year's advertising campaign, the company's accountant has prepared and presented Mr. Ro with the following data for the current year, 19x2:

Cost Schedule

Variable costs:	
Direct labor	$ 8.00/pipe
Direct material	3.25/pipe
Variable overhead	2.50/pipe
Total variable costs	$13.75/pipe
Fixed costs	
Manufacturing	$ 25,000
Selling	40,000
Administrative	70,000
Total fixed costs	$135,000
Selling price, per pipe:	$25.00
Expected sales, 19x2 (20,000 units):	$500,000
Tax rate: 40%	

Mr. Ro has set the sales target for 19x3 at a level of $550,000 (or 22,000 pipes).

Required:

1. What is the projected after-tax net income for 19x2?
2. What is the break-even point in units for 19x2?
3. Mr. Ro believes an additional selling expense of $11,250 for advertising in 19x3, with all other costs remaining constant, will be necessary to attain the sales target. What will be the after-tax net income for 19x3 if the additional $11,250 is spent?
4. What will be the break-even point in dollar sales for 19x3 if the additional $11,250 is spent on advertising?
5. If the additional $11,250 is spent on advertising in 19x3, what is the required sales level in dollar sales to equal 19x2's after-tax net income?
6. At a sales level of 22,000 units, what is the maximum amount which can be spent on advertising if an after-tax net income of $60,000 is desired?

8-19. Distinctions between contribution and functional approaches. The Dischinger Company provides you with the following miscellaneous data regarding operations in 19x2:

Sales	$100,000
Direct material used	40,000
Direct labor	15,000
Fixed manufacturing overhead	20,000
Fixed selling and administrative expenses	10,000
Gross profit	20,000
Net loss	5,000

There are no beginning or ending inventories.

Required:

Prepare the following:

1. Variable selling and administrative expenses.
2. Contribution margin in dollars.
3. Variable manufacturing overhead.
4. Break-even point in sales dollars.
5. Manufacturing cost of goods sold.

8-20. Distinctions between contribution and functional approaches. The Dietz Corporation provides you with the following miscellaneous data regarding operations for 19x4:

Break-even point (in sales dollars)	$ 66,667
Direct material used	22,000
Gross profit	25,000
Contribution margin	30,000
Direct labor	30,000
Sales	100,000
Variable manufacturing overhead	5,000

There are no beginning or ending inventories.

Required:

Prepare the following:

1. Fixed manufacturing overhead.
2. Variable selling and administrative expenses.
3. Fixed selling and administrative expenses.

8-21. Case study of cost-volume-profit relationships; analysis of financial statements. The Knapp Company is a processor of a Bacardi-mix concentrate. Sales are made principally to liquor distributors throughout the country.

The company's income statements for the past year and the coming year are being analyzed by top management.

KNAPP COMPANY
Income Statements

	For the Year 19x1 Just Ended		For the Year 19x2 Tentative Budget	
Sales 1,500,000 gallons in 19x1		$900,000		$1,000,000
Cost of goods sold:				
Direct material	$450,000		$495,000	
Direct labor	90,000		99,000	
Factory overhead:				
Variable	18,000		19,800	
Fixed	50,000	608,000	50,000	663,800
Gross margin		$292,000		$ 336,200
Selling expenses:				
Variable:				
Sales commissions (based on dollar sales)	$ 45,000		$ 50,000	
Shipping and other	90,000		99,000	
Fixed: salaries, advertising, etc.	110,000		138,000	
Administrative expenses:				
Variable	12,000		13,200	
Fixed	40,000	297,000	40,000	340,200
Net income		$ − 5,000		$ − 4,000

Required:

Consider each requirement independently.

Unless otherwise stated, assume that all unit costs of inputs like material and labor are unchanged. Also, assume that efficiency is unchanged—that is, the labor and quantity of material consumed per unit of output are unchanged. Unless otherwise stated, assume that there are no changes in fixed costs.

1. The president has just returned from a management conference at a local university, where he heard an accounting professor criticize conventional income statements. The professor had asserted that knowledge of cost behavior patterns was of key importance in determining managerial strategies. The president now feels that the income statement should be recast to harmonize with cost-volume-profit analysis—that is, the statement should have three major sections: sales, variable costs, and fixed costs. Using the 19x1 data, prepare such a statement, showing the contribution margin as well as net income.
2. Comment on the changes in each item in the income statement. What are the most likely causes for each increase? For example, have selling prices been changed for 19x2? How do sales commissions fluctuate in relation to units sold or in relation to dollar sales?
3. The president is unimpressed with the 19x2 budget: "We need to take a fresh look in order to begin moving toward profitable operations. Let's tear up the 19x2 budget, concentrate on 19x1 results, and prepare a new comparative 19x2 budget under each of the following assumptions:
   a. A 5 percent average price cut will increase unit sales by 20 percent.
   b. A 5 percent average price increase will decrease unit sales by 10 percent.

c. A sales commission rate of 10 percent and a $3\frac{1}{3}$ percent price increase will boost unit sales by 10 percent."

Prepare the budgets for 19x2, using a contribution-margin format and three columns. Assume that there are no changes in fixed costs.

4. The advertising manager maintains that the advertising budget should be increased by $100,000 and that prices should be increased by 10 percent. Resulting unit sales will soar by 25 percent. What would be the expected operating income under such circumstances?

5. A nearby distillery has offered to buy 300,000 gallons in 19x2, if the unit price is low enough. The Knapp Company would not have to incur sales commissions or shipping costs on this special order, and regular business would be undisturbed. Assuming that 19x2's regular operations will be exactly like 19x1's, what unit price should be quoted in order for the Knapp Company to earn an operating income of $5,000 in 19x2?

6. The company chemist wants to add a special ingredient, an exotic flavoring that will add 2¢ per gallon to the Bacardi-mix costs. He also wants to replace the ordinary grenadine now used, which costs 3¢ per gallon of mix, with a more exquisite type costing 4¢ per gallon. Assuming no other changes in cost behavior, how many units must be sold to earn an operating income of $5,000 in 19x2?

Flexible Budgets
and Standards for Control

9

The essence of control is feedback—the comparison of actual performance with planned performance. Flexible budgets and standard costs are major attention-directing techniques for planning and for providing feedback regarding individual costs. Throughout this chapter, to stress some basic ideas, we shall continue to assume that all costs are either variable or fixed; in the next chapter, we shall consider various cost behavior patterns in more detail.

FLEXIBLE BUDGETS

Static Budget Comparisons

As Chapter 6 shows, budgets may be developed on a company-wide basis to cover all activities, from sales to direct materials to sweeping compounds, and from spending on a new plant to expected drains on petty cash. A budget may be expressed on an accrual basis or on a cash-flow basis; it may be highly condensed or exceedingly detailed. All the budgets discussed in Chapter 6 are **static** (inflexible). To illustrate: A typical master planning budget is a plan tailored to a single target volume level of, say, 100,000 units. All results would be compared with the original plan, regardless of changes in ensuing conditions—even though, for example, volume turns out to be 90,000 units instead of the original 100,000.

In contrast, **flexible** budgets, also called **variable** budgets, have the following distinguishing features: (a) They are prepared for a range of activity instead of a single level; (b) They supply a dynamic basis for comparison because they are automatically geared to changes in volume. The flexible-budget approach says, "Give me any activity level you choose, and I'll provide a budget tailored to that particular volume."

EXHIBIT 9-1
DOMINION COMPANY
Performance Report Using Static Budget
For the Month Ending June 30, 19x1

	MASTER (STATIC) BUDGET	ACTUAL	VARIANCE
Units	9,000	7,000	2,000
Sales	$216,000	$168,000	$48,000 U
Variable costs:			
Direct material	$ 27,000	$ 21,350	$ 5,650 F
Direct labor	72,000	61,500	10,500 F
Labor to transport materials internally and provide general support	14,400	11,100	3,300 F
Idle time	3,600	3,550	50 F
Cleanup time	2,700	2,500	200 F
Other indirect labor	900	800	100 F
Miscellaneous supplies	5,400	4,700	700 F
Variable manufacturing costs	$126,000	$105,500	$20,500 F
Shipping expenses (selling)	5,400	5,000	400 F
Xerox, telephone, etc. (administrative)	1,800	2,000	200 U
Total variable costs	$133,200	$112,500	$20,700 F
Contribution margin	$ 82,800	$ 55,500	$27,300 U
Fixed costs:			
Factory supervision	$ 14,400	$ 14,700	$ 300 U
Rent of factory	5,000	5,000	—
Depreciation of factory equipment	15,000	15,000	—
Other fixed factory costs	2,600	2,600	—
Fixed manufacturing costs	$ 37,000	$ 37,300	$ 300 U
Fixed selling and administrative costs	33,000	33,000	—
Total fixed costs	$ 70,000	$ 70,300	$ 300 U
Operating income (loss)	$ 12,800	$ (14,800)	$27,600 U

F = Favorable cost variances occur when actual costs are less than budgeted costs.
U = Unfavorable cost variances occur when actual costs are greater than budgeted costs.

To understand this distinction better, let us examine a simplified illustration. Suppose that the Dominion Company, a one-department firm, manufactured and sold a special kind of carry-on flight luggage that required several hand operations. The product had some variations, but it was essentially viewed as a single product bearing one selling price.

The master budget for the forthcoming month included the condensed income statement shown in Exhibit 9-1, Column 1. The actual results are in Column 2. The master budget called for the production and sales of 9,000 units, but only 7,000 units were actually produced and sold. There were no beginning or ending inventories.

The master budget was based on detailed expectations for the given month, including a careful forecast of sales. The **performance report** in Exhibit 9-1 compares the actual results with the master budget. *Performance report* is a general term that usually means a comparison of actual results with some budget. In particular, note that the volume of activity, as measured by sales, was substantially below the budget. The budget in Exhibit 9-1 is an example of a *static* budget.

Exhibit 9-1 is difficult to analyze. Clearly, sales are below expectations, but the favorable variances regarding the variable costs are deceptive. Considering the lower than projected level of activity, was cost control really satisfactory? The comparison of actual results with a static budget does not give much help in answering that question.

Flexible Budget Comparisons

As president of the Dominion Company, you probably would want a performance report that better pinpoints some major variances between the master budget and the actual results. To get a better basis for analysis, a flexible budget is introduced. The flexible budget is based on an adequate knowledge of cost behavior patterns. It is essentially a set of budgets that may be tailored to any level of activity. Ideally, the flexible budget is compiled after obtaining a detailed analysis of how each cost fluctuates in relation to changes in activity. Exhibit 9-2 shows how a flexible budget might appear.

The costs in Exhibit 9-2 may be graphed, as in Exhibit 9-3. Although we have assumed that the graph is valid for the range of 7,000 to 9,000 units, costs are unlikely to behave in accordance with such a pat formula on either side of this range. Inasmuch as the activity was 7,000 units, the pertinent flexible budget is in the 7,000-unit column of Exhibit 9-2.

Need to Isolate Variances

Pause a moment to reflect on the analytical problem. The company had an original plan, and the president may seek an explanation of why the plan was not achieved; in other words, a manager may desire a more penetrating analysis of the variances in Exhibit 9-1. The extent of the analysis

EXHIBIT 9-2
DOMINION COMPANY
Flexible Budget
For the Month Ending June 30, 19x1

	BUDGET FORMULA PER UNIT	VARIOUS LEVELS OF ACTIVITY		
Units	—	7,000	8,000	9,000
Sales	$24.00	$168,000	$192,000	$216,000
Variable costs:				
Direct material	$ 3.00	$ 21,000	$ 24,000	$ 27,000
Direct labor	8.00	56,000	64,000	72,000
Labor to transport materials internally and provide general support	1.60	11,200	12,800	14,400
Idle time	.40	2,800	3,200	3,600
Cleanup time	.30	2,100	2,400	2,700
Other indirect labor	.10	700	800	900
Miscellaneous supplies	.60	4,200	4,800	5,400
Variable manufacturing costs	$14.00	$ 98,000	$112,000	$126,000
Shipping expenses (selling)	.60	4,200	4,800	5,400
Xerox, telephone, etc.	.20	1,400	1,600	1,800
Total variable costs	$14.80	$103,600	$118,400	$133,200
Contribution margin	$ 9.20	$ 64,400	$ 73,600	$ 82,800
Fixed costs:				
Factory supervision		$ 14,400	$ 14,400	$ 14,400
Rent of factory		5,000	5,000	5,000
Depreciation of factory equipment		15,000	15,000	15,000
Other fixed factory costs		2,600	2,600	2,600
Fixed manufacturing costs		$ 37,000	$ 37,000	$ 37,000
Fixed selling and adminis-trative costs		33,000	33,000	33,000
Total fixed costs*		$ 70,000	$ 70,000	$ 70,000
Operating income (loss)		$ (5,600)	$ 3,600	$ 12,800

*Note that the budget formula for fixed costs is $70,000 per month. Therefore, the budget formula for total costs is $14.80 per unit plus $70,000 per month. The graph in Exhibit 9-3 portrays these relationships.

EXHIBIT 9-3
DOMINION CO.
Graph of Flexible Budget of Costs

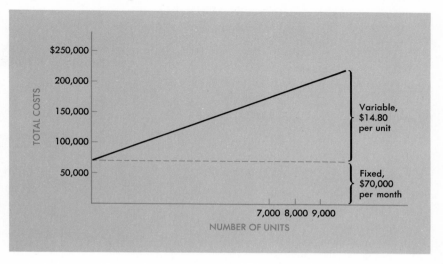

may become quite detailed. However, as a start, consider how the variances may be divided into two major categories:

1. Variances from a revenue target (sometimes called a volume target or, in the case of a production manager, a scheduled production target).[1] In this book, this variance will be called a *marketing variance,* although its label will vary from company to company. It emphasizes the idea that the marketing function usually has the primary responsibility for reaching the sales level called for in the master budget.

2. Variances arising from changes in unit prices (or unit costs) and from inefficient utilization of inputs, here called *price* and *efficiency* variances.

The trouble with the static budget, as Exhibit 9-1 shows, is its failure to distinguish between these two facets of a manager's performance. However, Exhibit 9-4 gives a condensed view of how these variances can be isolated by the use of a flexible budget.

Column 2 in Exhibit 9-4 focuses on the marketing variance. It shows

---

[1]Sometimes this is generically called an *effectiveness* variance, as distinguished from all other measures, which are loosely called *efficiency* variances. Effectiveness is the accomplishment of a predetermined objective. Efficiency is an optimum relationship between input and output. Given any level of output, did the manager control his inputs as he should have? Performance may be both effective and efficient, but either condition can occur without the other. For example, a company may set 200,000 units as a production objective. Subsequently, because of material shortages, only 150,000 units may be produced with 100 percent efficiency—performance would be ineffective but efficient. In contrast, 200,000 units may be produced on schedule but with a considerable waste of labor and materials—performance would be effective but inefficient.

EXHIBIT 9-4
DOMINION COMPANY
Summary of Performance
For the Month Ending June 30, 19x1

	(1) MASTER BUDGET*	(2) (1)–(3) MARKETING VARIANCE	(3) FLEXIBLE BUDGET FOR OUTPUT ATTAINED†	(4) (3)–(5) VARIANCES BECAUSE OF PRICE CHANGES AND INEFFICIENCY**	(5) RESULTS AT ACTUAL PRICES*
Physical units	9,000	2,000	7,000	—	7,000
Sales	$216,000	$48,000	$168,000	$ —	$168,000
Variable costs	133,200	29,600	103,600	8,900 U	112,500
Contribution margin	$ 82,800	$18,400	$ 64,400	$8,900 U	$ 55,500
Fixed costs	70,000	—	70,000	300 U	70,300
Operating income	$ 12,800	$18,400 U	$ (5,600)	$9,200 U	$ (14,800)

U = Unfavorable
 * = Figures are from Exhibit 9-1
 † = Figures are from the 7,000-unit column in Exhibit 9-2
** = Figures are shown in more detail in Exhibit 9-5.

that the underachievement of sales by 2,000 units and $48,000 resulted in an $18,400 decrease in attained contribution margin and hence an $18,400 decrease in operating income. Note that unit prices are held constant in this part of the analysis—that is, the net marketing variance is computed by using the budgeted contribution margin per unit:

Net marketing variance = Budgeted unit contribution margin ×
Difference between the master budgeted sales
in units and the actual sales in units

= $9.20 × (9,000 − 7,000) = $18,400,
unfavorable

Without the flexible budget in Column 3, this marketing variance cannot be isolated.

Column 4 focuses on the variances arising from price changes and inefficient uses of inputs. Again, without the flexible budget in Column 3, these variances cannot be separated from the effects of changes in sales volume.

If the president wants to pursue his analysis of cost control beyond the summary in Exhibit 9-4, he may be helped by the cost performance report in Exhibit 9-5. Even if the president were not interested in probing further, some lower-level managers may be so inclined. Exhibit 9-5 gives a line-by-line sizeup, showing how most of the costs which had favorable

EXHIBIT 9-5

DOMINION COMPANY

Cost Control Performance Report

For the Month Ending June 30, 19x1

(To show that the format of these reports is not uniform, the actual costs incurred are in the first column and the budgeted amounts are in the second column; the reverse order was shown in Exhibit 9-1.)

	ACTUAL COSTS INCURRED	FLEXIBLE BUDGET*	FLEXIBLE BUDGET VARIANCE†	EXPLANATION
Units	7,000	7,000	—	
Variable costs:				
Direct material	21,350	21,000	$ 350 U	Lower price, higher usage
Direct labor	61,500	56,000	5,500 U	Higher price, higher usage
Labor to transport materials internally and provide general support	11,100	11,200	100 F	
Idle time	3,550	2,800	750 U	Excessive machine breakdowns
Cleanup time	2,500	2,100	400 U	Needs more investigation
Other indirect labor	800	700	100 U	
Miscellaneous supplies	4,700	4,200	500 U	Higher price, higher usage
Variable manufacturing costs	$105,500	$ 98,000	$7,500 U	
Shipping expenses (selling)	5,000	4,200	800 U	Use of air freight
Xerox, telephone, etc.	2,000	1,400	600 U	Needs more investigation
Total variable costs	$112,500	$103,600	$8,900 U	
Fixed costs:				
Factory supervision	$ 14,700	$ 14,400	$ 300 U	Unanticipated raise
Rent of factory	5,000	5,000	—	
Depreciation of factory equipment	15,000	15,000	—	
Other fixed factory costs	2,600	2,600	—	
Fixed manufacturing costs	$ 37,300	$ 37,000	$ 300 U	
Fixed selling and administrative costs	33,000	33,000	—	
Total fixed costs	$ 70,300	$ 70,000	$ 300 U	
Total variable and fixed costs	$182,800	$173,600	$9,200 U	

F = Favorable   U = Unfavorable

*From 7,000-unit column in Exhibit 9-2

†This represents a line-by-line breakdown of the variances in column 4 of Exhibit 9-4

variances when a static budget was used as a basis for comparison have, in reality, unfavorable variances. These "flexible budget variances" may be analyzed in even more depth by being subdivided further, at least for the more important material and labor costs, as the next section shows.

STANDARDS FOR MATERIAL AND LABOR

Standard costs are the building blocks of a budgeting and feedback system. They are carefully predetermined costs—targets that should be achieved.

Difference Between Standards and Budgets

What is the difference between a standard amount and a budget amount? If standards are currently attainable, as they are assumed to be in this book, there is no conceptual difference. The term **standard cost,** as it is most widely used, is a unit concept; for example, the standard cost of direct material shown in Exhibit 9-2 is $3 per unit. The term **budgeted cost,** as it is most widely used, is a total concept; that is, the budgeted cost of material is $21,000 if 7,000 units are to be produced at a standard cost of $3 per unit. It may be helpful to think of a standard as a budget for the production of a single unit. In many companies, the terms **budgeted performance** and **standard performance** are used interchangeably.

In practice, direct material and direct labor are often said to be controlled with the help of *standard costs,* whereas all other costs are usually said to be controlled with the help of **departmental overhead budgets.** This distinction probably arose because of different timing and control techniques for various costs. Direct material and direct labor are generally relatively costly, and are easily identifiable for control purposes. Therefore, techniques for planning and controlling these costs are relatively refined. Overhead costs are combinations of many individual items, none of which justifies an elaborate control system. In consequence, use of direct material may be closely watched on an hourly basis; direct labor, on a daily basis; and factory overhead, on a weekly or monthly basis.

All this leads to the following straightforward approach (using assumed figures), which we will pursue throughout the remainder of this book. The *standard* is a *unit* idea; the *budget* is a *total* idea. Using the data in Exhibit 9-2:

	Standards	*Budget for 7,000 units*
Direct material	$3 per finished unit*	$21,000
Direct labor	$8 per finished unit†	56,000
Other costs (detailed)	Various	96,600

*Assume that five pounds is the standard allowance for producing one unit. The standard price per pound is 60¢.

†Assume that two hours is the standard allowance for producing one unit. The standard labor rate is $4 per hour.

The study of past behavior patterns is typically a fundamental step in formulating a standard or a budgeted cost. Although the study of past cost behavior is a useful starting point, a budgeted cost should not be merely an extension of past experience. Inefficiencies may be reflected in prior costs. Changes in technology, equipment, and methods also limit the usefulness of comparisons with the past. Also, performance should be judged in relation to some currently attainable goal, one that may be reached by skilled, diligent, superior effort. **Concern with the past is justified only insofar as it helps prediction.** Management wishes to plan what costs *should be,* not what costs *have been.*

Current Attainability: The Most
Widely Used Standard

What standard of expected performance should be used? Should it be so severe that it is rarely, if ever, attained? Should it be attainable 50 percent of the time? Eighty percent? Twenty percent? Individuals who have worked a lifetime in setting standards for performance cannot agree, so there are no universal answers to these questions.

Two types of standards deserve mention here, *perfection standards* and *currently attainable standards.* Perfection standards (often also called *ideal standards*) are expressions of the absolute minimum costs possible under the best conceivable conditions, using existing specifications and equipment. No provision is made for shrinkage, spoilage, machine breakdowns, and the like. Those who favor this approach maintain that the resulting unfavorable variances will constantly remind managers of the perpetual need for improvement in all phases of operations. These standards are not widely used, however, because they have an adverse effect on employee motivation. Employees tend to ignore unreasonable goals.

Currently attainable standards are those that can be achieved by *very efficient* operations. Expectations are set high enough so that employees regard their fulfillment as possible, though perhaps not probable. Allowances are made for normal shrinkage, waste, and machine breakdowns. Variances tend to be unfavorable, but managers accept the standards as being reasonable goals.

The major reasons for using currently attainable standards are:

1. The resulting standard costs serve multiple purposes. For example, the same cost may be used for cash budgeting, inventory valuation, and budgeting departmental performance. In contrast, perfection standards cannot be used *per se* for cash budgeting, because financial planning will be thrown off.[2]

---

[2]If standards are not currently attainable because they are ideal or outdated, the amount budgeted for financial (cash) planning purposes has to differ from the standard. Otherwise, projected income and cash disbursements will be forecasted incorrectly. In such cases, ideal or outdated standards may be used for compiling performance reports, but "ex-

2. They have a desirable motivational impact on employees. The standard represents reasonable future performance, not fanciful ideal goals or antiquated goals geared to past performance.

Price and Efficiency Variances

The assessment of performance is facilitated by separating the items that are subject to the manager's direct influence from those that are not. The general approach is to separate *price* factors from *efficiency* factors. Price factors are less subject to immediate control than are efficiency factors, principally because of external forces, such as general economic conditions and unforeseeable price changes. Even when price factors are regarded as outside of company control, it is still desirable to isolate them to obtain a sharper focus on the efficient usage of the goods or services in question.

To see how the analysis of variances can be pursued more fully, reconsider the direct material and direct labor in Exhibit 9-5. The flexible budget variances can be subdivided into two major types: *price* and *efficiency*.[3]

To demonstrate this general approach for direct material and direct labor, we continue our illustration and assume that the following actually occurred:

Direct material: 36,810 pounds were used at an actual unit price of 58¢, for a total actual cost of $21,350.
Direct labor: 15,000 hours were used at an actual hourly rate of $4.10.

The budget variance for materials may be analyzed as follows:

Price variance = Actual quantity used × Difference between the actual unit price and the standard unit price
= 36,810 pounds × ($.58 − $.60)
= $736 *F*

Efficiency variance = Standard unit price × Difference between the actual pounds used and the standard allowance for the finished units produced
= $.60 × [36,810 − (7,000 units × 5 pounds per unit)]

---

pected variances" are stipulated in the master budget for financial planning. For example, if unusually strict labor standards are used, the standard cost per finished unit may be $8 despite the fact that top management anticipates an unfavorable performance variance of 40¢ per unit. In the master budget, the total labor costs would be $8.40 per unit: $8 plus an expected variance of 40¢.

[3]Price and efficiency will be used throughout this book to describe these two classes of variances. In practice, the price variance is often called a *rate* variance when it is used in conjunction with labor. Similarly, the efficiency variance is often called a *usage* or *quantity* variance when it is used in conjunction with materials.

$$= \$.60 \times (36{,}810 - 35{,}000)$$
$$= \$.60 \times 1{,}810 = \$1{,}086 \ U$$

Budget variance explained $=$ Price variance $+$ Efficiency variance
$$= \$736 \ F + \$1{,}086 \ U = \$350 \ U$$

Variance analysis does *not* provide any answers. But it raises questions, provides clues, and directs attention. For instance, one possible explanation, among many, for this set of variances is that a manager might have made a trade-off and lost—that is, he might have purchased, at a favorable price, some materials that were slightly substandard, resulting in excessive waste as indicated by the unfavorable efficiency variance.

The analysis for direct labor is similar:

Price variance $\qquad = 15{,}000 \text{ hours} \times (\$4.10 - \$4.00)$
$\qquad\qquad\qquad\quad = 15{,}000 \times \$.10 = \$1{,}500 \ U$

Efficiency variance $\qquad = \$4.00 \times [15{,}000 - (7{,}000 \text{ units} \times$
$\qquad\qquad\qquad\quad 2 \text{ allowed hours per unit})]$
$\qquad\qquad\qquad\quad = \$4.00 \times 1{,}000 = \$4{,}000 \ U$

Budget variance explained $= \$1{,}500 \ U + \$4{,}000 \ U = \$5{,}500 \ U$

Evidently, direct labor warrants further investigation, because it is easily the largest variance of all.

A General Approach

Exhibit 9-6 presents the foregoing analysis in a format that deserves close study. The general approach is at the top of the exhibit; the specific applications then follow. Even though the exhibit may seem unnecessarily complex at first, its repeated use will solidify your understanding of variance analysis. Of course, the other budget variances in Exhibit 9-5 could be further analyzed in the same manner in which direct material and direct labor are analyzed in Exhibit 9-6. The pursuit of such a detailed investigation depends on the manager's perceptions as to whether the extra benefits will exceed the extra cost of such detective work.

Limitations of Price and Efficiency Variances

The division of variances into two neat categories of "price" and "efficiency" is a good first step. However, it is a crude split, and its limitations should be kept in mind. In particular, the individual overhead items may be hard to subdivide in this way. For instance, the flexible budget for supplies is budgeted in Exhibit 9-5 at $4,200, based on a formula of 60¢ per unit.

In practice, a simple but fragile assumption underlies the usual

EXHIBIT 9-6
General Approach to Analysis of Variable Cost Variances

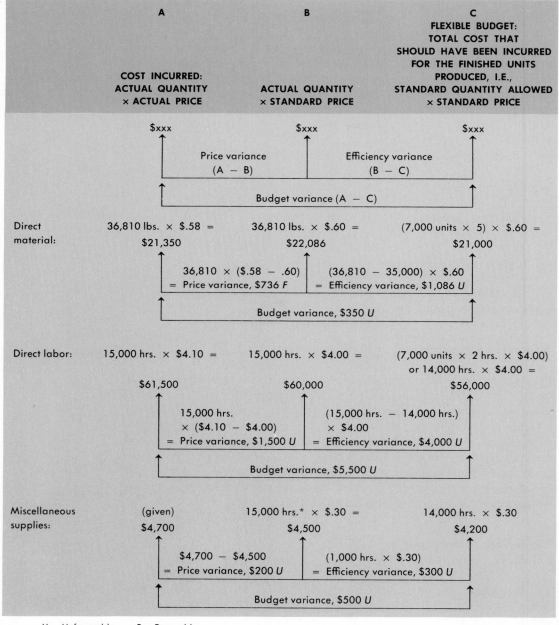

	A	B	C
	COST INCURRED: **ACTUAL QUANTITY** **× ACTUAL PRICE**	**ACTUAL QUANTITY** **× STANDARD PRICE**	**FLEXIBLE BUDGET:** **TOTAL COST THAT** **SHOULD HAVE BEEN INCURRED** **FOR THE FINISHED UNITS** **PRODUCED, I.E.,** **STANDARD QUANTITY ALLOWED** **× STANDARD PRICE**

$xxx $xxx $xxx

Price variance (A − B)   Efficiency variance (B − C)

Budget variance (A − C)

Direct material:
36,810 lbs. × $.58 = $21,350   36,810 lbs. × $.60 = $22,086   (7,000 units × 5) × $.60 = $21,000

36,810 × ($.58 − .60) = Price variance, $736 F   (36,810 − 35,000) × $.60 = Efficiency variance, $1,086 U

Budget variance, $350 U

Direct labor:
15,000 hrs. × $4.10 = $61,500   15,000 hrs. × $4.00 = $60,000   (7,000 units × 2 hrs. × $4.00) or 14,000 hrs. × $4.00 = $56,000

15,000 hrs. × ($4.10 − $4.00) = Price variance, $1,500 U   (15,000 hrs. − 14,000 hrs.) × $4.00 = Efficiency variance, $4,000 U

Budget variance, $5,500 U

Miscellaneous supplies:
(given) $4,700   15,000 hrs.* × $.30 = $4,500   14,000 hrs. × $.30 = $4,200

$4,700 − $4,500 = Price variance, $200 U   (1,000 hrs. × $.30) = Efficiency variance, $300 U

Budget variance, $500 U

U = Unfavorable   F = Favorable
*For comments, see the section, "Limitations of Price and Efficiency Variances," in text.

efficiency variance computation for variable overhead items: Variable overhead costs fluctuate in direct proportion to direct labor-hours. Therefore, the efficiency variance for a variable overhead item like supplies is a measure of the extra overhead (or savings) incurred *solely* because the actual *direct labor-hours* used differed from the standard hours allowed:

Overhead efficiency variance = Standard overhead rate per hour ×
(Actual direct labor-hours − Standard
direct labor-hours allowed)
= $.30 × (15,000 − 14,000)
= $300 unfavorable

Because direct labor was inefficiently used by 1,000 hours under this approach, we would expect the related usage of supplies to be proportionately excessive solely because of labor inefficiency. However, whether, in fact, this direct relationship exists depends on specific circumstances.

To recapitulate, let us investigate why there was a $500 unfavorable supplies variance in Exhibit 9-5. The analysis in Exhibit 9-6 implies:

Actual costs		$4,700
Efficiency variance—The amount that would be expected to be incurred *because of the inefficient use of direct labor,* 1,000 hrs. × $.30 =	$300	
Price variance—The amount unexplained by the efficiency variance. It could arise from unit price changes for various supplies—but it could also arise simply from the general waste and sloppy use of these supplies. In short, this, too, could be partially or solely traceable to *more inefficiency,* even though it is labeled as a price variance. (Incidentally, for this reason, many practitioners call this type of overhead variance a *spending* variance rather than a price variance.)	200	
Budget variance		500
Budgeted amount in flexible budget		$4,200

Above all, the limitations of these analyses of variances should be underscored. The *only* way to discover why overhead performance did not agree with a budget is to investigate possible causes, line item by line item. However, the price-efficiency distinctions provide a handy springboard for a more rigorous analysis.

CONTROLLABILITY AND VARIANCES

Need for Price Variances

In most companies, the *acquisition* of materials or merchandise entails different control decisions than their *use.* The purchasing executive of a manufacturing company worries about getting raw materials at favorable prices, whereas the production executive concentrates on using them efficiently. The merchandise manager of a large grocery company will be responsible for skillful buying of foodstuffs, but the store manager will be responsible for their sale and for minimizing losses from shrinkage, shop-lifting, and the like.

At departmental levels, budgets are often constructed to highlight particular responsibilities. For example, the purchasing officer may be made responsible for price variances and the production manager's "actual" costs may be based on standard unit prices entirely rather than on actual unit prices. That is, the production manager's budget could be compiled on the basis of standard quantities multiplied by standard prices, and his "actual" results compiled on the basis of actual quantities multiplied by standard prices. Then his variance would be solely an efficiency variance. When one executive is responsible for prices and the other for efficient usage, each will then be evaluated with a measuring stick that is not marred by uncontrollable factors.

Purchases of Merchandise or Raw Materials

The buyers in retail stores and the purchasing executives in wholesale and manufacturing companies usually plan their purchases in accordance with forthcoming demand. Their objective is to obtain the correct number of items, of the appropriate quality, at the right time and at the right price. Unsatisfactory performance can usually be traced to failure to meet one or more of these requirements (e.g., an incorrect number of items might be ordered, the quality might be inferior, or the unit price might be high).

The most common example of an unsatisfactory purchase is acquisition at a price not equal to the standard price. (Ordinarily, the purchasing agent is given little discretion over the quantities to be purchased, though in exceptional circumstances he may have permission to buy a huge lot at a bargain price.) A performance report for a purchasing department using standard prices might include the following:

Actual Quantity Purchased	Type	Actual Price	Standard Price	Total Actual	Total Budgeted	Purchase Price Variance
1,000 lbs.	Material A	$1.10	$1.00	$1,100	$1,000	$100 (*Unfavorable*)
500 sq. ft.	Material B	3.70	4.00	1,850	2,000	150 (*Favorable*)

From the viewpoint of control, nearly all variances should be measured as soon as is feasible. The longer the delay, the more stale will be the data and the fewer the opportunities for corrections. In some companies, price variances are computed when the original purchase order is sent to the supplier; in others, the most feasible time for measuring is upon receipt of the supplier's invoice.

The responsibility for price variances usually rests with the purchasing officer. Price variances are often regarded as measures of forecasting ability rather than of failure to buy at specified prices. Some control over the price variance is obtainable by getting many quotations, buying in economical lots, taking advantage of cash discounts, and selecting the most economical means of delivery. Price variances may lead to decisions to change suppliers or freight carriers.

Failure to meet price standards may result from a sudden rush of sales orders or from unanticipated changes in production schedules, which in turn may require the purchasing officer to buy at uneconomical prices or to request delivery by air freight. In such cases, the responsibility may rest with the sales manager or the head of production scheduling, rather than with the purchasing officer.

Labor Price Variances

In most companies, because of union contracts or other predictable factors, labor prices can be foreseen with much greater accuracy than can prices of materials. Therefore, labor price variances tend to be relatively insignificant.

Labor, unlike material and supplies, cannot ordinarily be stored for later use. The acquisition and use of labor occur simultaneously. For these reasons, labor rate variances are usually charged to the same manager who is responsible for labor usage.

Labor price variances may be traceable to faulty predictions of the labor rates. However, the more likely causes include: (1) the use of a single average standard labor price for a given operation that is, in fact, performed by individuals earning slightly different rates because of seniority; (2) the assignment of a worker earning, perhaps, $6 per hour to a given operation that should be appointed to a less skilled worker earning, say, $4 per hour; and (3) the payment of hourly rates, instead of prescribed piece rates, because of low productivity.

Causes of Efficiency Variances

The general approach to analyzing efficiency variances is probably best exemplified by the control of direct materials in standard cost systems. The budget of the production department manager is usually based on a **standard formula** or a Standard Bill of Materials (Exhibit 9-7). This is a specification of the physical quantities allowed for producing a specified number of acceptable finished units. These quantities are then compared to the quantities actually used.

What does the manager do with the variances? He seeks explanations for their existence. Common causes of efficiency variances include: improper handling, inferior quality of material, poor workmanship, changes in methods, new workmen, slow machines, broken cutting tools, and faulty blueprints.

EXHIBIT 9-7
Standard Bill of Materials

STANDARD BILL OF MATERIALS		
Assembly No. 4xy Description: Card table		
Part Number	**Quantity**	**Description**
A 403	4	Steel legs
A 501	1	Table top
P 42	16 sq. ft.	Plastic cover
P 48	6 oz.	Adhesive
B 5	1	Bolt kit

Control Procedures

There are many ways of systematizing the control of material quantity variances. One popular way is to issue direct material only in response to a Standard Bill of Materials (Exhibit 9-7). As manufacturing proceeds, additional material may be obtained only by submitting a special **excess materials requisition.** From the latter, the material efficiency variance is compiled.

Labor efficiency variances are usually followed carefully by foremen, who scrutinize work tickets. These coded tickets may have a number showing the department, another number showing the particular operation (e.g., the work-step, such as milling, boring, grinding), and another number showing the cause of the variance.

Trade-offs Among Variances

As was mentioned earlier, managers often have opportunities to take advantage of bargain purchases or to combine available resources in a way that will save overall costs. For example, a quantity of a raw material having a few inferior characteristics (perhaps a different grade of lumber or shade of color) may be consciously acquired at an unusually low price. This material may cause unusually heavy spoilage or excessive labor hours when used to produce a finished piece that will meet standard quality specifications. Nevertheless, the manager may have enough discretion to proceed. His aim would be to reduce the total costs of manufacturing by trading off favorable price variances against expected unfavorable efficiency variances.

A standard cost system should not be a straitjacket that prevents the manager from looking at the overall company objectives. Too often, each unfavorable variance is regarded as, ipso facto, bad; and each favorable variance is regarded as, ipso facto, good. If the manager guesses wrong, and the unfavorable efficiency variances exceed the favorable price variance, the decision to make the bargain purchase was unfavorable despite the favorable label pinned on the price variance. Similarly, if the manager guesses correctly so that the favorable price variance exceeds the unfavorable efficiency variances, the decision was favorable despite the unfavorable label pinned on the efficiency variances. The point is that there are too many interdependencies among activities; an "unfavorable" or a "favorable" label should not lead the manager to jump to conclusions about what happened. By themselves, such labels merely raise questions and provide clues. They are attention directors, not answer givers.

When to Investigate Variances

When should variances be investigated? Frequently the answer to such a question is based on subjective judgments, hunches, guesses, and rules of thumb. The most troublesome aspect of feedback is deciding when a variance is significant enough to warrant management's attention. For some items, a small deviation may prompt follow-up. For other items, a minimum dollar amount or 5, 10, or 25 percent deviations from budget may be necessary before investigations commence. Of course, a 4 percent variance in a $1 million material cost may deserve more attention than a 20 percent variance in a $10,000 repair cost. Therefore, rules such as "Investigate all variances exceeding $5,000, or 25 percent of standard cost, whichever is lower" are common.

Variance analysis is subject to the same cost-benefit test as other phases of an information system. The trouble with the foregoing rules of thumb is that they are too frequently based on subjective assessments, guesses, or hunches. The field of statistics offers tools to help reduce these subjective features of variance analysis. These tools help answer the cost-benefit question, and they help separate variances caused by random events from variances that are controllable.

Accounting systems have traditionally implied that a standard is a single acceptable measure. Practically, the accountant (and everybody else) realizes that the standard is a *band* or *range* of possible acceptable outcomes. Consequently, he expects variances to fluctuate randomly within some normal limits.

A random variance, by definition, calls for no corrective action to an existing process. In short, random variances are attributable to chance rather than to management's implementation decisions.

SUMMARY

Management is best aided by carefully prepared standards and budgets representing what *should* be accomplished. These standards should be based on material specifications and on work measurement rather than on past performance, because the latter too often conceals past inefficiencies.

Currently attainable standards are the most widely used because they usually have the most desirable motivational impact and because they may be used for a variety of accounting purposes, including financial planning, as well as for monitoring departmental performance.

When standards are currently attainable, there is no logical difference between standards and budgets. A standard is a *unit* concept, whereas a budget is a *total* concept. In a sense, the standard is the budget for one unit.

Flexible budgets are geared to changing levels of activity rather than to a single static level. They may be tailored to a particular level of sales or production volume—*before* or *after* the fact. They tell how much cost *should be* or *should have been* incurred for any level *of output,* which is usually expressed either in product units of output or in standard direct labor hours allowed for that output.

The evaluation of performance is aided by a feedback comparison of actual results with budgeted expectations. Flexible budget variances are often divided into price and efficiency variances. In practice, the efficiency factors are more important because they are subject to more direct management influence than are prices of materials or labor.

There is a similarity in approach to the control of all costs that are regarded as variable. The *price* variance is the *difference in price multiplied by actual quantity*. The efficiency variance is the *difference in quantity multiplied by standard price.*

Variances raise questions; they do not provide answers. The analysis and follow-up of variances are the keys to successful management control. Variances provide clues, jog memories, and open pertinent avenues for management investigation. If managers do not do anything with the variances, then either the reporting system needs overhauling or the managers need to be educated and convinced of the benefits that can be derived from a careful analysis of the variances.

Variance analysis is subject to the same cost-benefit test as other phases of an information system. The decision on whether to investigate a variance depends on expected net benefits.

Chapter 15, which may be studied now if desired, probes the analysis of variances in more depth, particularly with respect to fixed overhead and inventories.

SUMMARY PROBLEM FOR YOUR REVIEW

Problem

The following questions are based on the data contained in the illustration used in the chapter:

1. Suppose that actual production and sales were 8,500 units instead of

7,000 units. (a) Compute the marketing variance. Is the performance of the marketing function the sole explanation for this variance? Why? (b) Using a flexible budget, compute the budgeted contribution margin, the budgeted operating income, budgeted direct material, and budgeted direct labor.

285
Flexible Budgets and
Standards for
Control

2. Suppose the following were the actual results for the production of 8,500 units:

Direct material: 46,000 pounds were used at an actual unit price of 55¢, for a total actual cost of $25,300.

Direct labor: 16,500 hours were used at an actual hourly rate of $4.20, for a total actual cost of $69,300.

Compute the flexible budget variance and the price and efficiency variances for direct material and direct labor. Present your answers in the form shown in Exhibit 9-6.

3. Suppose that the company is organized so that the purchasing manager bears primary responsibility for the acquisition prices of materials, and the production manager bears the primary responsibility for efficiency but no responsibility for unit prices. Assume the same facts as in Requirement 2, except that the purchasing manager acquired 60,000 pounds of materials. This means that there is an ending inventory of 14,000 pounds. Would your variance analysis of materials in (2) change? Why? Show computations to support your answer.

Solution

1. (a) Marketing variance = Budgeted unit contribution margin × Difference between the master-budgeted sales in units and the actual sales in units

$$= \$9.20 \times (9,000 - 8,500) = \$4,600, \, U$$

This variance is labeled as a marketing variance because it quantifies the impact on net income of the deviation from an original sales target—while holding price and efficiency factors constant. Of course, the failure to reach target sales may be traceable to a number of causes beyond the control of the marketing force, including strikes, material shortages, and storms.

(b) The budget formulas in Exhibit 9-2 are the basis for the following answers:

Budgeted contribution margin = $9.20 × 8,500 = $78,200
Budgeted operating income = $78,200 − $70,000 fixed costs = $8,200
Budgeted direct material = $3.00 × 8,500 = $25,500
Budgeted direct labor = $8.00 × 8,500 = $68,000

2.

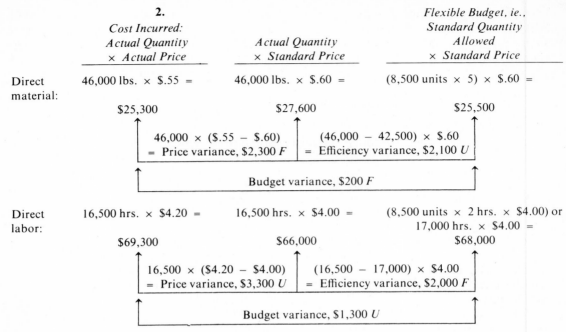

	Cost Incurred: Actual Quantity × Actual Price	Actual Quantity × Standard Price	Flexible Budget, ie., Standard Quantity Allowed × Standard Price
Direct material:	46,000 lbs. × $.55 = $25,300	46,000 lbs. × $.60 = $27,600	(8,500 units × 5) × $.60 = $25,500

46,000 × ($.55 − $.60)
= Price variance, $2,300 F   (46,000 − 42,500) × $.60
= Efficiency variance, $2,100 U

Budget variance, $200 F

	16,500 hrs. × $4.20 = $69,300	16,500 hrs. × $4.00 = $66,000	(8,500 units × 2 hrs. × $4.00) or 17,000 hrs. × $4.00 = $68,000
Direct labor:			

16,500 × ($4.20 − $4.00)
= Price variance, $3,300 U   (16,500 − 17,000) × $4.00
= Efficiency variance, $2,000 F

Budget variance, $1,300 U

3. Whether the variance analysis in Part (2) would change depends on how the information system is designed. In many organizations, price variances for materials are isolated at the most logical control point—time of purchase rather than time of use. In turn, the production or operating departments that later use the materials are always charged at some predetermined so-called budget or standard unit price, never at actual unit prices. Under this procedure the price variance analysis would be conducted in the purchasing department and the efficiency variance analysis in the production department. This represents a slight modification of the approach in Part (2) as follows:

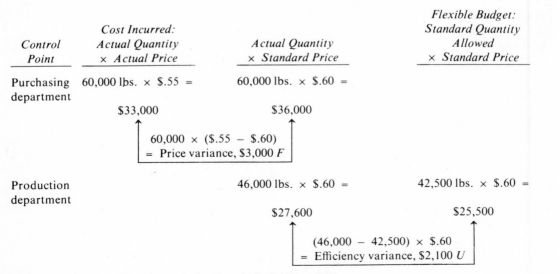

Control Point	Cost Incurred: Actual Quantity × Actual Price	Actual Quantity × Standard Price	Flexible Budget: Standard Quantity Allowed × Standard Price
Purchasing department	60,000 lbs. × $.55 = $33,000	60,000 lbs. × $.60 = $36,000	

60,000 × ($.55 − $.60)
= Price variance, $3,000 F

Production department		46,000 lbs. × $.60 = $27,600	42,500 lbs. × $.60 = $25,500

(46,000 − 42,500) × $.60
= Efficiency variance, $2,100 U

Note that the efficiency variance is the same in Parts (2) and (3).

The usual breakdown of variances into price and efficiency is not theoretically perfect because there may be a small mutual price-efficiency effect. A production foreman and a purchasing agent might argue over the following situation. The direct material is 1,000 pounds @ $1, and is intended to produce 1,000 good finished units. The performance report shows the use of 1,150 pounds @ $1.20 to produce 1,000 good finished units.

The ordinary analysis of variances would appear as follows:

Actual quantity × Actual price or 1,150 × $1.20 = $1,380
Price
variance = Difference in price × Actual pounds
= ($1.20 − $1) × 1,150 = $230 *U*

(Continued on next page.)

EXHIBIT 9-8
Graphic Analysis of Variances

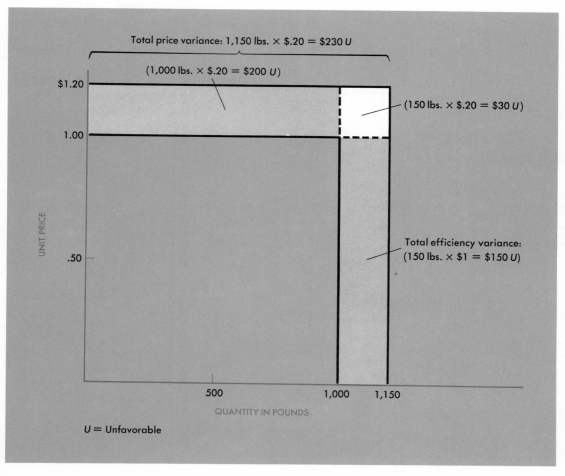

U = Unfavorable

Quantity
variance = Difference in quantity × Standard price
$$= (1{,}150 - 1{,}000) \times \$1 = \qquad \underline{150\ \ U}$$
Total variance explained $\qquad\qquad\qquad\qquad \underline{380\ \ U}$
Standard quantity allowed for units produced ×
Standard price = $1{,}000 \times \$1 = \qquad\qquad \underline{\underline{\$1{,}000}}$

The small area in the upper right-hand corner of the graphic analysis (Exhibit 9-8) may be the area of controversy. The purchasing officer might readily accept responsibility for the price variance on the 1,000 pounds in the standard allowance, but he might claim that the extra $30 which is buried in his $230 total variance is more properly attributable to the production foreman. After all, if the foreman had produced in accordance with the standard, the extra 150 pounds would not have been needed. But this distinction is not often made, simply because it usually involves a small sum. However, we should be aware that the conventional variance analysis, which includes the joint price-efficiency variance ($30, in this case) as a part of an overall price variance, has logical deficiencies.

In practice, the efficiency variance is considered much more important than the price variance because the manager can exert more direct influence over the efficiency variance. Consequently, the performance report on efficiency should minimize the possibility of the production manager's criticisms of any accounting or measurement methods. Joint price-efficiency variance is less likely to cause arguments if it is buried in the total price variance than if it is buried in the efficiency variance.

ASSIGNMENT MATERIAL

Fundamental Assignment Material

9-1. Terminology: Define: *currently attainable standards; standard cost; price variance; rate variance; bill of materials; quantity variance; usage variance; flexible budget; variable budget; static budget; spending variance; efficiency variance; excess material requisitions;* and *master operations lists.*

9-2.[4] Flexible and static budgets. Orange Transportation Company executives have had trouble interpreting operating performance for a number of years. The company has used a budget based on detailed expectations for the forthcoming quarter. For example, the condensed performance report for a recent quarter for a midwestern branch was (in dollars):

	Budget	Actual	Variance
Net revenue	10,000,000	9,500,000	500,000 U
Fuel	200,000	196,000	4,000 F
Repairs and maintenance	100,000	98,000	2,000 F
Supplies and miscellaneous	1,000,000	985,000	15,000 F
Variable payroll	6,700,000	6,500,000	200,000 F
Total variable costs*	8,000,000	7,779,000	221,000 F

[4]Problems 9-36 or 9-37 may be used instead of 9-2 and 9-3.

Supervision	200,000	200,000	—
Rent	200,000	200,000	—
Depreciation	600,000	600,000	—
Other fixed costs	200,000	200,000	—
Total fixed costs	1,200,000	1,200,000	—
Total costs charged against revenue	9,200,000	8,979,000	221,000 *F*
Operating income	800,000	521,000	279,000 *U*

U = Unfavorable   *F* = Favorable

*For purposes of this analysis, assume that all these costs are totally variable. In practice, many are mixed and have to be subdivided into variable and fixed components before a meaningful analysis can be made. Also assume that the prices and mix of services remain unchanged.

Although the branch manager was upset about not obtaining enough revenue, he was happy that his control performance was favorable; otherwise his net operating income would be even worse.

His immediate superior, the Vice-President for Operations, was totally unhappy and remarked: "I can see some merit in comparing actual performance with budgeted performance because we can see whether actual revenue coincided with our best guess for budget purposes. But I can't see how this performance report helps me evaluate the cost control performance of the department head."

Required:

1. Prepare a columnar flexible budget for expected costs at $9, $10, and $11 million levels of revenue. Include both variable and fixed costs in your budget.
2. Express Requirement 1 in formula form.
3. Prepare a condensed summary similar to Exhibit 9-4 that might better trace the effects on operating income of the deviations of actual results from the original plans.

9-3. Similarity of direct labor and variable overhead variances. The Fram Company has had great difficulty controlling costs during the past three years. Last month, a standard cost and flexible budget system was installed. A condensation of results for a department follows:

	Expected Behavior per Standard Direct Labor-Hour	Total Budget Variance
Lubricants	$ .30	$200 *F*
Other supplies	.20	150 *U*
Rework	.40	300 *U*
Other indirect labor	.50	300 *U*
Total variable overhead	$1.40	$550 *U*

F = Favorable   *U* = Unfavorable

The department had initially planned to manufacture 6,000 units in 4,000 standard direct labor-hours allowed. However, material shortage and a heat wave resulted in the production of 5,400 units in 3,900 actual direct labor-hours. The standard wage rate is $3.50 per hour, which was 20¢ higher than the actual average hourly rate.

Required:

1. Prepare a detailed performance report with two major sections: direct labor and variable overhead.
2. Prepare a summary analysis of price and efficiency variances for direct labor and for variable overhead, using the format of Exhibit 9-6.
3. Explain the similarities and differences between the direct labor and variable overhead variances. What are some of the likely causes of the overhead variances?

Additional Assignment Material

9-4. What are standard costs? Why is their use preferable to comparisons of actual data with past data?

9-5. "Direct material and direct labor may be included in a flexible budget." Do you agree? Explain.

9-6. Why should a budgeted cost not be merely an extension of past experience?

9-7. Distinguish between perfection and currently attainable standards.

9-8. What is the difference between a standard amount and a budget amount?

9-9. What are expected variances?

9-10. "Price variances should be computed even if prices are regarded as outside of company control." Do you agree? Explain.

9-11. "Failure to meet price standards is the responsibility of the purchasing officer." Do you agree? Explain.

9-12. Why do labor price variances tend to be insignificant?

9-13. What are the key questions in the analysis and follow-up of variances?

9-14. What are some common causes of quantity variances?

9-15. Why is the joint price-quantity variance buried in the price variance rather than in the quantity variance?

9-16. What two basic questions must be asked in approaching the control of all costs?

9-17. Why do the techniques for controlling overhead differ from those for controlling direct material and direct labor?

9-18. "The flex in the flexible budget relates solely to variable costs." Do you agree? Explain.

9-19. How does the overhead price variance differ from the labor price variance?

9-20. Why are standard hours superior to actual hours as an index of activity?

9-21. Federal park service. The Federal Park Service prepared the following budget for one of its national parks for 19x4:

Revenue from fees	$4,000,000
Variable costs (miscellaneous)	400,000
Contribution margin	$3,600,000
Fixed costs (miscellaneous)	3,600,000
Operating income	$ 0

The fees were based on an average of 50,000 vehicle-admission days (vehicles multiplied by number of days in parks) per week for the twenty-week season, multiplied by average entry and other fees of $4 per vehicle-admission day.

The season was booming for the first four weeks. However, there was a wave of thievery and violence during the fifth week. Grizzly bears killed four campers during the sixth week and two during the seventh week. As a result, the number of visitors to the parks dropped sharply during the remainder of the season.

Total revenue fell by $1,000,000. Moreover, extra rangers and police had to be hired at a cost of $200,000. The latter was regarded as a fixed cost.

Required:

Prepare a columnar summary of performance, showing the original budget, marketing variance, and actual results.

9-22. Explanation of variance in income. The Instil Company makes a variety of products that result in standard contribution margins averaging 30 percent of dollar sales and average unit selling prices of $8. Average productivity is three units per standard direct labor-hour. The master budget for 19x1 had predicted sales of 500,000 units, but only 460,000 units were produced and sold. As many as 156,000 actual direct labor-hours were used to produce the 460,000 units.

Fixed manufacturing costs were $700,000 and fixed nonmanufacturing costs were $300,000. There were no beginning or ending inventories.

The president was upset because the budgeted net income of $200,000 was not attained, particularly since the only budget variances were unfavorable variable cost efficiency variances amounting to merely $6,000.

Required:

1. What is the net income for the year?
2. Explain fully why the target net income was not achieved. Use a presentation similar to Exhibit 9-4.

9-23. Explanation of variance in income. The Sarah Company based its master budget for 19x2 on an expected sales volume of 110,000 units, at an average unit selling price of $25. Costs were expected to be:

Standard Variable Costs per Unit		*Total Fixed Costs*	
Direct material	$ 9.00		
Direct labor	5.00	Manufacturing	$600,000
Factory overhead	1.00	Nonmanufacturing	250,000
Order filling	.75	Total fixed costs	$850,000
Administrative	.25		
Total variable costs per unit	$16.00		

Standard costs and flexible budgets were used. There were no beginning or ending inventories. During 19x2, 97,000 units were produced and sold. The only variances were an unfavorable efficiency variance for direct labor ($15,000) and variable factory overhead ($3,000).

Required:

Prepare two sets of reports: (a) a summary of performance similar to Exhibit 9-4, and (b) a cost control performance report similar to Exhibit 9-5.

9-24. Explanation of variance in income. The Ilima Company had been unable to change its formal records in accordance with more liberal direct labor efficiency specifications for 19x2. Instead, the company provided for an "expected direct labor efficiency variance" of $10,000, unfavorable, in its master budget. Expected net income was $60,000, based on expected production and sales of 100,000 units at an average unit contribution margin of $2. Total fixed expenses for the year, budgeted and actual, were $130,000.

Actual results proceeded exactly according to plan until the last quarter of the year, which was marked by a general lull in business conditions plus some weakness in prices. Ilima had to cut selling prices on the final 20,000 units sold by an average of 20¢ per unit without being able to cut unit variable costs. The company scheduled, produced, and sold a total of 92,000 units for the year. There were no beginning or ending inventories.

Required:

Complete the following schedule:

1. Master-budgeted net income $XXX
2. Actual net income   XXX
   Variance to be explained $XXX

   Explained as follows:
3. Marketing variance (describe fully) $XXX
4. Other variances, if any (describe fully)   XXX
   Total variance explained $XXX

9-25. Comparing budgeted and actual performance. The Reliance Company recently constructed a factory that can manufacture 100,000 units of a product per year. The forecasted demand averaged 84,000 units per year over a planning horizon of fifteen years. The bigger plant was built because management decided that this was the most economical way to prepare for growth and seasonality in demand.

The sales forecast used in a master budget for 19x1 was 90,000 units. Average productivity is one-half unit per direct labor-hour, but it took 164,000 labor-hours to produce the 78,000 units that were sold.

The average unit selling price was $32. There were no beginning or ending inventories. The standard direct labor rate was $6 per hour. Standard direct material was $8 per unit and standard variable overhead was $2 per hour. Variable nonmanufacturing costs were $1 per unit. Fixed manufacturing costs were $400,000 and fixed nonmanufacturing costs were $200,000.

All prices, rates, and fixed costs were incurred as foreseen in the master budget, except that the advertising budget allowance was underspent by $40,000 and actual material prices on the last 10,000 units produced were $9 per unit.

Required:

1. Present a schedule of the marketing variance, material price variance, efficiency variances, and advertising variances. Show your computations.
2. Prepare two sets of reports: (a) a summary of performance similar to Exhibit 9-4 and (b) a cost-control performance report similar to Exhibit 9-5.
3. Suppose there were no variable or fixed-cost variances whatsoever. Compute the budgeted net income if the master-budgeted level were at the average long-run demand of 84,000 units. What is the break-even point? What alternatives should management explore to increase profitability?

9-26. Reconstructing financial statements. On New Year's Eve, December 31, 19x1, a fire partially destroyed the records of the Valentino Manufacturing Company. You are asked to prepare a summary of performance similar to Exhibit 9-4 for the year 19x1 based on scattered data.

Production and sales were 52,000 units. The unfavorable marketing variance, based on the unit contribution margin, was $40,000. The average selling price was $20 per unit. Total actual operating income was $17,000. The standard contribution margin per unit was $5. Budgeted and actual fixed costs were the same. Efficiency variances were $43,000, unfavorable.

9-27. Efficiency variances. Assume that 10,000 units of a particular item were produced. Suppose that the standard direct material allowance is two pounds per unit, at a cost per pound of $2. Actually, 21,000 pounds of materials (input) were used to produce the 10,000 units (output).

Similarly, assume that it is supposed to take four direct labor hours to produce one unit, and that the standard hourly labor cost is $3. But 41,000 hours (input) were used to produce the 10,000 units.

Required:

Compute the efficiency variances for direct material and direct labor.

9-28. Straightforward variance analysis. The Dixon Company uses a standard cost system. The month's data regarding its single product follows:

Variable overhead rate, $.90 per hour
Standard direct labor cost, $4 per hour
Standard material cost, $1 per pound
Standard pounds of material in a finished unit, 3
Standard direct labor-hours per finished unit, 5
Material purchased and used, 6,700 lbs.
Direct labor costs incurred, 11,000 hours, $41,800
Variable overhead costs incurred, $9,500
Finished units produced, 2,000
Actual material cost, $.90 per pound

Required:

Prepare schedules of all variances, using the format of Exhibit 9-6.

9-29. Variance analysis. The Wayne Company uses standard costs and a flexible budget. The purchasing agent is responsible for material price variances, and the production manager is responsible for all other variances.

Operating data for the past week are summarized as follows:

Finished units produced: 5,000.

Direct material: Purchases, 10,000 lbs. @ $1.50. Standard price, $1.60 per lb.
Used, 5,400 lbs. Standard allowed per unit produced, 1 lb.

Direct labor: Actual costs, 8,000 hours @ $3.05, or $24,400.
Standard allowed per good unit produced, 1½ hours.
Standard price per direct labor hour $3.

Variable manufacturing overhead: Actual costs, $8,800. Budget formula is $1 per standard direct labor-hour.

Required:

1. a. Material purchase price variance.
   b. Material efficiency variance.
   c. Direct labor price variance.
   d. Direct labor efficiency variance.
   e. Variable manufacturing overhead price variance.
   f. Variable manufacturing overhead efficiency variance.

   (*Hint:* For a format, see part (3) of the solution to the Summary Problem for Your Review.)

2. a. What is the budget allowance for direct labor?
   b. Would it be any different if production were 6,000 good units?

9-30. Labor variances. The City of New York has a sign shop where street signs of all kinds are manufactured and repaired. The manager of the shop uses standards to judge performance. However, because a clerk mistakenly discarded some labor records, the manager has only partial data for October. The manager knew that the total direct labor variance was $880, favorable, and that the standard labor price was $6 per hour. Moreover, a recent pay raise had produced an unfavorable labor price variance for October of $320. The actual hours of input were 1,600.

Required:

1. Find the actual labor price per hour.
2. Determine the standard hours allowed for work done.

9-31. Variable overhead variances. You have been asked to prepare an analysis of the overhead costs in the billing department of a hospital. As an initial step, you prepare a summary of some events that bear on overhead for the most recent period. The variable overhead budget variance was $4,000, unfavorable. The standard variable overhead price per billing was 5¢. Ten bills per hour is regarded as standard productivity per clerk. The total overhead incurred was $168,500, of which $110,000 was fixed. There were no variances for fixed overhead. The variable overhead price variance was $2,000, favorable.

Required:

Find the following:

1. Variable overhead efficiency variance.
2. Actual hours of input.
3. Standard hours allowed for work done.

9-32. Review problem on standards and flexible budgets; answers provided. The Alphonse Company makes a variety of leather goods. It uses standard costs and a flexible budget to aid planning and control. Budgeted variable overhead at a 60,000-direct-labor-hour level is $36,000.

During April, the company had an unfavorable variable overhead efficiency variance of $1,200. Material purchases were $322,500. Actual direct labor costs incurred were $187,600. The direct labor efficiency variance was $6,000, unfavorable. The actual average wage price was 20¢ lower than the average standard wage price.

The company uses a variable overhead rate of 20 percent of standard direct labor *cost* for flexible budgeting purposes. Actual variable overhead for the month was $41,000.

Required:

Prepare the following items; then use *U* or *F* to indicate whether requested variances are favorable or unfavorable.

1. Standard direct labor cost per hour.
2. Actual direct labor-hours worked.
3. Total direct labor price variance.
4. Total flexible budget for direct labor costs.
5. Total direct labor variance.
6. Variable overhead price variance in total.

Answers to Problem 9-32:

1. $3. The variable overhead price is 60¢, obtained by dividing $36,000 by 60,000 hours. Therefore, the direct labor price must be 60¢ ÷ .20 = $3.
2. 67,000 hours. Actual costs, $187,600 ÷ ($3 − 20¢) = 67,000 hours.
3. $13,400 *F*. 67,000 actual hours × 20¢ = $13,400.
4. $195,000. Efficiency variance was $6,000, unfavorable. Therefore, excess hours must have been $6,000 ÷ $3 = $2,000. Consequently, standard hours allowed must be 67,000 − 2,000 = 65,000. Flexible budget = 65,000 × $3 = $195,000.
5. $7,400 *F*. $195,000 − $187,600 = $7,400 *F*; or $13,400 *F* − $6,000 *U* = $7,400 *F*.
6. $800 *U*. Flexible budget = 65,000 × 60¢ = $39,000. Total variance = $41,000 − $39,000 = $2,000 *U*. Price variance = $2,000 − $1,200 efficiency variance = $800 *U*.

9-33. Review problem on standards and flexible budgets. The Haber Company uses a flexible budget and standard costs to aid planning and control. At a 60,000-direct-labor-hour level, budgeted variable overhead is $30,000 and budgeted direct labor is $240,000.

The following are some results for August:

Variable overhead budget variance	$ 12,500 *U*
Variable overhead efficiency variance	9,500 *U*
Actual direct labor costs incurred	294,000
Material purchase price variance	
(based on goods purchased)	16,000 *F*
Material efficiency variance	9,000 *U*

The standard price per pound of direct material is $1.50. The standard allowance is one pound of direct material for each unit of finished product. Ninety thousand finished units of product were produced during August. There was no beginning or ending work in process. In July, the material efficiency variance was

$1,000, favorable, and the purchase price variance was 20¢ per pound unfavorable. In August, the purchase price variance was 10¢ per pound.

In July, labor troubles caused an immense slowdown in the pace of production. There had been an unfavorable direct labor efficiency variance of $60,000; there was no labor price variance. These troubles had persisted in August—some workers quit. Their replacements had to be hired at higher rates (prices) which had to be extended to all workers. The actual average wage rate in August exceeded the standard average wage rate by 20¢ per hour.

Required:

Establish the following for the month of August:

1. Total pounds of direct material purchased.
2. Total number of pounds of excess material usage.
3. Variable overhead price variance.
4. Total number of actual hours worked.
5. Total number of standard hours allowed for the finished units produced.

9-34. **Combined or joint price-quantity variance and incentives.** The Brisbane Company had an incentive system that rewarded managers each Christmas for cost savings on materials. The manager of purchasing received 10 percent of any favorable price variance accumulated for the fiscal year ending November 30. Similarly, the production manager received 10 percent of the favorable efficiency (quantity) variances. In addition, each manager received 10 percent of the favorable net material variances. Note, however, that all variances were included in the computations, that is, an unfavorable variance in one month would offset a favorable variance in another month.

In the opinion of the company president, this system had worked reasonably well in past years. Of course, because of the sensitivity of the incentive system, the standards were carefully specified and adjusted each quarter. Only minimal inventories were kept at any time. Bonuses had varied from zero to 20 percent of the managers' base salaries. The purchasing manager's base salary for a recent fiscal year ending November 30 was $24,000; the production manager's was $30,000.

The operating results on Material A for a recent month were:

Purchase-price variance	$ 72,000 U
Efficiency variance	36,000 U
Net material variance	$108,000 U

Two pounds of Material A was the standard quantity allowed for every unit of a particular finished product, a chemical used in petroleum refining. One hundred thousand units of the chemical had been manufactured. The average price actually paid for Material A was 30¢ per pound in excess of the standard price.

Required:

1. What number of pounds of Material A was purchased?
2. Find the standard price per pound of Material A.
3. What is the total standard cost allowed for material components of the finished product?
4. As the purchasing manager, what is your opinion of the bonus system? Would your answer be the same if the actual raw-material price paid had been 70¢ per pound? Explain fully.

5. As the production manager, what is your opinion of the bonus system? Why?
6. Why is part of the bonus dependent on the net material variance?
7. Assume that some bonus system tied to variance analysis is maintained. What changes would you recommend?

9-35. **Comprehensive variance analysis.** (CMA adapted.) The Carberg Corporation manufactures and sells a single product. The cost system used by the company is a standard cost system. The standard variable cost per unit of product is shown below:

Material—one pound plastic @ $2.00	$ 2.00
Direct labor, 1.6 hours @ $4.00	6.40
Variable overhead cost	3.00
	$11.40

The variable overhead cost per unit was calculated from the following annual overhead cost budget for a 60,000-unit volume.

Variable overhead cost:

Indirect labor 30,000 hours @ $4.00..............	$120,000
Supplies—Oil 60,000 gallons @ $.50	30,000
Allocated variable service department costs	30,000
Total variable overhead cost	$180,000

The charges to the manufacturing department for November, when 5,000 units were produced, are given below:

Material 5,300 pounds @ $2.00...................	$10,600
Direct labor 8,200 hours @ $4.10................	33,620
Indirect labor 2,400 hours @ $4.10..............	9,840
Supplies—Oil 6,000 gallons @ $0.55	3,300
Allocated variable service department costs	3,200
Total variable costs..............................	$60,560

The purchasing department normally buys approximately the same quantity as is used in production during a month. In November, 5,200 pounds were purchased at a price of $2.10 per pound.

Required:
1. Calculate the following variances from standard costs for the data given:
   a. material purchase price
   b. material efficiency
   c. direct labor price
   d. direct labor efficiency
   e. overhead budget
2. The company has divided its responsibilities so that the purchasing department is responsible for the price at which material and supplies are purchased, and the manufacturing department is responsible for the quantities of material used. Does this division of responsibilities solve the conflict between price and efficiency variances? Explain your answer.
3. Prepare a report which details the overhead budget variance. The report, which will be given to the manufacturing department manager, should display only

that part of the variance that is the responsibility of the manager and should highlight the information in ways that would be useful to him in evaluating departmental performance and when considering corrective action.

9-36. Review of major points in chapter. The following questions are based on the data contained in the illustration used in the chapter:

1. Suppose that actual production and sales were 8,000 units instead of 7,000 units. (a) Compute the marketing variance. Is the performance of the marketing function the sole explanation for this variance? Why? (b) Using a flexible budget, compute the budgeted contribution margin, the budgeted operating income, budgeted direct material, and budgeted direct labor.
2. Suppose the following were the actual results for the production of 8,000 units:

Direct material: 42,000 pounds were used at an actual unit price of 56¢, for a total actual cost of $23,520.
Direct labor: 16,500 hours were used at an actual hourly rate of $4.10, for a total actual cost of $67,650.

Compute the flexible budget variance and the price and efficiency variances for direct materials and direct labor. Present your answers in the form shown in Exhibit 9-6.

3. Suppose that the company is organized so that the purchasing manager bears primary responsibility for the acquisition prices of materials, and the production manager bears the primary responsibility for efficiency but no responsibility for unit prices. Assume the same facts as in part (2), except that the purchasing manager acquired 60,000 pounds of materials. This means that there is an ending inventory of 18,000 pounds. Would your variance analysis of materials in part (2) change? Why? Show your computations.

9-37. Review of major points in chapter. The master budget income statement for 19x2 for the Merced Company was:

Sales (1,000,000 units @ $3)		$3,000,000
Variable charges:		
Direct material @ $.50	$ 500,000	
Direct labor @ $1	1,000,000	
Variable factory overhead @ $.20	200,000	
Selling @ $.30	300,000	
Administrative @ $.10	100,000	2,100,000
Contribution margin @ $.90		$ 900,000
Fixed charges:		
Manufacturing	$ 300,000	
Other	500,000	800,000
Budgeted net income		$ 100,000

Results from 19x2 did not fulfill expectations. Only 940,000 units were produced and sold. Average productivity was supposed to be four units per direct labor-hour. Direct material price and efficiency variances totaled $30,000, unfavorable. Actual direct labor-hours were 250,000. There was a favorable direct labor price variance of $25,000. The variable overhead price variance was

$10,000, favorable. Variable overhead cost behavior was most closely related to fluctuations in direct labor-hours.

Negotiations with tax assessors resulted in lower property taxes than anticipated. Fixed charges had a favorable budget variance of $15,000.

There were no beginning or ending inventories, or variable selling and administrative cost variances.

Required:

1. Quantify the following variances in dollars, and show your computations:
   a. Marketing variance.
   b. Direct labor efficiency variance.
   c. Variable factory overhead efficiency variance.
   d. Variable factory overhead budget variance.
2. Prepare two sets of reports: (a) a summary of performance similar to Exhibit 9-4 and (b) a cost-control performance report similar to Exhibit 9-5.

SUGGESTED READING

Beyer, R. and D. Trawicki, *Profitability Accounting for Planning and Control,* 2nd ed. (New York: The Ronald Press Company, 1972). Especially strong in the area of flexible budgeting.

Variations of Cost Behavior Patterns   10

When we refer to "cost behavior patterns," we generally mean the relationship of total costs to changes in the volume of activity. Until this chapter, we have concentrated on two basic linear-cost behavior patterns: variable and fixed. Now we shall examine some variations of these patterns that have been developed in response to decision needs. First, we shall examine some distinctions that have proven useful for planning and control. Then we shall explore the complex problem of how to determine cost behavior patterns so that predictions and evaluations may be made as accurately as is feasible.

ENGINEERED, DISCRETIONARY, AND COMMITTED COSTS

During the 1960's, a classification of costs evolved as follows:

Variable costs:	*Fixed costs:*
Engineered	Discretionary
Discretionary*	Committed

      *Only a few variable costs belong in the discretionary classification, as explained below.

We shall discuss these costs in reverse order, beginning with fixed committed costs.

Fixed Costs and Capacity

Fixed costs, also called **capacity costs,** measure the capacity for manufacturing, sales, administration, and research. They reflect the capability for sustaining a planned volume of activity.

The size of fixed costs is influenced by long-run marketing conditions, technology, and the methods and strategies of management. Examples of the methods and strategies of management include sales salaries versus sales commissions and one-shift versus two-shift operations. Fixed costs are often the result of a trade-off decision whereby lower variable costs are attained in exchange for higher fixed costs. For example, automatic equipment may be acquired to reduce labor costs.

Generally, a heavier proportion of fixed to variable costs lessens management's ability to respond to short-run changes in economic conditions and opportunities. Still, unwillingness to incur fixed costs reveals an aversion to risk that may exclude a company from profitable ventures. For instance, the launching of new products often requires very large fixed costs for research, advertising, equipment, and working capital.

Committed Fixed Costs

For planning and control, fixed costs may be usefully subdivided into committed and discretionary costs. **Committed fixed costs** consist largely of those fixed costs that arise from the possession of plant, of equipment, and of a basic organization. Examples are depreciation, property taxes, rent, insurance, and the salaries of key personnel. These costs are affected primarily by long-run sales forecasts that, in turn, indicate the long-run capacity needs.

The behavior of committed fixed costs may best be viewed by assuming a zero volume of activity in an enterprise that fully expects to resume normal activity (for example, during a strike or a shortage of materials that forces a complete shutdown of activity). The committed fixed costs are all those organization and plant costs that continue to be incurred and that cannot be reduced without injuring the organization's competence to meet long-range goals. Committed fixed costs are the least responsive of the fixed costs, because they tend to be less affected by month-to-month and year-to-year decisions.

In planning, the focus is on the impact of these costs over a number of years. Such planning usually requires tailoring the capacity to future demand for the organization's products in the most economical manner. For example, should the store size be 50,000 square feet, or 80,000 or 100,000? Should the gasoline station have one, or two, or more stalls for servicing automobiles? Such decisions usually involve selecting the point of optimal trade-off between present and future operating costs—that is, constructing excess capacity now may save costs in the long run, because construction costs per square foot may be much higher later. On the other hand, if the forecast demand never develops, the organization may own facilities that are unnecessarily idle.

These decisions regarding capital expenditures are generally shown in an annual budget called the **capital budget** or **capital-spending budget.** As you recall, the *master budget* is based primarily on the annual sales forecast, the cornerstone of budgeting. Similarly, all capital-spending decisions are ultimately based on long-range sales forecasts. Capital budgeting is discussed in Chapter 13.

Once buildings are erected and equipment is installed, little can be done in day-to-day operations to affect the *total level* of committed costs. From a control standpoint, the objective is usually to increase current utilization of facilities, because this will ordinarily increase net income.

There is another aspect to the control problem, however. A follow-up, or audit, is needed to find out how well the ensuing utilization harmonizes with the decision that authorized the facilities in the first place. The latter approach helps management to evaluate the wisdom of its past long-range decisions and, in turn, should improve the quality of future decisions.

Discretionary Fixed Costs

Discretionary fixed costs (sometimes called **managed** or **programmed costs**) are fixed costs (a) that arise from periodic (usually yearly) appropriation decisions that directly reflect top-management policies regarding the maximum permissible amounts to be incurred, and (b) that do not have a demonstrable optimum relationship between inputs (as measured by the costs) and outputs (as measured by sales, services, or production). Discretionary costs may have no particular relation to volume of activity. Examples are research and development, advertising, sales promotion, donations, management consulting fees, and many employee-training programs. Conceivably, these costs could be reduced almost entirely for a given year in dire times, whereas the committed costs would be much more difficult to reduce.

Discretionary fixed costs are decided upon by management at the start of the budget period. Goals are selected, the means for their attainment are chosen, the maximum expense to be incurred is specified, and the total amount to be spent is appropriated. For example, a company may appropriate $5 million for an advertising campaign. The company's advertising agency is unlikely to exceed that amount, nor is it likely to spend much less than $5 million in trying to attain the company goals. In the give-and-take process of preparing the master budget, the discretionary costs are the most likely to be revised.

Discretionary fixed costs represent an assortment of manufacturing, selling, administrative, and research items. For example, a large portion of discretionary fixed costs may consist of salaries for salesmen, accountants, clerks, and engineers, and often appear in the income statement lumped under the heading "General Selling and Administrative Expense." As in the case of committed costs, the resources acquired should be carefully planned and fully utilized if net income is to be maximized. Unlike committed costs, discretionary costs can be influenced more easily from period to period. It is also harder to measure the utilization of resources acquired via discretionary costs, principally because the results of services like creative personnel, advertising, research, and training programs are much more difficult to isolate and quantify than the results of utilizing plant and equipment to make products.

The behavior of some discretionary fixed costs is easy to delineate. Advertising, research, donations, and training programs, for example, are usually formulated with certain objectives in mind. The execution of such projects is measured by comparing total expenditures with the appropriation. Because the tendency is to spend the entire appropriation, the resulting dollar variances are generally trivial. But planning is far more important than this kind of day-to-day control. The perfect execution of an advertising program—in the sense that the full amount authorized was spent in specified media at predetermined times—will be fruitless if the advertisements are unimaginative and lifeless and if they reach the wrong audience.

The most noteworthy aspect of discretionary fixed costs is that, unlike most other costs, they are not subject to ordinary engineering input-output analysis. For example, an optimum relationship between inputs and outputs can be specified for direct materials because it takes three pounds or five gallons or two square feet to make a finished product. In contrast, we are usually unsure of the "correct" amount of advertising, research, management training, donations, and management consulting costs.

Engineered and Discretionary Variable Costs

An **engineered cost** is any cost that has an explicit, specified physical relationship with a selected measure of activity. Most variable costs fit this classification. An "engineered" variable cost exists when an optimum relationship between inputs and outputs has been carefully determined. In fact, efficiency has been defined as just such an optimum relationship. For example, an automobile may have exact specifications: one battery, one radiator, two fan belts, and so forth. Direct material and direct labor are prime examples of engineered costs.

Many managers and accountants tend to use "variable cost" and "engineered cost" interchangeably, as if they were synonomous terms. Most of the time, this is a harmless error. However, as noted at the start of the chapter, although most variable costs are engineered, some fit a discretionary classification; depending on management policy, there may be other costs that will go up and down with sales (or production) merely because management has predetermined that the organization can afford to spend a certain percentage of the sales dollar for items like research, donations, and advertising. These costs would have a graphical pattern of variability, but not for the same reasons as direct materials or direct labor. An increase in such costs may be due to management's authorization to spend "because we can afford it" rather than because there is an engineered cause-and-effect relationship between such costs and sales.

Classifying Particular Costs

From time to time, you will undoubtedly find these distinctions between engineered, discretionary, and committed costs to be useful. However, these are subjective decisions, so expect some ambiguity as to whether a given cost is, say, committed or discretionary. For example, the salaries of supervisory or other highly prized personnel that would be kept on the payroll at zero activity levels are often regarded as committed costs; but some organizations may classify them as discretionary costs. Arguments about whether such costs are committed or discretionary are a waste of time—these matters must be settled on a case-by-case basis. In a particular organization, quick agreement regarding an appropriate classification is usually possible.

WORK MEASUREMENT

Measurement Needed for Control

Engineering and accounting techniques for planning and control were initially developed for manufacturing rather than for nonmanufacturing activities. This occurred because inputs and outputs in the manufacturing areas are easier to identify and measure. The measurement of direct material consumed and finished units produced is straightforward. However, much more difficult is a measurement for relating the inputs of advertising and sales-promotion activity to the outputs of sales or contribution margins.

As the input-output relationships become less defined, management tends to abandon any formal work measurement techniques and, instead, relies almost wholly on the individual and his supervisor for successful control. Consequently, cost control is approached from a discretionary cost rather than from an engineered cost (work measurement) viewpoint, especially in many areas of nonmanufacturing.

Despite the difficulties of implementation, work measurement is getting more attention from organizations as they seek to improve their efficiency. This approach is based on a fundamental premise: Permanent improvement in any performance is impossible unless the work is measured. In recent years, work measurement has extended into selling and into administrative clerical areas.

Work measurement is the careful analysis of a task, its size, the methods used in its performance, and its efficiency. Its objective is to determine the work load in an operation and the number of workers needed to perform that work efficiently. The techniques used include time and motion study, observation of a random sample of the work (work sampling), and the estimation, by a work-measurement analyst and a line supervisor, of the amount of time required for the work (time analysis). The workload is expressed in *control-factor units* which are used in formulating the budget.

For example, the control-factor units in a payroll department might include operations performed on time cards, on notices of change in the labor rate, on notices of employee promotion, on new employment and termination reports, and on routine weekly and monthly reports. All of these would be weighed. The estimated workload would then be used for determining the required labor force and budgetary allowance.

Another example of work measurement is the physical handling of goods in warehousing, shipping, receiving, or shelving. In these instances, a **standard handling unit** may be formulated. The standard handling unit may be a case of goods; then barrels, packages, sacks, and other items "may be expressed as multiple or fractional handling units according to their time-of-handling relationship to that of the case of goods (the standard unit)."[1]

The activity measure used as a budget base may be sales dollars, product units, cases, tons, or some other unit that best reflects cost influence:

Operation	*Unit of Measure (Control-Factor Unit)*
Billing	Lines per hour
Warehouse labor	Pounds or cases handled per day
Packing	Pieces packed per hour
Posting accounts receivable	Postings per hour
Mailing	Pieces mailed per hour

Standards for certain order-filling activities such as packing or driving a truck may necessarily be less refined than for such manufacturing activities as assembly work, but they still provide the best available formal tool for planning and control. For example, short-interval scheduling has been attempted; this technique routes all work through a supervisor, who batches the work in hourly lots. This develops standards, controls backlogs, and provides close follow-up.[2]

The measurement of work often spurs controversy, because employees do not usually welcome more stringent monitoring of their productivity. Despite some delicate problems of human relations, there is an increasing tendency for work measurement to be applied in office, transportation, and other nonmanufacturing activities.

---

[1]Charles H. Sevin, *Marketing Productivity Analysis* (New York: McGraw-Hill Book Company, Inc.) p. 21.

[2]Vincent Melore, "Cutting Payroll Costs in Manufacturing Staffs," *Management Services,* Vol. 1, No. 3, 24.

Budgeting of Order-filling and Administrative Costs: Two Approaches

There is much disagreement about how order-filling and many clerical costs should be controlled. Advocates of work measurement favor a more rigorous approach, which essentially regards these costs as engineered. In contrast, a discretionary-fixed-cost approach is more often found in practice.

Assume that ten payroll clerks are employed, and that each clerk's operating efficiency *should be* the processing of the payroll records of 500 employees per month. In the month of June, the payroll records of 4,700 individuals were processed by these ten clerks. Each clerk earns $600 per month. The variances shown by the engineered-cost approach and the discretionary-fixed-cost approach are tabulated below and graphed in Exhibit 10-1.

The Engineered Cost Approach: Perfection Standards

The engineered cost approach to this situation is to base the budget formula on the unit cost of the individual pay record processed—$600 ÷ 500 records, or $1.20. Therefore, the budget allowance for payroll-clerk labor would be $1.20 × 4,700, or $5,640. Assume that the ten employees worked throughout the month. The following performance report would be prepared:

	Actual Cost	*Flexible Budget: Total Standard Quantity Allowed for Good Units Produced*	*Budget Variance*
Payroll-clerk labor	$6,000 (10 × $600)	$5,640 (4,700 × $1.20)	$360 *U*

EXHIBIT 10-1

	BUDGET AS AN ENGINEERED COST (PERFECTION)	BUDGET AS A DISCRETIONARY COST (CURRENTLY ATTAINABLE)
Actual cost incurred	$6,000	$6,000
Budget allowance	5,640*	6,000
Variance	360 *U*	0

*Rate = $6,000 ÷ 5,000 records or $1.20 per record; total = 4,700 records @ $1.20 = $5,640.

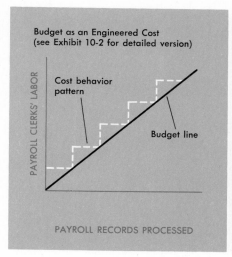

Budget as an Engineered Cost
(see Exhibit 10-2 for detailed version)

PAYROLL CLERKS' LABOR

Cost behavior pattern

Budget line

PAYROLL RECORDS PROCESSED

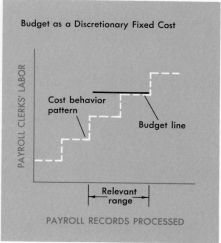

Budget as a Discretionary Fixed Cost

PAYROLL CLERKS' LABOR

Cost behavior pattern

Budget line

Relevant range

PAYROLL RECORDS PROCESSED

A graphic representation of what has occurred (Exhibit 10-2) may yield insight.

Essentially, two decisions must be made in this operation. The first is a policy decision: How many clerks do we need? How flexible should we be? How divisible is the task? Should we use part-time help? Should we hire and fire as the volume of work fluctuates? The implication of these questions is that once the hiring decision is made, the total costs incurred can be predicted easily—$6,000 in our example.

The second decision concentrates on day-to-day control, on how efficiently the given resources are being utilized. The work-measurement approach is an explicit and formal attempt to measure the utilization of resources by:

1. Assuming a proportionately variable budget and the complete divisibility of the workload into small units. Note that the budget line on the graph in Exhibit 10-2 is proportionately variable, despite the fact that the costs are really incurred in steps.

2. Generating a budget variance that assumes a comparison of actual costs with a perfection standard—the cost that would be incurred if payroll-clerk labor could be turned on and off like a faucet. In this case, the variance of $360 informs management that there was overstaffing (that is, the tenth step was only partially utilized). The workload capability was 5,000 pay records, not the 4,700 actually processed. The extra cost of $360 resulted from operating in a way that does not attain the lowest possible cost, even though this may not be the result of a conscious decision but merely the effect of producing the volume that satisfies the monthly changes in demand.

Such an approach provides a measure ($360) of the amount that management is currently investing to provide stability in the work force.

EXHIBIT 10-2
Engineered Costs and Variances

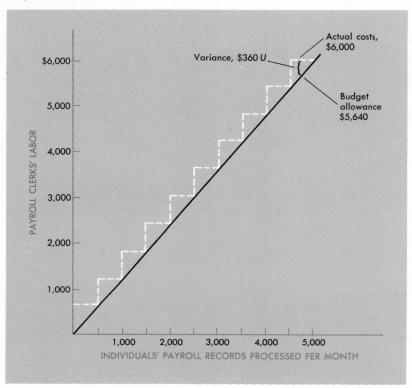

Advocates of work measurement maintain that such an approach is the only reliable way to satisfy management's desire to plan and control such costs. The use of a tight budget based on perfection standards generates variances that upon investigation will reveal either or both of the following: (a) faulty use or underutilization of available personnel (for instance, perhaps 5,000 individual payroll records had to be processed, and other clerks or supervisors had to pitch in to get all the work done); (b) the cost of a management policy of deliberately retaining personnel to service long-run needs even though the volume of the current workload is insufficient (for instance, the maximum work available for payroll clerical labor may be 4,700 individual payroll records and the individual work may have been performed with complete efficiency).

Critics of work measurement will often assert that such a formal approach is not worth its cost because strong labor unions and other forces prevent managers from fine-tuning the size of the work force. In response, the defenders of work measurement will assert that managers must know the costs of various labor policies. For instance, if the cost of overstaffing becomes exorbitant, the pertinent provisions in a labor contract may become key bargaining issues when the contract is about to be renewed.

Work-measurement techniques are not used in the vast majority of organizations. Consequently, the tendency is to rely on the experience of the department head and his superior for judging the size of the work force needed to carry out the department's functions. There is a genuine reluctance to overhire because there is a corresponding slowness in discharging or laying off people when volume slackens. As a result, temporary peak loads are often met by hiring temporary workers or by having the regular employees work overtime.

In most cases, the relevant range of activity during the budget period can be predicted with assurance, and the work force needed for the marketing and administrative functions can be readily determined. If management refuses, consciously or unconsciously, to rigidly control costs in accordance with short-run fluctuations in activity, these costs become discretionary—that is, their total amount is relatively fixed and unresponsive to short-run variations in volume.

Hence, there is a conflict between common practice and the objective of work measurement, which is to treat most costs as engineered and to therefore subject them to short-range management control. The moral is that management's attitudes and its planning and controlling decisions often determine whether a cost is discretionary fixed or engineered variable. A change in policy can transform a fixed cost into a variable cost, and vice versa.

Moreover, management may regard a cost as a discretionary fixed cost for "cash-planning purposes" in the preparation of the master budget, but may use the engineered cost approach for "control purposes" in the preparation of flexible budgets for departmental performance evaluation. These two views may be reconciled within the same overall system. In our example, a master budget conceivably could include the following item:

Payroll-clerk labor:
Flexible budget allowance for departmental control	$5,640
Expected flexible budget variance (due to deliberate overstaffing)	360
Total budget allowance for cash planning	$6,000

The common impression, which is reinforced by work-measurement approaches, is that control should be constantly exerted to be effective. However, the National Association of Accountants comments:

> In one company, where considerable study had been devoted to determining how costs ought to be affected by volume changes, it was concluded that certain costs (e.g., maintenance) which management had attempted to con-

trol with current volume could better be controlled as managed [i.e., discretionary] capacity costs. While this conclusion was contrary to management's impression that it was desirable to control costs with current volume wherever possible, trials showed savings when all relevant factors including quality and reliability of services were included in the comparison.[3]

Follow-up of Discretionary Fixed Costs

Thus, we see that control may be exercised (a) in the commonly accepted sense of the day-to-day follow-up that is associated with engineered costs, and (b) in the special sense of periodically evaluating an expenditure, relating it to the objectives sought, and carefully planning the total amount of the cost for the ensuing period. The latter approach does not mean that day-to-day follow-up is neglected; follow-up is necessary to see that the resources made available are being used fully and efficiently. It does mean that perceptive planning is stressed and that daily control is de-emphasized. Reliance is placed more on hiring capable people and less on frequent checking up.

The practical effects of the discretionary fixed-cost approach are that the budgeted costs and the actual costs tend to be very close, so that resulting budget variances are small. Follow-ups to see that the available resources are being fully and efficiently utilized are regarded as the managers' responsibility, a duty that can be carried through by face-to-face control and by records of physical quantities (for example, pounds handled per day in a warehouse, pieces mailed per hour in a mailing room) that do not have to be formally integrated into the accounting records in dollar terms.

Difficulties in Applying Work Measurement

The success of the work-measurement, engineered-cost approach to order filling and administrative costs is limited by the nature of the work being performed. Attempts have been made to measure the work of legal personnel and claims adjusters in insurance companies, of economists in a Federal Reserve Bank, and of stockboys in retail stores. Such attempts have achieved only limited success because of (a) the inability to develop a satisfactory control-factor unit, (b) the diversity of tasks and objectives of such personnel, or (c) the difficulty of measuring the output of lawyers or economists.

For example, consider the attempt to measure the work of clerks and stockboys in a food store. Their tasks are routine and repetitive, but they are often splintered. Attempts at measuring employee work have shown volatile results. Such results indicate that there are opportunities for

---

[3] *Accounting for Costs of Capacity,* N.A.A. Research Report No. 39, p. 13.

better utilization of personnel. The trouble is that each employee usually performs a variety of tasks on a variety of items. He may unpack, price mark, stock shelves, operate a cash register, bag groceries, cart groceries to automobiles, sweep floors, and watch for shoplifters.

Control-factor units may be satisfactorily established for each individual task, but the comparison of results must be made with care. For instance, a comparison showed that in one store, productivity was fourteen cases of frozen food per man-hour for receiving, price marking, and displaying; in another, the productivity was twenty-two cases per hour.[4] These results may prompt investigation in the low-productivity store, but other factors may narrow the apparent difference in productivity. Such overstaffing may occur because, after experimentation, the store manager has decided that his local competitive situation requires a certain number of clerks and stockboys to service customers. Merchandise characteristics are secondary, and the "case per hour" figure may reflect a more leisurely work pace simply because the alternative is idle time during a certain span of the day. The point is that an able store manager, one who can see the jointness of the problem and who is willing to experiment and to compare his practices with those of other stores, is still the key to successful operations. Work measurement is helpful, because measurement is a first step toward control. But it is only a step.

DETERMINING HOW COSTS BEHAVE

Objectives Provide the Framework

The process of determining cost behavior patterns (cost functions) should be viewed from the perspective of the sensitivity of the results to the decision. Ideally, the decision maker wants to know the "true" or "exact" impact of a variety of actions and events on costs. In the vast majority of instances, that impact cannot be known with certainty. Instead, the statistician or accountant provides some cost function (for example, $y = bx$) that is a simplification of the underlying relationships.

The central question is whether the resulting approximation, which is nearly always a linear function, is good enough for the purpose at hand. The answer to that question is often difficult to establish with much confidence. Nevertheless, it is a cost-and-value-of-information question that cannot be avoided. By the very act of using the cost function, the manager has made an information decision. He may have faced the decision squarely and explicitly by saying, "Yes, I can use this cost function for my prediction rather than a simpler or more complicated cost function." Or he may have reached the same conclusion implicitly, by proceeding with the given function with no questions asked. For example, when a man-

[4]*The Economics of Frozen Foods,* McKinsey-Birds Eye Study, General Foods Corporation (White Plains, N. Y., 1964), p. 37.

ager uses an overhead rate of $2 per direct labor-hour as a part of the accumulation of costs for a pricing decision—even though he knows that overhead is affected by labor-hours, machine-hours, weight of materials, dimensions of materials, and weather conditions—he has made an information decision. He has decided that the simple $2 cost function is good enough for his purpose. In his mind, his pricing decision would not be sufficiently affected by a more complicated cost function to justify its added cost.

Two common simplifications are widely used in the determination of cost functions. First, linear approximations to cost functions are considered "good enough," even though nonlinear behavior is more likely. Second, a common assumption is that cost behavior can be sufficiently explained by one independent variable (such as labor-hours) rather than by more than one (for instance, labor-hours, machine-hours, and dimensions of materials). Of course, whether these simplifications provide sufficiently accurate approximations of underlying relationships is a question that can be answered only in actual situations on a case-by-case basis.

Linearity and Cost Functions

Almost without exception, accountants and managers use linear-cost functions to approximate the relationships of total costs to a given range of inputs or outputs. There are several assumptions that are sufficient conditions for linearity to exist when total costs are related to output.

1. The technological relationships between inputs and outputs must be linear; for example, each unit of finished product must contain the same amount of raw materials.

2. The inputs acquired must equal the inputs used; for example, each worker hired must be fully utilized.

3. The cost of acquiring each input must be a linear function of the quantity acquired; for example, the unit price of raw materials must be identical regardless of the amount purchased.

The relevant range of output under consideration may permit a linearity assumption within specified limits of output. Beyond that point, the cost of production may increase much faster or slower than the assumed linear rate.

Step-Cost Functions

Nonlinear cost behavior can be caused by a variety of circumstances. For example, suppliers may offer quantity discounts on some inputs; other inputs may require higher prices in order to bid scarce resources away from competitors; some inputs (like most workers) may not be obtainable in fractional quantities, even though they may be used in fractional quantities; there may be economies or diseconomies of scale; and so forth.

For example, consider the step-cost function in Exhibit 10-3.

EXHIBIT 10-3
Step-Cost Function

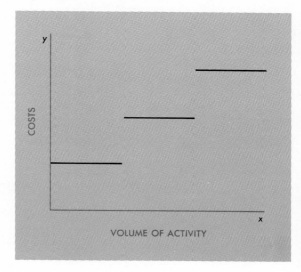

The utilizing of an input is a step-cost function if the cost of the input is constant over various ranges of output, but it increases by discrete amounts as activity moves from one range to the next. This step-like behavior occurs when the input is acquired in discrete quantities but is used in fractional quantities. For example, employees may be hired for the week, but the firm may need them only for some fraction of that week.

As compared with the clerical step-cost function in Exhibit 10-2, the steps in Exhibit 10-3 are higher and wider. The width and height of the steps may vary among the types of labor services—for instance, the number of hours worked by each direct laborer may be closely geared to production. Therefore, direct labor cost steps may be so narrow and so small that they approximate the proportionately variable cost typically shown as the budget line; to see this, compare the step-cost function in Exhibit 10-3 with the budget line, which is drawn as a proportionately variable cost.

Of course, a different approach may be taken if the steps widen. Exhibit 10-4 demonstrates how supervision costs may have wider steps. Here a fixed-cost approximation would be more accurate than a variable-cost approximation for the bulk of the relevant range under consideration.

EXHIBIT 10-4
Step-Cost Function
Supervision Costs

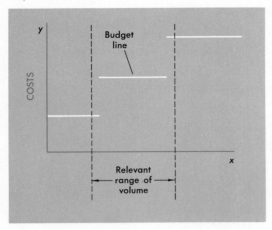

Other Nonlinear Cost Functions

Raw material costs often have nonlinear behavior, as the graphs in Exhibit 10-5 show. The first graph is an example of an upward-sloping supply curve, where the purchase price per unit soars as demand increases. In contrast, the second graph is an example of the effect of quantity discounts, where the purchase price per unit declines at specified break points as quantities purchased increase.

EXHIBIT 10-5
Two Examples of Nonlinear Raw Material Costs

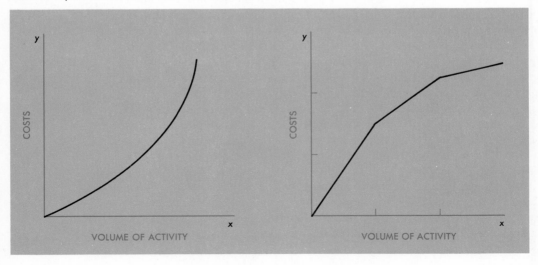

To approximate cost functions, *relationships* are sought between the activities and the costs incurred. The preferable cost function is the one that facilitates the most accurate prediction of changes in costs—the one that depicts persistent relationships, regardless of whether particular causes or effects can be established with assurance.

The following guides should help you to obtain accurate approximations of cost functions:

1. To the extent that physical relationships are observable, use them. The engineered-cost approach described earlier is an example of heavy reliance on observed technical relationships between inputs and outputs.

2. To the extent that relationships can be implicitly established via logic and knowledge of operations, use them—preferably in conjunction with step 3. Managers frequently use their knowledge of operations to choose a particular relationship between the independent variable (e.g., the volume of activity) and the dependent variable (e.g., the cost to be predicted). For example, power or repairs may be more closely related to machine hours than to direct labor hours.

3. To the extent that relationships can be explicitly established by appropriate statistical techniques such as regression analysis (described later), use them. The use of step 3 is a check on step 2, but the use of step 2 is also a check on step 3. Note that knowledge of cost accounting and operations is needed for intelligent regression analysis. For example, repairs are often made when output is low because the machines can be taken out of service at these times. Therefore, regression analysis would show repair costs going down as output increases, whereas managers and engineers know that the *timing* of the repair is deceptive—that the true cause-and-effect relationship is a tendency for most repair costs to increase as activity increases. Consequently, these costs should be analyzed separately, or else the true extent of variability of costs with output will be masked.[5]

Five Methods of Linear Approximation

There are at least five methods of approximating cost functions: (**a**) **account analysis,** (**b**) **high-low points,** (**c**) **visual fit,** (**d**) **simple regression, and** (**e**) **multiple regression.** These methods are not mutually exclusive; frequently, two or more methods are used to prevent major blunders. In many organizations, each of these five methods is used in succession over the years as the need for more accurate approximations becomes evident.

In account analysis, the analyst proceeds through the accounts, one by one, and classifies each into one of two categories, variable or fixed. In

[5]George J. Benston, "Multiple Regression Analysis of Cost Behavior," *Accounting Review,* Vol. XLI, No. 4, 668.

so doing, he may use his past experience intuitively and nothing else. More likely, he will at least study how total costs behave over a few periods before making judgments.

An examination of the accounts is obviously a necessary first step, no matter whether cost functions are approximated by means of simple inspection of the accounts or multiple regression. Familiarity with the data is needed to avoid the analytical pitfalls that abound in regression analysis.

A major disadvantage of the account classification method is its inherent subjectivity. The high-low method is slightly less subjective because at least it employs a series of samples and relies on two of their results, the highest cost and the lowest cost. It will be illustrated in a subsequent section.

The visual-fit, simple-regression, and multiple-regression methods have a distinct advantage because all sample points are used in determining the cost function. A visual fit is applied by drawing a straight line through the cost points on a scatter diagram, which consists of a plotting on a graph of individual dots that represent various experienced costs at various activity levels.

There are no objective tests to assure that the line fitted visually is the most accurate representation of the underlying data. Consequently, regression analysis is a more systematic approach.[6] Under certain assumptions, it has measures of probable error. Regression analysis refers to the measurement of the average amount of change in one variable (e.g., shipping cost) that is associated with unit increases in the amounts of one or more other variables. When only two variables are studied (e.g., shipping costs in relation to units shipped), the analysis is called **simple regression;** when more than two variables are studied (e.g., shipping costs in relation to units shipped and to the weight of those units shipped), it is called **multiple regression.**[7]

ILLUSTRATION OF DETERMINING A COST FUNCTION

Mixed Costs

As the name implies, a mixed cost has both fixed and variable elements (see Exhibit 10-6). The fixed element represents the minimum cost of supplying a service. The variable element is that portion of the mixed cost which is influenced by changes in activity. An example of a mixed cost is the rental of a delivery truck for a fixed cost per month plus a variable cost based on mileage. The variable element is that portion of

---

[6]For elaboration, see Charles T. Horngren, *Cost Accounting: A Managerial Emphasis,* 3rd ed. (Englewood Cliffs, N.J.: Prentice-Hall, Inc., 1972), Chapter 24.

[7]For elaboration, see Benston, *op. cit.,* 657–72.

EXHIBIT 10-6

Mixed Cost

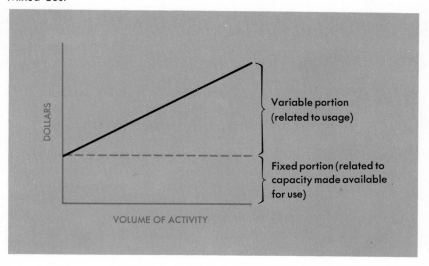

the mixed cost which is influenced by changes in activity (e.g., repairs, power, and some clerical costs).

Ideally, there should be no accounts for mixed costs. All such costs should be subdivided into two accounts, one for the variable portion and one for the fixed portion. In practice, these distinctions are rarely made in the recording process, because of the difficulty of analyzing day-to-day cost data into variable and fixed sections. Costs like power, indirect labor, repairs, and maintenance are generally accounted for in total. It is generally very difficult to decide, as such costs are incurred, whether a particular invoice or work ticket represents a variable or fixed item. Moreover, even if it were possible to make such distinctions, the advantages might not be worth the additional clerical effort and costs. Whenever cost classifications are too refined, the perpetual problem of getting accurate source documents is intensified.

In sum, mixed costs are merely a blend of two unlike cost behavior patterns; they do not entail new conceptual approaches. Anybody who obtains a working knowledge of the planning and controlling of variable and fixed costs, separately, can adapt to a mixed-cost situation when necessary.

In practice, where a report is divided into two main cost classifications, variable and fixed, mixed costs tend to be included in the variable category even though they may not have purely variable behavior. At first glance, such arbitrary classification may seem undesirable and misleading. However, within a particular organization, the users of the reports usually have an intimate knowledge of the fundamental characteristics of the cost in question. Therefore, they can temper their interpretation accordingly.

Budgeting Mixed Costs

How should mixed costs be budgeted? Ideally, of course, their variable and fixed elements should be isolated and budgeted separately. One widely practiced method is a budget formula which contains both a fixed and a variable element. For example, repairs for delivery trucks might be budgeted at $15 per month plus 1¢ per mile.

The estimation of mixed-cost behavior patterns preferably should begin with a scatter chart of past cost levels, a graph on which costs are plotted to show various historical costs. Exhibit 10-7 is a scatter diagram for the costs of machine repairs. A line is fitted to the points, either visually or by the statistical method of simple regression (described in the Appendix to this chapter). The intersection of the line with the vertical axis indicates the amount of the intercept at $x = 0$.

The concept of a relevant range was discussed in Chapter 7 and elsewhere. In the present context, the relevant range should be perceived as the span of activity that encompasses the observed relationships. Note especially that the relevant range rarely includes zero activity. Therefore, rather than thinking of the intercept (the fixed component) as a fixed cost, think of it merely as the intercept at $x = 0$. The value of the constant term is not the expected cost at zero activity; it is only the result of a regression line fitted to the available data. Too often, cost analysts unjustifiably extrapolate beyond the relevant range.

The scatter diagram is probably the most important single tool available for estimating the past behavior of costs. A careful scrutiny of such a diagram by knowledgeable managers will yield many insights about cost behavior that cannot be obtained by using statistical formulas. The indiscriminate use of data without such scrutiny will tend to overlook the past quirks in behavior that are obvious to the observer of a scatter diagram. These quirks, such as strikes, material shortages, inclement weather, and clerical errors in accruals or classifications, must be eliminated or adjusted before a useful estimate of behavior can be formulated. Moreover, seeming inconsistencies in the data on a scatter diagram may indicate that factors other than volume or activity have also significantly affected cost behavior. This may necessitate the use of more sophisticated techniques.

In industry, a crucial assumption is commonly made when cost behavior is estimated: Costs go up and down solely because of fluctuations in the volume of one causative factor. Such an assumption may be practical and adequate in many cases, but it is a simplification that may prove dangerous. **There is frequently more than one causative factor:** for example, product mix, material yield, weather, sizes of production runs, number of setups, weight, time, and so forth. For instance, the costs of a shipping department may be affected not only by the numbers of orders processed; other influences may be weather and the weight of the units. If these factors are important, even the least squares method described in

EXHIBIT 10-7

Scatter diagram—costs of machine repairs

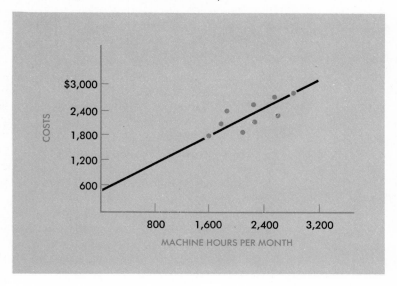

the Appendix at the end of the chapter would be inadequate. Multiple regression should then be used because it measures the influence of more than one factor on costs. Computers have made multiple-regression analysis economically feasible, so we can expect to see such analysis used more widely. Although regression analysis is a valuable tool for management, it has many pitfalls and should be conducted only by analysts who have adequate statistical skills.

For our purposes, we can get an introductory grasp of the overall problems without using such advanced statistical techniques.

High-Low Method

The High-Low Method (Exhibit 10-8) requires the plotting of two points, representing the highest cost and the lowest cost, respectively, over the contemplated relevant range.

A solid line is used to connect the high point and the low point. This line is extended back to intersect the vertical axis at the height at which the fixed portion of the cost has been plotted ($480 in Exhibit 10-8). The slope, or rate of change, of the line (80¢ per machine-hour) represents the variable portion of the mixed cost. Thus, the formula that depicts the behavior of this cost over the relevant range is $480 per month plus 80¢ per machine-hour.

The same results could be computed by using the following algebraic technique:

$$\text{Variable rate} = \frac{\text{Change in mixed cost}}{\text{Change in machine-hours}}$$

$$= \frac{\$2,720 - \$1,760}{2,800 - 1,600} = \frac{\$960}{1,200} = \$.80 \text{ per machine-hour} \quad (1)$$

Fixed overhead component
= Total mixed cost less variable component $\qquad$ (2)
At 1,600-hour level of activity:
= $\$1,760 - \$.80(1,600) = \$1,760 - \$1,280 = \$480$
At 2,800-hour level of activity:
= $\$2,720 - \$.80(2,800) = \$2,720 - \$2,240 = \$480$
Cost formula = $\$480$ per month plus $\$.80$ per machine-hour $\qquad$ (3)

Such cost formulas are only the *first step* in the budgetary process. The budgeted figures are expected future data, so cost formulas must be altered to reflect anticipated changes in prices, efficiency, technology, and other influential factors. Also, the high-low method must be used cautiously, if at all, in practice because two such measurements can rarely pinpoint an accurate cost behavior pattern over a wide range of volume.

EXHIBIT 10-8
High-Low Method of Estimating Costs

	Machine repairs	
Volume of activity	Machine hours per month	Cost
High	2,800	$2,720
Low	1,600	1,760

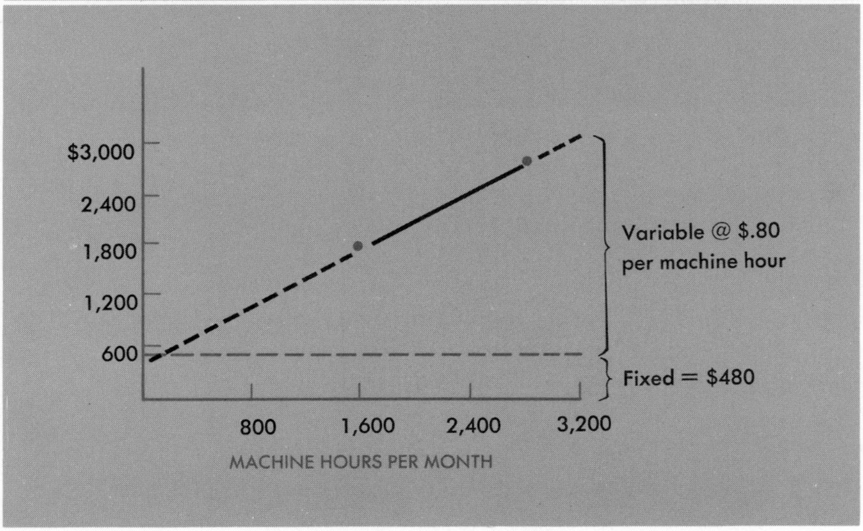

The division of costs into engineered, discretionary, and committed categories highlights the major factors that influence cost incurrence. Management policies often determine whether a cost will be planned and controlled as an engineered cost or as a discretionary cost.

Predictions of how costs will behave in response to various actions usually have an important bearing on a wide number of decisions. The cost function used to make these predictions is usually a simplification of underlying relationships. Whether this simplification is justified depends on how sensitive the manager's decisions are to the errors that the simplifications may generate. In some cases, additional accuracy may not make any difference; in other cases, it may be significant. The choice of a cost function is a decision concerning the cost and value of information.

Two common assumptions are widely used in cost analysis. First, cost behavior can be sufficiently explained by one independent variable. Second, linear approximations to cost functions are "good enough" for most purposes. The following guides for cost estimation and prediction should be used:

1. To the extent that physical relationships are observable, use them.
2. To the extent that relationships can be implicitly established by means of logic and knowledge of operations, use them—preferably in conjunction with step 3.
3. To the extent that relationships can be explicitly established via regression analysis, use them. The use of step 3 is a check on step 2. This step should never be taken before step 2 is performed.

Regression analysis is the most systematic approach to cost estimation. Unlike other approaches, it has measures of probable error and it can be applied when there are several independent variables instead of one. Nevertheless, regression has many assumptions and pitfalls, so professional help should be sought when it is applied.

The job of cost analysis is quickly complicated in the real world by a variety of causal factors that underlie any particular result. Modern cost accounting offers useful techniques, although they sometimes seem too crude for the task at hand. Measurement frequently seems to be performed with a yardstick rather than with a micrometer. But a yardstick is sufficient for many measurement problems for which a micrometer is either unnecessary or impractical.

SUMMARY PROBLEMS FOR YOUR REVIEW

Problem One

The Alic Company has many small accounts receivable. Work measurement of billing labor has shown that a billing clerk can process 2,000 customers' accounts per month. The company employs thirty billing clerks at an annual salary of $9,600 each. The outlook for next year is for a decline in the number of customers, from 59,900 to 56,300 per month.

Required:

1. Assume that management has decided to continue to employ the thirty clerks despite the expected drop in billings. Show two approaches, the engineered-cost approach and the discretionary-fixed-cost approach, to the budgeting of billing labor. Show how the *performance report* for the year would appear under each approach.

2. Some managers favor using tight budgets as motivating devices for controlling operations. In these cases, the managers really expect an unfavorable variance and must allow, in financial planning, for such a variance so that adequate cash will be available as needed. What would be the budgeted variance, also sometimes called expected variance, in this instance?

3. Assume that the workers are reasonably efficient. (a) Interpret the budget variances under the engineered-cost approach and the discretionary-fixed-cost approach. (b) What should management do to exert better control over clerical costs?

Problem Two

The Delite Company has its own power plant. All costs related to the production of power have been charged to a single account, Power. We know that the total cost for power was $24,000 in one month and $28,000 in another month. Total machine hours in those months were 120,000 and 160,000, respectively. Express the cost behavior pattern of the Power account in formula form.

Solution to Problem One

1. Engineered-cost approach:

Standard Unit Rate = $9,600 ÷ 2,000 = $4.80 per customer per year

or = $.40 per customer per month

	Actual Cost	*Flexible Budget: Total Standard Quantity Allowed for Good Units Produced ×* *Standard Unit Rate*	*Budget Variance*
Billing-clerk labor	(30 × $9,600) $288,000	(56,300 × $.40 × 12 months) $270,240	$17,760 *U*

Discretionary-fixed-cost approach:

	Actual Cost	*Budget*	*Budget Variance*
Billing-clerk labor	$288,000	$288,000	—

2. The budgeted variance would be $17,760, unfavorable. The master budget for financial planning must provide for labor costs of $288,000; therefore, if the engineered-cost approach were being used for control, the master budget might specify:

Billing-clerk labor:

Control-budget allowance	$274,240
Expected control-budget variance	17,760
Total budget allowance for financial planning	$280,000

3. As the chapter explains, management decisions and policies are often of determining importance in categorizing a cost as fixed or variable. If management refuses, as in this case, to control costs rigidly in accordance with short-run fluctuations in activity, these costs are discretionary. The $17,760 variance represents the price that management, consciously or unconsciously, is willing to pay currently in order to maintain a stable work force geared to management's ideas of "normal needs."

Management should be given an approximation of such an extra cost. There is no single "right way" to keep management informed on such matters. Two approaches were demonstrated in the previous parts of this problem. The important point is that clerical workloads and capability must be measured before effective control may be exerted. Such measures may be formal or informal. The latter is often achieved through a supervisor's regular observation, so that he knows how efficiently work is being performed.

Solution to Problem Two

$$\text{Variable rate} = \frac{\text{Change in mixed cost}}{\text{Change in volume}} = \frac{\$28,000 - \$24,000}{160,000 - 120,000}$$

$$= \frac{\$4,000}{40,000} = \$.10 \text{ per machine hour}$$

Fixed component = Total mixed cost less variable component
At 160,000-hour level = $28,000 − $.10(160,000) = $12,000
Or, at 120,000-hour level = $24,000 − $.10(120,000) = $12,000
Cost formula = $12,000 per month + $.10 per machine hour

APPENDIX

Method of Least Squares

The method of least squares is the most accurate device for formulating the *past behavior* of a mixed cost.

The line itself is not plotted visually, however; it is located by means of two simultaneous linear equations:

$$\Sigma XY = a\Sigma X + b\Sigma X^2 \qquad (1)$$

$$\Sigma Y = na + b\Sigma X \qquad (2)$$

where a is the fixed component, b is the variable cost rate, X is the activity measure, Y is the mixed cost, n is the number of observations, and Σ means summation.

For example, assume that nine monthly observations of power costs are to be used as a basis for developing a budget formula. A scatter diagram indicates a mixed-cost behavior in the form $Y = a + bX$. Computa-

EXHIBIT 10-9

Least-Squares Computation of Budget Formula
for Mixed Cost

MONTH	MACHINE HOURS X	TOTAL MIXED COST Y	XY	X^2
1	22	$ 23	$ 506	484
2	23	25	575	529
3	19	20	380	361
4	12	20	240	144
5	12	20	240	144
6	9	15	135	81
7	7	14	98	49
8	11	14	154	121
9	14	16	224	196
	129	$167	$2,552	2,109

Source: *Adapted from* Separating and Using Costs As Fixed and Variable, N.A.A., Bulletin,
Accounting Practice Report No. 10 (New York, June, 1960), p. 13. For a more thorough explanation,
see any basic text in statistics or Charles T. Horngren, *Cost Accounting: A Managerial Emphasis*,
3rd ed., (Englewood Cliffs, N.J.: Prentice-Hall, Inc., 1972), Chapter 24.

tion of the budget formula by the method of least squares is shown in
Exhibit 10-9. The answer is: Total cost $9.82 per month + 60.9 cents per
machine hour. Substitute the values from Exhibit 10-9 into Equations 1
and 2:

$$\$2,552 = 129a + 2,109b \quad (1)$$
$$\$ \ 167 = \ 9a + \ 129b \quad (2)$$

Multiply Equation 1 by 3 $\quad \$7,656 = 387a + 6,327b$

Multiply Equation 2 by 43 $\quad \$7,181 = 387a + 5,547b$

Subtract: $\quad \$ \ 475 = 780b$

$$b = \$.609$$

Substitute $.609 for b in Equation 2 $\quad \$ \ 167 = 9a + 129(\$.609)$

$$a = \$9.82$$

Therefore, fixed cost is $9.82 and variable cost is 60.9¢ per machine hour.
A scatter diagram also should be prepared to see whether the derived
line seems to fit the existing cost data to a satisfactory degree. If not, then
factors other than volume or activity have also significantly affected total
cost behavior. In such instances, multiple regression techniques may
have to be used.

Fundamental Assignment Material

10-1. Terminology: Define: *committed costs; discretionary costs; managed costs; appropriation; order-getting cost;* and *order-filling cost.*

10-2. Clerical costs and the budgeting of variances. The Milwaukee Company has many small accounts receivable. Work measurement of billing labor has shown that a billing clerk can process 2,000 customers' accounts per month. The company employs thirty billing clerks at an annual salary of $4,800 each. Next year's outlook is for a decline in the number of customers, from 59,900 to 56,300 per month.

1. Assume that management has decided to continue to employ the thirty clerks despite the drop in billings. Show two approaches, the engineered-cost approach and the discretionary-cost approach, to the budgeting of billing labor. Show how the *performance report* for the year would appear under each approach.
2. Assume that the workers are reasonably efficient. (a) Interpret the budget variances under the engineered-cost approach and the discretionary-cost approach. (b) What should management do to exert better control over clerical costs?
3. Some managers favor using tight budgets as motivating devices for controlling operations. In these cases, the managers really expect an unfavorable variance and must allow, in financial planning, for such a variance so that adequate cash will be available as needed. What would be the budgeted variance, also sometimes called *expected variance,* in this instance?

10-3. Classification of cost behavior. Identify the following as (a) proportionately variable costs; (b) committed fixed costs; (c) discretionary fixed costs; (d) mixed costs; (e) step costs. More than one letter can be used in an answer. If in doubt, write a short explanation of why doubt exists.

1. Straight-line depreciation on a building.
2. Fork-lift truck operators' wages. One operator is needed for every 5,000 tons of steel sold monthly by a steel warehouse.
3. Property taxes on plant and equipment.
4. Advertising costs.
5. Research costs.
6. Total rental costs of salesmen's automobiles. Charge is a flat $60 per month plus 5¢ per mile.
7. Salesmen's total compensation, including salaries and commissions.
8. Total repairs and maintenance.
9. Foremen's salaries. A new foreman is added for every ten workers employed.
10. Management consulting costs.
11. Public accounting fees.
12. Management training costs.

10-4. Division of mixed costs into variable and fixed components. The president and the controller of the Tramer Transformer Company have agreed that refinement of the company cost classifications will aid planning and control decisions. They have asked you to approximate the formula for variable and fixed-cost behavior of repairs and maintenance from the following sparse data:

Monthly Activity in Direct Labor-Hours	Monthly Repair and Maintenance Costs Incurred
3,000	$1,700
5,000	2,300

Additional Assignment Material

10-5. Why are fixed costs also called capacity costs?

10-6. How do committed costs differ from discretionary costs?

10-7. How do the methods and philosophies of management affect cost behavior?

10-8. "Ideally, there should be no accounts for mixed costs." Explain.

10-9. Describe how mixed costs are budgeted.

10-10. "Variable costs are those that should fluctuate directly in proportion to sales." Do you agree? Explain.

10-11. How does the basic behavior of the cost of raw materials differ from that of clerical services?

10-12. "For practical budgeting purposes, costs do not have to be strictly variable in order to be regarded as variable." Explain.

10-13. "The objective in controlling step costs is to attain activity at the highest volume for any given step." Explain.

10-14. What is the primary determinant of the level of committed costs?

10-15. What is the primary determinant of the level of discretionary costs?

10-16. "Planning is far more important than day-to-day control of discretionary costs." Do you agree? Explain.

10-17. Distinguish between order getting and order filling.

10-18. When are planning and control techniques most effective?

10-19. What is the central purpose of analyzing order-getting costs?

10-20. What is the best single gauge of a salesman's effectiveness?

10-21. What is work measurement?

10-22. Why are committed costs the stickiest of the fixed costs?

10-23. "An unfavorable variance for discretionary costs would measure the failure to spend the entire appropriation." Do you agree? Explain.

10-24. **Identifying cost behavior patterns.** At a seminar, a cost accountant spoke on the classification of different kinds of cost behavior.

Mr. Fons, a hospital administrator who heard the lecture, identified several hospital costs and classified them. After his classification, Mr. Fons presented you with the following list of costs and asked you to classify their behavior as one of the following: variable; step; mixed; discretionary fixed; or committed fixed:

1. Straight-line depreciation of operating room equipment.
2. Costs incurred by Dr. X. Cise in cancer research.
3. Costs of services of Better-Run Hospital Consultant Firm.
4. Repairs made on hospital furniture.
5. Nursing supervisors' salaries (a supervisor is added for each forty-five nursing personnel).
6. Leasing costs of X-ray equipment ($7,500 a year plus $1\frac{1}{2}$ ¢ per film).
7. Training costs of an administrative resident.
8. Blue Cross insurance for all full-time employees.

10-25. Separation of hospital X-ray mixed costs into variable and fixed components. A staff meeting has been called at the High G. Dephicit Memorial Hospital by the new administrator, Buck Saver. Mr. Saver has examined the income statement and is particularly interested in the X-ray department. The chief radiologist, Dr. I. C. Throoyou, has demanded an increase in prices to cover the increased repair costs because of the opening of an outpatient clinic. He claims it is costing more per X-ray for this expense.

Mr. Saver asks the controller, Mr. Adam Upp, to approximate the fundamental variable and fixed-cost behavior of repairs and maintenance for the X-ray department and to prepare a graphic report he can present to Dr. Throoyou. Data for the relevant range follow:

	X-rays per Month	Monthly Repair and Maintenance Cost Incurred
Low volume	6,000	$3,400
High volume	10,000	5,400

Required:

As the controller, prepare the requested information.

10-26. Gilroy Business College, a private institution, is preparing a budgeted income statement for the coming academic year ending August 31, 19x4. Tuition revenue for the past two years ending August 31 were 19x3, $500,000; and 19x2, $550,000. Total expenses in 19x3 were $510,000 and in 19x2 were $530,000. No tuition rate changes occurred in 19x2 or 19x3, nor are any expected to occur in 19x4. Tuition revenue is expected to be $520,000 for the year ending August 31, 19x4. What net income should be budgeted for next year, assuming that the implied-cost behavior patterns remain unchanged?

10-27. Various cost behavior patterns. (CPA adapted.) Select the graph on page 328 that matches the numbered factory-cost or expense data. You are to indicate by letter which of the graphs best fits each of the situations or items described.

The vertical axes of the graphs represent *total* dollars of expense and the horizontal axes represent production. In each case, the zero point is at the intersection of the two axes. The graphs may be used more than once.

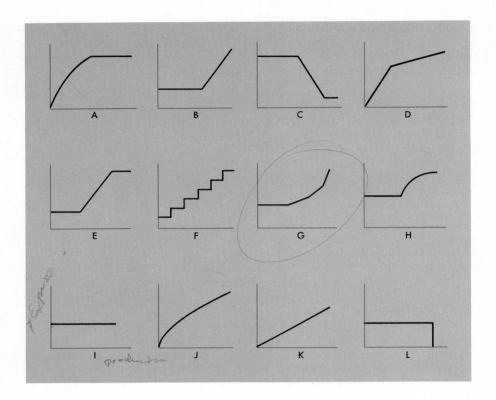

K 1. Depreciation of equipment, where the amount of depreciation charged is computed by the machine-hours method.

B 2. Electricity bill—a flat fixed charge, plus a variable cost after a certain number of kilowatt hours are used.

G 3. City water bill, which is computed as follows:

First 1,000,000 gallons or less	$1,000 flat fee
Next 10,000 gallons	.003 per gallon used
Next 10,000 gallons	.006 per gallon used
Next 10,000 gallons	.009 per gallon used
etc.	etc.

J 4. Cost of lubricant for machines, where cost per unit decreases with each pound of lubricant used (for example, if one pound is used, the cost is $10; if two pounds are used, the cost is $19.98; if three pounds are used, the cost is $29.94) with a minimum cost per pound of $9.25.

I 5. Depreciation of equipment, where the amount is computed by the straight-line method. When the depreciation rate was established, it was anticipated that the obsolescence factor would be greater than the wear-and-tear factor.

L 6. Rent on a factory building donated by the city, where the agreement calls for a fixed-fee payment unless 200,000 man-hours are worked, in which case no rent need be paid.

F 7. Salaries of repairmen, where one repairman is needed for every 1,000 machine-

328

hours or less (that is, 0 to 1,000 hours requires one repairman, 1,001 to 2,000 hours requires two repairmen, and so forth).

D 8. Federal unemployment compensation taxes for the year, where labor force is constant in number throughout the year (average annual salary is $6,000 per worker). Maximum salary subject to tax is $3,000 per employee.

K 9. Cost of raw materials used.

C 10. Rent on a factory building donated by county, where agreement calls for rent of $100,000 less $1 for each direct labor-hour worked in excess of 200,000 hours, but minimum rental payment of $20,000 must be paid.

10-28. Work Measurement. The Fremont Company has installed a work measurement program for its billing operations. A standard billing cost of 50¢ per bill has been used, based on hourly labor rates of $4 and an average processing rate of eight bills of ten lines each per hour. Each clerk has a 7½-hour work day and a five-day workweek.

The supervisor has received the following report of performance from his superior, the office manager, Mr. Davis, for a recent four-week period regarding his clerks:

	Actual	Budget	Variance Amount	Variance Equivalent Persons
Billing labor (5 clerks)	$3,000	(3,700 bills × $.50) $1,850	$1,150 U	1.9

The supervisor knows that he must explain the unfavorable variance and offer suggestions on how to avoid such an unfavorable variance in the future. Because of a recession, the office manager is under severe pressure to cut staff. In fact, he had penciled a question on the report, "Looks as if we can get along with two less clerks?"

Anticipating the pressures, the supervisor had taken a careful random sample of 400 of the 3,700 bills that were prepared during the period under review. His count of the lines in the sample totaled 5,200.

Required:

As the supervisor, prepare a one-page explanation of the $1,150 unfavorable variance, together with your remedial suggestions.

10-29. Flexible budgets and wages. The administrator of the Mavis Hotel has established a budget for the laundry department. The department's equipment consists of a washer that can process 500 pounds an hour. For every 100 pounds of linen processed, soap costs of 15¢ and water costs of 5¢ are incurred. One man operates the laundry. He works eight hours daily, six days per week, at $2 per hour.

The depreciation on the machine is $1,950 per year. The budget drawn by the administrator calls for $100 of overhead to be charged to the laundry for every four-week period. When the budget was established, the administrator thought that the expenses for the normal volume of linen would be $802 for a four-week period, including fixed expenses.

During the last four weeks, the laundry processed 72,000 pounds of linen, and incurred $814 in expenses, of which $145 was for soap, and $35 was for water. The man in charge of the laundry says he is doing a good job, because the budget calls for expenses of $802, and he incurred only $814.

Required:

1. What volume of laundry did the administrator use for his $802 budget for the four-week period?
2. Prepare a performance report that will give the administrator a method for evaluating the laundry.

10-30. Guaranteed minimum wages and cost behavior patterns. (Prepared by the author and adapted for use in a CPA examination.) The Lavin Company had a contract with a labor union that guaranteed a minimum wage of $500 payable monthly to direct laborers with at least twelve years of service. One hundred workers qualified for such coverage at the beginning of 19x1. All direct-labor employees are paid $5 per hour.

The budget for 19x1 was based on the usage of 400,000 hours of direct labor, a total of $2,000,000. Of this amount, $600,000 (100 men × $500 × 12 months) was regarded as fixed.

Data on performance for the first three months of 19x1 follow:

	January	*February*	*March*
Direct labor-hours actually worked	22,000	32,000	42,000
Standard direct labor-hours allowed*	22,000	32,000	42,000
Direct labor costs budgeted	$127,000	$162,000	$197,000
Direct labor costs incurred	110,000	160,000	210,000
Variance (*U* = Unfavorable, *F* = favorable)	17,000 *F*	2,000 *F*	13,000 *U*

*Note that perfect efficiency is being assumed.

The factory manager was perplexed by the results, which showed favorable variances when production was low and unfavorable variances when production was high. He felt that his control over labor costs was consistently good.

Required:

1. Why did the variances arise? Explain, using amounts and diagrams as necessary.
2. Does this direct-labor budget provide a basis for evaluating direct-labor performance? Explain, assuming that only 5,000 standard and actual hours were utilized in a given month. What variances would arise under the approach used in Requirement 1? Under the approach you recommend?
3. Suppose that 5,500 actual hours were used, but that only 5,000 standard hours were allowed for the work accomplished. What variances would arise under the approach used in Requirement 1? Under the approach you recommend?

10-31. Rudiments of least-square analysis. (Adapted from an analysis prepared by Robert Keyes). Assume that train-miles y traveled (and costs) are a function of the gross ton-miles x (tons times miles) of work to be performed. The records show:

Date	(x) Gross Ton-miles (Thousands)	(y) Train-miles
10-1	800	350
10-2	1,200	350
10-3	400	150
10-4	1,600	550

This example is used only to illustrate the methods that can be used for determining similar information. If, as in this instance, the number of observations is small, additional analysis should be performed to determine whether the results are reliable.

Required:

1. Draw a scatter diagram.
2. Use simple regression to fit a line to the data. What is the equation of the line? Plot the line.

10-32. Interpretation of regression coefficient. A manager learned about linear regression techniques at an evening college course. He decided to apply regression in his study of repair costs in his plant. He plotted twenty-four points for the past twenty-four months and fitted a least-squares line, where

$$\text{Total repair cost per month} = \$80,000 - \$.50x$$

where x = number of machine hours worked.

He was baffled because the result was nonsense. Apparently, the more the machines were run, the less the repair costs. He decided that regression was a useless technique.

Required:

Why was the puzzling regression coefficient negative? Do you agree with the manager's conclusions regarding regression? Explain.

10-33. Account analysis and cause and effect. The costs of maintenance of way and structures (M of W & S) are incurred by a railroad to continue in usable condition the fixed facilities employed in the carrier's railway operations. These costs are usually very material in relation to revenue and net income. A substantial portion of M of W & S costs is incurred on a cyclical program. For example, the costs are influenced by the tonnage that moves over the road for periods of up to or more than ten years. The costs are also influenced by management policy decisions and other nontraffic factors.

Required:

1. What are likely to be heavy influences (the influential independent variables) on the M of W & S costs for any given year? Be as specific as possible.
2. If M of W & S costs were estimated by simple regression using a measure of traffic (such as train-miles or gross ton-miles) as the independent variable, will the variable-cost portion (the b-coefficient) tend to be too high or too low? Why?

10-34. Method of least squares and sales forecasts. (SIA adapted.) The Progressive Company, Ltd., has recorded the following sales since its inception in 19x2:

19m2	$ 10,000
19m3	20,000
19m4	30,000
19m5	45,000
19m6	70,000
19m7	90,000
19m8	125,000
19m9	150,000
19n0	180,000
19n1	220,000
19n2	270,000

Required:

1. Calculate 19n3 sales, using the least-squares method.
2. If the directors have determined from an outside consultant that the cyclical factor in 19n4 will cause sales to be 10 percent above the forecast trend, what will they amount to?

10-35. Nonlinear cost behavior. Assume that total overhead cost depends on only one variable, direct labor-hours. The actual-cost behavior pattern is the non-linear function represented by curve (N) in the graph. Through statistical analysis or historical experience, we have the four points A, B, C, and D. If we use linear regression or visual fit, we are likely to obtain a linear relationship. Our budgeted overhead curve will be represented by line (L).

Suppose Foreman Smith controls direct labor, Manager Jones controls overhead, and Manager Johnson controls the whole plant. At the end of the period, actual hours are $0h_a$, actual overhead is $0e$, and the standard hours allowed for the work done are $0h_s$.

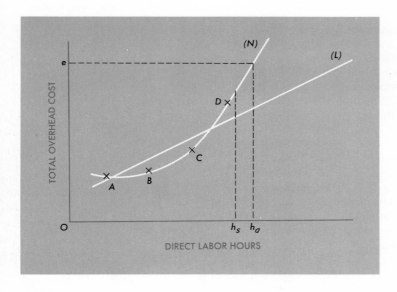

Required:

1. Suppose that the budget were based on line (L). Use the graph to measure the amount of the spending variance (call it ge), the efficiency variance (call it hg), and the budget variance (he).
2. Suppose that the budget were based on line (N). Would your answers to Requirement 1 be different? How? Be specific.
3. Compare your answers to those of Requirements 1 and 2. What are the likely effects on the attitudes of the three managers if line (L) is used as the basis for budgeting?

10-36. Two independent variables. Suppose that the cost behavior pattern of overhead is linear but two-dimensional—that is, cost incurrence depends on two independent variables, direct labor-hours, x_1, and machine-hours, x_2. For example, there may be two subdepartments, one heavily automated and one extremely labor-intensive. Therefore, the actual-cost behavior pattern is:

$$\text{Total overhead} = a + bx_1 + cx_2$$

where a = fixed costs, b = rate per direct labor-hour, and c = rate per machine-hour.

Using the traditional approach, the controller has examined the cost behavior of total overhead in relation to x_1 and x_2. He has decided to compute a budgeted-overhead function that is based on direct labor-hours:

$$\text{Budgeted total overhead} = a + bx$$

The results for the most recent reporting period appear on the following graph:

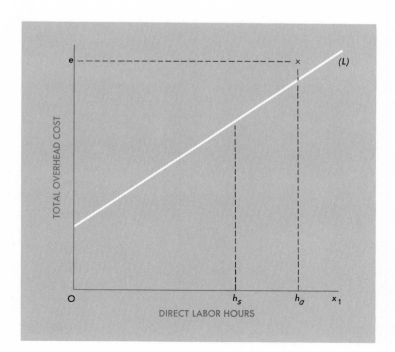

The budget is based on line (L). At the end of the period, actual hours are $0h_a$, the standard hours allowed for the work done are $0h_s$, and actual overhead is $0e$. Smith controls direct labor, James controls machine-hours, and Johnson is responsible for total overhead.

Required:

1. Use the graph to measure the amount of the spending variance (call it ge), the efficiency variance (call it gh), and the budget variance (he). Which of the three managers is ordinarily held responsible for each variance?
2. What are the likely effects on the attitudes of the three managers if line (L) is used as a basis for budgeting?

SUGGESTED READING

Beyer, R. and D. Trawicki, *Profitability Accounting for Planning and Control.* 2nd Ed. (New York: The Ronald Press Company, 1972).

Motivation, Responsibility Accounting, and Cost Allocation

11

This chapter takes an overview of the problem of management control and the design of control systems. It emphasizes behavioral factors, introduces responsibility accounting, and examines the imposing difficulties of cost allocation.

GOAL CONGRUENCE AND MOTIVATION

How should managers and accountants judge a given management accounting system? We need some criteria, some benchmarks to gauge the quality of a planning and control system. Too often, criteria concentrate on physical or data-processing aspects, emphasizing the detection of fraud and compliance with various legal requirements. However, such criteria are incomplete because they overlook the central purpose of a management control system. The primary question to ask about the benefit of such a system is whether it encourages managers, when working in their own best interests as they perceive them, to act simultaneously in harmony with the overall objectives of top management. This benefit has been called **goal congruence,** whereby goals and subgoals are specified to induce (or at least not discourage) decisions that will blend with top-management goals.

In turn, goal congruence requires **motivation,** which can be defined as the need to achieve some selected goal and the resulting drive that influences action toward that goal. There are two aspects of motivation: direction and strength—that is, top managers want subunit managers not only to *aim* toward top-management goals, but also to *strive* for them, to have a strong desire to reach them.

Obtaining goal congruence is essentially a behavioral problem. The incessant focus is on the motivational impact of a particular accounting system or method versus another system or method. For example, consider the following commonly encountered questions. Should standards and budgets be relatively tight or loose? Should performance be judged on the basis of sales, gross profit, contribution to fixed costs, net income, return on investment, or on some other basis? Should central corporate costs be fully allocated to divisions and departments? There are no clear-cut answers to these questions. A method that works well in one organization may flop in the next. Nevertheless, the answers must be framed in terms of the predicted motivational impact of the various alternatives. It may seem strange to view accounting systems in terms of their behavioral effects, but the task of the accountant is more complex, more ill-structured, and more affected by the human aspects than many people believe at first glance. A simple awareness of the importance of goal congruence and the motivational impact of systems is at least a first step toward getting a perspective on the design of accounting systems and the selection of accounting techniques.

Underlying all of this, of course, is the most basic decision of all. When a manager chooses a particular system, he is confronted with a decision regarding the cost and value of information. He must weigh the relative costs and benefits, given the particular circumstances of the specific organization that is considering one variety of control system over others. The trade-offs of costs and benefits form the dominant criterion for systems design and appraisal.

TOP-MANAGEMENT OBJECTIVES

To evaluate the accounting system for planning and control, the manager and the systems designer must begin by determining top management's stated (or unstated) objectives. For example, top management may *state* that the objective of the organization is the maximization of long-run earnings. Nevertheless, management may *act* so that the objective is really to "maximize reported earnings for next year regardless of other consequences."

The system should be judged in relation to how well any *given* objective is achieved. For example, top managers may specify that earnings for the following year should be $50 million. They may use the accounting system to communicate and enforce this objective. Near the end of the year, if the earnings prospects are gloomy, top managers may exert immense pressure to reach the budgeted target. To reach the earnings objective, subordinates may be inclined to reduce current expenses by postponing outlays for maintenance, sales promotion, or research, even though such decisions could cripple future earning power.

We may deplore these decisions, but our criticism should be aimed at top management's choice of objectives rather than at the system. Given the objective, the accounting system performed admirably as the helpmate of top management. The system should be judged in light of the objectives, whatever they may be.

There are assorted ways to reach top-management objectives. Some principal ways follow:

1. Use of multiple goals.
2. Acceptance of system goals as personal goals.
3. Design of organization structure to pinpoint responsibility.
4. Provision of timely, accurate, relevant data to guide acquisition and utilization of resources.

These means of motivation and coordination to obtain goal congruence will be discussed in the following four major sections. We should find these ideas useful when we then consider problems of cost allocation.

USE OF MULTIPLE GOALS

Various multiple goals are often specified as a way of giving operational meaning to some lofty overall goal. The specification must be concrete enough so that managers understand what is expected; this usually requires some form of measurement. For example, the General Electric Company has stressed multiple goals by stating that organizational performance will be measured in the following eight areas:

1. Profitability
2. Market position
3. Productivity
4. Product leadership
5. Personnel development
6. Employee attitudes
7. Public responsibility
8. Balance between short-range and long-range goals

Note that the first goal, profitability, usually is measured in terms of a single year's results. The thrust of the other goals is to offset the inclination of managers to maximize short-run profits to the detriment of long-run profits.

Overstress on any single goal, whether it be short-run profits or some other goal, usually does not promote long-run profitability. Instead, coordination of goals is blocked; one goal may be achieved while others are neglected.

Example. As already mentioned, there are many questionable ways to improve short-run performance. Examples include stinting on repairs, quality control, advertising, research, or training. A manager may successfully exert pressure on employees for more productivity for short spurts of time. This may have some unfavorable long-run overtones.

Example. Litton's business-equipment group has been ill-starred for a long time—perhaps ever since Litton entered the field with its acquisition of Monroe in 1958 ... the pretax profit margin on sales is 7 to 9 percent. By comparison, the average for the business-equipment industry is 20 percent.

Contrary to what might be expected from its record in other fields, Litton so far has rarely been at the forefront of business-machine technology. One reason, ironically, may have been an overemphasis on immediate profits. By tying managers' incentives to their current return on gross assets, Litton may have inadvertently discouraged them from spending enough on research and development.[1]

Example. An executive of a major corporation described the following situation. Central headquarters ordered all plants to reduce their inventories of supplies from a ninety-day to a sixty-day level. Subsequently, the internal audit staff discovered two interesting developments. Two of the plant managers really rode hard on the inventory amounts and achieved the requested reduction. In the first plant, the employees threw the factory supplies out the back door. In the second plant, their consciences hurt. They did not throw the supplies out. Instead, they hid the items throughout the plant.

Example. The Moscow Cable Company decided to reduce copper wastage, and actually slashed waste by 60 percent in a given year. But top management in the central government noticed that the company produced copper scrap worth only $40,000 instead of the $100,000 originally budgeted. The goals were so uncoordinated that the plant was fined $45,000 for not meeting the budget of $100,000 in scrap.

ACCEPTANCE OF SYSTEM GOALS AS PERSONAL GOALS

Acceptance Is the Key

Another means of attaining goal congruence is to get top-management goals accepted by managers as their personal goals. It is not enough for the system to specify subgoals so that they harmonize with top-management goals. Individual managers must *accept* the subgoals as their personal goals. In this way, managers, working in their best self-interest as they perceive it, will make goal-congruent decisions. For example, how important is conformity to a budget prediction? If conformity is accepted by the manager as being important, and the accounting feedback is regarded as the most important source of information regarding his own appraisal of self-worth (for example, it tells him, "I am competent"), then the budget will be a crucial part of the control system.

Of course, the accounting system is only one of many control systems that influence an individual's behavior. Society as a whole can be

[1]William S. Rukeyser, "Litton Down to Earth," *Fortune,* April, 1968.

viewed as a control system, and various institutions can impinge on an individual's values and reactions. For example, a person can be affected by his family, religion, profession, company, department, and so forth. This point may be obvious, but it is not trivial.

The budgetary accountant may try to influence the individual's acceptance of goals. However, his influence may be overwhelmed by the values of society and the feedback information from other sources. Furthermore, in practice it is very hard to detect and allow for the variations in perceived individual self-worths. For example, the design of budget systems for professional personnel, such as research scientists, is often particularly difficult. This is undoubtedly partially attributable to the phenomenon that perceived self-worth may be little affected by the formal control system *per se*. In short, propositions such as "It's important to adhere to budget" may be relatively unimportant to a researcher. Moreover, his feedback sources are more likely to be informal than formal. The opinions of co-workers and external critics may count heavily.

Thus, although the motivational effects of accounting systems are often weighty, in some parts of the organization they may simply be unimportant. Personal goals, to the extent that acceptance of goals(such as budget goals) can be affected by formal systems within the organization, are likely to be heavily influenced by how higher executives support the system. Without massive top-management backing, the goals specified by the system, which should aim at goal congruence, are less likely to gain acceptance as personal goals. Note, too, that acceptance is the key; acceptance may be best achieved in some cases by participatory processes and in other cases by authoritative processes.

Slack: A Universal Behavioral Problem

The budgetary process entails the setting of goals. If the budget is overemphasized or viewed as a rigid monitor of performance, managers and employees are induced toward behavior that is usually not consonant with the typical goals of the organization as a whole. When the budget is administered too rigidly, a manager is sometimes inhibited from incurring a departmental cost that will exceed the budget ceiling but that will clearly produce a net benefit for the organization as a whole and the department. Another example of incongruent behavior is frequently found in not-for-profit organizations, which usually stipulate a spending limit. This creates a philosophy of "We'd better spend it or we'll lose it," which does not lead to long-range cost reduction. Similarly, managers in industry are often disinclined to reduce costs because this leads to cuts in budget allowances for future periods. In other words, cost-cutting performance now may generate temporary praise or rewards but will make the job tougher later because the future budget will not be as easy to attain.

The personal goals of managers (personal income, size of staff, esteem, power) will often lead to a "bargained" budget, whereby managers intentionally create *slack* as a protective device.[2] Slack can be defined in a cost context as the difference between the minimum necessary costs and the actual costs of the firm. (Slack may be called *padding* in some organizations.) This seeking of slack permeates all budgeting in every conceivable sort of organization. Little has been done to counteract it.

An example of the attempt to reduce slack is the widespread use of lump-sum rewards to managers and other employees for "permanent" cost-savings. Another example is allowing the manager to "keep" the saving, in the form of not tightening the budget for a specified subsequent span of one to three years. Therefore, even though the old cost budget of $100,000 should be decreased to $90,000 because of the discovery of a new production method, the cut may be postponed for a year or more. Despite these attempts at counteraction, slack remains as one of the major unsolved problems in budgetary control.

Of course, the ruthless elimination of slack is probably undesirable because it would result in too much inflexibility in decision making. There may be an unknown and unmeasurable optimal amount of slack for every organization.

ORGANIZATION STRUCTURE AND PINPOINTING RESPONSIBILITY

Responsibility Accounting Approach

Another principal way of promoting goal congruence is to tailor the accounting system to the organization in order to strengthen motivation. The design of an organizational structure and a control system should be interdependent. Practically, however, the organizational structure is often regarded as a given when systems are modified or constructed. To work optimally, top managers subdivide activities and stipulate a hierarchy of managers who oversee some predetermined sphere of activities and who have some latitude to make decisions in that sphere. The sphere of responsibility may be termed a cost center; or, if the manager must also make decisions about sales or investments, the responsibility sphere may be in the form of a profit center or investment center. Some type of responsibility accounting usually accompanies this delegation of decision making.

The impact of the responsibility-accounting approach is described in the following:

> The sales department requests a rush production. The plant scheduler argues that it will disrupt his production and cost a substantial though not

---

[2]M. Schiff and A. Lewin, "Where Traditional Budgeting Fails," *Financial Executive,* Vol. XXXVI, No. 5, 51–62; and "The Impact of People on Budgets," *The Accounting Review,* Vol. XLV, No. 2 (April 1970), 259–69.

clearly determined amount of money. The answer coming from sales is: "Do you want to take the responsibility of losing the X Company as a customer?" Of course the production scheduler does not want to take such a responsibility, and he gives up, but not before a heavy exchange of arguments and the accumulation of a substantial backlog of ill feeling. Analysis of the payroll in the assembly department, determining the costs involved in getting out rush orders, eliminated the cause for argument. Henceforth, any rush order was accepted with a smile by the production scheduler, who made sure that the extra cost would be duly recorded and charged to the sales department—"no questions asked." As a result, the tension created by rush orders disappeared completely; and, somehow, the number of rush orders requested by the sales department was progressively reduced to an insignificant level.[3]

Ideally, particular revenues and costs are recorded and automatically traced to the one individual in the organization who shoulders primary responsibility for the item. He is in the best position to evaluate and to influence a situation—to exert control. In practice, the diffusion of control throughout the organization complicates the task of collecting relevant data by responsibility centers. The organizational networks, the communication patterns, and the decision-making processes are complex—far too complex to yield either pat answers or an ideal management accounting system.

Illustration of Responsibility Accounting

The simplified organization chart in Exhibit 11-1 will be the basis for our illustration. We will concentrate on the manufacturing phase of the business. The lines of responsibility are easily seen in Exhibit 11-2, which is an overall view of responsibility reporting. Starting with the supervisor of the machining department and working toward the top, we shall see how these reports may be integrated through three levels of responsibility.

Exhibit 11-3 shows the same relationships as those in Exhibit 11-2, but in greater detail. All the variances shown may be subdivided for further analysis, either in these reports or in more detailed reports.

Note that each of these three responsibility reports furnishes the department head with figures on only those items subject to his control. Items not subject to his control are removed from these performance reports; he should not receive data that may clutter and confuse his decision making.

Trace the $72,000 total from the machining department report in Exhibit 11-3 to the production vice-president's report. The vice-president's report merely summarizes the reports of the three individuals under his jurisdiction. He may also want copies of the detailed statements of each supervisor responsible to him.

---

[3]Raymond Villers, "Control and Freedom in a Decentralized Company," *Harvard Business Review*, Vol. XXXII, No. 2, 95.

EXHIBIT 11-1
Lustre Co.: Simplified Organization Chart

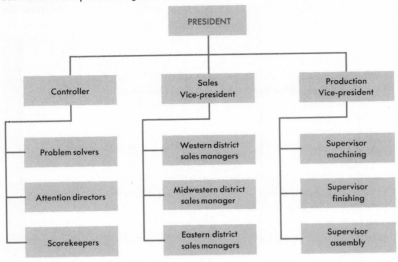

EXHIBIT 11-2
Responsibility Reporting at Various Management Levels

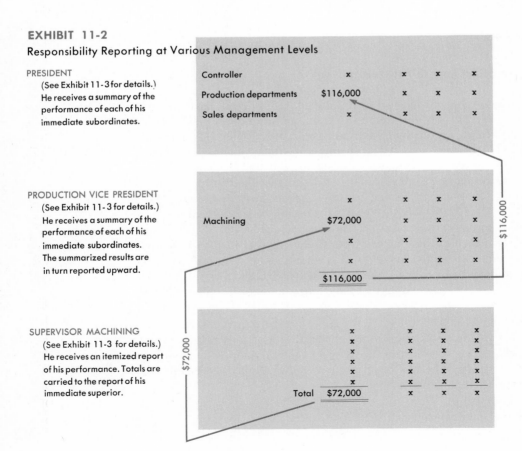

PRESIDENT

(See Exhibit 11-3 for details.) He receives a summary of the performance of each of his immediate subordinates.

Controller	x	x	x	x
Production departments	$116,000	x	x	x
Sales departments	x	x	x	x

PRODUCTION VICE PRESIDENT

(See Exhibit 11-3 for details.) He receives a summary of the performance of each of his immediate subordinates. The summarized results are in turn reported upward.

	x	x	x	x
Machining	$72,000	x	x	x
	x	x	x	x
	x	x	x	x
	$116,000			

$116,000

SUPERVISOR MACHINING

(See Exhibit 11-3 for details.) He receives an itemized report of his performance. Totals are carried to the report of his immediate superior.

$72,000

	x	x	x	x
	x	x	x	x
	x	x	x	x
	x	x	x	x
	x	x	x	x
	x	x	x	x
Total	$72,000	x	x	x

EXHIBIT 11-3

LUSTRE CO.
President's Monthly Responsibility
Performance Report

	BUDGET		VARIANCE: FAVORABLE, (UNFAVORABLE)	
	THIS MONTH	YEAR TO DATE	THIS MONTH	YEAR TO DATE
President's office	$ 6,000	$ 20,000	$ 100	$ 400
Controller	4,000	13,000	(200)	(1,000)
Production vice-president	116,000	377,000	(8,950)	(20,600)
Sales vice-president	40,000	130,000	(1,000)	(4,000)
Total controllable costs	$166,000	$540,000	$(10,050)	(25,200)

Production Vice-President's
Monthly Responsibility
Performance Report

	BUDGET		VARIANCE: FAVORABLE, (UNFAVORABLE)	
	THIS MONTH	YEAR TO DATE	THIS MONTH	YEAR TO DATE
Vice-president's office	$ 9,000	$ 29,000	$ (1,000)	$ (1,000)
Machining department	72,000	236,000	(2,950)	(11,600)
Finishing department	15,000	50,000	(2,000)	(3,000)
Assembly department	20,000	62,000	(3,000)	(5,000)
Total controllable costs	$116,000	$377,000	$ (8,950)	$(20,600)

Machining Department
Supervisor's Monthly Responsibility
Performance Report

	BUDGET		VARIANCE: FAVORABLE, (UNFAVORABLE)	
	THIS MONTH	YEAR TO DATE	THIS MONTH	YEAR TO DATE
Direct material	$ 40,000	$140,000	$ (1,000)	$ (4,000)
Direct labor	25,000	75,000	(2,000)	(7,000)
Setup	4,000	12,000	400	100
Rework	2,000	6,000	(200)	(300)
Supplies	200	600	(40)	(100)
Small tools	300	900	(50)	(100)
Other	500	1,500	(60)	(200)
Total controllable costs	$ 72,000	$236,000	$ (2,950)	$(11,600)

Also trace the $116,000 total from the production vice-president's report to the president's report. His summary report includes data for his own office plus a summarization of the entire company's current cost-control performance.

To simplify the illustration, only engineered costs are shown in the exhibits. However, an individual manager may exert control over many discretionary costs, which could also be included, separately labeled.

Format of Feedback Reports

This set of illustrative reports shows only the budgeted amount and the variance, which is defined as the difference between the budgeted and the actual amounts. This places the focus on the variances and illustrates *management by exception,* which means that the executive's attention is concentrated on the important deviations from budgeted items. In this way, managers do not waste time on those parts of the reports that reflect smoothly running phases of operations.

Of course, this illustration is only one possible means of presenting a report of performance. Another common reporting method shows three sets of dollar figures instead of two sets. Moreover, the variances could also be expressed in terms of percentages of budgeted amounts. For example, direct labor in the machining department could appear as follows:

	Budget		Actual Results		Variance: Favorable, (Unfavorable)		Variance: Percent of Budgeted Amount	
	This Month	*Year to Date*	*This Month*	*Year to Date*	*This Month*	*Year to Date*	*This Month*	*Year to Date*
Direct labor	$25,000	$75,000	$27,000	$82,000	$(2,000)	$(7,000)	(8.0%)	(9.4%)

The full performance report would contain a similar line-by-line analysis of all items. The exact format adopted in a particular organization depends heavily on user preferences.

Cooperation Versus Competition

A fragile balance must be struck between careful delineation of responsibility on the one hand, and a too-rigid separation of responsibility on the other hand. Buck passing is a pervasive tendency that is supposedly minimized when responsibility is fixed unequivocally.

> **Example.** A large utility used to hire college graduates and rotate them among all departments in the company during a two-year training program. Their salaries were not assigned to the departments, and individual managers took little interest in the trainees. But now it assigns the trainee to a definite department that fits his primary interest, where he is given direct

responsibility as soon as possible. Both the trainees and the managers are much more satisfied with the new responsibility arrangement.

But often the motivational impact boomerangs; too much falls between the chairs. Managers often wear blinders and concentrate more than ever on their individual worlds. Family cooperation is replaced by intracompany competition.

> **Example.** Two departments performed successive operations in a line-production process making automobile frames. The frames were transferred from the first to the second department via an overhead conveyor system. Because of machine breakdowns in his department, the Department 2 manager requested the Department 1 manager to slow down production. He refused, and the frames had to be removed from the conveyor and stacked to await further processing. A bitter squabble ensued regarding which department should bear the extra labor cost of stacking the frames.

Definition of Controllable Costs

Responsibility accounting has a natural appeal because it specifies a boundary of operations and distinguishes between controllable and uncontrollable costs. It is easy to say that a manager's performance should be judged on the basis of only those items subject to his control. But experienced cost accountants and managers will testify that it is far from easy to decide whether an item is controllable or uncontrollable. Moreover, there are shades of influence—an item may be controllable in whole or in part. Therefore, do not expect to get a crystal-clear, practical concept of a controllable cost. It does not exist. Still, accountants must grapple with this problem, even though their approaches are often coarse.

The concept of a controllable cost is associated with the implementation of decisions. It is a critical underpinning of the ideas of responsibility accounting. The basic idea is that only humans can influence the level of cost incurrence. The focus is on the activity or organization unit under the supervision of an individual. Controllable costs are those that may be directly regulated at a given level of management authority. Put another way, controllable costs are those that are directly influenced by a *manager* within a *given time span.*

The definition has two important ingredients. First, we cannot distinguish controllable from uncontrollable costs without specifying a level and scope of management authority. In other words, we must circumscribe the activity or organizational unit that is under the direction of the manager. For example, insurance costs on machinery may not be controllable by the manager of a producing department. However, such costs may indeed be controllable by the manager of the insurance department.

Second, the time-period assumption is important. If the time period were long enough, virtually all costs would be controllable by somebody in the organization. On the other hand, as the time period shortens, very few costs may be controllable. In the insurance example, note that the cost of a one-year insurance policy might not be controllable, even by the insurance manager, if the time period for evaluation were a week or a month instead of a year. In contrast, the rent on a building having a thirty-year lease could be viewed as controllable by the building and facilities manager if the time period used for evaluation were thirty years.

Determining Controllability or Responsibility

The main trouble for the designer of a responsibility accounting system is that controllability is a matter of degree: (a) There are usually few costs that are clearly the *sole* responsibility of one person; and (b) the time-period problem is almost impossible to solve for many costs. Although controllability may often be difficult to pinpoint, responsibility account-ing nevertheless clings to a tough-minded approach. It asks: Who is the one person in the organization with the most decision-making power over the item in question? This is usually the executive who most closely super-vises the day-to-day activities that influence that cost. He typically has the authority to accept or reject the material or service in question. There-fore, he must bear the responsibility, and so must his superiors.

If the manager is responsible for both the acquisition and the use of the service, the cost should be deemed as controllable by him. However, the diffusion of control throughout the organization complicates the task of collecting data by responsibility centers. For example, raw-material *prices* may be most affected by the decisions of the purchasing officer, whereas raw-material *usage* may be most strongly influenced by the pro-duction supervisor.

As Chapter 9 (pp. 279–80) showed in detail, the management ac-countant approaches this problem by charging the production department for raw materials at predetermined unit prices rather than actual unit prices. In this way, month-to-month price fluctuations do not affect the performance of the production supervisor. Predetermined prices (most often called *budgeted* or *standard* prices) are frequently utilized so that performance measures may exclude the possible misleading effects of changes in unit prices.

The whole complex problem of allocating indirect costs to depart-ments, territories, products, and other cost objects, as we shall see later in this chapter, illustrates how messy the idea of fixing responsibility or controllability can become. There are many instances when a manager can indirectly influence the amount of cost incurred. For instance, if a repair and maintenance department renders service to many departments, the level of repair costs borne by any production supervisor for nonrou-tine repairs can be affected by the wage rates in the repair department, the efficiency of the repair work force, the supervisory skills of the repair foreman, the efficiency of the production workers, the timing and care of the ordinary repairs done by regular production personnel, and so on.

Reporting Controllable and
Uncontrollable Items

347

**Motivation,
Responsibility
Accounting, and
Cost Allocation**

In a given situation, therefore, some costs may be regarded as controllable with various degrees of influence and others as uncontrollable. Most advocates of responsibility accounting favor excluding the uncontrollable items from a performance report. For example, the report for a shop foreman's department would contain only his controllable costs. Such items as property taxes and rent would not appear on his report; from his standpoint, these are uncontrollable costs.

The countervailing view is that uncontrollable items that are indirectly caused by the existence of the foreman's department should be included in his report. In this way, managers become aware of the whole organization and its costs. The behavioral implication of this idea is that some managers in the organization influence almost every cost; by also assigning that cost to some other executives in the organization, these executives will be more inclined to influence the manager who has primary control over the cost.

> **Example.** A president of a large corporation insists that central basic research costs be fully allocated to all divisions despite objections about uncontrollability. His goal is to force division managers' interests toward such research activity. The basic question is whether the accounting system is the best vehicle for reaching such an objective. Indiscriminate cost allocations may undermine the confidence of the managers in the entire accounting system.

But there is also a pitfall here. There can be overdependence on an accounting system as being the prime means of motivation and the final word on the appraisal of performance. Although the system may play a necessary role in coordination and motivation, its many limitations deserve recognition, too, particularly in matters of cost allocations. A common complaint of managers, often marked by tones of discouragement, is that they are being unfairly charged with uncontrollable costs. In any event, if management insists that both controllable and uncontrollable costs appear on the same report, these costs should not be mingled indiscriminately.

The Time Period and Control

The influence of the time period on determining whether a cost is controllable is a vexing problem. Too often, managers are inclined to oversimplify by assuming that variable costs are controllable and fixed costs are uncontrollable. Such thinking may lead to erroneous conclusions. For example, rent is uncontrollable by the assembly foreman, but it may be controllable by, say, the executive vice-president, who is assigned the responsibility of choosing plant facilities and of deciding whether to own or rent. Moreover, managers frequently have the option of trading off variable for fixed costs—for example, by purchasing labor-saving devices.

Some of the most severe analytical difficulties arise because of the existence of long-run costs like depreciation. How, for example, should depreciation be regarded in a situation where (a) a department already has all its needed equipment, (b) the current department manager has inherited the equipment from his predecessor, and (c) the life of the equipment is long? In such a situation, the main control must be exerted at the time of acquisition of the equipment; once incurred, the level of cost may be hard to influence for many years. Later in this chapter, Exhibit 11-4 shows a possible way to report costs so that these long-run committed costs are sharply differentiated from other costs that are subject to short-run decisions.

PROVISION OF TIMELY, ACCURATE, RELEVANT DATA

Data must be timely, accurate, and relevant to help managers make optimal decisions about the acquisition and utilization of resources. Here we concentrate on accuracy and relevancy, the two aspects that have the most bearing on the motivational influences of a system.

Accurate Scorekeeping

Textbooks do not devote much space to the problems of obtaining accurate source documents. Yet this is easily one of the most pervasive, everlasting problems in collecting information. An accounting system cannot help managers predict and make decisions if its scorekeeping is haphazard.

Pressures may spur managers to encourage their subordinates to record time erroneously or to tinker with scrap or usage reports.

> **Example.** The maintenance crews of one telephone company regularly performed recurring short-term maintenance and repair work on various projects. At other times, the same crews would be concerned with huge construction projects—installing or building plant and equipment. The company had weekly reports on performance of the regular maintenance work, but had only loose control over the construction projects. An investigation disclosed that the foremen were encouraging the workmen to boost the time on the construction projects and to understate the time on the regular maintenance projects. Thus the foremen's performance on the latter always looked good. The situation was corrected when the emphases on maintenance and on construction were balanced so that both were currently budgeted and controlled.

Again, accurate record keeping is essentially a problem of motivation. The accountant and manager should be more sensitive to possible errors, more aware of the futility of trying to get usage of time and materials reported accurately in small increments, and more conscious of the natural tendency of individuals to report their activities so as to minimize their personal bother and maximize their own showing.[4] The hazard of trying to get extremely detailed reports extends not only to lack of confidence in individual reports themselves but to the likelihood of generating monumental contempt for the entire system.

Top managers can induce accurate scorekeeping if they can persuade subordinates that the documents are important for decision making. Again we see the need for active management support:

> **Example.** A firm of civil engineers has surveying jobs throughout California that are largely obtained by firm price quotations. A key to profitability is the ability to predict how much time will be required for the various subtasks on the job. The president of the firm feels so strongly about the need for feedback that his field crew managers must mail daily time reports to the central office. If they are not received on the day expected, the president immediately phones to find out why.

Intelligent Analysis of Relevant Data

The accounting system should produce information that leads managers toward correct decisions regarding either evaluation of performance or selection among courses of action. Intelligent analysis of costs is often dependent on explicit distinctions between cost behavior patterns, which is more likely to be achieved via the contribution approach than via traditional methods. The general tendency toward indiscriminate full-cost allocations raises analytical dangers.

> **Example.** A bakery distributed its products through route salesmen, each of whom loaded a truck with an assortment of products in the morning and spent the day calling on customers in an assigned territory. Believing that some items were more profitable than others, management asked for an analysis of product costs and sales. The accountants to whom the task was assigned allocated all manufacturing and marketing costs to products to obtain a net profit for each product. The resulting figures indicated that some of the products were being sold at a loss, and management discontinued these products. However, when this change was put into effect, the company's overall profit declined. It was then seen that, by dropping some products, sales revenues had been reduced without commensurate reduction in costs because the joint manufacturing costs and route sales costs had to be continued in order to make and sell remaining products.[5]

The foregoing example demonstrates the importance of knowing how various costs behave. Intelligent cost analysis is impossible unless

---

[4]Also see Sam E. Scharff, "The Industrial Engineer and the Cost Accountant," *N.A.A. Bulletin*, Vol. XLII, No. 7, Section 1, for more examples.

[5]Walter B. McFarland, "The Field of Management Accounting," *N.A.A. Bulletin*, Vol. XLV, No. 10, Sec. 3, 19.

the manager can distinguish among controllable and uncontrollable costs, variable and fixed costs, and separable and joint costs. Moreover, he must be able to interpret unit costs wisely.

THE CONTRIBUTION APPROACH TO COST ALLOCATION

Cost allocation, the tracing of costs to cost objects, is an inescapable problem in nearly all organizations. Various organizations use diverse terminology to describe this tracing procedure: cost allocation, assignment, apportionment, reapportionment, and distribution. We use *cost allocation* here, but be alert for variations in terms. Although the answers often are not clearly right or wrong, at least we shall become acquainted with the dimensions of the problem of cost allocation.

Stress on Cost Behavior Patterns

The most frequently encountered cost objects are responsibility centers or products. Cost objects can be any *segment* (a line of activity or part of an organization) for which a separate computation of costs is sought. The contribution approach provides a valuable general framework for cost allocation because it is applicable to all types of cost objects and because it spotlights the cost behavior patterns that are nearly always essential for evaluating performance and making decisions.

Exhibit 11-4 illustrates the contribution approach to cost allocation. This is an unusually important exhibit because it provides a sweeping glimpse of how accounting information may be organized to facilitate decisions and their implementation. The stress is on cost behavior patterns. Failure to distinguish cost behavior patterns is an obstacle to clarity in cost analysis.

Revenues, Variable Costs, and Contribution Margins

The allocation of revenue and of variable costs is usually straightforward, because each item is directly and specifically identifiable with a given segment of activity. The Contribution Margin, Line (a) in Exhibit 11-4, is particularly helpful for predicting the impact on income of short-run changes in volume. Changes in income may be quickly calculated by multiplying the change in units by the unit contribution margin or by multiplying the increment in dollar sales by the contribution-margin ratio. For example, suppose the contribution-margin ratio of meats is $120 ÷ $300 = 40 percent. The increase in net income resulting from a $20 increase in sales can be readily computed as .40 × $20, or $8.

EXHIBIT 11-4

The Contribution Approach:
Model Income Statement, by Segments*
(In thousands of dollars)

| | RETAIL FOOD COMPANY AS A WHOLE | COMPANY BREAKDOWN INTO TWO DIVISIONS | | POSSIBLE BREAKDOWN OF BRANCH B ONLY | | | | POSSIBLE BREAKDOWN OF BRANCH B, MEATS ONLY | | |
		BRANCH A	BRANCH B	NOT ALLOCATED†	GROCERIES	PRODUCE	MEATS	NOT ALLOCATED†	STORE 1	STORE 2
Net sales	$4,000	$1,500	$2,500	—	$1,300	$300	$900	—	$600	$300
Variable costs:										
Cost of merchandise sold	$3,000	$1,100	$1,900	—	$1,000	$230	$670	—	$450	$220
Variable operating expenses	260	100	160	—	100	10	50	—	35	15
Total variable costs	$3,260	$1,200	$2,060	—	$1,100	$240	$720	—	$485	$235
(a) Contribution margin	$ 740	$ 300	$ 440	—	$ 200	$ 60	$180	—	$115	$ 65
Less: Fixed costs controllable by segment managers**	260	100	160	$ 20	40	10	90	$ 30	35	25
(b) Contribution controllable by segment managers	$ 480	$ 200	$ 280	$(20)	$ 160	$ 50	$ 90	$(30)	$ 80	$ 40
Less: Fixed costs controllable by others‡	200	90	110	20	40	10	40	10	22	8
(c) Contribution by segments	$ 280	$ 110	$ 170	$(40)	$ 120	$ 40	$ 50	$(40)	$ 58	$ 32
Less: Unallocated costs***	100									
(d) Income before income taxes	$ 180									

*Three different types of segments are illustrated here: branches, product lines, and stores. As you read across, note that the focus becomes narrower: from Branch A and B, to Branch B only, to Meats in Branch B only.

†Only those costs clearly identifiable to a product line should be allocated.

**Examples are certain advertising, sales promotion, salesmen's salaries, management consulting, training and supervision costs.

‡Examples are depreciation, property taxes, insurance, and perhaps the segment manager's salary.

***These costs are not clearly or practically allocable to any segment except by some highly questionable allocation base.

Unallocated Costs

An unallocated cost is common to all the segments in question and is not clearly or practically assignable except on some questionable basis. Examples of unallocated costs may be the salaries of the president and other top officers, basic research and development, and some central corporate costs like public relations or corporate-image advertising. These are usually fixed costs.

Discretionary and committed costs may or may not be allocated, *depending on the segments in question.*

In Exhibit 11-4, a retail food company's outlay for a newspaper advertisement may easily be identified with a territorial branch in a territorial income statement. The cost of the advertisement may also be readily split between groceries, produce, and meats. However, allocating the cost between the stores is more questionable. Consequently, it may be unallocated in an income statement by stores.

Similarly, the salary of a branch meat merchandise manager may be directly identified with a breakdown of the branch's activities by product lines, but the same cost may be unallocable to individual stores. Thus, a given cost may be allocated with respect to one segment of the organization and unallocated with respect to another.

Contribution Controllable by Segment Managers

As Chapter 16 explains more fully, a distinction should be made between the performance of the segment manager and the performance of the segment as an economic investment. That distinction is keyed in the form of subtotals (b) and (c) in Exhibit 11-4. Our earlier discussion of controllability and uncontrollability stressed how performance may be affected by factors that are subject to varying degrees of influence by a particular manager.

The reason for this distinction comes sharply into focus if you consider that many companies deliberately assign their best manager to their least profitable divisions with the hope that improvements will be forthcoming. Unless some discrimination is made between the manager and the responsibility center as an economic entity, the skillful manager will be reluctant to accept assignments to troublesome responsibilities. Sometimes it takes a miracle worker to get a limping segment up to a minimally acceptable level of income.

What version of income is most appropriate for judging performance by division managers or product managers? The controllable contribution, keyed as item (b) in Exhibit 11-4, should be helpful, especially when it is interpreted in conjunction with the contribution margin. This will happen because most top managers can influence many fixed costs, particularly *discretionary fixed costs.* (Examples of these costs are given in Exhibit 11-4.) The incurrence of discretionary costs may have interacting effects on variable costs. For example, heavier outlays for maintenance, engineering, or management consulting may reduce repairs, increase machine speeds, heighten labor productivity, and so forth. Also, decisions on advertising, research, and sales-promotion budgets are necessarily related to expected impacts on sales volumes.

The line between controllable and uncontrollable costs must be drawn on a company-by-company basis. For example, some managements may prefer to have depreciation on some classes of plant and equipment deducted when item (2), the controllable contribution, is computed. Getting agreement as to these classifications may be bothersome, but it is not a Herculean task.

Tailor Making of Income Statements

The income statement in Exhibit 11-4 has four measures of performance, ranging from contribution margin through income before income taxes. There is nothing hallowed about these four illustrative measures; some organizations may want to use only two or three such measures. Income statements should be custom designed for management's use.

Furthermore, as a section in Chapter 10 ("Classifying Particular Costs") stressed, some questions will always arise about the appropriate classification or allocation of a particular cost. These issues usually can be resolved in a number of ways, as long as the managers involved understand the issues and the necessity for being arbitrary occasionally.

Contribution by Segments and Income Before Income Taxes

Contribution by segments, item (c) in Exhibit 11-4, is computed after deducting the fixed cost classified as uncontrollable by the managers in the short run. Although this figure may be helpful as a crude indicator of long-run segment profitability as an economic investment, it should definitely not influence appraisals of current performance of managers.

Income before taxes, item (d) in Exhibit 11-4, may sometimes be a helpful gauge of the long-run earning power of a whole company. However, it may be misleading to refine this ultimate measure by breaking it into segments (and still have the whole equal the sum of the parts).

It is difficult to see how segment performance can be judged on the basis of income after deductions for a "fair" share of general company costs over which the segment manager exerts no influence. Examples of such costs would be central-research and central-headquarters costs, including salaries of the president and other high officers. Unless the general company costs are clearly traceable to segments, allocation serves no useful purpose and should not be made. Therefore, income is not computed by segments in Exhibit 11-4.

This refusal to allocate some costs is the most controversial aspect of the contribution approach to the income statement. Accountants and managers are used to the whole being completely broken down into neat parts that can be added up again to equal the whole. In traditional segment income statements, all costs are fully allocated, so that the segments show final net incomes that can be summed to equal the net income for the company as a whole.

Of course, if management prefers a whole-equals-the-sum-of-its-parts net income statement, the unallocated costs may be allocated so that the segments show income figures that will cross-add to equal the income for the company as a whole. The important point is that the contribution approach distinguishes between various degrees of objectivity in cost allocations. As you read downward in Exhibit 11-4, you become less and less confident about the validity and accuracy of the cost allocations. A dozen independent accountants will be most likely to agree on how the variable costs should be allocated and least likely to agree on whether and how the unallocated costs should be accounted for.

Reports by Product Lines and Territories

The most widely used detailed operating statements are tabulated by product lines and by sales territories. The emphasis depends on the organization of the marketing function. Some companies have distinct product lines with separate sales forces and separate advertising programs, and their operating reports emphasize contributions by products. Other companies make a multitude of products that are promoted by brand-name advertising and that are all sold by the same salesmen. Their operating reports emphasize territorial or district sales and contributions to profit.

CHOOSING AMONG VARIOUS COST-ALLOCATION BASES

Allocation of Costs of Service Departments

The difficulties of allocation among departments are even more imposing than allocations to divisions and product lines. Although fine lines are hard to draw, departments may be usefully divided into two broad classes: (1) operating (line) departments and (2) service (staff) departments. Examples of the former are machining, drill press, other production departments, and sales departments. Service departments are those that exist solely to aid the operating departments by rendering specialized assistance or advice with certain phases of the work (e.g., internal auditing, personnel, production control, accounting, research, materials handling, maintenance and repair). Under responsibility accounting, service department costs are usually charged initially to the service department. Difficulties arise as to (1) whether all costs of all service departments should then be reallocated to the other operating and service departments benefiting therefrom, and (2) what basis is most justifiable for measuring such benefits received or services rendered.

Regarding point (1), service department costs are indeed generally reallocated. However, are there any service departments whose costs should not be allocated even though they clearly benefit the other parts of the organization? Consider the internal auditing department or the legal department as examples. Ordinarily, where the other department managers have no discretion over their consumption of such services, the argument in favor of reallocation rests on the idea that the costs should be assigned to those departments benefited and that managers generally do not get overly concerned about such allocations as long as all departments are subject to a uniform cost-reallocation procedure. The argument against the reallocation of such costs rests on the idea that no costs should be reallocated to a manager unless he has some direct influence over the services he receives.

In some organizations, however, operating managers may have much control over their usage of such services. Charging for the auditing or legal services on the basis of the amount provided may discourage their use even though such use may be very desirable from the standpoint of the organization as a whole. In such instances, either no charge may be made, or a flat annual fee may be charged regardless of the quantity of services consumed. For instance, a large automobile manufacturing company does not charge for its internal auditing services because it wants to encourage its managers to utilize such services.

As a general rule, the same objective will be attained by allocating a flat sum to the various departments regardless of actual use. A possible advantage of the latter is its retainer-fee effect, where the user feels that he is paying for the service in any event so he had better take advantage of its availability. Of course, there is always the danger that a few managers may demand too much of what they would then regard as a "free" service. Then some priority system must be instituted, and a method of charging on the basis of services consumed usually is finally adopted.

Some managers maintain that the effects of allocation procedures on the morale of operating departments are given too much attention. There are also important effects on the morale of the service-department employees—that is, unless the other departments are charged with service department costs, the service department staff is less likely to feel that it has the status of first-class citizenship as an integral part of the organization.

Procedures for Reallocation

As you probably suspect, there are many ways to reallocate service-department costs. They all are compromises, practical approximations of the ideal results which may be visualized in any given company as being theoretically best. The steps are as follows:

1. Service-department budgets are prepared by the department for the forth-coming year in light of expected levels of activity.
2. Exhibit 11-5 illustrates that there is a wide variety of bases for cost alloca-tion and reallocation. These bases are seldom changed. The choice of a base depends on a policy decision regarding the most likely trail between cause and effect or a historical study of persistent relationships that pro-vide a reliable basis for cost predictions.
3. Reallocation cost rates are developed by dividing the service-department budgets by the reallocation base chosen. For example:

$$\text{Building and grounds reallocation rate} = \frac{\text{Budgeted building and grounds department costs}}{\text{Reallocation base: number of square feet}}$$

Then the costs are reallocated to the producing departments on the basis of square feet occupied.

EXHIBIT 11-5

Typical Bases for Reallocation of Service-Department
Costs to Production Departments

SERVICE DEPARTMENT	BASE FOR REALLOCATION OF COSTS
Building Grounds	Square footage or cubic footage
Cafeteria	Number of workers
Cost Accounting	Labor hours
Engineering	*Analysis of services rendered each department; labor hours
Maintenance	Direct charges on basis of materials used plus hours worked for each department
Material Handling	Units carried; tonnage; hours of service rendered
Medical	Number of employees; labor hours; number of cases
Personnel or Employment	Number of workers; rate of labor turnover; number of workers hired; *analysis of time spent for each department
Production Planning and Control	Machine-hours; labor-hours; analysis of services rendered
Power	Metered usage; capacity of equipment; machine-hours; formula weighting capacity and machine-hours
Receiving, Shipping, and Stores	Pounds handled; requisitions; receiving slips; issues
Tool Room	Requisitions

*Sometimes detailed analyses or surveys are made of services rendered over two, six, or twelve months; the results of the "sample" are used as a basis for reallocation until conditions warrant another sample survey.

Some Complications

Exhibit 11-5 is a widely used straightforward approach to reallocation of service-department costs. Such a method ignores the following complicating factors that are sometimes allowed for in more refined systems:[6]

1. Certain items within a service department's budget may obviously be reallocated in a manner different from the rest of the items. Such items are culled and are assigned on a basis different from that used for other costs in the same service department. For example, the costs of a special cleanup work force under the jurisdiction of the Building and Grounds Department may be separately assigned to the Machining Department, if its work is confined to cleaning there.
2. There is always mutual or reciprocal service between service departments. For example, Personnel serves Buildings and Grounds, and vice versa. This reciprocity can be taken into account. Some companies use a sequential reallocation plan, whereby reallocation begins with the department that renders service to the greatest number of other service departments. Once a service department's costs have been reallocated, no subsequent service department costs are recirculated. Other companies use the theoretically most accurate method for reallocating reciprocal service: simultaneous linear equations that are quickly solved by digital computers.

Services Used and Facilities Provided

Services used is usually a clear-cut cause of cost incurrence: power, repairs, computers, and so on. But too often, no distinction is made between the variable costs and the fixed costs of such services. This lumping may result in allocations that portray inaccurate cause-and-effect relationships, particularly where fixed costs are significant. Although variable costs of such services may fluctuate in proportion to fluctuations in the services used during a given period, the fixed costs are more likely to be affected by long-range decisions.

The use of separate cost-allocation rates for variable and fixed costs is an attempt to recognize some differences in cause-and-effect relationships. Variable costs might be allocated on the basis of *services utilized.* Fixed costs might be allocated via a predetermined periodic lump sum for providing a fundamental *capacity to serve,* based on the needs of the operating departments that initially justified the incurring of the fixed costs. This may be maximum capacity or perhaps some "normal" percentage of maximum capacity.

The fixed costs of service departments usually arise because service departments must have a basic capability to provide for the fundamental demands of consuming departments. Therefore, to the extent feasible, such costs might be reallocated in accordance with the plans that generated such fixed commitments. Again, the reallocation depends on deci-

[6]For elaboration, see Charles T. Horngren, *Cost Accounting: A Managerial Emphasis,* 3rd ed. (Englewood Cliffs, N.J.: Prentice-Hall, Inc., 1972), Chapter 12.

sion needs. For example, what factors influence the equipping of power service departments or maintenance departments? If they are equipped with key men and machinery so that they may meet the peak needs of production departments, then the peak activity levels of the production departments should be the basis for reallocations of costs. If, on the other hand, they are equipped to meet the long-run average needs, then the "normal" level of activity in each production department should be the basis for reallocations of costs. Finally, if they are equipped because of the whims of the president, there is no preferable base for allocation.

How to Allocate for Planning and Control

The following guidelines should help in deciding on what procedures to use for reallocating service-department or division costs:

1. Plan and control the costs of service departments or divisions just like those of operating departments or divisions. The fundamental distinctions between variable- and fixed-cost behavior patterns should be preserved. Flexible budgets and standards should be used wherever feasible.
2. Use predetermined or budgeted unit prices or rates, not actual unit prices or rates, to charge departments.
3. Do not allow charges to a specific department to depend on how much of the service is being consumed by other departments.
4. Where feasible, use a dual system that distinguishes between variable and fixed costs.
5. Where feasible, charge on the basis of predetermined standard or budgeted times allowed for services rendered. This is especially applicable to routine service. In this way, the operating department is responsible for the overall quantity of services consumed, but not directly for fluctuations in unit prices or efficiency.

These points are illustrated in Problem Two of the Summary Problems for your Review at the end of this chapter.

Beware of Full Reallocation of Actual Costs

Many companies fully reallocate all service-department costs monthly on the basis of actual hours and costs used in servicing the needs of the operating departments. The rate used is obtained by dividing the total actual costs of the service department by the total hours actually used by the operating departments.

Consider the following example. There are two operating departments and one service department. The actual monthly costs of the service department are reallocated on the basis of the total machine-hours actually worked by the operating departments as shown at the top of Exhibit 11-6, for a 10,000-hour level. Note that the basic-cost behavior pattern of the service department is $6,000 monthly plus 40¢ per machine-hour used in the operating departments.

EXHIBIT 11-6
Reallocations of Service-Department Costs

AT A 10,000-MACHINE-HOUR LEVEL OF THE PRODUCTION DEPARTMENTS:	
Actual costs = $6,000 + $.40 (10,000 hours)	= $10,000
Rate per hour = $10,000 ÷ 10,000 = $1.00	
To Department 1: 5,000 hrs. × $1.00	= $ 5,000
To Department 2: 5,000 hrs. × $1.00	= 5,000
Total reallocated	$10,000

AT AN 8,000-MACHINE-HOUR LEVEL:	
Actual costs = $6,000 + $.40 (8,000 hours)	= $ 9,200
Rate per hour = $9,200 ÷ 8,000 hours = $1.15	
To Department 1: 5,000 hrs. × $1.15	= $ 5,750
To Department 2: 3,000 hrs. × $1.15	= 3,450
Total reallocated	$ 9,200

But suppose that one of the operating departments worked only 3,000 hours instead of 5,000 hours. The next section of Exhibit 11-6 shows the new results.

Note that there are two basic faults in fully reallocating costs on an actual basis instead of on a standard basis. First, a specific period's charges to an operating department depend on how much of the service is being consumed by the *other* operating department(s). In this example, given the same utilization of services as measured by the total labor-hours it actually incurred, Department 1 had 15 percent more costs (an increase from $5,000 to $5,750) solely because Department 2's volume declined.

Second, the amount charged is dependent on factors not directly subject to the control of the operating managers: the unit price and the efficiency of the services rendered. Frequently, operating managers do not complain so much about the allocation base used as they do about the total costs incurred by the service departments. If this service-department manager does not properly control his costs, his inefficiencies or high rates are routinely passed along to the producing departments.

Ability to Bear

When cause-and-effect relationships are impossible to establish, accountants and managers often resort to arbitrary bases. An often-misused base is actual sales dollars or gross margins or some other "ability-to-bear" base that often has a most tenuous causal relationship to the costs being allocated. The costs of administrative and central corporate effort are frequently independent of the results obtained, in the sense that the costs are budgeted by management discretion or in relation to sales *targets*. The point is that sales dollars may be a good surrogate for establishing cause-and-effect relationships, but there should always be a serious examination of whether a better base is available or whether any allocation is indeed warranted.

The use of revenue or sales as a base is a clear example of an "ability-to-bear" philosophy as contrasted with a services-rendered or benefits-received approach. A survey by the National Industrial Conference Board showed that 41 of 109 companies surveyed used actual sales as the sole base for allocating central expenses to divisions.[7] Sales is frequently a last resort in the search for a common denominator. The costs of efforts are independent of the results actually obtained in the sense that the costs are programmed by management, not determined by sales. Moreover, the allocation of costs on the basis of dollar sales entails circular reasoning— that is, the costs per segment are determined by relative sales per segment. For example, examine the effects in the following situation (figures represent millions of dollars):

	Product				
Year 1	*A*	*B*	*C*	*Total*	
Sales	$100	$100	$100	$300	(100%)
Costs allocated by dollar sales	$ 10	$ 10	$ 10	$ 30	(10%)

Assume that the dollar volume of *A* and *B* rises considerably. However, the direct costs and sales of Product *C* do not change. The total costs to be allocated on the basis of dollar sales are also unchanged.

	Product				
Year 2	*A*	*B*	*C*	*Total*	
Sales	$137.5	$137.5	$100.0	$375.0	(100%)
Costs allocated by dollar sales	$ 11.0	$ 11.0	$ 8.0	$ 30.0	(8%)

The ratio between the costs allocated on the basis of dollar sales and total sales was reduced in the second year to 8 percent ($30 ÷ $375), as compared with 10 percent ($30 ÷ $300) in the first year. This resulted in less cost being allocated to Product *C*, despite the fact that its unit volume and directly attributable costs were the same as for the first year. So the product that did the worst is relieved of costs without any reference to underlying causal relationships.

Advertising is a prime example of a cost that is typically allocated on

[7] *Allocating Corporate Expenses,* Studies in Business Policy, No. 108 (New York: National Industrial Conference Board), 13. This book has a good overall discussion of this topic.

the basis of dollar sales. Basing allocation on dollar sales *achieved* may be questionable, because the unsuccessful product or territory may be unjustifiably relieved of costs. However, there is some merit in basing allocation on *potential* sales or purchasing power available in a particular territory or for a particular product. For example, there would be a consistent relationship between the advertising costs and sales volume in each territory if all territories were equally efficient. If, however, a manager has poor outlets or a weak sales staff, one of the indicators would be a high ratio of advertising to sales.

FULLY ALLOCATED VERSUS PARTIALLY ALLOCATED COSTS

In nearly all organizations, every manager seems to get involved at some point in his career in a controversy regarding whether costs should be fully allocated to a department, product, or some other cost object. Costs are allocated ultimately for the purpose of decision making. The key question is, What difference does it make whether costs are allocated one way or the other? Most often, managers seek some prediction of the impact on costs of a particular decision to add a unit of product or render a service. And most often, they are unsure about the impact. They realize that *neither* a partially allocated cost or fully allocated cost is likely to provide the most accurate answer in a given decision.

Little is known in practice about the effects of alternative cost allocations on management decisions. If "accurate" costs are too illusive or too expensive to obtain, how do managers grope with their uncertainty? The heavy use of averages and the widespread tendency toward full allocations of costs are the practical means of estimating overall effects. A decision to produce a given batch of product may not, by itself, be causing an increase in a particular cost at its given moment of production. But its cumulative, indirect effects do indeed cause increases in costs. These cumulative effects are approximated by applying fully allocated unit costs to products rather than partially allocated costs. The unanswered question is, How accurate are such approximations? By implication, those who favor the full allocation of costs regardless of the lack of verifiable relationships are saying that the danger of overstatement of cost is less than that of understatement. For example, if costs are fully allocated, managers are less likely to cut prices, to underbid, to be inefficient, to overexpand, and so on. The heavy use of full-cost allocations is indicative that such assertions are widely believed, but we have only hearsay evidence to support either side of the argument.

In any event, in choosing whether and how to allocate costs, accountants and managers must focus on motivation; they must predict how one method of allocation will influence decisions as compared to another method of allocation.

SUMMARY

The success of the management-control system can be affected by both its technical perfection and by nontechnical factors that influence management behavior. Accounting records, budgets, standards, and reports are inanimate objects. By themselves, they are neither good nor bad. Whether they help or hinder strictly depends on how skillfully they are used by managers.

The trade-offs of the benefits and cost of information form the basic criterion for systems design and appraisal. Motivation is the dominant consideration in pinpointing the value or benefits of a management-control system. Above all, the system should promote goal congruence by encouraging managers to act in harmony with top-management objectives. Among the questions that seem particularly important are:

1. Does the system specify goals and subgoals which encourage behavior that blends with top-management goals?

2. Are the goals as specified by top management and through the system accepted by managers as their personal goals?

3. Is the accounting system tailored to the organizational structure to strengthen motivation?

4. Does the system properly guide managers in the acquisition and utilization of resources by providing accurate, timely, relevant data?

Subquestions deserving consideration would cover such commonly encountered difficulties as the overemphasis on a subgoal; the overemphasis on short-run performance; failure to pinpoint responsibility; cooperation versus competition; the lack of distinction between controllable and uncontrollable costs; limitations of records as motivation devices; inaccurate source documents; and faulty cost analysis.

The contribution approach to the income statement and to the problems of cost allocation is accounting's most effective method for helping management to evaluate performance and make decisions. Allocations are made with thoughtful regard for the purpose of the information being compiled. Various subdivisions of net income are drawn for different purposes. The contribution approach distinguishes sharply between various degrees of objectivity in cost allocations.

Where feasible, fixed costs of service departments should be reallocated by using predetermined monthly lump sums for providing a basic capacity to serve. Variable costs should be reallocated by using a predetermined standard unit rate for the services utilized.

The complexity of a cost-allocation method should be influenced by how the results of the alternative allocation methods affect decisions. Full-cost allocations are widespread, apparently because accountants and managers feel that these methods generally induce better decisions than partial-cost allocations.

Problem One

Review the section on the contribution approach to cost allocation, especially Exhibit 11-4.

Problem Two

Examine Exhibit 11-6 and the accompanying text. Suppose that the service department's fundamental readiness to serve was based on long-run expected activity of 4,000 machine-hours per month in Department 1 and 6,000 hours in Department 2. The company decided to reallocate fixed cost on a predetermined lump-sum basis and variable costs on a predetermined standard cost-per-hour basis.

1. Show the reallocations to both departments at a 10,000-hour level and an 8,000-hour level as indicated in Exhibit 11-6. Compare the results with those in Exhibit 11-6. Explain the differences.
2. Suppose that the service department had inefficiencies and price and rate changes at a 10,000-hour level. The service department incurred costs of $11,000 instead of the $10,000 originally budgeted. How would this change the cost reallocations under the method in Exhibit 11-6 and under the alternative method? Be specific.

Solution to Problem One

See Exhibit 11-4.

Solution to Problem Two

1. Fixed costs allocated on a 4/10 and 6/10 basis, or (.4 × $6,000) and (.6 × $6,000) respectively. Variable costs allocated at 40¢ per machine-hour.

> *At a 10,000-hour level:*
> To Department 1: $2,400 + ($.40 × 5,000) = $ 4,400
> To Department 2: $3,600 + ($.40 × 5,000) =   5,600
> Total reallocated $10,000

> *At an 8,000-hour level:*
> To Department 1: $2,400 + ($.40 × 5,000) = $ 4,400
> To Department 2: $3,600 + ($.40 × 3,000) =   4,800
> Total reallocated $ 9,200

The rates used in Exhibit 11-6 were combined and not predetermined. In other words, no distinction was made between variable and fixed costs, and the single combined unit rate was computed after the fact—after the actual hours used were tallied.

In contrast, a flexible budget was used in this recommended alternative analysis. Note that the charges to Department 1 do not depend on how much service is being consumed by Department 2. The $4,400 charge to Department 1 depends solely on the 5,000 hours consumed by Department 1, whereas in Exhibit 11-6, Department 1's charges went up from $5,000 to $5,750 solely because of a decrease in usage by Department 2.

2. In Exhibit 11-6, costs would go up by 10 percent for both Departments 1 and 2. Under the alternative method, the extra $1,000 would not be reallocated. The amount would remain charged to the service department as a $1,000 variance to be explained by the manager who had the most direct influence over such cost incurrence.

ASSIGNMENT MATERIAL

Fundamental Assignment Material

11-1. Terminology: Define: *responsibility accounting; profitability accounting; activity accounting; controllable cost; segment; allocation; separable cost; joint cost; and common cost.*

11-2. Responsibility of purchasing agent. Acme Manufacturing Company has received an order for 500 special parts which will require modifications of stock part No. 1739. There is a penalty clause on the order—$200 a day for every day delivery is late. It will cost the company $2 less per unit to purchase and process raw materials for the special part than to rework standard part No. 1739.

Mr. Smith, the purchasing agent, is responsible for securing the raw material in time to meet the scheduled delivery date. Mr. Smith places the order and receives an acceptable delivery date from his supplier. He checks up several times and does everything in his power to insure prompt delivery of the raw material.

On the delivery date specified by the supplier, Mr. Smith is notified that the raw material was damaged in packaging and will be delivered four days late. As a result, the special order will also be four days late. Consequently, an $800 penalty must be paid by Acme Company.

What department should bear the $800 penalty? Why?

11-3. Using revenue as a basis for allocating costs. The Southwest Transportation Company has had a long-standing policy of fully allocating all costs to its various divisions. Among the costs allocated were general and administrative costs in central headquarters consisting of office salaries, executive salaries, travel expense, accounting costs, office supplies, donations, rents, depreciation, postage, and similar items.

All these costs were difficult to trace directly to the individual divisions benefited, so they were allocated on the basis of the total revenue of each of the divisions. The same basis was used for allocating general advertising and miscellaneous selling costs. For example, in 19x3 the following allocations were made:

| | Divisions | | | |
	A	*B*	*C*	*Total*
Revenue (in millions)	$50.0	$40.0	$10.0	$100.0
Costs allocated on the basis of revenue	6.0	4.8	1.2	12.0

In 19x4, Division *A*'s revenue was expected to rise. But the division encountered severe competitive conditions; its revenue remained at $50 million. In

contrast, Division C enjoyed explosive growth in traffic because of the completion
of several huge factories in its area; its revenue rose to $30 million. Division B's
revenue remained unchanged. Careful supervision kept the total costs allocated
on the basis of revenue at $12 million.

365
Motivation,
Responsibility
Accounting, and
Cost Allocation

Required:

1. What costs will be allocated to each division in 19x4?
2. Using the results in Requirement 1, comment on the limitations of using revenue as a basis for cost allocation.

   11-4. **Reallocation of costs.** Trans Company has two operating departments
(A and B) and one service department. The actual monthly costs of the service
department are reallocated on the basis of the net ton-miles operated. The bud-
geted-cost behavior pattern of the service department is $200,000 monthly plus
50¢ per 1,000 ton-miles operated in Departments A and B.

Required:

1. In May, Trans Company handled 300,000,000 ton-miles of traffic, half in each
operating department. The actual costs of the service department were precisely as budgeted. How much cost would be reallocated to each department?
2. Suppose that in Requirement 1 Department B handled only 90,000,000 ton-
miles instead of 150,000,000. Department A handled 150,000,000 ton-miles.
Also suppose that the actual costs of the service department were precisely as
budgeted for this lower level of activity. How much cost would be reallocated
to each department?
3. Suppose that in Requirement 1 the actual costs of the service department were
$420,000 because of various inefficiencies and unfavorable but controllable rate
or price changes in various items. How much cost would be reallocated to each
department? Does such reallocation seem justified? If, not, what improvement
in the reallocation procedure would you suggest?
4. Suppose that various investment outlays for space and equipment in the service
department were made to provide a basic maximum capacity to serve other
departments under the assumption that Department A would operate at a
maximum monthly level of 160,000,000 ton-miles and Department B at a level
of 200,000,000 ton-miles. In Requirement 2, suppose fixed costs are reallocated via a predetermined monthly lump sum for providing a basic maximum
capacity to serve; variable costs are reallocated via a predetermined standard
rate per 1,000 ton-miles. How much cost would be reallocated to each department? What are the advantages of this method over other methods?

Additional Assignment Material

11-5. "There are corporate objectives other than profit." Name four.

11-6. What is the most important question in judging the effectiveness of a
measure of performance?

11-7. What eight areas has General Electric Company used to avoid overemphasis of one performance measure?

11-8. Give three examples of how managers may improve short-run performance to the detriment of long-run results.

11-9. Illustrate how a measurement system may engender faulty cost analysis.

11-10. What three guides are basic to the accountant's work in current planning and control?

11-11. What are the most glaring sources of error in source documents?

11-12. Why is attention-directing such an important accounting function?

11-13. "Collecting relevant data by responsibility centers is difficult." Why?

11-14. "Variable costs are controllable and fixed costs are uncontrollable." Do you agree? Explain.

11-15. "Managers may trade off variable for fixed costs." Give three examples.

11-16. What two major factors influence controllability?

11-17. Describe three guides to deciding how costs should be charged to a responsibility center.

11-18. "Material costs are controllable by a production department foreman." Do you agree? Explain.

11-19. Give examples of segments, as described in this chapter.

11-20. Distinguish between a separable cost and a joint (common) cost.

11-21. "The contribution margin is the best measure of short-run performance." Do you agree? Why?

11-22. What is the most controversial aspect of the contribution approach to cost allocation?

11-23. Give two guides to cost allocation.

11-24. "A commonly misused basis for allocation is dollar sales." Explain.

11-25. How should national advertising costs be allocated to territories?

11-26. **Cost classifications.** Construct a chart with the following headings:

			Controllable Cost		
	Product Cost	Variable Cost	By Sales Vice-President	By Assembly Supervisor	By Production Vice-President
Salesmen's commissions					
Direct material					
Machining department—direct labor					
Finishing department—supplies					
Sales vice-president's salary					
Straight-line depreciation—equipment in assembly department					
Management consulting fee for improving labor methods in assembly department					

Assume the same organization chart as shown in Exhibit 11-1. For each account, answer "yes" or "no" as to whether the cost is a product cost, a variable cost, and a cost controllable by the three officers indicated. Thus, you will have five answers, entered horizontally, for each account.

11-27. Responsibility accounting. (CMA adapted.) Listed below are three charges found on the monthly report of a division which manufactures and sells products primarily to outside companies. Division performance is evaluated by the use of return on investment. You are to state which, if any, of the following charges are consistent with the "responsibility accounting" concept, and support each answer with a brief explanation:

1. A charge for general corporation administration at 10 percent of division sales.
2. A charge for the use of the corporate computer facility. The charge is determined by taking actual annual computer department costs and allocating an amount to each user on the ratio of its use to total corporation use.
3. A charge for goods purchased from another division. The charge is based upon the competitive market price for the goods.

11-28. Effects of misclassification. (CMA adapted.) Assume that a department manager performs the timekeeping function for a manufacturing department. From time to time, analysis of overhead and direct labor variances have shown that the department manager has deliberately misclassified labor-hours (e.g., listed direct labor-hours as indirect labor-hours and vice versa) so that only one of the two labor variances is unfavorable. It is not feasible economically to hire a separate timekeeper. What should the company do, if anything, to resolve this problem?

11-29. Responsibility accounting. (CMA adapted.) The Fillep Company operates a standard cost system. The variances for each department are calculated and reported to the department manager. It is expected that the manager will use the information to improve his operations and recognize that it is used by his superiors when they are evaluating his performance.

John Smith was recently appointed manager of the assembly department of the company. He has complained that the system as designed is disadvantageous to his department. Included among the variances charged to the departments is one for rejected units. The inspection occurs at the end of the assembly department. The inspectors attempt to identify the cause of the rejection so that the department where the error occurred can be charged with it. But not all errors can be easily identified with a department. The non-identified units are totalled and apportioned to the departments according to the number of identified errors. The variance for rejected units in each department is a combination of the errors caused by the department plus a portion of the unidentified causes of rejects.

Required:

1. Is John Smith's claim valid? Explain the reason(s) for your answer.
2. What would you recommend the company do to solve its problem with John Smith and his complaint?

11-30. Motivation and salesmen's behavior. The Frank James Brush Company is a small local firm with three salesmen. Mr. James, being unable to decide on a payment plan for his salesmen, has assigned a different payment plan to each of his salesmen for a six-month period. The three plans assigned are:

Plan *A:* A flat salary of $400 per month.

Plan *B:* No base salary, but a $600 bonus if a monthly sales norm is met, plus 5 percent commission on sales over the norm of $10,000.

Plan *C:* A base salary of $200 per month, plus 25 percent commission on sales over the norm.

The sales record for the past six months is:

	Salesmen		
	1	*2*	*3*
January	$10,000	$10,200	$ 6,000
February	10,000	10,000	14,000
March	10,000	9,700	6,000
April	10,000	10,100	15,000
May	10,000	10,150	6,000
June	10,000	9,850	13,000

Required:

1. Analyze the sales patterns. Which payment plan (*A, B,* or *C*) was probably given to salesman No. 1, No. 2, and No. 3, respectively?
2. Which plan would be most desired by a person who desires to maximize personal income?
3. Which of the three plans, if any, should Mr. James adopt on a permanent basis?

11-31. Commission plan for new-car salesmen. As an automobile dealer, you are faced with the problem of formulating a new-car salesmen's commissions plan. You have listed the following alternatives:

(a) Commissions based on a flat percentage of dollar sales.
(b) Commissions based on varying percentages of dollar sales. The higher the sales price of a deal, the higher the commission rate. Also, commissions will differ, depending on various accessories sold.
(c) Commissions based on net profit after allocation of a fair share of all operating expenses.

Required:

Evaluate these alternatives. Are there other methods which deserve consideration?

11-32. Responsibility for a stable employment policy. The Fast-Weld Metal Fabricating Company has been manufacturing machine tools for a number of years and has an industry-wide reputation for doing high-quality work. The company has been faced with irregularity of output over the years. It has been company policy to lay off welders as soon as there was insufficient work to keep them busy, and to rehire them when demand warranted. The company, however, now has poor labor relations and finds it very difficult to hire good welders because of its lay-off policy. Consequently, the quality of the work has been continually declining.

The plant manager has proposed that the welders, who earn $6 per hour, be retained during slow periods to do menial plant maintenance work which is normally performed by men earning $3.85 per hour in the plant maintenance department.

You, as controller, must decide the most meaningful accounting procedure to handle the wages of the welders doing plant maintenance work. What department or departments should be charged with this work, and at what rate? Discuss the implications of your plan.

11-33. Salesmen's compensation plan. You are sales manager of a manufacturing firm whose sales are subject to month-to-month variations, depending upon the individual salesman's efforts. A new salary plus bonus plan has been in effect for four months and you are reviewing a sales performance report. The plan provides for a base salary of $400 per month, a $500 bonus each month if the salesman's monthly quota is met, and an additional commission of 5 percent on all sales over the monthly quota.

		Salesman A	Salesman B	Salesman C
January	Quota	$30,000	$10,000	$50,000
	Actual	10,000	10,000	60,000
February	Quota	$10,300	$10,300	$61,800
	Actual	20,000	10,300	40,000
March	Quota	$20,600	$10,600	$41,200
	Actual	35,000	5,000	60,000
April	Quota	$36,050	$ 5,150	$61,800
	Actual	15,000	5,200	37,000

Evaluate the compensation plan. Be specific. What changes would you recommend?

11-34. Responsibility accounting, profit centers, and the contribution approach. Consider the following data for the year's operations of an automobile dealer:

Sales of vehicles	$2,000,000
Sales of parts and service	500,000
Cost of vehicle sales	1,600,000
Parts and service materials	150,000
Parts and service labor	200,000
Parts and service overhead	50,000
General dealership overhead	100,000
Advertising of vehicles	100,000
Sales commissions, vehicles	40,000
Sales salaries, vehicles	50,000

The president of the dealership has long regarded the markup on material and labor for the parts and service activity as the amount which is supposed to cover all parts and service overhead plus all general overhead of the dealership. In other words, the parts and service department is viewed as a cost-recovery operation, and the sales of vehicles as the income-producing activity.

Required:
1. Prepare a departmentalized operating statement that harmonizes with the views of the president.
2. Prepare an alternative operating statement that would reflect a different view of the dealership operations. Assume that $10,000 and $50,000 of the $100,000 general overhead can be allocated with confidence to the parts and service

department and to sales of vehicles, respectively. The remaining $40,000 cannot be allocated except in some highly arbitrary manner.
3. Comment on the relative merits of Requirements 1 and 2.

11-35. Divisional contribution, performance, and segment margins. The president of the Midwestern Railroad wants to obtain an overview of his operations, particularly with respect to comparing freight and passenger business. He has heard about some new "contribution" approaches to cost allocations that emphasize cost behavior patterns and so-called *contribution margins, contributions controllable by segment managers,* and *contributions by segments.* Pertinent data for the year ended December 31, 19x2, follow:

Total revenue was $100 million, of which $90 million was freight traffic and $10 million was passenger traffic. Half of the latter was generated by Division 1; 40 percent by Division 2; and 10 percent by Division 3.

Total variable costs were $56,000,000, of which $44 million was freight traffic. Of the $12 million allocable to passenger traffic, $4.4, $3.7, and $3.9 million could be allocated to Divisions 1, 2, and 3, respectively.

Total separable discretionary fixed costs were $10,000,000, of which $9,500,000 applied to freight traffic. Of the remainder, $100,000 could not be allocated to specific divisions, although it was clearly traceable to passenger traffic in general. Divisions 1, 2, and 3 should be allocated $300,000, $70,000, and $30,000, respectively.

Total separable committed costs, which were not regarded as being controllable by segment managers, were $30,000,000, of which 90 percent was allocable to freight traffic. Of the 10 percent traceable to passenger traffic, Divisions 1, 2, and 3 should be allocated $1,800,000, $420,000, and $180,000, respectively; the balance was unallocable to a specific division.

The joint fixed costs not clearly allocable to any part of the company amounted to $1,000,000.

Required:

1. The president asks you to prepare statements, dividing the data for the company as a whole between the freight and passenger traffic and then subdividing the passenger traffic into three divisions.
2. Some competing railroads actively promote a series of one-day sight-seeing tours on summer weekends. Most often, these tours are timed so that the cars with the tourists are hitched on with regularly scheduled passenger trains.
   What costs are relevant for making decisions to run such tours? Other railroads, facing the same general cost picture, refuse to conduct such sight-seeing tours. Why?
3. For purposes of this analysis, even though the numbers may be unrealistic, suppose that Division 2's figures represented a specific run for a train instead of a division. Suppose further that the railroad has petitioned government authorities for permission to drop Division 2. What would be the effect on overall company net income for 19x3, assuming that the figures are accurate and that 19x3 operations are in all other respects a duplication of 19x2 operations?

11-36. Reallocation of costs. The repairs and maintenance department served two operating departments. The budgeted costs for the service department were $20,000 monthly plus 20¢ per machine hour used in the operating departments.

Required:

1. Suppose that the actual costs of the repair and maintenance department were exactly in accordance with the flexible budget at an activity level of 100,000 machine hours, 50,000 in Department A and 50,000 in Department B. Reallocate the total costs on the basis of the total hours used.

2. Suppose in Requirement 1 that actual costs were exactly in accordance with the flexible budget at an activity level of 70,000 hours, 20,000 in A and 50,000 in B. Reallocate the total costs on the basis of the total hours used, as you did in Requirement 1. What are the weaknesses of using total actual hours as a base?

3. Suppose that the repair department's fundamental capability to serve was based on long-run expected activity of 60,000 machine-hours in Department A and 40,000 in Department B. The company decided to reallocate fixed costs on a predetermined lump-sum basis based on capability to serve, and variable costs on a predetermined cost-per-hour-used basis. Show the allocations to both departments at the 100,000-hour level and the 70,000-hour levels described in Requirements 1 and 2. Compare the results with those in Requirements 1 and 2. Explain the difference.

4. Suppose that the service department had price and rate changes and miscellaneous inefficiencies at the 100,000-hour level in Requirement 1. The service department incurred costs of $46,000 instead of the $40,000 originally budgeted. How would this change the cost reallocations for the 100,000-hour level in Requirements 1 and 3. Be specific.

11-37. Product-line and territorial income statements. The Delvin Company shows the following results for the year 19x1:

Sales	$1,000,000	100.0%
Manufacturing costs of goods sold	$ 675,000	67.5%
Selling and advertising*	220,000	22.0%
Administrative (all nonvariable)	35,000	3.5%
Total expenses	$ 930,000	93.0%
Net income before income taxes	$ 70,000	7.0%

*All nonvariable, except for $40,000 freight-out cost.

The sales manager has asked you to prepare statements that will help him assess the company efforts by product line and by territories. You have gathered the following information:

	Product			Territory		
	A	B	C	North	Central	Eastern
Sales*	25%	40%	35%			
Product A				50%	20%	30%
Product B				15%	70%	15%
Product C				14/35	8/35	13/35
Variable manufacturing and packaging costs†	68%	55%	60%			

	Product			Territory		
	A	*B*	*C*	*North*	*Central*	*Eastern*
Nonvariable separable costs:						
Manufacturing	15,000	14,000	21,000		(not allocated)	
Selling and advertising	40,000	18,000	42,000	48,000	32,000	40,000
Freight out		(not allocated)		13,000	9,000	18,000

Note. All items not directly allocated were considered joint or common costs.

*Percent of company sales.
†Percent of product sales.

Required:

1. Prepare a product-line income statement, showing the results for the company as a whole in the first column and the results for the three products in adjoining columns. Show a contribution margin and a product margin, as well as net income.
2. Repeat Requirement 1 on a territorial basis. Show a contribution margin and a territory margin.
3. Should salesmen's commissions be based on contribution margins, product margins, territorial margins, net income, or dollar sales? Explain.

11-38. Reallocation of personnel department costs. The costs of operating the personnel department of the Kuffle Transportation Company are reallocated to three operating departments on the basis of total labor-hours. The results for 19x1 were:

	Personnel	*1*	*2*	*3*
Personnel department costs	$(300,000)	$100,000	$100,000	$100,000
Total labor-hours		500,000	500,000	500,000

In 19x2, the activity of Department 1 was severely restricted between March and October, requiring many layoffs, much employee counseling, and the hiring of many new employees in October. Operations returned to normal in November and December.

The costs of the personnel department in 19x2 were $300,000. The total labor-hours worked in the operating departments were 250,000, 500,000 and 500,000, respectively.

Required:

1. Reallocate the costs for 19x2 using total labor-hours as a base.
2. As the manager of Department 2, what comments would you make about the charges. What would be a better base for reallocation?

11-39. Dual reallocation. The power plant that services all factory departments has a budget for the forthcoming year. This budget has been expressed in the following terms, for a normal month:

Factory Departments	Kilowatt-Hours Needed at Practical Capacity Production Volume*	Average Expected Monthly Usage
A	10,000	8,000
B	20,000	9,000
X	12,000	7,000
Y	8,000	6,000
Totals	50,000	30,000

*This was the most influential factor in planning the size of the power plant.

The expected monthly costs for operating the department during the budget year are $15,000—$6,000 variable and $9,000 fixed.

Required:

1. What dollar amounts should be reapportioned to each department? Show three different sets of answers.
2. Which method do you prefer? Why?

11-40. Multiple goals and profitability.[8] The following are multiple goals of the General Electric Company:

1. Profitability
2. Market position
3. Productivity
4. Product leadership
5. Personnel development
6. Employee attitudes
7. Public responsibility
8. Balance between short-range and long-range goals

General Electric is a Goliath corporation with sales of about $11 billion and assets of $7 billion in 1973. It had approximately 170 responsibility centers called "departments," but that is a deceiving term. In most other companies, these departments would be called divisions. For example, some GE departments have sales of over $300 million.

Each department manager's performance is evaluated annually in relation to the specified multiple goals. A special measurements group was set up in 1952 to devise ways of quantifying accomplishments in each of the areas. In this way, the evaluation of performance would become more objective as the various measures were developed and improved.

Required:

1. How would you measure performance in each of these areas? Be specific.
2. Can the other goals be encompassed as ingredients of a formal measure of profitability? In other words, can profitability *per se* be defined to include the other goals?

11-41. Responsibility accounting and control of costs. The Witmer Company develops, manufactures, and markets several product lines of low-cost consumer goods. Top management of the company is attempting to evaluate the

[8]Adapted from a problem originally appearing in R. H. Hassler and Neil E. Harlan, *Cases in Controllership* (Englewood Cliffs, N.J.: Prentice-Hall, Inc.).

present method and a new method of charging the different production departments for the services they receive from one of the engineering departments, which is called Manufacturing Engineering Services (MES).

The function of MES, which consists of about thirty engineers and ten draftsmen, is to reduce the costs of producing the different products of the company by improving machine and manufacturing process design, while maintaining the required level of quality. The MES manager reports to the engineering supervisor, who reports to the vice-president of manufacturing. The MES manager may increase or decrease the number of engineers under him. He is evaluated on the basis of several variables, one of which is the annual incremental savings to the company brought about by his department in excess of the costs of operating his department. These costs consist of actual salaries, a share of corporate overhead, the cost of office supplies used by his department, and a cost of capital charge. An individual engineer is evaluated on the basis of the ratio of the annual savings he effects to his annual salary. The salary range of an engineer is defined by his personnel classification; there are four classifications, and promotion from one classification to another depends on the approval of a panel that includes both production and engineering personnel.

Production-department managers report to a production supervisor, who reports to the vice-president of manufacturing. The production department for each product line is treated as a profit center, and engineering services are provided at a cost, according to the following plan. When a production department manager and an engineer agree on a possible project to improve production efficiency, they sign a contract that specifies the scope of the project, the estimated savings to be realized, the probability of success, and the number of engineering man-hours of each personnel classification required. The charge to the particular production department is determined by the product of the number of man-hours required multiplied by the "classification rate" for each personnel classification. This rate depends on the average salary for the classification involved and a share of the engineering department's other costs. An engineer is expected to spend at least 85 percent of his time on specific, contracted projects; the remainder may be used for preliminary investigations of potential cost-saving projects or self-improving study. A recent survey showed that production managers have a high degree of confidence in the MES engineers.

A new plan has been proposed to top management, in which no charge will be made to production departments for engineering services. In all other respects the new system will be identical to the present. Production managers will continue to request engineering services as under the present plan. Proponents of the new plan say that, under it, production managers will take greater advantage of existing engineering talent. Regardless of how engineering services are accounted for, the company is committed to the idea of production departments as profit centers.

Required:

Evaluate the strong and weak points of the present and proposed plans. Will the company tend to hire the optimal quantity of engineering talent? Will this engineering talent be used as effectively as possible?

11-42. Allocation of computer costs. Roger, Inc., is an international ethical pharmaceutical manufacturer that specializes in hormone research and the development and marketing of hormone-base products. The twenty-two different wholly owned subsidiaries and separate divisions that comprise the organization are highly decentralized, but they receive overall direction from a small corporate staff at parent-corporation headquarters in Palo Alto. The laboratories division, research division, and all corporate offices are located at the home-office site. Each of the divisional functional areas operates as a cost center; for example, labs accounting, labs production, labs sales, research accounting, and research operations are separate cost centers. Corporate purchasing, employee relations, office services, and computer (EDP) systems also function as individual cost centers, and they provide their services to Research, Labs, and the other divisions as necessary.

Until recently, no costs of the corporate-service cost centers were allocated to the divisional cost centers; they were simply lumped together as central corporate overhead. Recently, however, it was decided to start charging the operating units (that is, the cost centers) for their EDP usage. Prior to this time, EDP services were simply requested as desired by the cost centers; priorities were determined by negotiations, with ultimate recourse to an EDP control committee (each cost center was represented); and all charges were absorbed as corporate overhead.

EDP systems comprise both systems-programming services and computer operations. In the current "charge-back" system, the EDP director prepares a budget at the start of each quarter based upon his estimates of user demand. Using full absorption costing, he then computes an hourly charge rate, which he promulgates to the user cost centers. The users prepare their budgets utilizing his charge rate and their estimates of the services they think they will be needing. When a user desires to undertake any specific project or use EDP services, he negotiates an agreement with EDP on the hours (thus cost) that he will be charged. The user is free to reject the EDP "bid" and obtain outside services if he does not feel the EDP job estimates are reasonable. Also, since many projects last a year or more but service agreements are arranged on a quarterly basis, the user can drop a project in midstream at the end of a quarter if his overall budget should become too tight. If the actual hours needed to complete a given job exceed those contracted for, the EDP center must absorb the extra cost as an unfavorable overhead variance.

The performance of all cost centers is evaluated on the basis of how closely their actual results match budget. Thus the EDP director must not only be sure that his actual expenditures coincide with those that were budgeted, but that he is able to bill other centers for all his actual charges. He must be sure that he contracts for enough projects from the users to absorb his budget.

The shift to the charge-back method was imposed by the corporate financial vice-president for the "purpose of putting control and responsibility for expenditures where the benefits are received." The vice-president also felt the move was necessary to avoid a "mushrooming of the EDP group" and to make users more aware of the costs they were incurring. An additional factor mentioned was an almost irresistible tide of "allocationism" prevalent in local industry because of the overpowering influence of government contracting there. He does feel he will resist allocating the other services, however, with the possible exception of the printing and reproduction function, which has grown to be quite costly in the last few years. The major rationale for not allocating the other services is that they are all uniform, predictable functions, whereas the EDP services are more spasmodic and project-oriented.

The head of the EDP group is strongly opposed to the new system. He believes that there is "too much lip service paid to the specialized nature of computers" and that the new system is reducing the effectiveness of the EDP group to the corporation as a whole. He and several of the user-directors believe the shift was simply a political maneuver on the part of the VP to consolidate the EDP empire under the aegis of the corporate staff. The head of the EDP group believes

EXHIBIT 11-7

R. G. BARRY CORPORATION AND SUBSIDIARIES PRO FORMA
(Conventional and Human-Resource Accounting)

Balance Sheet

ASSETS	1972 CONVENTIONAL AND HUMAN RESOURCE	1972 CONVENTIONAL ONLY
Total current assets	$16,408	$16,408
Net property, plant and equipment	3,371	3,371
Excess of purchase price over net Assets acquired	1,288	1,288
Deferred financing costs	183	183
Net investments in human resources	**1,779**	—
Other assets	232	232
	$23,264*	$21,484

LIABILITIES AND STOCKHOLDERS' EQUITY		
Total current liabilities	3,218	3,218
Long term debt, excluding current installments	7,285	7,285
Deferred compensation	116	116
Deferred federal income tax based upon full tax deduction for human resource costs	**889**	—
Stockholders' equity:		
Capital stock	1,818	1,818
Additional capital in excess of par value	5,047	5,047
Retained earnings:		
Financial	3,998	3,998
Human resources	**889**	—
	$23,264	$21,484

Statement of Income

Net sales	$39,162	$39,162
Cost of sales	25,667	25,667
Gross profit	13,494	13,494
Selling, general and administrative expenses	10,190	10,190
Operating income	3,303	3,303
Interest expense	549	549
Income before Federal income taxes	2,754	2,754
Net increase in human-resource investment	**218**	—
Adjusted income before Federal income taxes	2,973	2,754
Federal income taxes	1,414	1,305
Net income	$ 1,558	$ 1,449

*(000's deleted, so totals may appear slightly inaccurate.)

376

a nonchargeable system administered by the EDP control committee would yield better results.

Required:

1. What are the motivational and operational effects of this change on users, EDP group, and corporation?
2. Evaluate the impact of having coexistence of allocated and nonallocated services.
3. Evaluate the operation of this particular allocation system.

11-43. Human-resource accounting. The Barry Corporation is a producer of leisure footwear in Columbus, Ohio. The company has been a pioneer in so-called "human-resource accounting," an outgrowth of research conducted by Rensis Likert, a social psychologist, and others.

For many years, Likert has stressed that accounting systems encourage the misuse of human resources because of undue emphasis on short-run profits. According to Likert, the attempts to maximize immediate earnings have induced managers to exert too much pressure for productivity and to have uneconomical layoffs and discharges. Why? Because increases in employee turnover and later additional spending for hiring and training more than offset the immediate savings. Likert advocates incorporating human-resource accounting as part of the formal accounting system.

Many variations of human-resource accounting are possible. The Barry Corporation has taken a minimum step by recording as assets the outlays for recruiting and training managers. These investments in human assets are then amortized over the expected useful lives of the employees.

Data from the human-resource system have not yet been incorporated in the company's audited financial statements. Nevertheless, as seen in Exhibit 11-7, the company's annual reports contain a *supplementary* balance sheet and income statement that shows the human-resource effects.

Required:

1. Were new investments in human assets during 1972 undertaken more rapidly than they were written off? Explain, using the figures given in Exhibit 11-7.
2. Do you favor implementing human-resource accounting for internal-reporting purposes? Why do you think Likert prefers human-resource accounting to the use of less formal measures, such as employee-attitude surveys, absenteeism, employee-turnover rates, and so on? Be specific.

Relevant Costs and the Contribution Approach to Problem Solving

12

Managers' problem-solving decisions pervade a variety of areas and different spans of time. Examples are dropping or adding products, setting prices, selecting equipment, selling manufactured products or processing them further, and making parts internally or buying them from outside suppliers. Unique factors bear on particular decisions. However, there is a general approach that will help the executive make wise decisions in *any* problem-solving situation. The term "relevant" has been overworked in recent years; nevertheless the general approach herein will be labeled as the **relevant-cost approach.** Coupled with the contribution approach, the ability to distinguish relevant items from irrelevant items is the key to wise problem solving.

Throughout this chapter, in order to concentrate on a few major points, we shall ignore the time value of money (which is discussed in Chapter 13) and income taxes (which are discussed in Chapter 14).

THE ACCOUNTANT'S ROLE IN SPECIAL DECISIONS

Accuracy and Relevance

Accountants have an important role in the problem-solving process, not as the decision makers but as collectors and reporters of relevant data. Their reports must provide valid data—numbers that measure the quantities which are pertinent to the decision at hand. Many managers want the accountant to offer recommendations about the proper decision, even though the final choice always rests with the operating executive.

The distinction between precision and relevance should be kept in
mind. Ideally, the data should be *precise* (accurate) and *relevant* (pertinent). However, as we shall see, figures can be precise but irrelevant, or
imprecise but relevant. For example, the president's salary may be
$100,000 per year, to the penny, but may have no bearing on the question
of whether to make or buy a certain part needed in production.

Qualitative and Quantitative Factors

The aspects of each alternative may be divided into two broad categories,
qualitative and **quantitative.** Qualitative factors are those whose measurement in dollars and cents is difficult and imprecise; yet a qualitative factor
may easily be given more weight than a measurable saving in cost. For
example, the opposition of a militant union to new labor-saving machinery may cause an executive to defer or even reject completely the contemplated installation. Or, the chance to manufacture a component one-
self for less than the supplier's selling price may be rejected because of
the company's long-run dependency on the supplier for other subassemblies. Quantitative factors are those which may more easily be reduced to
dollars and cents—for example, projected costs of alternative materials,
of direct labor, and of overhead. The accountant, statistician, and mathe-
matician try to express as many decision factors as feasible in quantitative
terms. This approach reduces the number of qualitative factors to be
judged.

MEANING OF RELEVANCE: THE MAJOR CONCEPTUAL LESSON

Problem solving is essentially decision making—choosing among several
courses of action. The available courses of action are the result of an
often time-consuming formal or informal search and screening process,
perhaps carried on by a company team which includes engineers, accountants, and operating executives.

The accountant's role in problem solving is primarily that of a technical expert on cost analysis. His responsibility is to be certain that the
manager is guided by relevant data, information that will lead him to the
best decision.

Consider the final stages of the decision-making process. Two (or
more) courses of action are aligned, and a comparison is made. The decision is based on the difference in the effect of the two on future performance. The key question is, What difference does it make? The relevant
information is that **expected future data** which will **differ** among alternatives.

The ideas in the previous paragraph deserve elaboration because
they have such wide application. Historical, or past, data have no direct
bearing on the decision. Historical data may be helpful in the formulation of predictions, but past figures, in themselves, are irrelevant simply

because they are not the expected future data that managers must use in intelligent decision making. Decisions affect the future. Nothing can alter what has already happened; all past costs are down the drain as far as current or future decisions are concerned.

Of the expected future data, only those that will differ between alternatives are relevant. Any item is irrelevant if it will remain the same regardless of the alternative selected. For instance, if the department manager's salary will be the same regardless of the products stocked, his salary is irrelevant to the selection of products.

The following examples will help us summarize the sharp distinctions needed for proper cost analysis for special decisions.

You habitually buy gasoline from either of two nearby gasoline stations. Yesterday you noticed that one station is selling gasoline at 60¢ per gallon; the other, at 58¢. Your automobile needs gasoline, and, in making your choice of stations, you *assume* that these prices are unchanged. The relevant costs are 60¢ and 58¢, the expected future costs that will differ between the alternatives. You use your past experience (i.e., what you observed yesterday) for predicting today's price. Note that the relevant cost is not what you paid in the past, or what you observed yesterday, but what you *expect to pay* when you drive in to get gasoline. This cost meets our two criteria: (a) it is the expected future cost; and (b) it differs between the alternatives.

You may also plan to have your car lubricated. The recent price at each station was $4.50 and this is what you anticipate paying. This expected future cost is irrelevant because it will be the same under either alternative. It does not meet our second criterion.

Exhibit 12-1 sketches the decision process and uses the following decision as an illustration. A manufacturer is thinking of using aluminum instead of copper in a line of desk lamps. The cost of direct material will decrease from 30¢ to 20¢. The elaborate mechanism in Exhibit 12-1 seems unnecessary for this decision. After all, the analysis in a nutshell is:

	Aluminum	*Copper*	*Difference*
Direct material	$.20	$.30	$.10

The cost of copper used for this comparison undoubtedly came from historical-cost records, but note that the relevant costs in the above analysis are both expected future costs.

The direct labor cost will continue to be 70¢ per unit regardless of the material used. It is irrelevant because our second criterion—an element of difference between the alternatives—is not met. Therefore, we can safely exclude direct labor from our cost comparisons. Of course, many companies would not bother to exclude direct labor. In such a case, the following comparison would be made:

	Aluminum	*Copper*	*Difference*
Direct material	$.20	$.30	$.10
Direct labor	.70	.70	—

EXHIBIT 12-1
Decision Process and Role of Information

The decision is whether to use aluminum instead of copper.

The objective is to minimize costs.

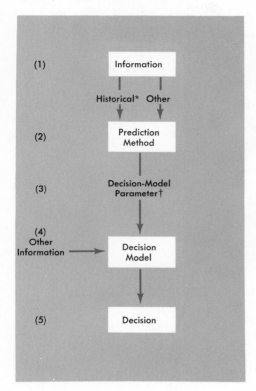

(1)   Information

Historical*   Other

(2)   Prediction Method

(3)   Decision-Model Parameter†

(4) Other Information →   Decision Model

(5)   Decision

Historical direct material costs were $.30 per unit. Direct labor costs were $.70 per unit, and will not be affected by the switch in materials.

Use the information together with an assessment of probabilities as a basis for predicting the future costs of direct material and direct labor. Direct material unit costs are expected to be $.20

COST COMPARISON PER UNIT

	Aluminum	Copper
Direct material	$.20	$.30

The *expected future* costs are the outputs of the prediction method and are inputs of the decision model together with other quantitative and qualitative information.

*Note that historical data may be relevant for prediction methods.

†Historical data are never relevant *per se* for decision models. Only those expected future data that are different are really relevant. For instance, in this example, direct material makes a difference and direct labor does not. Therefore, under our *definition* here, direct labor is irrelevant.

There is no harm in including irrelevant items in a formal analysis, provided that they are included properly. However, clarity is usually enhanced by confining the reports to the relevant items only.

If you view the decision process in Exhibit 12-1 in perspective, the role of historical costs becomes evident. Although they are never inputs to the decision model (the method for making the choice), historical costs are frequently the chief inputs to prediction methods. For example, statistical regression (a formal study of past cost behavior) may be used as a basis for predicting a future cost; but the predicted costs, not the historical costs, are the inputs to the cost comparisons that form the decision model.

Exhibit 12-2 summarizes the relationships between relevance and irrelevance and the decision model. Note that although historical costs are

EXHIBIT 12-2

Summary of Definition of Relevant Costs

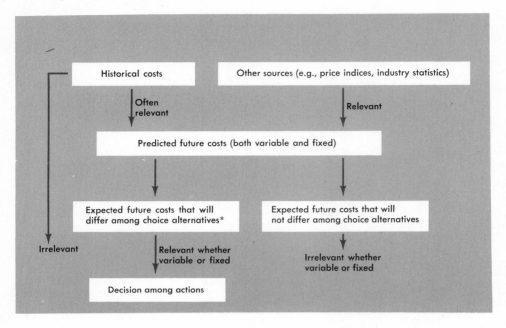

*The time value of money is ignored here, but it is discussed in the next chapter. Strictly interpreted, differences in future data are affected by both magnitude and timing. Therefore, expected future data with the same magnitude but different timing can be relevant.

often used as a guide to prediction, they are irrelevant *per se* to the decision itself.

This is the major conceptual lesson in this chapter. The remainder of the chapter will show how this notion of relevant costs combined with the contribution approach may be applied to various particular decisions. Note that the analytical approach is consistent regardless of the particular decision encountered.

THE CONTRIBUTION APPROACH TO SPECIAL DECISIONS

We have already seen that the contribution approach to preparing income statements facilitates evaluation of performance. Now we shall see how the same approach facilitates analysis for special decisions regarding (1) joint products; (2) the deletion or addition of product lines, departments, or territories; (3) the acceptance of orders or emphasis of products in relation to available capacity; (4) the making or buying of products; and (5) the thorny, everlasting problem of pricing a product.

Joint Product Costs and
Incremental Costs

383

**Relevant Costs and
the Contribution
Approach to
Problem Solving**

Joint product cost is the term most often used to describe the costs of manufactured goods that are produced by a single process and that are not identifiable as different individual products up to a certain stage of production known as the **split-off point.** Examples include chemicals, lumber, petroleum products, flour milling, copper mining, meat packing, leather tanning, soap making, and gas manufacturing. A meat-packing company cannot kill a sirloin steak; it has to slaughter a steer, which supplies various cuts of dressed meat, hides, and trimmings.

Joint product costs are the costs of a single process, or a series of processes, that simultaneously produces two or more products of significant sales value. There are many elaborate schemes for assigning these joint costs to the various products. Most are based on the relative sales value of the products. But managers need not be overly concerned with how various joint products are costed for inventory purposes.

No technique for allocating joint product costs is applicable to decisions of whether a product should be sold at the split-off point or processed further. When a product results from a joint process, the decision to process further is not influenced either by the size of the joint costs or the portion of the joint costs that is assigned to the particular product. Joint costs are irrelevant to these decisions.

Suppose that a company produces two petroleum products, *X* and *Y*, as a result of a particular joint process. Data are given in Exhibit 12-3.

EXHIBIT 12-3

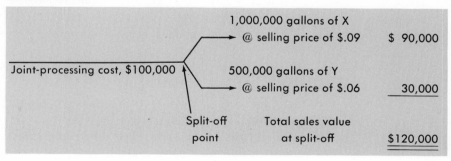

1,000,000 gallons of X
@ selling price of $.09 $ 90,000

Joint-processing cost, $100,000

500,000 gallons of Y
@ selling price of $.06   30,000

Split-off   Total sales value
point   at split-off $120,000

The 500,000 gallons of *Y* can be processed further and sold as high-octane gasoline at an additional cost of 8¢ per gallon for manufacturing and distribution. The net sales price of the high-octane gasoline would be 16¢ per gallon.

Product *X* will be sold at the split-off point, but management is undecided about Product *Y*. Should *Y* be sold or should it be processed into high-octane gasoline? The joint costs must be incurred to reach the split-off point, so they are completely irrelevant to the question of whether to sell or process further.[1] The sure-fire approach that will yield valid results is to concentrate on the *additional* costs and revenue after split-off (as shown in Exhibit 12-4).

EXHIBIT 12-4

	SELL AT SPLIT-OFF	PROCESS FURTHER	DIFFERENCE
Revenue	$30,000	$80,000	$50,000
Separable costs beyond split-off, @ $.08	—	40,000	40,000
Income effects	$30,000	$40,000	$10,000

Briefly, it is profitable to extend processing or to incur additional distribution costs on a joint product if the difference in revenue exceeds the difference in expenses (including the cost of capital, which will be discussed in Chapter 13).

Two important points deserve mentioning here. First, the allocation of joint costs would not affect the decision, as Exhibit 12-5 demonstrates.

EXHIBIT 12-5

	(1) SELL AT SPLIT-OFF	(2) PROCESS FURTHER	(3) INCREMENT OR DIFFERENTIAL
Joint costs, no matter how allocated	(same for each alternative)		
Revenue	$30,000	$80,000	$50,000
Separable costs	—	40,000	40,000
Income effects	$30,000	$40,000	$10,000

Second, the title of the last column in Exhibit 12-5 contains terms that are frequently encountered in cost analysis for special decisions. **Incremental costs** (sometimes called **differential costs**) are, in any given situation, the difference between the total cost of each alternative. In this situation, the *incremental revenue* is $50,000, the *incremental cost* is

---

[1]Conventional methods of joint cost allocation should be ignored. They are useful for inventory costing purposes *only*. Not only are they irrelevant, they may be downright misleading. Costing by gallonage would show allocated joint cost of $.06667 per gallon ($100,000 ÷ 1,500,000 gallons). This would indicate that Product Y is a loss product. Costing by relative sales value would show a profit for both products at split-off. Product X would bear $75,000 of the joint cost ($90,000/$120,000 × $100,000), and Product Y, $25,000 ($30,000/$120,000 × $100,000). Clearly, the indicated profitability of the individual products depends on the method used for allocating a joint cost which is unallocable by its nature: Product X cannot be obtained without obtaining Product Y, and vice versa.

$40,000, and the *incremental income* is $10,000. Each is the difference between the corresponding items under the alternatives being considered. An analysis that shows only the differences is called an *incremental analysis,* and in it only Column 3 would be shown. In a *total analysis,* all three columns are shown. The choice of an incremental or a total analysis is a matter of individual preference.

Deletion or Addition of Products or Departments

Consider a discount department store that has three major departments: groceries, general merchandise, and drugs. Management is considering dropping groceries, which have consistently shown a net loss. The present annual net income follows:

		Departments		
	Total	Groceries	General Merchandise	Drugs
		(In thousands of dollars)		
Sales	$1,900	$1,000	$800	$100
Variable cost of goods sold and expenses	1,420	800	560	60
Contribution margin	$ 480(25%)	$ 200(20%)	$240(30%)	$ 40(40%)
Fixed expenses (salaries, depreciation, insurance, property taxes etc.)				
Separable*	$ 265	$ 150	$100	$ 15
Joint—but allocated	180	60	100	20
Total fixed expenses	$ 445	$ 210	$200	$ 35
Net income	$ 35	$ (10)	$ 40	$ 5

*Includes department salaries and other separable costs which could be avoided by not operating the specific department.

Assume that the alternatives are to drop or continue the grocery department. Assume further that the total assets invested will not be affected by the decision. The vacated space will be idle. Which alternative would you recommend?

Income Statements	A Keep Groceries	B Drop Groceries	A − B Difference
Sales	$1,900	$900	$1,000
Variable expenses	1,420	620	800
Contribution margin	$ 480	$280	$ 200
Separable fixed expenses	265	115	150
Profit contribution to joint space and other costs	$ 215	$165	$ 50
Joint space and other costs	180	180	—
Net income	$ 35	$(15)	$ 50

The preceding analysis shows that matters would be worse, rather than better, if groceries were dropped and the vacated facilities left idle. In short, as the income statement shows, groceries bring in a contribution margin of $200,000—$50,000 more than the $150,000 separable fixed expenses which would be saved by closing the grocery department.

Assume now that the space made available by the dropping of groceries would be used by an expanded general merchandise department. The space would be occupied by merchandise that would increase sales by $500,000, generate a 30 percent contribution-margin percentage, and have separable fixed costs of $70,000. The operating picture would then be improved by an increase in net income of $30,000—from $35,000 to $65,000.

	Total	General Merchandise	Drugs
		(In thousands of dollars)	
Sales	$1,400	$800 + $500	$100
Variable expenses	970	560 + 350	60
Contribution margin	$ 430	$240 + $150	$ 40
Separable fixed expenses	185	100 + 70	15
Profit contribution to joint space and other costs	$ 245	$140 $ 80	$ 25
Joint space and other costs*	180		
Net income	$ 65		

*Former grocery fixed costs, which were allocations of joint costs that will continue regardless of how the space is occupied.

As the following summary analysis demonstrates, the objective is to obtain, from a given amount of space or capacity, the maximum contribution to the payment of those costs that remain unaffected by the nature of the product sold:

	Profit Contribution of Given Space		
	Groceries	*Expansion of General Merchandise*	*Difference*
Sales	$1,000	$500	$500 *U*
Variable expenses	800	350	450 *F*
Contribution margin	$ 200	$150	$ 50 *U*
Directly separable fixed expense	150	70	80 *F*
Profit contribution to joint space costs	$ 50	$ 80	$ 30 F

F = Favorable difference resulting from replacing groceries with general merchandise.
U = Unfavorable difference.

In this case, the general merchandise will not achieve the dollar sales volume that groceries will, but the higher markups and the lower wages (mostly because of the diminished need for stocking and checkout clerks) will bring more favorable net results.

Contribution to Profit per Unit
of Limiting Factor

When a multiple-product plant is being operated at capacity, decisions as to which orders to accept must often be made. The contribution approach is also applicable here, because the product to be pushed or the order to be accepted is the one that makes the biggest *total* profit contribution per unit of the limiting factor.

The contribution approach must be used wisely, however. Sometimes, a major pitfall is the erroneous tendency to favor those products with the biggest contribution-margin ratios per sales dollar.

Assume that a company has two products:

	Product	
Per Unit	*A*	*B*
Selling price	$20	$30
Variable costs	16	21
Contribution margin	$ 4	$ 9
Contribution-margin ratio	20%	30%

Which product is more profitable? Product *B* apparently is more profitable than *A:* however, one important fact has been purposely withheld—the time that it takes to produce each product. If 10,000 hours of capacity are available, and three units of *A* can be produced per hour in contrast to one unit of *B,* your choice would be *A,* because it contributes the most profit per hour, the **limiting, critical,** or **scarce factor** in this example:

	A	B
Contribution margin per hour	$12	$9
Total contribution for 10,000 hours	$120,000	$90,000

The limiting, critical, or scarce factor is that item which restricts or constrains the production or sale of a given product. **Thus the criterion for maximizing profits, for a given capacity, is to obtain the greatest possible contribution to profit per unit of the limiting or critical factor.** The limiting factor in the above example may be machine-hours or labor-hours. In the discount store example, it was square feet of floor space. It may be cubic feet of display space. In such cases, a ratio such as the conventional gross-profit percentage (gross profit ÷ selling price) is an insufficient clue to profitability because profits also depend on the stock turnover (number of times the average inventory is sold per year).

The success of the suburban discount department stores illustrates the concept of the contribution to profit per unit of limiting factor. These stores have been satisfied with subnormal markups because they have been able to increase turnover and thus increase the contribution to profit per unit of space (Exhibit 12-6).

EXHIBIT 12-6

	REGULAR DEPARTMENT STORE	DISCOUNT DEPARTMENT STORE
Retail price	$4.00	$3.50
Cost of merchandise	3.00	3.00
Contribution to profit per unit	$1.00 (25%)	$ .50 (14+%)
Units sold per year	10,000	22,000
Total contribution to profit, assuming the same space allotment in both stores	$10,000	$11,000

Make or Buy and Idle Facilities

Manufacturers are often confronted with the question of whether to make or buy a product—whether, for example, to manufacture their own parts and subassemblies or buy them from vendors. The qualitative factors may be of paramount importance. Sometimes the manufacture of parts requires special know-how, unusually skilled labor, rare materials, and the like. The desire to control the quality of parts is often the determining factor in the decision to make them. Then, too, companies hesitate to destroy mutually advantageous long-run relationships by erratic order giving, which results from making parts during slack times and buying them during prosperous times. They may have difficulty in obtaining any parts during boom times, when there are shortages of material and workers and no shortage of sales orders.

What are the quantitative factors relevant to the decision of whether to make or buy? The answer, again, depends on the context. A key factor is whether there are idle facilities. Many companies make parts only when their facilities cannot be used to better advantage.

Assume that the following costs are reported:

Cost of Making Part No. 300

	Total cost for 10,000 units	Cost Per Unit
Direct material	$10,000	$1
Direct labor	80,000	8
Variable overhead	40,000	4
Fixed overhead, separable	20,000	2
Fixed overhead, joint but allocated	30,000	3
Total costs	$180,000	$18

Another manufacturer offers to sell B Company the same part for $16. Should B Company make or buy the part?

Although the above figures seemingly indicate that the company should buy, the answer is rarely obvious. The key question is the difference in expected future costs as between the alternatives. If the $3 fixed overhead assigned to each unit represents those costs (e.g., depreciation, property taxes, insurance, reapportioned executive salaries) that will continue regardless of the decision, the entire $3 becomes irrelevant.

Again, it is risky to say categorically that only the variable costs are relevant. Perhaps all of the $2 of directly identifiable fixed costs will be saved if the parts are bought instead of made. In other words, fixed costs that may be avoided in the future are relevant.

For the moment, let us assume that the capacity now used to make parts will become idle if the parts are purchased. The relevant computations follow:

	Per Unit		Totals	
	Make	Buy	Make	Buy
Direct material	$ 1		$ 10,000	
Direct labor	8		80,000	
Variable overhead	4		40,000	
Fixed overhead that can be avoided by not making	2		20,000	
Total relevant costs	$15	$16	$150,000	$160,000
Difference in favor of making		$1		$10,000

Essence of Make or Buy: Opportunity Cost

Fundamentally, the choice in the preceding example is not whether to make or buy; it is how best to utilize available facilities. Although the data indicate that making the part is the better choice, the figures are not conclusive—primarily because we have no idea of what can be done with the manufacturing facilities if the component is bought. Only if the released facilities are to remain idle are the above figures valid.

On the other hand, if the released facilities can be used advantageously in some other manufacturing activity or can be rented out, these additional alternatives should be considered. Suppose that the decision to manufacture entailed the rejection of an opportunity to rent the given capacity to another manufacturer for $5,000 annually. The two courses of action in the preceding example have become three, and can be analyzed in the following summary form:

	Make	Buy and Not Rent	Buy and Rent
Obtaining of parts	$150,000	$160,000	$160,000
Rent revenue	—	—	(5,000)
Total relevant costs	$150,000	$160,000	$155,000

Alternatively, the opportunity-cost approach yields the same difference in results, but the format of the analysis differs:

	Make	Buy
Obtaining of parts	$150,000	$160,000
Opportunity cost: rent foregone	5,000	
Total relevant costs	$155,000	$160,000

An **opportunity cost** is the measurable sacrifice in rejecting an alternative; it is the maximum amount foregone by forsaking an alternative; it is the maximum earning that might have been obtained if the productive good, service, or capacity had been applied to some alternative use. The opportunity cost of making the parts is the sacrifice of the chance to get $5,000 rental. A common example of an opportunity cost would be that arising from the personal decisions made by many managers who quit their jobs to enter business for themselves. Their opportunity cost is their foregone salary.

Note that opportunity costs are not ordinarily incorporated in formal accounting systems. Such costs represent incomes foregone by rejecting alternatives; therefore, opportunity costs do not involve cash receipts or outlays. Accountants usually confine their recording to those events that ultimately involve exchanges of assets. Accountants confine their history to alternatives selected rather than those rejected, primarily because of the impracticality or impossibility of accumulating meaningful data on what might have been.

Policy Making for Make or Buy

Costs must be related to time. A cost which is fixed over a short period is variable over a longer period. Profits may increase momentarily by applying the contribution-margin approach to decisions but, over the long run, profits may suffer by inordinate use of such an approach. Thus, companies develop long-run policies for the use of capacity:

> One company stated that it solicits subcontract work for other manufacturers during periods when sales of its own products do not fully utilize the plant, but that such work cannot be carried on regularly without expansion of its plant. The profit margin on subcontracts is not sufficiently large to cover these additional costs and hence work is accepted only when other business is lacking. The same company sometimes meets a period of high volume by purchasing parts or having them made by subcontractors. While the cost of such parts is usually higher than the cost to make them in the company's own plant, the additional cost is less than it would be if they were made on equipment which could be used only part of the time.[2]

[2] *The Analysis of Cost-Volume-Profit Relationships,* National Association of Accountants, Research Series No. 17, p. 552.

Factors that Influence Prices

391

**Relevant Costs and
the Contribution
Approach to
Problem Solving**

Many businessmen say that they use cost-plus pricing—that is, they compute an average unit cost and add a "reasonable" markup which will generate an adequate return on investment. This entails circular reasoning because price, which influences sales volume, is based upon full cost, which in turn is partly determined by the underlying volume of sales. Also, the plus in cost-plus is rarely an unalterable markup. Its magnitude depends on the behavior of competitors and customers. There are three major factors that influence pricing decisions: customers, competitors, and costs.

Customers always have an alternative source of supply, can substitute one material for another, and may make a part rather than buy it if the vendor's prices are too high.

Competitors will usually react to price changes made by their rivals. Tinkering with prices is usually most heavily influenced by the price setter's expectations of competitors' reactions.

The maximum price that may be charged is the one that does not drive the customer away. The minimum price is zero; companies may give out free samples to gain entry into a market. A more practical guide is that, in the short run, the *minimum* price to be quoted, *subject to consideration of long-run effects,* should be the costs that may be avoided by not landing the order—often all variable costs.

Guiding Decisions: Target Pricing

When a company has little influence over price, it usually sells at the market price and tries, by controlling costs, to achieve profitable operations. When a company can set its own prices, its procedures are often a combination of shrewd guessing and mysterious folklore. Often the first step is to accumulate costs and add a markup. This is the target price. Subsequent adjustments may be made "in light of market conditions."

There are many ways to arrive at the same target price. They simply reflect different arrangements of the components of the same income statement.

However, when it is used intelligently, the contribution approach has distinct advantages over the traditional approach, which fails to highlight different cost behavior patterns:

First, the contribution approach offers more detailed information than the traditional full-costing approach because variable- and fixed-cost behavior patterns are explicitly delineated. Because the contribution approach is sensitive to cost-volume-profit relationships, it is a better, easier basis for developing pricing formulas.

Second, a normal or target-pricing formula can be as easily developed by the contribution approach as by traditional full-costing approaches. Consider the facts in Exhibit 12-7. Note that under traditional approaches the target markup percentage (66.7 percent) is often expressed

EXHIBIT 12-7

Comparison of Contribution Approach
and Traditional Approach to Pricing

BUDGETED INCOME STATEMENT	CONTRIBUTION APPROACH		
		PERCENT OF SALES	PERCENT OF TOTAL VARIABLE COSTS
Sales		$100,000	100	200
Variable factory cost of goods sold	$40,000			
Variable selling and administrative expenses	10,000	50,000	50	100
Contribution margin		$ 50,000	50	100
Fixed costs:				
Factory costs	$20,000			
Selling and administrative costs	20,000	40,000	40	80
Target net income		$ 10,000	10	20

Note: To obtain a target net income of $10,000, the target or normal markup percentage must be $50,000 ÷ $50,000 = 100 percent of total variable costs.

BUDGETED INCOME STATEMENT	TRADITIONAL APPROACH		
		PERCENT OF SALES	PERCENT OF FACTORY COST OF GOODS SOLD
Sales	$100,000	100	166.7
Factory cost of goods sold*	60,000	60	100.0
Gross profit	$ 40,000	40	66.7
Operating expenses†	30,000	30	50.0
Target net income	$ 10,000	10	16.7

*Includes fixed costs of $20,000
†Includes fixed costs of $20,000

Note: To obtain a target net income of $10,000, the target or normal markup percentage must be $40,000 ÷ $60,000 = 66.7 percent of manufacturing cost.

as a percentage of total manufacturing costs. In contrast, under the contribution approach the target markup percentage could also be expressed as 100 percent of total variable costs. Under *either* approach, the pricing decision maker will have a formula that will lead him toward the *same* target price. If he is unable to obtain such a price consistently, the company will not achieve its $10,000-income objectives or its desired net income percentage of sales.

Third, the contribution approach offers insight into the short-run versus long-run effects of cutting prices on special orders. For example, assume the same cost behavior patterns as in Exhibit 12-7. Assume further that a customer offers $540 for some units that would have an ordinary target price of $1,000. Should the offer be accepted? No categorical answer can be given, but more information relevant to a decision can be generated by the contribution approach:

	Traditional Approach	Contribution Approach
Sales price	$540	$540
Factory cost of goods sold	600	
Total variable costs		500
Apparent decrease in net income	$ – 60	
Contribution margin		$ 40

Compare the two approaches. Under the traditional approach, the decision maker has no direct knowledge of cost-volume-profit relationships. He makes his decision by hunch. On the surface, the offer is definitely unattractive because the price of $540 is $60 below factory costs.

Under the contribution approach, the decision maker sees a short-run advantage of $40 from accepting the offer. Fixed costs will be unaffected by whatever decision is made and net income will increase by $40. Still, there are long-run effects to consider. Will acceptance of the offer undermine the long-run price structure? In other words, is the short-run advantage of $40 more than offset by high probable long-run financial disadvantages? The decision maker may think so and may reject the offer. But—and this is important—by doing so he is, in effect, saying that *he is willing to forego $40 now in order to protect his long-run market advantages.* Generally, he can assess problems of this sort by asking whether the probability of long-run benefits is worth an "investment" equal to the foregone contribution margin ($40 in this case). Under traditional approaches, he must ordinarily conduct a special study to find the immediate effects; under the contribution approach, he has a system that will routinely provide such information.

Our general theme of different costs for different purposes also extends into the area of pricing. To say that the contribution approach or traditional approach provides the best guide to pricing decisions is a dangerous oversimplification of one of the most perplexing problems in business. Lack of understanding and judgment can lead to unprofitable pricing regardless of the kind of cost data available or cost-accounting system used.

Frequently, managers are reluctant to employ a contribution approach because of fears that variable costs will be substituted indiscriminately for full costs and will therefore lead to suicidal price cutting. This should *not* occur if the data are used wisely. However, if top management perceives a pronounced danger of underpricing when variable-cost data are revealed, they may justifiably prefer a full-cost approach to guiding pricing decisions.

A complete discussion of pricing is beyond the scope of this book. However, a contribution approach should clarify the major classes of information that bear on the pricing decision.

Robinson-Patman Act

The pricing decision is further complicated by the Robinson-Patman Act, which forbids quoting different prices to competing customers unless such price discrimination is justified by differences in costs of manufacturing, sale, or delivery. Decisions of courts and of the Federal Trade Commission have been based on allocation of full cost rather than on computation of incremental or differential cost.

Most of these price differentials are justified by differences in distribution costs (e.g., advertising, warehousing, and freight), rather than by differences in manufacturing costs. Companies with flexible-pricing policies need to keep thorough records of distribution costs in order to be able to answer any government inquiries. However, cost justification is only one aspect of these cases. In most instances, it has been overshadowed by the issues of lessening competition and price cutting in good faith.

IRRELEVANCE OF PAST COSTS

As defined earlier, a relevant cost is (a) an expected future cost that will (b) differ between alternatives. The contribution aspect of relevant-cost analysis has shown that those expected future costs that will not differ among alternatives are irrelevant. Now we return to the idea that all past costs are also irrelevant.

Obsolete Inventory

A company has 100 obsolete missile parts that are carried in inventory at a manufacturing cost of $100,000. The parts can be: (1) remachined for $30,000, and then sold for $50,000; or (2) scrapped for $5,000. Which should be done?

This is an unfortunate situation; yet the $100,000 cost is irrelevant to the decision to remachine or scrap. The only relevant factors are the expected future revenue and costs:

	Remachine	Scrap	Difference
Expected future revenue	$ 50,000	$ 5,000	$45,000
Expected future costs	30,000	—	30,000
Relevant excess of revenue over costs	$ 20,000	$ 5,000	$15,000
Accumulated historical inventory costs*	100,000	100,000	—
Net overall loss on project	$(80,000)	$(95,000)	$15,000

*Irrelevant because it is not an element of difference as between the alternatives.

We could completely ignore the historical cost and still arrive at the $15,000 difference, the key figure in the analysis.

Book Value of Old Equipment

For now, we shall not consider all aspects of equipment-replacement decisions, but we shall turn to one widely misunderstood facet of the replacement problem—the role of the book value of the old equipment. Suppose that an old machine originally cost $10,000, has accumulated depreciation of $6,000, and has four years of useful life remaining. It can be sold for $2,500 cash now, but will have no disposal value at the end of the four years. A new machine, which (to simplify the analysis) will also have a useful life of four years, is available for $6,000. The new machine will reduce cash operating costs (maintenance, power, repairs, coolants, and the like) from $5,000 to $3,000 annually, but it will have no disposal value at the end of four years. Prepare a comparative analysis of the two alternatives.

The most widely misunderstood facet of replacement analysis is the role of the book value of the old equipment in the decision. The book value, in this context, is sometimes called a *sunk cost,* which is really just another term for historical or past cost. All historical costs are always irrelevant. Therefore the book value of the old equipment is always irrelevant in replacement decisions. At one time or another, we all like to think that we can soothe our wounded pride arising from having made a bad purchase decision by using the item instead of replacing it. The fallacy here is in erroneously thinking that a current or future action can influence the long-run impact of a past outlay. All past costs are down the drain. *Nothing* can change what has already happened.

We can apply our definition of relevance to four commonly encountered items:

1. *Book value of old equipment.* Irrelevant, because it is a past (historical) cost. Therefore, depreciation on old equipment is irrelevant.

2. *Disposal value of old equipment.* Relevant (ordinarily), because it is an expected future inflow that usually differs between alternatives.

3. *Gain or loss on disposal.* This is the algebraic difference between 1 and 2. It is therefore a meaningless combination of book value, which is always

irrelevant, and disposal value, which is usually relevant. The combination form, *loss* (or *gain*) *on disposal,* blurs the distinction between the irrelevant book value and the relevant disposal value. Consequently, it is best to think of each separately.[3]

4. *Cost of new equipment.* Relevant, because it is an expected future outflow that will differ between alternatives. Therefore, depreciation on new equipment is relevant.

Exhibit 12-8 should clarify the above assertions. Book value of old equipment is irrelevant regardless of the decision-making technique used. The "difference" columns in Exhibit 12-8 show that book value of old equipment is not an element of difference between alternatives and could be completely ignored without changing the $1,125 difference in average annual net income. No matter what the *timing* of the charge against revenue, the *amount* charged is still $4,000, regardless of any available alternative. In either event, the undepreciated cost will be written off with the same ultimate effect on profit.[4] The $4,000 creeps into the income

[3] For simplicity, we ignore income tax considerations and the effects of the interest value of money in this chapter. But book value is irrelevant even if income taxes are considered, because the relevant item is then the tax cash flow, not the book value. Using the approach in Exhibit 12-1, the book value is essential information for the *prediction method,* but the expected future income tax cash outflows are the relevant information for the *decision model.* The prediction method would be: Disposal value, $2,500 − Book value, $4,000 = Loss on disposal, $1,500. If the income tax rate is 50 percent, the income tax cash saving would be $750. This $750 would be the expected future cash flow that is relevant input to the decision model. For elaboration, see Chapter 14.

[4] We are deliberately ignoring income tax factors for the time being. If income taxes are considered, the *timing* of the writing off of fixed-asset costs may influence income tax payments. In this example, there will be a small real difference: the present value of $40,000 as a tax deduction now versus the present value of a $10,000 tax deduction each year for four years. But this difference in *future* income tax flows is the *relevant* item—not the book value of the old fixed asset *per se.* See Chapter 14.

EXHIBIT 12-8

Cost Comparison—Replacement of Equipment
Including Relevant and Irrelevant Items

	FOUR YEARS TOGETHER			ANNUALIZED (DIVIDED BY 4)		
	KEEP	REPLACE	DIFFERENCE	KEEP	REPLACE	DIFFERENCE
Cash operating costs	$20,000	$12,000	$ 8,000	$ 5,000	$ 3,000	$ 2,000
Old equipment (book value):						
Periodic write-off as depreciation	4,000	—	—	1,000	—	—
or						
Lump-sum write-off		4,000*	—	—	1,000	
Disposal value	—	−2,500*	2,500	—	−625	625
New machine, written off						
periodically as depreciation	—	6,000	−6,000	—	1,500	−1,500
Total costs	$24,000	$19,500	$ 4,500	$ 6,000	$ 4,875	$ 1,125

*In a formal income statement, these two items would be combined as "loss on disposal" of $1,500.

statement either as a $4,000 offset against the $2,500 proceeds to obtain the $1,500 *loss on disposal* in one year, or as $1,000 depreciation in each of four years. But how it appears is irrelevant to the replacement decision. In contrast, the $1,500 annual depreciation on the new equipment *is* relevant because the total $6,000 depreciation may be avoided by not replacing.

Note the motivational factors here. A manager may be reluctant to replace simply because the large loss on disposal will severely harm his profit performance in the first year. Many managers and accountants would not replace the old machine because it would entail recognizing a $1,500 "loss on disposal," whereas retention would allow spreading the $4,000 over four years in the form of "depreciation expense" (a more appealing term than "loss on disposal"). This demonstrates how overemphasis on short-run income may conflict with the objective of maximizing income over the long run.

The advantage of replacement is $4,500 for the four years together; the average annual advantage is $1,125.

Examining Alternatives Over the Long Run

The foregoing is the first example that has looked beyond one year. A useful technique is to view the alternatives over their entire lives and then to compute annual average results. In this way, peculiar nonrecurring items (such as loss on disposal) will not obstruct the long-run view that must necessarily be taken in almost all special managerial decisions.

Exhibit 12-9 concentrates on relevant items only. Note that the same answer (the $4,500 net difference) will be produced even though the book value is completely omitted from the calculations. The only relevant items are the cash operating costs, the disposal value of the old equipment, and the depreciation on the new equipment.

Finally, the amount of the book value will not affect the answer. To prove this, suppose the book value of the old equipment is $500,000 rather

EXHIBIT 12-9
Cost Comparison—Replacement of Equipment,
Relevant Items Only

	FOUR YEARS TOGETHER			ANNUALIZED (DIVIDED BY 4)		
	KEEP	REPLACE	DIFFERENCE	KEEP	REPLACE	DIFFERENCE
Cash operating costs	$20,000	$12,000	$ 8,000	$5,000	$3,000	$2,000
Disposal value of old equipment	—	−2,500	2,500	—	−625	625
Depreciation—new equipment	—	6,000	−6,000	—	1,500	−1,500
Total relevant costs	$20,000	$15,500	$ 4,500	$5,000	$3,875	$1,125

than $4,000. Your final answer will not be changed. The cumulative advantage of replacement would still be $4,500. (If you are in doubt, rework this example, using $500,000 as the book value.)

IRRELEVANCE OF FUTURE COSTS THAT WILL NOT DIFFER

The past costs in the preceding two examples were not an element of difference between the alternatives. As was noted, the $100,000 inventory and the $4,000 book value were included under both alternatives and were irrelevant because they were the same for all alternatives under consideration.

There are also expected *future* costs that may be irrelevant because they will be the same under all feasible alternatives. These, too, may be safely ignored for a particular decision. The cost of lubrication and the direct labor cost in our initial examples in the chapter are illustrations of expected future costs that will not be affected by the decision at hand.

Other examples include many fixed costs that will be unaffected by such considerations as whether Machine *A* or Machine *B* is selected, or whether a special order is accepted. However, it is not merely a case of saying that fixed costs are irrelevant and variable costs are relevant. We have already seen that variable costs (lubrication and direct labor in our first two examples) can be irrelevant and, in our preceding example, that fixed costs (cost of new equipment) can be relevant. Fixed costs are relevant whenever they differ under the alternatives at hand.

BEWARE OF UNIT COSTS

Unit costs should be analyzed with care in decision making. There are two major ways to go wrong: (a) the inclusion of irrelevant costs, such as the $3 allocation of joint costs in the make-or-buy example which would result in a unit cost of $18 instead of the relevant unit cost of $15; and (b) comparisons of unit costs not computed on the same basis, as the following example demonstrates. Generally, it is advisable to use total costs rather than unit costs. Then, if desired, the totals may be unitized. Machinery salesmen, for example, often brag about the low unit costs of using the new machines. Sometimes, they neglect to point out that the unit costs are based on outputs far in excess of the volume of activity of their prospective customer.

Assume that a new $100,000 machine with a five-year life can produce 100,000 units a year at a variable cost of $1 per unit, as opposed to a variable cost per unit of $1.50 with an old machine. Is the new machine a worthwhile acquisition?

It is attractive at first glance. If the customer produces 100,000 units, unit-cost comparisons would be valid, provided that new depreciation is also considered. Assume that the disposal value of the old equipment is zero. Because depreciation is an allocation of historical cost, the depreciation on the old machine is irrelevant. In contrast, the depreciation on the new machine is relevant because the new machine entails a future cost that can be avoided by not acquiring it.

	Old Machine	New Machine
Units	100,000	100,000
Variable costs	$150,000	$100,000
Straight-line depreciation	—	20,000
Total relevant costs	$150,000	$120,000
Unit relevant costs	$ 1.50	$ 1.20

However, if the customer's expected volume is only 30,000 units a year, the unit costs change:

	Old Machine	New Machine
Units	30,000	30,000
Variable costs	$45,000	$30,000
Straight-line depreciation	—	20,000
Total relevant costs	$45,000	$50,000
Unit relevant costs	$ 1.50	$ 1.6667

THE PROBLEM OF UNCERTAINTY

It is vitally important to recognize that throughout this chapter and the next, dollar amounts of future sales and operating costs are assumed in order to highlight and to simplify various important points. In practice, the forecasting of these key figures is generally the most difficult aspect of decision analysis. For elaboration, see Chapter 17.

SUMMARY

The accountant's role in problem solving is primarily that of a technical expert on cost analysis. His responsibility is to be certain that the manager uses *relevant data* in guiding his decisions. Accountants and managers must have a penetrating understanding of relevant costs.

To be relevant to a particular decision, a cost must meet two criteria:

(1) it must be an expected *future* cost; and (2) it must be an element of *difference* as between the alternatives. All *past (historical* or *sunk)* costs are in themselves irrelevant to any decision about the future, although they often provide the best available basis for the prediction of expected future data.

The combination of the relevant costing and contribution approaches is a fundamental framework, based on economic analysis, that may be applied to a vast range of problems. The following are among the more important generalizations regarding various decisions:

1. Joint product costs are irrelevant in decisions about whether to sell at split-off or process further.

2. Incremental costs or differential costs are the differences in the total costs under each alternative.

3. The key to obtaining the maximum profit from a given capacity is to obtain the greatest possible contribution to profit per unit of the limiting or scarce factor.

4. Make-or-buy decisions are, fundamentally, examples of obtaining the most profitable utilization of given facilities.

5: Sometimes the notion of an opportunity cost is helpful in cost analysis. An opportunity cost is the maximum sacrifice in rejecting an alternative; it is the maximum earning that might have been obtained if the productive good, service, or capacity had been applied to some alternative use. The opportunity-cost approach does not affect the important final differences between the courses of action, but the format of the analysis differs.

6. The contribution approach to pricing offers more helpful information because the foregone contribution can be quantified as the investment currently being made to protect long-run benefits.

7. The book value of old equipment is always irrelevant in replacement decisions. This cost is often called a *sunk cost.* Disposal value, however, is generally relevant.

8. Generally, it is advisable to use total costs, rather than unit costs, in cost analysis.

SUMMARY PROBLEM FOR YOUR REVIEW

Problem

Exhibit 12-10 contains data for the Block Company for the year which has just ended. The company makes parts which are used in the final assembly of its finished product.

EXHIBIT 12-10

	A + B COMPANY AS A WHOLE	A FINISHED PRODUCT*	B PARTS
Sales: 100,000 units, @ $100	$10,000,000		
Variable costs:			
Direct material	$ 4,900,000	$4,400,000	$ 500,000
Direct labor	700,000	400,000	300,000
Variable factory overhead	300,000	100,000	200,000
Other variable costs	100,000	100,000	—
Sales commissions, @ 10%			
of sales	1,000,000	1,000,000	—
Total variable costs	$ 7,000,000	$6,000,000	$1,000,000
Contribution margin	$ 3,000,000		
Separable discretionary costs	$ 1,800,000	$1,450,000	$ 350,000
Separable committed costs	500,000	450,000	50,000
Joint discretionary and			
committed costs	400,000	320,000	80,000
Total fixed costs	$ 2,700,000	$2,220,000	$ 480,000
Operating income	$ 300,000		

*Not including the cost of parts (Column B).

Required:

1. During the year, a prospective customer in an unrelated market offered $82,000 for 1,000 finished units. The latter would be in addition to the 100,000 units sold. The regular sales commission rate would have been paid. The president rejected the order because "it was below our costs of $97 per unit." What would operating income have been if the order had been accepted?

2. A supplier offered to manufacture the year's supply of 100,000 parts for $13.50 each. What would be the effect on operating income if the Block Company purchased rather than made the parts? Assume that the separable discretionary costs assigned to parts would have been avoided if the parts were purchased.

3. The company could have purchased the parts for $13.50 each and used the vacated space for the manufacture of a deluxe version of their major product. Assume that 20,000 deluxe units could have been made (and sold in addition to the 100,000 regular units) at a unit variable cost of $70, exclusive of parts and exclusive of the 10 percent sales commission. The sales price would have been $110. The fixed costs pertaining to the parts would have continued, including the $350,000 separable discretionary costs, because these costs related primarily to the manufacturing facilities utilized. What would operating income have been if Block bought the necessary parts and made and sold the deluxe units?

Solution

1. Costs of filling special order:

Direct material	$49,000
Direct labor	7,000
Variable factory overhead	3,000
Other variable cost	1,000
Sales commission, @ 10% of $82,000	8,200
Total variable costs	$68,200
Selling price	82,000
Contribution margin	$13,800

Net income would have been $300,000 + $13,800, or $313,800, if the order had been accepted. In a sense, the decision to reject the offer implies that the Block Company is willing to invest $13,800 in immediate gains foregone (an opportunity cost) in order to preserve the long-run selling-price structure.

2. Assuming that the $350,000 separable discretionary costs could have been avoided by not making the parts and that the other fixed costs would have been continued, the alternatives can be summarized as follows:

	Make	*Buy*
Purchase cost		$1,350,000
Variable costs	$1,000,000	
Separable discretionary costs	350,000	
Total relevant costs	$1,350,000	$1,350,000

If the facilities used for parts were to become idle, the Block Company would be indifferent as to whether to make or buy. Operating income would be unaffected.

3.

Sales would increase by 20,000 units, @ $110		$2,200,000
Variable costs exclusive of parts would increase by 20,000 units, @ $70	$1,400,000	
Plus the sales commission, 10% of $2,200,000	220,000	1,620,000
Contribution margin on 20,000 units		$ 580,000
Parts: 120,000 rather than 100,000 would be needed		
Buy 120,000, @ $13.50	$1,620,000	
Make 100,000, @ $10 (only the variable costs are relevant)	1,000,000	
Excess cost of outside purchase		620,000
Fixed costs, unchanged		—
Disadvantage of making deluxe units		$ (40,000)

Operating income would decline to $260,000 ($300,000 — $40,000, the disadvantage of selling the deluxe units). The deluxe units bring in a contribution margin of $580,000, but the additional costs of buying rather than making parts is $620,000, leading to a net disadvantage of $40,000.

ASSIGNMENT MATERIAL

Fundamental Assignment Material

12-1. Terminology. Define: *qualitative factor; relevant data for decision making; sunk cost; historical cost; joint product costs; incremental cost; differential cost; and opportunity cost.*

12-2. Role of old equipment in replacement. On January 2, 19x1, the Clarion Company installed a brand-new $81,000 special molding machine for producing a new product. The product and the machine have an expected life of three years. The machine's expected disposal value at the end of three years is zero.

On January 3, 19x1, Jim Swaze, a star salesman for a machine tool manufacturer, tells Mr. Clarion: "I wish I had known earlier of your purchase plans. I can supply you with a technically superior machine for $100,000. The old machine can be sold for $16,000. I guarantee that our machine will save $35,000 per year in cash operating costs, although it too will have no disposal value at the end of three years."

Mr. Clarion examines some technical data. Although he has confidence in Swaze's claims, Clarion contends: "I'm locked in now. My alternatives are clear: (a) disposal will result in a loss; (b) keeping and using the 'old' equipment avoids such a loss. I have brains enough to avoid a loss when my other alternative is recognizing a loss. We've got to use that equipment till we get our money out of it."

The annual operating costs of the old machine are expected to be $60,000, exclusive of depreciation. Sales, all in cash, will be $900,000 per year. Other annual cash expenses will be $800,000 regardless of this decision. Assume that the equipment in question is the company's only fixed asset. Note that the facts in this problem are probed more deeply in Problems 13-4 and 14-3.

Required:

Ignore income taxes and the time value of money.

1. Prepare statements of cash receipts and disbursements as they would appear in each of the next three years under both alternatives. What is the total net difference in cash flow for the three years?
2. Prepare income statements as they would appear in each of the next three years under both alternatives. Assume straight-line depreciation. What is the total difference in net income for the three years?
3. Assume that the cost of the "old" equipment was $1,000,000 rather than $81,000. Would the net difference computed in Requirements 1 and 2 change? Explain.
4. As Jim Swaze, reply to Clarion's contentions.
5. What are the irrelevant items in each of your presentations for Requirement 1 and 2? Why are they irrelevant?

12-3. **Unit costs and choice of most profitable product.** The Frange Corporation sells two molding powders, known as *A* and *B*. A detail of the unit income and costs is as follows:

	Product	
	A	*B*
Selling price	$12	$20
Direct material	$ 2	$ 4
Direct labor	2	1
Variable factory overhead*	2	4
Fixed factory overhead*	2	4
Total cost of goods sold	$ 8	$13
Gross profit per unit	$ 4	$ 7

*On a machine-hour basis.

As far as can be determined, the sales outlook is such that the plant could operate at full capacity on either or both products. Both *A* and *B* are processed through the same cost centers. Selling costs are completely fixed and may be ignored.

Which product should be produced? If more than one should be produced, indicate the proportions of each. Explain your answer briefly.

Additional Assignment Material

12-4. "The distinction between precision and relevancy should be kept in mind." Explain.

12-5. Distinguish between the quantitative and qualitative aspects of decisions.

12-6. "Any future cost is relevant." Do you agree? Explain.

12-7. Why are historical or past data irrelevant in special decisions?

12-8. Which of the following items are relevant in replacement decisions? Explain.
   a. Book value of old equipment.
   b. Disposal value of old equipment.
   c. Cost of new equipment.

12-9. "No technique applicable to the problem of joint product costing should be used for management decisions regarding whether a product should be sold at the split-off point or processed further." Explain. Do you agree?

12-10. "Incremental cost is the addition to costs from the manufacture of one unit." Do you agree? Explain.

12-11. Give four examples of limiting or scarce factors.

12-12. "A ratio such as the conventional gross profit percentage is an insufficient clue to profitability." Do you agree? Explain.

12-13. "I had a chance to rent my summer cottage for two weeks for $150. But I chose to have it idle. I didn't want strangers living in my summer house." What term in this chapter describes the $150? Why?

12-14. "Accountants do not formally record opportunity costs in the accounting records." Why?

12-15. There are two major reasons why unit costs should be analyzed with care in decision making. What are they?

12-16. What three major factors influence pricing decisions?

12-17. Why are customers one of the three factors influencing prices?

12-18. "I don't believe in assigning only variable costs to a job for guiding pricing. This results in suicidal underpricing." Do you agree? Why?

12-19. Special order. The Prudent Company manufactures quality party hats. The current operating level, which is below full capacity of 110,000 units per year, indicates the following results for the year:

	Total	Per Unit
Sales—80,000 units @ $1.00	$80,000	$1.0000
Manufacturing cost of goods sold*	65,000	.8125
Gross profit or gross margin	$15,000	$ .1875
Selling and other expenses†	12,000	.1500
Operating income	$ 3,000	$ .0375

*Includes fixed costs of $25,000.
†Includes fixed costs of $8,000. The remaining $4,000 consists only of shipping expenses of 5¢ per unit.

A mail-order company has offered to buy 20,000 units @ 75¢. The buyer will pay for the shipping expenses. The president of Prudent is reluctant to accept the order because the 75¢ price is below the $.8125 factory unit cost. Should the offer be accepted? Explain, showing your computations.

12-20. Special order. (CMA adapted.) George Jackson operates a small machine shop. He manufactures one standard product available from many other similar businesses and he also manufactures products to customer order. His accountant prepared the annual income statement shown below:

	Custom Sales	Standard Sales	Total
Sales	$50,000	$25,000	$75,000
Material	$10,000	$8,000	$18,000
Labor	20,000	9,000	29,000
Depreciation	6,300	3,600	9,900
Power	700	400	1,100
Rent	6,000	1,000	7,000
Heat and light	600	100	700
Other	400	900	1,300
	$44,000	$23,000	$67,000
	$ 6,000	$ 2,000	$ 8,000

The depreciation charges are for machines used in the respective product lines. The power charge is apportioned on the estimate of power consumed. The rent is for the building space which has been leased for ten years at $7,000 per year. The rent and heat and light are apportioned to the product lines based on amount of floor space occupied. All other costs are current expenses identified with the product line causing them.

A valued custom-parts customer has asked Mr. Jackson if he would manufacture 5,000 special units for him. Mr. Jackson is working at capacity and would have to give up some other business in order to take this business. He can't renege on custom orders already agreed to, but he could reduce the output of his standard product about one-half for one year while producing the specially requested custom part. The customer is willing to pay $7 for each part. The material cost will be about $2.00 per unit and the labor will be $3.60 per unit. Mr. Jackson will have to spend $2,000 for a special device which will be discarded when the job is done.

Required:

1. Calculate and present the following costs related to the 5,000-unit custom order:
   a. The incremental cost of the order.
   b. The full cost of the order.
   c. The opportunity cost of taking the order.
2. Should Mr. Jackson take the order? Explain your answer.

12-21. Utilization of passenger jets. In 19x2, Continental Air Lines, Inc., filled 50 percent of the available seats on its Boeing 707 jet flights, a record about 15 percent below the national average.

Continental could have eliminated 4 percent of its runs and raised its average load considerably. But the improved load factor would have reduced profits. Give reasons for or against this elimination. What factors should influence an airline's scheduling policies?

When you answer this question, suppose that Continental had a basic package of 3,000 flights per month that had an average of 100 seats available per flight. Also suppose that 52 percent of the seats were filled at an average ticket price of $50 per flight. Variable costs are about 70 percent of revenue.

Continental also had a marginal package of 120 flights per month that had an average of 100 seats available per flight. Suppose that only 20 percent of the seats were filled at an average ticket price of $40 per flight. Variable costs are about 50% of this revenue. Prepare a tabulation of the basic package, marginal package, and total package, showing percentage of seats filled, revenue, variable expenses, and contribution margin.

12-22. Effects of new technology. A large automobile parts plant was constructed four years ago in an Ohio city served by two railroads. The PC Railroad purchased forty specialized sixty-foot freight cars as a direct result of the additional traffic generated by the new plant. The investment was based on an estimated useful life of twenty years.

Now the competing railroad has offered to service the plant with new 86-foot freight cars which would enable more efficient shipping operations at the plant. The automobile company has threatened to switch carriers unless PC Railroad buys ten new 86-foot freight cars.

The PC marketing management wants to buy the new cars, but PC operating management says: "The new investment is undesirable. It really consists of the new outlay plus the loss on the old freight cars. The old cars must be written down to a low salvage value if they cannot be used as originally intended."

Required:

Evaluate the comments. What is the correct conceptual approach to the quantitative analysis in this decision?

12-23. Profit per unit of space.

1. Several successful chains of discount department stores have merchandising policies that differ considerably from the traditional downtown department stores. Name some characteristics of these discount stores that have contributed to their success.
2. Food chains have typically regarded, perhaps, 20 percent of selling price as an average target gross profit on canned goods and similar grocery items. What are the limitations of such an approach? Be specific.

12-24. Selection of product for special promotion.

The Bost Company produces three delicious snacks, Wheatly, Cornly, and Oatly. A two-month sales promotion, during which a trinket costing 6¢ will be given away with the purchase of a box of one of the snacks, is being planned. The snack to be promoted is being selected on the basis of the following figures:

	Wheatly	Cornly	Oatly
Regular selling price, per box	25¢	20¢	30¢
Standard cost of sales	22¢	14¢	26¢
Contribution-margin ratio	20%	40%	30%
Anticipated increase in sales because of trinket	200,000 boxes	110,000 boxes	80,000 boxes

Required:

Which product should be chosen? Present appropriate figures to support your answer.

12-25. Meaning of allocation of joint costs.

1. Examine the illustration on joint costs which appears in this chapter. Suppose the joint costs were allocated on a gallonage basis. Prepare an income statement by product line on the assumption that Product Y was (a) sold at split-off, or (b) was processed further.
2. Repeat Requirement 1, assuming that the joint costs were allocated on the basis of relative sales values at split-off.
3. Which set of income statements is more meaningful, those in Requirement 1 or in 2? Why?

12-26. Joint products: sell or process further.

The Burns Company produced three joint products at a joint cost of $100,000. These products were processed further and sold as follows:

Product	Sales	Additional Processing Costs
A	$245,000	$200,000
B	330,000	300,000
C	175,000	100,000

The company has had a opportunity to sell at split-off directly to other processors. If that alternative had been selected, sales would have been: *A*, $56,000; *B*, $28,000; and *C*, $56,000.

The company expects to operate at the same level of production and sales in the forthcoming year.

Required:

Consider all the available information, and assume that all costs incurred after split-off are variable.

1. Could the company increase net income by altering its processing decisions? If so, what would be the expected overall net income?
2. Which products should be processed further and which should be sold at split-off?

12-27. Joint costs and decisions. A petrochemical company has a batch process whereby 1,000 gallons of a raw material is transformed into 100 pounds of *X-1* and 400 pounds of *X-2*. Although the joint costs of their production is $900, both products are worthless at their split-off point. Additional separable costs of $250 are necessary to give *X-1* a sales value of $750 as Product *A*. Similarly, additional separable costs of $100 are necessary to give *X-2* a sales value of $750.

Required:

You are in charge of the batch process and the marketing of both products. (Show your computations for each answer.)

1. (a) Assuming that you believe in assigning joint costs on a physical basis, allocate the total profit of $250 per batch to Products *A* and *B*.
   (b) Would you stop processing one of the products? Why?
2. (a) Assuming that you believe in assigning joint costs on a relative sales value basis, allocate the total profit of $250 per batch to Products *A* and *B*. If there is no market for *X-1* and *X-2* at their split-off point, a relative sales value is usually imputed by taking the ultimate sales values at the point of sale and working backward to obtain approximated "synthetic" relative sales values at the split-off point. These synthetic values are then used as weights for allocating the joint costs to the products.
   (b) You have internal product-profitability reports in which joint costs are assigned on a relative sales value basis. Your chief engineer says that, after seeing these reports, he has developed a method of obtaining more of Product *B* and correspondingly less of Product *A* from each batch, without changing the per pound cost factors. Would you approve this new method? Why? What would the overall net profit be if fifty more pounds of *B* were produced and fifty less pounds of *A*?

12-28. Elimination of drug-store departments: joint effects. A small drug store owner is considering dropping all services and items that are not of a pharmaceutical nature. This includes the lunch counter and various sundries (candy, magazines, stationery, cosmetics, etc.).

Other small store owners have reported that, after dropping the lunch counter, drug sales declined 10 percent and sundry sales fell 5 percent. Still others reported that after they dropped sundry items, drug sales dropped 5 percent and lunch counter sales decreased 5 percent.

At present, the store employs two pharmacists at yearly salaries of $12,000 and a counter clerk at $4,000 a year. Past experience has shown that one pharmacist is required for every $46,000 of drug sales.

In 19x4, sales and cost of goods sold were as follows:

	Drugs	Lunch Counter	Sundries
Sales	$90,000	$8,000	$15,000
Cost of goods sold	45,000	7,000	12,000

The lunch-counter employee spends about 30 percent of his time handling sundry items. If he were eliminated, a pharmacist would have to handle the sundry sales. Drug sales would decrease 1 percent as a result of inconvenience to the customers. It would not be feasible to operate the counter without a counter man.

Required:

1. What is the operating income of each operation?
2. Should any operation be dropped? What would be the saving, or the loss?
3. Assume that the owner considered the lunch counter a complete nuisance and has closed it. However, in an effort to regain lost drug sales, he is now considering cutting prices on certain manufactured drugs. He estimates that these discounts would amount to $1,000 a year, but that they would increase gross current drug sales by $10,000. This course of action would have an insignificant effect on sundry sales other than the effects already considered in Requirement 2. Sould he cut the prices?

12-29. **Make or buy.** The Fram Company's old equipment for making subassemblies is worn out. The company is considering two courses of action: (a) completely replacing the old equipment with new equipment, or (b) buying subassemblies from a reliable outside supplier who has quoted a unit price of $1 on a seven-year contract for a minimum of 50,000 units per year.

Production was 60,000 units in each of the past two years. Future needs for the next seven years are not expected to fluctuate beyond 50,000 to 70,000 units per year. Cost records for the past two years reveal the following unit costs of manufacturing the subassembly:

Direct material	$ .25	.25	.25
Direct labor	.40	·15	.10
Variable overhead	.10		.05
Fixed overhead (including $.10 depreciation and $.10 for supervision and other direct departmental fixed overhead)	.25	.25	.40
	$1.00	.65	.80

The new equipment will cost $188,000 cash, will last seven years, and will have a disposal value of $20,000. The current disposal value of the old equipment is $10,000.

The salesman for the new equipment has summarized his position as follows: The increase in machine speeds will reduce direct labor and variable overhead by 35¢ per unit. Consider last year's experience of one of your major competitors with identical equipment. They produced 100,000 units under operating conditions very comparable to yours and showed the following unit costs:

Direct material	$.25
Direct labor	.10
Variable overhead	.05
Fixed overhead, including $.24 depreciation	.40
	$.80

Required:

For purposes of this case, assume that any idle facilities cannot be put to alternative use. Also assume that 5¢ of the old Fram unit cost is allocated fixed overhead that will be unaffected by the decision.

1. The president asks you to compare the alternatives on a total annual cost basis and on a per unit basis for annual needs of 60,000 units. Which alternative seems more attractive?

2. Would your answer to Requirement 1 change if the needs were 50,000 units? 70,000 units? At what volume level would Fram be indifferent between make and buy. Show your computations.

3. What factors, other than the above, should the accountant bring to the attention of management to assist them in making their decision? Include the considerations that might be applied to the outside supplier.

For additional analysis, see Problem 13-31 and Problem 14-26.

12-30. Make or buy. (CMA adapted.) The Vernom Corporation, which produces and sells to wholesalers a highly successful line of summer lotions and insect repellents, has decided to diversify in order to stabilize sales throughout the year. A natural area for the company to consider is the production of winter lotions and creams to prevent dry and chapped skin.

After considerable research, a winter products line has been developed. However, because of the conservative nature of the company management, Vernom's president has decided to introduce only one of the new products for this coming winter. If the product is a success, further expansion in future years will be initiated.

The product selected (called Chap-Off) is a lip balm that will be sold in a lipstick-type tube. The product will be sold to wholesalers in boxes of twenty-four tubes for $8 per box. Because of available capacity, no additional fixed charges will be incurred to produce the product. However, a $100,000 fixed charge will be absorbed by the product to allocate a fair share of the company's present fixed costs to the new product.

Using the estimated sales and production of 100,000 boxes of Chap-Off as the expected volume, the accounting department has developed the following costs per box:

Direct labor	$2.00
Direct material	3.00
Total overhead	1.50
Total	$6.50

Vernom has approached a cosmetics manufacturer to discuss the possibility of purchasing the tubes for Chap-Off. The purchase price of the empty tubes from the cosmetics manufacturer would be 90¢ per twenty-four tubes. If the Vernom Corporation accepts the purchase proposal, it is predicted that direct labor and variable overhead costs would be reduced by 10 percent and direct material costs would be reduced by 20 percent.

Required:

1. Should the Vernom Corporation make or buy the tubes? Show calculations to support your answer.
2. What would be the minimum purchase price acceptable to the Vernom Corporation for the tubes? Support your answer with an appropriate explanation.
3. Instead of sales of 100,000 boxes, revised estimates show sales volume at 125,000 boxes. At this new volume, additional equipment, at an annual rental of $10,000, must be acquired to manufacture the tubes. However, this incremental cost would be the only additional fixed cost required even if sales increased to 300,000 boxes. (The 300,000 level is the goal for the third year of production.) Under these circumstances, should the Vernom Corporation make or buy the tubes? Show calculations to support your answer.
4. The company has the option of making and buying at the same time. What would be your answer to Requirement 3 if this alternative was considered? Show calculations to support your answer.
5. What nonquantifiable factors should the Vernom Corporation consider in determining whether they should make or buy the lipstick-type tubes?

12-31. **Costs of operating an automobile.** Here are typical costs of operating a salesman's car for 30,000 miles in a year:

Gasoline, 2,000 gallons @ 40¢	$ 800
Oil changes and lubrication, 5 @ $10	50
Tire wear (based on life of 20,000 miles; a new set of 4 costs $100)	150
Regular maintenance and repair	210
Auto insurance	290
Washing and waxing	100
Licenses	100
Garage rent and parking fees	300
Depreciation ($3,800 − $1,800) ÷ 2-year life	1,000
	$3,000

Unit cost is $3,000 ÷ 30,000 miles or 10¢ per mile.

Required:

1. If the salesman drives 20,000 miles per year, what would be the average unit cost per mile? If he drives 40,000 miles?
2. The salesman takes his car on a 200-mile journey with a friend who agrees to share the cost of the trip. How much should the friend pay?
3. The salesman's wife wants a similar car for shopping and other errands that the husband now performs. If he buys the second car, it will be driven 4,000 miles per year, but suppose the total mileage of the two cars taken together would still be 30,000 miles. What would the annual cost of operating the second car be? The average unit cost? What costs are relevant? Why?
4. List other possible costs of car ownership that are not included in the above tabulation.
5. What costs are relevant to the question of selling the car at the end of one year (market value, $2,500) and using other means of transportation?

6. Assume that the salesman has no car. What costs are relevant to the question of buying the car described rather than using other means of transportation?

12-32. Accepting a low bid. The Vittetaw Company, a maker of a variety of metal and plastic products, is in the midst of a business downturn and is saddled with many idle facilities. The National Hospital Supply Company has approached Vittetaw to produce 300,000 nonslide serving trays. National will pay $1.20 each.

Vittetaw predicts that its variable costs will be $1.30 each. However, its fixed costs, which had been averaging $1 per unit on a variety of other products, will now be spread over twice as much volume. The president commented, "Sure, we'll lose 10¢ each on the variable costs, but we'll gain 50¢ per unit by spreading our fixed costs. Therefore, we should take the offer because it represents an advantage of 40¢ per unit."

Required:

Do you agree with the president? Why? Use figures to support your answer.

12-33. Various costing techniques for pricing. Budgeted income statement items for the Doyle Company include: sales, $1,200,000; total factory cost of goods sold, $900,000; total selling and administrative expenses, $200,000; operating income, $100,000; direct material, $350,000; direct labor, $200,000; fixed factory overhead, $300,000; and variable selling and administrative expenses, $100,000.

Operations were exactly in accordance with the budget. Target selling prices were achieved on every order.

Required:

1. Prepare two income statements for the year, one with a traditional format and a second with a contribution format. Show alternate percentage breakdowns of major items.
2. For an item with total variable costs of $583 (including variable selling and administrative costs) and total factory costs of $750, what markup percentage would be used on a price-quotation sheet that would yield the same target price under (a) the contribution approach and (b) the traditional approach? Under (a), the percentage would be based on some version of variable costs; under (b), percentage would be on some version of full costs.
3. During the year, the president personally rejected an offer of $8,500 for some items whose total factory cost of goods was $9,000. The president said, "We never take orders for less than cost." What was the effect of his decision on net income for the year? Did he make a wise decision? Explain.

12-34. Cost analysis and pricing. The budget for the Bright Printing Company for 19x2 follows:

Sales		$1,000,000
Direct material	$180,000	
Direct labor	320,000	
Overhead	400,000	900,000
Net income		$ 100,000

The company typically uses a so-called cost-plus pricing system. Direct material and direct labor are computed, overhead is added at a rate of 125 percent of direct labor, and one-ninth of the total cost is added to obtain the selling price.

Mr. Bright has placed a $10,000 bid on a particularly large order with a cost of $1,800 direct material and $3,200 direct labor. The customer informs him that he can have the business for $8,900, take it or leave it. If Mr. Bright accepts the order, total sales for 19x2 will be $1,008,900.

Mr. Bright refuses the order, saying: "I sell on a cost-plus basis. It is bad policy to accept orders at below cost. I would lose $100 on the job."

The company's annual fixed overhead is $160,000.

Required:

1. What would net income have been with the order? Without the order? Show your computations.
2. Give a short description of a contribution approach to pricing that Bright might follow. Include a stipulation of the pricing formula that Bright should routinely use if he hopes to obtain a target net income of $100,000.

12-35. Profit planning in a developing country. The subsidiary of a multinational drug company was the largest firm in a developing nation's pharmaceutical industry (comprising some thirty manufacturers) with sales in the vicinity of $20 million. The manufacturing operation consisted primarily of processing and packing imported bulk materials into finished products. The ninety-eight finished products were made from some fifty different kinds of raw (bulk) materials, almost all of which were imported. The firm had its own well-trained "detail" sales force and distribution network.

The subsidiary had grown rapidly after commencing operations in the mid-1950's and became the largest company in terms of sales in 1966 after overtaking its British rival. Although sales had grown phenomenally, the profit performance of the subsidiary had been relatively poor as measured by profits as a percentage of sales. The first president of the company had stressed sales and volume and had provided the sales force with all the financial benefits and assistance possible. His successor, in an effort to improve profitability, had concentrated on reducing costs.

The country in which the subsidiary was located was typical of many developing nations in that it suffered from severe foreign-exchange problems. Some 80 percent of the foreign exchange available was devoted to the import of food and defense equipment, the remainder being made available for all other imports, including drugs. The amount of foreign exchange available was rationed by industry and by company on a six-month basis. Firms then received permits of $X of foreign exchange which they could use to import materials (not available in the country) in any quantities and in any combination. The permitted amount for each company could vary by significant amounts, but planning beyond a six-month period was almost impossible.

The foreign-exchange limitation made the market for drugs in the country a seller's market. The government kept a close watch on prices, and the pharmaceutical industry was extremely sensitive to arousing public hostility due to pricing as had been the case in some other developing countries. The task, therefore, was to find a straightforward technique—which did not require sophisticated quantitative skills—that could be used as a guide to maximizing profits.

There are practically no constraints in manufacturing and a wide range in production quantities of the ninety-eight different products is possible. For the purpose of this problem assume that any product can be dropped if necessary.

Required:

The following information was chosen at random. Rank the products in order of desired production and sales effort. Explain your ranking:

	Per Unit of Product		
	A	B	C
Selling price (in dollar equivalents)	$10.50	$12.00	$8.00
Cost of imported materials	2.00	1.00	1.00
Variable costs of production and selling*	2.50	5.00	2.00

*Excluding imported materials.

12-36. Relevant cost analysis. The following are the unit costs of making and selling a single product at a normal level of 5,000 units per month and a current unit selling price of $75:

Manufacturing costs:	
Direct material	$20
Direct labor	12
Variable overhead	8
Fixed overhead	
(total for the year, $300,000)	5
Selling and administrative expenses:	
Variable	15
Fixed (total for the year, $540,000)	9

Required:

Consider each requirement separately. Label all computations, and present your solutions in a form that will be comprehensible to the company president.

1. This product is usually sold at a rate of 60,000 units per year. It is predicted that a rise in price to $80 will decrease volume by 5 percent. How much may advertising be increased under this plan without having annual net profit fall below the current level?

2. The company has received a proposal from an outside supplier to make and ship this item directly to the company's customers, as sales orders are forwarded. Variable selling and administrative costs would fall 40 percent. If the supplier's proposal is accepted, the company will use its own plant to produce a new product. The new product would be sold through manufacturers' agents at a 10 percent commission based on a selling price of $20 each. The cost characteristics of this product, based on predicted yearly normal volume, are as follows:

	Per Unit
Direct material	$ 3
Direct labor	6
Variable overhead	4
Fixed overhead	3
Manufacturing costs	$16
Selling and administrative expenses:	
Variable	10% of selling price
Fixed	$ 1

What is the maximum price per unit that the company can afford to pay to the supplier for subcontracting the entire old product? Assume the following:

(a) Total fixed factory overhead and total fixed selling expenses will not change if the new product line is added.

(b) The supplier's proposal will not be considered unless the present annual net income can be maintained.

(c) Selling price of the old product will remain unchanged.

12-37. Dispute about defense contract. During the late 1960's and early 1970's, fury arose in Washington, D.C., about the scenario involved in developing weapons. The frequently encountered situation was begun by the contractor signing a fixed-price contract with the Defense Department. Later, the contractor encountered cost problems and managed to renegotiate the contract at a higher price. The Pentagon's budget soared, and Congressmen demanded a tougher posture.

In 1969, Grumman Corporation agreed to build as many as 313 F-14 Tomcat fighter-bombers at a price of $16.8 million each. The Navy ordered various production lots, and eighty-six planes were in various stages of completion at the end of 1972. However, when the Navy placed an order for forty-eight more planes in late 1972, Grumman announced that it would not deliver the planes at that price. The company claimed that it was losing $1 million each on the eighty-six planes already in production. Furthermore, building forty-eight more planes at contract prices would cause the company to lose another $105 million and threaten its survival. The company's sales during the first nine months of 1972 were $45 million; its net income was $1.4 million.

The company chairman claimed that the rising costs were not the company's fault. He blamed unexpectedly fast inflation and the phasing out of other government work (including the lunar module for Apollo), not the "bad management" and "inefficiencies" that critics had attributed to another troubled defense contractor, Lockheed.

Required:

1. Elaborate on the reasoning of the company chairman. What has the phasing out of other government work got to do with the F-14 contract? Be specific.
2. If you were Senator Proxmire, a habitual critic of defense contracting, what would be your major argument against renegotiation?

SELECTED TOPICS
FOR
FURTHER STUDY

Capital Budgeting 13

Should we replace the equipment? Should we add this product to our line? Managers must make these and similar decisions having long-range implications; they are called capital-budgeting decisions. Many different decision models are used for capital budgeting. In this chapter, we deal mostly with the accountant's problem-solving function; we compare the uses and limitations of various capital-budgeting models, with particular emphasis on relevant-cost analysis.

CONTRASTING PURPOSES OF INTERNAL ACCOUNTING

At this stage, we again focus on purpose. Income determination and the planning and controlling of operations primarily have a **current time-period** orientation. Special decisions and long-range planning primarily have a **project** orientation. These distinctions can be illustrated with a chart like that in Exhibit 13-1.

The project and time-period orientations of Exhibit 13-1 represent two distinct cross sections of the total corporate assets. The vertical dimension signifies the total investment (assets) of the company, which may be subdivided into divisions, product lines, departments, buildings, a fleet of trucks, or a machine. These parts of an organization's resources are individual *projects,* or investment decisions. The horizontal dimension represents successive years in a company's life.

The shaded horizontal rectangle for Project *P* shows that many projects entail commitments over a prolonged span of time, not just one year.

EXHIBIT 13-1

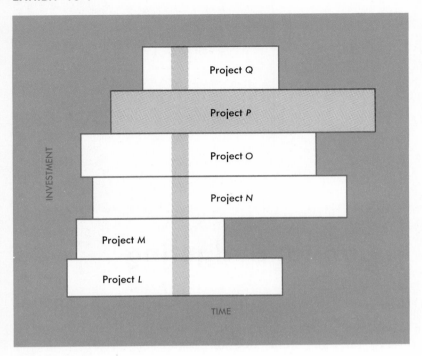

The focus is on a single cross section, a lone investment venture, throughout its life. The interest that can be earned over a period of time (i.e., the time value of money) often looms large in special decisions and in long-range planning.

The shaded vertical rectangle illustrates the focus of income determination and current planning and control. The cross-sectional emphasis is upon the company's overall performance and status for a year or less. The time period is relatively short, and the interest value of money is usually not directly involved.

The point is that our ordinary accounting systems and techniques have been designed to determine the cost and income of products for current planning and control. There is a great danger of using the existing general-purpose accounting system incorrectly—that is, of using data indiscriminately for solving special problems.

So in this chapter, we shall shift gears. We shall take a fresh look at the purpose of the special decision, and then decide what models seem best for achieving that purpose.

DEFINITION OF CAPITAL BUDGETING

Capital budgeting is long-term planning for making and financing proposed capital outlays. Most expenditures for plant, equipment, and other long-lived assets affect operations over a series of years. They are large, permanent commitments that influence long-run flexibility and earning power. Decisions in this area are among the most difficult, primarily because the future to be foreseen is distant and hard to predict. Because the unknowable factors are many, it is imperative that all the knowable factors be collected and properly measured before a decision is reached.

The profitability of a business decision depends on two vital factors: (1) future net increases in cash inflows or net savings in cash outflows and (2) required investment. Thus, a chance to receive an annual return of $5,000 on a bond or stock can be judged only in relation to how much money need be committed to obtain the $5,000. If the required capital is $10,000, the $5,000 (50 percent) return may be extremely appealing. If the required investment is $1 million, the $5,000 ($\frac{1}{2}$ percent) return probably will be unappealing. Depending on risk and available alternatives, individuals and corporate investors usually have some notion of a minimum rate of return that would make various projects desirable investments.

The quantitative approach to the selection of projects generally compares predicted cash flows with the required investments. Thus, all projects whose rate of return exceeds the minimum rate of return would be desirable, and vice versa. A project with an expected return of 25 percent would ordinarily be more desirable than one of 12 percent. The problem of choosing the minimum acceptable rate of return (more a problem of finance than of accounting) is extremely complex.[1] In this book, we shall assume that the minimum acceptable rate of return is given to the accountant by management, and that it represents the rate that can be earned by the best alternative uses of investment capital.

There are several different ways of approaching the capital-budgeting decision. Although we shall discuss (a) discounted cash flow, (b) payback, and (c) the unadjusted rate of return, we shall concentrate on discounted cash flow because it is conceptually superior to the others.

DISCOUNTED CASH FLOW

Time Value of Money

The old adage that a bird in the hand is worth two in the bush is applicable to the management of money. A dollar in the hand today is worth more than a dollar to be received (or spent) five years from today, because the use of money has a cost (interest), just as the use of a building or an automobile may have a cost (rent). **Because the discounted-cash-flow method explicitly and automatically weighs the time value of money, it is the best method to use for long-range decisions.**

---

[1]For an excellent discussion, see the chapter on cost of capital in James C. Van Horne, *Financial Management and Policy,* 3rd. ed. (Englewood Cliffs, N.J.: Prentice-Hall, Inc., 1974).

Another major aspect of the cash-flow method is its focus on *cash* inflows and outflows rather than on *net income* as computed in the conventional accounting sense. As we shall see, the student without a strong accounting background has an advantage here. He does not have to unlearn the accrual concepts of accounting, which the accounting student often incorrectly tries to inject into discounted-cash-flow analysis.

There are two main variations of the discounted-cash-flow method: (a) time-adjusted rate of return; and (b) net present value. A brief summary of the tables and formulas used is included in Appendix B at the end of this book. Do not be frightened by the mathematics of compound interest. We shall confine our study to present value tables, which may seem imposing but which are simple enough to be taught in many grade-school arithmetic courses. *Before reading on, be sure you understand Appendix B, which starts on page 597.*

The following example will be used to illustrate the concepts:

A manager is contemplating the rearrangement of assembly-line facilities. Because of rapid technological changes in the industry, he is using a four-year planning horizon as a basis for deciding whether to invest in the facilities for rearrangement, which should result in cash operating savings of $2,000 per year. In other words, the useful life of this project is four years, after which the facilities will be abandoned or rearranged again.

Required:

1. If the plant rearrangement will cost $6,074 now, what is the time-adjusted rate of return on the project?

2. If the minimum desired rate of return is 10 percent, and the plant rearrangement will cost $6,074, what is the project's net present value? How much more would the manager be willing to invest and still earn 10 percent on the project?

Requirement 1 deals with the time-adjusted rate of return, which we shall consider first.

Time-Adjusted Rate of Return

The time-adjusted rate of return has been defined as "the maximum rate of interest that could be paid for the capital employed over the life of an investment without loss on the project."[2] This rate corresponds to the effective rate of interest so widely computed for bonds, purchased or sold at discounts or premiums. Alternatively, the rate of return can be defined as the discount rate that makes the present value of a project equal to the cost of the project.

[2]*Return on Capital as a Guide to Managerial Decisions*, National Association of Accountants, Research Report No. 35 (New York), p. 57.

EXHIBIT 13-2

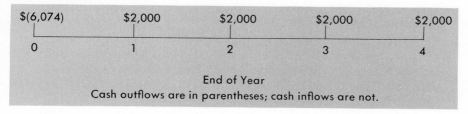

$(6,074) $2,000 $2,000 $2,000 $2,000

| 0 | 1 | 2 | 3 | 4 |

End of Year

Cash outflows are in parentheses; cash inflows are not.

EXHIBIT 13-3
Two Proofs of Time-Adjusted Rate of Return

Original investment, $6,074
Useful life, 4 years
Annual cash inflow from operations, $2,000
Rate of return (selected by trial-and-error methods), 12 percent

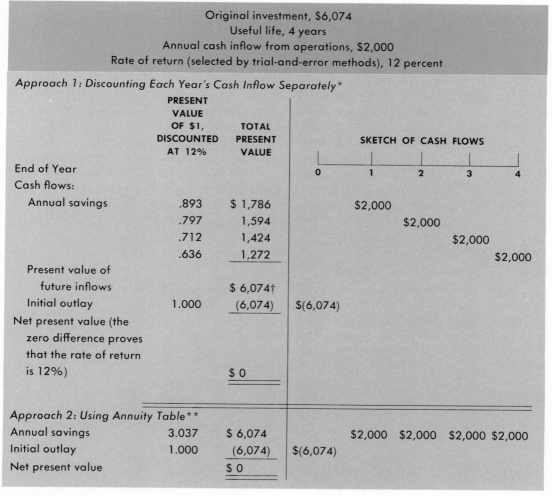

Approach 1: Discounting Each Year's Cash Inflow Separately*

End of Year	PRESENT VALUE OF $1, DISCOUNTED AT 12%	TOTAL PRESENT VALUE	SKETCH OF CASH FLOWS
Cash flows:			0 1 2 3 4
Annual savings	.893	$ 1,786	$2,000
	.797	1,594	$2,000
	.712	1,424	$2,000
	.636	1,272	$2,000
Present value of future inflows		$ 6,074†	
Initial outlay	1.000	(6,074)	$(6,074)
Net present value (the zero difference proves that the rate of return is 12%)		$ 0	

Approach 2: Using Annuity Table**

Annual savings	3.037	$ 6,074	$2,000 $2,000 $2,000 $2,000
Initial outlay	1.000	(6,074)	$(6,074)
Net present value		$ 0	

*Present values from Table 1, Appendix B (p. 601).
†Sum is really $6,076, but is rounded.
**Present values of annuity from Table 2, Appendix B (p. 602).

Compare Table 2 with Table 1 in Appendix B. Note that Table 1 is the fundamental table, and Table 2 can only be used as a short-cut when uniform cash flows occur; that is, Table 2 accomplishes in one computation what Table 1 accomplishes in four computations. Table 2 is really compiled by using the basic present value factors in Table 1; for example, 3.037 is equal to the sum (rounded) of .893 + .797 + .712 + .636.

The cash flows relating to our rearrangement problem are shown in Exhibit 13-2. The discounted-cash-flow analysis of these cash flows is shown in Exhibit 13-3.

The exhibit shows that $6,074 is the present value, at a rate of return of 12 percent, of a four-year stream of inflows of $2,000 in cash. Twelve percent is the rate that equates the amount invested ($6,074) with the present value of the cash inflows ($2,000 per year for four years). In other words, if money were borrowed at an effective interest rate of 12 percent, the cash inflow produced by the project would exactly repay the hypothetical loan plus the interest over the four years. If the cost of capital (minimum desired rate of return on the capital) is less than 12 percent, the project will be desirable. If the cost of capital exceeds 12 percent, the cash inflow will be insufficient to pay the interest and repay the principal of the hypothetical loan. Therefore, 12 percent is the time-adjusted rate of return for this project.

Explanation of Compound Interest

The time-adjusted rate of return is computed on the basis of the cash in use from period to period, rather than on the original investment. Exhibit 13-4 shows that the return is 12 percent of the cash invested during the year. After 12 percent of the cash invested is deducted, the remainder is the recovery of the original investment. Over the four years, the cash inflow equals the recovery of the original investment plus annual interest, at the rate of 12 percent of the unrecovered capital. In Exhibit 13-4, at the end of Year 1, the $2,000 cash inflow represents a 12 percent ($729) return

EXHIBIT 13-4

Rationale of Time-Adjusted Rate of Return

Note: Same data as in Exhibit 13-3: Original investment, $6,074; Useful life, 4 years; Annual cash inflow from operations $2,000; Rate of return, 12 percent. Unrecovered investment at the beginning of each year earns interest for the whole year. Annual cash inflows are received at the end of each year.

YEAR	(A) UNRECOVERED INVESTMENT AT BEGINNING OF YEAR	(B) ANNUAL CASH INFLOW	(C) RETURN: 12% PER YEAR (A) × 12%	(D) AMOUNT OF INVESTMENT RECOVERED AT END OF YEAR (B) − (C)	(E) UNRECOVERED INVESTMENT AT END OF YEAR (A) − (D)
1	$6,074	$2,000	$729	$1,271	$4,803
2	4,803	2,000	576	1,424	3,379
3	3,379	2,000	405	1,595	1,784
4	1,784	2,000	216*	1,784	0

*Rounded.

on the $6,074 unrecovered investment at the beginning of Year 1 *plus* a $1,271 recovery of principal.

This difficult point warrants another illustration. Assume that a company is considering investing in a project with a two-year life and no residual value. Cash inflow will be equal payments of $4,000 at the end of each of the two years. How much would the company be willing to invest to earn a time-adjusted rate of return of 8 percent? A quick glance at the table for the present value of $1 (Appendix B, Table 1) will reveal:

$4,000 received at end of Year 1 ($4,000 × .926) = $3,704
$4,000 received at end of Year 2 ($4,000 × .857) = $3,428
Total present value $7,132

The following is an analysis of the computations that are automatically considered in the construction of present value tables.

Year	Investment at Beginning of Year	Operating Cash Inflow	Return, @ 8% per Year	Amount of Investment Received at End of Year	Unrecovered Investment at End of Year
1	$7,132	$4,000	.08 × $7,132 = $571	$4,000 − $571 = $3,429	$7,132 − $3,429 = $3,703
2	3,703	4,000	.08 × 3,703 = $297	$4,000 − $297 = $3,703	$3,703 − $3,703 = 0

A study of the above calculations will demonstrate that discounted-cash-flow techniques and tables have built into them the provisions for recovery of investment.

Depreciation and Discounted Cash Flow

Students are often mystified by the apparent exclusion of depreciation from discounted-cash-flow computations. A common homework error is to deduct depreciation. This is a misunderstanding of one of the basic ideas involved in the concept of the time-adjusted rate of return. Because the discounted cash flow approach is fundamentally based on inflows and outflows of *cash* and not on the *accrual* concepts of revenues and expenses, no adjustments should be made to the cash flows for the periodic allocation of cost called depreciation expense (which is not a cash flow). In the discounted-cash-flow approach, the initial cost of an asset is usually regarded as a *lump-sum* outflow of cash at time zero. **Therefore, it is wrong to deduct depreciation from operating cash inflows before consulting present value tables.** To deduct periodic depreciation would be a double-counting of a cost that has already been considered as a lump-sum outflow.

How to Compute the Return

The mechanics of computing the time-adjusted rate of return are not too imposing when the annual cash inflows are uniform. In Exhibit 13-3, the following equation is used:

$6,074 = Present value of annuity of $2,000 at X percent for 4 years, or what factor F in Table 2 (page 602) will satisfy the following equation:

$$\$6,074 = \$2,000\ F$$

$$F = 3.037$$

On the Period 4 line of Table 2, find the column that is closest to 3.037. It happens to be exactly 12 percent.

But suppose that the cash inflow were $1,800 instead of $2,000:

$$\$6,074 = \$1,800\ F$$

$$F = 3.374$$

On the Period 4 line of Table 2, the column closest to 3.374 is 8 percent. This may be close enough for most purposes. To obtain a more accurate rate, interpolation is needed:

	Present Value Factors	
6%	3.465	3.465
True rate		3.374
8%	3.312	
Difference	.153	.091

$$\text{True rate} = 6\% + \frac{.091}{.153}(2\%) = 7.2\%$$

These hand computations become more complex when the cash inflows and outflows are not uniform. Then trial-and-error methods are needed. See the Appendix to this chapter for examples. Of course, in practice, canned computer programs are commonly available for such computations.

Net Present Value

Another type of discounted-cash-flow approach may be called the **net present value method.** As we just saw, computing the exact time-adjusted rate of return entails trial and error and, sometimes, cumbersome hand calculations and interpolations within a compound-interest table. In contrast, the net present value method assumes some minimum desired rate of return. All expected future cash flows are discounted to the present, using this minimum desired rate. If the result is positive, the project is desirable, and vice versa.

Requirement 2 of our example will be used to demonstrate the net

EXHIBIT 13-5

Net Present Value Technique

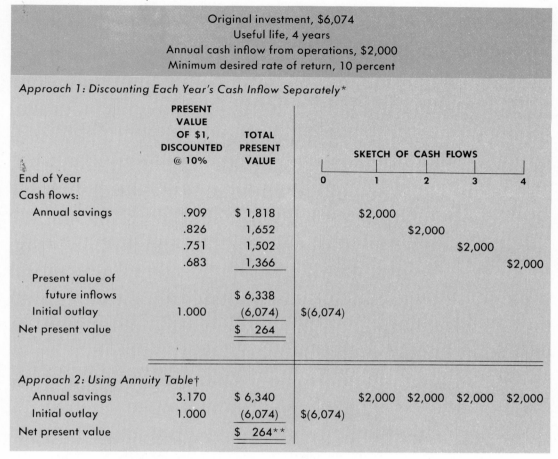

Original investment, $6,074
Useful life, 4 years
Annual cash inflow from operations, $2,000
Minimum desired rate of return, 10 percent

Approach 1: Discounting Each Year's Cash Inflow Separately*

	PRESENT VALUE OF $1, DISCOUNTED @ 10%	TOTAL PRESENT VALUE	SKETCH OF CASH FLOWS				
			0	1	2	3	4
End of Year							
Cash flows:							
Annual savings	.909	$ 1,818		$2,000			
	.826	1,652			$2,000		
	.751	1,502				$2,000	
	.683	1,366					$2,000
Present value of future inflows		$ 6,338					
Initial outlay	1.000	(6,074)	$(6,074)				
Net present value		$ 264					

Approach 2: Using Annuity Table†

Annual savings	3.170	$ 6,340		$2,000 $2,000 $2,000 $2,000		
Initial outlay	1.000	(6,074)	$(6,074)			
Net present value		$ 264**				

*Present values from Table 1, Appendix B at the end of the book.
†Present annuity values from Table 2.
**Rounded.

present value approach. The problem assumes that the rearrangement will cost $6,074. Exhibit 13-5 shows a net present value of $264, so the investment is desirable. The manager would be able to invest $264 more, or a total of $6,338 (i.e., $6,074 + $264), and still earn 10 percent on the project.

The higher the minimum desired rate of return, the less the manager would be willing to invest in this project. At a rate of 16 percent, the net present value would be $−478 (i.e., $2,000 × 2.798 = $5,596, which is $478 less than the required investment of $6,074). (Present value factor, 2.798, is taken from Table 2, p. 602.) When the desired rate of return is 16 percent, rather than 10 percent, the project is undesirable at a price of $6,074.

Review of Decision Rules

Review the basic ideas of discounted cash flow. The decision maker cannot readily compare an outflow of $6,074 with a series of future inflows of $2,000 each because the outflows and inflows do not occur simultaneously. The net present value model expresses all amounts in equivalent terms (in today's dollars at time zero). An interest rate is used to measure the decision maker's time preference for money. At a rate of 12 percent, the comparison can be shown as follows:

Outflow in today's dollars	$(6,074)
Inflow equivalent in today's dollars @ 12%	6,074
Net present value	$ 0

Therefore, at a time preference for money of 12 percent, the decision maker is indifferent about having $6,074 now or a stream of four annual inflows of $2,000 each. If the interest rate were 16 percent, the decision maker would find the project unattractive because the net present value would be negative:

Outflow	$(6,074)
Inflow equivalent in today's dollars @ 16% =	
$2,000 × 2.798 (from Table 2) =	5,596
Net present value	$(478)

We can summarize the decision rules offered by these two models as follows:

Time-Adjusted Rate of Return

1. Using present value tables, compute the time-adjusted rate of return by trial-and-error interpolation.
2. If this rate equals or exceeds the minimum desired rate of return, accept the project; if not, reject the project.

Net Present Value

1. Calculate the net present value, using the minimum desired rate of return as the discount rate.
2. If the net present value is zero or positive, accept the project; if negative, reject the project.

Two Simplifying Assumptions

Two simplifying assumptions are being made here and throughout this book:

a. For simplicity in the use of tables, all operating cash inflows or outflows are assumed to take place at the *end* of the years in question. This is unrealistic because such cash flows ordinarily occur irregularly throughout

the given year, rather than in lump sums at the end of the year. Compound-interest tables especially tailored for these more realistic conditions are available, but we shall not consider them here.

429
Capital Budgeting

b. We assume that the cost of capital is known, is given; it is the minimum
desired rate of return, an opportunity investment rate on alternative uses
of the funds to be invested. The cost of capital is discussed in literature
on finance;[3] but experts do not agree on how it should be computed. Cost
of capital is usually a long-run weighted average based on both debt and
equity. In any event, the cost of capital is *not* "interest expense" on
borrowed money as the accountant usually conceives it. For example, a
mortgage-free house still has a cost of capital—the maximum amount
that could be earned with the proceeds if the house were sold.

UNCERTAINTY AND SENSITIVITY ANALYSIS

In this and other chapters, we almost always work with the expected
values (single dollar amounts) of cash flows in order to emphasize and
simplify various important points. These cash flows are subject to varying
degrees of risk or uncertainty; risk or uncertainty is defined here as the
possibility that the actual cash flow will deviate from the expected cash
flow. Nevertheless, as a minimum, a manager must make some prediction
of the probable outcome of various alternative projects. These expected
values really should be analyzed in conjunction with probability distributions, as we see in Chapter 17. However, to stress the fundamental differences among various decision models, in this chapter we deal only with
the expected values.

Sensitivity analysis is a widely used approach to the problem of uncertainty. Sensitivity analysis is a technique that measures how the basic
forecasted results in a decision model will be affected by changes in the
critical data inputs that influence those results. In the context of capital
budgeting, sensitivity analysis answers the question: "How will my rate of
return or net present value be changed if the useful life or the cash flows
that I used for its computation are inaccurate?"

Sensitivity analysis is best understood by example. Suppose in Exhibit 13-5 that the cash inflows were $1,500 annually instead of $2,000.
What would be the net present value? The annuity factor of 3.170 would
be multiplied by $1,500, producing a gross present value of $4,755 and a
negative net present value of $4,755 − $6,074, or $−1,319. Alternatively,
management may want to know how far cash inflows will have to fall to
break even on the investment. In this context, "break even" means the
point of indifference, the point where the net present value is zero:

> Let X = annual cash inflows and let net present value = 0
> Then $0 = 3.170(X) − 6,074$
> $X = \$1,916$

---

[3]Van Horne, *op. cit.*

Thus, cash inflows can drop only $84 ($2,000 − $1,916) annually to reach the point of indifference regarding the investment.

Another critical factor is useful life. If useful life were only three years, the gross present value would be $2,000 multiplied by 2.487 (from the Period 3 row in Table 2), or $4,974, again producing a negative net present value, $4,974 − $6,074, or $−1,100.

These calculations can also be used in testing the sensitivity of rates of return. As we saw in the section on "How to Compute the Return," a fall in the annual cash inflow from $2,000 to $1,800 reduces the rate of return from 12 percent to 7.2 percent.

Of course, sensitivity analysis works both ways. It can measure the potential increases in net present value or rate of return as well as the decreases. The major contribution of sensitivity analysis is that it provides an immediate financial measure of the consequences of possible errors in forecasting. Therefore, it can be very useful because it helps focus on those decisions which may be very sensitive indeed, and it eases the manager's mind about those decisions that are not so sensitive.

In addition, sensitivity analysis is applicable to the comparison of various capital-budgeting decision models. In other words, the results under the discounted-cash-flow model may be compared to the results, using the same basic data, generated under simpler models like payback and unadjusted rate of return.

THE NET PRESENT VALUE COMPARISON OF TWO PROJECTS

Incremental versus Total Project Approach

The mechanics of compound interest may appear formidable to those readers who are encountering them for the first time. However, a little practice with the interest tables should easily clarify the mechanical aspect. More important, we shall now combine some relevant cost analysis with the discounted-cash-flow approach. Consider the following example:

A company owns a packaging machine, which was purchased three years ago for $56,000. It has a remaining useful life of five years, but will require a major overhaul at the end of two more years of life, at a cost of $10,000. Its disposal value now is $20,000; in five years, its disposal value is expected to be $8,000, assuming that the $10,000 major overhaul will be done on schedule. The cash operating costs of this machine are expected to be $40,000 annually.

A salesman has offered a substitute machine for $51,000, or for $31,000 plus the old machine. The new machine will reduce annual cash operating costs by $10,000, will not require any overhauls, will have a useful life of five years, and will have a disposal value of $3,000.

Required:

Assume that the minimum desired rate of return is 14 percent. Using the net present value technique, show whether the new machine should be purchased, using: (1) a total project approach; (2) an incremental approach. Try to solve before examining the solution.

A difficult part of long-range decision making is the structuring of the data. We want to see the effects of each alternative on future cash flows. The focus here is on bona fide cash transactions, not on opportunity costs. Using an opportunity cost approach may yield the same answers, but repeated classroom experimentation with various analytical methods has convinced the author that the following steps are likely to be the clearest:

Step 1. Arrange the relevant cash flows by project, so that a sharp distinction is made between total project flows and incremental flows. The incremental flows are merely algebraic differences between two alternatives. (There are always at least two alternatives. One is the status quo—i.e., doing nothing.) Exhibit 13-6 shows how the cash flows for each alternative are sketched.

Step 2. Discount the expected cash flows and choose the project with the least cost or the greatest benefit. Both the total project approach and the incremental approach are illustrated in Exhibit 13-6. Which approach you use is a matter of preference. However, to develop confidence in this area, you should work with both at the start. One approach can serve as proof of the accuracy of the other. In this example, the $8,425 net difference in favor of replacement is the ultimate result under either approach.

Analysis of Typical Items under Discounted Cash Flow

1. **Future disposal values.** The disposal values at the date of termination of a project is an increase in the cash inflow in the year of disposal. Errors in forecasting disposal value are usually not crucial because the present value is usually small.

2. **Current disposal values and required investment.** There are a number of correct ways to analyze this item, all of which will have the same ultimate effect on the decision. Probably the simplest way was illustrated in Example 2, where the $20,000 was offset against the $51,000 purchase price, and the actual cash outgo was shown. Generally, the required investment is most easily measured by offsetting the disposal value of the old assets against the gross cost of the new assets.

3. **Investments in receivables and inventories.** Investments in receivables, inventories, and intangible assets are basically no different than investments in plant and equipment. In the discounted-cash-flow model, the initial outlays are entered in the sketch of cash flows at time zero. At the end of the useful life of the project, the original outlays for machines may not be recouped at all or may be partially recouped in the amount of the salvage values. In contrast, the entire original investments in receivables

EXHIBIT 13-6
Total Project versus Incremental Approach to Net Present Value

	PRESENT VALUE DISCOUNT FACTOR, @ 14%	TOTAL PRESENT VALUE	\		SKETCH OF CASH FLOWS				
End of Year			0	1	2	3	4	5
TOTAL PROJECT APPROACH								
A. Replace								
Recurring cash operating costs, using an annuity table*	3.433	$(102,990)		($30,000)	($30,000)	($30,000)	($30,000)	($30,000)
Disposal value, end of Year 5	.519	1,557						3,000
Initial required investment	1.000	(31,000)	($31,000)					
Present value of net cash outflows		$(132,433)						
B. Keep								
Recurring cash operating costs, using an annuity table*	3.433	$(137,320)		($40,000)	($40,000)	($40,000)	($40,000)	($40,000)
Overhaul, end of Year 2	.769	(7,690)			(10,000)			
Disposal value, end of Year 5	.519	4,152						8,000
Present value of net cash outflows		$(140,858)						
Difference in favor of replacement		$ 8,425						
INCREMENTAL APPROACH								
A − B Analysis Confined to Differences								
Recurring cash operating savings, using an annuity table*	3.433	$ 34,330		$10,000	$10,000	$10,000	$10,000	$10,000
Overhaul avoided, end of Year 2	.769	7,690			$10,000			
Difference in disposal values, end of Year 5	.519	(2,595)						(5,000)
Incremental initial investment	1.000	(31,000)	($31,000)					
Net present value of replacement		$ 8,425						

*Table 2, p. 602.

and inventories are usually recouped. Therefore, except for their expected "disposal" values being different, all investments are typically regarded as outflows at time zero, and their disposal values are regarded as inflows at the end of the project's useful life.

4. Book value and depreciation. Depreciation is a phenomenon of accrual accounting that entails an allocation of cost, not a specific cash outlay. Depreciation and book value are ignored in discounted-cash-flow approaches for the reasons mentioned earlier in this chapter.

5. Income taxes. In practice, comparison between alternatives is best made after considering tax effects, because the tax impact may alter the picture. (The effects of income taxes are considered in Chapter 14 and may be studied now if desired.)

6. Overhead analysis. In relevant cost analysis, only the overhead that will differ between alternatives is pertinent. There is need for careful study of the fixed overhead under the available alternatives. In practice, this is an extremely difficult phase of cost analysis, because it is hard to relate the individual costs to any single project.

7. Unequal lives. Where projects have unequal lives, comparisons may be made either over the useful life of the longer-lived project or over the useful life of the shorter-lived project. For our purposes, we will estimate what the residual values will be at the end of the longer-lived project. We must also assume a reinvestment at the end of the shorter-lived project. This makes sense primarily because the decision maker should extend his time horizon as far as possible. If he is considering a longer-lived project, he should give serious consideration to what would be done in the time interval between the termination dates of the shorter-lived and longer-lived projects.

8. Mutually exclusive projects. When the projects are mutually exclusive, so that the acceptance of one automatically entails the rejection of the other (e.g., buying Dodge or Ford trucks), the project which maximizes wealth measured in net present value in dollars should be undertaken.

9. A word of caution. The foregoing material has been an *introduction* to the area of capital budgeting, which is, in practice, complicated by a variety of factors: unequal lives; major differences in the size of alternative investments; peculiarities in time-adjusted rate-of-return computations; various ways of allowing for uncertainty (see Chapter 17); changes, over time, in desired rates of return; the indivisibility of projects in relation to a fixed overall capital budget appropriation; and more. These niceties are beyond the scope of this introduction to capital budgeting, but the Suggested Readings at the end of the chapter will help you pursue the subject in more depth.

OTHER MODELS FOR ANALYZING LONG-RANGE DECISIONS

Although discounted-cash-flow models for business decisions are being increasingly used, they are still relatively new, having been developed and applied for the first time on any wide scale in the 1950's. There are other models with which the manager should be at least somewhat familiar, because they are entrenched in many businesses.[4]

The models we are about to discuss are conceptually inferior to discounted-cash-flow approaches. Then why do we bother studying them? First, because changes in business practice occur slowly. Second, because where older models such as payback are in use, they should be used properly, even if there are better models available. The situation is similar to using a pocket knife instead of a scalpel for removing a person's appendix. If the pocket knife is used by a knowledgeable and skilled surgeon, the chances for success are much better than if it is used by a bumbling layman.

Of course, as always, the accountant and manager face a cost and value-of-information decision when they choose a decision model. Reluctance to use discounted-cash-flow models may be justified if the more familiar payback model or other models lead to the same investment decisions.

One existing technique may be called the **emergency-persuasion method.** No formal planning is used. Fixed assets are operated until they crumble, product lines are carried until they are obliterated by competition, and requests by a manager for authorization of capital outlays are judged on the basis of his past operating performance regardless of its relevance to the decision at hand. These approaches to capital budgeting are examples of the unscientific management that often leads to bankruptcy.

Payback Model

Payback, or **payout,** or **payoff,** is the measure of the time it will take to recoup, in the form of cash inflow from operations, the initial dollars of outlay. Assume that $12,000 is spent for a machine with an estimated useful life of eight years. Annual savings of $4,000 in cash outflow are expected from operations. Depreciation is ignored. The payback calculations follow:

[4]Thomas Klammer, "Empirical Evidence of the Adoption of Sophisticated Capital Budgeting Techniques," *The Journal of Business,* Vol. VL, No. 3 (October 1972), surveyed 369 large firms and received 184 responses. Fifty-seven percent of the firms responding indicated that they use discounted-cash-flow techniques in 1970, as compared with only 19 percent in 1959:

	Percentage Using in:		
	1970	*1964*	*1959*
Discounting	57	38	19
Accounting rate of return	26	30	34
Payback	12	24	34
Urgency	5	8	13
	100	100	100

$$P = \frac{I}{O} = \frac{\$12,000}{\$4,000} = 3 \text{ years} \qquad (1)$$

where P is the payback time; I is the initial incremental amount of outlay; and O is the uniform annual incremental cash inflow from operations.

The payback model or method, by itself, does *not* measure profitability; it measures how quickly investment dollars may be recouped. This is its major weakness, because a shorter payback time does not necessarily mean that one project is preferable to another.

For instance, assume that an alternative to the $12,000 machine is a $10,000 machine whose operation will also result in a reduction of $4,000 annually in cash outflow. Then

$$P_1 = \frac{\$12,000}{\$4,000} = 3.0 \text{ years}$$

$$P_2 = \frac{\$10,000}{\$4,000} = 2.5 \text{ years}$$

The payback criterion indicates that the $10,000 machine is more desirable. However, one fact about the $10,000 machine has been purposely withheld. Its useful life is only 2.5 years. Ignoring the impact of compound interest for the moment, the $10,000 machine results in zero benefit, while the $12,000 machine generates cash inflows for five years beyond its payback period.

The main objective in investing is profit, not the recapturing of the initial outlay. If a company wants to recover its outlay fast, it need not spend in the first place. Then no waiting time is necessary; the payback time is zero.

The payback approach may also be applied to the data in Exhibit 13-6. What is the payback time?

$$P = \frac{I}{O} = \frac{\$31,000}{\$10,000} = 3.1 \text{ years}$$

However, the formula may be used with assurance only when there are uniform cash inflows from operations. In this instance, $10,000 is saved by avoiding an overhaul at the end of the second year. When cash inflows are not uniform, the payback computation must take a cumulative form—that is, each year's net cash flows are accumulated until the initial investment is recouped:

Year	Initial Investment	Net Cash Inflows Each Year	Accumulated
0	$31,000	—	—
1	—	$10,000	$10,000
2	—	20,000	30,000
2.1	—	1,000	31,000

The payback time is slightly beyond the second year. Straight-line interpolation within the third year reveals that the final $1,000 needed to recoup the investment would be forthcoming in 2.1 years.

Appendix 13-B at the end of this chapter has additional comments on payback.

Unadjusted Rate-of-Return Model

The label for this model or method is not uniform. It is also known as the **accounting model,** the **financial statement model,** the **book value model,** the **rate-of-return on assets model,** and the **approximate rate-of-return model.** Its computations supposedly dovetail most closely with conventional accounting models of calculating income and required investment. However, the dovetailing objective is not easily attained because the purposes of the computations differ. The most troublesome aspects are depreciation and decisions concerning capitalization versus expense. For example, advertising and research are usually expensed, even though they often may be viewed as long-range investments.

The equations for the unadjusted rate of return are:

$$\text{Unadjusted rate of return} = \frac{\text{Increase in future average annual net income}}{\text{Initial increase in required investment}} \quad (2)$$

$$R = \frac{O - D}{I} \quad (3)$$

where R = Average annual rate of return on initial additional investment
O = Average annual incremental cash inflow from operations
D = Incremental average annual depreciation
I = Initial incremental amount invested

Assume the same facts as in our payback illustration: cost of machine, $12,000; useful life, eight years; estimated disposal value, zero; and expected annual savings in annual cash outflow from operations, $4,000. Substitute these values in Equation 3:

$$R = \frac{\$4,000 - \$1,500}{\$12,000} = 20.83\%$$

Weighing Dollars Differently

The unadjusted model ignores the time value of money. Expected future dollars are unrealistically and erroneously regarded as equal to present dollars. The discounted-cash-flow model explicitly allows for the force of interest and the exact timing of cash flows. In contrast, the unadjusted model is based on **annual averages.** To illustrate, consider a petroleum

EXHIBIT 13-7

Comparison of Unadjusted Rates of Return
and Time-Adjusted Rates of Return

	EXPANSION OF EXISTING GASOLINE STATION	OIL WELL	NEW GASOLINE STATION
Initial investment	$ 90,000	$ 90,000	$ 90,000
Cash inflows from operations:			
Year 1	$ 40,000	$ 80,000	$ 20,000
Year 2	40,000	30,000	40,000
Year 3	40,000	10,000	60,000
Totals	$120,000	$120,000	$120,000
Average annual cash inflow	$ 40,000	$ 40,000	$ 40,000
Less: Average annual depreciation ($90,000 ÷ 3)	30,000	30,000	30,000
Increase in average annual net income	$ 10,000	$ 10,000	$ 10,000
Unadjusted rate of return on initial investment	11.1%	11.1%	11.1%
Time-adjusted rate of return, using discounted cash flow	16.0%*	23.2%*	13.8%*

*Computed by trial-and-error approaches using Tables 1 and 2, pp. 601, 602. See the Appendix to this chapter for a detailed explanation.

company with three potential projects: an expansion of an existing gasoline station, an oil well, and a new gasoline station. To simplify the calculations, assume a three-year life for each project. Exhibit 13-7 summarizes the comparisons. Note that the unadjusted rate of return would indicate that all three projects are equally desirable and that the time-adjusted rate of return properly discriminates in favor of earlier cash inflows.

Thus, the conflict of purposes is highlighted in Exhibit 13-7. The unadjusted model utilizes concepts of capital and income that were originally designed for the quite different purpose of accounting for periodic income and financial position. In the unadjusted model, the initial capital calculation is subject to questionable asset-versus-expense decisions (e.g., allocation of costs of research or of sales promotion outlays), while the effects of interest on the timing of cash flows may be ignored. The resulting unadjusted rate of return may be far from the real mark.[5]

[5]For illustrations of the details, subtleties, and complexities of the unadjusted (accounting) rate of return see Charles T. Horngren, *Cost Accounting: A Managerial Emphasis,* 3rd ed. (Englewood Cliffs, N.J.: Prentice-Hall, Inc., 1972), Chapters 11 and 13.

Postaudit

The unadjusted model usually facilitates follow-up, because the same approach is used in the forecast as is used in the accounts. Yet exceptions to this ideal situation often occur. The most common exceptions arise from the inclusion in the forecast of some initial investment items that are not handled in the same manner in the subsequent accounting records. For example, the accounting for trade-ins and disposal values varies considerably. In practice, spot checks are frequently used on key items.

Another means of reconciling the two models is to use the discounted-cash-flow model for decision making but simultaneously compute its anticipated effects on accounting net income. The latter is then used as a basis for following up and auditing the capital-budgeting decision.

Conflict of Models and Evaluating Performance

The use of the conventional accrual accounting model for evaluating performance is a stumbling block to the implementation of present value models for capital-budgeting decisions. To illustrate, the manager of a division of a huge company took a course in management accounting in an executive program. He learned about discounted cash flow. He was convinced that such a model would lead to decisions that would better achieve the long-range profit goals of the company.

When he returned to his company, he was more frustrated than ever. Top management used the overall rate of return of his division to judge his performance. Each year, divisional net income was divided by average divisional assets to obtain his rate of return on investment (ROI). Such a measure usually inhibits investments in plant and equipment which might be clearly attractive using the present value models. Why? Because a huge investment often inordinately boosts depreciation in the early years under accelerated depreciation methods, thus reducing the numerator in the ROI computation. Also, the denominator is increased substantially by the initial cost of the new assets. As one manager said, "Top management is always giving me hell about my new flour mill, even though I know it is the most efficient we've got regardless of what the figures say."

Obviously, there is an inconsistency between citing present value models as being best for capital-budgeting decisions and then using quite different models for monitoring subsequent performance. As long as such practices continue, managers will frequently be tempted to make decisions which may be nonoptimal under the present value criterion but optimal, at least over short or intermediate spans of time, under conventional methods of evaluating operating performance. Such temptations become more pronounced when managers are subject to regular transfers and promotions. For a deeper exploration of this issue, see the appendix to Chapter 16.

Product costing, income determination, and the planning and controlling of operations have a current time-period orientation. Special decisions and long-range planning have primarily a project orientation. There is a danger in using ordinary accounting data for special purposes. Discounted-cash-flow techniques have been developed for the making of special decisions and for long-range planning because the time value of money becomes extremely important when projects extend beyond one or two years.

The field of capital budgeting is important because lump-sum expenditures on long-life projects have far-reaching effects on profit and on a business's flexibility. It is imperative that management develop its plans carefully and base them on reliable forecasting procedures. Capital budgeting is long-term planning for proposed capital outlays and their financing. Projects are accepted if their rate of return exceeds a minimum desired rate of return.

Because the discounted-cash-flow model explicitly and automatically weighs the time value of money, it is the best method to use for long-range decisions. The overriding goal is maximum long-run net cash inflows.

The discounted-cash-flow model has two variations: time-adjusted rate of return and net present value. Both models take into account the timing of cash flows and are thus superior to other methods.

The payback model is the most widely used approach to capital-spending decisions. It is simple and easily understood, but it neglects profitability.

The unadjusted rate-of-return model is also widely used in capital budgeting, although it is conceptually inferior to discounted-cash-flow models. It fails to recognize explicitly the time value of money. Instead, the unadjusted model depends on averaging techniques that may yield inaccurate answers, particularly when cash flows are not uniform through the life of a project.

A serious practical impediment to the adoption of discounted-cash-flow models is the widespread use of conventional accrual models for evaluating performance. Frequently, the optimal decision under discounted cash flow will not produce a good showing in the early years, when performance is computed under conventional accounting methods. For example, heavy depreciation charges and the expensing rather than capitalizing of initial development costs will hurt reported income for the first year.

SUMMARY PROBLEM FOR YOUR REVIEW

Problem

A toy manufacturer who specializes in making fad items has just developed a $50,000 molding machine for automatically producing a special toy. The machine has been used to produce one unit. It is planned to depreciate the $50,000 original cost evenly over four years, after which time production of the toy will be stopped.

Suddenly a machine salesman appears. He has a new machine which is ideally suited for producing this toy. His automatic machine is distinctly superior. It reduces the cost of material by 10 percent and produces twice as many units per hour. It will cost $44,000 and will have zero disposal value at the end of four years.

Production and sales would continue to be at a rate of 25,000 per year for four years; annual sales will be $90,000. The scrap value of the toy company's machine is now $5,000 and will be $2,600 four years from now. Both machines will be useless after the 100,000-unit total market potential is exhausted.

With its present equipment, the company's annual expenses will be: direct materials, $10,000; direct labor, $20,000; and variable factory overhead, $15,000. Fixed factory overhead, exclusive of depreciation, is $7,500 annually, and fixed selling and administrative expenses are $12,000 annually.

Required:

1. Assume that the minimum rate of return desired is 18 percent. Using discounted-cash-flow techniques, show whether the new equipment should be purchased. Use a total project approach and an incremental approach. What is the role of the book value of the old equipment in the analysis?
2. What is the payback period for the new equipment?
3. As the manager who developed the $50,000 molding machine, you are trying to justify not buying the new $44,000 machine. You question the accuracy of the expected cash operating savings. By how much must these cash savings fall before the point of indifference, the point where net present value of the project is zero, is reached? Ignore income taxes.

Solution

1. The first step is to analyze all relevant operating cash flows and align them with the appropriate alternative:

Schedule of Annual Operating Cash Outflows

	(1) Present Situation	(2) New Situation	(3) Increment
Sales (irrelevant)			
Expenses:			
Direct material	$10,000	$ 9,000	$ 1,000
Direct labor	20,000	10,000	10,000
Variable overhead	15,000	7,500	7,500
Fixed overhead (irrelevant)			
Selling and administrative expenses (irrelevant)			
Total relevant operating cash outflows	$45,000	$26,500	$18,500

The next step is to sketch the *other* relevant cash flows, as shown in Exhibit 13-8. Either the total project approach or the incremental approach results in the same $9,423 net present value in favor of replacement.

Note that the book value of the old machine is irrelevant, and so is completely ignored. In the light of subsequent events, nobody will deny that the

EXHIBIT 13-8
Solution to Requirement 1
of Summary Problem for Your Review

	PRESENT VALUE DISCOUNT FACTOR, @ 18%	TOTAL PRESENT VALUE	SKETCH OF CASH FLOWS				
End of Year			0	1	2	3	4
TOTAL PROJECT APPROACH							
A. New Situation							
Recurring cash operating costs, using an annuity table*	2.690	$ (71,285)		($26,500)	($26,500)	($26,500)	($26,500)
Disposal value of old equipment now	1.000	5,000	$ 5,000				
Cost of new equipment	1.000	(44,000)	($44,000)				
Present value of net cash outflows		$(110,285)					
B. Present Situation							
Recurring cash operating costs, using an annuity table	2.690	$(121,050)		($45,000)	($45,000)	($45,000)	($45,000)
Disposal value of old equipment four years hence	.516	1,342					$ 2,600
Present value of net cash outflows		$(119,708)					
Difference in favor of replacement		$ 9,423					
INCREMENTAL APPROACH							
A − B Analysis Confined to Differences							
Recurring cash operating savings, using an annuity table*	2.690	$ 49,765		$18,500	$18,500	$18,500	$18,500
Disposal value of old equipment now	1.000	5,000	$ 5,000				
Cost of new equipment	1.000	(44,000)	($44,000)				
Disposal value of old equipment foregone four years hence	.516	(1,342)					$(2,600)
Net present value of replacement		$ 9,423					

*From Table 2, p. 602.

original $50,000 investment could have been avoided, with a little luck or fore-sight. But nothing can be done to alter the past. The next question is whether the company will nevertheless be better off by buying the new machine. Management would have been much happier had the $50,000 never been spent in the first place, but the original mistake should not be compounded by keeping the old machine.

2. The payback formula can be used because the operating savings are uniform:

$$P = \frac{I}{O} = \frac{\$44,000 - \$5,000}{\$18,500} = 2.1 \text{ years}$$

3. This is an example of sensitivity analysis:

Let X = annual cash savings and let net present value = O
Then O = 2.690(X) + $5,000 − $44,000 − $1,342

(Note that the $5,000, $44,000, and $1,342 are at the bottom of Exhibit 13-8.)

$$2.690X = \$40,342$$
$$X = \$14,997$$

If the annual savings fall $3,503, from the estimated $18,500 to $14,997, the point of indifference will be reached. Rounding errors may affect the computation slightly.

An alternative way to get the same answer would be to divide the net present value of $9,423 (see bottom of Exhibit 13-8) by 2.690, obtaining $3,503, the amount of the annual difference in savings that will eliminate the $9,423 of net present value.

APPENDIX 13-A:
CALCULATIONS OF TIME-ADJUSTED RATES OF
RETURN (DATA ARE FROM EXHIBIT 13-7)

Expansion

$90,000 = Present value of annuity of $40,000 at x percent for three years, or what factor F in the table of the present values of an annuity will satisfy the following equation:
$90,000 = $40,000 F
F = $90,000 ÷ $40,000 = 2.250

Now, on the Year 3 line of Table 2 (p. 602), find the column that is closest to 2.250. You will find that 2.250 is extremely close to a rate of return of 16 percent—so close that straight-line interpolation is unnecessary between 14 percent and 16 percent. Therefore, the time-adjusted rate of return is 16 percent.

Trial-and-error methods must be used to calculate the rate of return that will equate the future cash flows with the $90,000 initial investment. As a start, note that the 16 percent rate was applicable to a uniform annual cash inflow. But now use Table 1, p. 601, because the flows are not uniform, and try a higher rate, 22 percent, because you know that the cash inflows are coming in more quickly than under the uniform inflow:

		Trial at 22 Percent		Trial at 24 Percent	
Year	Cash Inflows	Present Value Factor	Total Present Value	Present Value Factor	Total Present Value
1	$80,000	.820	$65,000	.806	$64,480
2	30,000	.672	20,160	.650	19,500
3	10,000	.551	5,510	.524	5,240
			$91,270		$89,220

The true rate lies somewhere between 22 and 24 percent and can be approximated by straight-line interpolation.

Interpolation	Total Present Values	
22%	$91,270	$91,270
True rate		90,000
24%	89,220	
Difference	$ 2,050	$ 1,270

Therefore

$$\text{True rate} = 22\% + \frac{1,270}{2,050} \times 2\%$$

$$= 22\% + 1.2\% = 23.2\%$$

New Gasoline Station

In contrast to the oil-well project, this venture will have slowly increasing cash inflows. The trial rate should be much lower than the 16 percent rate applicable to the expansion project. Let us try 12 percent.

		Trial at 12 Percent		Trial at 14 Percent	
Year	Cash Inflows	Present Value Factor	Total Present Value	Present Value Factor	Total Present Value
1	$20,000	.893	$17,860	.877	$17,540
2	40,000	.797	31,880	.769	30,760
3	60,000	.712	42,720	.675	40,500
			$92,460		$89,300

Interpolation	*Total Present Values*	
12%	$92,460	$92,460
True rate		90,000
14%	89,300	
	$ 3,160	$ 2,460

$$\text{True rate} = 12\% + \frac{2,460}{3,160} \times 2\%$$

$$= 12\% + 1.8\% = 13.8\%$$

APPENDIX 13-B: VARIATIONS OF PAYBACK

The Bail-Out Factor: A Better Approach to Payback

The typical payback computation tries to answer the question: "How soon will it be before I can recoup my investment *if operations proceed as planned?*" However, a more fundamental question is: "Which of the competing projects has the best bail-out protection if things go wrong? In other words, which has the least risk?" To answer such a question, we must consider the salvage value of the equipment throughout its life, an item that is ignored in the usual payback computations. For instance, salvage values of general-purpose equipment far exceed those of special-purpose equipment. If such salvage values are considered, the payback times may look radically different than if they are ignored.

Payback Reciprocal

Businessmen have tempered their use of the payback model, the most widely used approach to capital budgeting, with common sense. They have used it in conjunction with estimated useful life. The payback model may yield satisfactory indications of relative profitability, provided that the following two criteria are both met:

a. Uniform cash inflows from operations occur throughout the project's useful life.

b. The useful life of the project must be at least twice the payback time.

Coupling these criteria with the payback time effects a crude approximation of the relative time-adjusted profitability of various projects. The payback time is thus no longer being used alone, a dangerous approach that may lead to wrong decisions.

For example, consider our $12,000 machine with the eight-year life where the payback time was three years:

$$\text{Payback reciprocal} = \frac{O}{I} = \frac{\$4,000}{\$12,000} = .333, \text{ or } 33\%$$

$$\text{or} = \frac{1}{3 \text{ years}} = .333, \text{ or } 33\%$$

This percentage is a crude approximation of the time-adjusted rate of return, which is calculated as follows:

$$\$12,000 = 4,000\,F$$
$$F = 3.000 \text{ (note this is the payback time)}$$

In Table 2, the Period 8 row indicates that the time-adjusted rate is slightly under 30 percent, so the reciprocal provided a fairly accurate approximation.

However, if the machine's useful life is only five years, the reciprocal is no longer accurate. The reciprocal is still 33 percent, but the time adjusted-rate (see the Period 5 line in Table 2) is approximately 20 percent. This demonstrates why the useful life must be at least twice the payback period.

Exhibit 13-9 demonstrates various combinations of payback period and time-adjusted rates of return. The table is based on one designed by a company that uses the payback period in approximating the rate of return.

The reciprocal always provides too high an estimate of the time-adjusted rate. In general, the payback reciprocal becomes more accurate as the interest rate gets higher or as the useful life gets longer and longer beyond the payback time.

EXHIBIT 13-9
Table for Approximating Rate of Return

USEFUL LIFE IN YEARS	TIME-ADJUSTED RATE OF RETURN (PERCENT)										
3	0										
4	15	11	7	3							
5	23	19	15	12	9	6	4	2	0		
6	27	23	20	17	15	12	10	8	6	3	0
7	29	26	23	20	18	15	13	11	10	7	4
8	30	27	25	22	20	18	16	14	12	10	8
9	31	28	26	23	21	19	18	16	15	12	10
10	32	29	27	24	22	21	19	18	16	14	11
15	33	30	28	25	25	23	22	20	19	16	15
20	33	30	28	26	25	23	22	20	19	18	16
Over 20	33	31	29	27	26	25	23	21	20	19	17
Payback period in years	3	$3\frac{1}{4}$	$3\frac{1}{2}$	$3\frac{3}{4}$	4	$4\frac{1}{4}$	$4\frac{1}{2}$	$4\frac{3}{4}$	5	$5\frac{1}{2}$	6

Source: Adapted from N.A.A. Research Report 35, Return on Capital as a Guide to Managerial Decisions, p. 76.

Example 1. Project savings expected to last ten years; computed payback period is five years (a payback reciprocal of 20 percent). Enter table at ten-year row and five-year column. Table shows 16 percent time-adjusted rate of return.

Example 2. Project savings expected to last twelve years. Computed payback period is 4.7 years. Enter table using nearest values—that is, use ten years for savings and 4¾ years for payback period. Table shows 18 percent time-adjusted rate of return. For more accurate computations, interpolation may be used.

ASSIGNMENT MATERIAL

Special Note: Ignore income taxes. The effects of income taxes are considered in Chapter 14.

Fundamental Assignment Material

13-1. Terminology. Define: *capital budgeting; time-adjusted rate of return; net present value method; payback; payout; payoff; unadjusted rate of return; accounting method; book-value method; total project approach;* and *incremental approach.*

13-2. Exercises in compound interest: answers supplied.[6] Use the appropriate interest tables to compute the following:

a. It is your sixty-fifth birthday. You plan to work five more years before retiring. Then you want to take $5,000 for a round-the-world tour. What lump sum do you have to invest now in order to accumulate the $5,000? Assume that your minimum desired rate of return is:
   (1) 4 percent, compounded annually.
   (2) 10 percent, compounded annually.
   (3) 20 percent, compounded annually.
b. You want to spend $500 on a vacation at the end of each of the next five years. What lump sum do you have to invest now in order to take the five vacations? Assume that your minimum desired rate of return is:
   (1) 4 percent, compounded annually.
   (2) 10 percent, compounded annually.
   (3) 20 percent, compounded annually.
c. At age sixty, you find that your employer is moving to another location. You receive termination pay of $5,000. You have some savings and wonder whether to retire now.
   (1) If you invest the $5,000 now at 4 percent, compounded annually, how much money can you withdraw from your account each year so that at the end of five years there will be a zero balance?
   (2) If you invest it at 10 percent?
d. At 16 percent, compounded annually, which of the following plans is more desirable in terms of present values? Show computations to support your answer.

[6]The answers appear at the end of the assignment material for this chapter.

	Annual Cash Inflows	
Year	Mining	Farming
1	$10,000	$ 2,000
2	8,000	4,000
3	6,000	6,000
4	4,000	8,000
5	2,000	10,000
	$30,000	$30,000

13-3. Comparison of capital budgeting techniques. The Putnam Company is considering the purchase of a new packaging machine at a cost of $20,000. It should save $4,000 in cash operating costs per year. Its estimated useful life is eight years, and it will have zero disposal value.

Required:

1. What is the payback time?
2. Compute the net present value if the minimum rate of return desired is 10 percent. Should the company buy? Why?
3. Establish the time-adjusted rate of return.

13-4. Replacement of equipment. Refer to Problem 12-2. Assume that the new equipment will cost $100,000 in cash, and that the old machine cost $81,000 and can be sold now for $16,000 cash.

Required:

1. Compute the net present value of the proposed investment in new equipment, assuming that the minimum desired rate of return is 10 percent.
2. What will be the time-adjusted rate of return?
3. How long is the payback period?

13-5. Sensitivity analysis. The All Directions Railroad is considering the replacement of an old power jack tamper used in the maintenance of track with a new improved version that should save $5,000 per year in net cash operating costs.

The old equipment has zero disposal value, but it could be used indefinitely. The estimated useful life of the new equipment is twelve years and it will cost $20,000.

Required:

1. What is the payback time?
2. Compute the time-adjusted rate of return.
3. Management is unsure about the useful life. What would be the rate of return if the useful life were (a) six years instead of twelve and (b) twenty years instead of twelve?
4. Suppose the life will be twelve years but the savings will be $3,000 per year instead of $5,000. What would be the rate of return?
5. Suppose the annual savings will be $4,000 for six years. What would be the rate of return?

Additional Assignment Material

13-6. "Doublecounting occurs if depreciation is separately considered in discounted-cash-flow analysis." Do you agree? Explain.

13-7. "Problem solving is project-oriented rather than time-period-oriented." Explain.

13-8. Why is capital budgeting likely to receive increasing attention?

13-9. Why is discounted cash flow a superior method for capital budgeting?

13-10. Why should depreciation be excluded from discounted-cash-flow computations?

13-11. Can net present value ever be negative? Why?

13-12. "The higher the minimum rate of return desired, the higher the price that a company will be willing to pay for cost-saving equipment." Do you agree? Explain.

13-13. Why should the incremental approach to alternatives always lead to the same decision as the total project approach?

13-14. "Current disposal values of equipment are always relevant to a replacement decision." Do you agree? Explain.

13-15. "Discounted-cash-flow approaches will not work if the competing projects have unequal lives." Do you agree? Explain.

13-16. Some perceptive observer in ancient times said, "A little knowledge is a dangerous thing." How might this apply in capital budgeting?

13-17. State a rule that can serve as a general guide to capital budgeting decisions.

13-18. "If discounted-cash-flow approaches are superior to the payback and the accounting methods, why should we bother to learn the others? All it does is confuse things." Answer this contention.

13-19. What is the basic flaw in the payback method?

13-20. How can the payback method be adjusted to yield satisfactory indications of relative profitability?

13-21. Compare the unadjusted rate of return approach and the discounted-cash-flow approach to the time value of money.

13-22. **New equipment.** The Acme Company has offered to sell some new packaging equipment to the Zenith Company. The list price is $40,000, but Acme has agreed to accept some old equipment in trade. A trade-in allowance of $6,000 was agreed upon. The old equipment was carried at a book value of $7,700 and could be sold outright for $5,000 cash. Cash operating savings are expected to be $5,000 annually for the next twelve years. The minimum desired rate of return is 12 percent. The old equipment has a remaining useful life of twelve years. Both the old and new equipment will have zero disposal values twelve years from now.

Required:

Should Zenith buy the new equipment? Show your computations, using the net present value method. Ignore income taxes.

13-23. **Illustration of trial-and-error method of computing rate of return.** Study Exhibit 13-3. Suppose the annual cash inflow will be $2,500 rather than $2,000.

13-24. Cafeteria facilities. The cafeteria of an office building is open 250 days a year. It offers typical cafeteria-line service. At the noon meal (open to the public), serving-line facilities can accommodate 200 people per hour for the two-hour serving period. The average customer has a thirty-minute lunch hour. Serving facilities are unable to handle the overflow of noon customers with the result that, daily, 200 dissatisfied customers who do not wish to stand in line choose to eat elsewhere. Projected over a year, this results in a considerable loss to the cafeteria.

To tap this excess demand, the cafeteria is considering two alternatives: (a) installing two vending machines, at a cost of $5,000 apiece; or (b) completely revamping present serving-line facilities with new equipment, at a cost of $80,000. The vending machines and serving-line equipment have a useful life of ten years and will be depreciated on a straight-line basis. The minimum desired rate of return for the cafeteria is 10 percent. The average sale is $1.50, with a contribution margin of 30 percent. This will remain the same if new serving-line facilities are installed.

Data for alternative *a* (vending machines) are as follows:

Service cost per year is $300; salvage value of each machine at the end of ten years is $500. The price of a sandwich is 80¢; salad, 30¢; dessert, 20¢; milk or coffee 20¢. Contribution margin is 20 percent. It is estimated that 60 percent of the dissatisfied customers will use the vending machines and will have a full lunch. The estimated salvage value of the present equipment will net $2,000 at the end of the ten-year period.

Data for alternative *b* (new serving-line facilities) are as follows:

Yearly salary for an extra clerk is $4,000; salvage value of old equipment is $5,000; salvage value of new equipment, at the end of ten years, is $10,000; cost of dismantling old equipment is $1,000. It is estimated that all the previously dissatisfied customers will use the new facilities.

All other costs are the same under both alternatives and need not be considered.

Required:

Using the discounted-cash-flow model, which is the better alternative?

13-25. Replacement decision for railway equipment. The Milwaukee Railroad is considering replacement of a Kalamazoo Power Jack Tamper, used for maintenance of track, with a new automatic raising device which can be attached to a production tamper.

The present power jack tamper cost $18,000 five years ago and has an estimated life of twelve years. A year from now the machine will require a major overhaul estimated to cost $5,000. It can be disposed of now via an outright cash sale for $2,500. There will be no value at the end of twelve years.

The automatic raising attachment has a delivered selling price of $24,000 and an estimated life of twelve years. Because of anticipated future developments in combined maintenance machines, it is felt that the machine should be disposed of at the end of the seventh year to take advantage of newly developed machines. Estimated sale value at end of seven years is $5,000.

Tests have shown that the automatic raising machine will produce a more uniform surface on the track than the power jack tamper now in use. The new equipment will eliminate one laborer whose annual salary is $9,500.

Track maintenance work is seasonal and the equipment normally works from May 1 to October 31 each year. Machine operators and laborers are transferred to other work after October 31, at the same rate of pay.

The salesman claims that the annual normal maintenance of the new machine will run about $1,000 per year. Because the automatic raising machine is more complicated than the manually operated machine, it is felt that it will require a thorough overhaul at the end of the fourth year at an estimated cost of $7,000.

Records show the annual normal maintenance of the Kalamazoo machine to be $1,200. Fuel consumption of the two machines is equal.

Should the Milwaukee keep or replace the Kalamazoo Power Jack Tamper? A 10 percent rate of return is desired.

The railroad is not currently paying any income tax.

13-26. Cost-volume-profit analysis and discounted cash flow. (CPA adapted.) Thorne Transit, Inc. has decided to inaugurate express bus service between its headquarters city and a nearby suburb (one-way fare, 50¢) and is considering the purchase of either 32- or 52-passenger buses, on which pertinent estimates are as follows:

	32-Passenger Bus	52-Passenger Bus
Number of each to be purchased	6	4
Useful life	8 years	8 years
Purchase price of each bus (Paid on delivery)	$80,000	$110,000
Mileage per gallon	10	7½
Salvage value per bus	$ 6,000	$ 7,000
Drivers' hourly wage	$ 3.50	$ 4.20
Price per gallon of gasoline	$ .30	$ .30
Other annual cash expenses	$ 4,000	$ 3,000

During the four daily rush hours all buses will be in service and are expected to operate at full capacity (state law prohibits standees) in both directions of the route, each bus covering the route twelve times (six round trips) during that period. During the remainder of the sixteen-hour day, 500 passengers would be carried and Thorne would operate only four buses on the route. Part-time drivers would be employed to drive the extra hours during the rush hours. A bus traveling the route all day would go 480 miles and one traveling only during rush hours would go 120 miles a day during the 260-day year.

Required:
1. Prepare a schedule showing the computation of estimated annual revenue of the new route for both alternatives.
2. Prepare a schedule showing the computation of estimated annual drivers' wages for both alternatives.
3. Prepare a schedule showing the computation of estimated annual cost of gasoline for both alternatives.
4. Assume that your computations in parts 1, 2, and 3 are as follows:

	32- Passenger Bus	52- Passenger Bus
Estimated revenues	$365,000	$390,000
Estimated drivers' wages	67,000	68,000
Estimated cost of gasoline	16,000	18,000

Assuming that a minimum rate of return of 12 percent before income taxes is desired and that all annual cash flows occur at the end of the year, prepare a schedule showing the computation of the present values of net cash flows for the eight-year period; include the cost of buses and the proceeds from their disposition under both alternatives, but disregard the effect of income taxes. The following data are relevant:

Year	Present Value of $1.00 Due at the End of the Indicated Year Discounted at 12%	Present Value of $1.00 Due Annually at the End of Each Year Discounted at 12%
1.......	.89	.89
2.......	.80	1.69
3.......	.71	2.40
4.......	.64	3.04
5.......	.57	3.61
6.......	.51	4.11
7.......	.45	4.56
8.......	.40	4.97

13-27. Minimizing transportation costs. The Wegener Company produces industrial and residential lighting fixtures at its manufacturing facility located in Los Angeles. Shipment of company products to an eastern warehouse is presently handled by common carriers at a rate of 10¢ per pound of fixtures. The warehouse is located in Cleveland, 2,500 miles from Los Angeles.

The treasurer of Wegener Company is presently considering whether to purchase a truck for transporting products to the eastern warehouse. The following data on the truck are available:

Purchase price	$25,000
Useful life	5 years
Salvage value after 5 years	$5,000
Capacity of truck	10,000 lbs.
Cash costs of operating truck	$.40 per mile

The treasurer feels that an investment in this truck is particularly attractive because of his successful negotiation with X Company to back-haul X's products from Cleveland to Los Angeles on every return trip from the warehouse. X has agreed to pay Wegener $1,200 per load of X's products hauled from Cleveland to Los Angeles up to and including 100 loads per year.

Wegener's marketing manager has estimated that 500,000 pounds of fixtures will have to be shipped to the eastern warehouse each year for the next five years. The truck will be fully loaded on each round trip.

Ignore income taxes. For income tax effects, see Problem 14-20.

Required:

1. Assume that Wegener requires a minimum rate of return of 20 percent. Should the truck be purchased? Show computations to support your answer.
2. What is the minimum number of trips that must be guaranteed by the X Company to make the deal acceptable to Wegener, based on the above numbers alone?
3. What qualitative factors might influence your decision? Be specific.

13-28. Uses of warehouse: review of Chapters 12 and 13.

a. The Miller Company is currently leasing one of its warehouses to another company for $3,000 per year, on a month-to-month basis.
b. The estimated sales value of the warehouse is $12,000. This price is likely to remain unchanged indefinitely—even if a contemplated public expressway results in the building's condemnation. The building originally cost $20,000 and is being depreciated at $500 annually. Its net book value is $9,000.
c. The Miller Company is seriously considering converting the warehouse into a retail outlet for selling furniture at ridiculously low discount prices. Such an endeavor would entail remodeling, at a cost of $15,000. The remodeling would be extremely modest because the major attraction will be flimsy furniture at rock-bottom prices. The remodeling can be accomplished over a single weekend.
d. The inventory, cash, and receivables needed to open and sustain the retail outlet would be $50,000. This total is fully recoverable whenever operations terminate.
e. The president, who paid an expressway engineer $1,000 to discover when and where the expressway will be built, is virtually certain that the warehouse will be available for no more than four years. He has asked you to give him an analysis of whether the company should continue to lease the warehouse or convert it to a retail outlet, assuming that the minimum annual rate of return desired is 14 percent over a four-year planning horizon. Estimated annual operating data, exclusive of depreciation, are:

f. Sales	$200,000
g. Operating expenses	177,000
h. Nonrecurring sales promotion costs at *beginning* of Year 1	20,000
i. Nonrecurring termination costs at *end* of Year 4	10,000

The president has definitely decided not to sell the warehouse until forced to by condemnation proceedings.

Required:

1. Show how you would handle the *individual* items on the company's analysis form, which is set up as follows:

		Net Present Value	Cash Flows in Year				
Item	Description		0	1	2	3	4
a.							
b.							
.							
.							
.							
h.							
i.		‾‾‾‾‾					
		═════					

Use the following present value factors: P.V. of $1 = .60 and the P.V. of an annuity of $1 = 2.9. Ignore income taxes. If you think an item is irrelevant, leave the space blank.

2. After analyzing all the relevant data, compute the net present value. Indicate which course of action, based on the data alone, should be taken.

13-29. Investment in machine and working capital. The Brinow Company has an old machine with a net disposal value of $10,000 now and $4,000 five years from now. A new Speedee machine is offered for $60,000 cash or $50,000 with a trade-in. The new machine will result in annual operating cash outflow of $40,000 as compared with the old machine's annual outflow of $50,000. The disposal value of the new machine five years hence will be $4,000.

Because the new machine will produce output more rapidly, the average investment in inventories will be $160,000 by using the new machine instead of $200,000.

The minimum desired rate of return is 20 percent. The company uses discounted-cash-flow techniques to guide these decisions.

Required:

Should the Speedee machine be acquired? Show your calculations. Company procedures require the computing of the present value of each alternative. The most desirable alternative is the one with the least cost. Assume P.V. of $1 at 20 percent for five years, .40; P.V. of annuity of $1 at 20 percent for five years, 3.00.

13-30. Evaluation of payback method. The Knickel Oil Company has two methods of evaluating the attractiveness of oil-drilling proposals, the *payback method* and so-called *cumulative profitability method.* The supervisor of drilling explained to some visitors that the most recent project, which was begun two days previously, will have an investment of $108,000, a nine-month payback time, and a cumulative profitability ratio of 2.3.

When asked to explain the latter, he replied, "We take the total expected production over the life of the well and figure the overall profitability by dividing its associated cash inflow by the original investment."

Required:

1. What was the expected cash inflow from operations for the first year?
2. What was the total expected cash inflow from operations for the useful life of the project?

3. Evaluate the validity of the computation in Requirement 2 in comparison with (a) the payback model, and (b) the discounted-cash-flow model. Be specific. This is the most important part of the problem.

13-31. Make or buy, discounted cash flow, and unadjusted rate of return. Refer to Problem 12-29, requirement 1.

1. Using a net present value analysis, which alternative is most attractive? Assume that the minimum rate of return desired is 8 percent.
2. Using the unadjusted (accounting) rate-of-return method, what is the rate of return on the initial investment?

13-32. Comparison of unadjusted method and time-adjusted method. Tony's Pizza Company makes and sells frozen pizzas to local retail outlets. Tony just inherited $10,000 and has decided to invest it in the business. He is trying to decide between:

Alternative *a:* Buy a $10,000 contract, payable immediately, from a local reputable sales promotion agency. The agency would provide various advertising services, as specified in the contract, over the next ten years. Tony is convinced that the sales promotion would increase cash inflow from operations, through increased volume, by $2,000 a year for the first five years, and by $1,000 per year thereafter. There would be no effect after the ten years had elapsed.

Alternative *b:* Buy new mixing and packaging equipment, at a cost of $10,000, which would reduce operating cash outflows by $1,500 per year for the next ten years. The equipment would have zero salvage value at the end of the ten years.

Ignore any tax effect.

Required:

1. Compute the rates of return on initial investment by the unadjusted (accounting) method for both alternatives.
2. Compute the rates of return by the discounted-cash-flow model for both alternatives.
3. Are the rates of return different under the discounted-cash-flow model? Explain.

13-33. New equipment and analysis of operating costs: unadjusted rate of return. The processing department of Fay Company has incurred the following costs in producing 150,000 units, which is normal volume, during the past year:

Variable	$100,000
Fixed	50,000
	$150,000

The department has been offered some new processing equipment. The salesman says that the new equipment will reduce unit costs by 20¢. The department's old equipment has a remaining useful life of five years, has zero disposal value now, and is being depreciated on a straight-line basis at $5,000 annually. The new equipment's straight-line depreciation would be $30,000 annually. It would last five years and have no disposal value. The salesman pointed out that overall unit costs now are $1, whereas the new equipment is being used by one of Fay's competitors to produce an identical product at a unit cost of 80¢, computed as follows:

Variable costs	$ 80,000
Fixed costs*	80,000
Total costs	$160,000
Divide by units produced	200,000
Cost per unit	$.80

*Fixed costs include $30,000 depreciation on the new equipment. Fay's supervisory payroll is $10,000 less than this competitor's.

The salesman stated that a saving of 20¢ per unit would add $30,000 to Fay's annual net income.

Required:

1. Show *specifically* how the salesman computed Fay's costs and prospective savings.
2. As adviser to the Fay Company, evaluate the salesman's contentions and prepare a quantitative summary to support your recommendations for Fay's best course of action. Include the unadjusted rate-of-return method and the net present value method in your evaluation. Assume that Fay's minimum desired rate of return is 10 percent.

13-34. **Payback reciprocal.** Refer to Problem 13-5. Appendix 13-B and Professor Myron Gordon have pointed out that the payback reciprocal can be a crude approximation of the true rate of return where (a) the project life is at least twice the payback period, and (b) the cash earnings or savings are uniformly received in equal amounts throughout the investment's life. The payback reciprocal, using the original data, will be $5,000 ÷ $20,000, or 25 percent.

Required:

1. How close is this to the time-adjusted rate of return?
2. Compute the payback reciprocals for 3(a) and 3(b) in Problem 13-5. How close are they to the time-adjusted rates of return?
3. Compute the payback reciprocals for (4) and (5) in Problem 13-5. How close are they to the time-adjusted rates of return?

13-35. **Replacement decision.** The Eastern Railroad has been operating a dining car on its single passenger train. Yearly operations have shown a consistent loss, as follows:

Revenue (in cash)		$100,000
Expenses for food, supplies, etc. (in cash)	$50,000	
Salaries	60,000	110,000
Net loss (ignore depreciation on the dining car itself)		($10,000)

The Auto-Vend Company has offered to sell automatic vending machines to Eastern for $22,000, less a $3,000 trade-in allowance on old equipment that can be sold outright for $3,000 cash and that is now used in the dining-car operation.

The useful life of the vending equipment is estimated at ten years, with zero scrap value. The equipment will serve 50 percent more food than the dining car handled, but prices will be 50 percent less. A catering company will completely service and supply the machines. The variety of food will be the same as that which prevailed for the dining car. The catering company will pay 10 percent of gross receipts to the Eastern Company and will bear all costs of food, repairs, etc. All dining-car employees will be discharged. Their termination pay will total $5,000. However, an attendant who has some general knowledge of vending machines will be needed for one shift per day. The annual cost to Eastern for the attendant will be $6,500.

The railroad will definitely not abandon its food service. The old equipment will have zero scrap value at the end of ten years.

Required:

Using the above data, carefully compute the following. Label computations. Ignore income taxes.

1. How long is the payback period?
2. Compute the incremental net present value, in dollars, of the proposed investment. Assume a minimum desired rate of return of 20 percent.
3. Management is very uncertain about the prospective revenue from the vending equipment. Suppose the Eastern share of the gross receipts amounted to $2,500. Repeat the computations in Requirements 1 and 2.
4. What would be the minimum amount of annual revenue from the new equipment that Eastern should have to justify making the investment? Show computations to support your answer.

13-36. Discounted cash flow and evaluation of performance. John Castleman, the general manager of a division of a huge, highly diversified company, recently attended an executive-training program. He learned about discounted-cash-flow analysis, and he became convinced that it was the best available guide for making long-range investment decisions.

However, upon returning to his company, he became frustrated. He wanted to use the discounted-cash-flow technique, but top management had a long-standing policy of evaluating divisional management performance largely on the basis of its rate of return as calculated by dividing divisional net income by the net book value of total divisional assets. Therefore, in his own best interests and in accordance with the specifications of his superiors, he had to make decisions that he felt were not really the most desirable in terms of maximizing what he considered to be the "true" rate of return (that is, the discounted-cash-flow rate). Ignore income taxes.

Required:

1. Suppose Mr. Castleman had an opportunity to invest $30,000 cash in some automated machinery with a useful life of three years and a scrap value of zero. The expected cash savings per year were $12,060. Compute the time-adjusted rate of return.
2. Show the effect on net income for each of the three years, assuming straight-line depreciation. Also show the rate of return based on the beginning balance of the net book value of the fixed asset for each year.
3. Repeat Requirement 2, assuming sum-of-the-years'-digits depreciation.
4. Top management has indicated a minimum desired rate of return of 10 percent. After examining the above results, Mr. Castleman was more baffled than ever. He just could not see why he should invest in the machinery if his net

The professor reacted: "The basic trouble is not confined to your company. Many companies now insist that their managers use discounted-cash-flow techniques for appraising investment opportunities, but they use conventional accounting techniques for judging operating performance. In short, one 'model' is supposed to be used for planning, but another model is used for control.

"A possible solution is to use a compound-interest method of depreciation for evaluating subsequent performance. The compound-interest method is based on the same model as the discounted-cash-flow technique—that is, each receipt ($12,060 in this case) consists of interest on the beginning investment balance plus the recovery of principal. For example, the $12,060 cash savings during the first year would be analyzed as consisting of 'interest' of 10 percent of $30,000, or $3,000, plus a recovery of principal ('depreciation') of $9,060."

Repeat Requirement 2, assuming the compound-interest method of depreciation.

5. Contrast the pattern of depreciation in Requirement 4 with the other methods. Why is industry reluctant to use the compound-interest method of depreciation? What other means might be used to reconcile the two models described in 4?

13-37. Sensitivity of capital budgeting and inflation. The president of the Haywood Company, a London manufacturer, is considering whether to invest £100,000 in some automatic equipment that will last five years, have zero scrap value, and produce cash savings in materials and labor usage as follows, using 19x0 prices and wage rates (in pounds sterling):

Year	19x1	19x2	19x3	19x4	19x5
	20,000	20,000	30,000	30,000	20,000

The minimum desired rate of return, which embodies an element attributable to inflation, is 12 percent per year. For purposes of this problem, assume that the present values of £1 at the end of each year are .89, .80, .71, .64, and .57, respectively.

Required:

1. Compute the net present value of the project, using the above data.
2. Ms. Haywood is virtually certain that inflation will continue, although she is uncertain about its degree. She hopes that government control over prices and wages will dampen inflation, but she thinks that the existing rate of inflation, 6 percent annually, will prevail over the next five years. She wants to pinpoint price changes more precisely with respect to the materials and labor question, but she thinks 6 percent is probably as good an overall guess as any.

One pound invested at time zero will grow as follows, if the rates of interest are (rounded to the second decimal place):

End of Period	4%	6%	8%
1	1.04	1.06	1.08
2	1.08	1.12	1.17
3	1.12	1.19	1.26
4	1.17	1.26	1.36
5	1.22	1.34	1.47

Compute the net present value of the project, using the above data and an inflation rate of 6 percent throughout the five-year period.

3. Compare your results in Requirements 1 and 2. What generalizations seem warranted?

13-38. Effects of currency devaluation and qualitative factors. Phelan Glass Manufacturing Company is a large producer of high-quality crystal glassware in Dublin, Ireland. Its glassware is sold entirely on the export market, mostly in the United States and France. A small research group within the company had recently been investigating a new glass coating that, when applied to aluminum cooking ware, gave a finish which was cheap yet colorful, heat resistant, unbreakable, and non-stick. Patents on the process had been obtained by the company in many countries, including France and the U.S.

Mr. Phelan, the president, has ordered a market-research program to determine the approximate sales potential of the new product. At a conference called to discuss the product, he asked his marketing manager, "Why not kick off the meeting by telling us what the market-research fellows have come up with?"

John: "Basically, we can sell this new thing in the U.S. and France—tariffs and competition make other countries unfeasible. In those two countries, the new line will tie in well with our present lines, since it will have the same high-quality image and be sold through the same distribution channels, over which we have strong influence in both countries. As accurately as we can predict, for the first five years, the net additional cash inflows by the new line will be $560,000 per year in the U.S. market, and 1,680,000 Francs in the French market. For the second five years, the average annual contribution will be only half of these figures, as the product line begins to decline. After ten years, other finishes and techniques will be taking over, so we plan on phasing the product out by the end of ten years. By the way, £1 equals $2.8, and £1 equals 14.0 Francs."

The president then asked Jim Wood, the production manager, to describe what plant commitment would be involved.

Jim: "My predictions, based on the production levels that John is talking about, show that, apart from land, the total cost of buildings and normal equipment needed will be about £1.1 million. In addition to this, the glazing furnace and controls will have to be purchased in the U.S. for an estimated additional $2.1 million (dollars). I included installation of the furnace in the £1.1 million. The useful life should be ten years. The predicted value of the building at the end of ten years is £.8 million; of all equipment, zero."

The possible plant location was then discussed by the president. Adjoining the present factory was a five-acre site that would just be large enough for the proposed plant. It had been left over when the present factory had been built years ago. This site had been landscaped into a recreation area and park; it had won numerous awards for Phelan Glass for "best plant layout" competitions. Furthermore, it housed changing rooms and a football field for the factory's own football team, composed of amateur players among the company's 2,500 workers. Most large companies had such a football team, and Phelan Glass had among the best in the country—a fact in which most company workers took great pride.

Mr. Phelan was quite concerned that this area would have to go, because he felt that the image of the "well-groomed factory" was good employee and public relations. When the personnel manager had been informed of the proposal, he had flatly stated that the workers' high morale, for which the company was famous, "would disappear along with the football facilities." Investigation showed that another site, suitable for either a building or conversion to a football facility, was available five miles away at a cost of £90,000.

At this stage, the president turned to Patricia O'Shea, who had recently obtained a degree in management, and said, "Pat, you've been listening to us for the last few hours. We don't want to take on any project at present that does not give us a rate of return of 10 percent or more. Why don't you take our facts and predictions and give us your recommendations at our meeting tomorrow."

Required:

1. As Patricia, how accurate do you feel the predictions given in the cases are likely to be? What other information would you look for, if any?
2. Using the given data and predictions as the best available, would you recommend that the project be undertaken? Show computations in sterling. Assume that the value of the building sites will be unchanged over the next few years. Suppose that you favor proceeding. What would be your recommendation on the "site" problem?
3. Patricia finished her analysis late in the evening. Early next morning, she glanced at the morning newspaper. She was startled to read the banner headline: *"POUND DEVALUED 14.3% LAST NIGHT."* The story stated that now £1 equalled $2.4, and £1 equalled 12 Francs.

Does this news affect your recommendations? If so, what recommendations will you make to the management group?

Solutions to Exercises in Compound Interest, Problem 13-2.

The general approach to these exercises centers about one fundamental question: Which of the two basic tables am I dealing with? No calculations should be made until after this question is answered with assurance. If you made any errors, it is possible that you used the wrong table.

a. From Table 1 in appendix, p. 601.
   (1) $4,110
   (2) $3,105
   (3) $2,010

The $5,000 is an *amount* or *future worth*. You want the present value of that amount:

$$PV = \frac{S}{(1 + i)^n}$$

The conversion factor, $\frac{1}{(1 + i)^n}$, is on line 5 of Table 1.

Substituting:

$$PV = \$5,000\,(.822) = \$4,110 \qquad (1)$$
$$PV = \$5,000\,(.621) = \$3,105 \qquad (2)$$
$$PV = \$5,000\,(.402) = \$2,010 \qquad (3)$$

Note that the higher the interest rate, the lower the present value.

b. From Table 2, p. 602.
   (1) $2,226.00
   (2) $1,895.50
   (3) $1,495.50

The $500 withdrawal is a uniform annual amount, an annuity. You need to find the present value of an annuity for five years:

$$PV_A = \text{Annual withdrawal}\,(F), \text{ where } F \text{ is the conversion factor.}$$

Substituting:

$$PV_A = \$500\,(4.452) = \$2,226.00 \tag{1}$$
$$PV_A = \$500\,(3.791) = \$1,895.50 \tag{2}$$
$$PV_A = \$500\,(2.991) = \$1,495.50 \tag{3}$$

c. From Table 2:
  (1) $1,120.82
  (2) $1,318.91

You have $5,000, the present value of your contemplated annuity. You must find the annuity that will just exhaust the invested principal in five years:

$$PV_A = \text{Annual withdrawal}\,(F) \tag{1}$$

$$\$5,000 = \text{Annual withdrawal}\,(4.452)$$
$$\text{Annual withdrawal} = \$5,000 \div 4.452$$
$$= \$1,120.82$$

$$\$5,000 = \text{Annual withdrawal}\,(3.791) \tag{2}$$
$$\text{Annual withdrawal} = \$5,000 \div 3.791$$
$$= \$1,318.91$$

d. From Table 1: Mining is preferable; its present value exceeds farming by $3,852.

Year	Present Value Factors @ 16 Percent from Table 1	Present Value of Mining	Present Value of Farming
1	.862	$ 8,620	$ 1,724
2	.743	5,944	2,972
3	.641	3,846	3,846
4	.552	2,208	4,416
5	.476	952	4,760
		$21,570	$17,718

Note that the nearer dollars are more valuable than the distant dollars.

SUGGESTED READINGS

Financial Analysis to Guide Capital Expenditure Decisions, National Association of Accountants, Research Report No. 43. New York, 1967. Has a good bibliography.

Bierman, H., and S. Smidt, *The Capital Budgeting Decision,* 3rd ed. (New York: The Macmillan Company, 1971).

Morris, William T., *The Capacity Decision System* (Homewood, Ill.: Richard D. Irwin, Inc., 1967).

Van Horne, James C., *Financial Management and Policy,* 3rd ed. (Englewood Cliffs, N.J.: Prentice-Hall, Inc., 1974).

Impact of Income Taxes on Management Planning

14

Income taxes influence nearly all business decisions. In this chapter, we show how income taxes may be reckoned with in decision making. Our focus is on corporations, rather than on individuals or partnerships.

Managers have an obligation to avoid income taxes. Avoidance is not evasion. Avoidance is the use of legal means to minimize tax payments; evasion is the use of illegal means. Income tax problems are often exceedingly complex, so qualified counsel should be sought whenever the slightest doubt exists.

We are especially concerned with the effect of income taxes on depreciation and on capital-budgeting decisions. However, other topics will also be explored—the tax effects of last-in, first-out inventory valuations, or charitable contributions, and some miscellaneous matters. Obviously, in one chapter we can only scratch the surface of this vast and complicated subject.

INCOME TAXES AND CAPITAL BUDGETING

General Characteristics

Income taxes are cash disbursements. Income taxes can influence the **amount** and/or the **timing** of cash flows. Their basic role in capital budgeting is no different from any other cash disbursement. However, taxes tend to narrow the cash differences between projects. Cash savings in operations will cause an increase in net taxable income and, thus, an increase in tax outlays. A 60 percent income tax rate reduces the net attractiveness of $1,000,000 in cash operating savings to $400,000.

Federal income tax rates on ordinary corporate net income, as of 1974, were 22 percent on the first $25,000 and 48 percent on the excess. These rates are sometimes subject to additional surcharges, which may vary from year to year. State income tax rates vary considerably. In many instances, state plus federal income tax rates are more than 50 percent. We use a 60 percent rate in several examples to facilitate computations.

Effects of Depreciation Deductions

Exhibit 14-1 shows the interrelationship of net income before taxes, income taxes, and depreciation. Please examine this exhibit carefully before reading on. Assume that the company has a single fixed asset, purchased for $100,000 cash, which has a four-year life and zero disposal value. The purchase cost, less the estimated disposal value, is tax-deductible in the form of yearly depreciation. Depreciation deductions (and similar deduc-

EXHIBIT 14-1
Basic Analysis of Income Statement,
Income Taxes, and Cash Flows

TRADITIONAL INCOME STATEMENT	
(S) Sales	$130,000
(E) Less: Expenses, excluding depreciation	$ 70,000
(D) Depreciation (straight line)	25,000
Total expenses	$ 95,000
Net income before taxes	$ 35,000
(T) Income taxes @ 60%	21,000
(I) Net income after taxes	$ 14,000

Net after-tax cash inflow from operations is

$$\text{either } S - E - T = \$130{,}000 - \$70{,}000 - \$21{,}000 = \$39{,}000$$
$$\text{or } I + D = \quad \$14{,}000 + \$25{,}000 = \$39{,}000$$

ANALYSIS OF THE ABOVE FOR CAPITAL BUDGETING	
(S − E) Cash inflow from operations: $130,000 −$70,000 =	$ 60,000
Income tax effects, @ 60%	36,000
After-tax effects of cash inflow from operations	$ 24,000
Effect of depreciation:	
(D) Straight-line depreciation: $100,000 ÷ 4 = $25,000	
Income tax savings @ 60%	15,000
Total cash effects	$ 39,000

EXHIBIT 14-2

After-Tax Effects of Depreciation

Assume: Original cost of equipment $100,000; four-year life; zero disposal value; annual cash inflow from operations, $60,000; income tax rate, 60 percent; minimum desired after-tax rate of return, 12 percent.

Straight-Line Depreciation

Annual depreciation: $100,000 ÷ 4 = $25,000
Savings in income tax disbursements,
@ 60% = .60 × $25,000 = $15,000

	12% DISCOUNT FACTOR, FROM APPROPRIATE TABLES	TOTAL PRESENT VALUE, @ 12%	YEAR 0	1	2	3	4
	3.037	$45,555	$ —	$15,000	$15,000	$15,000	$15,000

Sum-of-the-Years'-Digits Depreciation

YEAR	MULTIPLIER*	DEPRECIATION DEDUCTION	INCOME TAX SAVINGS, @ 60%	12% DISCOUNT FACTOR, FROM APPROPRIATE TABLES	TOTAL PRESENT VALUE, @ 12%	YEAR 0	1	2	3	4
1	4/10	$40,000	$24,000	.893	$21,432	—	$24,000			
2	3/10	30,000	18,000	.797	14,346			$18,000		
3	2/10	20,000	12,000	.712	8,544				$12,000	
4	1/10	10,000	6,000	.636	3,816					$ 6,000
					$48,138					

*The denominator for the sum-of-the-years'-digits method is:

$$1 + 2 + 3 + 4 = 10$$

or

$$S = \frac{n(n + 1)}{2} \quad (1)$$

$$S = \frac{4(4 + 1)}{2} = 4 \times 2.5 = 10$$

where S = sum of the digits
n = years of estimated useful life

tions that are noncash expenses when deducted) have been aptly called **tax shields** because they protect that amount of income from taxation.

As Exhibit 14-2 shows, the asset represents a valuable future tax deduction of $100,000. The present value of this deduction depends directly on its specific yearly effects on future income-tax payments. Therefore, the present value is influenced by the depreciation method selected, the tax rates, and the discount rate.

The Best Depreciation Method

The three most popular depreciation methods are straight-line depreciation, sum-of-the-years' digits, and the double-declining balance. The effects of the first two are shown in Exhibit 14-2. Note that the present value of the income tax savings is greater if straight-line depreciation is *not* used. The general decision rule is to select accelerated methods because, as compared with the straight-line method, they maximize the present values of income tax savings. The cumulative *dollar* tax bills may not change when the years are taken together, but the early write-offs defer tax outlays to future periods. The measure of the latter advantage depends on the rate of return that can be gained from funds that otherwise would have been paid as income taxes. The mottoes in income tax planning are: When there is a legal choice, take the deduction sooner rather than later; and recognize taxable income later rather than sooner.

Comprehensive Illustration: Effects
of Income Taxes on Cash Flow

The easiest way to visualize the effects of income taxes on cash flow is by a step-by-step analysis of a concrete situation. The following illustration is the same one used in the example in Chapter 13 (p. 430). However, an after-tax discount rate is now going to be used, and all income tax effects —including gains and losses on disposals—will now be considered.

A company owns a packaging machine, which was purchased three years ago for $56,000. It has a remaining useful life of five years, providing that it has a major overhaul, at the end of two more years of life, at a cost of $10,000, fully deductible in that year for income tax purposes. Its disposal value now is $20,000; in five years, its disposal value will be $8,000. The cash operating costs of this machine are expected to continue at $40,000 annually. The company has not used a residual value in allocating depreciation for tax purposes. Accumulated straight-line depreciation is $21,000.

A manufacturer has offered a substitute machine for $51,000 in cash. The new machine will reduce annual cash operating costs by $10,000, will not require any overhauls, will have a useful life of five years, and will have a disposal value of $3,000. The company would use sum-of-the-years'-digits depreciation for tax purposes, with no provision for residual value.

Assume that the minimum desired rate of return, after taxes, is 6 percent. Using the net present value technique, show whether the new machine should be purchased: (a) under a total project approach; (b) under an incremental approach. Assume that income tax rates are 60 percent on ordinary income. Assume that all taxes are paid in the same year in which the taxable income is earned. Also, assume that the zero residual values used for tax purposes will not be challenged by the Internal Revenue Service.

Exhibits 14-3 and 14-4 show the complete solution. The following steps are recommended. The pertinent income tax aspects will be considered as each step is discussed.

Step 1. General Approach. Review the example in Chapter 13 (p. 430). The general approach to these decisions is unchanged by income tax considerations.

Step 2. Cash Operating Costs and Depreciation. Cash operating costs and their income tax effects are separated from the depreciation effects. **These can be combined, if preferred.** However, the approach illustrated facilitates comparisons of alternative depreciation effects and permits the use of annuity tables for the cash operating costs when they do not differ from year to year.

This illustration, in which we assume that any given cash flows and related tax flows occur in the same period, could be refined to account for any possible lags. For instance, the pretax operating cash inflows may occur in Year 1, and some related tax outflows may not occur until April in Year 2. For simplicity, we are neglecting this possibility.

Step 3. Disposals of Equipment. In general, gains and losses on disposals of equipment are taxed in the same way as ordinary gains and losses.[1]

Exhibit 14-3 is an analysis of the alternative dispositions of the asset. Disposal at the end of Year 5 entails the cash effect of the selling price, subject to a 60 percent tax. The tax is on the *gain,* the excess of the selling price over book value; the book value was zero in this case.

Immediate replacement entails the disposal of the old equipment at a loss. This loss is fully deductible from current income, so the cash flow computations become a bit more subtle. The net loss must be computed to isolate its effect on current income tax, but the total cash inflow effect is the selling price plus the current income tax benefit.

[1]In this case, the old equipment was sold outright. Where there is a trade-in of old equipment for new equipment of like kind, special income tax rules result in the gain or loss being added to, or deducted from, the capitalized value of the new equipment. The gain or loss is not recognized in the year of disposal. Instead, it is spread over the life of the new asset as an adjustment of the new depreciation charges.

Before 1962, gains from disposal of equipment were taxed at the existing capital gains rate, 25 percent. Since then, the general rule has been that gain on sale of equipment is not a capital gain except in special circumstances. This complicates the effect on taxes of gains arising on disposal, frequently resulting in part of the gain being taxed at ordinary income tax rates and part at capital gain rates. For simplicity, this chapter does not introduce the latter complication.

EXHIBIT 14-3

After-tax Analysis of Equipment Replacement:
Total Project Approach

End of year			PRESENT VALUE DISCOUNT FACTORS, @ 6%	TOTAL PRESENT VALUE
(A) Replace				
Recurring cash operating costs		$30,000		
Income tax savings, @ 60%		18,000		
After-tax cash operating costs		$12,000	4.212	$(50,544)

Depreciation deductions (sum of digits
$1 + 2 + 3 + 4 + 5 = 15$)

YEAR	MULTIPLIED BY $51,000	DEDUCTION	INCOME TAX SAVINGS, @ 60%			
1	5/15	$17,000	$10,200	.943		9,619
2	4/15	13,600	8,160	.890		7,262
3	3/15	10,200	6,120	.840		5,141
4	2/15	6,800	4,080	.792		3,231
5	1/15	3,400	2,040	.747		1,524

Residual value, all subject to tax
because book value will be zero, $3,000
Less: 60% income tax 1,800

Net cash inflow			$ 1,200	.747		896

SKETCH OF CASH FLOWS

	0	1	2	3	4	5
		($12,000)	($12,000)	($12,000)	($12,000)	($12,000)
		10,200	8,160	6,120	4,080	2,040
						1,200

Initial required investment, actual cash
outflow: $51,000 — $51,000 | 1.000 | (51,000) | ($51,000)

Disposal of old equipment:
Book value now:
$56,000 − $21,000 = $35,000
Selling price — $20,000
Net loss — $15,000
Tax savings — × .60 — 9,000

Net immediate cash effects, including
tax saving — $29,000 | 1.000 | 29,000 | 29,000

Total present value of all cash flows — $(44,871)

(B) Keep

Description	Amount	PV factor	Total PV	Year 0	Year 1	Year 2	Year 3	Year 4
Recurring cash operating costs	$40,000							
Income tax savings, @ 60%	24,000							
After-tax cash operating costs	$16,000	4.212	$(67,392)		($16,000)	($16,000)	($16,000)	($16,000)
Savings in income tax disbursements because of depreciation, @ 60% = .60 × $7,000	4,200	4.212	17,690		4,200	4,200	4,200	4,200
Residual value, all subject to tax	$ 8,000							
Less: 60% income tax	4,800							
Net cash inflow	$ 3,200	.747	2,390					3,200
Overhaul, end of Year 2	$10,000							
Income tax savings, @ 60%	6,000							
Net effect on cash flow	$ 4,000	.890	(3,560)			(4,000)		
Total present value of all cash flows			$(50,872)					
Difference in favor of replacement			$ 6,001					

EXHIBIT 14-4

After-tax Analysis of Equipment Replacement
Incremental Approach

	PRESENT VALUE DISCOUNT FACTORS, @ 6%	TOTAL PRESENT VALUES	SKETCH OF CASH FLOWS 0	1	2	3	4	5
End of year								
Analysis Confined to Differences between (A) and (B) in Exhibit 14-3:								
Recurring operating savings,								
$40,000 − $30,000		$10,000						
Income tax, @ 60%		6,000						
After-tax operating savings	4.212	$ 16,848		$4,000	$4,000	$4,000	$4,000	$4,000

Differences in depreciation:

YEAR	REPLACE	KEEP	DIFFERENCE	INCOME TAX EFFECT, @ 60%	PRESENT VALUE DISCOUNT FACTORS, @ 6%	TOTAL PRESENT VALUES	SKETCH 0	1	2	3	4	5
1	$17,000	$7,000	$10,000	$6,000	.943	5,658		6,000				
2	13,600	7,000	6,600	3,960	.890	3,524			3,960			
3	10,200	7,000	3,200	1,920	.840	1,614				1,920		
4	6,800	7,000	(200)	(120)	.792	(95)					(120)	
5	3,400	7,000	(3,600)	(2,160)	.747	(1,614)						(2,160)

		PRESENT VALUE DISCOUNT FACTORS, @ 6%	TOTAL PRESENT VALUES	SKETCH 0	1	2	3	4	5
Difference in disposal value, end of Year 5									
(see Exhibit 14-3 for details):									
$1,200 − $3,200 = $(2,000)		.747	(1,494)						(2,000)
Overhaul avoided, end of Year 2, net of tax effects		.890	3,560			4,000			
Incremental initial investment									
(see Exhibit 14-3 for details): $51,000 − $29,000		1.000	(22,000)	($22,000)					
Net present value of replacement			$ 6,001						

Step 4. Total Project or Incremental Approach? The relative merits of the project and the incremental approaches were discussed in Chapter 13. Exhibits 14-3 and 14-4 demonstrate these approaches. Either yields the same net answer in favor of replacement. Note, however, that the incremental approach rapidly becomes unwieldy when computations become intricate. This becomes even more apparent when three or more alternatives are being considered.

Income Tax Complications

In the foregoing illustration, believe it or not, we deliberately avoided many possible income tax complications. As all taxpaying citizens know, income taxes are affected by many intricacies, including progressive tax rates, loss carrybacks and carryforwards, a variety of depreciation options, state income taxes, short- and long-term gains, distinctions between capital assets and other assets, offsets of losses against related gains, exchanges of property of like kind, exempt income, and so forth. Moreover, most depreciable asset purchases in the 1960's and 1970's have qualified for an "investment tax credit," which is generally an immediate income tax credit of 7 percent of the initial cost. This credit is a lump-sum reduction of the income tax cash outflow at time zero or in Year 1. Furthermore, the full original cost, less the estimated disposal value, is deductible in the form of yearly depreciation.[2]

Keep in mind that miscellaneous changes in the tax law occur each year. For example, the investment tax credit has been suspended, reinstated, and changed in many respects through the years.

MISCELLANEOUS TAX PLANNING MATTERS

Form of Organization

The corporation is a distinct business entity subject to separate corporate income taxes. In contrast, individual proprietorships and partnerships are not separate entities for income tax purposes. Instead, their income is attributed to the owners as individuals regardless of whether they make any cash withdrawals from the business. These distinctions are shown in Exhibit 14-5.

For a corporation, reasonable salaries paid to officers who are also stockholders are deductible for income tax purposes. For partnerships or proprietorships, no deductions are allowed for owners' salaries or for interest expense on invested ownership capital.

Corporate income is subject to double taxation. First, it is taxed to

---

[2]For a book-length discussion of these and other complications, see W. L. Raby, *The Income Tax and Business Decisions*, 2nd ed. (Englewood Cliffs, N.J.: Prentice-Hall, Inc., 1972).

EXHIBIT 14-5

Diagram of Tax Effects of Form of Business Organization

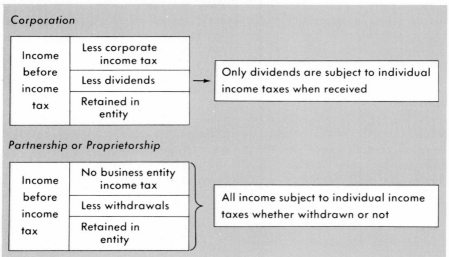

the separate entity. Second, any cash dividends are taxed to the individual at the recipient's income tax rate.

What form of business organization should be chosen? The answer depends on a myriad of legal and tax considerations, including the extent of personal liability of the owners for business debts, ease of transfer of ownership, and expected life of the business. But the personal income tax bracket of the owners is often paramount. For example, suppose an individual with a marginal income tax rate of 70 percent (because of other income) is considering how to organize his solely owned business.

Operating data may be analyzed as follows:

	Corporation		Proprietorship (or Partnership)	
Sales (all for cash)		$200,000		$200,000
Operating expenses:				
Owner's salary	$ 20,000 (a)		$ 20,000 (b)	
Other expenses	150,000 (a)	170,000	150,000 (a)	170,000
Income before income taxes		$ 30,000		$ 30,000
Corporate income tax				
22% on first $25,000	$ 5,500			
48% on excess of $5,000	2,400	7,900		—
Net income		$ 22,100		$ 30,000 (b)
Cash dividends		$ 22,100	Withdrawals	30,000
Net income retained		$ —		$ —

(a) For simplicity, assume these are all cash expenses.

(b) Note that these amounts can be any number without affecting the personal income tax liability. "Salaries" and withdrawals are irrelevant as far as income tax liability is concerned. In this case, the proprietor will be subject to personal income taxes on the entity income of $30,000 plus the $20,000 owner's salary.

Incidentally, partnerships must file information returns disclosing the determination of net income and the share of each partner. However, under the income tax law, proprietorships and partnerships are regarded as a conduit through which taxable income flows to the owners. Thus, although salaries paid to proprietors and partners are deducted here in computing entity income, they must be reported as income by the recipients on their personal tax returns. In essence, then, the income tax laws would regard the entity income shown here ($30,000) and the owner's salary ($20,000) as arbitrary splits of a $50,000 income taxable to the owner. Therefore, if the owner wants to label the entity income as $40,000 and the salary as $10,000, it makes no difference regarding his taxable income, which will be $50,000 regardless. Furthermore, if the owner withdraws zero or $100,000, his taxable income will still be $50,000.

If the personal income tax brackets are low, the non-corporate forms may become more attractive. But high-bracket taxpayers will almost always find the corporate form more attractive if they do not need cash dividends. The tabulations in Exhibit 14-6 illustrate that the need for high dividends will favor using the proprietorship form, and little need for dividends will favor the corporate form of organization.[3]

Note that if heavy cash dividends are paid, the corporate form has no income tax advantage to the owner. If no cash dividends are paid, the corporate form is advantageous to an owner in a high tax bracket.

The remainder of this chapter will focus on planning for corporate taxes. However, unless specifically stated otherwise, most of the points are applicable to personal taxes and to any form of business organization.

Changes in Income Tax Rates

During World War II and the Korean War, the United States imposed an excess profits tax which considerably boosted effective income tax rates. At the time, the prospect of changes in income tax rates in a given year or series of years influenced management planning extensively. If income taxes were going to rise in the next year, the tendency would be to postpone certain expenses (e.g., repairs, advertising, legal services, purchases of supplies not usually inventoried) and to accelerate revenue recognition by boosting production to fill any existing orders before the higher tax rates took effect.

[3]Of course, there must be a legitimate business purpose, such as expansion of the corporation, for not paying dividends. Otherwise, penalty taxes are imposed on unjustified retentions of earnings.

EXHIBIT 14-6

Tax Effects on Form of Business Organization
(Data from text)

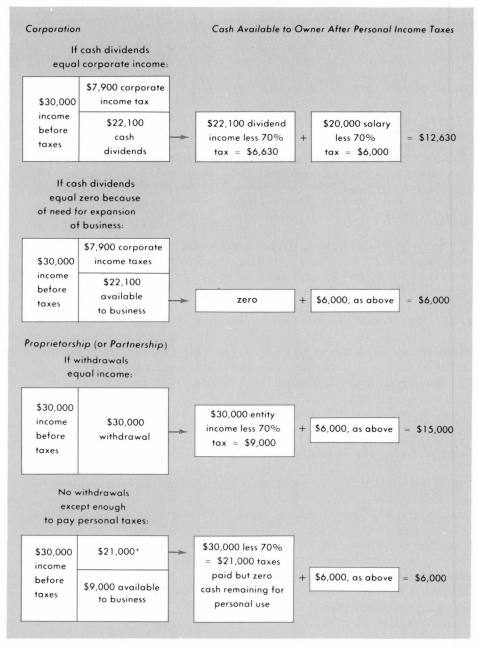

*The assumption is that proprietorship cash is used to pay all taxes on proprietorship income. Tax on proprietorship is based on total proprietorship income regardless of withdrawals.

Lifo or Fifo

The income tax planner does not have to be directly concerned with the relative conceptual merits of Lifo (last-in, first-out) or Fifo (first-in, first-out) inventory methods. The most desirable inventory method is that which postpones income tax payments, perhaps permanently. For instance, an expansion coupled with increasing price levels favors Lifo rather than Fifo; under Lifo, the highest (most recent) costs will be released to expense sooner rather than later.

The adoption of Lifo by one-third of the large American companies is directly attributable to the income tax benefits rather than to the conceptual justification of more "realistic" income measures so often cited. The only tax-planning reasons for not adopting Lifo would be: (1) the negligible prospect of income tax savings because of expected long-run declines in prices; (2) stability of prices; and (3) insignificance of inventories to particular organizations, such as service businesses.

If the prices of inventory are expected to rise, a company should adopt Lifo. The annual savings in cash flow will have compound effects and will result in a substantial financial advantage. Raby illustrates these effects as follows:

> Assume an effective income tax rate of 50 percent and after-tax rate of return of 7 percent. Inventory is $1,000,000 at time of adoption of Lifo. Prices increase in a straight line, so that inventory in Year 1 is $1,100,000 under Fifo but still $1,000,000 under Lifo; in Year 2 Fifo inventory is $1,200,000; in Year 3, $1,300,000; and so forth throughout 20 years. Meanwhile, Lifo inventory stays at $1,000,000, and income tax savings of $50,000 annually, invested at 7 percent compounded annually, will accumulate to $2,049,750 more assets under Lifo.[4]

Effect of Lifo on Purchase Decisions

When prices are rising, it may be advantageous—subject to prudent restraint as to maximum and minimum inventory levels—to buy unusually heavy amounts of inventory near year-end, particularly if income tax rates are likely to fall. For example, assume that a company has made the following transactions during 19x1, its first year in business:

Sales: 10 units, @ $5   Purchases: 8 units, @ $2
                                        3 units, @ $3

Decision: Buy six more units, near year-end, @ $4? Current income tax rates, 50 percent, are expected to decline to 40 percent next year. Prices on inventory are not expected to decline next year.

[4]*Ibid.*, p. 226.

	Comparison of Alternatives	
	Do Not Buy	*Buy 6 More Units*
Sales: 10 units, @ $5	$50	$50
Cost of goods sold (Lifo basis):		
3 units, @ $3 = $ 9		
7 units, @ $2 = 14	23	
or		
6 units, @ $4 = $24		
3 units, @ $3 = 9		
1 unit, @ $2 = 2		35
Gross margin	$27	$15

Tax savings: 50 percent of ($27 − $15) = $6 this year. The effects on later years' taxes will depend on inventory levels, prices, and tax rates.

Tax savings can be generated because Lifo permits management to influence immediate net income by its purchasing decisions. In contrast, Fifo results would be unaffected by this decision:

	Do Not Buy	*Buy 6 More Units*
Sales	$50	$50
Cost of goods sold (Fifo basis):		
8 units, @ $2 = $16		
2 units, @ $3 = 6	22	22
Gross margin	$28	$28

Contributions of Property Rather Than Cash

Donations to qualifying charitable, educational, and similar institutions are generally deductible, up to specified maximum limits, in computing income taxes. Giving property (such as marketable securities or land) rather than cash is more beneficial to both the donor and the donee. The reason is that any increase in the value of the property is not taxed, but the tax deduction is the fair market value of the contributed asset. For example:

Market price	$400,000
Cost of property	100,000
Capital gain	$300,000
Capital gain tax, @ 30%	$ 90,000*

*For corporations, a capital gain on qualifying assets held more than six months is subject to tax at a rate of 30 percent, rather than at ordinary income tax rates. The tax law specifies which assets are subject to the capital gains rate (the most notable are land and marketable securities). Gains on sales of inventories and receivables are taxed at ordinary rates, while gains on sales of depreciable property are also taxed as ordinary income in many cases.

	Sell, and Donate Cash	Donate Outright
Income tax effects of contribution:		
Deduction	$310,000	$400,000
Assumed income tax rate of 50%	×.50	×.50
Income tax savings	$155,000	$200,000
Charitable institution can receive:		
Cash = $400,000 in cash − $90,000 tax, or	$310,000	
Property, and then sell it for cash		$400,000

As the tabulation shows, compared to a cash donation, the direct dona-tion of property can enable the donor to reap larger tax savings while the donee also receives a larger benefit. Therefore, charitable institutions have tried to attract donations by stressing the tax-saving features of giving property rather than cash.

Operating Losses

The net operating loss of a corporation may be used to offset net income by being carried back to each of the three preceding years and carried forward to each of the five following years. This sequence must be fol-lowed strictly. No part of a given year's loss may be used to offset the second preceding year's income until all of the third preceding year's in-come has been absorbed. In short, a net operating loss enables the cor-poration to obtain tax refunds related to past years' operations or to reduce tax disbursements in future years.

The tax effects of a 19x4 net operating loss may be illustrated as follows (note that any loss carryforward unused after five years becomes nondeductible):

	Net Income (Loss)	19x4 Carryback or Carryforward	Taxable Income
19x1	$ 5,000	$ (5,000)	—
19x2	15,000	(15,000)	—
19x3	35,000	(35,000)	—
19x4	(100,000)	—	—
19x5	5,000	(5,000)	—
19x6	8,000	(8,000)	—
19x7	10,000	(10,000)	—
19x8	10,000	(10,000)	—
19x9	5,000	(5,000)	—
Used		(93,000)	
Unused and nondeductible		(7,000)	
Accounted for		(100,000)	

Strangely enough, a company may properly view a loss carry-forward as an "asset," for planning purposes. It represents a valuable tax deduction as long as profitable operations are forthcoming. If the tax rate is 48 percent, a loss carryforward of $100,000 represents future tax savings of $48,000. In certain cases, this may prompt corporations to buy other profitable companies at higher-than-usual prices.

Suppose that Company A has a potential net operating cash inflow of $200,000 per year for the next five years. Suppose further that two companies, X and Y, are interested in buying Company A. Company X has a $1,000,000 net operating loss carryforward that can be offset against the next five years' net taxable income. Company Y has no such loss carryforward. Both companies are willing to buy all the capital stock of Company A at a price not to exceed the present value of the five years' after-tax cash inflows, discounted at 8 percent. What are the maximum prices that Company X and Company Y are willing to pay? Calculations follow:

Company Y

After-tax net cash inflow of Company A is $200,000 less .48(200,000)	=	$104,000
Present value of an annuity of $1, @ 8%, for 5 years	×	3.993
Maximum price		$415,272

Company X

After-tax net cash inflow of Company A would be the entire $200,000, because of the loss carried forward		$200,000
Present value of an annuity of $1, @ 8%, for 5 years	×	3.993
Maximum price		$798,600

The relevance of the loss carryforward in the Company X analysis depends on the available alternatives. Perhaps the carryforward can be used to offset Company X's future taxable income—that is, there is danger of double-counting the carryforward. It cannot be used to offset both the Company A income and the Company X income.

Tax-Free Interest

Interest on the bonds issued by a city, state, and certain nonprofit organizations is nontaxable to the investor. Because of this feature, such bonds have a lower pretax yield than industrial bonds. However, the high-bracket taxpayer and corporations will usually find tax-exempt bonds more attractive:

	Industrial Bond: Coupon Rate, 8%	Municipal Bond: Coupon Rate, 5%
Investment in bonds	$100,000	$100,000
Interest income before taxes	$ 8,000	$ 5,000
Income taxes, @ 50%	4,000	—
Net income, after taxes	$ 4,000	$ 5,000

Corporate Capital Gains and Losses

Investments in stocks and bonds are usually cited as a common example of capital assets. The Internal Revenue Service defines capital assets negatively as being all assets except inventory, trade receivables, copy-rights, depreciable property, and real property used in a trade or business.

Unless a corporation has an operating loss, the gains from the sale of capital assets are taxed at a maximum of 30 percent. A corporation cannot deduct any part of a net capital loss in the year incurred. The loss may be carried back to each of three years before the loss year and then may be carried forward and offset against capital gains for a limit of five succeeding years.

The technicalities of carrybacks and carryforwards are not too im-portant for our purposes. However, because the usual incremental corporate-tax rate is 48 percent, and the long-term capital gain rate is no higher than 30 percent, tax planners try to have taxable income treated as capital gains rather than as ordinary income.

Capital Gains Alternative

Depreciable property and real property used in a trade or business are not capital assets. Nevertheless, a special rule regarding these "Section 1231 assets" permits treating certain gains as capital gains and certain losses as ordinary losses. If net gains exceed net losses, all the gains and losses are regarded as long-term capital gains and losses. If net losses exceed net gains, all the gains and losses are regarded as ordinary. Because the losses offset the gains dollar for dollar, the shrewd tax planner tries to time his transactions so that losses occur in one year and gains in another.

For example, assume that a company owns two parcels of land. One parcel can be sold at a capital gain of $500,000, the other at a capital loss of $500,000. If both are sold in the same year, the loss would offset the gain, and there would be no impact on taxes. If they are sold in separate years, the tax bill would be 25 percent of $500,000 in one year, or $125,000, and lower (assuming an ordinary tax rate of 48 percent) by $240,000 in the next year. The second strategy would save the company $115,000 in income tax disbursements.

Other General Considerations

Purchases of assets. When a group of assets is acquired for a single overall price, care must be taken to see that as much of the total cost as possible is allocated to those assets whose costs will eventually be deductible for income-tax purposes. Otherwise, the excess of the total cost over those parts allocated is assigned to land and/or goodwill, which are not subject to amortization for income tax purposes.

Use of debt in the capital structure. Interest is deductible as an expense; dividends are not. Therefore, the relative after-tax cash drains on corporations favor using as much debt in the capital structure as seems prudent. Assume a 50 percent tax rate:

	Pretax Cost	*After-tax Cost*
4% Bonds payable	4%	2%
6% Preferred stock	6%	6%

Research and development. There is conceptual merit in capitalizing many research costs. From a tax-planning standpoint, however, research costs should be deducted as quickly as possible.

Cash versus accrual accounting methods. The cash method of accounting allows more discretion in the timing of revenue and expense than the accrual method. However, where inventories exist, companies must use the accrual basis.

Deferral of income. Among the many ways of deferring income are installment sales methods, whereby income is geared to cash receipts rather than point of sale.

For example, a furniture store's taxable income for its first year in business could be computed as follows:

	Regular Basis	*Installment Basis*
Installment sales	$500,000	
Cost of goods sold	300,000	
Gross profit, @ 40%	$200,000	$160,000*
Expenses	150,000	150,000
Net taxable income	$ 50,000	$ 10,000

*Forty percent of current installment collections of $400,000. Unrealized gross profit is 40 percent of ending receivables: 40 percent of $100,000, or $40,000.

If the owner chooses to report income on the installment basis, income tax on the uncollected gross profit—which is 40 percent of $100,000 (i.e., $500,000 − $400,000), or $40,000—is deferred.

Also available is the discretionary timing of shipments. At year-end, shipment at December 31 or January 1 can have a significant impact on income taxes, because the sale can be included in either year.

Impact of Income
Taxes on
Management
Planning

Dividends received. Corporations can generally deduct 85 percent of dividends received from taxable domestic corporations; in other words, only 15 percent of the dividend is taxable to the recipient. This provision enhances the attractiveness of investing excess cash in common stock rather than in federal or corporate bonds, whose interest is fully taxable.

Desirability of Losses

The often heard expression, "What the heck, it's deductible," sometimes warps perspective. Even though losses bring income-tax savings and gains bring additional income taxes, gains are still more desirable than losses. For example, business land (see earlier section, "Capital Gains Alternative") that cost $300,000 a few years ago and that is sold now, would have the following effect at two different selling prices:

	Gain		Loss	
Selling price	$1,000,000	$1,000,000	$100,000	$100,000
Cost	300,000		300,000	
Gain (loss)	$ 700,000		$(200,000)	
Tax, @ 30% of $700,000		210,000		
Tax savings, @ 60% of $200,000				120,000
Net cash effect		$ 790,000		$220,000

SUMMARY

Income tax is a significant cost of conducting business. No accountant or manager should be indifferent to its impact. Income taxes may be necessary evils, but this does not mean that management should be resigned to tax burdens. Intelligent planning, assisted by expert advice, can minimize income taxes.

Income taxes are sometimes too influential in business decisions. Their effects may be overemphasized. The ogre of the income tax may reduce the emphasis on efficiency and may unduly hamper risk taking. Income tax is only one of a number of variables that bear on business administration.

SUMMARY PROBLEM FOR YOUR REVIEW

Problem

The Flan Company estimates that it can save $2,500 per year in annual cash operating costs for the next five years if it buys a special-purpose machine at a cost of $9,000. Residual value is expected to be $1,000, although no residual value is being provided for in using sum-of-the-years'-digits depreciation for tax purposes. The minimum desired rate of return, after taxes, is 10 percent. Income tax rates are 40 percent on ordinary income. Using discounted-cash-flow techniques, show whether the investment is desirable.

Solution

		Present Value Discount Factors, @ 10%	Total Present Values	Sketch of Cash Flows

		Present Value Discount Factors, @ 10%	Total Present Values	0	1	2	3	4	5
End of year									
Recurring cash operating savings	$2,500								
Income taxes, @ 40%	1,000								
After-tax cash operating savings	$1,500	3.791	$ 5,686		$1,500	$1,500	$1,500	$1,500	$1,500

Depreciation: Sum-of-the-years' digits,
  1 + 2 + 3 + 4 + 5 = 15

Year	Multiplied by $9,000	Deduction	Income Tax Savings, @ 40%							
1	5/15	$3,000	$1,200	.909	1,091	1,200				
2	4/15	2,400	960	.826	793		960			
3	3/15	1,800	720	.751	541			720		
4	2/15	1,200	480	.683	328				480	
5	1/15	600	240	.621	149					240

Residual value, all subject to tax because book value will be zero	$1,000				
Less: 40% income tax on disposal gain*	400				
Net cash inflow	$ 600	.621	373		600
Initial required investment			(9,000)	(9,000)	
Net present value of all cash flows			$(39)		

*Assume that ordinary income tax rates, not capital gains rates, apply.

There is a net disadvantage in purchasing because the net present value is slightly negative, indicating a time-adjusted rate of return a shade below the minimum desired rate of 10 percent.

Fundamental Assignment Material

14-1. Income taxes and disposal of assets. Assume that income tax rates are 60 percent.

1. The book value of an old machine is $20,000. It is to be sold for $8,000. What is the effect of this decision on cash flows, after taxes?
2. The book value of an old machine is $10,000. It is to be sold for $13,000. What is the effect on cash flows, after taxes, of this decision?

14-2. Equipment purchase. The Morax Company expects to save $6,000 in cash operating costs for each of the next four years if it buys a special machine at a cost of $20,000. Residual value is expected to be $1,000, although no residual value is being provided for in using the sum-of-the-years'-digits depreciation method for tax purposes. A major overhaul, costing $1,000, will occur at the end of the second year and is fully deductible, in that year, for income tax purposes. The minimum desired rate of return, after taxes is 8 percent. Income tax rates are 60 percent. Using discounted-cash-flow techniques, show whether the investment is desirable.

14-3. Income taxes and replacement of equipment. Refer to Problem 12-2. Assume that income tax rates are 60 percent. The minimum desired rate of return, after taxes, is 6 percent. Using the net present value technique, show whether the proposed equipment should be purchased. Present your solution on both a total approach and an incremental approach. For illustrative purposes, assume that old equipment would have been depreciated on a straight-line basis and the proposed equipment on a sum-of-the-years'-digits basis.

Additional Assignment Material

14-4. Distinguish between tax avoidance and tax evasion.

14-5. "Tax planning is unimportant because the total income tax bill will be the same in the long run, regardless of short-run maneuvering." Do you agree? Explain.

14-6. What are the major influences on the present value of a tax deduction?

14-7. Explain why accelerated depreciation methods are superior to straight-line methods for income tax purposes.

14-8. "Immediate disposal of equipment, rather than its continued use, results in a full tax deduction of the undepreciated cost now—rather than having such a deduction spread over future years in the form of annual depreciation." Do you agree? Explain, using the $35,000 cost of old equipment in Exhibit 14-3 as a basis for your discussion.

14-9. Name some income tax complications that were ignored in Exhibits 14-3 and 14-4.

14-10. What is an investment credit?

14-11. Why does Lifo save income taxes when prices are rising?

14-12. "If income tax rates are likely to rise, the tendency would be to increase year-end purchases of inventory under Lifo." Do you agree? Explain.

14-13. Why have charitable institutions tried to attract donations in the form of property rather than cash?

14-14. How was it possible that the drug companies' net income was increased in 1962 by their contribution to the ransom of Cuban prisoners?

14-15. "A loss carryforward has an economic value." Explain.

14-16. Effects of Lifo on purchase decisions. Solve Problem 5-39.

14-17. Effects of Lifo and Fifo. Solve Problem 5-40.

14-18. Switch from Lifo to Fifo. Effective January 1, 1970, Chrysler Corporation adopted the Fifo method for inventories previously valued by the Lifo method. The 1970 annual report stated: "This ... makes the financial statements with respect to inventory valuation comparable with those of the other United States automobile manufacturers."

The Wall Street Journal reported:

> The change improved Chrysler's 1970 financial results several ways. Besides narrowing the 1970 loss by $20 million it improved Chrysler's working capital. The change also made the comparison with 1969 earnings look somewhat more favorable because, upon restatement, Chrysler's 1969 profit was raised only $10.2 million from the original figures.
>
> Finally, the change helped Chrysler's balance sheet by boosting inventories, and thus current assets, by $150 million at the end of 1970 over what they would have been under LIFO. As Chrysler's profit has collapsed over the last two years and its financial position tightened, auto analysts have eyed warily Chrysler's shrinking ratio of current assets to current liabilities.
>
> Chrysler's current liabilities shrank last year because it was able to pay off sizable amounts of short-term debt with the help of a $200 million long-term financing last winter. Chrysler's short-term debt stood at $374 million at year-end, down from $477 million a year earlier but up slightly from $370 million on Sept. 30. Chrysler's cash and marketable securities shrank during the year to $156.4 million at year-end, down from $309.3 million a year earlier and $220 million on Sept. 30.
>
> To get the improvements in its balance sheet and results, however, Chrysler paid a price. Roger Helder, vice president and comptroller, said Chrysler owed the government $53 million in tax savings it accumulated by using the LIFO method since it switched from FIFO in 1957. The major advantage of LIFO is that it holds down profit and thus tax liabilities. The other three major auto makers stayed on the FIFO method. Mr. Helder said Chrysler now has to pay back that $53 million to the government over 20 years, which will boost Chrysler's tax bills about $3 million a year.

Required:

Given the content of this text chapter, do you think the Chrysler decision to switch from Lifo to Fifo was beneficial to its stockholders? Explain, being as specific and using as much data as you can.

14-19. Donations of property rather than cash. The Fantasy Company has 100 shares of Florence common stock that were acquired four years ago at $70 per share. Current market price is $120 per share. Income tax rates are 60 percent on ordinary income and 25 percent on capital gains. Compare the effects on Fantasy's income taxes of: (1) selling the stock and donating the net cash after taxes to a university, and (2) donating the stock outright. How much cash will the university net under each plan, assuming that all donations of property are immediately converted into cash?

14-20. Minimizing transportation costs. Refer to Assignment 13-27, but ignore the requirements there and make the following assumptions:

a. Wegener requires a minimum 10 percent after-tax rate of return.
b. A 40 percent tax rate.
c. Sum-of-the-year's-digits depreciation with an allowance for the $5,000 salvage value of the truck.
d. No investment tax credit.

Required:

1. Should the truck be purchased? Show computations to support your answer.
2. What qualitative factors might influence your decision? Be specific.

14-21. Routine capital budgeting. (CMA adapted.) The Baxter Company manufactures toys and other short-lived fad-type items.

The research and development department came up with an item that would make a good promotional gift for office-equipment dealers. Aggressive and effective effort by Baxter's sales personnel has resulted in almost firm commitments for this product for the next three years. It is expected that the product's value will be exhausted by that time.

In order to produce the quantity demanded, Baxter will need to buy additional machinery and rent some additional space. It appears that about 25,000 square feet will be needed. As much as 12,500 square feet of presently unused, but leased, space is available now. (Baxter's present lease with ten years to run costs $3 a foot.) There is another 12,500 square feet adjoining the Baxter facility which Baxter will rent for three years at $4.00 per square foot per year if it decides to make this product.

The equipment will be purchased for about $900,000. It will require $30,000 in modifications, $60,000 for installation, and $90,000 for testing; all of these activities will be done by a firm of engineers hired by Baxter. All of the expenditures will be paid for on January 1, 19x3.

The equipment should have a salvage value of about $180,000 at the end of the third year. No additional general overhead costs are expected to be incurred.

The following estimates of revenues and expenses for this product for the three years have been developed.

	19x3	19x4	19x5
Sales	$1,000,000	$1,600,000	$800,000
Material, labor and incurred overhead	400,000	750,000	350,000
Assigned general overhead	40,000	75,000	35,000
Rent	87,500	87,500	87,500
Depreciation	450,000	300,000	150,000
	$ 977,500	$1,212,500	$622,500

	19x3	19x4	19x5
Income before tax	$ 22,500	$ 387,500	$177,500
Income tax (40%)........................	9,000	155,000	71,000
	$ 13,500	$ 232,500	$106,500

Required:

1. Prepare a schedule which shows the incremental, after-tax cash flows for this project.
2. If the company requires a two-year payback period for its investment, would it undertake this project? Show your supporting calculations clearly.
3. A newly hired business-school graduate recommends that the company consider the use of the net present value analysis to study this project. If the company sets a required rate of return of 20 percent after taxes, will this project be accepted? Show your supporting calculations clearly. (Assume that all operating revenues and expenses occur at the end of the year.)

Discount Factors for 20% (Rounded off)

Period	Present Value of $1.00	Present Value of $1.00 per period received at end of period
1	.83	.83
2	.69	1.52
3	.58	2.10
4	.48	2.58

14-22. Loss carryforward and purchase of a business. Company *G*'s potential net operating cash inflow, before taxes, for the next five years is $500,000 annually. Two companies, *P* and *Q,* are interested in buying all of the capital stock of Company *G*. Company *P* has a $2,500,000 net operating loss which it can carry forward to offset the next five years' net taxable income. Company *Q* has no such loss carryforward. Both companies are willing to buy all the capital stock of Company *G* at a price not to exceed the present value of the five years' cash inflow after taxes, discounted at 10 percent.

Required:

What are the maximum prices that Company *P* and Company *Q* are willing to pay? Show your calculations. The ordinary income tax rate is 40 percent and the capital gains rate is 25 percent.

14-23. Timing of gains and losses. A company owns 10,000 shares each of the common stock of Company *A* and Company *B*. The Company *A* stock was acquired ten years ago for $100,000. It can now be sold for $400,000. The Company *B* stock was purchased five years ago for $900,000. It can now be sold for $600,000. It is now near the end of year 19x1. Capital gains tax rate is 30 percent, and ordinary income tax rate is 40 percent.

Required:

1. If all the stock were sold in 19x1, what would be the effect on income taxes?
2. If the Company *B* stock were sold in 19x1, and the Company *A* stock were sold

in 19x2, what would be the effect on income taxes? Assume that these are the only transactions affecting capital gains or losses. Which strategy will save the most income taxes? How much would be saved?

14-24. Corporate capital gains and losses. A corporation disposed of an investment in the common stock of a subsidiary for $500,000 on December 1, 19x3. The investment had cost $600,000 in 19x1. The company had no capital gain in 19x4, a $30,000 capital gain in 19x5, and a $45,000 capital gain in 19x8.

Required:

Tabulate the effect on each tax return for 19x3 through 19x8 of the sale of the investment in 19x3. Show the amount of the loss carryforward that is exhausted at the end of 19x8.

14-25. Form of organization. *X* and *Y* are attempting to decide whether to organize their new business as a corporation or as a partnership. Each will invest $100,000 and will receive annual compensation for services of $20,000 each. Sales will be $900,000 and cash expenses other than owners' salaries will be $760,000. All plant assets are rented, so there is no depreciation.

Each owner is in a 60 percent marginal income tax bracket. The corporate tax rate is 22 percent on the first $25,000 of income and 48 percent on the excess.

Required:

1. Suppose that dividends or withdrawals are equal to net income. What is the income subject to tax for the corporation? The partnership? How much cash will be available to the business and to each owner after taxes?
2. Suppose that no dividends are paid. Suppose also that the withdrawals of the partners are equal to the salary equivalent of $20,000 each plus an additional withdrawal for payment of additional income taxes on the portion of partnership income that is not withdrawn. For the corporation and the partnership forms of organization, compute the cash available to each owner after taxes and the cash available to the business for expansion.

14-26. Income taxes and make or buy. Refer to Problem 12-29, Requirement 1. Assume a tax rate of 40 percent. The minimum desired rate of return, after taxes, is 6 percent. Using the net present value technique, show whether the proposed purchase from the outside supplier is desirable. Use both a total project approach and an incremental approach. Assume straight-line depreciation.

14-27. Tax shield and depreciation methods. A company has just paid $42,000 for some equipment that will have a six-year life and no residual value. The minimum rate of return desired, after taxes, is 10 percent.

The president has attended a management conference luncheon where an accounting professor adamantly stated: "Not using accelerated depreciation for tax purposes is outright financial stupidity." The president has a perpetual fear of rises in income tax rates and has favored straight-line depreciation "to have greater deductions against future income when taxes are higher."

He is having second thoughts now, and has asked you to prepare a financial analysis of the dollar benefits of using sum-of-the-years'-digits depreciation instead of straight-line depreciation under the following assumptions: (a) income tax rates of 60 percent throughout the coming six years, and (b) income tax rates of 60 percent for the first three years and 80 percent for the subsequent three years.

14-28. Comprehensive problem on equipment replacement. A manufacturer who specializes in making aircraft parts developed a $68,000 special-purpose molding machine for automatically producing a special part. The machine will be useless after the total market potential, spread evenly over four years, is exhausted. The machine has been used for one year. The $68,000 original cost is being depreciated on a straight-line basis.

At the beginning of the second year, a machine salesman offers a new machine which is vastly more efficient. It will cost $45,000, will reduce annual cash operating costs from $45,000 to $26,500, and will have zero disposal value at the end of three years. Sum-of-the-years' digits would be the depreciation method used for tax purposes for this machine.

The scrap value of the old machine is $30,000 now and will be $2,000 three years from now; however, no scrap value has been provided for in calculating straight-line depreciation for tax purposes.

Required:

Assume that income tax rates are 60 percent. The minimum rate of return desired, after taxes, is 8 percent. Using the net present value technique, show whether the new machine should be purchased: (a) under a total project approach, and (b) under an incremental approach.

Overhead Application: Direct and Absorption Costing

15

The day-to-day operations of an accounting system have a twofold purpose: (1) planning and control, hereafter for brevity's sake often called *control,* and (2) product costing. Chapters 8 and 9 concentrated on planning and control, and this chapter gives an overview of product costing by building on the ideas of Chapter 9.

Thus far, we have paid little attention to the product costing-income determination purpose of an accounting system. Management makes policy decisions, at one time or another, regarding methods of product costing. Because such decisions affect the way net income will be determined, managers should know the various approaches to product costing. Moreover, as we have seen previously, a knowledge of product-costing techniques will enhance a manager's understanding of his product costs, particularly when the latter are used for pricing and evaluating product lines.

We shall concentrate on two major variations of standard product costing, although there are several other product-costing methods in use that do not employ standard costs. However, an understanding of standard product costing is readily transferable to any other method that might be encountered.

ROLE OF UNIT COSTS

The basic objective of product costing is to trace the total manufacturing costs incurred for a given time period to the units produced. This tracing procedure is frequently called the **application** of costs to product. Most often, this is accomplished by heavy use of unit costs. Consider a rudimentary example:

Total manufacturing costs for 10,000 units	$48,000
Divided by the number of units produced	÷ 10,000
Equals cost per unit	$4.80

Suppose that 9,000 units are sold for $10 each and 1,000 units remain in ending inventory. The unit cost facilitates the application of costs to the units in ending inventory and the units sold. An income statement might have the following details:

Sales (9,000 @ $10)		$90,000
Less: Cost of goods sold:		
Beginning inventory (assume none)	$ 0	
Cost of goods manufactured, 10,000 @ $4.80	48,000	
Cost of goods available for sale	$48,000	
Ending inventory, 1,000 @ $4.80	4,800	
Cost of goods sold, 9,000 @ $4.80		43,200
Gross profit		$46,800

DIRECT VERSUS ABSORPTION COSTING

Accounting for Fixed Manufacturing Overhead

The foregoing example lumped all manufacturing costs together. In practice, unit costs are usually developed for various subclassifications of manufacturing costs. In this way, unit costs can be used to accumulate the costs of a variety of products that may utilize differing amounts of productive resources such as material and labor.

Two major methods of product costing will be compared in this chapter: direct costing (the contribution approach), and absorption costing (the functional or traditional approach). These methods differ in only one conceptual respect: *Fixed manufacturing overhead is excluded from the cost of products under direct costing but included in the cost of products under absorption costing.* In other words, direct costing signifies that fixed factory overhead is not inventoried. In contrast, absorption costing signifies that fixed factory overhead is inventoried.

Absorption costing is much more widely used than direct costing, although the growing use of the contribution approach in performance measurement and cost analysis has led to increasing use of direct costing for internal-reporting purposes. Neither the public accounting profession nor the Internal Revenue Service has approved of direct costing for external-reporting purposes.

Direct costing is more accurately called **variable** or **marginal costing,**

EXHIBIT 15-1

Comparison of Flow of Costs

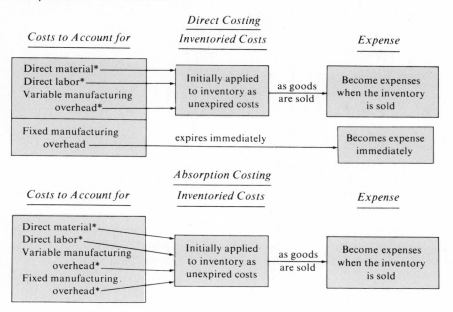

*As goods are manufactured, the costs are "applied" to inventory usually via the use of unit costs.

because in substance it applies only the *variable* production costs to the product. As Exhibit 15-1 shows, **fixed manufacturing overhead is regarded as an expired cost to be immediately charged against sales rather than as an unexpired cost to be held back as inventory and charged against sales later as a part of cost of goods sold.**

To make these ideas more concrete, let us examine the following example. The Tolman Company had the following operating character-istics in 19x4 and 19x5:

Basic production data at standard cost

Direct material	$1.30
Direct labor	1.50
Variable manufacturing overhead	.20
Standard variable costs per unit	$3.00
Fixed manufacturing overhead	$150,000

Sales price, $5.00 per unit.
Selling and administrative expense is assumed for simplicity as being all fixed at $65,000 yearly, except for sales commissions at 5% of dollar sales.

	19x4	19x5
In units:		
Opening inventory	—	30,000
Production	170,000	140,000
Sales	140,000	160,000
Ending inventory	30,000	10,000

There were no variances from the standard variable manufacturing costs, and fixed manufacturing overhead incurred was exactly $150,000 per year.

Required:

1. Prepare income statements for 19x4 and 19x5 under direct costing.
2. Prepare income statements for 19x4 and 19x5 under absorption costing.
3. Show a reconciliation of the difference in net income for 19x4, 19x5, and the two years as a whole.

The solution to this problem will be explained, step by step, in subsequent sections. The solution to Requirement 1 is in Exhibit 15-2, to Requirement 2 in Exhibit 15-3, and to Requirement 3 in Exhibit 15-5.

EXHIBIT 15-2

Direct Costing

TOLMAN COMPANY

Comparative Income Statements (in thousands of dollars)

For the Year 19x4 and 19x5

(Data are in text)

		19x4	19x5
Sales	(1)	700	800
Opening inventory—at standard variable cost of $3.00		—	90
Add variable cost of goods manufactured at standard		510	420
Available for sale		510	510
Deduct ending inventory—at standard variable cost of $3.00		90	30
Variable manufacturing cost of goods sold		420	480
Variable selling expenses—at 5% of dollar sales		35	40
Total variable expenses	(2)	455	520
Contribution margin	(3) = (1) − (2)	245	280
Fixed factory overhead		150	150
Fixed selling and administrative expenses		65	65
Total fixed expenses	(4)	215	215
Net income	(3) − (4)	30	65

Direct-Costing Method

491
**Overhead
Application:
Direct and
Absorption Costing**

The solution to Requirement 1 is shown in Exhibit 15-2. It has a familiar contribution-approach format, the same format introduced in Chapter 8. The only new characteristic of Exhibit 15-2 is the presence of a detailed calculation of cost of goods sold, which is affected by changes in the beginning and ending inventories. (In contrast, the income statements in Chapters 8 through 12 assumed that there were no changes in the beginning and ending inventories.)

The costs of the product are accounted for by applying all variable manufacturing costs to the goods produced at a rate of $3 per unit; thus, inventories are valued at standard variable costs. In contrast, fixed manufacturing costs are not applied to any products but are regarded as expired costs as actually incurred.

EXHIBIT 15-3
Absorption Costing
TOLMAN COMPANY
Comparative Income Statements (in thousands of dollars)
For the Year 19x4 and 19x5
(Data are in text)

	19x4	19x5
Sales	700	800
Opening inventory—at standard absorption cost of $4.00	—	120
Cost of goods manufactured at standard of $4.00	680	560
Available for sale	680	680
Deduct ending inventory at standard absorption cost of $4.00	120	40
Cost of goods sold—at standard	560	640
Gross profit at standard	140	160
Volume variance*	20 F	10 U
Gross margin or gross profit—at "actual"	160	150
Selling and administrative expenses	100	105
Net income	60	45

*Computation of volume variance based on denominator volume of 150,000 units:

19x4	$20,000 F	(170,000 − 150,000) × $1.00
19x5	10,000 U	(150,000 − 140,000) × $1.00
Two years together	$10,000 F	(310,000 − 300,000) × $1.00

U-Unfavorable
F-Favorable

Absorption-Costing Method

Exhibit 15-3 contains the following highlights of standard absorption costing.

1. The unit product cost is $4, not $3, because variable manufacturing costs ($3) plus fixed manufacturing overhead ($1) are applied to product.

2. The $1 predetermined application rate for fixed overhead was based on a denominator of 150,000 units ($150,000 ÷ 150,000 = $1). A volume variance appears whenever actual production (140,000 units in 19x5) deviates from the level of activity selected as the denominator for computing the predetermined product-costing rate. As the footnote in Exhibit 15-3 indicates, the measure of the variance is $1 multiplied by the difference between the actual volume of output and the denominator volume.

3. Volume variances (and other variances) are usually accounted for as expired costs. They are often accounted for as adjustments that convert the gross profit at standard to gross profit at "actual."

The first of these points has already been explained. The volume variance and the disposition of variances will be discussed in subsequent sections.

FIXED OVERHEAD AND ABSORPTION COSTS OF PRODUCT

Comparison of Purposes

The planning and control objectives (here called the *control* purposes) of management are aided by the flexible budgets and standards described in Chapter 9. The flexible budget may be viewed as a *control budget* because it is primarily designed to help managers by quantifying expectations and then comparing results with those expectations. In addition to the control purpose, a management accounting system tries to trace costs to products.

Reflect on the control-budgeting purpose and product-costing purpose in relation to accounting for variable costs. As Chapter 9 demonstrated, variable costs are *budgeted* with the following behavior pattern in mind:

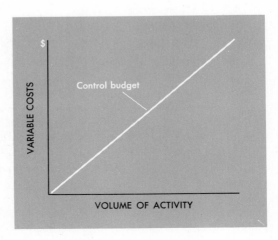

However, *product costing* must also be accomplished. This is not an insuperable problem where variable costs are encountered because, as the volume of production goes up, the *total* variable costs rise in proportion. Therefore, if we were to draw two lines on the graph of variable costs, one for the control budget purpose and the other for the product-costing purpose, the two lines would be superimposed:

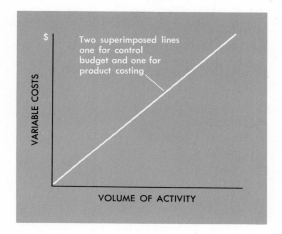

Because fixed costs have different cost behavior patterns than variable costs, they require special analysis. As we saw in Exhibits 15-1 and 15-2, fixed costs are immediately charged as expired costs under direct costing. In contrast, as Exhibits 15-1 and 15-3 showed, absorption costing applies fixed manufacturing costs to the product. For control-budget purposes, fixed costs may be plotted as follows:

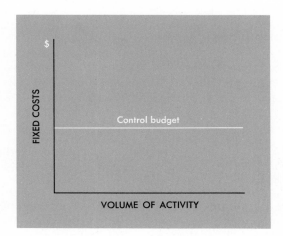

By definition, *total* fixed overhead does not change over wide ranges of activity. However, if these costs are applied to product under absorption costing, what unit cost should be used? The unit cost depends on the activity level chosen as the denominator in the computation; the higher the level of activity, the lower the unit cost. The costing difficulty is magnified because management usually desires a single representative standard fixed cost for a product despite month-to-month changes in production volume.

If we were to draw two lines on the graph of fixed costs, one for the control budget and one for absorption product costing, they would not be superimposed:

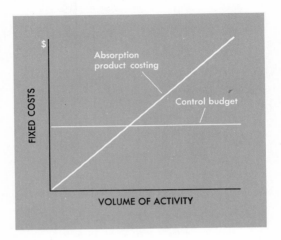

This graph dramatizes how the two purposes differ. The control-budget purpose regards fixed costs in a straightforward manner, viewing them in accordance with their actual cost behavior pattern. In contrast, as the graph indicates, the absorption product-costing approach views these fixed costs as though they have a variable cost behavior pattern.

Role of the Denominator

To obtain a single standard product cost for pricing and inventory uses, a selection of an appropriate activity (often called *volume*) level is necessary. A predetermined rate for applying fixed overhead is computed as follows:

$$\text{Predetermined fixed factory-overhead rate for applying costs to product} = \frac{\text{Budgeted fixed factory overhead}}{\text{Some preselected activity level for the year}}$$

Typically, a denominator level is chosen at the beginning of a year and then it is used without alteration throughout the year. Moreover, the same denominator level may be used for more than one year, as Exhibit 15-3 demonstrates. The solution in Exhibit 15-3 is based on a fixed overhead rate computed as follows:

$$\text{Fixed overhead rate} = \frac{\$150,000 \text{ (budget for the year)}}{150,000 \text{ units (the chosen denom-}} = \$1.00$$
$$\text{inator level of activity for}$$
$$\text{the year)}$$

If fixed costs are large, the preselected denominator level can have a significant effect on the unit costs of the product. In our example:

Total Budgeted Fixed Overhead	Total Activity	Predetermined Fixed Overhead Rate for Product Costing	Predetermined Variable Costs for Product Costing	Absorption Cost Per Product Unit
$150,000	100,000	$1.50	$3.00	$4.50
150,000	140,000	1.07	3.00	4.07
150,000	150,000	1.00	3.00	4.00
150,000	160,000	.94	3.00	3.94
150,000	170,000	.88	3.00	3.88
150,000	200,000	.75	3.00	3.75

Selecting the Denominator Level

The selection of an appropriate denominator level for the predetermination of fixed overhead rates is a matter of judgment; a dozen independent accountants or engineers would probably decide on a dozen different denominator levels based on the same set of available facts. Thus, the standard product cost would differ, depending on who sets the rate for fixed overhead. Some managers favor using the expected actual activity for the year in question; others favor using some longer-run approximation of "normal" activity; and others favor using maximum or full capacity as the denominator.

Although fixed overhead rates are important for product costing and long-run pricing, such rates *have limited significance for control purposes.* At the lower levels of supervision, almost no fixed costs are under direct control; even at higher levels of supervision, few fixed costs are controllable within wide ranges of anticipated activity.

Nature of Volume Variance

An activity or volume variance arises whenever the actual activity deviates from the activity level selected as the denominator for computing the predetermined product-costing rate.

The volume variance is the conventional measure of the cost of departing from the level of activity originally used to set the overhead rate.[1]

---

[1]Do not confuse the volume variance described here with the marketing variance described in Chapter 9. The volume variance arises because of the peculiarities of historical cost accounting for fixed overhead in an absorption cost system. In contrast, the marketing

Most companies consider volume variances to be beyond immediate control, although sometimes the top sales executive has to do some explaining or investigating. Sometimes failure to reach the denominator volume is caused by idleness due to poor production scheduling, unusual machine breakdowns, shortages of skilled workers, strikes, storms, and the like.

There is no volume variance for variable overhead. The concept of volume variance arises for fixed overhead because of the conflict between accounting for control (by budgets) and accounting for product costing (by application rates). Note carefully that the fixed overhead budget serves the control purpose whereas the development of a product-costing rate results in the treatment of fixed overhead *as if it were* a variable cost. In other words, the applied line in Exhibit 15-4 is artificial in the sense that, for product-costing purposes, it seemingly transforms a fixed cost

---

variance in Chapter 9 is an entirely separate measure. It aims at estimating the effects on profit of deviating from an original master budget. It is the budgeted unit contribution margin multiplied by the difference between the master budgeted sales in units and the actual sales in units.

EXHIBIT 15-4

Volume Variance for 19x5
(Data are from Exhibit 15-2)

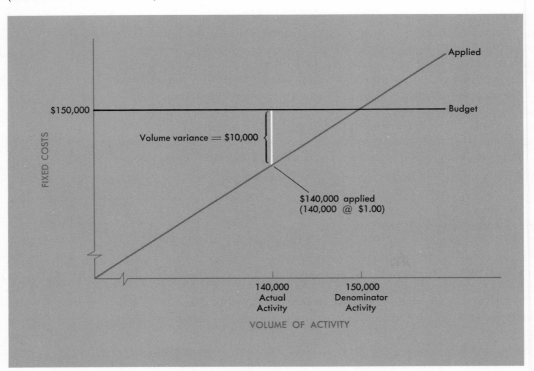

into a variable cost. This bit of magic forcefully illustrates the distinction between accounting for control and accounting for product costing.

To summarize, volume variance arises because the actual activity level achieved frequently does not coincide with the activity level used as a denominator for selecting a predetermined product-costing rate for fixed factory overhead.

1. When denominator activity and actual activity are identical, there is no volume variance.
2. When actual activity is less than denominator activity, the volume variance is unfavorable. It is measured in Exhibit 15-4 as follows:

(Denominator Activity − Actual Activity) × Predetermined Fixed-
Overhead Rate = Volume Variance
(150,000 hours − 140,000 hours) × $1.00 = $10,000

or

Budget minus Applied = Volume Variance
$150,000 − $140,000 = $10,000

3. Where actual activity exceeds denominator activity, as was the case in 19x4, the volume variance is favorable because it is an index of better-than-expected utilization of facilities.

Note, too, that the dollar amount of the volume variance depends on what activity level was selected to determine the application rate. In our example, suppose that 200,000 units were selected as the denominator volume level. The predetermined rate would have been $150,000 divided by 200,000, or 75¢. A subsequent volume of 170,000 hours would result in what volume variance for 19x4? (Compute it before reading on.) The variance would be 30,000 hours multiplied by 75¢, or $22,500, unfavorable, as compared with the $20,000 favorable variance now shown in Exhibit 15-3. This shows how the choice of the volume-level denominator can radically affect the analysis and unit costs for product-costing purposes. That is why you may find it helpful to think of the volume variance as a "denominator variance."

Above all, we should recognize that fixed costs are simply not divisible like variable costs; they come in big chunks and they are related to the provision of big chunks of production or sales capability rather than to the production or sale of a single unit of product.

There are conflicting views on how fixed overhead variances are best analyzed. Obviously, the "best" way is the one that provides management with the most insight into its company's operations. Consequently, overhead analysis varies from company to company. In many companies volume variances are most usefully expressed in physical terms only. For instance, a volume variance could be expressed in machine-hours or kilowatt-hours.

RECONCILIATION OF DIRECT COSTING AND ABSORPTION COSTING

Exhibit 15-5 contains a reconciliation of the net incomes shown in Exhibit 15-2 and 15-3. The difference can be explained in a shortcut way by multiplying the fixed overhead product-costing rate by the *change* in the total units in the beginning and ending inventories. Consider 19x5: The change in units was 20,000, so the difference in net income would be 20,000 units multiplied by $1.00 = $20,000.

EXHIBIT 15-5
Reconciliation of Net Income Under Direct Costing and Absorption Costing

	19x4	19x5	TOGETHER
Net income under:			
Absorption costing (see Exhibit 15-3)	$60,000	$45,000	$105,000
Direct costing (see Exhibit 15-2)	30,000	65,000	95,000
Difference to be explained	$30,000	$−20,000	$ 10,000
The difference can be reconciled by multiplying the fixed overhead rate by the *change* in the total inventory units:			
Fixed overhead rate	$1.00	$1.00	$1.00
Change in inventory units:			
Opening inventory	—	30,000	—
Ending inventory	30,000	10,000	10,000
Change	$30,000	$−20,000	$ 10,000
Difference in net income explained	$30,000	$−20,000	$ 10,000

Exhibit 15-6 gives a more complete explanation of the difference in results. It traces the $30,000 of fixed costs held over from 19x4 under absorption costing, and shows how the 19x5 income statement must bear these costs as well as the new costs of 19x5 (except for $10,000 lodged in the ending inventory of 19x5).

EFFECT OF OTHER VARIANCES

So far, our example has deliberately ignored the possibility of any variance except the volume variance, which arises solely because of fixed overhead in an absorption-costing situation. Now we will introduce other variances that were previously discussed in Chapter 9. Let us assume some additional facts for 19x5:

EXHIBIT 15-6

Tracing of Fixed Manufacturing Costs During 19x5
(Data are from Exhibits 15-2 and 15-3)

Note that net income must be $20,000 lower under absorption costing than under direct costing because $170,000 of fixed costs expire rather than $150,000.

DIRECT COSTING— INVENTORIED COSTS

COSTS TO ACCOUNT FOR		EXPENSE IN 19x5
No fixed overhead was unexpired in 19x4		
Fixed overhead of $150,000 actually incurred in 19x5	expires immediately ——————→	$150,000

ABSORPTION COSTING— INVENTORIED COSTS

COSTS TO ACCOUNT FOR		EXPENSE IN 19x5
Fixed overhead of $30,000 was held as unexpired cost at end of 19x4 ——→	Fixed overhead included in beginning inventory, 30,000 units × $1.00 = $ 30,000	
Fixed overhead of $150,000: Applied to product $140,000 ——→	Additions to inventory, 140,000 units × $1.00 = 140,000	
	Available for sale 170,000 units $170,000	
	160,000 units sold 160,000	Part of cost of goods sold, at standard ——→ $160,000
	Ending inventory 10,000 units $ 10,000	expires
Not applied to product, $10,000, expired as a volume variance ———————→	expires immediately ———————→	Volume variance 10,000
		Expired costs $170,000

499

Direct material variances	None
Direct labor variances	$ 34,000 U
Variable manufacturing overhead variances	$ 3,000 U
Fixed overhead budget-control variance	$ 7,000 U
Supporting data (which are analyzed in the appendix to this chapter):	
Standard direct labor-hours allowed for 140,000 units produced	35,000
Standard direct labor rate per hour	$6.00
Actual direct labor-hours of input	40,000
Actual direct labor rate per hour	$6.10
Variable manufacturing overhead actually incurred	$ 31,000
Fixed manufacturing overhead actually incurred	$157,000

Exhibit 15-7 contains the income statement under absorption costing that incorporates these new facts. These new variances hurt income by $44,000 because, like the volume variance, they are all charged against income in 19x5.

EXHIBIT 15-7
Absorption Costing
Modification of Exhibit 15-3 for 19x5
(Additional facts are in text)

Sales		$800
Opening inventory at standard	$120	
Cost of goods manufactured at standard	560	
Available for sale	$680	
Deduct ending inventory at standard	40	
Cost of goods sold at standard		640
Gross profit at standard		$160
Net variances for standard variable manufacturing costs ($34,000 + $3,000), unfavorable	$ 37	
Fixed overhead budget control variance, unfavorable	7	
Volume variance (arises only because of fixed overhead), unfavorable	10	
Total variances		54
Gross profit at "actual"		$106
Selling and administrative expenses		105
Net income		$ 1

DISPOSITION OF STANDARD COST VARIANCES

The advocates of standard costing, particularly when the standards are viewed as being currently attainable, contend that variances are by and large subject to current control. Therefore, variances are not inventoriable and should be considered as adjustments to the income of the period instead of being prorated over inventories and cost of goods sold. In this way, inventory valuations will be more representative of desirable and attainable costs.

The countervailing view favors a proration of the variances over inventories and cost of goods sold. In this way, inventory valuations will be more representative of the "actual" costs incurred to obtain the products. In practice, variances are usually not prorated because the managers who use standard cost systems favor the views in the preceding paragraph.

Therefore, in practice, all variances are typically regarded as adjustments to current income. The form of the disposition is unimportant. Exhibit 15-7 shows the variances as a component of the computation of gross profit at "actual." The variances could also appear as a completely separate section elsewhere in the income statement. This helps to distinguish between product costing (that is, the cost of goods sold, at standard) and loss recognition (unfavorable variances are "lost" or "expired" costs because they represent waste and inefficiency that do not justify them as inventoriable costs).

SUMMARY

Standard cost accounting systems are usually designed to satisfy *control* and *product-costing* purposes simultaneously. Many varieties of product costing are in use. For years, manufacturing companies regularly have used a version of absorption costing, which includes fixed factory overhead as a part of the cost of product. In contrast, direct costing, which is more accurately called *variable costing,* charges fixed factory overhead to the period immediately—that is, fixed overhead is excluded from inventories. Absorption costing continues to be much more widely used than direct costing, although the growing use of the contribution approach in performance measurement has led to increasing use of direct costing.

The volume variance, which might better be called the denominator variance, is linked with absorption costing, not direct costing. It arises from the conflict between the control-budget purpose and the product-costing purpose of cost accounting. The volume variance is measured by the predetermined fixed overhead rate multiplied by the difference between denominator volume and actual volume.

Standard costing uses fully predetermined product costs for direct material, direct labor, and factory overhead. If the standards are currently attainable, the variances are not inventoried. Instead, they are directly charged or credited to current operations.

Problems

1. Reconsider Exhibits 15-2 and 15-3. Suppose in 19x5 that production was 145,000 units instead of 140,000 units, but sales were 160,000 units. Also assume that the net variances for all variable manufacturing costs were $37,000, unfavorable. Regard these variances as adjustments to standard cost of goods sold. Also assume that actual fixed costs were $157,000. Prepare income statements for 19x5 under direct costing and under absorption costing.
2. Explain why net income was different under direct costing and absorption costing. Show your calculations.
3. Without regard to Requirement 1, would direct costing or absorption costing give a manager more leeway in influencing his short-run net income through production-scheduling decisions? Why?

Solutions

1. See Exhibits 15-8 and 15-9. Note that the ending inventory will be 15,000 instead of 10,000 units.

EXHIBIT 15-8

TOLMAN COMPANY

Income Statement (Direct Costing)

For the Year 19x5

(In thousands of dollars)

Sales			$800
Opening inventory—at variable standard cost			
of $3.00	$ 90		
Add variable cost of goods manufactured	435		
Available for sale	525		
Deduct ending inventory—at variable standard			
cost of $3.00	45		
Variable cost of goods sold, at standard		$480	
Net variances for all variable costs, unfavorable		37	
Variable cost of goods sold, at actual		517	
Variable selling expenses—at 5% of dollar sales		40	
Total variable costs charged against sales			557
Contribution margin			243
Fixed factory overhead		157*	
Fixed selling and administrative expenses		65	
Total fixed expenses			222
Net income			$ 21†

*This could be shown in two lines, $150,000 budget plus $7,000 variance.

†The difference between this and the $65,000 net income in Exhibit 15-2 occurs because of the $37,000 unfavorable variable cost variances and the $7,000 unfavorable fixed-cost control-budget variance.

EXHIBIT 15-9
TOLMAN COMPANY
Income Statement (Absorption Costing)
For the Year 19x5
(in thousands of dollars)

Sales		$800
Opening inventory at standard cost of $4.00	$120	
Cost of goods manufactured at standard	580	
Available for sale	700	
Deduct ending inventory at standard	60	
Cost of goods sold at standard	640	
Net variances for all variable manufacturing		
costs, unfavorable	$37	
Fixed factory overhead budget-control		
variance, unfavorable	7	
Volume variance, unfavorable	5*	
Total variances	49	
Cost of goods sold at actual		689†
Gross profit at "actual"		111
Selling and administrative expenses		
Variable	40	
Fixed	65	105
Net income		$ 6**

*Volume variance is $1.00 × (150,000 denominator volume − 145,000 actual production).

†This format differs slightly from Exhibit 15-7. The difference is deliberate; it illustrates that the formats of income statements are not rigid.

**Compare this result with the $1,000 net income in Exhibit 15-7. The *only* difference is traceable to the *production* of 145,000 units instead of 140,000 units, resulting in an unfavorable volume variance of $5,000 instead of $10,000.

2. Decline in inventory levels is 30,000 − 15,000, or 15,000 units. The fixed-overhead rate per unit in absorption costing is $1. Therefore, $15,000 more of fixed overhead was charged against operations under absorption costing than under direct costing. Generally, when inventories decline, absorption costing will show less income than direct costing; when inventories rise, absorption costing will show more income than direct costing.

3. Some version of absorption costing will give a manager more leeway in influencing his net income via production scheduling. Net income will fluctuate in harmony with changes in net sales under direct costing, but it is influenced by both production and sales under absorption costing. For example, compare the direct costing in Exhibits 15-2 and 15-8. As Note 2 to Exhibit 15-8 indicates, the net income may be affected by assorted variances (but not the volume variance) under direct costing, but production scheduling *per se* will have no effect on net income. On the other hand, compare the net income of Exhibits 15-7 and 15-9. As Note 3 to Exhibit 15-9 explains, production scheduling as

well as sales influence net income. Production was 145,000 rather than 140,000 units. So $5,000 of fixed overhead became a part of ending inventory (an asset) instead of part of the volume variance (an expense)—that is, the volume variance is $5,000 lower and the ending inventory contains $5,000 more fixed overhead in Exhibit 15-9 than in Exhibit 15-7.

APPENDIX: COMPARISONS OF VOLUME VARIANCES WITH OTHER VARIANCES

Volume Variance Is Unique

The only new variance introduced in this chapter is the volume variance, which arises because fixed overhead accounting must serve two masters: the budget-control purpose and the product-costing purpose. Let us examine these variances in perspective by using the approach originally demonstrated in Exhibit 9-6. The results of the approach are in Exhibit 15-10, which deserves your careful study, particularly Notes 1 and 2. Please ponder the exhibit before reading on.

Exhibit 15-11 provides a graphical comparison of the variable and fixed overhead that were analyzed in Exhibit 15-10. Note how the control-budget line and the product-costing line (the applied line) are super-imposed in the graph for variable overhead but differ in the graph for fixed overhead.

Efficiency Variance for Fixed Overhead?

Incidentally, there are many views on how fixed overhead variances are best analyzed. The position taken in this chapter has been to distinguish between fixed and variable overhead as separate management problems. In contrast, some accountants favor analyzing variable and fixed costs in a parallel manner. For instance, an efficiency variance for fixed overhead is often computed, just as it is for other variable costs:

Efficiency variance = Hourly fixed overhead rate × (Actual hours of input − Standard hours allowed for units produced)[2]

[2]Some accountants favor computing volume variance on the basis of the difference between the fixed overhead budget ($150,000) and (actual hours worked × fixed overhead rate). In this example, the volume variance would then become $150,000 − (40,000 × $4), or $10,000, favorable. The remaining variance of $20,000, unfavorable [(actual hours − standard hours) × $1 overhead rate] is sometimes called the fixed overhead *efficiency* or *effectiveness* variance—the measure of the ineffective use or waste of facilities because of off-standard labor performance. This breakdown of the volume variance really attempts to separate the cost of *misused* facilities from the cost of *unused* facilities.

The author thinks this refinement is unnecessary in most cases because (a) in the short run, total fixed costs incurred are *not* changed by efficiency changes, and (b) if the budget uses standard hours as a base, the *volume* variance is more logically calculated by comparing standard hours worked with the denominator volume that was used as a basis for setting the predetermined overhead rate.

EXHIBIT 15-10

Analysis of Variances
(data are from text)

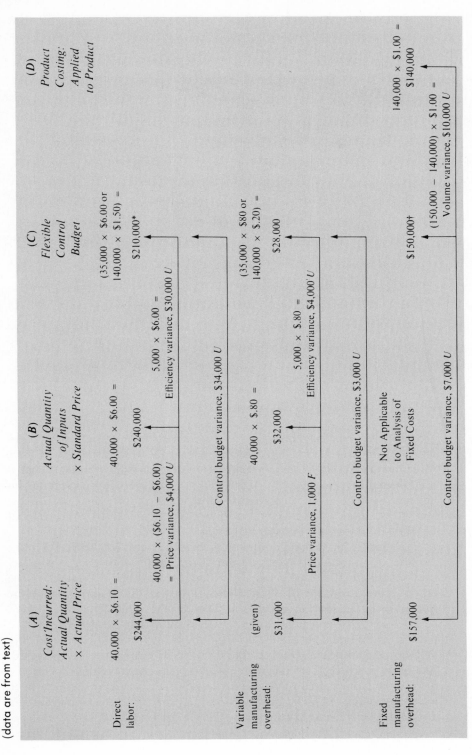

	(A) Cost Incurred: Actual Quantity × Actual Price	(B) Actual Quantity of Inputs × Standard Price	(C) Flexible Control Budget	(D) Product Costing: Applied to Product
Direct labor:	40,000 × $6.10 = $244,000	40,000 × $6.00 = $240,000	(35,000 × $6.00 or 140,000 × $1.50) = $210,000*	140,000 × $1.00 = $140,000

40,000 × ($6.10 − $6.00) = Price variance, $4,000 U

5,000 × $6.00 = Efficiency variance, $30,000 U

Control budget variance, $34,000 U

| Variable manufacturing overhead: | (given) $31,000 | 40,000 × $.80 = $32,000 | (35,000 × $80 or 140,000 × $.20) = $28,000 | |

Price variance, 1,000 F

5,000 × $.80 = Efficiency variance, $4,000 U

Control budget variance, $3,000 U

| Fixed manufacturing overhead: | $157,000 | Not Applicable to Analysis of Fixed Costs | $150,000† | |

(150,000 − 140,000) × $1.00 = Volume variance, $10,000 U

Control budget variance, $7,000 U

U = Unfavorable   F = Favorable

*Note especially that the control budget for variable costs rises and falls in direct proportion to production. Note also that the control budget purpose and the product costing purpose harmonize completely; the total costs in the flexible budget will always agree with the standard variable costs applied to product because they are based on standard costs per unit multiplied by units produced.

†In contrast with variable costs, the control budget total will always be the same regardless of the units produced. However, the control budget purpose and the product costing purpose conflict; whenever actual production differs from denominator production, the standard costs applied to product will differ from the control budget. This difference is the volume variance.

EXHIBIT 15-11

Comparison of Control and Product-Costing Purposes,
Variable Overhead and Fixed Overhead (Not to scale)

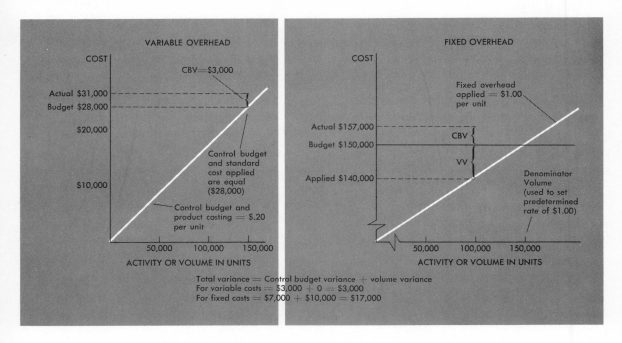

VARIABLE OVERHEAD

COST

CBV = $3,000

Actual $31,000

Budget $28,000

$20,000

Control budget
and standard
cost applied
are equal
($28,000)

$10,000

Control budget and
product costing = $.20
per unit

50,000   100,000   150,000

ACTIVITY OR VOLUME IN UNITS

FIXED OVERHEAD

COST

Fixed overhead
applied = $1.00
per unit

Actual $157,000

CBV

Budget $150,000

VV

Applied $140,000

Denominator
Volume
(used to set
predetermined
rate of $1.00)

50,000   100,000   150,000

ACTIVITY OR VOLUME IN UNITS

Total variance = Control budget variance + volume variance
For variable costs = $3,000 + 0 = $3,000
For fixed costs = $7,000 + $10,000 = $17,000

However, the resulting variance is very different from the efficiency variances for material, labor, and variable overhead. Efficient usage of these three factors can affect actual cost, but short-run fixed overhead cost is not affected by efficiency. Furthermore, the managers responsible for inefficiency will be aware of its existence through reports on variable-cost control, so there is little to gain from expressing ineffective utilization of facilities in historical-dollar terms.

Finally, what is the economic significance of unit fixed costs? Unlike variable costs, total fixed costs do not change in the short run as production or sales fluctuate. Management would obtain a better measure of the cost of underutilization of physical facilities by trying to approximate the related lost-contribution margins instead of the related historical fixed costs. Fixed-cost incurrence often involves lump-sum outlays based on a pattern of expected recoupment. But ineffective utilization of existing facilities has no bearing on the amount of fixed costs currently incurred. The economic effects of the inability to reach target volume levels are often directly measured by lost-contribution margins, even if these have to be approximated. The historical-cost approach fails to emphasize the distinction between *fixed-cost incurrence,* on the one hand, and the objective of *maximizing the total contribution margin,* on the other hand. These are separable management problems, and the utilization of existing capacity is more closely related to the latter.

For instance, the activity variance in our example was computed at $10,000 by multiplying a unit fixed cost of $1 by the 10,000-unit difference between the 150,000 units of denominator activity and 140,000 units produced. This $10,000 figure may be helpful in the sense that management is alerted in some crude way to the probable costs of failure to produce 150,000 units. But the more relevant information is the lost-contribution margins that pertain to the 10,000 units. This information may not be so easy to obtain. The lost-contribution margins may be zero in those cases where there are no opportunities to obtain any contribution margin from alternative uses of available capacity; in other cases, however, the lost-contribution margins may be substantial. For example, if demand is high, the breakdown of key equipment may cost a company many thousands of dollars in lost-contribution margins. Unfortunately, in these cases, existing accounting systems would show volume variances based on the unitized fixed costs and entirely ignore any lost-contribution margins.

ASSIGNMENT MATERIAL

Fundamental Assignment Material

15-1. Terminology. Define: *absorption costing; direct costing; variable costing; marginal costing; standard absorption costing;* and *standard direct costing.*

15-2. Comparison of direct costing and absorption costing. From the following information pertaining to a year's operation, answer the questions below:

Units produced	2,400
Units sold	2,000
Selling and administrative expenses (all fixed)	$ 800
Fixed manufacturing overhead	2,400
Variable manufacturing overhead	1,100
Direct labor	3,400
Direct material used	2,700
All beginning inventories	-0-
Gross margin (gross profit)	2,000
Direct materials inventory, end	300
Work in process inventory, end	-0-

Required:

1. What is the ending finished goods inventory cost under traditional-costing procedures (absorption costing)?
2. What is the ending finished goods inventory cost under variable-costing procedures (direct costing)?
3. Would net income be higher or lower under direct costing? By how much? Why? (Answer: $400 lower.)

15-3. Extension of chapter illustration. Reconsider Exhibits 15-2 and 15-3. Suppose that in 19x5 production was 156,000 units instead of 140,000 units, and sales were 150,000 units. Also assume that the net variances for all variable manufacturing costs were $24,000, unfavorable. Also assume that actual fixed manufacturing costs were $157,000.

Required:
1. Prepare income statements for 19x5 under direct costing and under absorption costing. Use a format similar to Exhibits 15-8 and 15-9.
2. Explain why net income was different under direct costing and absorption costing. Show your calculations.

15-4. Extension of appendix illustration. Study the analysis of variances in Exhibit 15-10. Suppose that production is 156,000 units. Also assume:

Standard direct labor-hours allowed per unit produced	.25
Standard direct labor rate per hour	$6.00
Actual direct labor-hours of input	42,000
Actual direct labor rate per hour	$6.10
Variable manufacturing overhead actually incurred	$33,000
Fixed manufacturing overhead actually incurred	$157,000

Required:
Prepare an analysis of variances similar to that shown in Exhibit 15-10.

Additional Assignment Material

15-5. "Direct costing means that only direct material and direct labor are inventoried." Do you agree? Why?

15-6. Why do advocates of currently attainable standard costs as a method for product costing claim that it is conceptually superior to actual costing?

15-7. "Absorption costing regards more categories of costs as product costs." Explain. Be specific.

15-8. "Direct costing is used in several corporate annual reports." Do you agree? Explain.

15-9. How is fixed overhead applied to product?

15-10. Define the *volume variance* as conventionally measured.

15-11. "The dollar amount of the volume variance depends on what activity level was chosen to determine the application rate." Explain.

15-12. Why is it artificial to unitize fixed costs?

15-13. "The fixed cost per unit is directly affected by the denominator selected." Do you agree? Explain.

15-14. Comparison of direct and absorption costing over five years. Two corporations are hotly competitive in the manufacture and sale of farm machinery. Their sales volume, production volume, and their fixed indirect manufacturing costs have been practically identical.

Companies A and B	19x1	19x2	19x3	19x4	19x5
Units produced	100,000	100,000	105,000	90,000	90,000
Units sold	90,000	90,000	100,000	100,000	95,000
Fixed indirect manufacturing costs	$100,000	$105,000	$105,000	$105,000	$100,000

Company *A* uses absorption costing, and Company *B* uses direct costing. For each of the five years, would Company *A*'s net income be higher or lower than Company *B*'s? Assume that neither company had inventories at the beginning of 19x1. Assume that there is a first-in, first-out flow of costs.

15-15. **Comparison of direct costing and absorption costing.** From the following information pertaining to a year's operations, answer the questions below:

Units sold	1,000
Units produced	1,100
Fixed manufacturing overhead	$2,200
Variable manufacturing overhead	500
Selling and administrative expenses (all fixed)	900
Direct labor	4,000
Direct material used	2,100
Beginning inventories	-0-
Contribution margin	4,000
Direct material inventory, end	1,000

There are no work-in-process inventories.

Required:
1. What is the ending finished goods inventory cost under traditional-costing procedures (absorption costing)?
2. What is the ending finished goods inventory cost under variable-costing procedures (direct costing)?

15-16. **All-fixed costs.** (Suggested by Raymond P. Marple.) The Marple Company has built a massive water-desalting factory next to an ocean. The factory is completely automated. It has its own source of power, light, heat, etc. The salt water costs nothing. All producing and other operating costs are fixed; they do not vary with output because the volume is governed by adjusting a few dials on a control panel. The employees have flat annual salaries.

The desalted water is not sold to household consumers. It has a special taste that appeals to local breweries, distilleries, and soft-drink manufacturers. The price, 10¢ per gallon, is expected to remain unchanged for quite some time.

The following are data regarding the first two years of operations:

	In Gallons		Costs (All Fixed)	
	Sales	Production	Manufacturing	Other
19x1	5,000,000	10,000,000	$450,000	$100,000
19x2	5,000,000	0	450,000	100,000

Orders can be processed in four hours, so management decided, in early 19x2, to gear production strictly to sales.

Required:

1. Prepare three-column income statements for 19x1, for 19x2, and for the two years together using (a) direct costing and (b) absorption costing.
2. What is the break-even point under (a) direct costing and (b) absorption costing?
3. What inventory costs would be carried on the balance sheets on December 31, 19x1 and 19x2, under each method?
4. Comment on your answers in Requirements 1 and 2. Which costing method appears more useful?

15-17. Semifixed costs. The McFarland Company differs from the Marple Company (described in Problem 15-16) in only one respect: it has both variable and fixed manufacturing costs. Its variable costs are $.025 per gallon and its fixed manufacturing costs are $225,000 per year.

Required:

1. Using the same data as in the previous problem, except for the change in production cost behavior, prepare three-column income statements for 19x1, for 19x2, and for the two years together using (a) direct costing and (b) absorption costing.
2. Why did McFarland earn a profit for the two-year period while Marple suffered a loss?
3. What inventory costs would be carried on the balance sheets on December 31, 19x1 and 19x2, under each method?

15-18. Fundamentals of overhead variances. The Green Company is installing an absorption standard cost system and a flexible overhead budget. Standard costs have been recently developed for its only product and are as follows:

Direct material, 2 pounds @ $15	$30
Direct labor, 6 hours @ $6	36
Variable overhead, 6 hours @ $1	6
Fixed overhead	?
Standard cost per unit of finished product	$?

Denominator activity (expected activity) is expressed as 12,000 standard direct labor hours per month. Fixed overhead is expected to be $18,000 per month.

Required:

1. Calculate the proper fixed overhead rate per standard direct labor hour and per unit.
2. Graph the following for activity from zero to 15,000 hours:
   (a) Budgeted variable overhead.
   (b) Variable overhead applied to product.
3. Graph the following for activity from zero to 15,000 hours:
   (a) Budgeted fixed overhead.
   (b) Fixed overhead applied to product.
4. Assume that 10,000 standard direct labor hours are allowed for the output during a given month. Actual variable overhead of $10,200 was incurred; actual fixed overhead amounted to $18,500. Calculate the:
   (a) Fixed overhead control budget variance.
   (b) Fixed overhead volume variance.
   (c) Variable overhead control budget variance.

5. Assume that 12,500 standard direct labor-hours are allowed for the output during a given month. Actual overhead incurred amounted to $29,900, $18,900 of which was fixed. Calculate the:
  (a) Variable overhead control budget variance.
  (b) Fixed overhead volume variance.
  (c) Fixed overhead control budget variance.

15-19. Analysis of fixed overhead; various activity levels. The fixed overhead items of the lathe department of Costanzo Company include for the month of January, 19x4:

Item	Actual	Budget
Supervision	$ 900	$ 800
Depreciation—Plant	750	750
Depreciation—Equipment	1,750	1,750
Property taxes	350	400
Insurance—Factory	400	300
	$4,150	$4,000

Expected activity for the lathe department is 1,000 standard hours per month. Practical capacity is 1,600 standard hours per month. Standard hours allowed for work done (good units actually produced) were 1,250.

Required:

1. Prepare a summary analysis of fixed overhead variances using expected activity as the activity base.
2. Prepare a summary analysis of fixed overhead variances using practical capacity as the activity base.
3. Explain why the control-budget variances in Requirements 1 and 2 are identical whereas the volume variances are different.

15-20. Characteristics of fixed overhead variances. Mitchell Company executives have studied their operations carefully and have been using a standard cost system for years. They are now formulating currently attainable standards for 19x1. They agree that the standards for direct material will amount to $10 per finished unit produced and that the standards for direct labor and variable overhead are to be $4 and $1 per direct labor-hour, respectively. Total fixed overhead is expected to be $600,000. Two hours of direct labor is the standard time for finishing one unit of finished product.

Required:

1. Graph the budgeted fixed overhead for 400,000 to 800,000 standard-allowed direct labor-hours of activity, assuming that the total budget will not change over that activity level. What would be the appropriate product-costing rate per standard direct labor-hour for fixed overhead if denominator activity is 500,000 hours? Graph the applied overhead line.
2. Assume that 250,000 units of product were produced. How much fixed overhead would be applied to product? Would there be a volume variance? Why? Assume that 200,000 units were produced. Would there be a volume variance? Why? Show the latter volume variance on a graph. In your own words, define *volume variance*. Why does it arise? Can a volume variance exist for variable overhead? Why?
3. Assume that 220,000 units are produced. Fixed overhead costs incurred were

$617,000. What is the fixed overhead control-budget variance? Volume variance? Use the analytical technique illustrated in the chapter.

4. Ignore Requirements 2 and 3. In Requirement 1, what would be the appropriate product-costing rate per standard direct labor-hour for fixed overhead if denominator activity is estimated at 400,000 hours? 600,000 hours? 800,000 hours? Draw a graph showing budgeted fixed overhead and three "applied" lines, using the three rates just calculated. If 200,000 units are produced, and the denominator activity is 600,000 standard direct labor-hours, what is the volume variance? Now compare this with the volume variance in your answer to Requirement 2. Explain.

5. Specifically, what are the implications in Requirements 1 and 4 regarding (a) the setting of product-costing rates for fixed overhead, (b) the meaning of budget and volume variances, and (c) the major differences in planning and control techniques for variable and fixed costs?

15-21. Standard absorption and standard direct costing. Coleman Company has the following results for a certain year. All variances are written off as additions to (or deductions from) the standard cost of goods sold. Find the unknowns, designated by letters.

Sales: 200,000 units, @ $22	$4,400,000	
Net variance for standard variable manufacturing costs	$ 36,000,	unfavorable
Variable standard cost of goods manufactured	$ 10	per unit
Variable selling and administrative expenses	$ 2	per unit
Fixed selling and administrative expenses	$1,000,000	
Fixed manufacturing overhead	$ 240,000	
Maximum capacity per year	240,000	units
Denominator volume for year	200,000	units
Beginning inventory of finished goods	30,000	units
Ending inventory of finished goods	10,000	units
Beginning inventory: direct-costing basis	*a*	
Contribution margin	*b*	
Net income: direct-costing basis	*c*	
Beginning inventory: absorption-costing basis	*d*	
Gross margin	*e*	
Net income: absorption-costing basis	*f*	

15-22. Direct costing and standard costing. The following data refer to the operations of the Rebholz Company during 19x5:

Costs:	
Standard variable costs per unit:	
Material and labor	$4.50
Factory overhead	1.00
	$5.50
Fixed costs (budgeted and actual):	
Production	$250,000
Selling and administrative	100,000
	$350,000

Operating data:

Plant capacity	100,000 units
Sales	95,000 units
Production	90,000 units

Total material and labor and variable-overhead variances from standard is $4,500, unfavorable. Selling price per unit is $10.

Overhead under absorption costing is applied at rates based on 100 percent of capacity. All variances and underabsorbed overhead are charged as additions to standard cost of goods sold.

Required:

1. Prepare tabular calculations of income for the Rebholz Company for 19x5 on (a) an absorption-cost basis and (b) a direct-costing basis.
2. Indicate how the two schedules of Requirement 1 can be reconciled.
3. How would the income figures for Requirement 1 have differed if production had been 95,000 units and sales 90,000 units? (Show calculations to support your answer.)

15-23. Direct costing for external reporting. (CMA adapted.) The S. T. Shire Company uses direct costing for internal-management purposes and absorption costing for external-reporting purposes. Thus, at the end of each year financial information must be converted from direct costing to absorption costing in order to satisfy external requirements.

At the end of 19x1 it was anticipated that sales would rise 20 percent the next year. Therefore, production was increased from 20,000 units to 24,000 units to meet this expected demand. However, economic conditions kept the sales level at 20,000 units for both years.

The following data pertain to 19x1 and 19x2:

	19x1	19x2
Selling price per unit	$ 30	$ 30
Sales (units)	20,000	20,000
Beginning inventory (units)	2,000	2,000
Production (units)	20,000	24,000
Ending inventory (units)	2,000	6,000
Unfavorable labor, materials and variable		
overhead variances (total)	$ 5,000	$ 4,000

Standard variable costs per unit for 19x1 and 19x2:

Labor	$ 7.50
Material	4.50
Variable overhead	3.00
	$15.00

Annual fixed costs for 19x1 and 19x2
(Budgeted and Actual):

Production	$ 90,000
Selling and administrative	100,000
	$190,000

The overhead rate under absorption costing is based upon practical plant capacity which is 30,000 units per year. All variances and under- or over-absorbed overhead are included in cost of goods sold.

All taxes are to be ignored.

Required:

1. Present the income statement based on direct costing for 19x2.
2. Present the income statement based on absorption costing for 19x2.
3. Explain the difference, if any, in the net income figures.
4. The company finds it worthwhile to develop its internal financial data on a direct-cost basis. What advantages and disadvantages are attributed to direct costing for internal purposes?
5. There are many who believe that direct costing is appropriate for external reporting and there are many who oppose its use for external reporting. What arguments for and against the use of direct costing might be advanced for its use in external reporting?

15-24. **Fill in the blanks.**

	Factory Overhead	
	Fixed	Variable
Actual incurred	$5,500	$10,800
Budget for standard hours allowed	5,000	9,000
Applied	4,800	9,000
Budget for actual hours worked	5,000	9,800

From the above information fill in the blanks below:

	Fixed $_____
The control budget variance is $_____	Variable $_____
	Fixed $_____
The volume variance is $_____	Variable $_____
	Fixed $_____
The price variance is $_____	Variable $_____
	Fixed $_____
The efficiency variance is $_____	Variable $_____

Mark your variances *F* for favorable and *U* for unfavorable.

15-25. **Comprehensive, straightforward problem on standard cost system.** The Mellor Company uses a standard cost system. The month's data regarding its single product follow:

Fixed overhead costs incurred, $6,150
Variable overhead applied at $.90 per hour
Standard direct labor cost, $4 per hour
Denominator production per month, 2,500 units
Standard direct labor-hours per finished unit, 5
Direct labor costs incurred, 11,000 hours, $41,800
Variable overhead costs incurred, $9,500
Fixed overhead budget variance, $100, favorable
Finished units produced, 2,000

Required:

Prepare schedules of all variances.

**Overhead
Application:
Direct and
Absorption Costing**

15-26. Analysis of variances. (CPA adapted.) The Groomer Company manufactures two products, florimene and glyoxide, used in the plastics industry. The company uses a flexible budget in its standard cost system to develop variances. Selected data follow:

	Florimene	Glyoxide
Data on standard costs:		
Raw material per unit	3 pounds at $1.00 per pound	4 pounds at $1.10 per pound
Direct labor per unit	5 hours at $2.00 per hour	6 hours at $2.50 per hour
Variable factory overhead per unit	$3.20 per direct labor hour	$3.50 per direct labor hour
Fixed factory overhead per month	$20,700	$26,520
Denominator activity per month	5,750 direct labor hours	7,800 direct labor hours
Units produced in September ...	1,000	1,200
Costs incurred for September:		
Raw material	3,100 pounds at $.90 per pound	4,700 pounds at $1.15 per pound
Direct labor	4,900 hours at $1.95 per hour	7,400 hours at $2.55 per hour
Variable factory overhead	$16,170	$25,234
Fixed factory overhead	$20,930	$26,400

Required:

Select the best answer for each of the following items. Show computations to support your answer.

1. The total variances (that is, the difference between total costs incurred and total standard costs applied to product) to be explained for both products for September are
   a. Florimene, $255, favorable; Glyoxide, $909, unfavorable.
   b. Florimene, $7,050, favorable; Glyoxide, $6,080, favorable.
   c. Florimene, $4,605, favorable; Glyoxide, $3,431, favorable.
   d. Florimene, $2,445, unfavorable; Glyoxide, $2,949, unfavorable.
   e. None of the above.
2. The labor efficiency variances for both products for September are
   a. Florimene, $195, favorable; Glyoxide, $510, unfavorable.
   b. Florimene, $1,700, favorable; Glyoxide, $1,000, favorable.
   c. Florimene, $200, favorable; Glyoxide, $500, unfavorable.
   d. Florimene, $195, favorable; Glyoxide, $510 favorable.
   e. None of the above.

3. The labor price (rate) variances for both products for September are
    a. Florimene, $245, favorable; Glyoxide, $370, unfavorable.
    b. Florimene, $200, favorable; Glyoxide, $500, unfavorable.
    c. Florimene, $1,945, favorable; Glyoxide, $630 favorable.
    d. Florimene, $245, unfavorable; Glyoxide, $370, favorable.
    e. None of the above.
4. The "price" variances for variable overhead for both products for September are
    a. Florimene, $490, unfavorable; Glyoxide, $666, favorable.
    b. Florimene, $167, unfavorable; Glyoxide, $35, unfavorable.
    c. Florimene, $170, unfavorable; Glyoxide, $34, unfavorable.
    d. Florimene, $1,900, favorable; Glyoxide, $1,960, favorable.
    e. None of the above.

15-27. Comparing the performance of two plants. On your first day as assistant to the president of Holland Systems, Inc., your in-box contains the following memo:

> To: Assistant to the President
> From: The President
> Subject: Mickey Mouse Watch Situation
>
> This note is to bring you up-to-date on one of our acquisition problem areas. Market research detected the current nostalgia wave almost a year ago and concluded that HSI should acquire a position in this market. Research data showed that Mickey Mouse Watches could become profitable ($2 contribution margin on a $5 sales price) at a volume of 100,000 units per plant if they became popular again. Consequently, we picked up closed-down facilities on each coast, staffed them, and asked them to keep us posted on operations.
>
> Friday I got preliminary information from accounting that is unclear. I want you to find out why their Cost of goods sold are far apart and how we should have them report in the future to avoid confusion. This is particularly important in the Mickey Mouse case as market projections look bad and we may have to close one plant. I guess we'll close the West Coast plant unless you can show otherwise.

Preliminary Accounting Report

	East	*West*
Sales	$500,000	$500,000
Cost of goods sold	300,000	480,000
Gross margin	$200,000	$ 20,000
Administration costs (fixed)	20,000	20,000
Net income	$180,000	$ 0
Production	200,000 units	100,000 units
Variances (included in Cost of goods sold)	$180,000, favorable	$ 90,000, unfavorable

Required:

Reconstruct the given income statements in as much detail as possible. Then explain in detail why the income statements differ, and clarify the situation confronting the president. Assume that there are no price or efficiency variances.

15-28. Inventory measures, production scheduling, and evaluating divisional performance. The Mark Company stresses competition between the heads of its various divisions and rewards stellar performance with year-end bonuses that vary between 5 and 10 percent of division net operating income (before considering the bonus or income taxes). The divisional managers have great discretion in setting production schedules.

Division Y produces and sells a product for which there is a longstanding demand but which can have marked seasonal and year-to-year fluctuations. On November 30, 19x2, George Craft, the Division Y manager, is preparing a production schedule for December. The following data are available for January 1 through November 30:

Beginning inventory, January 1, in units	10,000
Sales price, per unit	$ 500
Total fixed costs incurred for manufacturing	$11,000,000
Total fixed costs: other (not inventoriable)	$11,000,000
Total variable costs for manufacturing	$22,000,000
Total other variable costs (fluctuate with units sold)	$ 5,000,000
Units produced	110,000
Units sold	100,000
Variances	None

Production in October and November was 10,000 units each month. Practical capacity is 12,000 units per month. Maximum available storage space for inventory is 25,000 units. The sales outlook, for December through February, is 6,000 units monthly. In order to retain a core of key employees, monthly production cannot be scheduled at less than 4,000 units without special permission from the president. Inventory is never to be less than 10,000 units.

The denominator used for applying fixed factory overhead is regarded as 120,000 units annually. The company uses a standard absorption-costing system. All variances are disposed of at year-end as an adjustment to standard cost of goods sold.

Required:

1. Given the restrictions as stated, and assuming that the manager wants to maximize the company's net income for 19x2:
   (a) How many units should be scheduled for production in December?
   (b) What net operating income will be reported for 19x2 as a whole, assuming that the implied cost behavior patterns will continue in December as they did throughout the year, to date? Show your computations.
   (c) If December production is scheduled at 4,000 units, what would reported net income be?
2. Assume that standard direct costing is used rather than standard absorption costing.
   (a) What would net income for 19x2 be, assuming that the December production schedule is the one in Requirement 1, part (a)?

(b) Assuming that December production was 4,000 units?

(c) Reconcile the net incomes in this Requirement with those in Requirement 1.

3. From the viewpoint of the long-run interests of the company as a whole, what production schedule should the division manager set? Explain fully. Include in your explanation a comparison of the motivating influence of absorption and direct costing in this situation.

4. Assume standard absorption costing. The manager wants to maximize his after-income-tax performance over the long run. Given the data at the beginning of the problem, assume that income tax rates will be halved in 19x3. Assume also that year-end write-offs of variances are acceptable for income tax purposes.

How many units should be scheduled for production in December? Why?

Decentralization, Performance Measurement, and Transfer Pricing

16

Responsibility accounting, as Chapter 11 explained, helps measure performance by focusing on the cost items subject to an individual's control. The basic ideas of responsibility accounting have been extended beyond cost centers to profit centers and investment centers. We shall now examine the nature of these centers and the major accounting problems that occur in the measurement of performance. We shall be particularly concerned with two widely used measures: (1) rate of return on investment (hereafter often called ROI) and (2) transfer prices.

COST CENTERS, PROFIT CENTERS, AND INVESTMENT CENTERS

A *cost center* is the smallest segment of activity or area of responsibility for which costs are accumulated. Typically, cost centers are departments, but in some instances a department may contain several cost centers. For example, although an assembly department may be supervised by one foreman, it may contain several assembly lines. Sometimes each assembly line is regarded as a separate cost center with its own assistant foreman.

A *profit center* is a segment of a business, often called a division, that is responsible for both revenue and expenses. An *investment center* goes a step further; its success is measured not only by its income but also by relating that income to its invested capital. In practice, the term *investment center* is not widely used. Instead, *profit center* is used indiscriminately to describe segments that are always assigned responsibility for revenue and expenses but may or may not be assigned responsibility for the related invested capital.

Relative Freedom to Make Decisions

To reach their objectives, top managers face two general difficulties: (1) how to divide activities and responsibilities and (2) how to coordinate subunits. Inevitably, the power to make decisions is distributed among managers. Organizations are often characterized as being decentralized or centralized according to how widely this power is distributed. Decentralization is a matter of degree. Total decentralization means minimum constraints and maximum freedom to make decisions. At the other extreme of the continuum, total centralization means maximum constraints and minimum freedom.

Benefits of Decentralization

In practice, organizations are seldom totally centralized or decentralized. How should top managers decide on how much decentralization is desirable? Conceptually, top managers try to choose a degree of decentralization that optimally achieves their overall objectives, that maximizes benefits over costs. Practically, top managers cannot quantify the benefits or the costs. Still, this cost-benefit approach identifies the central issue of organizational design as a choice along a continuum:

Centralized   Decentralized

The benefits of decentralization are claimed to include:

1. Better decisions are likely because the manager of the subunit can react quickly to local conditions.
2. The burden of processing a massive volume of decisions is distributed so that all the decisions are collectively optimized. Moreover, top managers are more likely to have time for strategic planning.
3. Greater freedom heightens incentives because managers have more control over the factors that affect the measures of their performance.
4. Greater freedom induces more frequent checks on outside market forces. This built-in check is more likely to spot opportunities and uneconomic activities sooner rather than later.
5. More decision making over a wide spectrum provides better training for executives as they rise in the organization.
6. Greater freedom bestows higher status and a more desirable motivational effect.

All these claimed advantages are benefits because they are supposed to result in larger gross increases in profits than would occur in a more heavily centralized organization.

Costs of Decentralization

The largest cost of decentralization is probably dysfunctional decision making—where the benefit to one subunit is more than offset by the costs or loss of benefit to other subunits. Dysfunctional decisions are most probable where the subunits are highly interdependent so that a decision in one part of an organization influences the decisions or performance of another part. For example, parts and raw materials made by one subunit must meet specifications and schedules of another subunit; two subunits may share or compete for computer services, management skills, or raw materials; they may sell in a common market (for instance, Buick and Oldsmobile) so that an action beneficial to one subunit may harm another and the organization as a whole. Moreover, if the performance evaluation mechanism is not carefully designed, long-run goals may be sacrificed to improve a short-run showing.

The costs of gathering and processing information often increase. Transfer pricing is an example. A centralized organization might impose a transfer price between subunits and might require all purchases or sales of a particular item to be made internally. In contrast, a decentralized organization might have managers negotiate a price and might allow them to buy and sell in outside markets. The decentralized approach often causes increases in costs of management time in negotiations and perhaps extra information gathering for making individual decisions. In addition, some central corporate services tend to be duplicated.

Comparison of Benefits and Costs

The foregoing benefits and costs lead to heavy decentralization of some functions and heavy centralization of other functions. For example, the controller's function may be heavily decentralized for many attention-directing and problem-solving purposes (such as preparing operating budgets and interpreting performance reports), but heavily centralized for other purposes (such as invoice processing and income tax planning).

Decentralization is likely to be most beneficial and least costly when the organizational units are independent. A subunit is independent to the extent that it can make decisions and obtain goal congruence without coordination with other subunits, does not buy or sell internally, and does not compete in the same markets with other subunits for either its input needs or customers.

Role of Profit Centers

Normally, the profit center is the major organizational device used to maximize decentralization. However, decentralization and the creation of profit centers are separate issues. There are two major myths about profit centers: First, profit centers and decentralization are interchangeable terms. Second, profit centers and decentralization are not applicable to small organizations. Each myth will be discussed in turn.

Although profit centers typically accompany decentralization, their existence does not necessarily mean that heavy decentralization also exists. The substance of decentralization is the freedom to make decisions; the form of decentralization is frequently the use of profit centers. While some organizations may have profit centers, their managers may have little leeway to make decisions. A manager may be restricted from buying or selling outside the organization, may have to obtain approval from central headquarters for every capital expenditure over $300, and may be forced to accept "advice" from the central staff. In other companies, which have only cost centers, managers may have enormous latitude to purchase or sell goods and services and to make capital outlays. In short, the degree of decentralization depends on the relative freedom to make decisions; the labels of **profit center** and **cost center** may be deceptive as clues to the amount of decentralization.

The second myth about decentralization and profit centers, based on superficial reasoning, is that they pertain only to large organizations. The most publicity seems to go to the corporate giants, but automobile dealers, medical centers, and retail department stores often thrive on decentralization and profit centers.

SYSTEMS DESIGN AND DECENTRALIZATION

When a manager chooses a particular management-control system, he is basically confronted with a decision regarding the cost and value of information—that is, what are the relative costs and benefits, given the particular circumstances of the specific organization that is considering one variety of control system versus other varieties. The trade-offs of costs and benefits form the dominant criterion for systems design and appraisal.

Three criteria are helpful for designing or judging a particular accounting system in a decentralized setting: (a) goal congruence, (b) performance evaluation, and (c) autonomy.[1] As you know, goal congruence focuses on the harmonizing of the objectives of the managers with the objectives of the organization as a whole. Evaluation of performance (feedback) is needed to help make predictions for future decisions, to appraise the abilities of the *manager,* and to assess the profitability of the capital invested in the organizational *subunit* as an economic investment. Moreover, the choice of various performance measures will have different influential effects on manager behavior. Finally, if top management wants to preserve a given decentralized structure, it must respect the subunits as decentralized entities.

Note that the common thread of these criteria is motivation. The aim is to find a system that will point the managers toward top-management goals. But pointing them in the right direction is only the first step.

---

[1] Joshua Ronen and George McKinney, "Transfer Pricing for Divisional Autonomy," *Journal of Accounting Research,* Spring 1970, pp. 100–101.

In addition, incentives must be provided that will spur managers toward those goals.

Consider the steps that must be taken by the control-system designer, who may be an accountant, a manager, or both. First, he must choose a measure of accomplishment that represents top-management objectives. This provides a conceptual structure. Should it be net income, rate of return on investment, contribution margin, sales, or some other measure? Second, whatever measure is chosen, the designer must then decide how to define such items as income or investment. Should income be based on variable or absorption costing? Should central corporate costs be allocated? Should investment consist of assets, or assets minus liabilities, or some other collection? Third, how should items be measured? Historical cost? Replacement cost? Realizable value? Fourth, what standards should be applied? Should all divisions be required to earn the same rate of return on all their investments? Fifth, what timing of feedback is needed? Quarterly? Annually? Should feedback on the performance of managers be timed differently from feedback on the performance of divisions as economic investments?

These five steps are not necessarily taken sequentially. Instead, the answers to these questions are interdependent. Taken together, they produce a particular control system that is supposed to be optimal for the specific organization as a whole. (We will explore these questions in subsequent sections.) Of course, the answers are not uniform. They depend on the particular needs of specific managers in a particular organization.

MEASURE THAT REPRESENTS TOP-MANAGEMENT OBJECTIVES

Role of Investment

What quantitative measure best represents top-management objectives? Income? Rate of return? Some other measure? Many managers are preoccupied with the measures of dollar sales, dollar profits, and profit margins (the ratio of profits to dollar sales). However, the ultimate test of profitability is not the absolute amount of profit or the relationship of profit to sales. The critical test is the relationship of profit to invested capital. The most popular way of expressing this relationship is via a rate of return on investment (ROI). The general concept of ROI is no different from that used for years in the financial markets. The desirability of an investment depends largely on its prospective ROI. If one borrower promises to pay 5 percent interest for a loan of $1,000, and another equally trustworthy borrower promises to pay $6\frac{1}{2}$ percent, the latter investment is deemed more desirable. Similarly, if one division can earn 5 percent on its assets, and another division can earn 9 percent *under comparable conditions,* the latter division is *ordinarily* deemed more efficient and effective.

The major advantage of the ROI technique is its focus on an often neglected phase of management responsibility—the required investment in assets. For a given company at a given time, there is a best level of investment in any asset—whether it be cash, receivables, physical plant, or inventories. Cash balances, for example, may be too large or too small. The principal cost of having too much cash is the sacrifice of possible earnings; idle cash earns nothing. The principal cost of having too little cash may be lost discounts on purchases or harm to one's credit standing. For every class of asset, then, there is an optimum level of investment which, along with optimum levels of investment in other assets, helps to maximize long-run profits.

The ROI measure blends together all the major ingredients of operating management's responsibility. ROI is probably the best single measure of performance. It can be compared with the rates of return of other divisions and with opportunities elsewhere, within or outside the company.

Most managers are well aware of the importance of gross-profit percentages and operating-profit percentages in relation to net sales. However, such percentages, considered by themselves, can be misleading. What counts is total dollar profits and the rate of return on investment:

Pretax operating rate of return
= Capital turnover × Operating margin percentage on sales

Pretax operating rate of return

$$= \frac{\text{Sales}}{\text{Invested capital}} \times \frac{\text{Operating income before interest and income taxes}}{\text{Sales}}$$

$$\text{Pretax operating rate of return} = \frac{\text{Operating income before interest and income taxes}}{\text{Invested capital}}$$

Concentrate on the components of these equations. If the objective is solely to maximize ROI, any action is beneficial which (1) increases sales; (2) decreases invested capital; or (3) decreases costs while holding the other two factors constant. In other words, turnover and margin percentages are the key factors. An improvement in either, without changing the other, will improve the rate of return on invested capital.

General Analytical Uses

Top management may decide upon a 30 percent rate of return as a target that will yield adequate rewards and yet not invite entry into the market by new competitors. How can this new return be achieved? The equations that follow summarize two approaches to the problem. All figures, other than percentages, are in millions of dollars.

	$\dfrac{\text{Sales}}{\text{Invested capital}}$	$\times$	$\dfrac{\begin{array}{c}\text{Operating}\\\text{income before}\\\text{interest and}\\\text{income taxes}\end{array}}{\text{Sales}}$	$=$	$\begin{array}{c}\text{Pretax}\\\text{operating}\\\text{rate of return}\end{array}$
Present outlook	$\dfrac{\$200}{\$50}$	$\times$	$\dfrac{\$14}{\$200}$		$= 14/50,\ \text{or } 28\%$
Alternatives: *A:* Increase margin by reducing expenses	$\dfrac{\$200}{\$50}$	$\times$	$\dfrac{\$15}{\$200}$		$= 15/50,\ \text{or } 30\%$
B: Decrease invested capital	$\dfrac{\$200}{\$46.67}$	$\times$	$\dfrac{\$14}{\$200}$		$= 14/46.67,\ \text{or } 30\%$

Alternative *A* demonstrates a popular way of improving performance. Margins may be increased by reducing expenses, as in this case, or by boosting selling prices.

Alternative *B* shows that controlling investments in assets may also improve performance. This means determining proper inventory levels, managing credit judiciously, and spending carefully on fixed assets. In other words, increasing the turnover of investment often means obtaining the most in dollar sales for every dollar of assets. For example, having too much inventory is sometimes worse than having too little. Turnover decreases and goods deteriorate or become obsolete, thus dragging the rate of return downward.

Let us not overlook the pervasive problem of balancing long-range and short-range goals, which was discussed in Chapter 11. For example, a manager could improve performance in the short run by reducing investment. Nevertheless, in some instances such action may be tantamount to eroding competitive position or liquidating market share. This is one of the toughest problems to solve in designing a control system.

ROI or Residual Income?

Earlier we saw that the ultimate test of profitability is the relationship of profit to invested capital. Until this point, our examples implied that the desired objective of management is the maximization of the rate of return on investment. But an investment center may be judged on what has been labeled *residual income* instead of on its rate of return. Residual income is the operating income of an investment center, less the "imputed" interest on the assets used by the center. The choice of whether to use ROI or residual income as a management objective will induce different decisions.

Compare the calculations for two identical divisions:

	Division A	Division B
(1) Operating income	$ 25,000	$ 25,000
(2) Imputed interest at 16% of assets		16,000
(3) Operating assets	100,000	100,000
ROI [(1) ÷ (3)]	25%	
Residual income [(1) − (2)]		9,000

The objective of maximizing residual income assumes that as long as the division earns a rate in excess of the charge for invested capital, the division should expand. The manager of Division B would expand as long as his incremental opportunities earned 16 percent or more on his incremental assets.

General Electric favors this approach because managers will concentrate on maximizing a number (dollars of residual income) rather than a percentage (rate of return). The objective of maximizing ROI may induce managers of highly profitable divisions to reject projects that, from the viewpoint of the corporation as a whole, should be accepted. For example, the manager of Division *A* would be reluctant to accept a new project with a 20 percent rate even though top management regards 16 percent as a minimum desired rate of return. In such a case, the residual-income approach would charge him 16 percent and he would be inclined to accept all projects that exceed that rate.

There is a parallel between the discounted-cash-flow methods in capital budgeting and the comparison of ROI and residual income. In Chapter 13, comparisons were made between the time-adjusted rate of return and the net present-value methods. The time-adjusted rate of return method is similar to the ROI method, and the net present-value method is similar to the residual-income method. Residual income changes the goal from "maximize ROI" to "maximize dollar return in excess of minimum desired ROI."

DISTINCTION BETWEEN MANAGERS AND INVESTMENTS

As Chapter 11 explained (see Exhibit 11-4), a distinction should be made between the performance of the division manager and the performance of the division as an investment by the corporation. The manager should be evaluated on the basis of his controllable performance (in many cases some controllable contribution in relation to controllable investment). For other decisions, "such as new investment or a withdrawal of funds from the division, the important thing is the success or failure of the divisional venture, not of the men who run it."[2]

This distinction helps clarify some vexing difficulties. For example, top management may want to use an investment base to gauge the eco-

---

[2] David Solomons, *Divisional Performance: Measurement and Control* (Homewood, Ill.: Richard D. Irwin, Inc., 1968), p. 84. Solomons also discusses residual income.

nomic performance of a retail store, but the *manager* may be best judged by focusing on income and forgetting about any investment allocations. If investment is assigned to the manager, the aim should be to assign controllable investment only. Controllability[3] depends on what *decisions* managers can make regarding the size of the investment base. In a highly decentralized company, for instance, the manager can influence the size of all his assets and can exercise judgment regarding the appropriate amount of short-term credit and perhaps some long-term credit.

DEFINITIONS OF INCOME

Contribution Approach

The selection of performance measures requires some concept or definition of income. A contribution approach can help distinguish between the performance of the division and the performance of the manager. Exhibit 11-4 shows a sample approach.

Income taxes are usually deducted for purposes of measuring the performance of the unit as an investment but not ordinarily for purposes of measuring the manager's performance *per se*. Of course, how income taxes are accounted for is highly dependent on who has the responsibility for income tax planning.

As will be explored in a later section called Measurement Alternatives, there is more to the issue of defining income than merely whether the contribution approach should be used. A more basic question is whether any form of historical-cost-related income should be used.

Allocating Costs and Assets to Divisions

Cost allocations affect income, and investment allocations affect rates of return. Chapter 11 concentrated on the problem of cost allocation, and the points made there apply also to the problems of asset allocation. Again, the aim is to allocate in a manner that will be goal-congruent, will provide incentive, and will recognize autonomy insofar as possible. Incidentally, as long as the managers feel that they are being treated uniformly, they tend to be more tolerant about the imperfections of the allocation. For example, should cash be included under controllable investment if the balances are strictly controlled by corporate headquarters? Arguments can be made for both sides, but the manager is usually regarded as being responsible for the volume of business generated by the division. In turn, this volume is likely to have a direct effect on the overall cash needs of the corporation.

A frequent criterion for allocation is avoidability. That is, the

---

[3]See Chapter 11 for an expanded discussion of controllability.

amount allocable to any given segment for the purpose of evaluating the division's performance is the amount that the corporation as a whole could avoid by not having that segment. Commonly used bases for allocation, when assets are not directly identifiable with a specific division, include:

Asset Class	*Possible Allocation Base*
Corporate cash	Budgeted cash needs
Receivables	Sales weighted by payment terms
Inventories	Budgeted sales or usage
Plant and equipment	Usage of services in terms of long-run forecasts of demand or area occupied

Where the allocation of an asset (such as central corporate facilities) would indeed be arbitrary, many managers feel that it is better not to allocate.

DEFINITIONS OF INVESTMENT

Possible Investment Bases

The base that is used for measuring invested capital may appropriately differ between companies and within segments of the same company. The alternative bases that may be used include:

1. **Total assets available.** This base includes all business assets, regardless of their individual purpose.

2. **Total assets employed.** This base excludes excess or idle assets, such as vacant land or construction in progress.

3. **Net working capital plus other assets.** This base is really the same as in part (1), except that current liabilities are deducted from the total assets available. In a sense, this represents an exclusion of that portion of current assets which is supplied by short-term creditors. The main justification for this base is that the manager often does have direct influence over the amount of short-term credit that he utilizes. An able manager should maximize the use of such credit, within some overall constraints to prevent endangering the company's credit standing.

4. **Stockholders' equity.** This base centers attention on the rate of return that will be earned by the business owners.

Comparison of Investment Bases

A possible base is stockholders' equity. Such a base is important to the owners, but it is not so significant to the operating manager. He is usually concerned with the utilization of assets, not with the long-term sources of assets. Business has two major management functions—operating and financing—and measurement of operating performance (how available assets are employed) should not be influenced by financing decisions (what sources of assets were selected). It would be invalid, for example, to use stockholders' equity as a basis for comparing the operating performance of two managers of similar companies, if one company is debt-free and the other debt-ridden.

For measuring the performance of division managers, one of the three asset bases listed above is almost always superior to stockholders' equity. If the division manager's mission is to utilize all assets as best he can without regard to their financing, then (1) is best. If top management directives force him to carry extra assets which are not currently productive, then (2) is best. If he has direct control over the amount of the division's short-term trade credit and bank loans, then (3) is best. In practice, (1) is used most often, although (3) is not far behind.[4] The figure used for total available assets should be the average amount during the period under review. This average might be computed by summing the beginning and ending balances and dividing by two; in other instances, a moving or weighted average may be needed to achieve accuracy.

MEASUREMENT ALTERNATIVES

Why Historical Cost?

How should we measure the assets that are included in the investment base? Should assets be valued at net book value, replacement cost, realizable value, or some other value? There is a propensity to have one investment measure serve many masters. Therefore, net book value[5] predominates, but its prevalence does not mean that it is necessarily correct. Of course, the correct but unsatisfying answer is: The relevant value depends on the decisions being affected and evaluated. These decisions often concern the evaluation of performance. They are decisions about the wisdom of past decisions; they require a follow-up of the historical cost and the predictions that were related thereto.

The use of traditional historical-cost-based-accounting measurements is subject to all the criticisms usually leveled at such practices, in-

[4]John J. Mauriel and Robert N. Anthony, "Misevaluation of Investment Center Performance," *Harvard Business Review* (March–April, 1966), pp. 98–105, summarize the practices of 2,658 companies. Forty-one percent deducted current external payables in arriving at the investment base.

[5]Mauriel and Anthony, *op. cit.,* report that 73 percent of the companies used net book value as their valuation measure and 18 percent used gross book value. Only 3 percent of the companies used some measure that departs from cost, such as insurance value or appraisal value.

cluding the overemphasis on short-run results and the ignoring of general and specific price-level changes.

Company accounting policies will have a telling impact on the amount of assets included in the investment base. For example, the variety of methods of accounting for inventories, leased assets, research, depreciation, patents, secret processes, trademarks, and advertising will have an important influence on the asset base.

Given the frequently cited infirmities of historical cost, why do organizations continue to use it for evaluating performance? There are several reasons. Some seem unjustifiable, while others make sense. Ignorance and inertia have been cited as two likely reasons. But overcoming ignorance is not costless. The basic job of control systems is to supply information. Information is gathered at a cost. The manager (and the accountant) must decide whether to seek (buy) more information. Numbers are routinely provided as clues regarding whether to buy more or "better" information. Most managers apparently have decided that a historical-cost system is good enough for the *routine* evaluation of managers—for providing feedback that will have the desired motivational effects and that will give clues to whether to invest or disinvest in a particular division. The investment decision is not made in a routine manner; therefore, it may be uneconomical to gather information on replacement costs or realizable value except as special needs arise. In other words, a system may be designed to help in the routine evaluation of managers, but the information that will provide for the evaluation of subunits as economic investments may be too expensive to collect repetitively.

Alternatives to Historical Cost

The weaknesses of historical cost are well-known (for examples, see Chapter 12). Are there some alternative measures that are superior, at least conceptually? The answer is yes, but the relevant measure depends on the particular decisions to be made or evaluated. Moreover, there are many alternative measures including:

1. **Present value.** The sum of the expected future cash flows discounted back to the current date at the appropriate rate of interest.

2. **Economic value.** The present value of an asset in existing use or contemplated use.

3. **Opportunity value.** The present value of the perceived "next-best" alternative use.

4. **Disposal value or exit value.** The value upon immediate sale, which may or may not be the next-best alternative.

5. **Replacement value or entry value.** Today's cost of obtaining similar assets that would produce the *same* expected operating cash flow as the existing asset.

Many terms are loosely used. Note particularly that *current value* and *market value* should be avoided because they are ambiguous in the literature and in discussions.

Suppose a division acquires new manufacturing equipment for $5 million. The equipment could be sold for perhaps $4 million on the day after installation. What value should be used for deciding whether to sell or hold the asset? How should the equipment be valued for measuring performance in Year 1? In Year 3? In Year 10?

If the manager examines an existing investment, he often considers three alternatives that may be likened to investments in securities. The economic value is always needed for these decisions. The required data are:

Disposal *(Sell)*	*Continuance* *(Hold)*	*Expansion* *(Buy More)*
Economic value compared to Disposal value	Economic value compared to Disposal value	Economic value compared to Required investment

In the example, the chances are high that the economic value exceeds the disposal value of $4 million. Moreover, the economic value must exceed the cost of $5 million for the investment to be profitable.

To evaluate economic performance, ideally the measure would be the change in economic value for a given span of time. Because economic value is difficult to determine objectively, replacement value is often accepted as a substitute. Although replacement value often is an objective way to evaluate subunit performance in an economic sense, managers frequently object to its use for evaluating their performance. Their decisions may not have nearly as much effect as outside forces on economic value or replacement value.

In any event, whether to use replacement costs or historical costs for routinely evaluating performance is essentially a cost and value of information decision. The systems designer and top management must decide if the extra time, trouble, and expense of evaluating performance based on replacement costs will generate sufficient benefits in the form of better incentives (motivation) and decisions than under an existing historical-cost system. A major part of an effort to use some nonhistorical-cost system is education, which is tremendously expensive.

Plant and Equipment: Gross or Net?

Because historical-cost investment measures are used most often in practice, there has been much discussion[6] about the relative merits of using

[6] *Return on Capital as a Guide to Managerial Decisions,* National Association of Accountants, Research Report No. 35, and David Solomons, *Divisional Performance,* pp. 134–42.

undepreciated cost (gross value) or net book value. Those who favor using gross assets claim that it facilitates comparisons among plants and divisions. If income decreases as a plant ages, the decline in earning power will be made evident, while the constantly decreasing net book value will reflect a possibly deceptive higher rate of return in later years. For this reason, du Pont and Monsanto use gross book value as a measure of their fixed assets when they compute rate of return. Eighteen percent of the companies surveyed[7] use gross book value.

One reason often cited for using undepreciated cost is that it partially compensates for the impact of the changing price level on historical cost. However, if a company desires to use replacement cost as a base, it should face the problem squarely by using appraisal values or specific price indexes. Reliance on gross book value is an unreliable means of approximating replacement value.

Solomons comments on the gross versus net book value debate:

> There is something inherently strange about the view that it is right to include fixed assets in a balance sheet at their depreciated value, but wrong to include them in a computation of capital at that value. The only reason for holding such a view is the irrational behavior of ROI when fixed assets are taken at book value rather than at cost. The proper remedy is to be found in the use of a compound interest method of depreciation, not in the abandonment of book value as a basis for valuing investment. If depreciation were handled in a theoretically correct manner (i.e., by the compound interest method), the decline in the book value of depreciating assets would not of itself disturb the stability of ROI.[8]

The proponents of using net book value as a measure maintain that it is less confusing because (a) it is consistent with the total assets shown on the conventional balance sheet, and (b) it is consistent with net income computations, which include deductions for depreciation. The major criticism of net book value is not peculiar to its use for ROI purposes. The critics say that historical cost does not represent a current economic sacrifice and is useless for making decisions about allocations of resources. On the other hand, as the appendix explains, if net book value is used in a manner that is consistent with the planning model, it can be useful for auditing past decisions and it might suffice for incentive purposes.

CHOOSING DESIRED RATES OF RETURN

Whatever their merits, neither the ROI nor the residual-income method avoids the question of cost of capital. The critical questions are (a) what minimum rates to specify; (b) when and by how much minimum rates should be altered; and (c) whether the same minimum rates should be

---

[7] Mauriel and Anthony, "Misevaluation," p. 101.

[8] David Solomons, *Divisional Performance,* p. 135. He discusses these issues at length on pp. 134–42.

used in each segment of the organization. If a uniform rate is used and many divisions are currently earning different rates, the use of a very low rate will surely drive ROI down toward such a rate. Moreover, frequent changes in the rate may be demoralizing as well as nonoptimal. For example, it might lead to acceptance of an 11 percent prospective return when the minimum rate is 11 percent, and rejection of a 15 percent prospective rate when the minimum rate is 16 percent.

Modern financial theory supports the use of different rates for different divisions.[9] Portfolio theory provides the analytical framework for the investment decision under uncertainty. The firm would be viewed as a collection of different classes of assets whose income streams bear different risks. The minimum desired rates of return are functions of risk. Various divisions face different risks. Therefore, a different minimum desired rate should be used for each division, based on the relative investment risks of each.

The use of different required rates for different divisions is apparently not widespread. The most extensive survey of practice in this area indicated an overwhelming tendency to use the same required rate for all divisions and for all classes of assets.[10] The use of uniform rates is probably attributable to the attitude that managers must be treated fairly (or uniformly unfairly). In this context, fairness means that the same required rate should apply to all divisions. Moreover, even the uniform use of different rates for different classes of assets (that is, one rate for investments in current assets and another rate for plant assets) may be perceived as unfair if divisions have different compositions of such assets.

The foregoing was a description of a central problem in guiding decisions and evaluating performance. Unfortunately, there is no pat solution. Researchers in economics and finance continue to quarrel about these issues. For our purposes, we explore the design of accounting systems given minimum required rates of return, however determined.

ALTERNATIVES OF TIMING

Accounting textbooks, including this one, do not discuss at length the problem of timing. However, timing is an important factor to consider when an information system is designed. For instance, the costs of gathering and processing information and the need for frequent feedback for controlling current operations may lead to using historical-cost measures rather than replacement costs. The need for replacement costs, realizable

---

[9]For a presentation of modern financial theory as it relates to accounting, see Ray Ball and Phillip Brown, "Portfolio Theory and Accounting," *Journal of Accounting Research,* Vol. 7, No. 2 (Autumn 1969), 300–323. They state (p. 313), "Thus there is some foundation to the practice of requiring different rates of return from different divisions, and similar rates from within each division.

[10]Mauriel and Anthony, in "Misevaluation," report that only 7 percent of the 258 respondents to this question used different rates.

values, and economic values tends to be less frequent, so the systems are not designed for providing such information routinely.

Admittedly, this point was made earlier in the chapter. Nevertheless, it is repeated here because it is a likely explanation of why actual practice seems to differ so markedly from what theory may prefer. The essence of the matter is that management seems unwilling to pay for more elegant information because its extra costs exceed its prospective benefits.

TRANSFER PRICING

Objectives of Transfer Pricing

Goods and services are often exchanged between various subunits. The value ascribed to these goods and services is often termed a transfer price. Although transfer prices are most often associated with profit centers, the allocation of service-department costs to production departments is really a form of transfer pricing.

How do you judge whether a transfer-pricing scheme can be improved? An earlier section proposed three criteria: goal congruence, performance evaluation, and autonomy. The goal is to have transfer prices impel subunit managers toward top-management goals. As you might expect, each criterion may conflict with the others. For example, there is a pervasive temptation to direct a manager from above in order to assure optimal decisions; but such direction undercuts the freedom of individual managers.

Market Prices

In many cases, market price is the most desirable transfer price because it fulfills all three criteria. The guidelines are: (a) a market or negotiated market price should be used; (b) the seller should have the option of not selling internally (because he may have more profitable opportunities for using his facilities to sell other products); and (c) an arbitration procedure should be available for settling disputes.

Where the intermediate market is competitive and where interdependencies of subunits are minimal, market prices typically establish the ceiling for transfer pricing. In many instances, a lower price may easily be justified, particularly when large purchases are made, when selling costs are less, or when an advantage is obtained through an exclusive supplier contract or through a cost-plus arrangement assuring profits in all cases. These situations lead to the notion of negotiated market prices, whereby the cost savings to the firm as a whole are split between the selling and buying divisions through bargaining.

Arbitrating or umpiring is sometimes necessary. However, its frequent use indicates a step toward centralization, because it usually elevates the decision to a representative of the organization as a whole.

Consequently, too much reliance on arbitration indicates the inability of the division managers to operate smoothly on a decentralized basis.

Many product parts are unique, a situation that causes considerable costs for preparing bids. If an outside supplier prepares a few bids and discovers that the internal supplier division always wins, the so-called resulting market prices either will not be forthcoming in the future or will be unreliable (and perhaps artificially high; after all, the bidder may submit a high price with little effort). Some companies deliberately purchase from outside suppliers to maintain alternate sources of supply and to provide a valid check on market prices.

The trouble with the use of market price is either that few markets are perfectly competitive or that no intermediate market exists for the exact product or service in question. A quoted price for a product is strictly comparable only if the credit terms, grade, quality, delivery terms, and auxiliary services are precisely the same. Moreover, isolated price quotations are sometimes temporary distress or dumping prices. Such prices can seldom be used as a basis for long-range planning, although they may be appropriate for monitoring short-term performance. In nearly all cases, however, temporary market prices are not applicable for repetitive, high-volume transactions, and they hurt the credibility of the so-called market transfer prices.

Inapplicability of Market Prices

The problems in transfer pricing would be trivial if the intermediate market price were widely applicable. But, too often, the intermediate markets are nonexistent, ill-structured, or imperfect. Furthermore, using market prices may be too costly strictly in terms of the need for the routine processing of market data. Therefore, market price is a special case rather than a universal guide.

Above all, transfer prices must be judged by using the three criteria simultaneously rather than one at a time. The answers are not ordinarily generated by economic analysis alone as it applies to a particular decision situation. For example, economic analysis can demonstrate that if no intermediate market exists, the correct transfer price is marginal cost. But division managers of supplying divisions are not gleeful about transferring at marginal cost because it does not enhance their measure of divisional performance and it impinges on their autonomy. The point is that forced transfers at a perceived economic-optimum transfer price may hurt the credibility of the overall decentralized system and may impede the obtaining of other wanted benefits.

As soon as alternate uses for capacity are considered, the transfer-pricing mechanism gets complicated. In practice, simple rules tend to be used (market, negotiated market, standard cost plus some markup) and unusual cases are negotiated. Whether such simplicity is optimal depends on the existence of profit opportunities and interdependencies among the segments of the company. The more opportunities and interdependencies, the more likely is the need for centralized control.

No Intermediate Market

Sometimes, specialized product components are not readily salable to or available from intermediate markets. In these cases, the economic interests of the organization as a whole are best served by transfers at the additional outlay costs of bringing the units to the point of transfer. In the short run, this is frequently approximated by so-called variable or marginal costs. However, the applicability of marginal cost is not widespread. The assumption of "no intermediate market" is a strong one and is indeed rare; conceivably, there is almost always the possibility of getting a part made to order on the outside. Moreover, even when there are idle facilities, there is almost always the alternative of using the facilities for making some other product. Still, let us examine the problem, because managers often perceive their situations as those of having no intermediate market, and they act accordingly.

An example may clarify the issue. Suppose that Supplier Division A is a profit center that sells a variety of products inside and outside the company. Suppose further that there is idle capacity and that Product X is a component of a finished product made by Division B. There is no intermediate market for Product X. Finally, suppose the variable cost of X is \$1, its full absorption cost is \$1.50, and Division A has an average markup on all its products of 60 percent of absorption cost.

Note the dilemma here. To benefit the organization as a whole, the supplying division should transfer the intermediate good at variable cost, because variable cost is the information needed for deciding on how many finished units should be produced. As the manager of the supplying division, how would you feel about such a rule? Unless you were totally generous, you probably would not be willing to transfer at a price of \$1. After all, the production of this part is essential to the overall company profit, so you are entitled to a share of that profit. In short, the transfer price of \$1 may seemingly be goal-congruent for the organization as a whole, but it may not lead to the wanted decisions because it fails to meet the other two criteria of performance evaluation and autonomy.

Dual Pricing

The dilemma may be met in various ways. The interdependence of the two divisions regarding this product may be overtly recognized by making a centralized decision and imposing the \$1 transfer price. In effect, this approach jettisons decentralization, at least for transactions in this product. Because most organizations are hybrids of centralization and decentralization anyway, this approach deserves serious consideration where such transfers are significant.

Alternatively, the seeming harshness of the foregoing authoritarian approach can be modified if organizations recognize that there is no necessity to have a *single* transfer price. The profit-center concept can be preserved more easily if one transfer price is used for one purpose (making the economic decision) and another for a second purpose (evaluation of performance). In our example, such a dual-pricing scheme could result in the transfer price to Division B being $1, while Division A is given credit for a synthetic market price of perhaps $2.40 ($1.50 plus 60 percent). Under this scheme, each division's performance would be enhanced by the transfer, and the $1 transfer price to Division B would induce the Division B manager to make the correct economic decisions from the viewpoint of the organization as a whole. Note that this dual-pricing plan essentially gives Division A a corporate subsidy. The profit for the company as a whole will be less than the sum of the divisional profits. Suppose that 100,000 units are transferred:

	Division A	
Sales to B @ $2.40	$240,000	
Variable costs @ $1.00	100,000	
Contribution	$140,000	

	Division B	
Sales of finished product @ $5		$500,000
Variable costs:		
Division A @ $1	$100,000	
Division B @ $3	300,000	400,000
Contribution		$100,000

Note that the contribution to the corporation as a whole is $100,000.

Prorating the Overall Contribution

If a dual transfer-pricing plan is unattractive because of its strangeness or for some other reason, another possibility is to impose a variable-cost transfer price but credit each division for a prorated share of the overall contribution to corporate profit. Suppose that 100,000 units were in question:

Sales of finished product @ $5		$500,000
Division A @ $1	$100,000	
Division B @ $3	300,000	400,000
Contribution to corporate profit		$100,000

The proration would probably be negotiated in any number of ways. Suppose that it were in proportion to the standard-variable costs incurred by each division. Then Division A would get credited for $25,000 and Division B for $75,000. In this way, Division A would be willing to transfer at $1, knowing that the transfers would somehow improve its showing as a profit center. Essentially, this is a standard-variable–cost-plus transfer-pricing system; the "plus" is a function of the overall contribution to corporate profit.

Imperfect Markets

Imperfect competition exists when one seller or buyer, *acting alone,* can exert an influence on the market price. If the intermediate market is imperfectly competitive, additional volume can be obtained only if selling prices are lowered. This means that the existing market price at a particular volume level is no longer applicable for the decision regarding how much to produce and sell. The additions to revenue will be less than the sales of the additional units at the new selling price because the new lower price will apply to the entire volume. For example, suppose the current selling price is $1 per unit and 80,000 units are being sold. The revenue is $80,000. A cut in price from $1 to $.90 may increase unit sales to 90,000. The increase in revenue is (10,000 × $.90) minus (80,000 × $.10, the loss in revenue on the 80,000 units), or $1,000. In these situations, the analyses can become exceedingly complex. The optimal transfer price from the viewpoint of the corporation as a whole is different for each situation, depending on the existence of cost interdependencies and demand interdependencies. An example of a cost interdependency is the case where the price of a certain raw material may be dependent on the total purchases by two or more divisions. An example of a demand interdependency is any vertically integrated operation where there is no intermediate market for a unique component part of a finished product. Then the total number of finished products sold is dependent on the total number of components available, and vice versa. The interests of the corporation as a whole are paramount, and where interdependencies are large, decentralization may be a nonoptimal form of organization.

Full-Cost Bases

There are no recent surveys of actual practices in transfer pricing. However, the use of full cost-plus is widespread. The intermediate transfers of products on the basis of accumulated cost typically mean that the supplying divisions are really cost centers rather than profit centers. If the transfers are based on actual costs, the performance of the receiving divisions would bear the accumulated efficiencies or inefficiencies of other divisions not subject to their control. Transfer prices that insure recovery of actual costs often fail to provide an incentive to control costs; therefore, some version of standard or budgeted costs is better than actual costs because it gives incentive to control costs.

Full standard costs may minimize the problem of inefficiency, but may lead to suboptimal decisions. For example, Division *A* may supply parts to Division *B* at a standard cost of $5, including a charge of $3 for fixed costs based on some normal activity level. (There may also be some "plus" added in a cost-plus transfer-pricing system.) Suppose that *A* and *B* have idle capacity and *B* has additional processing and selling costs of $4 per unit. *B* can obtain additional revenue of $8 per unit. *B* would refuse, because its performance would worsen at the rate of $1 per unit:

	Division B Performance	
Additional revenue		$8
Additional costs:		
Transfer price from *A*	$5	
Additional costs in *B*	4	9
Additional loss		−$1

But the entity as a whole would benefit:

	Entire Entity	
Additional revenue		$8
Additional costs:		
A	$2	
B	4	6
Additional profit		$2

This is a clear example of goal incongruence that is induced by a transfer price based on so-called full or average total costs. The transfer-pricing scheme has led *B* to regard the fixed costs in *A* as variable costs. From the viewpoint of the firm as a whole, this may lead to dysfunctional decisions.

Cost-Plus as a Synthetic Market Price

Despite the obvious limitations of the approach, transfer prices based on full cost, or on full cost plus some markup, are in common use. A major reason for the wide use of cost-based transfer pricing is its clarity and convenience. Moreover, the transferred product or service in question is often slightly different in quality or other characteristics from that available from outside sources. As a result, cost-plus pricing is often viewed as yielding a "satisfactory" approximation of an outside market price. Therefore, the resulting synthetic market price is regarded as a good practical substitute that is acceptable for both economic decisions and performance evaluation. The alternative—getting "real" market prices— is perceived as being too costly for incorporating into a routine control system.

Variable Cost Plus Lump Sum

Top management often wants the buyer-division manager to make month-to-month purchasing decisions based on the variable costs of the supplier division. Otherwise, as the example in the preceding section showed, the buyer division may be led toward the wrong decision. One way to satisfy the needs of the two divisions and the company as a whole is to transfer at a standard-variable cost. A separate predetermined lump-sum charge is made for fixed costs plus a lump-sum profit; this charge may be made annually or monthly. It is based on an annual expectation, not on actual purchases. In any event, the buyer's month-to-month decisions are not influenced by the supplier's fixed costs or the supplier's profit. Note that except for the profit, this was the approach recommended in Chapter 11 for the reallocation of service-department costs to operating departments.

THE NEED FOR MANY TRANSFER PRICES

Previous sections have already pointed out that there is seldom a single transfer price that will meet the three criteria that will induce the desired decisions. The "correct" transfer price depends on the economic and legal circumstances and the decision at hand. We may want one transfer price for motivation and a second for evaluation. Furthermore, the optimal price for either may differ from that employed for tax reporting or for other external needs.

Income taxes, property taxes, and tariffs often influence the setting of transfer prices so that the firm as a whole will benefit, even though the performance of a subunit may suffer under this set of prices. To minimize tariffs and domestic income taxes, a company may want to set an unusually low selling price for a domestic division that ships goods to foreign subsidiaries in countries where the prevailing tax rates are lower. To maximize tax deductions for percentage depletion allowances, which are based on revenue, a petroleum company may want to transfer crude oil to other subunits at as high a price as possible. As somebody in the oil industry once said, "Only fools and subsidiaries pay posted prices."

Transfer pricing is also influenced in some situations because of state fair-trade laws and national antitrust acts. Because of the differences in national tax structures around the world or because of the differences in the incomes of various divisions and subsidiaries, the firm may wish to shift profits and "dump" goods, if legally possible. These considerations are additional illustrations of the limits of decentralization where heavy interdependencies exist and of why the same company may use different transfer prices for different purposes.

WHY PROFIT CENTERS?

At this point, after studying all the weaknesses of profit centers and transfer prices, readers often jump to the conclusion that organizations should stay heavily centralized and use nothing fancier than flexible budgets. However, the conceptual perfection of a particular transfer price or profit center may be unimportant. Given our objectives, we seek the best feasible system in a specific organization.

As firms expand, control systems usually grow from systems of sheer physical observation, to simple historical recordkeeping, to static budgets, to flexible budgets and standards, and finally to some form of profit-center accounting. As these systems evolve, they usually build on one another. For example, a profit-center system often also has flexible budgets and standards.

Again and again, organizations have found flexible budgets and cost centers insufficient. These systems are a good first step, but profit centers and cost-plus transfer pricing have evolved in response to a need for more incentive toward top-management goals. For example, some top managers have found that cost-center managers aim at meeting a budget and keeping costs under control, and nothing more. When the cost centers are changed into profit centers, perhaps transferring goods at merely cost-plus prices, subunit managers continue to worry about costs, but they start worrying also about boosting production and about possible marketing needs. In these situations, nobody pretends that the "profit center" is an independent unit, but top managers often obtain the wanted goal congruence through profit centers more readily than through cost centers.

SUMMARY

As organizations grow, decentralization of some management functions becomes desirable. Decentralization immediately raises problems of obtaining decisions that are coordinated with the objectives of the organization as a whole. Ideally, planning and control systems should provide information that (a) aims managers toward decisions that are goal-congruent, (b) provides feedback (evaluation of performance) that improves incentive and future decisions, and (c) preserves autonomy. Note that the common thread of these criteria is motivation.

Many techniques like ROI or residual income fall far short of the ideal goals stipulated above. Nevertheless, in practice their conceptual shortcomings may be unimportant; often they are the best techniques available for obtaining the perceived top-management goals.

Despite the theoretical attractiveness of various nonhistorical-accounting methods, most managements have apparently decided that a historical-cost system is good enough for the *routine* evaluation of managers. Evidently, this crude approach provides the desired motivational effects and gives clues as to whether to invest or disinvest in a particular division. The investment decision is evidently not routine enough to justify gathering information regarding replacement costs or realizable values except as special needs arise.

Transfer-pricing systems are needed if decentralization is to be established in companies whose divisions exchange goods and services. Some version of market price as a transfer price will often best motivate managers toward optimal economic decisions; moreover, the evaluation of performance will then be consistent with the ideas of decentralization.

There is rarely a single transfer price that will serve all needs. Instead, there may be one transfer price for making a particular production decision, another for evaluating performance, and another for minimizing tariffs or income taxes.

Economic analysis can demonstrate that market price is not always the best guide to optimal decisions. In such instances, some centralization of control is needed to prevent dysfunctional decisions. If so, serious thought should be given to whether profit centers and decentralization provide the optimum organizational design. Above all, the perceived costs and benefits at alternative levels of decentralization should be explicitly considered when choosing a transfer-pricing scheme.

SUMMARY PROBLEMS FOR YOUR REVIEW

Problem One

You are given the following data regarding budgeted operations of a company division:

Average available assets:	
Receivables	$100,000
Inventories	300,000
Plant and equipment, net	200,000
	$600,000
Fixed overhead	$200,000
Variable costs	$1 per unit
Desired rate of return on average available assets	25%
Expected volume	100,000 units

Required:

1. a. What average unit sales price is needed to obtain the desired rate of return on average available assets?
   b. What would be the expected turnover of assets?
   c. What would be the net income percentage on dollar sales?
2. a. What rate of return would be earned on available assets if sales volume is 120,000 units?
   b. If sales volume is 80,000 units?
3. Assume that 30,000 units are to be sold to another division of the same company. The other division manager has balked at a tentative selling price of $4. He has offered $2.25, claiming that he can manufacture the units himself for that price. The manager of the selling division has examined his own data. He has decided that he could eliminate $40,000 of inventories, $60,000 of plant and equipment, and $20,000 of fixed overhead if he did not sell to the other division. Should he sell for $2.25? Show computations to support your answer.

Problem Two

A division has assets of $200,000 and operating income of $60,000.

1. What is the division's ROI?

2. If interest is imputed at 14 percent, what is the residual income?
3. What effects on management behavior can be expected if ROI is used to gauge performance?
4. What effects on management behavior can be expected if residual income is used to gauge performance?

Solution to Problem One

1. a. 25 percent of $600,000 = $150,000 target net income.

   Let X = Unit sales price
   Dollar sales = Variable expenses + Fixed expenses + Net income
   $100,000X$ = $100,000 ($1) + $200,000 + $150,000

$$X = \frac{\$450,000}{100,000} = \$4.50$$

   b. Expected asset turnover = $\dfrac{\$450,000}{\$600,000}$ = .75

   c. Net income percentage on dollar sales = $\dfrac{\$150,000}{\$450,000}$ = $33\frac{1}{3}$ percent

2. (a) and (b)

	Sales Volume		
Units	100,000*	120,000	80,000
Sales, @ $4.50	$450,000	$540,000	$360,000
Variable expenses, @ $1.00	$100,000	$120,000	$ 80,000
Fixed expenses	200,000	200,000	200,000
Total expenses	$300,000	$320,000	$280,000
Net income	$150,000	$220,000	$ 80,000
Rate of return on $600,000 assets	25.0%	36.7%	13.3%

*Column not required.

A summary analysis of these three cases, in equation form, follows:

	Net income percentage on sales	× Turnover	= Rate of return
Volume 100,000:	33.3%	× .75	= 25.0%
Volume 120,000:	40.7%	× .90	= 36.7%*
Volume 80,000:	22.2%	× .60	= 13.3%*

*Rounded.

3. Average available assets would decrease by $100,000, from $600,000 to $500,000. Fixed overhead would be $180,000, $200,000 − $20,000. Results would be:

	Sell 70,000 units	*Sell 100,000 units*	*Difference*
Sales, 70,000 units @ $4.50 and 30,000 @ $2.25	$315,000	$382,500	$67,500
Variable expenses, @ $1.00	$ 70,000	$100,000	$30,000
Fixed expenses	180,000	200,000	20,000
Total expenses	$250,000	$300,000	$50,000
Net income	$ 65,000	$ 82,500	$17,500
Rate of return on $500,000 and $600,000 assets, respectively	13.0%	13.7%	.7%

Based on the information given, he should sell at the $2.25 price. Both divisions and the company as a whole will benefit from such a decision. Although the original overall target rate of return of 25 percent is unattainable, the division will nevertheless earn a better rate of return with the intracompany business than without it. The additional units will earn an *incremental* rate of return which exceeds the 13.0 percent rate earned on 70,000 units. This incremental rate would be 17.5 percent (the additional net income of $17,500 divided by the additional investment of $100,000), and the overall rate of return would increase from 13.0 percent to 13.7 percent, as shown in the schedule above.

Despite this economic analysis, the manager may still decide against transferring goods at such a low price. For example, he may feel entitled to a higher profit. This would mean that the company would undoubtedly be worse off if the incremental costs of the other division are $2.25. Should top management interfere and force a transfer of $2.25? Such intervention would weaken the decentralization structure. Obviously, authoritarian action sometimes may be needed to prevent costly mistakes. But recurring interference and constraints simply transform a decentralized organization into a centralized organization. Of course, if managers repeatedly make costly dysfunctional decisions, the costs of decentralization may exceed the benefits. Then a more centralized organizational design may be desirable.

Solution to Problem Two

1. $60,000 ÷ $200,000 = 30%
2. $60,000 − .14($200,000) = $32,000
3. If ROI is used, the manager is prone to reject projects that do not earn an ROI of at least 30 percent. From the viewpoint of the organization as a whole, this may be undesirable because its best investment opportunities may lie in that division at a rate of, say, 22 percent. If a division is enjoying a high ROI, it is less likely to expand if it is judged via ROI than if it is judged via residual income.
4. If residual income is used, the manager is inclined to accept all projects whose expected ROI exceeds the minimum desired rate. His division is more likely to expand, because his goal is to maximize a dollar amount rather than a rate.

Need for Consistency Between Models

Ideally, the decision model used to make a capital-investment decision and the model used to judge subsequent performance would be consistent. However, in practice, we often find discounted-cash-flow (DCF) models being used for investment decisions and the accrual-accounting models being used for performance evaluation.

This conflict of models may lead to dysfunctional decisions. Managers are sometimes reluctant to make capital outlays that are justified by DCF methods but that lead to poor performance records in the first year or two after the outlay. This is especially likely if the outlay is subject to immediate write-off (for instance, product advertising, engineering development, and process improvement costs) or to accelerated-depreciation methods.

Compound Interest and Compatibility

How can compatibility be achieved? As explained in Chapter 13, DCF methods assume a capital-recovery factor that is related to funds in use. Suppose a company is considering investing in a project with a two-year life and no salvage value. Cash inflow will be equal payments of $4,000 at the end of each of the two years. If the company paid $7,132 for the project, present-value tables would reveal its time-adjusted rate of return as 8 percent. Each cash payment consists of "interest" (rate of return) plus recovery of principal.

Year	Investment at Beginning of Year	Operating Cash Inflow	(Interest) Return @ 8% per Year	(Depreciation) Amount of Investment Received at End of Year	(Net Book Value) Unrecovered Investment at End of Year
1	$7,132	$4,000	.08 × $7,132 = $571	$4,000 − $571 = $3,429	$7,132 − $3,429 = $3,703
2	3,703	4,000	.08 × $3,703 = $297	$4,000 − $297 = $3,703	$3,703 − $3,703 = 0

If subsequent performance were the same as had been forecast, the income statement based on the DCF model would be as shown in the first two columns on p. 546. For comparison, the results of using other depreciation methods are also shown.

The compound-interest method results in an increasing charge for depreciation over the useful life of the asset. But it does provide for a rate of return that dovetails with the assumptions in the DCF model. The comparison above shows how the commonly used depreciation models of

	Method of Depreciation					
	Compound-Interest		*Straight-Line*		*Sum-of-Years'-Digits*	
Year	1	2	1	2	1	2
Cash operating income	$4,000	$4,000	$4,000	$4,000	$4,000	$4,000
Depreciation	3,429[a]	3,703[a]	3,566[b]	3,566[b]	4,755[c]	2,377[c]
Net income	$ 571	$ 297	$ 434	$ 434	$(755)	$1,623
Investment base— beginning balance	$7,132	$3,703	$7,132	$3,566	$7,132	$2,377
Rate of return on beginning balance	8%	8%	6%	12%	−11%	68%

[a]See preceding table for computations.
[b]$7,132 ÷ 2 = $3,566 per year.
[c]Sum of digits = 1 + 2 = 3. Therefore, ⅔ × $7,132 = $4,755 for first year and ⅓ × $7,132 = $2,377 for second year.

accrual accounting procedure varying rates of return that have no relation to the DCF planning models.[11]

A residual-income approach to the compound-interest method would show:

	Year			
	1		*2*	
Cash operating income		$4,000		$4,000
Depreciation (based on original expectations)	$3,429		$3,703	
Imputed interest (at minimum desired rate)	571	4,000	297	4,000
		$ 0		$ 0

This example assumes that the 8 percent rate of return on this project is equal to the minimum desired rate that would be used in charging the division for its capital and in the computing of depreciation. Any cash flow that increased the rate of return would result in positive residual income. Assume that the cash flow was $4,500 and $3,800, respectively:

	Year			
	1		*2*	
Cash operating income		$4,500		$3,800
Depreciation (based on original expectations)	$3,429		$3,703	
Imputed interest	571	4,000	297	4,000
Residual income		$ 500		$−200

[11] For an elaboration of the differences, see Ezra Solomon, "Alternative Rate of Return Concepts and Their Implications for Utility Regulation," *The Bell Journal of Economics and Management Science,* Vol. 1, No. 1 (Spring 1970), 65–81.

Industry has rejected the compound-interest method of depreciation primarily because:

1. It usually produces an increasing charge over the useful life of an asset. Intuitively, however, managers do not see the justification for an increasing charge for depreciation if cash flows remain constant or decline.

2. The compound-interest method works clearly if projected annual operating cash flows are reasonably equal, but the implicit principal-recovery pattern is more difficult to compute and explain if projected cash flows differ markedly through the years.

3. The market values of particular assets do not coincide with the book values, particularly in the early years of use.

Until formal attempts are made to reconcile DCF models for planning with accrual-accounting models for control,[12] follow-up of investment decisions must rely on the sampling of projects or on a dual-planning scheme. In sampling, DCF decisions would be audited by gathering data, year by year, to see whether the specific cash-flow predictions proved accurate. In dual planning, the DCF decision would simultaneously be cast in the form of an accrual-accounting rate-of-return prediction; then the follow-up would be based on the accrual-accounting model.

ASSIGNMENT MATERIAL

Fundamental Assignment Material

16-1. Terminology. Define: *profit center; asset turnover; transfer price;* and *negotiated market prices.*

16-2. Rate of return on assets: transfer pricing. A company division manager has tentatively placed a selling price of $2 on his product. His division's asset and cost structure follows:

Cash	$ 10,000
Receivables	20,000
Inventories	70,000
Fixed assets, net	100,000
	$200,000

Fixed overhead	$80,000
Variable costs	$1.50 per unit
Desired rate of return on average assets available	20%

[12]For examples see H. Bierman, Jr., and T. R. Dyckman, *Managerial Cost Accounting* (New York: The Macmillan Company, 1971), pp. 365–81, and Alfred Rappaport, ed. *Information for Decision Making* (Englewood Cliffs, N.J.: Prentice-Hall, Inc., 1970).

Required:

1. a. How many units must he sell in order to obtain the desired rate of return?
   b. What would be the expected asset turnover?
   c. What would be the net income percentage on dollar sales?
2. a. What rate of return would be earned on available assets if the selling price were $1.90 and the sales volume 280,000 units?
   b. If the selling price were $2.20 and sales volume 200,000 units?
3. Assume that 40,000 of a normal total volume of 240,000 units are usually sold each year to another division of the same company. The two division managers are currently trying to agree on a transfer price for the coming year. The buying division manager has offered $1.80, claiming that he can buy the units from another company at that price. The selling division manager has decided that he can eliminate $10,000 of inventories, $10,000 of fixed assets, and $8,000 of fixed overhead if he does not sell to the other division. Should he sell for $1.80? Show computations to support your answer.
4. Assuming that all cost data originally given are correct and that the unit selling price is $1.80 for the intracompany business, at what price must the 200,000 other units be sold in order for the division to achieve the 20 percent desired rate of return?

16-3. **Choice of profitability measure, residual income, and motivation.** Suppose that the Solomons Company has the following relationships between net income and investment:

Investment (In millions of dollars)	Net Income (In dollars)		Investment (In millions of dollars)	Net Income (In dollars)	
	Case A	Case B		Case A	Case B
1	10,000	10,000	7	680,000	760,000
2	50,000	50,000	8	830,000	860,000
3	120,000	200,000	9	980,000	950,000
4	220,000	350,000	10	1,110,000	1,010,000
5	370,000	500,000	11	1,150,000	1,050,000
6	520,000	650,000	12	1,180,000	1,070,000

The minimum desired rate of return is 6 percent.

Required:

1. For *each* level of investment for Cases *A* and *B:*
   a. Compute the overall rate of return as measured by net income divided by investment (ROI).
   b. Compute the residual income as measured by net income less a capital charge of 6 percent on investment. Prepare your answer as a comparative table showing for each level:

		Case A		Case B	
Total Investment Level	6% Return	ROI	Residual Income	ROI	Residual Income

2. Explain any difference in potential effects on a manager's investment decisions that you detect between Case *A* and Case *B*. That is, will ROI and residual

income lead to the same decisions? What is the essential conceptual difference between the maximization of ROI and the maximization of residual income as management goals?

16-4. **Transfer-pricing dispute.** A transportation-equipment manufacturer, Chalmers Corporation, is heavily decentralized. Each division head has full authority on all decisions regarding sales to internal or external customers. Division *P* has always acquired a certain equipment component from Division *S*. However, when informed that Division *S* was increasing its unit price to $220, Division *P*'s management decided to purchase the component from outside suppliers at a price of $200.

Division *S* had recently acquired some specialized equipment that was used primarily to make this component. The manager cited the resulting high depreciation charges as the justification for the price boost. He asked the president of the company to instruct Division *P* to buy from *S* at the $220 price. He supplied the following:

P's annual purchases of component	2,000 units
S's variable costs per unit	$ 190
S's fixed costs per unit	$ 20

Required:

1. Suppose that there are no alternative uses of the *S* facilities. Will the company as a whole benefit if *P* buys from the outside suppliers for $200 per unit? Show computations to support your answer.
2. Suppose that internal facilities of *S* would not otherwise be idle. The equipment and other facilities would be assigned to other production operations which would otherwise require an additional annual outlay of $29,000. Should *P* purchase from outsiders at $200 per unit?
3. Suppose that there are no alternative uses for *S*'s internal facilities and that the selling price of outsiders drops $15. Should *P* purchase from outsiders?
4. As the president, how would you respond to the request of the manager of *S*? Would your response differ, depending on the specific situations described in Requirements 1 through 3 above? Why?

Additional Assignment Material

16-5. Distinguish between a profit center and a cost center.

16-6. What is the major benefit of the ROI technique for measuring performance?

16-7. "There is an optimum level of investment in any asset." Explain.

16-8. "Just as there may be different costs for different purposes, there may be different rates of return for different purposes." Explain.

16-9. Why are cost-based transfer prices in common use?

16-10. Why are transfer-pricing systems needed?

16-11. Why are interest expense and income taxes ordinarily excluded in computing incomes which are related to asset bases?

16-12. **Simple calculations.** You are given the following data:

Sales	$100,000,000
Invested capital	$20,000,000
Return on investment	10%

Required:
1. Turnover of capital.
2. Net income.
3. Net income as a percentage of sales.

16-13. Comparison of asset and equity bases. Company *A* has assets of $1,000,000 and a long-term, 6 percent debt of $500,000. Company *B* has assets of $1,000,000 and no long-term debt. The annual operating income (before interest) of both companies is $200,000.

Required:
Compute the rate of return on:
1. Assets available.
2. Stockholders' equity.

Evaluate the relative merits of each base for appraising operating management.

16-14. Using gross or net book value of fixed assets. Assume that a particular plant acquires $400,000 of fixed assets with a useful life of four years and no residual value. Straight-line depreciation will be used. The plant manager is judged on income in relation to these fixed assets. Annual net income, after deducting depreciation, is $40,000.

Assume that sales, and all expenses except depreciation, are on a cash basis. Dividends equal net income. Thus, cash in the amount of the depreciation charge will accumulate each year. The plant manager's performance is judged in relation to fixed assets because all current assets, including cash, are considered under central-company control.

Required:
1. Prepare a comparative tabulation of the plant's rate of return and the company's overall rate of return based on:
   a. Gross (i.e., original cost) assets.
   b. Net book value of assets. Assume (unrealistically) that any cash accumulated remains idle.
2. Evaluate the relative merits of gross assets and net book value of assets as investment bases.

16-15. Margins and turnover. Return on investment is often expressed as the product of two components—capital turnover and margin on sales. You are considering investing in one of three companies, all in the same industry, and are given the following information:

	Company		
	X	*Y*	*Z*
Sales	$5,000,000	$ 2,500,000	$50,000,000
Income	500,000	250,000	250,000
Capital	2,000,000	20,000,000	20,000,000

Required:
1. Why would you desire the breakdown of return on investment into margin on sales and turnover on capital?
2. Compute the margin on sales, turnover on capital, and return on investment for the three companies, and comment on the relative performance on the companies as thoroughly as the data permit.

16-16. **ROI or residual income.** d'Anconia Copper is a large integrated conglomerate with shipping, metals, and mining operations throughout the world. The general manager of the ferrous metals division has been directed to submit his proposed capital budget for 19x1 for inclusion in the company-wide budget.

The division manager has for consideration all of the following projects which require an outlay of capital. All projects have equal risk.

Project	Investment Required	Return
1	$6,000,000	$1,380,000
2	2,400,000	768,000
3	1,750,000	245,000
4	1,200,000	216,000
5	800,000	160,000
6	350,000	98,000

The division manager must decide which of the projects to take. The company has a cost of capital of 15 percent. An amount of $15,000,000 is available to the division for investment purposes.

Required:
1. What will be the total investment, total return, return on capital invested, and residual income of the rational division manager if:
   a. The company has a rule that all projects promising at least 20 percent or more should be taken.
   b. The division manager is evaluated on his ability to maximize his return on capital invested (assume that this is a new division with no invested capital).
   c. The division manager is expected to maximize residual income as computed by using the 15 percent cost of capital.
2. Which of the three approaches will induce the most effective investment policy for the company as a whole?

16-17. **Different ways of evaluating divisional performance.** As the president of Excell Enterprises Company, you have been given the following measures of the performance of three divisions (in thousands of dollars):

	Net Assets		
	(1)	(2)	(3)
Division	Net Book Value	Net Replacement Value	Net Income
A	10,000	10,000	1,800
B	20,000	32,000	3,200
C	30,000	37,500	4,500

Required:
1. Compute for each division the rate of return and the residual income based on net book value and on net replacement value. For purposes of computing residual income, use 10 percent as the minimum desired rate of return.

2. Rank the performance of each division under each of the four different measures computed in Requirement 1.
3. What do these measures tell you about the performance of the division? Of the division manager? Which measure do you prefer? Why?

16-18. Transfer-pricing concession. (CMA adapted.) The Ajax Division of Gunnco Corporation, operating at capacity, has been asked by the Defco Division of Gunnco to supply it with Electrical Fitting No. 1726. Ajax sells this part to its regular customers for $7.50 each. Defco, which is operating at 50 percent capacity, is willing to pay $5 each for the fitting. Defco will put the fitting into a brake unit which it is manufacturing on essentially a cost-plus basis for a commercial airplane manufacturer.

Ajax has a variable cost of producing fitting No. 1726 of $4.25. The cost of the brake unit as being built by Defco is as follows:

Purchased parts—Outside vendors	$22.50
Ajax fitting—No. 1726	5.00
Other variable costs	14.00
Fixed overhead and administration	8.00
	$49.50

Defco believes the price concession is necessary to get the job.

The company uses return on investment and dollar profits in the measurement of division and division-manager performance.

Required:

1. Consider that you are the division controller of Ajax. Would you recommend that Ajax supply fitting No. 1726 to Defco? Why or why not? (Ignore any income tax issues.)
2. Would it be to the short-run economic advantage of the Gunnco Corporation for the Ajax Division to supply the Defco Division with fitting No. 1726 at $5 each? (Ignore any income tax issues.) Explain your answer.
3. Discuss the organizational and manager-behavior difficulties, if any, inherent in this situation. As the Gunnco controller, what would you advise the Gunnco Corporation president do in this situation?

16-19. Transfer pricing. Newmill Enterprises runs a chain of drive-in hamburger stands on Cape Cod during the ten-week summer season. The manager of each stand is told to act as if he owned the stand and is judged on his profit performance. Newmill Enterprises has rented a soft-ice-cream machine for the summer, to supply its stands with ice cream for their frappés. Rent for the machine is $500. Newmill is not allowed to sell ice cream to other dealers because it cannot obtain a dairy license. The manager of the ice-cream machine charges the stands $1 per gallon. Operating figures for the machine for the summer are as follows:

Sales to the stands (5,000 gallons at $1)		$5,000
Variable costs, @ $.40 per gallon	$2,000	
Fixed costs:		
Rental of machine	500	
Other fixed costs	1,500	4,000
Operating margin		$1,000

The manager of the Clam Bar, one of the Newmill drive-ins, is seeking permission to make a contract to buy ice cream from an outside supplier at 80¢ a gallon. The Clam Bar uses 1,000 gallons of soft-ice cream during the summer. Frank Redmond, controller of Newmill Enterprises, refers this request to you. You determine that the Other Fixed Costs of operating the machine will decrease by $300 if the Clam Bar purchases from an outside supplier. He wants an analysis of the request in terms of overall company objectives and an explanation of your conclusion.

16-20. Profit centers and transfer pricing in an automobile dealership. A large automobile dealership is installing a responsibility-accounting system and three profit centers: parts and service; new vehicles; and used vehicles. Each department manager has been told to run his shop as if he were in business for himself. However, there are interdepartmental dealings. For example:

a. The parts and service department prepares new cars for final delivery and repairs used cars prior to resale.
b. The used-car department's major source of inventory has been cars traded in in part payment for new cars.

The owner of the dealership has asked you to draft a company policy statement on transfer pricing, together with specific rules to be applied to the examples cited. He has told you that clarity is of paramount importance because your statement will be relied upon for settling transfer-pricing disputes.

16-21. Transfer pricing. The Never Die Division of Durable Motors Company produces 12-volt batteries for automobiles. It has been the sole supplier of batteries to the Automotive Division, and charges $10 per unit, the current market price for very large wholesale lots. The battery division also sells to outside retail outlets, at $12.50 per unit. Normally, outside sales amount to 25 percent of a total sales volume of 2,000,000 batteries per year. Typical combined annual data for the division follow:

Sales	$21,250,000
Variable costs, @ $8 per battery	$16,000,000
Fixed costs	2,000,000
Total costs	$18,000,000
Gross margin	$ 3,250,000

The Sure Life Battery Company, an entirely separate entity, has offered the Automotive Division comparable batteries at a firm price of $9 per unit. The Never Die Division claims that it can't possibly match this price because it could not earn any margin at $9.

Required:
1. Assume you are the manager of the Automotive Division. Comment on the Never Die Division's claim. Assume that normal outside volume cannot be increased.
2. The Never Die Division feels that it can increase outside sales by 1,500,000 batteries per year by increasing fixed costs by $2,000,000 and variable costs by $1 per unit, while reducing the selling price to $12. Assume that maximum capacity is 2,000,000 batteries per year. Should the division reject intracompany business and concentrate on outside sales?

16-22. Variable cost as a transfer price. A product's variable cost is $2 and its market value is $3 at a transfer point from Division S to Division P. Division P's variable cost of processing the product further is $2.25, and the selling price of the final product is $4.75.

Required:

1. Prepare a tabulation of the contribution margin per unit for Division P performance and overall performance under the two alternatives of (a) processing further and (b) selling to outsiders at the transfer point.
2. As Division P manager, which alternative would you choose? Explain.

16-23. Transfer pricing. Refer to Problem 16-4, requirement 1 only. Suppose that Division S could modify the component at an additional variable cost of $10 per unit and sell the 2,000 units to other customers for $225. Then would the entire company benefit if P purchased the 2,000 components from outsiders at $200 per unit?

16-24. Markup formulas and transfer pricing. The Gatos Machinery Company has recently been decentralized. Many profit centers have been formed. The transfer-pricing system stipulates that average market prices should govern intracompany sales; however, reductions of such prices should be made for any expenses that do not pertain to intracompany sales. Examples would be some selling, shipping, and credit expenses.

The Fantasy Division, a large intracompany supplier of more than 100 parts and assemblies, tried to develop a workable method for quoting intracompany prices. The task was complicated by the presence of many selling and manufacturing costs that were common to a number of products. The Fantasy Division finally suggested a flat markup above traceable manufacturing costs as a practical approximation of market price:

Sales to outsiders	$22,000,000
Less:	
Selling, shipping, credit, and customer service expenses not applicable to intracompany sales	2,000,000
Adjusted sales	$20,000,000
Traceable manufacturing costs	15,000,000
Markup	$ 5,000,000

Markup formula: $20,000,000 ÷ $15,000,000 = 133 percent of traceable manufacturing costs. The formula would be reviewed and adjusted every quarter.

Required:

What are the strengths and weaknesses of the proposed markup formula? Does the formula adhere to the company policy on transfer pricing?

16-25. Evaluation of transfer pricing policy. The Hewlett Corporation is a mammoth enterprise with more than fifty profit centers. A company-wide transfer-pricing rule states that a selling division must always sell to a buying division at bona fide market prices.

The S Division has been asked to quote prices on 20,000 standard parts (representing 10 percent of the S Division's practical capacity) which the B Division has ordered from time to time in past years. The S Division quoted a price of $20 each, which would bring S a $120,000 total contribution margin for the 20,000 parts. However, an outside supplier quoted a price of $16, and the S Division was forced by company policy to accept the order at that price.

Required:

1. By how much is the net income of the Hewlett Corporation affected by keeping the business inside at the $16 price rather than going outside at that price? How much total contribution margin will the S Division earn at the $16 price?

2. The practical capacity of the S Division is 200,000 machine-hours. Suppose that it takes one machine-hour to make one of the standard parts. Suppose further that the order is indivisible; that is, the S Division must make all 20,000 parts or none—it cannot accept a third or a half of the order. Suppose finally that only 20,000 machine-hours of capacity were available for this production.

   The S Division manager had also planned to submit a bid to an outside company for making 8,000 special parts at a selling price of $40 each, which would bring S a total contribution margin of $64,000 for the 8,000 parts. The manager felt virtually certain that he would get the order. It takes two machine-hours to make one special part. However, because he could not handle both orders, he delayed submitting his bid because of the B Division's need for the standard parts. In view of these circumstances, how were the S Division's and the Hewlett Corporation's net income affected by the decision to keep the standard parts order inside? How would you modify the transfer-pricing rule?

16-26. The pertinent transfer price. The Santa Rusa Company has two divisions, S and P. For one of the company's products, S Division produces a major subassembly, and P Division incorporates this subassembly into the final product. There is a market for both the subassembly and the final product, and the divisions have been delegated profit responsibility. The transfer price for the subassembly has been set at long-run average market price.

The following data are available to each division:

Estimated selling price for final product	$400
Long-run average selling price for inter-	
mediate product	300
Variable cost for completion in P Division	150
Variable cost in S Division	220

The manager of P Division has made the following calculation:

Selling price—final product		$400
Transferred-in cost (market)	$300	
Variable cost for completion	150	450
Contribution (loss) on product		$(50)

Required:

1. Should transfers be made to P Division if there is no excess capacity in S Division? Is market price the correct transfer price?

2. Assume that S Division's maximum capacity for this product is 1,000 units per month, and sales to the intermediate market are presently 800 units. Should 200 units be transferred to P Division? At what relevant transfer price?

16-27. Transfer pricing in different situations. The Neumann Company, Ltd., adopted a philosophy of decentralization several years ago. All the company's autonomous manufacturing divisions are located in Great Britain, where the company manufactures a wide range of electronic controls and automated machine tools. Nominally, all divisions of the company are conducted as separate enterprises, which must negotiate all orders independently with prospective purchasers. Each division is then responsible for its own profitability and return on investment. However, all divisions are required to consider' purchasing from other Neumann divisions whenever possible.

The Machine-Products Division (MPD), situated in London, manufactures small precision components that can be integrated with other Neumann components in a variety of automated systems. Both the components and the entire systems are generally quite profitable and in high demand by other Neumann divisions, as well as by independent purchasers. MPD is the only Neumann plant with the facilities to produce a very essential component, magnesium balance wheels. The market price for these items is £100, both in Great Britain and in the United States. However, an import duty of 10 percent (of the selling price without the duty) is charged on the import of this type of product into the United States. The MPD income statement for the last twelve months is as follows (in thousands of pounds):

Net sales		£1,100
Direct labor	£250	
Direct material	300	
Manufacturing overhead	250	800
Gross margin		300
Fixed selling expenses	100	
Fixed administrative expenses	80	180
Divisional profit		£120

The cost of a batch of balance wheels has been calculated in the following manner:

Direct labor	£25
Direct material	30
Manufacturing overhead*	25
Total cost	£80

*100% of direct labor.

When the company was decentralized, several assembly and marketing divisions were opened in new areas to expand the size of the markets for existing manufacturing divisions. These divisions were expected to be less profitable than other Neumann divisions, especially where import duties might necessitate more burdensome costs. One of these new marketing and assembly divisions (Middle Continental) was headquartered in Chicago under Mr. Gorot. Gorot had previously worked in London under the divisional manager for MPD, Mr. Miller, who was a 35-year veteran of the company. Even though Gorot had been a highly successful department head while in London, Miller had surreptitiously instigated a transfer for Gorot because of a personality conflict. Needless to say, Miller was quite unhappy to hear of Gorot's recent successes as head of Middle Continental while he himself was struggling to eliminate unfavorable capacity variances in the MPD.

Miller has been reluctant in the past to sell MPD components to other divisions at less than the domestic price; he sees no reason why he should make less profit than if he sold them in Great Britain. Furthermore, he has stated categorically, "I will not hurt my own profits to help that upstart in Chicago!"

One of the most important systems sold by Middle Continental requires the use of magnesium balance wheels. In the past, Gorot has been under some pressure to purchase balance wheels from MPD at a base price of £100 plus £10 import duty. This practice has unduly affected his profit performance, and he is necessarily eager to obtain permission to purchase these components from local suppliers.

Required:

1. As the divisional controller at MPD, you are asked by Miller for advice in response to a memorandum from Gorot that he has obtained permission to purchase balance wheels in the United States unless MPD lowers its price. What would you advise Miller to do? Why? For this and the next part, assume that the manufacturing overhead is totally variable.
2. After you have given your advice to Miller, he receives a cablegram from Gorot indicating that several manufacturers in the United States have reduced their price on balance wheels to £85. How would you change your advice, if at all? Why?
3. Several days later, you determine that half the manufacturing overhead is fixed cost. Would this cause you to alter any of your previous decisions? In what way?
4. About a year later, MPD is operating at maximum capacity. Gorot sends MPD another order for balance wheels at the previously negotiated price in Requirement 1. Would you now recommend that this price be accepted? Why?
5. If the Neumann Company were to eliminate its divisions, what company guidelines should be established for transfers of goods between segments of the company?
6. Two years later, you are promoted to the controller's office of the entire Neumann Company. You are then asked to advise your new superior on whether some firm guidelines should be established for the determination of transfer prices between divisions as they were organized in Requirements 1 through 4. What would you recommend? Why?

16-28. Conflict of accrual and DCF models. Using DCF analysis, the Malott Company invested $100,000 in plant and equipment having a useful life of six years and generating $22,961 in operating cash inflows each year. At the end of six years, the assets are scrapped at zero salvage value.

Required:

1. What is the time-adjusted rate of return?
2. Suppose straight-line depreciation is used as a basis for performance evaluation. What is the ROI for the first, fourth, and sixth years if ROI is based on the initial balance (gross investment base)? On net book value?
3. How closely do the answers in Requirement 2 approximate the time-adjusted rate of return? Why do they differ?

16-29. Conflict of accrual and DCF models. Solve Problem 13-36, which could logically have been placed here instead of at the end of Chapter 13.

16-30. Setting multiple objectives. Solve Problem 11-40, which could logically have been placed here.

16-31. Judging a control technique. Solve Problem 11-41, which could logically have been placed here.

16-32. Judging a control technique. Solve Problem 11-42, which could logically have been placed here.

16-33. Human-resources accounting. Solve Problem 11-43, which could logically have been placed here.

16-34. Role of economic value and replacement value. "To me, economic value is the only justifiable basis for measuring plant assets for purposes of evaluating performance. By economic value, I mean the present value of expected future services. Still, we do not even do this upon acquisition of new assets—this is, we may compute a positive net present value, using discounted cash flow; but we record the asset at no more than its cost. In this way, the excess present value is not shown in the initial balance sheet. Moreover, the use of replacement costs in subsequent years is also unlikely to result in showing economic values; the replacement cost will probably be less than the economic value at any given instant of an asset's life.

"Market values are totally unappealing to me because they represent a second-best alternative value—that is, they ordinarily represent the maximum amount obtainable from an alternative that has been rejected. Obviously, if the market value exceeds the economic value of the assets in use, they should be sold. However, in most instances, the opposite is true; market values of individual assets are far below their economic value in use.

"The obtaining and recording of total present values of individual assets based on discounted cash flow techniques is an infeasible alternative. I, therefore, conclude that replacement cost (less accumulated depreciation) of similar assets producing similar services is the best practical approximation of the economic value of the assets in use. Of course, it will facilitate the evaluation of the division's performance more easily than the division manager's performance."

Required:

Critically evaluate the above comments. Please do not wander; concentrate on the issues described by the quotation.

16-35. Transfer pricing and decisions. Prepare a response to the following letter. Assume that the Marketing Division is decentralized to the extent that its management has sole power to decide when to use Free Goods and what to buy—that is, if Free Goods are to be used, they may be acquired inside or outside the company. The decision to buy outside is dysfunctional because the price paid to outsiders will exceed the incremental costs to the overall company if an inside purchase were made. Moreover, if outside purchases of Free Goods are forbidden, at the very least the marketing manager could decide to conduct no promotions and thus avoid acquisitions of Free Goods from the manufacturing division.

Dear Professor_____:

I wonder if you might offer an opinion on this problem. My problem, I believe, is termed Lost Sales Realization (LSR) and how to account it.

In consumer package-goods marketing, we sometimes offer consumers Lavoris Mouthwash in special bottles with three additional ounces for the same price as the normal bottle, or offer the trade three free Vicks Cough Drops packages with the purchase of forty packages.

My company wants to cost me at the full manufacturer's selling price for these Free Goods, rather than at the actual cost of goods. This procedure encourages me to use other companies' goods as Free Goods since I can get better prices on them than my own—and for my company this becomes an out-of-pocket expenditure.

To be more specific on the pricing, let us suppose that three "extra-ounce" Lavoris bottles have the same ounces as four "normal" Lavoris bottles. The company will then charge me the full manufacturer's selling price of one bottle for every three extra-ounce bottles I sell, rather than just the extra cost of goods in producing the extra-ounce bottles. The prices and costs for a Lavoris bottle might breakout as:

Retail selling price	$1.50
Manufacturing selling price	1.00
Cost of goods "normal" bottle	.30
Additional cost of goods "extra-ounce" bottle	.03

Charging me $1.00 for what costs the company $.03 makes this promotional technique unaffordable for me.

While I realize that I am selling more of the product for the same price, in effect lowering the price of a normal bottle, I am taking in more total sales dollars—many more than the extra $.03 cost per bottle.

While I may be loading consumers with free Lavoris and robbing some from future sales, I know I am also attracting customers who would not normally buy the Lavoris brand. However, I could not afford to conduct research to conclusively prove the numbers due to the complexity of the market—muddy waters with continuous, various promotions.

Can you offer any direction or an opinion on this problem?

Sincerely,

G. Chalmers

Note: "Free Goods" are the extra inducements to customers to buy the regular product. For example, suppose Lavoris Mouthwash were available to customers in a normal bottle of nine ounces for a regular retail price of $1.50. When a special twelve-ounce bottle is offered for the same price, $1.50, the extra three ounces are referred to as Free Goods because they are "free" to the company's customers.

SUGGESTED READINGS

Anthony, R. N., J. Dearden, and R. F. Vancil, *Management Control Systems: Cases and Readings,* rev. ed. (Homewood, Ill.: Richard D. Irwin, Inc., 1972).

Goldschmidt, Yaaqov, *Information for Management Decisions* (Ithaca, N.Y., and London: Cornell University Press, 1970).

Horngren, Charles T., *Cost Accounting: A Managerial Emphasis,* 3rd ed. (Englewood Cliffs, N.J., Prentice-Hall, Inc. 1972), Chapters 6, 21, 22.

Morris, William T., *Decentralization in Management Systems* (Columbus, O.: Ohio State University Press, 1968).

Solomons, David, *Divisional Performance: Measurement and Control* (New York: Financial Executives Research Foundation, 1965). Reprinted in paperback form in 1968 by Richard D. Irwin, Inc.

Influences of   17
Quantitative Techniques on
Management Accounting

Because the branches of knowledge overlap, it is always an over-simplification to specify where the field of accounting starts and where it ends. Some accountants take the view that accounting should restrict itself to scorekeeping, the compilation of financial history. Others feel that if accountants do not move quickly to assimilate a working knowledge of computer technology and assorted mathematical techniques, their attention-directing and problem-solving functions will be seized by the burgeoning field of management science.

We need not be concerned with the controversy over what accounting is and what it is not. Regardless of its label, the subject matter of this chapter has a bearing on management planning and control and is therefore important to accountants and to managers. One of the marks of an educated man is his ability to recognize and accept changes that promise better ways of accomplishing objectives. The accountant is still the top quantitative expert in nearly all organizations, and few companies employ full-time mathematics specialists. To retain and improve his status, the accountant should be aware of how mathematical models may improve planning and control. The alert manager would naturally expect his accountants to keep abreast of the newer quantitative techniques.

This chapter is a survey. Technical competence in any of the areas mentioned can be achieved only by thorough specialized study. We shall explore decision theory and uncertainty, linear-programming models, and inventory-control models.

Formal Decision Models

A **model** is a depiction of the interrelationships among the recognized factors in a real situation. Most models spotlight the key interrelationships and deemphasize the unimportant factors. Models take many forms. Museums contain model rockets and model ships. Automobile companies distribute miniature model cars. Accountants continually work with accounting systems and financial reports which are models. Operations researchers principally use mathematical equations as models.

Decision models are often expressed in mathematical form. The careful use of mathematical models supplements hunches and implicit rules of thumb with explicit assumptions and criteria. Mathematical models have been criticized because they may oversimplify and ignore important underlying factors. Still, many examples of successful applications can be cited. For example, inventory-control and linear-programming models are widely used. The test of success is not whether mathematical models lead to perfect decisions, but whether such models lead to better decisions than via alternative techniques. How is this test applied? Sometimes it is difficult, but conceptually the test is to compare the net financial impact (after deducting the cost of accumulating the information used in the decision) of the decision generated by the mathematical model versus the net financial impact of the decision generated by other techniques. In other words, the relative attractiveness of using mathematical decision models is again subject to the cost and value of information test.

Decision theory is a complex, somewhat ill-defined body of knowledge developed by statisticians, mathematicians, economists, and psychologists that tries to prescribe how decisions should be made and to describe systematically what variables affect choices. The basic approach of decision theory has the following characteristics:

1. An organizational objective that can be quantified. This objective can take many forms. Most often, it is expressed as a maximization (or minimization) of some form of profit (or cost). This quantification is often called a *choice criterion* or an *objective function.* This objective function is used to evaluate the courses of action and to provide a basis for choosing the best alternative.

2. A set of the alternative courses of action under explicit consideration. This set of *actions* should be collectively exhaustive and mutually exclusive.

3. A set of all relevant events or *states,* or states of nature, that can occur. This set should also be collectively exhaustive and mutually exclusive. Therefore, only one of the states will actually occur.

4. A set of *probabilities* that describes the possibilities of the various states' occurrence.

5. A set of *payoffs* or *expected values* that describes the consequences of the various possible outcomes evaluated in terms of the objective function. These are conditionally dependent on a specific course of action and a specific state.

An example may clarify the essential ingredients of a formal model. Suppose a decision maker has two mutually exclusive and exhaustive alternative courses of action regarding the quality-control aspects of his project: accept or reject. He also predicts that two mutually exclusive and exhaustive states of nature will affect his payoffs. Either the product conforms to the quality standards, or it does not. The combinations of actions and states and their conditional payoffs can be presented in a *payoff table:*

Alternative Actions	*Alternative States of Nature*	
	Conform	*Nonconform*
Accept	$12[1]	$2[2]
Reject	$ 7[3]	$7[4]

Note: The superior figures in the table above relate to the corresponding numbers in the list which follows.

The conditional payoffs are assumed to take the pattern shown because:

1. Acceptance and conformance should bring the normal "contribution" to profit.

2. Acceptance and nonconformance eventually results in expensive rework after the product is processed through later stages.

3. Rejection and conformance results in unnecessary rework that reduces the normal contribution.

4. Rejection and nonconformance results in immediate necessary rework.

The payoff table includes three of the five ingredients of the formal model: actions, states, and payoffs. The other two ingredients are the probabilities and the choice criterion. Assume that the probability of conform is 0.6 and that of nonconform is 0.4. Assume also that the choice criterion is to maximize the expected value of the dollar payoff. Given this model, the decision maker would always accept the product, because the expected payoff $\bar{A}$ for each action is

$$\text{If Accept, } \bar{A} = \$12\,(0.6) + \$2\,(0.4) = \$8$$
$$\text{If Reject, } \bar{A} = \$7\,(0.6) + \$7\,(0.4) = \$7$$

An expected value is an arithmetic mean, a weighted average using the probabilities as weights. The formula is

$$\overline{A} = \sum_{x=1}^{n} A_x P_x$$

The accountant often provides much of the data that are included in these decision models. His understanding of the nature of decision models should have a direct effect on how he designs a formal information system.

Decisions Under Certainty

Decisions are frequently classified as those made under certainty and those under uncertainty. Certainty exists when there is absolutely no doubt about which state of nature will occur and when there is a single payoff for each possible action. The payoff table would appear as follows (data assumed):

Action	State
Buy A	−$1,000
Buy B	− 1,400
Buy C	− 1,900
Buy D	− 800

Note that there is only one column in the payoff table because there is only one possible state of nature. The decision obviously consists of choosing the action that will produce the greatest payoff (least cost). However, decisions under certainty are not *always* obvious. There are often countless alternative actions, each of which may offer certain payoffs. The problem is then finding the best one. For example, the problem of allocating twenty different job orders to twenty different machines, any one of which could do the job, can involve literally *billions* of different combinations. Each way of assigning these jobs is another possible action. This decision's payoff table would have only one *column,* because the costs of production using the various machines are assumed as known; however, it would have 2½ quintillion *rows*. This demonstrates that decision making under certainty can be more than just a trivial problem.[1]

When a payoff is certain, the prediction is a single point with no dispersion on either side. There is a 100 percent chance of occurrence; in other words, the probability is 1.0. For example, the expected cash inflow on a federal Treasury note might be, say, $4,000 for next year. This might be graphed as follows:

---

[1]See D. W. Miller and M. K. Starr, *Executive Decisions and Operations Research,* 2nd ed. (Englewood Cliffs, N.J.: Prentice-Hall, Inc., 1969), pp. 104–5. Their distinctions among certainty, risk, and uncertainty are used here.

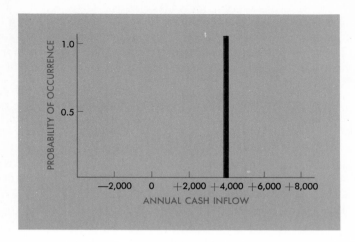

Decisions Under Risk or Uncertainty

Of course, the decision maker must frequently contend with uncertainty rather than certainty; he faces a number of possible states of nature. The distinction among various degrees of uncertainty centers on the degree of objectivity by which probabilities are assigned. The probabilities may be assigned with a high degree of objectivity.[2] That is, if the decision maker knows the probability of occurrence of each of a number of states of nature, his assignment of probabilities is "objective," because of mathematical proofs or the compilation of historical evidence. For example, the probability of obtaining a head in the toss of a symmetrical coin is 0.5; that of drawing a particular playing card from a well-shuffled deck, $\frac{1}{52}$. In a business, the probability of having a specified percentage of spoiled units may be assigned with great confidence, which is based on production experience with thousands of units.

If the decision maker has no basis in past experience or in mathematical proofs for assigning the probabilities of occurrence of the various states of nature, he must resort to the subjective assignment of probabilities. For example, the probability of the success or failure of a new product may have to be assessed without the help of any related experience. This assignment is subjective, because no two individuals assessing a situation will necessarily assign the same probabilities. Executives may be virtually certain about the *range* of possible states of nature or possible payoffs, but they may differ about the likelihoods of various possibilities within that range.

[2]This is sometimes called decision making under risk, as distinguished from decision making under certainty. See Miller and Starr, *op cit.,* p. 105. The distinction between risk and uncertainty in the current literature and in practice is so blurred that the terms are used interchangeably here.

The concept of uncertainty can be illustrated by considering two investment proposals on new projects.[3] The manager has carefully considered the risks. He has the following discrete probability distribution of expected cash flows for the next year (assume that the useful life of the project is one year):

Proposal A		Proposal B	
Probability	Cash Inflow	Probability	Cash Inflow
0.10	$3,000	0.10	$2,000
0.20	3,500	0.25	3,000
0.40	4,000	0.30	4,000
0.20	4,500	0.25	5,000
0.10	5,000	0.10	6,000

Expected Value and Standard Deviation

Exhibit 17-1 shows a graphical comparison of the probability distributions. The usual approach to this problem is to compute an expected value for each probability distribution.

The expected value of the cash inflow in Proposal A is

$$\overline{A} = 0.1(3,000) + 0.2(3,500) + 0.4(4,000) + 0.2(4,500) + 0.1(5,000)$$
$$= \$4,000$$

The expected value for the cash inflow in Proposal B is also $4,000:

$$\overline{A} = 0.1(2,000) + 0.25(3,000) + 0.3(4,000) + 0.25(5,000) + 0.1(6,000)$$
$$= \$4,000$$

Incidentally, the expected value of the cash inflow in the Federal Treasury note is also $4,000:

$$\overline{A} = 1.0(4,000) = \$4,000$$

Note that mere comparison of these $4,000 expected values is an oversimplification. These three single figures are not strictly comparable; one represents certainty, whereas the other two represent the expected values within their respective ranges. The decision maker must explicitly or implicitly (by "feel" or hunch) recognize that he is comparing figures that are really representations of probability distributions; otherwise the reporting of the expected value alone may mislead him.[4]

[3]James C. Van Horne, *Financial Management and Policy*, 3rd. ed. (Englewood Cliffs, N.J.: Prentice-Hall., Inc., 1974).

[4]For example, how would you feel about choosing between the following two investments? First, invest $10 today with a probability of 1.0 of obtaining $11 in two days. Second, invest $10 today with a probability of 0.5 of obtaining $22 in two days and 0.5 of obtaining $0. The expected value is $11 in both cases.

EXHIBIT 17-1. Comparison of Probability Distributions

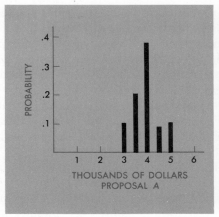

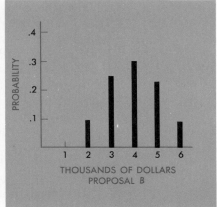

To give the decision maker more information, the accountant could provide the complete probability distribution for each proposal. However, often that course means flooding the manager with too much data for his comprehension. Therefore, a middle ground is often used. A summary measure of the underlying dispersion is supplied. The conventional measure of the dispersion of a probability distribution for a single variable is the standard deviation. The standard deviation is the square root of the mean of the squared deviations from the expected value:

$$\sigma = \sqrt{\sum_{x=1}^{n} (A_x - \overline{A})^2 P_x}$$

The standard deviation for Proposal A is smaller than that for Proposal B:

For A: $\sigma = [0.1(3{,}000 - 4{,}000)^2 + 0.2(3{,}500 - 4{,}000)^2$
$+ 0.4(4{,}000 - 4{,}000)^2 + 0.2(4{,}500 - 4{,}000)^2$
$+ 0.1(5{,}000 - 4{,}000)^2]^{1/2}$
$= [300{,}000]^{1/2} = \$548$

For B: $\sigma = [0.1(2{,}000 - 4{,}000)^2 + 0.25(3{,}000 - 4{,}000)^2$
$+ 0.3(4{,}000 - 4{,}000)^2 + 0.25(5{,}000 - 4{,}000)^2$
$+ 0.1(6{,}000 - 4{,}000)^2]^{1/2}$
$= [1{,}300{,}000]^{1/2} = \$1{,}140$

For the Treasury note: $\sigma = \sqrt{1.0(4{,}000 - 4{,}000)^2} = 0$

A measure of relative dispersion is the coefficient of variation, which is the standard deviation divided by expected value. The coefficient for Proposal B is $1{,}140 \div 4{,}000 = 0.29$; for A it is $548 \div 4{,}000 = 0.14$; and for the Treasury note it is $0 \div 4{,}000 = 0$. Therefore, because the coefficient is a relative measure of risk or uncertainty, B is said to have a greater degree of risk.

The Accountant and Uncertainty

Many accounting practitioners and businessmen shudder at the notion of using subjective probabilities to quantify things that are supposedly "intangible" or "unmeasurable" or "qualitative" or "unquantifiable." However, their position is weak, simply because decisions *do* have to be made. The attempts by statisticians, mathematicians, and modern accountants to measure the unmeasurable is an old and natural chore that scientists have performed for centuries. The use of subjective probabilities merely formalizes the intuitive judgments and hunches that businessmen so often use. It forces the decision maker to expose and evaluate what he may have done unconsciously for years.

Many statisticians and accountants favor presenting the entire probability distribution directly to the decision maker. Others first divide the information into a threefold classification of optimistic, middle, and pessimistic categories. Still others provide summary measures of dispersion, such as the standard deviation or the coefficient of variation. In any event, we are likely to see the accountant's formal recognition of uncertainty and probability distributions in his reporting. In this way, the information will portray underlying phenomena in a more straightforward fashion instead of as if there were only a world of certainty.

Example of General Approach to Uncertainty

An example of the general approach to dealing with uncertainty may clarify some of the preceding ideas.

Problem

Once a day, a retailer stocks bunches of fresh-cut flowers, each of which cost 40¢ and sells for $1. The retailer never cuts his price; leftovers are given to a nearby church. He estimates characteristics as follows:

Demand	Probability
0	0.05
1	0.20
2	0.40
3	0.25
4	0.10
5 or more	0.00
	1.00

Required:

He wants to know how many units he should stock in order to maximize profits. Try to solve before consulting the solution that follows.

Solution

The profit, per unit sold, is 60¢; the loss, per unit unsold, is 40¢. All the alternatives may be assessed in the following *payoff table*.

State of nature: Demand of	0	1	2	3	4	Expected Value (Payoff)
Probability of state:	0.05	0.20	0.40	0.25	0.10	
Actions, units purchased:						
0	$ 0	$ 0	$ 0	$ 0	$ 0	$ 0
1	− .40	.60	.60	.60	.60	.55
2	− .80	.20	1.20	1.20	1.20	.90
3	− 1.20	− .20	.80	1.80	1.80	.85
4	− 1.60	− .60	.40*	1.40	2.40	.55

*Example of computation: $(2 \times \$1.00) - (4 \times \$.40) = \$.40$

As was shown in an earlier section, the computation of expected value ($\overline{A}$) for each action is affected by the probability weights and the conditional payoff associated with each combination of actions and states.

$$\overline{A} \text{ (Stock 1)} = 0.05(-.40) + 0.20(.60) + 0.40(.60) + 0.25(.60) + 0.10(.60)$$
$$= \$.55$$

$$\overline{A} \text{ (Stock 2)} = 0.05(-.80) + 0.20(.20) + 0.40(1.20) + 0.25(1.20) + 0.10(1.20)$$
$$= \$.90$$

and so on.

To maximize expected payoff, the retailer should stock two units ($\overline{A} = \$.90$).

Obtaining Additional Information

Sometimes the executive is hesitant about making a decision. He would like to obtain more information before making a final choice. Some additional information is nearly always obtainable—at a price. Schlaifer[5] describes a technique for computing the maximum amount that should be paid for such additional information. The general idea is to compute the expected value under ideal circumstances—that is, circumstances that would permit the retailer to predict, with absolute certainty, the number of units to be sold on any given day. A payoff table *with perfect information* would appear as follows:

[5] Robert Schlaifer, *Analysis of Decisions Under Uncertainty* (New York: McGraw-Hill Book Company, 1969), pp. 585–88.

States of nature: Demand of	0	1	2	3	4	Expected Value (Payoff)
Probability of state:	0.05	0.20	0.40	0.25	0.10	
Actions, units purchased:						
0	$0					$ 0
1		$ .60				.12
2			$1.20			.48
3				$1.80		.45
4					$2.40	.24
Total expected value						$1.29

The total expected value with perfect information is computed as follows:

$$\overline{A} \text{ (Perfect Information)} = 0.05(0) + 0.20(.60) + 0.40(1.20) + 0.25(1.80) + 0.10(2.40) = \$1.29$$

In this table, it is assumed that the retailer will never err in his forecasts and that demand will fluctuate from zero to four exactly as indicated by the probabilities. The maximum day-in, day-out profit is $1.29. Consequently, the most he should be willing to pay for perfect advance information would be the difference between the expected value with perfect information and the expected value with existing information—$1.29 minus the $.90 E.V. computed in the previous example, or 39¢. Schlaifer calls the latter the expected value of perfect information, the top price the retailer should pay for additional knowledge.

In the real world, of course, the retailer would not pay 39¢, because no amount of additional information is likely to provide perfect knowledge. But businesses often obtain additional knowledge through sampling, and sampling costs money. The executive needs a method, such as the one described at length by Schlaifer, (a) of assessing the probable benefits, in relation to its cost, of additional information from sampling; and (b) of determining the best sample size. In the present example, no sampling technique would be attractive if its cost allocated to each day's operations exceeded 39¢.

LINEAR-PROGRAMMING MODELS

Characteristics

Linear programming is a potent mathematical approach to a group of business problems which contain many interacting variables and which basically involve the utilization of limited resources in such a way as to increase profit or decrease cost. There are nearly always limiting factors or scarce resources that are restrictions, restraints, or constraints on available alternatives. Linear programming has been applied to a vast number of business decisions, such as machine scheduling, product mix, raw material mix, scheduling flight crews, production routing, shipping schedules, transportation routes, blending gasoline, blending sausage ingredients, and designing transformers. In general, linear programming is the best available technique for combining materials, manpower, and facilities to best advantage, when all the relationships are approximately linear and many combinations are possible.

The Techniques, the Accountant, and the Manager

All of us are more or less familiar with linear equations (e.g., $X + 3 = 9$). We also know that simultaneous linear equations with two or three unknowns become progressively more difficult to solve with pencil and paper. Linear programming essentially involves: (1) constructing a set of simultaneous linear equations, which represent the model of the problem and which include many variables; and (2) solving the equations with the help of the digital computer.

The formulation of the equations—that is, the building of the model—is far more challenging than the mechanics of the solution. The model must be a valid and accurate portrayal of the problem. Computer programmers can then take the equations and process the solution.

As a minimum, accountants and executives should be able to recognize those types of problems in their organizations that are most susceptible to analysis by linear programming. Hopefully, the managers and accountants should be able to help in the construction of the model—i.e., in specifying the objectives, the constraints, and the variables. Ideally, they should understand the mathematics and should be able to talk comfortably with the operations researchers who are attempting to express their problem mathematically. However, the position taken here is that the accountant and the manager should concentrate on the formulation of the model and not worry too much about the technical intricacies of the solution. The latter may be delegated to the mathematicians; the ability to delegate the former is highly doubtful.

Product Mix

Machine 1 is available for twenty-four hours, and Machine 2 is available for twenty hours, for the processing of two products. Product X has a contribution margin of $2 per unit; Product Y, $1 per unit. These products must be sold in such combination that the quantity of X must be equal to or less than the quantity of Y. X requires six hours of time on Machine 1 and ten hours of time on Machine 2. Product Y requires four hours of time on Machine 1 only. What production combination will produce the maximum profit?

The linear-programming approach may be divided into four steps, although variations and shortcuts are available in unique situations, notably in transportation problems:

1. Formulate the objectives. The objective is usually to increase profit or decrease cost.

2. Determine the basic relationships, particularly the constraints.

3. Determine the feasible alternatives.

4. Compute the optimum solution.

Techniques may differ. In the uncomplicated situation in our example, the graphic approach is easiest to understand. In practice, the *simplex method* is used—a step-by-step process that is extremely efficient. Basically, the simplex method begins with one feasible solution and tests it

EXHIBIT 17-2
Linear Programming: Graphic Solution

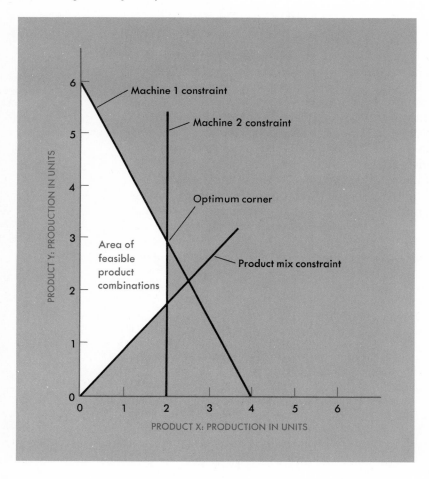

algebraically, by substitution, to see if it can be improved. These substitutions continue until further improvement is impossible. The optimum solution is therefore achieved.

These four steps may be applied to the example.

Step 1. **Formulate the objectives.** In our case, find the product combination that results in the maximum total contribution margin. Maximize:

$$\text{Total contribution margin} = \$2X + \$1Y \qquad (1)$$

This is called the objective function.

Step 2. **Determine the basic relationships.** The relationships may be depicted by the following inequalities:

For Machine 1:	$6X + 4Y \leq 24$
For Machine 2:	$10X \leq 20$
Sales of X and Y:	$X - Y \leq 0$
Because negative production is impossible:	$X \geq 0 \quad \text{and} \quad Y \geq 0$

The three solid lines in Exhibit 17-2 will help you to visualize the machine constraints and the product mix constraint.

Step 3. **Determine the feasible alternatives.** Alternatives are feasible if they are technically possible. We do not want to bother with computations for impossible solutions. The shaded area in Exhibit 17-2 shows the boundaries of the feasible product combinations.

Step 4. **Compute the optimum solution.** Steps 2 and 3 focused on physical relationships alone. We now return to the economic relationships expressed as the objective in Step 1. We test various feasible product combinations to see which one results in a maximum total contribution margin. It so happens that the best solution must lie on one of the corners of the Area of Feasible Product Combinations in Exhibit 17-2. The total contribution margin is calculated for each corner. The steps, which are similar to the simplex method, which uses digital computers, are:

a. Start with one possible combination.
b. Compute the profit.
c. Move to any other possible combination to see if it will improve the result in *b*. Keep moving from corner to corner until no further improvement is possible. (The simplex method is more efficient because it does not necessitate testing all possible combinations before finding the best solution.)

These steps are summarized below. They show that the optimum combination is two units of X and three units of Y:

Trial	Corner	Combination Product X	Product Y	$\$2X + \$1Y =$ Total contribution margin
1	0,0	0	0	$\$2(0) + \$1(0) = \$0$
2	0,6	0	6	$2(0) + 1(6) = 6$
3	2,3	2	3	$2(2) + 1(3) = 7$
4	2,2	2	2	$2(2) + 1(2) = 6$

Why must the best solution lie on a corner? Consider all possible combinations that will produce a total contribution margin of $1 ($2X + 1Y = \$1$). This is a straight line through (0,2) and (1,0). Other total contribution margins are represented by lines parallel to this one. Their associated total contribution margins increase the further the lines get from the origin. The optimum line is the one furthest from the origin which has a feasible point on it; intuitively, we know that this happens at a corner (2,3). Furthermore, if you put a ruler on the graph and move it parallel with the $1 line, the optimum corner becomes apparent.

As these trials show, the central problem of linear programming is to find the specific combination of variables that satisfies all constraints and achieves the objective sought. Moving from corner to corner (which is really moving from one possible solution to another) implies that the scarce resource, productive capacity, is being transferred between products. Each four-hour period that Machine 1 is productively used to produce one unit of Y may be sacrificed (i.e., given or traded) for one six-hour period required to produce one unit of X. Consider the exchange of twelve hours of time. This means that three units of Y will be traded for two units of X. Will this exchange add to profits? Yes:

Total contribution margin at corner (0,6)		$6
Additional contribution margin from Product X:		
2 units, @ $2	$4	
Lost contribution margin, Product Y:		
3 units, @ $1	3	
Net additional contribution margin		1
Total contribution margin at corner (2,3)		$7

These substitutions are a matter of trading a given contribution margin per unit of a limiting factor (i.e., a critical resource) for some other contribution margin per unit of a limiting factor. It is not simply a matter of comparing margins per unit of *product* and jumping to the conclusion that the production of Product X, which has the greater margin per unit of product, should be maximized.[6]

INVENTORY PLANNING AND CONTROL MODELS

Characteristics

Comprehensive inventory-planning and control systems have been successfully installed in many companies. The major objective of inventory management is to discover and maintain the optimum level of investment in the inventory. Inventories may be too high or too low. If too high,

[6]This point is also discussed in Chapter 12, pp. 387–388.

there are unnecessary carrying costs and risks of obsolescence. If too low, production may be disrupted or sales permanently lost. The optimum inventory level is that which minimizes all costs associated with inventory.

Exhibit 17-3 shows the many costs that must be considered. Some of these are not routinely recorded by the accounting system. For instance, operations researchers have had the challenging job of deciding the cost of an item being out of stock so that the seller's lack of inventory results in a lost order. Will the customer return later? Will he go elsewhere? Will he ever return? The appropriate cost is an opportunity cost—the profit lost on the orders lost.

EXHIBIT 17-3

Total Associated Costs of Inventories

Costs of Carrying
1. Desired rate of return on investment.*
2. Risk of obsolescence.
3. Space for storage.
4. Handling and transfer.
5. Clerical.
6. Personal property taxes.
7. Insurance.

plus

Cost of Not Carrying Enough
1. Foregone quantity discounts.*
2. Foregone fortuitous purchases.*
3. Contribution margins on lost sales.*
4. Loss of customer goodwill.*
5. Extra purchasing or transportation costs.
6. Extra costs of uneconomic production runs, overtime, setups, and training.

*Costs which ordinarily do not explicitly appear on formal accounting records.

The two main questions in inventory control are how much to order at a time and when to order. The two significant cost items tend to offset one another. The total costs of carrying, including interest, rise as orders grow in size, but the total costs of ordering, delivery, etc., decrease, and vice versa.

How Much to Order?

A key factor in inventory policy is computing the optimum size of either a normal purchase order for raw materials or a shop order for a production run. This optimum size is called the *economic-order quantity,* the size that will result in minimum total annual costs of the item in question. Consider this example:

Problem

A refrigerator manufacturer buys certain steel shelving in sets from outside suppliers at $4 per set. Total annual needs are 5,000 sets at a rate of twenty sets per working day.

The following cost data are available:

Desired annual return on inventory investment,		
10% × $4.00	$.40	
Rent, insurance, taxes, per unit per year	.10	
Carrying costs per unit per year		$ .50
Costs per purchase order:		
Clerical costs, stationery, postage, telephone, etc.		$10.00

What is the economic order quantity?

EXHIBIT 17-4

ANNUALIZED COSTS OF VARIOUS STANDARD ORDERS
(250 Working Days)

SYMBOLS					LEAST COST ↓	LEAST COST ↓				
E	Order size	50	100	200	400	500	600	800	1,000	5,000
$E/2$	Average inventory in units*	25	50	100	200	250	300	400	500	2,500
A/E	Number of purchase orders**	100	50	25	12.5	10	8.3	6.7	5	1
$S(E/2)$	Annual carrying cost @ $.50	$ 13	$ 25	$ 50	$100	$125	$150	$200	$ 250	$1,250
$P(A/E)$	Annual purchase-order cost @ 10.00	1,000	500	250	125	100	83	67	50	10
C	Total annual expenses	$1,013	$525	$300	$225	$225	$233	$267	$ 300	$1,260

E = Order size
A = Annual quantity used in units
S = Annual cost of carrying one unit in stock one year
P = Cost of placing an order
C = Total annual expenses

*Assume that stock is zero when each order arrives. (Even if a certain minimum inventory were assumed, it has no bearing on the choice here as long as the minimum is the same for each alternative.) Therefore, the average inventory relevant to the problem will be one-half the order quantity. For example, if 600 units are purchased, the inventory on arrival will contain 600. It will gradually diminish until no units are on hand. The average inventory would be 300; the storage cost, $.50 × 300 or $150.

**Number to meet the total annual need for 5,000 sets.

Solution

Exhibit 17-4 shows a tabulation of total costs under various alternatives. The column with the least cost will indicate the economic-order quantity.

Exhibit 17-4 shows minimum costs at two levels, 400 and 500 units. The next step would be to see if costs are lower somewhere between 400 and 500 units—say, at 450 units:

Average inventory, 225 × $.50   = $113 Carrying costs
Number of orders (5,000/450), 11.1 × $10 =   111 Purchase-order costs
                                         $224 Total annual expenses

The dollar differences here are extremely small, but the approach is important. The same approach may be shown in graphic form. See Exhibit 17-5. Note that in this case, total cost is at a minimum where total purchase-order cost and total carrying cost are equal.

Order-Size Formula

The graphic approach has been expressed in formula form. The total annual cost (for any case, not just this example) is differentiated with

EXHIBIT 17-5. Graphic Solution of Economic Lot Size

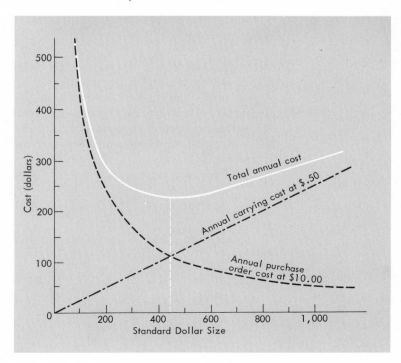

respect to order size. Where this derivative is zero, the minimum annual cost is attained. The widely used formula approach to the order-size problem may be expressed in a variety of ways, one of which follows:[7]

$$E = \sqrt{\frac{2AP}{S}}$$

where E = order size; A = annual quantity used in units; P = cost of placing an order; and S = annual cost of carrying one unit in stock for one year.

Substituting:

$$E = \sqrt{\frac{2(5,000)(\$10)}{\$.50}} = \sqrt{\frac{\$100,000}{\$.50}} = \sqrt{200,000}$$

$$E = 448, \text{ the economic order quantity}$$

As we may expect, the order size gets larger as A or P gets bigger or as S gets smaller.

Note in Exhibit 17-5 that the approach to economic lot-size centers on locating a minimum-cost *range* rather than a minimum-cost *point*. *The total-cost curve tends to flatten between 400 and 800 units.* In practice, there is a definite tendency to (a) find the range, and (b) select a lot size at the lower end of the range. In our example, there would be a tendency to select a lot size of 400 or slightly more.

When to Order?

Although we have seen how to compute economic order quantity, we have not yet answered another key question: When to order? This question is easy to answer only if we know the *lead time,* the time interval between placing an order and receiving delivery, know the economic-order quantity, and are *certain* of demand during lead time. The graph in Exhibit 17-6 will clarify the relationships between the following facts:

Economic order quantity	448 sets of steel shelving
Lead time	2 weeks
Average usage	100 sets per week

[7]The formula may be derived by expressing the tabular and graphic approaches as follows:

(1) $\quad C = \dfrac{AP}{E} + \dfrac{ES}{2}$ $\qquad$ (4) $\quad SE^2 = 2AP$

(2) $\quad \dfrac{dC}{dE} = \dfrac{-AP}{E^2} + \dfrac{S}{2}$ $\qquad$ (5) $\quad E^2 = \dfrac{2AP}{S}$

(3) Set $\dfrac{dC}{dE} = 0; \dfrac{S}{2} - \dfrac{AP}{E^2} = 0$ $\quad$ (6) $\quad E = \sqrt{\dfrac{2AP}{S}}$

EXHIBIT 17-6. Demand in Relation to Inventory Levels

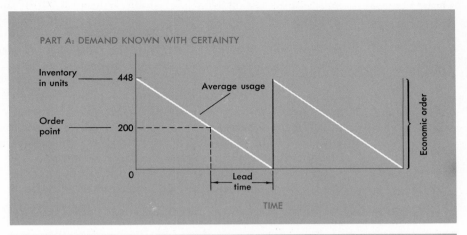

PART A: DEMAND KNOWN WITH CERTAINTY

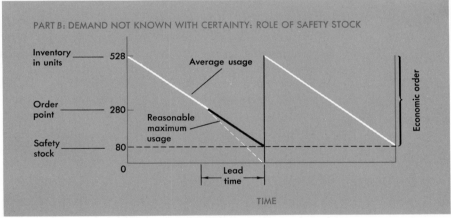

PART B: DEMAND NOT KNOWN WITH CERTAINTY: ROLE OF SAFETY STOCK

Exhibit 17-6, Part *A*, shows that the *reorder point*—the quantity level that automatically triggers a new order—is dependent on expected usage during lead time; that is, if shelving is being used at a rate of 100 sets per week and the lead time is two weeks, a new order would be placed when the inventory level reaches 200 sets.

Minimum Inventory: Safety Allowance

Our previous example assumed that 100 sets would be used per week—a demand pattern that was known with certainty. Businesses are seldom blessed with such accurate forecasting—instead, demand may fluctuate from day to day, from week to week, or from month to month. Thus, the company will run out of stock if there are sudden spurts in usage beyond 100 per week, delays in processing orders, or delivery delays. Obviously, then, nearly all companies must provide for some safety stock—some minimum or buffer inventory as a cushion against reasonable expected maximum usage. Part *B* of Exhibit 17-6 is based on the same facts as Part *A*, except that reasonable expected maximum usage is 140 sets per week. The safety stock would be eighty sets (excess usage of forty sets per week multiplied by two weeks). The reorder point is commonly computed as safety stock plus the average usage during the lead time.

The foregoing discussion of inventory control revolved around the so-called two-bin or constant order-quantity system: When inventory levels recede to *X*, then order *Y*. There is another widely used model in practice, the constant order-cycle system: For example, every month, review the inventory level on hand and order enough to bring the quantity on hand and on order up to some predetermined level of units. The reorder date is fixed, and the quantity ordered depends on the usage since the previous order and the outlook during the lead time. Demand forecasts and seasonal patterns also should be considered in specifying the size of orders during the year.

SUMMARY

Mathematical decision models are used increasingly, because they replace or supplement hunches with explicit assumptions and criteria. As these decision models become more widely utilized, accounting reports for decision making will tend to give more formal, explicit recognition of uncertainty. For example, the reporting of some measure of probability distributions is more likely.

Accountants often provide inputs to assorted decision models, such as linear-programming models and inventory-control models. Therefore, both accountants and managers need to understand the uses and limitations of the models.

SUMMARY PROBLEM FOR YOUR REVIEW

Problem

Review this chapter's examples on statistical-probability theory, linear programming, and inventory control by trying to solve them before studying their solutions.

ASSIGNMENT MATERIAL

Fundamental Assignment Material

17-1. Terminology. Define: *model; conditional value; expected value; payoff table; linear programming; economic standard order quantity; safety stock;* and *lead time.*

17-2. Influence of uncertainty in forecasts. The figures used in many examples and problems in the previous chapters were subject to uncertainty. For simplicity, the expected future amounts of sales, direct material, direct labor, and other operating costs were presented as if they were errorless predictions. For instance, in Example 1 in Chapter 13 (p. 422), we blithely said that a facilities rearrangement "should result in cash operating savings of $2,000 per year."

The industrial engineers who studied the situation had really prepared three estimates:

Event	Percentage Chance of Occurrence	Savings
Pessimistic	.1	$1,200
Most likely	.6	1,800
Optimistic	.3	2,500

Required:

Using an expected-value table, show how the estimate of $2,000 was probably computed.

17-3. Inventory levels and sales forecasting. Each day, an owner of a sidewalk stand stocks bunches of fresh flowers which cost 30¢ and sell for 50¢ each. Leftovers are given to a nearby hospital. Demand characteristics are:

Demand	Probability
Less than 20	.00
20	.10
21	.40
22	.30
23	.20
24 or more	.00

Required:

How many units should be stocked to maximize expected net income? Show your computations.

17-4. Costs and benefits of perfect information. If the owner of the stand in Assignment 17-3 were clairvoyant, so that he could perfectly forecast the demand each day and stock the exact number of flowers needed, what would be his expected profit per day? What is the maximum price that he should be willing to pay for perfect information?

17-5. Fundamental approach of linear programming. A company has two departments, machining and finishing. The company's two products require processing in each of two departments. Data follow:

Product	Contribution Margin per Unit	Daily Capacity in Units Department 1: Machining	Daily Capacity in Units Department 2: Finishing
A	$2.00	200	120
B	2.50	100	200

Severe shortages of material for Product B will limit its production to a maximum of ninety per day.

Required:

How many units of each product should be produced to obtain the maximum net income? Show the basic relationships as inequalities. Solve by using graphical analysis.

Additional Assignment Material

17-6. "The management accountant must be technically competent in computer technology and modern mathematics." Do you agree? Explain.

17-7. What are the distinguishing features of operations research?

17-8. What is a payoff table?

17-9. "OR is mainly a planning tool rather than a controlling tool." Why?

17-10. "Models must conform to reality in two major respects." Explain.

17-11. "Simulation is game playing in the world of make-believe. It has no practical value." Do you agree? Explain.

17-12. "I'm not certain what uncertainty is." Explain uncertainty briefly.

17-13. What is the difference between a conditional value and an expected value?

17-14. Consider the following probability distribution:

Daily Sales Event in Units	Probability
1,000	.1
1,500	.5
2,000	.2
2,500	.1
3,000	.1
	1.0

A student commented: "If a manager has perfect information, he will always sell 3,000 units." Do you agree? Explain.

17-15. Which of the following are linear equations?

$$x + y + 4z + 6a = 8c + 4m$$
$$x^2 = y$$
$$x^2 - y = 4$$
$$4c = 27$$

17-16. What is the minimum competence in linear programming that managers should have?

17-17. What is an infeasible alternative?

17-18. What are the four basic steps in linear programming?

17-19. "The major objective of inventory management is to minimize cash outlays for inventories." Do you agree? Explain.

17-20. What are the principal costs of having too much inventory? Too little inventory?

17-21. "The safety stock is the average amount of inventory used during lead time." Do you agree? Explain.

17-22. "If demand and lead time were known with certainty, no safety stock would be needed." Do you agree? Explain.

17-23. Production scheduling and linear programming. A factory can produce either Product A or Product B. Machine 1 can produce fifteen units of B or twenty units of A, per hour. Machine 2 can produce twenty units of B or twelve units of A, per hour. Machine 1 has a maximum capacity of 10,000 hours and Machine 2 has a maximum capacity of 8,000 hours.

Product A has a unit-contribution margin of 20¢; B, 16¢. There is an unlimited demand for either product; however, both products must be produced together through each machine in a combination such that the quantity of B is at least 20 percent of the quantity of A.

Required:

Which combination of products should be produced? Solve by graphic analysis. Express all relationships as inequalities.

17-24. Linear programming. A company manufactures two kinds of precision tools, C (cheap) and E (expensive). The contribution margin of C is $4 per unit, while E's contribution margin per unit is $5. The tools are produced in three operations: machining, assembling, and finishing. The following is the average time, in hours, required for each tool.

	Machining	Assembling	Finishing
C	1	5	3
E	2	4	2
Maximum time available for each operation	700	1,700	850

Required:

Assume that the time available can be allocated to either type of tool. Express the relationships as inequalities. Using graphic analysis, show which product mix will result in the maximum total contribution margin.

17-25. Linear programming and minimum cost. The local agricultural center has advised George Junker to spread at least 4,800 pounds of a special nitrogen fertilizer ingredient and at least 5,000 pounds of a special phosphate fertilizer ingredient in order to increase his crops. Neither ingredient is available in pure form.

A dealer has offered 100-pound bags of VIM @ $1 each. VIM contains the equivalent of twenty pounds of nitrogen and eighty pounds of phosphate. VOOM is also available in 100-pound bags, @ $3 each; it contains the equivalent of seventy-five pounds of nitrogen and twenty-five pounds of phosphate.

Required:

Express the relationships as inequalities. How many bags of VIM and VOOM should Junker buy in order to obtain the required fertilizer at minimum cost? Solve graphically.

17-26. Linear programming. (CMA adapted.)

Part A

The Witchell Corporation manufactures and sells three grades, *A, B,* and *C,* of a single wood product. Each grade must be processed through three phases—cutting, fitting, and finishing—before they are sold.

The following unit information is provided:

	A	B	C
Selling price	$10.00	$15.00	$20.00
Direct labor	5.00	6.00	9.00
Direct material	.70	.70	1.00
Variable overhead	1.00	1.20	1.80
Fixed overhead	.60	.72	1.08
Materials requirements in board feet	7	7	10
Labor requirements in hours			
Cutting	3/6	3/6	4/6
Fitting	1/6	1/6	2/6
Finishing	1/6	2/6	3/6

Only 5,000 board feet per week can be obtained.

The cutting department has 180 hours of labor available each week. The fitting and finishing departments each have 120 hours of labor available each week. No overtime is allowed.

Contract commitments require the company to make fifty units of *A* per week. In addition, company policy is to produce at least fifty additional units of *A* and fifty units of *B* and fifty units of *C* each week to actively remain in each of the three markets. Because of competition only 130 units of *C* can be sold each week.

Required:

Formulate and label the linear objective function and the constraint functions necessary to maximize the contribution margin.

Part B

The graph provided presents the constraint functions for a chair manufacturing company whose production problem can be solved by linear programming. The company earns $8 for each kitchen chair sold and $5 for each office chair sold.

Required:

1. What is the profit maximizing production schedule?
2. How did you select this production schedule?

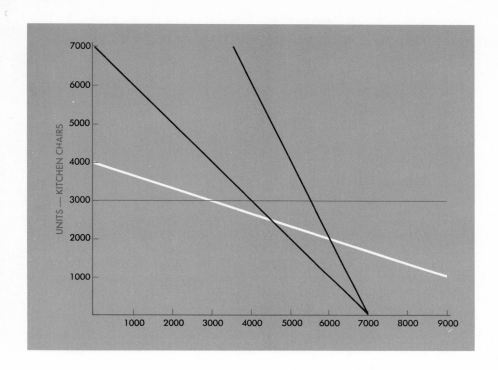

17-27. Probabilities and costs of rework versus costs of setup. The Schlaifer Company has an automatic machine ready and set to make a production run of 2,000 parts. For simplicity, only four events are assumed possible:

Faulty Parts	Probability
30	.6
200	.2
600	.1
900	.1

The incremental cost of reworking a faulty part is 20¢. An expert mechanic can check the setting. He can, without fail, bring the faulty parts down to thirty, but this is time-consuming and costs $25 per setting.

Should the setting be checked?

17-28. Probabilities: automatic or semiautomatic equipment. The Click Company is going to produce a new product. Two types of production equipment are being considered. The more costly equipment will result in lower labor and related variable costs:

Equipment	Total Original Cost	Salvage Value	Variable Costs, per Unit of Product
Semiautomatic	$40,000	—	$4
Automatic	95,000	—	3

Marketing executives believe that this unique product will be salable only over the next year. The unit selling price is $5. Their best estimate of potential sales follows:

Total Units	Probability
30,000	.2
50,000	.4
60,000	.2
70,000	.2

Required:

Prepare an analysis to indicate the best course of action.

17-29. Money on the table. The search for oil is a chancy and costly undertaking. For example, in December, 1972, the United States government sold a parcel of Louisiana offshore oil leases covering 536,000 acres for $1.6 billion dollars. The previous record was $900 million in the Alaska North Slope in 1969.

The leases are sold on blocks of acreage. Sealed bids are received on various blocks from joint ventures of several oil companies or from a single company. A news item concerning the bidding stated:

> The left-on-the-table aggregate this time came to a stunning $660 million or 40% of the winning total. By far, the most open-handed bidder was the group headed by Shell which grabbed fourteen tracts with bids totaling $230 million or more than twice the $93 million sum of the runner-up bids.

Required:

Describe what you think is meant by money-on-the-table. Why does it occur? Who collects it?

17-30. Probability assessment and new product. A new manager, Emil Frang, has just been hired by the Nattelle Company. He is considering the market potential for a new toy, Marvo, which, like many toys, may have great fad appeal.

Frang is experienced in the fad market and is well qualified to assess Marvo's chances for success. He is certain that sales will not be less than 25,000 units. Plant capacity limits total sales to a maximum of 80,000 units during Marvo's brief life. Frang thinks that there are two chances in five for a sales volume of 50,000 units. The probability that sales will exceed 50,000 units is four times the probability that they will be less than 50,000.

If sales are less than 50,000, he feels quite certain that they will be 25,000 units. If sales exceed 50,000, unit volumes of 60,000 and 80,000 are equally likely. A 70,000-unit volume is four times as likely as either. Variable production costs are $3 per unit, selling price is $5, and the special manufacturing equipment (which has no salvage value or alternate use) costs $125,000. Assume, for simplicity, that the above-mentioned are the only possible sales volumes.

Required:

Should Marvo be produced? Show detailed computations to support your answer.

17-31. Net present values, probabilities, and capital budgeting. At the recent stockholders meeting of a large utility company, the question of the profitability of the satellite communications project undertaken by the company was raised by a stockholder. The project was undertaken two years ago. The president stated that $10 million had been invested in the project in each of the previous years and that an equal amount must be invested in each of the next three years. There would be no income from the project until the total investment was completed. At that time the probability of receiving $4 million cash inflow from operations, would be .8; the probability of receiving $8 million in the second year after completion would be .7; the probability of receiving $15 million in the third year after completion would be .6; the probability of receiving $30 million for the following seven years would be .5.

This company expects a minimum rate of return of 10 percent on investments.

Required:

As a stockholder, would you have approved of this project when it was first undertaken? Support your answer with figures, using the net present value approach.

17-32. Long-distance phone calls. A memorandum from the president of Stanford University contained the following:

> As of October 20, 1972, the placement of person-to-person telephone calls from the University extensions will cease; rather, you are asked to place station-to-station calls instead . . . . We anticipate that this change in policy will save over $30,000 per year in toll charges.
>
> You will be interested to know that for the same cost approximately two station-to-station calls can be made for each person-to-person call. Further, a sampling of Stanford users indicates that there is the probability of $66\frac{2}{3}\%$ that a station-to-station call will be successfully completed the first time.

Required:

Using the data given, compute the annual Stanford long-distance phone bill for person-to-person calls before the new policy took effect. In all cases, assume that two station-to-station calls will obtain the desired person.

17-33. Evaluation of degree of risk: standard deviation and coefficient of variation. Suppose that you are the manager of a bottling company. You are trying to choose between two types of equipment, *F* and *G*. The proposals had the following discrete probability distributions of cash flows in each of the next four years:

Proposal F		Proposal G	
Probability	*Net Cash Inflow*	*Probability*	*Net Cash Inflow*
0.10	$3,000	0.10	$1,000
0.25	4,000	0.25	2,000
0.30	5,000	0.30	3,000
0.25	6,000	0.25	4,000
0.10	7,000	0.10	5,000

Required:

1. For each proposal, compute (a) the expected value of the cash inflows in each of the next three years, (b) the standard deviation, and (c) the coefficient of variation.
2. Which proposal has the greater degree of risk? Why?

17-34. Expected value, standard deviation, and risk. Suppose that the Van Horne Company is planning to invest in a common stock for one year. An investigation of the expected dividends and expected market price has been conducted. The probability distribution of expected returns for the year, as a percent, is:

Probability of Occurrence	Possible Return
0.05	.284
0.10	.224
0.20	.160
0.30	.100
0.20	.040
0.10	−.024
0.05	−.084

Required:

1. Compute the expected value of possible returns, the standard deviation of the probability distribution, and the coefficient of variation.
2. Van Horne could also earn 6 percent for certain on federal bonds. What is the standard deviation and coefficient of variation of such an investment?
3. Relate the computations in Requirement 1 with those in Requirement 2. That is, what role does the coefficient of variation play in determining the relative attractiveness of various investments?

17-35. Uncertainty and cost-volume-profit analysis. (This and the next problem are adapted from Robert K. Jaedicke and Alexander A. Robichek, "Cost-Volume-Profit Analysis under Conditions of Uncertainty," *The Accounting Review,* Vol. XXXIX, No. 4, 917–26.) The Jaedicke and Robichek Company is considering two new products to introduce. Either can be produced by using present facilities. Each product requires an increase in annual fixed expenses of $400,000. The products have the same selling price and the same variable cost per unit— $10 and $8, respectively.

Management, after studying past experience with similar products, has prepared the following subjective probability distribution:

Events (Units Demanded)	Probability— Product A	Probability— Product B
50,000	—	0.1
100,000	0.1	0.1
200,000	0.2	0.1
300,000	0.4	0.2
400,000	0.2	0.4
500,000	0.1	0.1
	1.00	1.00

Required:

1. What is the break-even point for each product?
2. Which product should be chosen? Why? Show your computations.
3. Suppose that management was absolutely certain that 300,000 units of Product B would be sold. Which product should be chosen? Why? What benefits are available to management from the provision of the complete probability distribution instead of just a lone expected value?

17-36. Uncertainty, choice of product, and cost-volume-profit analysis. You are a division manager of the *K* Company. You have conducted a study of the profit potential of three products:

	Products		
	1	*2*	*3*
Expected profit	$450,000	$450,000	$ 450,000
Standard deviation of profit	$500,000	$681,500	$1,253,000
The probability of:			
At least breaking even	0.816	0.745	0.641
Profit at least $250,000	0.655	0.615	0.564
Profit at least $600,000	0.382	0.413	0.456
Loss greater than $300,000	0.067	0.136	0.274

The expected contribution per unit for each product is $1,250, and the expected fixed expenses per year are $5,800,000, so each product has the same break-even quantity, 4,640 units.

Required:

Which product would you choose? Explain fully, including comparisons of the relative riskiness of the three products.

17-37. Cost and value of information. An oil-well driller, Mr. George, is thinking of investing $50,000 in an oil-well lease. He estimates the probability of finding a producing well as .4. Such a discovery would result in a net gain of $100,000 ($150,000 revenue—$50,000 cost). There is a .6 probability of not getting any oil, resulting in the complete loss of the $50,000.

Required:

1. What is the net expected value of investing?
2. Mr. George desires more information because of the vast uncertainty and the large costs of making a wrong decision. There would be an unrecoverable $50,000 outlay if no oil is found; there would be a $100,000 opportunity cost if he does not invest and the oil is really there. What is the most he should be willing to pay for perfect information regarding the presence or absence of oil? Explain.

17-38. Inventory control and television tubes. The Nemmers Company assembles private-brand television sets for a retail chain, under a contract requiring delivery of 100 sets per day for each of 250 business days per year. Each set requires a picture tube which Nemmers buys outside, for $20 each. The tubes are loaded on trucks at the supplier's factory door and are then delivered by a trucking service at a charge of $100 per trip, regardless of the size of the shipment. The cost of storing the tubes (including the desired rate of return on investment) is $2 per tube per year. Because production is stable throughout the year, the average inventory is one-half the size of the truck lot. Tabulate the relevant annual cost of various truck-lot sizes at 5, 10, 15, 25, 50, and 250 trips per year. Show your results graphically. (Note that the $20 unit cost of tubes is common to all alternatives and hence may be ignored.)

17-39. Reorder point. A utility company uses 5,000 tons of coal per year to generate power at one of its plants. The company orders 500 tons at a time. Lead time for the orders is five days, and the safety stock is a three-day supply. Usage is assumed to be constant over a 360-day year. Calculate the reorder point.

17-40. Payoff tables and perfect information. (CMA adapted.) Vendo, Inc. has been operating the concession stands at a university's football stadium. The university has had successful football teams for many years; as a result the stadium is always full. The university is located in an area which suffers no rain during the football season. From time to time, Vendo has found itself very short of hot dogs and at other times it has had many left. A review of the records of sales of the past nine seasons revealed the following frequency of hot dogs sold:

	Games
10,000 hot dogs	5
20,000 hot dogs	10
30,000 hot dogs	20
40,000 hot dogs	15
	50

Hot dogs sell for 50¢ each and cost Vendo 30¢ each. Unsold hot dogs are given to a local orphanage without charge.

Required:
1. Assuming that only the four quantities listed were ever sold and that the occurrences were random events, prepare a payoff table (ignore income taxes) to represent the four possible strategies of ordering 10,000; 20,000; 30,000; or 40,000 hot dogs.
2. Using the expected value decision rule, determine the best strategy.
3. What is the dollar value of perfect information?

17-41. Relevant costs of inventory planning; sensitivity analysis. (Prepared by G. A. Feltham.) The Super Corporation distributes widgets to the upper delta region of the Sunswop River. The demand for widgets is very constant and Super is able to predict the annual demand with considerable accuracy. The predicted demand for the next couple of years is 200,000 widgets per year.

Super purchases its widgets from a supplier in Calton at a price of $20 per widget. In order to transport the purchases from Calton to the upper delta region, Super must charter a ship. The charter services usually charge $1,000 per trip plus $2 per widget (this includes the cost of loading the ship). The ships have a capacity of 10,000 widgets. The placing of each order, including arranging for the ship, requires about five hours of employee time. It takes about a week for an order to arrive at the Super warehouse.

When a ship arrives at the Super warehouse, the widgets can be unloaded at a rate of twenty-five per hour per employee. The unloading equipment used by each employee is rented from a local supplier at a rate of $5 per hour. Supervisory time for each shipload is about four hours.

Super leases a large warehouse for storing the widgets; it has a capacity of 15,000 widgets. The employees working in the warehouse have several tasks:

a. Placing the widgets into storage, after they are unloaded, can be done at the rate of about forty per hour.
b. Checking, cleaning, etc., of the widgets in inventory requires about one-half hour per widget per year.
c. Removing a widget from inventory and preparing it for shipment to a customer requires about one-eighth hour.
d. Security guards, general maintenance, etc., require about 10,000 hours per year.

The average cost per hour of labor is approximately $10 (including fringe benefits). Super has developed the following prediction equation for its general overhead (excluding shipping materials, fringe benefits, and equipment rental):

Predicted overhead for the year = $1,000,000 + ($8 × Total labor-hours)

The materials used to ship one widget to a customer cost $1, and the delivery costs average out to about $2 per widget.

The company requires a before-tax rate of return of 20 percent on its investment.

Required:
1. Super has decided to base its ordering policy on an economic-order-quantity model. What amount should they order each time and what should they use as the reorder point? Show calculations to support your answer.
2. If the true overhead-prediction equation is

$800,000 + ($12 × Total labor-hours)

what is the opportunity cost of the prediction error? That is, compare (a) the optimal payoff given the actual magnitude of the parameters with (b) the actual payoff given the order quantity from Requirement 1 and the actual magnitude of the parameters. The difference is the opportunity cost of the prediction error.

APPENDICES

Recommended Readings

A

The following readings are suggested as an aid to those readers who want to pursue some topics in more depth than is possible in this book. Of course, many of the chapters have footnotes or suggested readings on a particular topic. Therefore, the specific chapters should be consulted for direct references.

There is a hazard in compiling a group of recommended readings. Inevitably, some worthwhile books or periodicals are overlooked. Moreover, such a list cannot include books published subsequent to the compilation here.

Professional journals are typically available in university libraries. *Management Accounting, Management Adviser,* and *The Financial Executive* tend to stress articles on management accounting. The *Journal of Accountancy* emphasizes financial accounting and is directed at the practicing CPA. The *Harvard Business Review* and *Fortune,* which are aimed at general managers, contain many articles on planning and control.

The Accounting Review and the *Journal of Accounting Research* cover all phases of accounting at a more theoretical level than the preceding publications.

The *Opinions* of the Accounting Principles Board are available from the American Institute of CPAs, 666 Fifth Avenue, New York, N.Y. 10019. The Institute also has a series of research studies on a variety of topics. The pronouncements of the Financial Accounting Standards Board are available from the Board's offices, High Ridge Park, Stamford, Connecticut 06905.

The Financial Executives Institute, 50 West 44th Street, New York, N.Y. and the National Association of Accountants, 505 Park Avenue, New York, N.Y. have long lists of accounting research publications.

There are many books on elementary management accounting. Also, many books entitled *Cost Accounting* stress a management approach, including those published since 1972 by Gerald Crowningshield (Houghton Mifflin), Nicholas Dopuch and Jacob Birnberg (Harcourt, Brace & World), Charles Horngren (Prentice-Hall), and Gordon Shillinglaw (Richard D. Irwin).

The following books on planning and control should be helpful:

Anthony, R. N., John Dearden, and Richard Vancil, *Management Control Systems,* Rev. ed. (Richard D. Irwin, 1972).

Beyer, Robert, and Donald Trawicki, *Profitability Accounting for Planning and Control,* 2nd ed. (Ronald Press, 1972).

Solomons, David, *Divisional Performance: Measurement and Control* (Homewood, Ill.: Richard D. Irwin, 1968). This book has an extensive bibliography. It is especially strong on transfer pricing.

Books of readings on management accounting topics published since 1969 include:

Anton, Hector R., and Peter A. Firmin (ed.), *Contemporary Issues in Cost Accounting* (2nd ed., Boston: Houghton Mifflin Company, 1972).

Benston, George J., *Contemporary Cost Accounting and Control* (Belmont, Cal.: Dickenson Publishing Company, Inc., 1970).

Bruns, William J., Jr., and Don T. De Coster, *Accounting and its Behavioral Implications* (McGraw-Hill Book Company, 1969).

Livingstone, John Leslie (ed.) *Management Planning and Control: Mathematical Models* (McGraw-Hill Book Company, 1970).

Rappaport, Alfred (ed.) *Information for Decision Making: Quantitative and Behavioral Dimensions* (Englewood Cliffs: Prentice-Hall, 1970).

Rosen, L. S., *Topics in Managerial Accounting* (McGraw-Hill Company of Canada, Ltd., 1970).

Schiff, Michael, and Arie Y. Lewin (ed.), *Behavioral Aspects of Accounting* (Englewood Cliffs, N.J.: Prentice-Hall, Inc., 1974).

Sundem, Gary L. (ed.), *Accounting for Managerial Decision Making* (Los Angeles: Melville Publishing Company, 1974).

Fundamentals
of Compound Interest
and the Use
of Present Value Tables

B

NATURE OF INTEREST

Interest is the cost of using money. It is the rental charge for cash, just as rental charges are often made for the use of automobiles or boats.

Interest does not always entail an outlay of cash. The concept of interest applies to ownership funds as well as to borrowed funds. The reason why interest must be considered on *all* funds in use, regardless of their source, is that the selection of one alternative necessarily commits funds which otherwise could be invested in some other opportunity. The measure of the interest in such cases is the return foregone by rejecting the alternative use. For instance, a wholly owned home or business asset is not cost-free. The funds so invested could alternatively be invested in government bonds or in some other venture. The measure of this opportunity cost depends on what alternative incomes are available.

Interest cost is often unimportant when short-term projects are under consideration, but it becomes extremely important when long-run plans are being considered. The longer the time span, the higher the interest or rental charge. If you place $10,000 in a savings account at 4 percent interest, compounded annually, the original $10,000 will grow to $10,400 at the end of Year 1 ($10,000 × 1.04); to $10,816 at the end of Year 2 ($10,400 × 1.04); to $11,249 at the end of Year 3 ($10,816 × 1.04); and to $21,911 at the end of Year 20 ($10,000 × 1.04^{20}). If the rate of interest were 10 percent compounded annually, the original $10,000 would grow to $13,310 at the end of Year 3, ($10,000 × 1.10^3); and to $67,276 at the end of Year 20 ($10,000 × 1.10^{20}).

Two basic tables are used in capital budgeting. The first table (Table 1, p. 601), the Present Value of $1, deals with a single lump-sum cash inflow or outflow at a given instant of time, the *end* of the period in question. An example should clarify the reasoning underlying the construction and use of the table.

Illustration: assume that a prominent corporation is issuing a three-year noninterest-bearing note payable which promises to pay a lump sum of $1,000 exactly three years from now. You desire a rate of return of exactly 6 percent, compounded annually. How much would you be willing to pay now for the three-year note? The situation is sketched as follows:

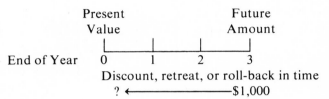

Let us examine the chart, period by period. First, let us assume that you are to purchase the $1,000 note at the end of Year 2 instead of at time zero. How much would you be willing to pay? If you wish to earn 6¢ annually on every $1 invested, you would want to receive $1.06 in one year for every $1 you invest today. Therefore, at the end of Year 2 you would be willing to pay $\frac{\$1.00}{\$1.06}$ × $1,000 for the right to receive $1,000 at the end of Year 3, or $.943 × $1,000 = $943. Let us enter this in a tabular calculation:

End of Year	Interest per Year	Cumulative Discount, Called Compound Discount	Present Value at the End of Year
3	$57	$ 57	$1,000
2	53	110	943
1	50	160	890
0	—	—	840

Note that what is really being done in the tabulation is a series of computations that could be formulated as follows:

$$PV_2 = \$1,000 \left[\frac{1.00}{1.06}\right] = \$943$$

$$PV_1 = \$1,000 \left[\frac{1.00}{(1.06)^2}\right] = \$890$$

$$PV_0 = \$1,000 \left[\frac{1.00}{(1.06)^3}\right] = \$840$$

This can be written as a formula for the present value of $1:

$$PV = \frac{S}{(1 + i)^n}$$

where PV = Present value at time zero; S = Future amount; i = Interest rate; and n = Number of periods.

Check the answers in the tabulation by using Table 1 (p. 601). For example, the Period 3 row and the 6 percent column show a factor of .840. Multiply this factor by the future cash flow, $1,000, to obtain its present value, $840.

Use Table 1 to obtain the present values of:

1. $1,600, @ 20 percent, at the end of 20 years.
2. $8,300, @ 10 percent, at the end of 12 years.
3. $8,000, @ 4 percent, at the end of 4 years.

   Answers:

1. $1,600 (.026) = $41.60.
2. $8,300 (.319) = $2,648.
3. $8,000 (.855) = $6,840.

TABLE 2: PRESENT VALUE OF AN ORDINARY ANNUITY OF $1

An ordinary annuity is a series of equal cash flows to take place at the *end* of successive periods of equal length. Assume that you buy a noninterest-bearing serial note from a corporation which promises to pay $1,000 at the end of each of three years. How much should you be willing to pay, if you desire a rate of return of 6 percent, compounded annually?

The tabulation below shows how the formula for PV_A, *the present value of an ordinary annuity,* is developed.

EXHIBIT B-1

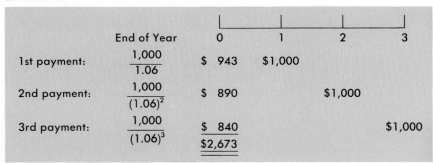

End of Year	0	1	2	3
1st payment: $\dfrac{1,000}{1.06}$	$ 943	$1,000		
2nd payment: $\dfrac{1,000}{(1.06)^2}$	$ 890		$1,000	
3rd payment: $\dfrac{1,000}{(1.06)^3}$	$ 840			$1,000
	$2,673			

$$PV_A = \text{Sum of present values of each item} \qquad (1)$$

For the general case, the present value of an ordinary annuity of $1 may be expressed as follows:

$$PV_A = \frac{1}{1+i} + \frac{1}{(1+i)^2} + \frac{1}{(1+i)^3} \qquad (2)$$

Substituting values from our illustration

$$PV_A = \frac{1}{1.06} + \frac{1}{(1.06)^2} + \frac{1}{(1.06)^3} \qquad (3)$$

Multiply by $\frac{1}{1.06}$:
$$PV_A\left(\frac{1}{1.06}\right) = \frac{1}{(1.06)^2} + \frac{1}{(1.06)^3} + \frac{1}{(1.06)^4} \qquad (4)$$

Subtract Equation 4 from Equation 3

$$PV_A - PV_A\left(\frac{1}{1.06}\right) = \frac{1}{1.06} - \frac{1}{(1.06)^4} \qquad (5)$$

Factor
$$PV_A\left(1 - \frac{1}{1.06}\right) = \frac{1}{1.06}\left[1 - \frac{1}{(1.06)^3}\right] \qquad (6)$$

or
$$PV_A\left(\frac{.06}{1.06}\right) = \frac{1}{1.06}\left[1 - \frac{1}{(1.06)^3}\right] \qquad (7)$$

Divide by $\frac{.06}{1.06}$
$$PV_A = \frac{1}{.06}\left[1 - \frac{1}{(1.06)^3}\right] \qquad (8)$$

The general formula for the present worth of an annuity is:

$$PV_A = \frac{1}{i}\left[1 - \frac{1}{(1+i)^n}\right] \qquad (9)$$

Solving
$$PV_A = \frac{1}{.06}(1 - .840) = \frac{.160}{.06} = 2.67 \qquad (10)$$

This formula is the basis for Table 2 (p. 602). Check the answer in the table. Minor differences are due to rounding.

Use Table 2 to obtain the present values of the following ordinary annuities.

1. $1,600 at 20 percent for 20 years.
2. $8,300 at 10 percent for 12 years.
3. $8,000 at 4 percent for 4 years.

Answers:

1. $1,600 (4.870) = $7,792.
2. $8,300 (6.814) = $56,556.
3. $8,000 (3.630) = $29,040.

TABLE 1:
Present Value of $1

$$PV = \frac{S}{(1+i)^n}$$

PERIODS	4%	6%	8%	10%	12%	14%	16%	18%	20%	22%	24%	26%	28%	30%	40%
1	0.962	0.943	0.926	0.909	0.893	0.877	0.862	0.847	0.833	0.820	0.806	0.794	0.781	0.769	0.714
2	0.925	0.890	0.857	0.826	0.797	0.769	0.743	0.718	0.694	0.672	0.650	0.630	0.610	0.592	0.510
3	0.889	0.840	0.794	0.751	0.712	0.675	0.641	0.609	0.579	0.551	0.524	0.500	0.477	0.455	0.364
4	0.855	0.792	0.735	0.683	0.636	0.592	0.552	0.516	0.482	0.451	0.423	0.397	0.373	0.350	0.260
5	0.822	0.747	0.681	0.621	0.567	0.519	0.476	0.437	0.402	0.370	0.341	0.315	0.291	0.269	0.186
6	0.790	0.705	0.630	0.564	0.507	0.456	0.410	0.370	0.335	0.303	0.275	0.250	0.227	0.207	0.133
7	0.760	0.665	0.583	0.513	0.452	0.400	0.354	0.314	0.279	0.249	0.222	0.198	0.178	0.159	0.095
8	0.731	0.627	0.540	0.467	0.404	0.351	0.305	0.266	0.233	0.204	0.179	0.157	0.139	0.123	0.068
9	0.703	0.592	0.500	0.424	0.361	0.308	0.263	0.225	0.194	0.167	0.144	0.125	0.108	0.094	0.048
10	0.676	0.558	0.463	0.386	0.322	0.270	0.227	0.191	0.162	0.137	0.116	0.099	0.085	0.073	0.035
11	0.650	0.527	0.429	0.350	0.287	0.237	0.195	0.162	0.135	0.112	0.094	0.079	0.066	0.056	0.025
12	0.625	0.497	0.397	0.319	0.257	0.208	0.168	0.137	0.112	0.092	0.076	0.062	0.052	0.043	0.018
13	0.601	0.469	0.368	0.290	0.229	0.182	0.145	0.116	0.093	0.075	0.061	0.050	0.040	0.033	0.013
14	0.577	0.442	0.340	0.263	0.205	0.160	0.125	0.099	0.078	0.062	0.049	0.039	0.032	0.025	0.009
15	0.555	0.417	0.315	0.239	0.183	0.140	0.108	0.084	0.065	0.051	0.040	0.031	0.025	0.020	0.006
16	0.534	0.394	0.292	0.218	0.163	0.123	0.093	0.071	0.054	0.042	0.032	0.025	0.019	0.015	0.005
17	0.513	0.371	0.270	0.198	0.146	0.108	0.080	0.060	0.045	0.034	0.026	0.020	0.015	0.012	0.003
18	0.494	0.350	0.250	0.180	0.130	0.095	0.069	0.051	0.038	0.028	0.021	0.016	0.012	0.009	0.002
19	0.475	0.331	0.232	0.164	0.116	0.083	0.060	0.043	0.031	0.023	0.017	0.012	0.009	0.007	0.002
20	0.456	0.312	0.215	0.149	0.104	0.073	0.051	0.037	0.026	0.019	0.014	0.010	0.007	0.005	0.001
21	0.439	0.294	0.199	0.135	0.093	0.064	0.044	0.031	0.022	0.015	0.011	0.008	0.006	0.004	0.001
22	0.422	0.278	0.184	0.123	0.083	0.056	0.038	0.026	0.018	0.013	0.009	0.006	0.004	0.003	0.001
23	0.406	0.262	0.170	0.112	0.074	0.049	0.033	0.022	0.015	0.010	0.007	0.005	0.003	0.002	
24	0.390	0.247	0.158	0.102	0.066	0.043	0.028	0.019	0.013	0.008	0.006	0.004	0.003	0.002	
25	0.375	0.233	0.146	0.092	0.059	0.038	0.024	0.016	0.010	0.007	0.005	0.003	0.002	0.001	
26	0.361	0.220	0.135	0.084	0.053	0.033	0.021	0.014	0.009	0.006	0.004	0.002	0.002	0.001	
27	0.347	0.207	0.125	0.076	0.047	0.029	0.018	0.011	0.007	0.005	0.003	0.002	0.001	0.001	
28	0.333	0.196	0.116	0.069	0.042	0.026	0.016	0.010	0.006	0.004	0.002	0.002	0.001	0.001	
29	0.321	0.185	0.107	0.063	0.037	0.022	0.014	0.008	0.005	0.003	0.002	0.001	0.001	0.001	
30	0.308	0.174	0.099	0.057	0.033	0.020	0.012	0.007	0.004	0.003	0.002	0.001	0.001	0.001	
40	0.208	0.097	0.046	0.022	0.011	0.005	0.003	0.001	0.001						

TABLE 2:
Present Value of Ordinary Annuity of $1

$$PV_A = \frac{1}{i}\left[1 - \frac{1}{(1+i)^n}\right]$$

PERIODS	4%	6%	8%	10%	12%	14%	16%	18%	20%	22%	24%	25%	26%	28%	30%	40%
1	0.962	0.943	0.926	0.909	0.893	0.877	0.862	0.847	0.833	0.820	0.806	0.800	0.794	0.781	0.769	0.714
2	1.886	1.833	1.783	1.736	1.690	1.647	1.605	1.566	1.528	1.492	1.457	1.440	1.424	1.392	1.361	1.224
3	2.775	2.673	2.577	2.487	2.402	2.322	2.246	2.174	2.106	2.042	1.981	1.952	1.923	1.868	1.816	1.589
4	3.630	3.465	3.312	3.170	3.037	2.914	2.798	2.690	2.589	2.494	2.404	2.362	2.320	2.241	2.166	1.849
5	4.452	4.212	3.993	3.791	3.605	3.433	3.274	3.127	2.991	2.864	2.745	2.689	2.635	2.532	2.436	2.035
6	5.242	4.917	4.623	4.355	4.111	3.889	3.685	3.498	3.326	3.167	3.020	2.951	2.885	2.759	2.643	2.168
7	6.002	5.582	5.206	4.868	4.564	4.288	4.039	3.812	3.605	3.416	3.242	3.161	3.083	2.937	2.802	2.263
8	6.733	6.210	5.747	5.335	4.968	4.639	4.344	4.078	3.837	3.619	3.421	3.329	3.241	3.076	2.925	2.331
9	7.435	6.802	6.247	5.759	5.328	4.946	4.607	4.303	4.031	3.786	3.566	3.463	3.366	3.184	3.019	2.379
10	8.111	7.360	6.710	6.145	5.650	5.216	4.833	4.494	4.192	3.923	3.682	3.571	3.465	3.269	3.092	2.414
11	8.760	7.887	7.139	6.495	5.988	5.453	5.029	4.656	4.327	4.035	3.776	3.656	3.544	3.335	3.147	2.438
12	9.385	8.384	7.536	6.814	6.194	5.660	5.197	4.793	4.439	4.127	3.851	3.725	3.606	3.387	3.190	2.456
13	9.986	8.853	7.904	7.103	6.424	5.842	5.342	4.910	4.533	4.203	3.912	3.780	3.656	3.427	3.223	2.468
14	10.563	9.295	8.244	7.367	6.628	6.002	5.468	5.008	4.611	4.265	3.962	3.824	3.695	3.459	3.249	2.477
15	11.118	9.712	8.559	7.606	6.811	6.142	5.575	5.092	4.675	4.315	4.001	3.859	3.726	3.483	3.268	2.484
16	11.652	10.106	8.851	7.824	6.974	6.265	5.669	5.162	4.730	4.357	4.033	3.887	3.751	3.503	3.283	2.489
17	12.166	10.477	9.122	8.022	7.120	6.373	5.749	5.222	4.775	4.391	4.059	3.910	3.771	3.518	3.295	2.492
18	12.659	10.828	9.372	8.201	7.250	6.467	5.818	5.273	4.812	4.419	4.080	3.928	3.786	3.529	3.304	2.494
19	13.134	11.158	9.604	8.365	7.366	6.550	5.877	5.316	4.844	4.442	4.097	3.942	3.799	3.539	3.311	2.496
20	13.590	11.470	9.818	8.514	7.469	6.623	5.929	5.353	4.870	4.460	4.110	3.954	3.808	3.546	3.316	2.497
21	14.029	11.764	10.017	8.649	7.562	6.687	5.973	5.384	4.891	4.476	4.121	3.963	3.816	3.551	3.320	2.498
22	14.451	12.042	10.201	8.772	7.645	6.743	6.001	5.410	4.909	4.488	4.130	3.970	3.822	3.556	3.323	2.498
23	14.857	12.303	10.371	8.883	7.718	6.792	6.044	5.432	4.925	4.499	4.137	3.976	3.827	3.559	3.325	2.499
24	15.247	12.550	10.529	8.985	7.784	6.835	6.073	5.451	4.937	4.507	4.143	3.981	3.831	3.562	3.327	2.499
25	15.622	12.783	10.675	9.077	7.843	6.873	6.097	5.467	4.948	4.514	4.147	3.985	3.834	3.564	3.329	2.499
26	15.983	13.003	10.810	9.161	7.896	6.906	6.118	5.480	4.956	4.520	4.151	3.988	3.837	3.566	3.330	2.500
27	16.330	13.211	10.935	9.237	7.943	6.935	6.136	5.492	4.964	4.524	4.154	3.990	3.839	3.567	3.331	2.500
28	16.663	13.406	11.051	9.307	7.984	6.961	6.152	5.502	4.970	4.528	4.157	3.992	3.840	3.568	3.331	2.500
29	16.984	13.591	11.158	9.370	8.022	6.983	6.166	5.510	4.975	4.531	4.159	3.994	3.841	3.569	3.332	2.500
30	17.292	13.765	11.258	9.427	8.055	7.003	6.177	5.517	4.979	4.534	4.160	3.995	3.842	3.569	3.332	2.500
40	19.793	15.046	11.925	9.779	8.244	7.105	6.234	5.548	4.997	4.544	4.166	3.999	3.846	3.571	3.333	2.500

Glossary

For a more elaborate description of each term, consult the chapter indicated in parentheses.

Absorption costing. That type of product costing which assigns fixed manufacturing overhead to the units produced as a product cost. Contrast with direct costing. (Chap. 15)

Account. Summary of the changes in a particular asset or equity. (Chap. 2)

Accounting method. See *Unadjusted rate of return.* (Chap. 13)

Accrual basis. A matching process whereby revenue is recognized as services are rendered and expenses are recognized as efforts are expended or services utilized to obtain the revenue. (Chap. 2)

Activity accounting. See *Responsibility accounting.* (Chap. 11)

Allocation. Assigning one or more items of cost or revenue to one or more segments of an organization according to benefits received, responsibilities, or other logical measure of use. (Chap. 11)

Appropriation. An authorization to spend up to a specified dollar ceiling. (Chap. 10)

Assets. Economic resources that are expected to benefit future activities. (Chap. 2)

Asset turnover. The ratio of sales to total assets available. (Chap. 16)

Attention directing. That function of the accountant's information-supplying task which focuses on problems in the operation of the firm or which points out imperfections or inefficiencies in certain areas of the firm's operation. (Chap. 1)

Balance Sheet. A statement of financial status at an instant of time. (Chap. 2)

Bill of materials. A specification of the quantities of direct material allowed for manufacturing a given quantity of output. (Chap. 9)

Book value. See *Net book value.* (Chap. 3)

Book value method. See *Unadjusted rate of return.* (Chap. 13)

Budget. A plan of action expressed in figures. (Chaps. 1, 6)

Capacity costs. An alternate term for fixed costs, emphasizing the fact that fixed costs are needed in order to provide operating facilities and an organization ready to produce and sell at a planned volume of activity. (Chap. 10)

Capital budgeting. Long-term planning for proposed capital outlays and their financing. (Chap. 13)

Capital surplus. The excess received over the par or stated or legal value of the shares issued. (Chap. 3)

Cash budget. A schedule of expected cash receipts and disbursements. (Chap. 6)

Cash flow. A general term that must be interpreted carefully. Most strictly, cash flow means inflows or outflows of cash. Frequently, the term is used loosely to represent funds provided by operations. (Chaps. 2, 13)

Committed costs. Those fixed costs arising from the possession of plant and equipment and a basic organization and thus affected primarily by long-run decisions as to the desired level of capacity. (Chap. 10)

Common cost. See *Joint cost.* (Chaps. 11, 12)

Comptroller. See *Controller.* (Chap. 1)

Conditional value. The value which will ensue if a particular event occurs. (Chap. 17)

Conservatism. Selecting that method of measurement which yields the gloomiest immediate results. (Chap. 2)

Consolidated financial statements. The combination of the financial positions and earnings reports of the parent company with those of various subsidiaries into an overall report as if they were a single entity. (Chap. 3)

Continuous budget. A budget which perpetually adds a month in the future as the month just ended is dropped. (Chap. 6)

Contribution approach. A method of preparing income statements which separates variable costs from fixed costs in order to emphasize the importance of cost behavior patterns for purposes of planning and control. (Chap. 8)

Contribution margin. Excess of sales price over variable expenses. Also called marginal income. May be expressed as a total, as a ratio, or on a per unit basis. (Chap. 7)

Controllable cost. A cost which may be directly regulated at a given level of managerial authority, either in the short run or in the long run. (Chap. 11)

Controller. The chief management accounting executive. Also spelled comptroller. (Chap. 1)

Controlling. Obtaining conformity to plans through action and evaluation. (Chap. 1)

Cost object. Any action or activity or product or part of an organization for which a separate determination of costs is desired. (Chap. 8)

Credit. An entry on the right side of an account. (Chap. 2)

Current assets. Cash plus those assets which are reasonably expected to be converted to cash or sold or consumed during the normal operating cycle. (Chap. 3)

Current liabilities. Liabilities that fall due within the coming year or within the normal operating cycle if longer than a year. (Chap. 3)

Currently attainable standards. Standards expressing a level of economic efficiency which can be reached with skilled, diligent, superior effort. (Chap. 9)

Debenture. A general claim against all unencumbered assets rather than a specific claim against particular assets. (Chap. 3)

Debit. An entry on the left side of an account. (Chap. 2)

Deferral method. Reflection in net income of an investment tax credit over the productive life of the asset acquired. Also see *Flow-through method.* (Chap. 5)

Deferred federal income taxes. A deferred credit in the balance sheet that represents the additional federal income taxes that would have been due if a company had not been allowed to deduct greater amounts for expenses (such as depreciation) for income tax reporting purposes than are recorded for financial reporting purposes. (Chap. 5)

Depreciation. The allocation of the original cost of plant, property, and equipment to the particular periods or products that benefit from the utilization of the assets. (Chap. 3)

Differential cost. See *Incremental cost.* (Chap. 12)

Direct costing. That type of product costing which charges fixed manufacturing overhead immediately against the revenue of the period in which it was incurred, without assigning it to specific units produced. Also called variable costing or marginal costing. (Chap. 16)

Direct labor. All labor which is obviously related and specifically and conveniently traceable to specific products. (Chap. 8)

Direct material. All raw material which is an integral part of the finished good and which can be conveniently assigned to specific physical units. (Chap. 8)

Discretionary costs. Those fixed costs that arise from periodic, usually yearly, appropriation decisions that directly reflect top management policies. Also called programmed costs and managed costs. (Chap. 10)

Earned surplus. See *Retained income.* (Chap. 2)

Earnings per share. Net income divided by the number of common shares outstanding. However, where preferred stock exists, the preferred dividends must be deducted in order to compute the net income applicable to common stock. (Chap. 3)

Economic standard order quantity. The amount of inventory which should be ordered at one time in order to minimize the associated annual costs of the inventory. (Chap. 17)

Efficiency variance. Quantity variance, applied to labor. (Chap. 9)

Entity. A specific area of attention and effort that is the focus of the accounting process. It may be a single corporation, a tax district, a department, a papermaking machine, or a consolidated group of many interrelated corporations. (Chap. 2)

Equities. The sources of the assets. (Chap. 2)

Equity method. A basis for carrying long-term investments at cost plus a prorata share of accumulated retained income since acquisition. (Chap. 3)

Excess material requisitions. A form to be filled out by the production staff to secure any materials needed in excess of the standard amount allotted for output. (Chap. 9)

Expected value. A weighted average of all the conditional values of an act. Each conditional value is weighted by its probability. (Chap. 17)

Expenses. Expired costs that are deducted from revenue for a given period. (Chap. 2)

Factory burden. See *Factory overhead.* (Chap. 8)

Factory overhead. All factory costs other than direct labor and direct material. Also called factory burden, indirect manufacturing costs, manufacturing overhead, and manufacturing expense. (Chap. 8)

First in, first out. The stock which is acquired earliest is assumed to be used first; the stock acquired latest is assumed to be still on hand. (Chap. 5)

Fixed cost. A cost which, for a given period of time and range of activity called the relevant range, *does not change in total* but becomes progressively smaller on a *per unit* basis as volume increases. (Chap. 7)

Flexible budget. A budget, often referring to overhead costs only, which is prepared for a range, rather than for a single level, of activity—one which can be automatically geared to changes in the level of volume. Also called variable budget. Direct material and direct labor are sometimes included in the flexible budget. (Chap. 9)

Flow-through method. Recognition in full in one year of the income benefits of an investment tax credit. Also see *Deferral method.* (Chap. 5)

Functional costing. Classifying costs by allocating them to the various functions performed, such as manufacturing, warehousing, delivery, billing, and so forth. (Chap. 8)

Fund. Setting aside a specific amount of cash or securities for a special purpose. (Chap. 3)

Funds provided by operations. The excess of revenue over all expenses requiring net working capital. (Chap. 4)

Funds statement. A statement of sources and applications of net working capital. (Chap. 4)

Going concern. The assumption that an entity will continue indefinitely or at least that it will not be liquidated in the near future. (Chap. 2)

Goodwill. The total purchase price of assets acquired in a lump-sum purchase that exceeds the total of the amounts that can be justifiably assigned to the individual assets. (Chap. 5)

Historical cost. See *Sunk cost.* (Chap. 12)

Ideal capacity. The absolute maximum number of units that could be produced in a given operating situation, with no allowance for work stoppages or repairs. Also called theoretical capacity. (Chap. 10)

Idle time. A classification of *indirect labor* which constitutes wages paid for unproductive time due to circumstances beyond the worker's control. (Chap. 8)

Income statement. A statement that evaluates the operating performance of the corporation by matching its accomplishments (revenue from customers, which usually is called sales) and efforts (cost of goods sold and other expenses). (Chap. 2)

Incremental approach. A method of determining which of two alternative courses of action is preferable by calculating the present value of the difference in net cash inflow between one alternative and the other. (Chap. 13)

Incremental cost. The difference in total cost between two alternatives. Also called differential cost. (Chap. 12)

Indirect manufacturing costs. See *Factory overhead.* (Chap. 8)

Internal rate of return. See *time-adjusted rate of return.* (Chap. 13)

Investment tax credit. Direct reductions of income taxes arising from the acquisition of depreciable assets. (Chap. 5)

Joint cost. A cost which is common to all the segments in question and which is not clearly or practically allocable except by some questionable allocation base. Also called common cost. (Chaps. 11, 12)

Joint product costs. Costs of two or more manufactured goods, of significant sales values, that are produced by a single process and that are not identifiable as individual products up to a certain stage of production, known as the split-off point. (Chap. 13)

Last in, first out. The stock acquired earliest is assumed to be still on hand; the stock acquired latest is assumed to have been used immediately. (Chap. 5)

Lead time. The time interval between placing an order and receiving delivery. (Chap. 17)

Liability. The economic obligation of the entity to outsiders. (Chap. 2)

Linear programming. A mathematical approach to a group of business problems which contain many interacting variables and which basically involve combining limited resources to maximize profits or minimize costs. (Chap. 17)

Line authority. Authority which is exerted downward over subordinates. (Chap. 1)

Managed costs. See *Programmed costs.* (Chap. 10)

Management by exception. The practice by the executive of focusing his attention mainly on significant deviations from expected results. It might also be called management by variance. (Chap. 1)

Management science. The formulation of mathematical and statistical models applied to decision making and the practical application of these models through the use of digital computers. (Chap. 17)

Manufacturing expenses. See *Factory overhead.* (Chap. 8)

Manufacturing overhead. See *Factory overhead.* (Chap. 8)

Marginal costing. See *Direct costing.* (Chap. 16)

Marginal income. See *Contribution margin.* (Chap. 7)

Marketing variance. The budgeted unit contribution margin multiplied by the difference between the master-budgeted sales in units and the actual sales in units. (Chap. 9)

Master budget. The budget which consolidates the organization's overall plans. (Chap. 6)

Master budgeted sales. That rate of activity employed in formulating the master budget for the period. (Chap. 6)

Matching. Establishing a relationship between efforts (expenses) and accomplishments (revenues). (Chap. 2)

Minority interest. The total shareholder interest (other than the parent's) in a subsidiary corporation. (Chap. 3)

Mixed cost. A cost that has both fixed and variable elements. (Chap. 10)

Negotiated market price. A transfer price negotiated by the buying and selling segments when there is no market mechanism to fix a price clearly relevant to the situation. (Chap. 16)

Net book value. The asset amount (usually unexpired cost) carried on the financial records of the organization. (Chap. 3)

Net present value method. A method of calculating the expected utility of a given project by discounting all expected future cash flows to the present, using some predetermined minimum desired rate of return. (Chap. 13)

Net working capital. The excess of current assets over current liabilities. (Chap. 4)

Normal activity. The rate of activity needed to meet average sales demand over a period long enough to encompass seasonal and cyclical fluctuations. (Chap. 15)

Object of costing. See *cost object.*

Objectivity. Accuracy that is supported by convincing evidence which can be verified by independent accountants. (Chap. 2)

Operations research. A diffused collection of mathematical and statistical models applied to decision making. (Chap. 17)

Opportunity cost. The maximum alternative earning that might have been obtained if the productive good, service, or capacity had been applied to some alternative use. (Chap. 12)

Order-filling cost. A marketing cost incurred in the storing, packing, shipping, billing, credit and collection, and in other similar aspects of selling merchandise. (Chap. 10)

Order-getting cost. A marketing cost incurred in the effort to attain a desired sales volume and mix. (Chap. 10)

Overabsorbed overhead. See *Overapplied overhead.* (Chap. 15)

Overapplied overhead. The excess of amount of overhead cost applied to product over the amount of overhead cost incurred. Also called overabsorbed overhead. (Chap. 15)

Overtime premium. A classification of *indirect labor costs,* consisting of the extra wages paid to *all* factory workers for overtime work. (Chap. 8)

Paid-in surplus. See *Capital surplus.* (Chap. 3)

Par value. The value printed on the face of the security certificate. (Chap. 3)

Payback. The measure of the time needed to recoup, in the form of cash inflow from operations, the initial dollars invested. Also called payout and payoff. (Chap. 13)

Payoff. See *Payback.* (Chap. 13)

Payoff table. A convenient technique for showing the total expected value of each of a number of contemplated acts in the light of the varying probabilities of the events which may take place and the varying values of each act under each of the events. (Chap. 17)

Payout. See *Payback.* (Chap. 13)

Performance report. The comparison of actual results with the budget. (Chap. 1)

PERT (Program Evaluation and Review Technique). A formal probabilistic diagram of the temporal interrelationships of a complex series of activities. (Chap. 17)

Planning. Selecting objectives and the means for their attainment. (Chap. 1)

Practical capacity. The maximum level at which the plant or department can realistically operate most efficiently, i.e., ideal capacity less allowances for unavoidable operating interruptions. Also called practical attainable capacity. (Chap. 15)

Preferred stock. Stock that has some priority over other shares regarding dividends or the distribution of assets upon liquidation. (Chap. 3)

Price variance. The difference between the actual price and the standard price, multiplied by the total number of items acquired. The term "price variance" is usually linked with direct material; the term "rate variance," which is conceptually similar to the price variance, is usually linked with direct labor. (Chap. 9)

Problem solving. That function of the accountant's information supplying task which expresses in concise, quantified terms the relative advantages and disadvantages to the firm of pursuing a possible future course of action, or the relative advantages of any one of several alternative methods of operation. (Chap. 1)

Profitability accounting. See *Responsibility accounting.* (Chap. 11)

Profit center. A segment of a business that is responsible for both revenue and expense. (Chap. 16)

Pro-forma statements. Forecasted financial statements. (Chap. 6)

Programmed costs. See *Discretionary costs.* (Chap. 10)

Qualitative factor. A factor which is of consequence but which cannot be measured precisely and easily in dollars. (Chap. 12)

Quantity variance. The standard price for a given resource, multiplied by the difference between the actual quantity used and the total standard quantity allowed for the number of good units produced. (Chap. 9)

Quote sheet. An analysis of costs used as a basis for determining selling prices. (Chap. 12)

Rate variance. The difference between actual wages paid and the standard wage rate, multiplied by the total actual hours of direct labor used. See *Price variance.* (Chap. 9)

Realization. The recognition of revenue. Generally, two tests must be met. First, the earning process must be virtually complete in that the goods or services must be fully rendered. Second, an exchange of resources evidenced by a market transaction must occur. (Chap. 2)

Reallocation. Allocation of the costs of operating the service departments to the various production departments in proportion to the relative benefits or services received by each production department. (Chap. 11)

Reapportionment. See *Reallocation.* (Chap. 11)

Relevant data for decision making. Expected future data which will differ as between alternatives. (Chap. 12)

Relevant range. The band of activity in which budgeted sales and expense relationships will be valid. (Chap. 7)

Reserve. Should not be confused with *fund. Reserve* has one of three meanings: (1) A restriction of dividend-paying power denoted by a specific subdivision of retained income. (2) An offset to an asset. (3) An estimate of a definite liability of indefinite or uncertain amount. (Chap. 3)

Residual income. The operating income of a profit center or investment center, less the "imputed" interest on the assets used by the center. (Chap. 16)

Responsibility accounting. A system of accounting which recognizes various responsibility centers throughout the organization and which reflects the plans and actions of each of these centers by allocating particular revenues and costs to the one having the pertinent responsibility. Also called profitability accounting and activity accounting. (Chap. 11)

Retained earnings. See *Retained income.* (Chap. 2)

Retained income. The accumulated increase in stockholders' equity arising from profitable operations. (Chap. 2)

Safety stock. A minimum inventory that provides a cushion against reasonably expected maximum demand and against variations in lead time. (Chap. 17)

Sales mix. The relative combination of the quantities of a variety of company products that compose total sales. (Chap. 7)

Scorekeeping. That data accumulation function of the accountant's information supplying task which enables both internal and external parties to evaluate the financial performance of the firm. (Chap. 1)

Segment. Any line of activity or part of an organization for which separate determination of costs and/or sales is wanted. (Chap. 11)

Segment margin. The contribution margin for each segment less all separable fixed costs, both discretionary and committed. A measure of long-run profitability. (Chap. 11)

Separable cost. A cost directly identifiable with a particular segment. (Chap. 11)

Service departments. Those departments that exist solely to aid the production departments by rendering specialized assistance with certain phases of the work. (Chap. 11)

Short-run performance margin. The contribution margin for each segment, less separable discretionary costs. (Chap. 11)

Source document. The original record of any transaction, internal or external, which occurs in the firm's operation. (Chaps. 1, 11)

Spending variance. Basically, a price variance applied to variable overhead. However, other factors besides price may influence the amount of the variance. (Chap. 9)

Staff authority. The authority to *advise* but not to command; it may be exerted laterally or upward. (Chap. 1)

Standard absorption costing. That type of product costing in which the cost of the finished unit is calculated as the sum of the costs of the standard allowances for the factory overhead, without reference to the costs actually incurred. (Chap. 16)

Standard cost. A carefully predetermined cost that should be attained, usually expressed per unit. (Chap. 9)

Standard direct costing. That type of product costing in which the cost of the finished unit is calculated as the sum of the costs of the *standard allowances* for the factors of production, *excluding* fixed factory overhead, which is treated as a period cost, and without reference to the costs actually incurred. (Chap. 16)

Statement of sources and applications of funds. See *Funds statement.* (Chap. 4)

Static budget. A budget prepared for only one level of activity and, consequently, one which does not adjust automatically to changes in the level of volume. (Chap. 9)

Step-variable costs. Those variable costs which change abruptly at intervals of activity because their acquisition comes in indivisible chunks. (Chap. 10)

Stockholders' equity. The excess of assets over liabilities. (Chap. 2)

Stock split. The issuance of additional shares for no consideration and under conditions indicating that the objective is to increase the number of outstanding shares for the purpose of reducing their unit market price. (Chap. 3)

Subordinated. A creditor claim that is junior to other creditor claims. (Chap. 3)

Subordinated debenture. See *Subordinated* and *Debenture.* (Chap. 3)

Sunk cost. A cost which has already been incurred and which, therefore, is irrelevant to the decision-making process. Also called historical cost. (Chap. 12)

Tax shield. Noncash items (e.g., depreciation) charged against income, thus protecting that amount from tax. (Chap. 14)

Time-adjusted rate of return. The rate of interest at which the present value of expected cash inflows from a particular project equals the present value of expected cash outflow of that same project. (Chap. 13)

Total project approach. A method of comparing two or more alternative courses of action by computing the total expected inflows and outflows of each alternative and then converting these flows to their present value by applying some predetermined minimum rate of return. (Chap. 13)

Trading on the equity. Using borrowed money at a fixed interest rate and/or paying preferred dividends in the hope of enhancing the rate of return on common stockholders' equity. (Chap. 4)

Transaction. Any event that affects the financial position or results of the organization; it is the happening that requires recording. (Chap. 2)

Transfer price. The price charged by one segment of an organization for a product or service which it supplies to another segment of the same organization. (Chap. 16)

Treasury stock. Outstanding stock that has subsequently been repurchased by the company. (Chap. 3)

Unadjusted rate of return. An expression of the utility of a given project as the ratio of the increase in future average annual net income to the initial increase in required investment. Also called book value method and accounting method. (Chap. 13)

Usage variance. Quantity variance applied to materials. (Chap. 9)

Variable budget. See *Flexible budget.* (Chap. 9)

Variable cost. A cost which is uniform *per unit*, but which fluctuates in total in direct proportion to changes in the related total activity or volume. (Chap. 7)

Variable costing. See *Direct costing.* (Chap. 16)

Variance. The deviation of actual results from the expected or budgeted result. (Chaps. 1 and 9)

Index